Common Core Mathematics Standards and Implementing Digital Technologies

Drew Polly
University of North Carolina at Charlotte, USA

A volume in the Advances in Educational
Technologies and Instructional Design

Information Science
REFERENCE
An Imprint of IGI Global

Managing Director:	Lindsay Johnston
Editorial Director:	Joel Gamon
Production Manager:	Jennifer Yoder
Publishing Systems Analyst:	Adrienne Freeland
Development Editor:	Monica Speca
Assistant Acquisitions Editor:	Kayla Wolfe
Typesetter:	Christina Henning
Cover Design:	Jason Mull

Published in the United States of America by
Information Science Reference (an imprint of IGI Global)
701 E. Chocolate Avenue
Hershey PA 17033
Tel: 717-533-8845
Fax: 717-533-8661
E-mail: cust@igi-global.com
Web site: http://www.igi-global.com

Library of Congress Cataloging-in-Publication Data

Common core mathematics standards and implementing digital technologies / Drew Polly, editor.
    pages cm
 Includes bibliographical references and index.
  Summary: "This book provides a critical discussion of educational standards in mathematics and how communication technologies can support the implementation of common practices across state lines"--Provided by publisher.
  ISBN 978-1-4666-4086-3 (hardcover) -- ISBN 978-1-4666-4087-0 (ebook) -- ISBN 978-1-4666-4088-7 (print & perpetual access) 1. Mathematics--Study and teaching. 2. Educational technology 3. Computer-assisted instruction. I. Polly, Drew, 1977- editor of compilation.
  QA135.6.C647 2013
  372.7'043021873--dc23
                        2013009203

This book is published in the IGI Global book series Advances in Educational Technologies and Instructional Design (ISSN: 2326-8905; eISSN: 2326-8913)

British Cataloguing in Publication Data
A Cataloguing in Publication record for this book is available from the British Library.

Advances in Educational Technologies and Instructional Design

Lawrence Tomei
Robert Morris University, USA

ISSN: 2326-8905
EISSN: 2326-8913

MISSION

Education has undergone, and continues to undergo, immense changes in the way it is enacted and distributed to both child and adult learners. From distance education, Massive-Open-Online-Courses (MOOCs), and electronic tablets in the classroom, technology is now an integral part of the educational experience and is also affecting the way educators communicate information to students.

The **Advances in Educational Technologies & Instructional Design (AETID) Book Series** is a resource where researchers, students, administrators, and educators alike can find the most updated research and theories regarding technology's integration within education and its effect on teaching as a practice.

COVERAGE

- Adaptive Learning
- Collaboration Tools
- Curriculum Development
- Digital Divide in Education
- E-Learning
- Game-Based Learning
- Hybrid Learning
- Instructional Design
- Social Media Effects on Education
- Web 2.0 and Education

IGI Global is currently accepting manuscripts for publication within this series. To submit a proposal for a volume in this series, please contact our Acquisition Editors at Acquisitions@igi-global.com or visit: http://www.igi-global.com/publish/.

Titles in this Series

For a list of additional titles in this series, please visit: www.igi-global.com

Cases on Educational Technology Planning, Design, and Implementation A Project Management Perspective
Angela D. Benson (University of Alabama, USA) Joi L. Moore (University of Missouri, USA) and Shahron Williams van Rooij (George Mason University, USA)
Information Science Reference ● copyright 2013 ● 328pp ● H/C (ISBN: 9781466642379) ● US $175.00 (our price)

Common Core Mathematics Standards and Implementing Digital Technologies
Drew Polly (University of North Carolina at Charlotte, USA)
Information Science Reference ● copyright 2013 ● 364pp ● H/C (ISBN: 9781466640863) ● US $175.00 (our price)

Technologies for Inclusive Education Beyond Traditional Integration Approaches
David Griol Barres (Carlos III University of Madrid, Spain) Zoraida Callejas Carrión (University of Granada, Spain) and Ramón López-Cózar Delgado (University of Granada, Spain)
Information Science Reference ● copyright 2013 ● 455pp ● H/C (ISBN: 9781466625303) ● US $175.00 (our price)

Cases on Interdisciplinary Research Trends in Science, Technology, Engineering, and Mathematics Studies on Urban Classrooms
Reneta D. Lansiquot (New York City College of Technology of the City University of New York, USA)
Information Science Reference ● copyright 2013 ● 412pp ● H/C (ISBN: 9781466622142) ● US $175.00 (our price)

Cases on Inquiry through Instructional Technology in Math and Science
Lesia Lennex (Morehead State University, USA) and Kimberely Fletcher Nettleton (Morehead State University, USA)
Information Science Reference ● copyright 2012 ● 696pp ● H/C (ISBN: 9781466600683) ● US $175.00 (our price)

Cases on Building Quality Distance Delivery Programs Strategies and Experiences
Stephanie Huffman (University of Central Arkansas, USA) Shelly Albritton (University of Central Arkansas, USA) Barbara Wilmes (University of Central Arkansas, USA) and Wendy Rickman (University of Central Arkansas, USA)
Information Science Reference ● copyright 2011 ● 348pp ● H/C (ISBN: 9781609601119) ● US $180.00 (our price)

Distinctive Distance Education Design Models for Differentiated Instruction
Richard G. Fuller (Robert Morris University, USA) Gary William Kuhne (Penn State University, USA) and Barbara A. Frey (D. Ed. University of Pittsburgh, USA)
Information Science Reference ● copyright 2011 ● 226pp ● H/C (ISBN: 9781615208654) ● US $180.00 (our price)

Designing Instruction for the Traditional, Adult, and Distance Learner A New Engine for Technology-Based Teaching
Lawrence A. Tomei (Robert Morris University, USA)
Information Science Reference ● copyright 2010 ● 470pp ● H/C (ISBN: 9781605668246) ● US $180.00 (our price)

IGI GLOBAL
DISSEMINATOR OF KNOWLEDGE
www.igi-global.com

701 E. Chocolate Ave., Hershey, PA 17033
Order online at www.igi-global.com or call 717-533-8845 x100
To place a standing order for titles released in this series, contact: cust@igi-global.com
Mon-Fri 8:00 am - 5:00 pm (est) or fax 24 hours a day 717-533-8661

Table of Contents

Section 1
Frameworks and Conceptual Orientations

Christian Hirsch, Western Michigan University, USA
Brin Keller, Michigan State University, USA
Nicole Fonger, Western Michigan University, USA
Alden Edson, Western Michigan University, USA

Chandra Hawley Orrill, University of Massachusetts Dartmouth, USA
Drew Polly, University of North Carolina at Charlotte, USA

Michelle Rutherford, Apex Learning, USA

P. Mark Taylor, Carson-Newman University, USA

Section 2
Content and Context

Detailed Table of Contents

Section 1
Frameworks and Conceptual Orientations

Christian Hirsch, Western Michigan University, USA
Brin Keller, Michigan State University, USA
Nicole Fonger, Western Michigan University, USA
Alden Edson, Western Michigan University, USA

Core Math Tools is an open-source suite of Java-based software tools that include general purpose tools—a spreadsheet, a computer algebra system, interactive (dynamic) geometry, data analysis, and simulation tools—together with topic-focused Custom Apps and Advanced Apps for triangle congruence and similarity, data modeling, linear programming, three-dimensional visualization, and more. Core Math Tools provides a unique linked tool set that supports the full range of contemporary high school mathematics. This design promotes the important mathematical practice of selecting and strategically using software tools. Accompanying the software is a Website at the National Council of Teachers of Mathematics (NCTM) providing content designed to help school districts meet the new Common Core State Standards for Mathematics (CCSSM). This chapter describes and illustrates use of the software in implementing rich tasks aligned with the CCSSM.

Chandra Hawley Orrill, University of Massachusetts Dartmouth, USA
Drew Polly, University of North Carolina at Charlotte, USA

Technology has the potential to support the creation and use of mathematical representations for exploring, reasoning about, and modeling cognitively demanding mathematical tasks. In this chapter, the authors argue that one of the key affordances of these dynamic representations is the synergistic relationship they can play with communication in the mathematics classroom. The authors highlight the ways in which technology-based representations can support mathematical communication in the classroom through a series of vignettes. They conclude with a discussion of the development of teachers' Technological Pedagogical and Content Knowledge (TPACK) for supporting the implementation of dynamic representations.

Chapter 3

Michelle Rutherford, Apex Learning, USA

Teachers and educators transitioning to the Common Core State Standards face a significant challenge of creating new lessons and resources, as well as formative assessments that match the increased rigor required. Teachers must ensure that each student achieves and demonstrates higher levels of understanding. Many aspects of this transition can be mitigated, supported, and enhanced through blended learning. Blended learning leverages digital curriculum to assist teachers in creating a student-centered learning experience while providing a curriculum that meets the new standards. Students receive individualized instruction at their own pace, achieve mastery, and experience success in high school. They are equipped with a deeper level of understanding and the critical thinking and problem solving skills needed to succeed in college and work.

Chapter 4

P. Mark Taylor, Carson-Newman University, USA

In the implementation of the Common Core State Standards, teacher educators have an unprecedented opportunity. Both preservice and inservice teachers are aware that they have much to learn about the effective implementation of the standards. This is especially true in light of the standards inclusion of technology on the list of tools, which students should be selecting and properly using. Action research can be an effective pedagogical tool for teacher educators to employ as we support teachers' learning about these technology tools for learning mathematics. Four levels of TPACK action research are suggested as a framework for teacher educators to use as they take advantage of this opportunity.

Section 2
Content and Context

Chapter 5

Azita Manouchehriazi, The Ohio State University, USA
Jennifer Czocher, Texas State University-San Marcos, USA
Ravi Somayajulu, Eastern Illinois University, USA
Yating Liu, Old Dominion University, USA
Pingping Zhang, The Ohio State University, USA
Jenna Tague, The Ohio State University, USA

In this longitudinal research project, the authors traced the impact of a mathematics enrichment program on a group of approximately 80 middle and high school students as they worked on mathematical explorations using interactive computer software for three years. The results indicate that learning environments designed for children supported their development of mathematical practices emphasized by the CCSMP while increasing their exposure to and understanding of content standards.

Chapter 6

Milan Sherman, Drake University, USA

This chapter discusses how the use of Dynamic Geometry Software (DGS) can be used to support students' engagement with the Standards for Mathematical Practice as outlined in Common Core State Standards for Mathematics (CCSS-M). In particular, the aim of this chapter is to (1) describe what students' strategic use of appropriate tools might entail in a DGS environment, and (2) argue that for students to engage in these practices in a DGS environment, they must construct meaning for and with these tools in the process of instrumental genesis. Illustrative examples are provided from three secondary mathematics classrooms, and the chapter concludes with recommendations for future research and teacher education in this area.

Chapter 7

Lisa Ames, Wood-Ridge High School, USA
Heejung An, William Paterson University, USA
Sandra Alon, William Paterson University, USA

The Common Core State Mathematics Standards (CCSSM) recommend that technology should be integrated into teaching and learning Mathematics. This chapter addresses how the Geometer's Sketchpad computer program can support students' thinking skills and learning outcomes in a high school geometry class, in particular for more effectively addressing the High School Geometry Standards (CCSSM: G.CO.10, G.CO. 11, and G.CO. 12). The findings from the study presented in this chapter indicate that this tool can help high school students increase their learning of geometry in terms of inductive reasoning and conceptual knowledge, but may not help improve students' motivation to learn geometry.

Chapter 8

D. Craig Schroeder, Fayette County Public Schools, USA
Carl W. Lee, University of Kentucky, USA

The Common Core State Standards for Mathematics include mathematical practices for modeling and also references to the appropriate use of technology. Several new dynamic programs can be leveraged using Technological Pedagogical Content Knowledge (TPACK) to enhance the conceptual and practical knowledge of students. The authors used Google SketchUp to develop understandings of 3-dimensional shapes and models. In the successful project, middle school students were introduced to the program, given small challenges, and then, as a culminating project, asked to model rooms within their school. The result was an exact replica of the schoolrooms and a project that could be used for virtual tours. This type of project-based learning can be implemented in most classrooms, even those in which the instructor has limited knowledge of SketchUp. Students were actively engaged throughout the instruction and were able to work with their peers and develop practical mathematical skills.

Shelby P. Morge, University of North Carolina Wilmington, USA

Mahnaz Moallem, University of North Carolina Wilmington, USA

Chris Gordon, University of North Carolina Wilmington, USA

Gene Tagliarini, University of North Carolina Wilmington, USA

Sridhar Narayan, University of North Carolina Wilmington, USA

The Common Core State Standards (CCSS) call for a change in the way mathematics is taught. The mathematical practices outlined by the CCSS call for mathematics as a problem-solving endeavor, rather than routine exercises and practice. A quick Web search can provide mathematics teachers with an abundance of workshops and courses, examples, and videos of the different mathematical practices to help them understand what they mean and look like in practice. However, those examples do not go far in changing the current culture of mathematics instruction. In this chapter, the authors discuss current US mathematics instructional practices and how the CCSS are asking for distinctly different teaching practices. In addition, the authors share how the innovative Using Squeak to Infuse Information Technology Project (USeIT) sidestepped traditional mathematics instructional approaches and utilized problem-solving activities and the development of computational models to support students' learning of STEM concepts. The authors illustrate how the design, development, and implementation of a Squeak Etoys and Problem-Based Learning (PBL) activity addresses the CCSS expectations for mathematics content, practice for learning, and assessment, and discuss what this means for mathematics teacher education and professional development.

Karina K. R. Hensberry, University of Colorado Boulder, USA

Ariel J. Paul, University of Colorado Boulder, USA

Emily B. Moore, University of Colorado Boulder, USA

Noah S. Podolefsky, University of Colorado Boulder, USA

Katherine K. Perkins, University of Colorado Boulder, USA

This chapter focuses on the design and use of interactive simulations as a powerful tool for learning mathematics. Since 2002, the PhET Interactive Simulations project at the University of Colorado Boulder (http://phet.colorado.edu) has been developing and studying the use of interactive simulations in teaching and learning STEM. While the project's initial work focused on science learning, the project now includes a significant effort in mathematics learning. In this chapter, the authors describe the PhET project, including theoretical perspective, design goals, and research-based simulation design principles. They demonstrate how these design principles are applied to simulations, describe how they support achievement of the Common Core State Standards for Mathematics (CCSSM), and provide supporting evidence from individual student interviews. Finally, the authors discuss various approaches to using these simulations in class and provide guidance on leveraging their capabilities to support knowledge construction in mathematics in a uniquely engaging and effective way.

Woong Lim, Kennesaw State University, USA
Dong-Gook Kim, Dalton State College, USA

This chapter reviews the roles of technology in statistics education and introduces technologies available for classroom use. A few concrete examples of how select technologies support the teaching of probability and statistics guided by the Common Core State Standards in Mathematics of high school Probability and Statistics (CCSSM-PS) are presented. The reality of the implementation of the CCSSM poses a rather exciting opportunity for all of us in mathematics education. It presents an opportunity to plan and create mathematics lessons based on good teaching strongly tied with technology. As the efficacy of the CCSSM-PS hinges on how teachers draw upon their content knowledge to facilitate student learning through technology, it is significant to provide professional development programs that help teachers infuse technology with the teaching of probability and statistics.

Karen Greenhaus, Consultant, Edtech Professional Development, USA

The Common Core State Standards for Mathematics (CCSSM) include overarching Standards for Mathematical Practice that cite dynamic geometry® software as one of the tools mathematically proficient students should know how to use strategically. Dynamic geometry software or more generally, dynamic mathematics software, provides visible and tangible representations of mathematical concepts that can be dragged and manipulated to discover underlying properties, investigate patterns and relationships, and develop deeper understandings of the concepts. The Geometer's Sketchpad®, TinkerPlots®, and Fathom® are examples of dynamic mathematics software. This chapter outlines how dynamic mathematics software supports the CCSSM. Specific mathematic content examples are described using these three resources to model the use of dynamic mathematics software for learning mathematics. Challenges for successfully integrating dynamic mathematics software are described with suggestions for training and support.

Section 3
Vignettes and Cases

Robin Magruder, University of Kentucky, USA
Margaret Mohr-Schroeder, University of Kentucky, USA

Virtual manipulatives provide benefits to students as they encounter the Common Core State Standards for Mathematics content and practice standards. The National Library of Virtual Manipulatives provides an abundant supply of virtual manipulatives for all K-12 grades and mathematics content areas. Specifically, in this chapter, the authors explore the use of Algebra Balance Scale manipulatives in a middle school mathematics classroom. Using virtual manipulatives increases understanding of the equal sign, algebraic symbols, and increases procedural and conceptual knowledge. In this chapter, the authors demonstrate how using virtual manipulatives helped middle school students to meet grade level content standards for solving equations in one variable. Additionally, practice standards, such as making sense of problems and persevering to solve them, modeling with mathematics, and using tools strategically through the use of virtual manipulatives are addressed. They conclude by considering practical issues related to incorporating virtual manipulatives in mathematics classrooms.

Chapter 14

Jessica Taylor Ivy, Mississippi State University, USA
Dana Pomykal Franz, Mississippi State University, USA

This chapter examines the practices and beliefs of two secondary mathematics teachers with similar demographic backgrounds. The influence of their practices and beliefs on teaching and student learning is considered through the lens of the TPACK Development Model and through evidence of student engagement in the Mathematical Practices. Even though they face common barriers to instructional technology integration, both teachers speak to their successes and positive impacts on student learning. Rich descriptions of conversations, classroom observations, and self-report survey data highlight critical contrasts between the practices of the two teachers. These differences represent the unique challenges faced by instructional technology researchers and other educational stakeholders. The purpose of this chapter is to highlight these subtle, yet far-reaching, areas of distinction in which the teachers unknowingly provide different levels of opportunity for teaching and learning in the mathematics classroom.

Chapter 15

Ayhan Kursat Erbas, Middle East Technical University, Turkey
Sarah Ledford, Kennesaw State University, USA
Chandra Hawley Orrill, University of Massachusetts Dartmouth, USA
Drew Polly, University of North Carolina at Charlotte, USA

As teachers prepare to teach the Common Core State Standards for Mathematics (CCSSM), students' exploration of patterns and relationships between numbers has gained more importance. Specifically, students' conceptual understanding of numerical patterns is critical in middle school, as it lays a groundwork for fostering mathematical thinking at all levels. Educational technologies can enhance student's explorations of patterns by providing opportunities to represent patterns, test conjectures, and make generalizations. In this chapter, the authors illustrate how spreadsheets can support students' explorations of both arithmetic and geometric patterns in the middle grades.

Chapter 16

Jayme Linton, Lenior-Rhyne University, USA
David Stegall, Newton-Connover City Schools, USA

This chapter seeks to answer the guiding question: How does the TPACK (Technological Pedagogical Content Knowledge) framework influence how technology can support the implementation of the Common Core Standards for Mathematical Practice? The authors provide an overview of the Standards for Mathematical Practice and an application of the TPACK framework to the Common Core State Standards for Mathematics. Classroom scenarios describe how teachers can use the TPACK framework to integrate technology into the Standards for Mathematical Practice from kindergarten to eighth grade. The authors conclude with implications for professional developers, teacher educators, and administrators as they work to develop teachers' TPACK and prepare teachers for implementing the Common Core State Standards for Mathematics.

The Common Core State Standards in Mathematics and English/Language Arts necessitate that teachers provide opportunities for their students to write about mathematical concepts in ways that extend beyond simply a summary of how students solve mathematical tasks. This study examined how mathematics journals in a fourth grade classroom supported students' mathematical experiences and reflected their understanding of concepts. Implications for the use of technology to support mathematics journals are also discussed.

Chapter 18

This chapter relates the classroom experiences of 44 teachers across the United States, implementing Investigations in Number, Data, and Space, an elementary school mathematics curriculum. These teachers participated in a "tryout" of Investigations for the Interactive Whiteboard with their students. Investigations for the Interactive Whiteboard was developed in collaboration by Pearson, TERC, and SMART Board. The teachers' reactions showcase how the use of this technology enhanced the teaching and learning of mathematics. These vignettes illuminate the essence of Common Core Standards for Mathematical Practice (CCSSI, 2010), which describe how students should engage with the mathematical skills and concepts of the Common Core Content. The use of the interactive whiteboard engaged all students, motivated them to participate beyond their norm, allowed modeling of the mathematics which opened access to all students, and encouraged students to explain, argue, and defend their ideas while listening to and critiquing others, the essences of the Standards for Mathematical Practice.

Section 4
Innovative Approaches to Teacher Education and Professional Development

This chapter describes how the authors have utilized digital graphics and Web 2.0 technologies to design an information technology environment, LessonSketch. In LessonSketch teachers can learn about mathematical practice in instruction through the transaction of representations of practice. The authors describe the main features of LessonSketch, its collection of lessons, and its authoring tools, and illustrate what teacher educators have done with them.

Chapter 20

This chapter addresses the need to prepare and support teachers of mathematics in order that they will be able to co-construct with their students classroom environments in which the Standards for Mathematical Practice as well as the content standards (CCSSM, 2010) are implemented fruitfully. Specifically, the chapter describes and illustrates design elements of learning environments with potential to positively impact pre- and in-service teachers' knowledge of mathematics, facility with technology, and beliefs about how mathematics may be learned. The practice of using appropriate tools strategically is highlighted; however, each of the practice standards is integral to a classroom environment which supports mathematical proficiency (National Research Council, 2001). This chapter examines and illustrates the explicit and intentional instructional design features of using provocative tasks, dynamic technology scaffolding, and sustained intellectual press, which together interact in classrooms to promote the mathematical practices and habits of mind explicated in the CCSSM.

Chapter 21

The purpose of this chapter is to present a framework for developing online professional development materials to support teachers as they adopt the Common Core standards. The framework builds conceptually from the principles associated with successful mathematics professional development on the teaching practices that support productive mathematical discourse in the classroom. The framework was applied to online materials developed from an emergent perspective (Cobb & Yackel, 1996) in the context of the Common Core fractions standards at the elementary level. Implications for the use of the framework to guide the selection, development, and implementation of mathematics professional development are discussed.

This chapter describes the process of developing Web-based resources to support elementary school teachers' implementation of the Common Core State Standards in Mathematics in a large urban school district in the southeastern United States. Based on a learner-centered approach to teacher professional development the authors describe a three-fold process of supporting teachers: providing opportunities for teachers to deepen their understanding of the CCSSM, providing curricular resources that align with the CCSSM, and providing ongoing support through teachers' implementation of the CCSSM. Implications for the development of Web-based resources and researching these types of endeavors are also shared.

This chapter focuses on how assessment for learning can be used to promote the development of student understanding of mathematics and mathematical practices as described in the Common Core State Standards for Mathematics while emphasizing the affordances of digital technologies. The mathematical focus centered on the families of functions connected to the mathematical practice of constructing viable arguments when using the digital technology tool, VoiceThread. The chapter describes an iterative model for implementing assessment for learning practices where VoiceThread gave voice to preservice teachers' mathematical justifications. Findings are taken from a study set in an algebra course designed for preservice elementary teachers working towards a minor in mathematics. Preservice teachers noted the positive impacts of using VoiceThread in improving their justification skills and the benefits of assessment for learning practices on their learning process.

Implementation of the Common Core State Standards in Mathematics has provided teacher educators a great opportunity to reexamine whether teacher preparation programs adequately provide the experiences to develop the base of knowledge and 21st century skills necessary to be effective teachers. The Mathematics TPACK Framework provides a roadmap for a series of pathways to integrate three knowledge components that are essential in teacher development: content knowledge, pedagogical knowledge, and technological knowledge. In this chapter, the authors examine how a teacher preparation program has evolved to integrate meaningful uses of digital technologies in content and pedagogy that are relevant to the teaching and learning of mathematics through the lens of implementing the Common Core State Standards.

The Standards for Mathematical Practice as delineated in the Common Core State Standards for Mathematics describe the processes, proficiencies, and habits of mind that students are expected to develop through their engagement with mathematics (Dacey & Polly, 2012). The purpose of this chapter is to discuss, anecdotally, how the iPad, a tablet computer designed by Apple ™, can be used to develop preservice teachers' understanding and implementation of the Standards for Mathematical Practice, most specifically Mathematical Practice Standard 3: Construct viable arguments and critique the reasoning of others. Under examination are the authors' experiences using the iPad as an observational tool during student teaching and as a teaching tool in their mathematics methods courses. The chapter concludes with suggestions for additional uses of the iPad to support preservice teachers as they work to develop their understanding of the Standards for Mathematical Practice.

Foreword

EDUCATIONAL TECHNOLOGY AND THE COMMON CORE MATHEMATICS STANDARDS

In 1958 I jumped into a mid-year assignment of teaching General Mathematics and Algebra I to students 3 to 5 years younger than me in rural Kansas. It was a marvelous adventure. There were no Common Core State Standards and no electronic technology to guide my students and me. We just had some textbooks, some common sense, and a mutual enthusiasm for school mathematics as we were experiencing it. Our technology was a chalkboard, pencils, and paper. It was the Sputnik era, and there was a media frenzy leading people to believe that whatever we were doing was totally inadequate. My students and I were rather untouched by all of that, however, and we went about doing the best we could with what we had and what we knew. I think we turned out pretty well.

Today, we have Common Core State Standards for mathematics, wonderful technology, and loads of advice from experts on what school mathematics should be. Are we better off? Of course. I would never want to go back to what we had before. What is the SAME, however, is that mathematics for students happens in the classroom when teacher and students make the most of what they have and use what they know to do their best. Common Core standards are great, but the political machine that created them and the state boards of education who adopted them are NOT in the classroom. It will be a teacher who makes sense of them with students. Likewise, computers, SMART boards, and calculators are wonderful, but it is up to teachers and their students to find appropriate uses for the technology to enable better learning of mathematics.

Mathematics educators for the most part have embraced the Common Core State Standards in mathematics – the grade level content standards and the eight standards for mathematical practices. Many mathematics educators have been active in exploring ways to assist teachers in implementing the standards. There is a recognition that education technologies appropriately used cannot only support the implementation of the content standards and standards of practice, but also that technology is modifying the mathematics we know and what it means to know mathematics.

This is a book about educational technology and the Common Core State Standards in Mathematics. It has come into being as professionals in mathematics education and educational technology as well as classroom teachers, professional development specialists, and developers of curriculum materials have worked to understand the standards, what it means to implement them, and ways that technology can lead to better mathematics experiences for students. It is a carefully crafted set of chapters by over 30 professionals to build a foundation for helping all of us in mathematics education navigate a shifting terrain of mathematics standards, technology innovations, and assessments. It is a welcome guide for helping us develop our own knowledge about the standards and how technology can facilitate implementation of the standards. Indeed, as we bring collective exploration of these issues it can help us move toward improved mathematics experiences for our students.

So, why am I writing the Foreword for this book? My journey with mathematics study and mathematics teaching has been going on for a long time and it has been interlaced with technology in a variety of ways. My courses on Mathematics with Technology[1] at the University of Georgia have helped prepare hundreds of teachers to incorporate technology into the mathematics explorations they do with their students. My course on Mathematics Problem Solving and its Website[2] is an evolving thing and quite consistent with CCSS mathematics standards. The InterMath Project with its Website[3] is also widely known for its integration of mathematical explorations and the use of technology.

Drew Polly, the editor, comes from a different background than me, but we share a similar vision of mathematics learned by doing, of technology becoming an integral part of the mathematics we learn, and of mathematics making sense for students in well-chosen tasks and activities. More important, Dr. Polly does not just relax in his ivory tower at the university. Rather, he spends a lot of time in classrooms working with the teachers he is guiding. That is, he goes to their workspace and works with them. Out of that has come the vision of this book as a tool to help teachers explore the use of technology, the common core state standards in mathematics, and doing mathematics with the students. This has led him to solicit and collect these various presentations in the book from people who share his sense of urgency for helping teachers and seeing the tremendous potential of various technologies.

To the audience and benefactors of this book, I suggest you have here the elements of a vision of what school mathematics classrooms could become with the enhanced understanding of mathematics using technology. The hard work is yet to be done, but this book gives a lot of useful direction for further work. There are challenges here for researchers, teacher educators, curriculum specialists, professional development specialists, and classroom teachers. Ultimately, it must culminate when teachers make sense of the CSSS, the technology, and the mathematics in classrooms where teachers and their students go about doing the best they can with what they have and what they know. This book is a start of that journey. Let the journey continue.

James W. Wilson
University of Georgia, USA

James W. Wilson *is a Professor of Mathematics Education at the University of Georgia. His mathematics education interests include mathematics problem solving, mathematics explorations with technology, mathematics teacher education, and mathematics assessment. He served as editor of the Journal for Research in Mathematics Education from 1977 to 1982 and was elected to the NCTM Board of Directors 1978 to 1981. In 2001, he received the NCTM Lifetime Achievement Award. He began teaching 55 years ago and is still excited about going to work each day. There have been 54 doctoral students to complete their doctorates at UGa with Jim as the major professor and still a few more to follow.*

ENDNOTES

[1] See http://Jwilson.coe.uga.edu/EMT668/EMT668.html

[2] See http://Jwilson.coe.uga.edu/EMT725/EMT725.html

[3] See http://InterMath.coe.uga.edu

Preface

As teachers and educational leaders in the United States continue through the early phases of implementing the Common Core State Standards for Mathematics (CCSSM), there is a need for educators to critically examine how to best support the implementation of both the Grade Level Content Standards and the eight Standards for Mathematical Practice. When we consider the potential that educational technologies and technological supports can have on mathematics teaching and learning, it is intuitive that we must consider how to best leverage these resources to support the teaching and learning processes.

This book aims to capture a wide variety of conceptual manuscripts, empirical pieces, as well as cases about how educational technologies can support the implementation of the CCSSM. To that end, this book is a compilation of some thought-provoking chapters written by a variety of mathematics educators, educational technologists, as well as representatives from K-12 schools and educational companies.

SECTION 1

In Section 1, "Frameworks and Conceptual Orientations," Hirsch and his colleagues provide a broad description of the potential power of the open-source suite of technologies called *Core Math Tools* and describe how they can support the mathematics teaching and learning processes in high school classrooms. In Chapter 2, Orrill and Polly present a framework about how technology and dynamic mathematical representations can support the communication of mathematical ideas in classrooms. As educational leaders focus more on how to support teachers' implementation of the Standards for Mathematical Practice, especially ones focused on communication, such as *Construct Viable Arguments* and *Attend to Precision*, the chapter provides examples of high-level mathematical tasks and details about how representations supported students' communication of mathematical ideas. In Chapter 3, Rutherford provides an overview of blended learning and implications for schools as resources become more digital and electronic. In Chapter 4, Taylor lays out a framework to support action research in their classroom in light of both the CCSSM and the framework Technological Pedagogical And Content Knowledge (TPACK). Taylor provides categories and possible questions for teachers to explore in order to more effectively examine their students' learning and their own teaching.

SECTION 2

Section 2, "Content and Context," provides a myriad of chapters that address how technology can support the teaching and learning of various concepts and learning environments. In Chapter 5, Manouchehri and colleagues provide an empirical study of how an interactive computer program over three years impacted middle school students' learning. They found that the program led to increased student understanding, provided struggling students with an entry point to cognitively demanding tasks, feedback on their performance, as well as successfully engaging them in mathematical inquiry. In Chapter 6, Sherman provides a description and examples of how Dynamic Geometry Software (DGS) can support students' development of geometric concepts. In Chapter 7, Ames and colleagues provide findings from a study in which they found that intensive use with Geometer's Sketchpad to explore mathematical tasks led to an increase in students' understanding of concepts. In Chapter 8, Schroeder and Lee describe a project in which middle grades students participated in several project-based learning tasks with Google Sketchup. They used Sketchup to complete a variety of mathematical tasks focused on modeling and manipulating 3-dimensional figures. In Chapter 9, Morge and her colleagues used a problem-based learning context and Squeak Etoys to engage learners in a variety of tasks focused on Science, Technology, Engineering, and Mathematics (STEM) concepts with a specific emphasis on mathematics and engineering.

In Chapter 10, Hensberry and her colleagues thoroughly describe the design and potential uses of the PhET interactive simulation project and how the various simulations (over 125) have been utilized to support students' learning. In Chapter 11 Lim and Kim provide a comprehensive overview of various technologies that can support students' work with statistics education in high schools. In Chapter 12, Greenhaus details how dynamic software, specifically Sketchpad®, Fathom®, and TinkerPlots® support the teaching and learning of the high school CCSSM.

SECTION 3

Section 3, "Cases and Vignettes," includes classroom-based cases and vignettes. In Chapter 13, Magruder and Mohr-Schroeder describe how a virtual manipulative was utilized to support middle school teachers' understanding of algebraic reasoning and the process of solving equations. In Chapter 14, Ivy and Franz use the TPACK framework to describe how high school students engaged in the CCSSM Standards for Mathematical Practice. In Chapter 15, Erbas and his colleagues provide a broad overview about how spreadsheets can support mathematical explorations and address the CCSSM Standards that focus on mathematical patterns and algebraic reasoning.

Chapters 16-18 include examples from elementary school classrooms. In Chapter 16, Linton and Stegall extrapolate how technology can support the implementation of the CCSSM Standards for Practice with examples from Grades Kindergarten through Grade 8. In Chapter 17 Martin and Polly share data from a study that examined how mathematics journals and writing across the curriculum supported students' mathematical understanding in elementary school. In Chapter 18, Boland shares the impact of Pearson's interactive whiteboard project focused on supporting teachers' work with the *Investigations in Number, Data, and Space* curricula.

SECTION 4

Section 4, "Innovative Approaches to Teacher Education and Professional Development," features examples about how technology is being leveraged to support teachers' and preservice teachers' understanding and implementation of the CCSSM. In Chapter 19, Herbst and his colleagues describe LessonSketch, a Web-based environment that allows preservice and practicing teachers to explore both the CCSSM content standards and the Standards for Mathematical Practice. In Chapter 20, Madden extrapolates how dynamic geometry software can be leveraged to create learning environments and learning experiences for preservice and inservice teachers' understanding of the CCSSM. Chapter 21 features Kopcha and Valentine's Web-based framework for supporting inservice teachers' implementation of the CCSSM through a suite of various professional development materials. In Chapter 22, LeHew and Polly share how technology was utilized in a large, urban school district to support elementary school teachers' implementation of the CCSSM. In Chapter 23, Browning and her colleagues describe a project where preservice teachers used VoiceThread to reason mathematically about mathematical tasks that they had solved and concepts that they were exploring. In Chapter 24, Borchelt and his colleagues show how their mathematics education program has been modified to include learning technologies aligned to the CC-SSM. In Chapter 25, Grassetti and Brookby describe how they have used iPads with preservice teachers to develop their mathematical understanding with an explicit focus on constructing viable arguments and critiquing the reasoning of others.

Drew Polly
University of North Carolina at Charlotte, USA

Section 1
Frameworks and Conceptual Orientations

Chapter 1
Core Math Tools:
Supporting Equitable Implementation of the Common Core State Standards for Mathematics

Christian Hirsch
Western Michigan University, USA

Nicole Fonger
Western Michigan University, USA

Brin Keller
Michigan State University, USA

Alden Edson
Western Michigan University, USA

ABSTRACT

Core Math Tools is an open-source suite of Java-based software tools that include general purpose tools—a spreadsheet, a computer algebra system, interactive (dynamic) geometry, data analysis, and simulation tools—together with topic-focused Custom Apps and Advanced Apps for triangle congruence and similarity, data modeling, linear programming, three-dimensional visualization, and more. Core Math Tools provides a unique linked tool set that supports the full range of contemporary high school mathematics. This design promotes the important mathematical practice of selecting and strategically using software tools. Accompanying the software is a Website at the National Council of Teachers of Mathematics (NCTM) providing content designed to help school districts meet the new Common Core State Standards for Mathematics (CCSSM). This chapter describes and illustrates use of the software in implementing rich tasks aligned with the CCSSM.

INTRODUCTION

It is essential that teachers and students have regular access to technologies that support and advance mathematical sense making, reasoning, problem solving, and communications. (National Council of Teachers of Mathematics, 2011)

The power and potential of computer technologies for enhancing student learning and understanding of mathematics has long been recognized (cf. Conference Board of the Mathematical Sciences, 1983; Fey et al., 1984; and more recently Fey, Cuoco, Kieran, McMullin, & Zbiek, 2003; Masalski, 2005; Zbiek Heid, Blume, & Dick,

DOI: 10.4018/978-1-4666-4086-3.ch001

2007). However, in spite of the considerable promise that computer technologies provide for the improvement of school mathematics, the fulfillment of that promise has been stymied by issues of finance, access, and equity, among others (Heid, 1997, 2005). These intermingled issues have been exacerbated by the economic recession that began in 2008 and that brought about often repeated and deep cuts in state-level funding of public schools. *Core Math Tools,* as described in this chapter, provides a viable solution to the problems of finance, access, and equity as related to the integration of mathematical software in high school mathematics.

BACKGROUND

Genesis of *Core Math Tools*

Core Math Tools has its roots in the research and development work of the Core-Plus Mathematics Project (CPMP). In particular, in pre-planning for the second edition of the CPMP four-year high school curriculum, surveys and interviews showed that although students using the first edition materials had access to graphing calculators in class, most did not have access to such technology outside of school. This in turn directly influenced teachers' assigned homework and overall course pacing, since most technology-intensive tasks had to be completed in class. On the other hand, pre-planning surveys revealed that students were increasingly using the Internet. As research and development began on the second edition, a decision was made to augment graphing calculator use with the use of computer technologies, specifically with a suite of Java-based software tools designed and developed by the project. Included were a spreadsheet, a computer algebra system (CAS), interactive geometry, data analysis, and simulation tools, together with topic-specific custom apps (Fey & Hirsch, 2007).

The team of mathematics educators working on the curriculum revision and software tools viewed the development process as an extended design experiment (Brown, 1992; Collins, 1992; Design-Based Research Collective, 2003; Gravemeijer, 1994) that included cycles of materials design, development, field testing, and revision. This process and the decision to fully incorporate use of the software in the instructional materials led to a richer, more engaging, and realistic problem-based curriculum. But equally important, we were able to maintain our commitment to access and equity in terms of technology use as evidenced in our field trials. These findings were substantiated by a Pew Internet and American Life Project (2009) survey that found that 95% of youth ages 14–17 were online, that 92% of families have a computer, and that 76% of those have high-speed Internet access. Reports from the field indicate that these percentages have continued to grow.

Common Core State Standards for Mathematics: Technology Expectations

The Common Core State Standards for Mathematics (CCSSM) released in June 2010 include Standards for Mathematical Practice in addition to content standards organized in conceptual categories. Among the eight identified mathematical practices is the disposition and skill to "Use appropriate tools strategically" (Common Core State Standards Initiative, 2010, p. 6). At the high school level these tools include:

A spreadsheet, a computer algebra system, a statistical package, or dynamic geometry software. Proficient students are sufficiently familiar with tools appropriate for their grade or course to make sound decisions about when each of these tools might be helpful. . . . They are able to use these tools to explore and deepen their understanding of concepts. (Common Core State Standards Initiative, 2010, p. 7)

Specific references to use of computer tools are cited in the conceptual categories of Algebra (three standards), Functions (four standards), Geometry (three standards), and Statistics and Probability (two standards). There are quite a few other content standards where technology tools would be potential "cognitive amplifiers" (Pea, 1987), as illustrated in Hart, Hirsch, and Keller (2007). The citation at the beginning of this section from the National Council of Teachers of Mathematics (NCTM) position statement on the use of technology published a year after the release of CCSSM identifies additional affordances of the use of technologies in teaching and learning school mathematics.

To provide teachers and students in U.S. school districts the technological tools to respond to these new expectations, in 2011 the first two named authors received a grant from the National Science Foundation to support re-purposing, refinement, and further development of the CPMP software so that it could be used with *any* CCSSM-oriented high school mathematics program. Through a partnership with the National Council of Teachers of Mathematics, the new CCSSM-oriented software, called *Core Math Tools* (CMT), is freely available at www.nctm.org/coremathtools. That partnership led to the creation of a Core Tools Task Force[1] that was very helpful in rethinking the design of the software and refining and further testing features of specific tools. The task force was also instrumental in developing a CMT portal within the NCTM Website that provides resources helpful to teachers in using the tools to effectively implement the CCSSM. Design and contents of the Website are elaborated in a later section.

Overview of *Core Math Tools*

The remainder of this chapter will provide an overview of the features of CMT and its Website; an example of how the software can be used to address key CCSSM practices and content in the context of mathematical modeling, itself both a mathematical practice and a conceptual domain; examples of CMT use as related to technology-specific content standards; and other affordances of CMT use as a mathematical habit of mind. As can be seen in Figure 1, in addition to the general purpose tools (Figure 1b), CMT Custom Apps and Advanced Apps (Figures 1c and 1d) focus on specific topics such as triangle congruence and similarity, data modeling, linear programming, vertex-edge graphs, voting methods and analysis, three-dimensional visualization, and more.

Using a common interface across the general purpose tools and apps reduces the steepness of the learning curve and promotes transfer among the various components. Visually (Figure 1b) one can see that CMT is organized around three major tool collections:

- **Algebra and Functions:** Includes an electronic spreadsheet and a CAS that produces tables and graphs of single- and two-variable functions; manipulates algebraic expressions, including those involving matrices; and solves equations and inequalities.
- **Geometry and Trigonometry:** Includes an interactive drawing tool for constructing, measuring, manipulating, and transforming geometric figures; a simple object-oriented programming language for creating animation effects; and a set of custom apps for studying geometric models of physical mechanisms, tessellations, and special properties of geometric figures.
- **Statistics and Probability:** Includes tools for graphic display and analysis of univariate and bivariate data, simulation of probabilistic situations, and mathematical modeling of quantitative relationships. The software contains an extensive collection of pre-loaded data sets that have been carefully selected to promote learning of specific content involving data and chance.

Figure 1. CMT initial screens

(a) Opening splash window

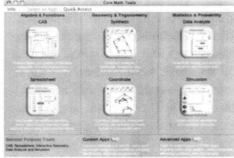

(b) General purpose tools

(c) Focused custom apps

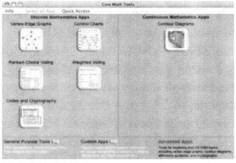

(d) Advanced topic apps

This visual organization of CMT is designed to highlight connections between the tools and the conceptual categories in the CCSSM. Using graphical images for each tool helps to support the choice of appropriate tools in inquiry, problem solving, and mathematical modeling. CMT affords access to each type of software tool identified in the mathematical practice of *using tools strategically*, and it does so within a learner-oriented interface.

In the individual tools themselves, we have attempted to bring together tested design elements and uses that span multiple forms of technology, as well as features unique to CMT. For example, the software permits a straightforward method of examining the role of parameters in function rules. While not a feature unique to CMT, finding such a feature in a software package that also permits data analysis or simulations or establishing triangle congruence and similarity conditions is unique. The collective and linked nature of the

software elevates the software from individual features for related mathematical tasks to a more coherent and integrated technology approach to school mathematics. For further information on the CMT general purpose tools and the custom and advanced apps, see www.nctm.org/coremathtools.

An example of a unique curriculum-inspired feature of CMT is its flexible handling of rotations about a point. In particular, CMT enables rotations in several different contexts: rotations about a point for exploring rotational symmetry of a figure, about a vertex of a triangle for establishing congruence of two triangles, about the origin for coordinate models, about midpoints of sides of triangles or quadrilaterals for tiling, and about any point in the plane for composition of transformations or for more general purposes.

As a final design note, teachers and students can access and use the software online in mathematics classrooms, in school and local libraries, at home, or at any other place that offers Internet access. The software can be freely downloaded to a user's class or home computer and is self-updating whenever connected to the Internet.

AFFORDANCES OF *CORE MATH TOOLS* FOR CURRICULUM MATERIALS DESIGN AND ENACTMENT

Curriculum materials matter. Begle (1973), Usiskin (1985), Robitaille and Travers (1992), Schmidt, McKnight, and Raizen (1997), and Schoenfeld (2002) provide evidence-based arguments that curriculum materials and the nature of their specific tasks are a strong determinant of what students learn and how they learn it.

Summarizing the Conference on Curriculum Design, Development, and Implementation in an Era of Common Core State Standards, Confrey and Krupa (2010) make the case that translation of the CCSSM into practice will require

...meaningful curriculum organizations that are problem-based, informed by international models, connected, consistent, coherent, and focused on both content and mathematical practices. These new models should exploit the capabilities of emerging digital technologies... with due attention to equity. (Confrey & Krupa, 2010)

In the remainder of this section and the next, we illustrate how problems focusing on both mathematical content and mathematical practices might be designed and enacted. The following example adapted from *Core-Plus Mathematics* Course 2 (Hirsch et al., 2008) illustrates the affordances of CMT in addressing the CCSSM mathematical practice and content standards of *modeling with mathematics.*

Optimal Refinery Location: *Drilling teams from oil companies search around the world for new*

sites to place oil wells. Increasingly, oil reserves are being discovered in offshore waters. The Gulf Oil Company has drilled two high-capacity wells in the Gulf of Mexico about 5 km and 9 km from shore and about 20 km apart.

The company needs to pipe oil from the two wells to one ore more new refineries on shore. Assume the oil wells project onto 20 km of shoreline that is nearly straight.

a. *How would you represent the problem?*
b. *What are important considerations in locating the refinery or refineries?*
c. *What is your best estimate for the location(s) of the refinery or refineries?*
d. *How did you decide on the location(s)?*
e. *How do you know you found optimal refinery location(s)?*

Students typically represent the problem situation as in Figure 2a and quickly decide that the goal is to minimize the cost of getting the crude oil to shore for refining. After some discussion, students propose that the optimal solution would be to build a single refinery on the shoreline and minimize the amount of piping from the two wells to the refinery. Using Interactive Geometry construction tools and the "select and drag feature" of the software, students are able to simulate locations of a refinery and dynamically test (as suggested by Figures 2b and 2c) for the minimum amount of piping required to connect the two wells to the refinery indicated by point P.

Students can use this simulation experience to abstract and formulate an algebraic model by observing if the distance from point A to the location of a proposed refinery at point P is x, thus the distance from the refinery to point B is $20 - x$ (Figure 2d). It follows that the length of piping required (without consideration of other conditions) is $\sqrt{x^2 + 25} + \sqrt{(20 - x)^2 + 81}$.

At this point, some students choose to use the algebraic representation to build and execute

Figure 2. Reasoning geometrically, numerically, and algebraically

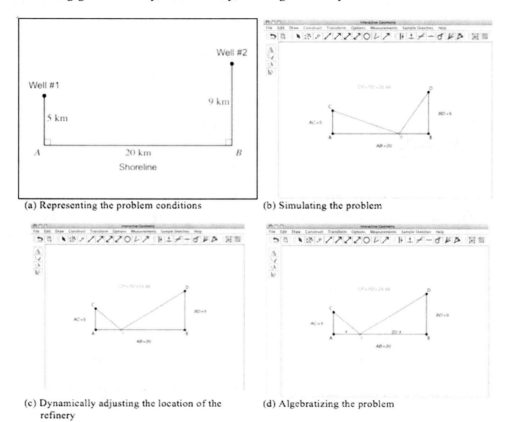

(a) Representing the problem conditions

(b) Simulating the problem

(c) Dynamically adjusting the location of the refinery

(d) Algebratizing the problem

a CMT spreadsheet (Figure 3a). Others use a function graph and trace capabilities of CMT to approximate a solution (Figure 3b). Some confirm their graphical solution by adjusting the x step size for the table and scanning the revised table of values.

Other students may choose to use the geometric representation and the transformation capabilities of CMT to find the reflection image (point D') of point D under a reflection across $\overline{AB}$ (Figure 3c). Note that $\overline{CD'}$ intersects $\overline{AB}$ at a point, say, R, a conjectured location for the refinery. To prove that the refinery should be located at point R, students show that $CR + RD$ is the minimal length satisfying the problem conditions. The method of proof varies among students. Some note that the reflection image of point R is itself

and since line reflections preserve segment lengths, the amount of piping is given by $CR + RD' = CD'$ and appeal to the fact that the shortest distance between two points is the length of the segment connecting them.

Other students, some with adroit teacher questioning, assume that a different point, on $\overline{AB}$, say Q, is the optimal location for the refinery. Using the Triangle Inequality, they argue that:

$$CQ + QD = CQ + QD' > CD' = CR + RD.$$

Once the location of the refinery has been determined, then the minimum length of piping can be found using the Pythagorean Theorem. Here $CD' = \sqrt{14^2 + 20^2} = \sqrt{596}$ or about 24.4 km as in Figure 3d. But now the mathematical

Figure 3. Modeling and strategic CMT use

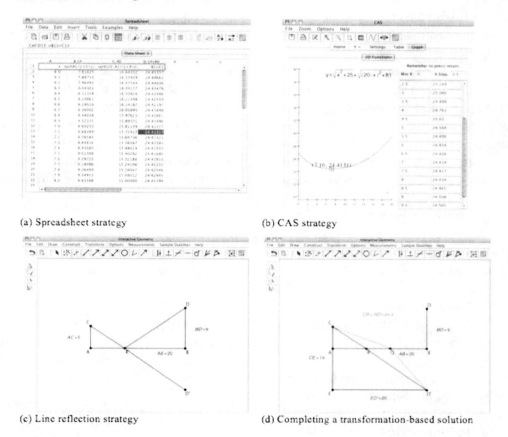

(a) Spreadsheet strategy

(b) CAS strategy

(c) Line reflection strategy

(d) Completing a transformation-based solution

solution must be interpreted back into the real-world context. How should the mathematical solution be adjusted from an actual contractor perspective?

This Optimal Refinery Location problem illustrates appropriate selection and strategic use of CMT for modeling a problem situation. It also illustrates that in a CMT environment, students are also influenced by their preference(s) for representation as discussed in Keller and Hirsch (1998). The reader is encouraged to consider the potential advantages of organizing a CCSSM-oriented curriculum around mathematical modeling by enumerating the mathematical practices and mathematical content standards that are addressed in the refinery location problem.

CMT SUPPORTING SPECIFIC CONTENT STANDARDS

The strategic selection and use of features of CMT will be elaborated in four additional examples that illustrate affordances of the software within specific CCSSM content domains and standards. Both general purpose tools and custom apps will be exemplified with screen shots to help demonstrate the diverse range of software capabilities. Connections between specific CMT tools and apps and the CCSSM standards that identify specific technology use will be addressed throughout this section. The potential of CMT to support the attainment of other CCSSM standards is also noted.

The first example features a CAS environment in which students work with symbolic representations to perform algebraic manipulations and to draw graphs and view tables for explicitly defined and implicitly defined functions. Connections to use of an interactive (dynamic) geometry environment are also made. Second, a specifically designed geometry app is showcased to illustrate an inquiry-oriented, transformations approach to congruence of triangles. In the third and fourth examples we illustrate the role of CMT in producing a variety of plots for both univariate and bivariate data, for modeling data patterns, for computing regression equations and correlations, and for simulating outcomes of a probabilistic situation.

Reasoning with Equations and Inequalities

In the CCSSM Reasoning with Equations and Inequalities domain (A-REI), students are expected to solve systems of equations in two variables algebraically and graphically. Consider the CCSSM standard that expects students to find the points of intersection between lines and circles (A-REI.7) and the following task, adapted from the Illustrative Mathematics Project (Illustrative Mathematics, 2012). As with the oil refinery problem, CMT provides students opportunities to make decisions regarding which specific tool(s) to strategically use in this task. As a suite of tools, CMT also acknowledges representation preferences students may have.

The Circle and the Line: *Draw the circle with equation $x^2 + y^2 = 1$ and the line with equation $y = 2x - 1$ on the same coordinates. Then find all the solutions to this system of equations.*

As shown in Figure 4a, students may decide to use the coordinate geometry tool in a dynamic geometry environment to draw the circle and the line, "construct" the intersections, and show coordinates for the two intersection points. Other students may decide to reason in a CAS environment where they may explore this problem in

various ways using tables, graphs, and algebraic reasoning.

In a CAS environment, students may use commands such as "factor," "expand," "simplify," and "solve" to find the intersection points algebraically. As shown in Figure 4b, students decide when it is beneficial to use various commands. In this process, students would provide mathematical justifications to reason between command inputs and their outputs. Students consider questions such as: Why did the solve command produce outputs of $x = 0$ or $x = \frac{4}{5}$? How can I justify that there are only two solutions for x? How did the solve command produce these two outputs algebraically? Students can also compare their algebraic solutions of $x = 0$ or $x = \frac{4}{5}$ to the intersection points $(0, -1)$ and $(0.8, 0.6)$ and make connections between their algebraic and graphical representations. Alternately, in a CAS environment, students might use the explicit equations of $y = \sqrt{1 - x^2}$ and $y = -\sqrt{1 - x^2}$ when reasoning with tables and graphs of the circle. As shown in Figure 4c, students might decide to examine a table on the x-interval $[-1,1]$ to see if corresponding y-values on the line are the same as corresponding y-values for either of the two equations that comprise the circle. By clicking on the intersection points to locate coordinates in a graphical representation, as shown in Figure 4d, students might verify that $(0, -1)$ and $(0.8, 0.6)$ are solutions to each equation.

Using CMT in different ways affords opportunities for students to be strategic users of technology and potentially amplify their thinking. As an extension of this task, some students investigate the general case of number of intersection points of a line and a circle by constructing dynamic general representations of lines and circles using sliders for parameters, a, b, and c in the equations $x^2 + y^2 = a$ and $y = bx + c$.

Figure 4. Various approaches to solving a system of nonlinear equations

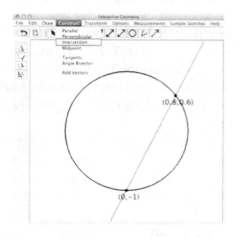

(a) Constructing intersection points

(b) Reasoning algebraically with a CAS

(c) Reasoning numerically using tables

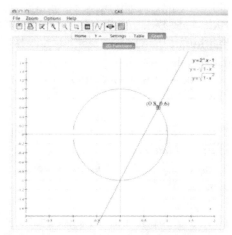

(d) Graphing equations to locate coordinates

The CAS general purpose tool allows one to manipulate symbolic expressions and equations, to compute results in approximate and exact forms, and to create, move between, and transform linked graphic and numeric representations of functions. For example, students can use the CAS to provide algebraic and graphical interpretations when exploring the effects on the graph of replacing $f(x)$ by $f(x) + k$, $kf(x)$, $f(kx)$, and $f(x + k)$ and for specific values of k, or find particular values of k given graphical representations (F-IF-3). In addition to the general tool, the Linear Programming custom app for Algebra and Functions allows students to analyze two-dimensional or three-dimensional linear programming problems by using constraint inequalities and an objective function to find the optimal value(s). Problems involving more than three variables can be examined using matrices in the CAS or numerically using a spreadsheet (A-REI.3; A-REI.6; 1A-REI.2).

Reasoning about Congruence

In CCSSM Geometry, high school students are to understand core ideas in geometry such as symmetry, similarity, and congruence through the perspective of rigid transformations or isometries. In a transformational approach to congruence, two figures are congruent if and only if there exists a sequence of rigid transformations that maps one figure onto the other. Students may explore different sequences of rigid transformations that will map a given figure onto another using the general purpose tools and custom apps in CMT (G-CO.2; G-CO.5). For example, the Transformations and Triangle Congruence custom app allows students to explore and test triangle congruence conditions such as the Side-Side-Side condition using different transformations. Since line reflections may be used to generate all other rigid transformations, this example will feature use of only the line reflection tool.

When Are Two Triangles Congruent? *Construct two triangles in which pairs of corresponding sides are the same length. Test if the two triangles are congruent.*

As shown in Figures 5a and 5b, students first create two triangles, $\triangle ABC$ and $\triangle DEF$, by changing lengths for each side, and explore using transformations to determine if $\triangle ABC$ can be mapped onto $\triangle DEF$ by a sequence of rigid motions. By clicking and dragging using the animated tool, students might drag a triangle to see, for example, if it is possible to make $\triangle ABC$ coincide with $\triangle DEF$. Alternatively, to find a sequence of line reflections that map $\triangle ABC$ onto $\triangle DEF$, students might begin by reflecting $\triangle ABC$ across the perpendicular bisector of $\overline{AD}$ (Figure 5c). If the triangles do not coincide, students can then use another reflection across the perpendicular bisector of $\overline{EB'}$ (Figure 5c). So the sequence of these two line reflections maps $\triangle ABC$

onto $\triangle DEF$. Therefore, $\triangle ABC \cong \triangle DEF$. Other students may recognize that the orientation of the two triangles is such that a translation may map $\triangle ABC$ onto $\triangle DEF$. This can be easily tested using the translation tool. The magnitude and direction of the translation is represented by a vector connecting a pre-image and image point, as shown in Figure 5d.

Comparing the approaches in Figures 5c and 5d suggests further experimentation enabling students to discover that the composite reflections across two parallel lines is a translation. As with all conjectures, students should be encouraged to justify (proof) their conjecture or provide a counterexample.

In addition to the Transformations and Triangle Congruence custom app, students can use the Transformations and Triangle Similarity custom app to explore whether two specified side or angle measures are sufficient to create similar triangles. Here a sequence of a size transformation followed by one or more rigid transformations is used to test the similarity of two triangles (G-SRT.2). Students may use two related tool environments in CMT: Synthetic and Coordinate Interactive Geometry. Using these general purpose tools, students may construct, measure, manipulate, transform, and animate geometric figures in a dynamic geometry environment (cf. G-CO.12).

Interpreting Data

In Interpreting Categorical and Quantitative Data (S-ID), Spreadsheet and Data Analysis general purpose tools afford both numerical and graphical options for displaying and analyzing univariate and bivariate data. The expansive collection of pre-loaded data sets can be accessed from both general purpose and custom apps across the Statistics and Probability and Algebra and Functions strands of CMT. The selection of data sets can be done to purposefully target the teaching and learning of particular statistical ideas such

Figure 5. Triangular congruence custom app to explore a sequence of rigid transformations that maps one triangle onto the other

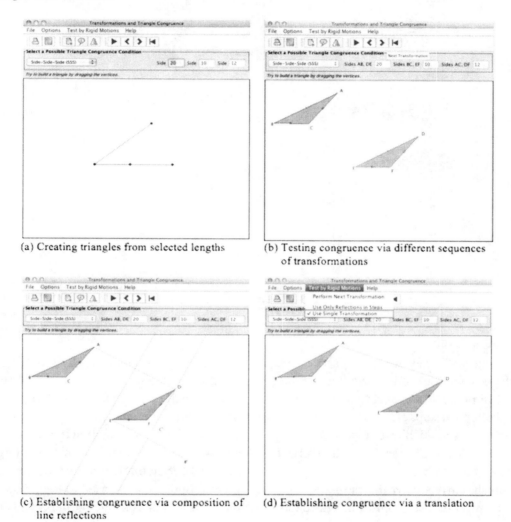

(a) Creating triangles from selected lengths

(b) Testing congruence via different sequences of transformations

(c) Establishing congruence via composition of line reflections

(d) Establishing congruence via a translation

as univariate plots, regression, residuals, or data transformations, among others (NCTM, 2012a).

Some bivariate quantitative data may lend themselves to the use of both univariate and bivariate data analysis. Consider the following problem adapted from NCTM (2012b):

Leg and Stride Length: *Examine the data in Figure 6 showing leg and stride measurements for 20 people from the Vine neighborhood walking group. Determine a relationship (if any) between these two variables.*

Taken as two separate discrete sets of univariate data, students may be inclined to summarize, represent, and interpret these data with comparative box-plots or histograms to analyze the shape center and spread of each individual variable (S-ID.1-3). Even before constructing plots of these variables, the context of the data set affords students an opportunity to make pre-

Figure 6. Sample leg and stride lengths of walkers

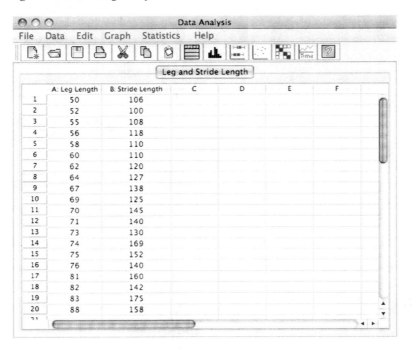

dictions about what they would expect to see. Should the distributions of leg length and stride length look similar? Would a particular plot type help to make comparisons of these variables more salient? Students should think critically about the utility of select displays of these data, and reflect on the choices they make.

Students should recognize that the use of comparative box plots or histograms limits the depth of inquiry into the relationship between two variables. See Figure 7a and Figure 7b, respectively. To build on this notion, students should consider what information is lost in a comparison of the individual variables. This may further motivate the need for a scatterplot to examine the bivariate data. The Data Analysis and Modeling tools each have specifically designed environments for regression modeling in a scatterplot graph window. Tools for correlation and/or regression analysis can be employed to explore this relationship and to make predictions about trends and patterns.

A number of options are available for examining the potential of a linear model (or other models such as exponential or power) with both user-defined drawing and a least squares regression line. The representation in Figure 7c shows a moveable modeling line for estimating a line of best fit. Some features such as the "exclude points" option can be used to toggle on and off the inclusion of possible outliers. To better understand how outliers affect regression models, it would be particularly important for students to interpret the meaning of the slope and y-intercepts of these models (S-ID.7). Plot information shown side-by-side with the graph also affords a combination of graphical and symbolic representations that can inform the interpretation of the correlation coefficient in such a linear situation (S-ID.8). Figure 7d illustrates the exclusion of an apparent outlier by displaying it in a different color. The updated regression line and equation appear in a second color next to additional plot information.

Figure 7. Univariate and bivariate graphical representations for the leg and stride length data

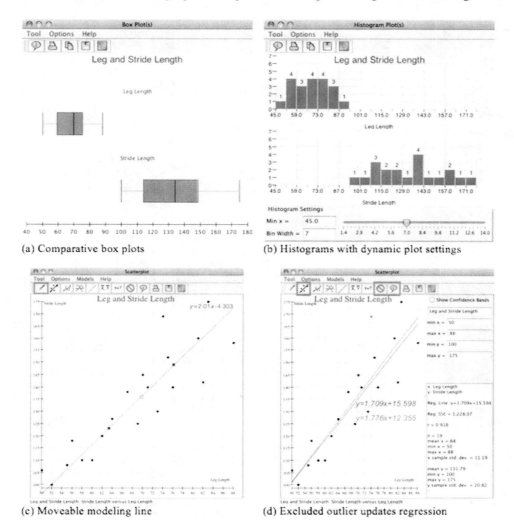

(a) Comparative box plots

(b) Histograms with dynamic plot settings

(c) Moveable modeling line

(d) Excluded outlier updates regression

Simulating Chance Situations

The Statistics and Probability strand is further exemplified with an example of using the CMT Simulation tool. The Simulation tool can be used to model and generate data for random processes such as flipping a coin, rolling a die, and generating random numbers. Consider the blood type scenario described in NCTM (2012c):

Waiting for Blood Donors: *Following the Memorial Day holiday weekend, the Plainwell blood center is in need of 4 pints of type B blood. Assuming that donors arrive independently and randomly, how many donors, on average, would the blood center have to test in order to obtain 4 donors with type B blood?*

Students can use the Simulation app to model this situation in several different ways as a compound event (7.SP.8). Figure 8 illustrates how to build the layers in the model and some quantitative and graphical results after conducting 1 and then 100 runs of the simulation. The first screen

Figure 8. Simulating waiting time for blood donors

(a) Build complex events

(b) Add layers to model in tree and bottom-up fashion

(c) Columns show results of one run

(d) A histogram for each visible layer of model (100 runs)

shots show which items in the Build menu were selected to create this compound event: "Create Custom Event," "Count Till See," then "Sum of" (See Figure 8a). The "Custom Event Editor" window, shown in Figure 8b, allows the user to specify the name of possible blood types and their frequency or weight of occurrence.

The use of simulation software such as that available in CMT should be done with a purpose in mind. Throughout their investigation of this situation, students should be encouraged to make predictions before running a simulation and to

carefully interpret the results of the simulation. For instance, they could begin by using the simulation controls to conduct one trial, then make sense of the quantitative results before conducting another (shown in Figure 8c). Reflection on the set-up and conduct of individual trials can also be extended to making connections to the theoretical model (S-IC.2). Prediction and reflection are important practices in using technology to learn and explore new concepts.

After making sense of the tabular results, students can conduct a large number of runs displaying the results in histograms to analyze trends in the distributions of the simulation data, as in Figure 8d. To strengthen students' representational fluency, students should be encouraged to make explicit connections among the numeric, graphic, and theoretical representations. Analogous to interpreting the simulation results in the numeric representation, the practices of predicting, acting (or building a model), and reflecting on the results can help students focus their attention on the connections between the use of software and the statistics and probability topics they are learning.

Knowledge of the available features in the suite of tools offered by CMT is an important prerequisite for making decisions about which tools are most appropriate in a given mathematical or statistical situation. Students' thinking about the use of these tools can be directed by the selection of appropriate tools, but also by predicting, acting on, and reflecting on their use of these tools and representations. Connections from mathematics and statistics content to specifically designed technology tools can be exemplified through rich, contextual tasks. The prior tasks illustrate a sample of the far-reaching applicability of CMT across the CCSSM. In the following section we discuss specific resources that will aid teachers in making effective instructional use of CMT.

CMT WEB PORTAL AND RESOURCES

Building a support structure that will enable teachers to capitalize on the affordances provided by *Core Math Tools* in effective implementation of the CCSSM will require continued time, effort, and expertise. The seed of such an effort has begun with the CMT portal at NCTM's Website. The Web portal provides initial concrete exemplars developed by NCTM's Core Tools Task Force of how CMT can be productively used to address important domain clusters and to provide guidance for implementing the Standards for Mathematical

Practice. These exemplars have been constructed by drawing upon Task Force members' experience in building similar resources for other NCTM initiatives.

One exemplar illustrates how CMT interactive geometry, a spreadsheet, and CAS tools can be utilized together in modeling an optimization problem. Another exemplar illustrates how a custom app for slicing and visualization of three-dimensional figures can be combined with the general purpose tools for geometry, data analysis, and CAS to develop quadratics and conic sections. Yet another example uses the simulation and data analysis apps to model the dynamics of meeting blood supply demands (cf. NCTM, 2012c). Like the problems and tasks in this chapter, the sample lessons provide an introduction to features of the software and their potential use to support student attainment of selected standards.

As familiarity with CMT grows, the portal provides further assistance by providing a compiled summary of details about the built-in data sets, two of which are shown in Figure 9a. The Website includes extended descriptions to help teachers in selecting appropriate data sets to address specific statistical concepts and methods. Details about each data set are organized into categories that match the organization in the software—univariate or bivariate, and categorical or quantitative. Figure 9b illustrates how the Web descriptions include potential uses such as identifying outliers, developing measures of center and spread, and making inferences about statistical differences. The database of descriptions increases the usability of the software with any CCSSM-oriented curriculum.

A completely revised Help system was constructed to help optimize student and teacher use of CMT. In the reorganization, we have increased the focus and visibility on mathematical content and mathematical actions to help students in selecting a tool. We have also sought to retain the familiarity of how one finds specific software features, as shown in the topics at a glance in

Figure 9. Built-in and additional web resource to support use of CMT

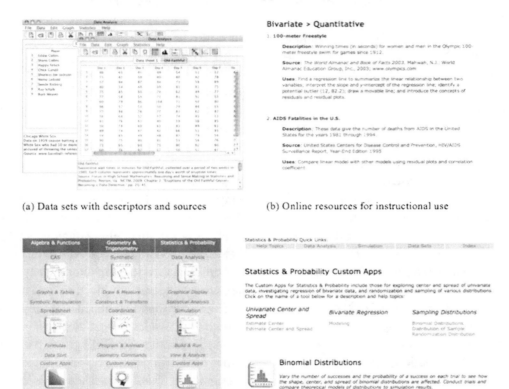

(a) Data sets with descriptors and sources   (b) Online resources for instructional use

(c) Help topics at a glance   (d) Detailed help with quick navigation options

Figure 9c. As with the software, the Help has multiple access points and paths to the content through hyperlinks and a navigation bar (e.g., see Figure 9d). The Help is available as a PDF under "Info" on the initial screens or from the Website. The PDF provides a simple familiar mechanism for searching and easily printing. Additional how-to content and video walk-throughs are planned. The Help represents a significant effort to increase the transparency between the software and the CCSSM.

As with similar ongoing NCTM initiatives, the task force hopes that this seedling Website will continue to grow both in diversity and robustness to match the scope of the software. The Website with its instructional exemplars, links to data set descriptors, and Help documentation, underscores some advantages of CMT over other existing free mathematical software in terms of the sheer mathematical and statistical scope of the resources and different points of access, use, time investment, and depth. CMT provides the value of several typically stand-alone software packages in a single linked software toolkit. Additionally, CMT is accompanied by focused features of a companion Website and app resources. An advantage of CMT is that these resources come bundled together in a reasonable and manageable form. Furthermore, CMT keeps a wider range of the types and uses of software at the forefront through a visual organization that emphasizes the mathematics and strategies. The visual interface is intended to keep the practice of "strategic use of technology" in the forefront as a habit of mind.

Figure 10. Connection and interplay among content, curriculum, and technology

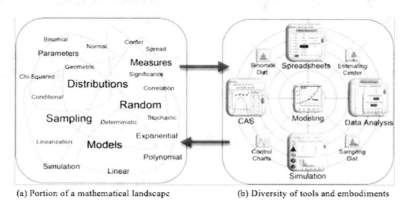

    (a) Portion of a mathematical landscape   (b) Diversity of tools and embodiments

CHALLENGES AND IMPLICATIONS

Throughout this chapter, we have highlighted some of the features and uses of *Core Math Tools* in CCSSM-oriented reasoning, problem solving, and modeling. We have attempted to bring together tested design elements and uses that span the collective and linked nature of the software, providing a more coherent and integrated technology approach to school mathematics. As we sought to create software for high school mathematics that embodies and encourages equitable enactment of the mathematical practices and standards envisioned by the CCSSM, in this section we discuss implications, challenges, and future directions for CMT in an era of CCSSM implementation.

Design and Enactment Challenges

CMT brings together a diverse suite of tools providing multiple entrance points and creating a multitude of paths to, from, and through the mathematical landscape. A challenge for both students and teachers is to build sufficient experience traversing the landscape to select an appropriate route. The choice of path depends upon the context and goals of the task. Consider the complex network of paths of data and distributions partially illustrated previously and in Figure 10. When calculating mean and variance for a given table of values, a data analysis tool is a natural fit and should be almost a reflex choice. However, a custom app exists for estimating these values graphically. But also, the spreadsheet and CAS can be used to compute them and to evaluate specific distributions such as a normal, binomial, or exponential (e.g., "=average(A1:A50)" or "binomialcdf(10,0.8,6)." Furthermore, these tools sometimes can be easier to use and often in a more direct manner than a data analysis tool in non-standard contexts, such as fitting data with a model not built-in to the software (e.g., $y = a + \dfrac{b}{x - c}$). Spreadsheets readily compute transformations of the data to linearize the data (e.g., $\left(Y_i - a\right)^{-1}$). The CAS can be used to fit data using an interactive graph with parameters a, b, and c. Central to navigating these paths is the ability to thinking numerically, graphically, symbolically, and dynamically.

Knowing the available mathematical and technological trails requires a wealth of experiences. A novice needs to know that a spreadsheet or data analysis tool will compute a chi-square (x^2) value for a contingency table or cross tabulation, while an expert might need to produce a table using the simulation tool (e.g., 7-SP.8c, S-IC.2, S-MD.1).

Spreadsheets are particularly valuable in modeling complex population growth or decline (S-M) where the outcomes may be dependent upon several conditions (e.g., harvesting, birth rate, maturity, morbidity rate) or other concurrent models such as food supply or environment. Spreadsheets are also useful in answering "what if" questions where multiple numeric answers are needed. An inherent challenge in our design and development work and in professional development for users is to provide a sufficient map to traverse this complexity while recognizing the flexibility in tool selection by either an individual or a curriculum.

Even where somewhat separate paths converge, as in the case of randomization (S-MD, S-IC.3), CMT frequently provides multiple embodiments. Randomization-related tools vary from the general purpose simulation tool to focused distribution custom apps. One custom app explores the "sampling" process, while another examines binomial distributions. Other paths are less visible, such as using the CAS to connect the binomial distributions to binomials for polynomials (e.g., "expand$((p+q)^{10})$" where p is probability of success). Yet other paths lead to new territory. For example, randomness is extended through an advanced app for control charts widely used in industry to monitor production processes.

A suite of tools is not sufficient to develop strategic selection and use of technology. Resources such as those on the CMT Website or the Illustrative Mathematics site can suggest new opportunities to both utilize different tools and exploit the juxtaposition of tools. Considerable work is needed to bring these illustrative examples to the forefront as work toward implementation of the CCSSM continues.

Implications for Teacher Education

With the needs of future teachers in mind, mathematics teacher educators should provide opportunities for teacher candidates... to explore and learn mathematics using technology in ways that build confidence and understanding of the technology and mathematics... model appropriate uses of a variety of established and new applications of technology as tools to develop a deep understanding of mathematics in varied contexts... make informed decisions about appropriate and effective uses of technology... [and] develop and practice teaching lessons that take advantage of the ability of the technology to enrich and enhance the learning of mathematics. (Association of Mathematics Teacher Educators, 2006, p. 2)

Supporting the NCTM's position statement on technology and teaching and learning, the previous citation by the Association of Mathematics Teacher Educators (AMTE) is still pertinent today to ensure that all mathematics teachers and teacher candidates have opportunities for integrating technology to enhance the teaching and learning of mathematics in an integrated, coherent, and equitable way. As discussed in this chapter, CMT provides a viable solution to the problems faced related to the integration of mathematical software in high school mathematics. Similarly, we believe that CMT is an affordable and accessible technology tool set for professional development providers and mathematics teacher educators when providing teachers support for understanding and implementing the CCSSM. In addition, the ease of access to CMT offers a viable option for supporting collaborations with mathematics teacher educators, professional development providers, and school district teachers from different states when implementing the CCSSM content and mathematical practices.

Mathematics educators at several universities are now examining the potential affordances of teacher candidates having access to the same CMT software in their on-campus learning as they will have in their intern and first-year teaching experiences, thus establishing a technology continuum from campus to classrooms. Equally important is that the open-source design of CMT ensures that students at those high schools will also have free access to CMT.

CONCLUSION

Core Math Tools was developed to provide equitable access to technological tools identified in the CCSSM as school districts and individual teachers plan for or initiate implementation of those standards. CMT was designed so that it could serve as a bridge among other mathematical and statistical software (free and commercial) and other technologies such as graphing calculators. The potential transfer of knowledge, including selection of tools to match tasks at hand, as well as the intended use of technology, guided the design and development of CMT throughout. Among the advantages of CMT are that the software is open-source, learner-oriented, flexible, can be used with any CCSSM-oriented high school mathematics program, and can be readily used by a wide range of teachers, students, and teacher educators at various levels of mathematical and technological maturity.

In closing, we note that simply having access to mathematical and statistical software tools like CMT is not sufficient. Curriculum materials that integrate that software and teachers with both the disposition toward, and knowledge of, using technology strategically play critical roles in mediating students' use of technological tools and what they ultimately learn (cf. King-Sears, 2009; Roschelle et al., 2010; Zbiek & Heid, 2012).

ACKNOWLEDGMENT

This chapter is based on work supported by the National Science Foundation (NSF) under Grants Nos. ESI-0137718, DRL-1020312, and DRL-1201917. Opinions expressed are those of the authors and do not necessarily reflect the views of the NSF. The authors would also like to acknowledge the creative contributions of James Laser (Western Michigan University) to the design and development of *Core Math Tools* and content for its portal at the NCTM website.

REFERENCES

Association of Mathematics Teacher Educators. (2006). *Preparing teachers to use technology to enhance the learning of mathematics: A position of the association of mathematics teacher educators*. Retrieved from http://www.amte.net/sites/all/themes/amte/resources/AMTETechnology-PositionStatement.pdf

Begle, E. G. (1973). Some lessons learned by SMSG. *Mathematics Teacher*, *66*, 207–214.

Brown, A. (1992). Design experiments: Theoretical and methodological challenges in creating complex interventions in classroom settings. *Journal of the Learning Sciences*, *2*(2), 141–178. doi:10.1207/s15327809jls0202_2.

Collins, A. (1992). Toward a design science of education. In Scanlon, E., & O'Shea, T. (Eds.), *New directions in educational technology* (pp. 15–22). New York: Springer-Verlag. doi:10.1007/978-3-642-77750-9_2.

Common Core State Standards Initiative (CCSSI). (2010). *Common core state standards for mathematics*. Washington, DC: National Governors Association Center for Best Practices and the Council of Chief State School Officers.

Conference Board of the Mathematical Sciences (CBMS). (1983). *The mathematical sciences curriculum K–12: What is still fundamental and what is not*. Report to National Science Board Commission on Precollege Education in Mathematics, Science, and Technology. Washington, DC: CBMS.

Confrey, J., & Krupa, E. E. (2010). *Curriculum design, development, and implementation in an era of common core state standards: Summary report of a conference.* Arlington, VA: Center for the Study of Mathematics Curriculum.

Design-Based Research Collective. (2003). Design-based research: An emerging paradigm for educational inquiry. *Educational Researcher, 32*(1), 5–8. doi:10.3102/0013189X032001005.

Fey, J. T., Atchison, W. F., Good, R. A., Heid, M. K., Johnson, J., Kantowski, M. G., & Rosen, L. P. (1984). *Computing and mathematics: The impact on secondary school curricula.* College Park, MD: National Council of Teachers of Mathematics and the University of Maryland.

Fey, J. T., Cuoco, A., Kieran, C., McMullin, L., & Zbiek, R. M. (Eds.). (2003). *Computer algebra systems in secondary school mathematics education.* Reston, VA: National Council of Teachers of Mathematics.

Fey, J. T., & Hirsch, C. R. (2007). The case of core-plus mathematics. In Hirsch, C. R. (Ed.), *Perspectives on the design and development of school mathematics curricula.* Reston, VA: National Council of Teachers of Mathematics.

Gravemeijer, K. (1994). Educational development and developmental research in mathematics education. *Journal for Research in Mathematics Education, 35*(5), 443–471. doi:10.2307/749485.

Hart, E. W., Hirsch, C. R., & Keller, S. A. (2007). Amplifying student learning in mathematics using curriculum-embedded Java-based software. In Martin, W. G., & Strutchens, M. (Eds.), *The learning of mathematics: 2007 yearbook of the national council of teachers of mathematics* (pp. 175–202). Reston, VA: NCTM.

Heid, M. K. (1997). The technological revolution and the reform of school mathematics. *American Journal of Education, 106*, 5–61. doi:10.1086/444175.

Heid, M. K. (2005). Technology in mathematics education: Tapping into visions of the future. In Masalski, W. J. (Ed.), *Technology-supported mathematics learning environments: Sixty-seventh yearbook of the national council of teachers of mathematics* (pp. 345–366). Reston, VA: NCTM.

Hirsch, C. R., Fey, J. T., Hart, E. W., Schoen, H., Watkins, A. E., & Ritsema, B. E., et al. (2008). *Core-plus mathematics: Course 2* (2nd ed.). Columbus, OH: Glencoe/McGraw-Hill.

Illustrative Mathematics. (2012). *A-REI the circle and the line.* Retrieved May 14, 2012, from http://illustrativemathematics.org/illustrations/223

Keller, B. A., & Hirsch, C. (1998). Student preferences for representations of functions. *International Journal of Mathematical Education in Science and Technology, 29*, 1–17. doi:10.1080/0020739980290101.

King-Sears, M. (2009). Universal design for learning: Technology and pedagogy. *Learning Disability Quarterly, 32*(4), 199–201.

Masalski, W. J. (Ed.). (2005). *Technology-supported mathematics learning environments: Sixty-seventh yearbook of the national council of teachers of mathematics.* Reston, VA: NCTM.

National Council of Teachers of Mathematics. (2011). *Technology in teaching and learning mathematics: A position statement of the national council of teachers of mathematics.* Retrieved from http://www.nctm.org/about/content.aspx?id=31734

National Council of Teachers of Mathematics. (2012a). *Data sets.* Retrieved May 14, 2012, from http://www.nctm.org/standards/content.aspx?id=32705

National Council of Teachers of Mathematics. (2012b). *Relating leg length to stride length.* Retrieved May 14, 2012, from http://www.nctm.org/uploadedFiles/Statistics%20and%20Probability%20Problem%202.pdf

National Council of Teachers of Mathematics. (2012c). *Waiting for blood donors.* Retrieved May 14, 2012, from http://www.nctm.org/uploaded-Files/Waiting%20for%20Donor_2(2).pdf

Pea, R. D. (1987). Cognitive technologies for mathematics education. In Schoenfeld, A. H. (Ed.), *Cognitive science and mathematics education* (pp. 89–122). Hillsdale, NJ: Lawrence Erlbaum Associates.

Pew Internet & American Life Project. (2009, September). *Parent-teen cell phone survey.* Retrieved from http://www.pewInternet.org/Reports/2009/Teens-and-Sexting/Survey/Topline.aspx

Robitaille, D. F., & Travers, K. J. (1992). International studies of achievement in mathematics. In Grouws, D. A. (Ed.), *Handbook of research on mathematics teaching and learning* (pp. 687–709). Reston, VA: National Council of Teachers of Mathematics.

Roschelle, J., Shechtman, N., Tatar, D., Hegedus, S., Hopkins, B., & Empson, S. et al. (2010). Integration of technology, curriculum, and professional development for advancing middle school mathematics: Three large-scale studies. *American Educational Research Journal, 47*(4), 833–878. doi:10.3102/0002831210367426.

Schmidt, W. H., McKnight, C. C., & Raizen, S. A. (1997). *A splintered vision: An investigation of U.S. science and mathematics education.* Dordrecht, Netherlands: Kluwer.

Schoenfeld, A. H. (2002). Making mathematics work for all children: Issues of standards, testing, and equity. *Educational Researcher, 31*(1), 13–25. doi:10.3102/0013189X031001013.

Usiskin, Z. (1985). We need another revolution in secondary school mathematics. In Hirsch, C. R. (Ed.), *The secondary school mathematics curriculum: 1985 yearbook of the national council of teachers of mathematics (NCTM)* (pp. 1–21). Reston, VA: NCTM.

Zbiek, R. M., & Heid, M. K. (2012). Using computer algebra systems to develop big ideas in mathematics with connections to the common core state standards for mathematics. In Hirsch, C. R., Lappan, G. T., & Reys, B. J. (Eds.), *Curriculum issues in an era of common core state standards for mathematics* (pp. 149–160). Reston, VA: National Council of Teachers of Mathematics.

Zbiek, R. M., Heid, M. K., Blume, G., & Dick, T. P. (2007). Research on technology in mathematics education: The perspective of constructs. In Lester, F. K. Jr., (Ed.), *Second handbook of research on mathematics teaching and learning* (pp. 1169–1207). Charlotte, NC: Information Age.

KEY TERMS AND DEFINITIONS

Cognitive Amplifiers: Cognitive tools such as written language and more recently digital technologies that amplify cognitive processes.

Common Core State Standards Initiative: A national education initiative organized by the National Governors Association and the Council of Chief State School Officers to collaborate with states in developing Common Core State Standards for grade K–12 Mathematics and English Language Arts that would then be adopted by the states as a means to bring alignment of learning expectations across the nation.

Core Math Tools: A suite of interactive software tools for algebra and functions, geometry and trigonometry, and statistics and probability, downloadable from http://www.nctm.org/coremathtools/. The tools are appropriate for use with any high school mathematics curriculum and compatible with the Common Core State Standards for Mathematics in terms of content and mathematical practices.

Curriculum-Based Software: Software developed concurrently with the development of curriculum materials through an extended design experiment.

Equitable Access to Technology: Closing the "digital divide" or educational gap between the economically advantaged and disadvantaged, providing students and schools with physical access to technology resources, maintenance, and services not otherwise available.

Mathematical Modeling: A systematic process of mathematically representing an applied problem situation, analyzing or solving the corresponding mathematical representation, and then interpreting and evaluating the solution in terms of the original problem.

Online Resources: Internet-based resources for supporting implementation of the CCSSM, including designed Web sites and Web portals that offer links to lessons, exemplar extended descriptions of available materials, and technology tools.

Strategic User of Tools: One who makes informed decisions about which tool or tools to use and why; the decision is based on knowledge of available tools and consideration of the appropriateness for the mathematical context and representation types in question.

ENDNOTES

[1] Members of the NCTM Core Tools Task Force were Fred Dillon (Strongsville High School, Ohio); Christian Hirsch, Chair (Western Michigan University); Patrick Hopfensperger (University of Wisconsin–Milwaukee); Brin Keller (Michigan State University); Henry Kepner (Emeritus, University of Wisconsin–Milwaukee); Gary Martin (Auburn University); Rose Mary Zbiek (Pennsylvania State University); David Barnes (NCTM Liaison).

Chapter 2
Supporting Mathematical Communication through Technology

Chandra Hawley Orrill
University of Massachusetts Dartmouth, USA

Drew Polly
University of North Carolina at Charlotte, USA

ABSTRACT

Technology has the potential to support the creation and use of mathematical representations for exploring, reasoning about, and modeling cognitively demanding mathematical tasks. In this chapter, the authors argue that one of the key affordances of these dynamic representations is the synergistic relationship they can play with communication in the mathematics classroom. The authors highlight the ways in which technology-based representations can support mathematical communication in the classroom through a series of vignettes. They conclude with a discussion of the development of teachers' Technological Pedagogical and Content Knowledge (TPACK) for supporting the implementation of dynamic representations.

INTRODUCTION

Communication and representation play prominent roles in modern mathematics education. They are incorporated as goals in standards documents from the mathematics education community (NCTM, 2000, 2006) and policymakers (National Governor's Association/Chief Council of State School Officers, 2010; U.S. Department of Education, 2008). Specifically, the new Common Core State Standards for Mathematics (Common Core; NGA/CCSSO, 2010), adopted by 45 states, includes *Standards for Mathematical Practice*, that embody processes all K-12 teachers are expected to consistently enact in their classroom. One avenue for addressing communication and representation

DOI: 10.4018/978-1-4666-4086-3.ch002

in the mathematics classroom involves the use of cognitively-demanding mathematical tasks that benefit from students' interactions with digital mathematical representations as a medium for fostering communication (Henningsen & Stein, 1997; Huferd-Ackles, Fuson, & Sherin, 2004; Orill & Polly, 2012).

Digital technologies have potential to support teachers' enactment of mathematical practices by supporting students' creation of mathematical representations, their modeling of mathematical situations, and their computation within the context of exploring cognitively-demanding mathematical tasks (Battista & Clements, 2007; Clements & Battista, 2001; Wenglinsky, 1998; Zbiek, Heid, Blume, & Dick, 2007). Technologies, such as Geometer's Sketchpad (Johnson, 2002; Leong & Lim-Teo, 2003), spreadsheets (Erbas, Ledford, Orrill, & Polly, 2005), and virtual manipulatives (Polly, 2011; Steen, Brooks, & Lyon, 2006) allow students to create dynamic representations, which they can construct and manipulate to deeply explore mathematical concepts in ways that are impractical or impossible outside of the digital environment. Further, the use of these technologies has been empirically linked to gains in students' mathematical understanding (e.g. Polly, 2008; Bitter & Hatfield, 1994; Leong & Lim-Teo, 2003; Roberts, 1980; Steen, Brooks, & Lyon, 2006; Wenglinsky, 1998).

In this chapter, we examine the synergistic relationship between digital, dynamic representations and the communication they support. To do this, we provide snapshots of classroom learning in which dynamic representations support meaningful communication. Through these snapshots, we provide insight into four different ways that dynamic representation can support meaningful conversations about mathematics and students' development of related Standards for Mathematical Practice from the Common Core State Standards for Mathematics. We conclude by exploring the interplay between communication, technology, representation, and cognitive

demand of mathematical tasks. We also consider the implications for teacher knowledge if creating communication-rich, technology-enhanced, representationally-rich classrooms is our goal.

BACKGROUND

In this section, we explain how technology-based representations and communication are interconnected in the mathematics classroom. In order to situate this view, we present a brief overview of the literature on the importance of communication in the mathematics classroom followed by a discussion of the role of representations in promoting mathematical learning. We work from a position that mathematical learning is best achieved through the use of high cognitively demanding tasks (Stein, Grover, & Henningsen, 1996), therefore we also discuss representations in these contexts. We end the section by examining the promise of dynamic representations to support communication in mathematics classrooms.

Communication

Communication in mathematics classrooms is done through verbal, drawn, and written means. Naturally, discussion is a critical component of communication. The role of discussion in supporting student learning is prevalent and persuasive in the mathematics education literature (e.g., Franke, Kazemi, & Battey, 2007). The *Principles and Standards for School Mathematics* (PSSM; NCTM, 2000), the Common Core State Standards (Common Core) and findings from a variety of research (e.g., Boston & Smith, 2009; Cobb, Yackel, & McClain, 2000; Hufferd-Ackles, Fuson, & Sherin, 2004; Ryve, 2006; van Es & Sherin, 2008) confirm the importance of communication in the mathematics classroom. For example, the Common Core outlines two important Standards of Practice that specifically require mathematical sharing among students in the classroom.

First, the Common Core asserts that students at all grades should engage in constructing viable arguments about mathematics as well as critiquing the arguments of others. Second, the Standards of Practice focus on developing precision, which is grounded in communication of mathematical ideas between participants. Of particular interest to our assertions about the role of representations, the precision standard explicitly calls for students to "communicate precisely to others" (Chief Council of State School Officers (CCSSO), 2010, p. 7).

The focus on discourse in mathematics is grounded in constructivist and socio-constructivist perspectives on learning. These theories assert that sense making and learning are explicitly linked to collaboration and communication among learners who become participants in broader communities of learning (Cobb, 1994; Cobb, Wood, & Yackel 1993). Hufferd-Ackles, Fuson, & Sherin (2004) explained that in a constructivist classroom, "participants consider all members of the community to be constructing their own knowledge and reflecting on and discussing this knowledge" (p. 83). In short, learning is a communication-based endeavor as a student can neither learn to build an effective argument nor critique another's argument without engaging in some kind of interaction with the other learner(s) and/or the teacher.

A growing body of research has demonstrated that the kinds of communication had in the mathematics classroom matters (Cobb, et al., 2000; van Es & Sherin, 2008). Researchers have found that having deeply meaningful mathematically-grounded discussions is critical for learning (e.g., Kazemi & Stipek, 2001; Wood, Williams, & McNeal, 2006). That is having a classroom in which students are generally discussing mathematics yields lower levels of success than classrooms in which the discussions are grounded in argumentation, conjecture-testing, and other high cognitive demand activities (Stein, Engle, Smith, & Hughes, 2008). For example, this is a contrast between students' discussion focused on what they did to solve a task versus their discussion of why they did

it. It is also a contrast between students reporting their answers and explaining their approach in light of other approaches already shared, which requires a synthesis and evaluation (e.g., Wood, Williams, & McNeal, 2006). This research suggests that students need opportunities to explain their own thinking as well as engage with others' thinking, compare it to their own, and adapt their own thinking from that interaction.

Cognitive Demand

Cognitively demanding tasks provide students with the opportunities to explore, create mathematical representations, and communicate their mathematical thinking with both their classmates and their teacher. Reform-oriented approaches to mathematics teaching and learning advocate that teachers rely on cognitively demanding tasks as a basis for developing students' mathematical understanding (Boston & Smith, 2009; Hiebert et al., 1996; NCTM, 2000; Schoenfeld, 2002; Stein, Grover, & Henningsen, 1996). Smith and Stein (1998) established a framework for mathematical tasks focused on cognitive demand. These tasks are naturally supported by mathematical representations that can support reasoning and sensemaking. For example, Procedures with Mathematical Connections tasks involve mathematical computations and procedures, but require students to generate multiple representations or solve tasks in multiple ways. Consider the following tasks:

Find 1/6 of 1/2 using pattern blocks and one other representation. Draw your answer and explain your solution in terms of your representations and an equation (Smith & Stein, 1998).

Pattern blocks (real or virtual) can be used to model this situation so that a student can reason through it. Further, the student could rely on that model to clearly communicate his or her thinking to the class and to tie the pattern-block model to the equation.

Doing Mathematics tasks are non-routine problems that "require complex and non-algorithmic thinking" (Smith & Stein, 1998, p. 348). Students must determine how to solve the task, generate mathematical representations and communicate their mathematical thinking. Consider the following Doing Mathematics task:

There are 36 chairs in the room. If you want to put an equal number of chairs in each row, what are the different arrangements that you can make? Show your solution using both pictures and equations. Explain how you know that you have found all of the possible arrangements.

Students could generate various mathematical representations using arrays, a set model with groups of chairs, or by drawing various floor plans of the chairs. In order to satisfy the expectation of equations, students would be matching their representations to finding factors of 36, and then communicating their reasoning about how they know that they have found all of the factors of 36.

Representation

Students need opportunities to create and reason with mathematical representations while exploring tasks. Mathematical representations provide vehicles to make sense of problems, create a means for communicating mathematical ideas, and provide opportunities for learners of varying abilities to engage with problems from multiple entry points (Friedlander & Tabach, 2001; Preston & Garner, 2003). Representations also provide a means for students to connect the real world with the abstract world of symbols and numerals. Similarly, representations of various kinds can be included in the toolbox of approaches students use to strategically address a new situation. Further, representations serve as a pedagogical content tool (Rasmussen & Marrongelle, 2006) that can serve

as a vehicle for the teacher to move mathematical thinking further through discussion around it. Because of their potential as problem-solving tools, representations have been promoted widely in various curricular documents including the PSSM (NCTM, 2000) and the Common Core Standards (NGA/CCSSO, 2010).

Dynamic representations are particularly promising as supports for learning because of their dynamic affordances. That is, dynamic representations allow a means for students to actively interact with the mathematics. Students can make mathematical conjectures and test them immediately and they can "see" the situation from various perspectives, are particularly interesting because they enable a more interactive approach to mathematics. Of particular interest are the class of computer-based tools that support interactive engagement with mathematics in ways that allow the normally-unseeable to become seen. These include dynamic geometry tools that allow shapes to be created and explored; microworlds that allow engagement in modeling of and conjecture testing about different mathematical relationships; and tools that shift the work of calculating to the computer while supporting the student in finding patterns, making conjectures, and predicting results. As one example, Clements and Battista (1989) found that students who had completed computer-based Logo activities had more conceptually-oriented and mathematically specific views of geometric concepts, such as angles, than their peers. For example, non-Logo students referred to an angle as a corner, while Logo students talked about angles as turns and rotations. In summarizing research on the use of dynamic representations for supporting learning about fractions, Olive and Lobato (2008) noted that, "With static pictures the part is either embedded in the whole or is drawn separate from the whole...Using a computer tool that provides the child with the ability to dynamically pull a part out of a partitioned whole while leaving the whole intact, the child can enact the disembedding operation that is necessary to make the part-to-whole comparison." (p. 6). Examples such as these highlighting the advantages of moving toward dynamic representations are prevalent in the mathematics education literature.

In summary, representations are powerful tools for supporting reasoning about mathematical situations that are cognitively demanding. Dynamic representations extend the possibilities of representations by creating an environment in which students can move elements around that would be fixed in a paper-based environment, support calculation or presentation of a large number of examples to allow for pattern analysis, or otherwise engage students with mathematics in ways that are complicated or impossible in a paper-based environment.

Bringing Communication and Representation Together

Representations are tools for reasoning about mathematics that can also foster communication between and among the classroom participants about mathematical ideas. That is, they become the tools of social negotiation (e.g., Ares, Stroup, & Schademan, 2009). Social negotiation implies not just that there is discussion in a classroom, but that the discussion leads to the development of a shared understanding of the concept of interest. By using dynamic representations, participants in the classroom can easily make, test, and refine conjectures in an effort to move the collective understanding forward because the technology allows easy testing of a variety of mathematical conjectures.

To build a shared understanding of mathematics, all of the participants in the discussion need to be able to focus on the same ideas. In classrooms without representations, discussion is too often dominated by indefinite pronouns such as "that" or "it" because students are still developing their abilities to communicate precise ideas. This use of pronouns obscures the idea or concept being

discussed in ways that may lead different members of the same discussion to be discussing different things. By utilizing dynamic representations of the mathematics, we are invoking a set of artifacts to support the description and testing of ideas in ways that allow others to actually see those ideas and provide explicit explanations of them—and the teacher can reinforce the ongoing development of the needed mathematical language that will ultimately allow conversation without the representation. Further, the nature of dynamic representations allows them to be used to explore "what if" questions as they arise in the discussion and the invoking of representations allow teachers to better understand students' reasoning to better understand where their limitations might be as well as to highlight connections between and among those ideas in ways that build meaningful mathematical connections. Finally, digital represnetations allow generalization across sets of individual representations in such a way that allows aggregation of specific cases, thus supporting generalization from pattern identification rather than from guessing (e.g., Hegedus & Penuel, 2008).

In the next section, we present examples from our work in a variety of mathematical settings that illustrate the relationship between dynamic representations and communication. In each example, we highlight only certain affordances of the dynamic representations from our previous discussion. However, as these examples come from real classrooms – in elementary and middle schools, graduate courses, and professional development – they are rich and inevitably address a number of the affordances listed prior.

ROLE OF DYNAMIC REPRESENTATIONS IN CLASSROOMS

In this section, we present examples dynamic representations being used to enhance communication in the context of cognitively demanding mathematics. We focus on four specific roles representations can play in promoting learning: connecting multiple approaches, testing conjectures, socially negotiating meaning, and uncovering limitations in understanding. The examples are provided as illustrations of this interplay but are by no means exhaustive in terms of the myriad ways representation and communication interact. We conclude this section by highlighting some of the specific relationship types we have observed in our efforts with students and teachers.

Connecting Multiple Approaches

Dynamic representations provide students to explore a task from multiple perspectives and use multiple approaches to unpack the mathematical concepts embedded within the task. For example consider this task from a fifth grade classroom, " You have a rectangular-shaped room that you need to partition into three sections. Only two of the sections can be the same size and shape. Also, all of the sections must have 4 right angles. What are the different ways that you can partition the room? Write an equation for each way that shows how you split the room.

The class began by using an online virtual Geoboard on a computer. Many virtual Geoboards are available online for free, including the one used by students from the National Library of Virtual Manipulatives (http://nlvm. usu.edu/en/nav/frames_asid_172_g_2_t_3. html?open=activities). The students worked in pairs on this task sharing a computer. Figure 1 shows the work of Hector and Lina, two students who only used a 4 unit by 3 unit rectangle for the size of their room. As they worked, they talked to me (Polly) about their work.

Polly: *Tell me about how you chose the size of your rooms?*

Hector: *We knew that a 4 by 3 rectangle would give us 12 square units inside. This would make the fractions very easy to calculate when we have to write our equations.*

Figure 1. Student work for Hector and Lina

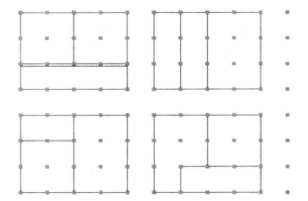

Lina: *By using 12 square units we just need to count the area of each of our sections to figure out the numerator for each of our fractions.*
Polly: *What about the denominators?*
Lina: *They will always be 12 since the total area is 12 square units.*

While Hector and Lina worked with rectangles that had an area of 12 square units, Tyrone and Kim worked with various sized rectangles (Figure 2). Shown next, they partitioned each rectangle with two sections that were one unit wide and one larger section on the right. When they were asked to explain their work, they commented:

Tyrone: *Since we knew that we had to partition rectangles into 3 different sections that we*

Figure 2. Student work for Tyrone and Kim

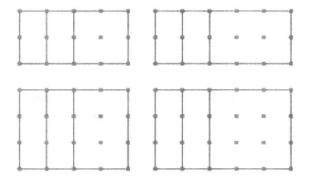

could make the first two sections the same and just modify the size of the third section.
Kim: *For our bottom rectangles we just made them a little bit longer than the top two rectangles.*

In an effort to see if students could make the connection from partitioning the shapes to determining the fraction, I asked them:

Polly: *In each of the top rectangles the two sections on the left are the same size. Would the fraction for those shapes be the same for each rectangle?*
Kim: *They should be.*
Polly: *Let's find out.*

Tyrone and Kim both count the number of square units in the large squares and then in each smaller section. They are recording numbers after they count each part.

Kim: *The rectangle in the top left has 8 square units and the 2 sections on the left each take up 2 of the 8 sections which is two-eighths of the whole rectangle.*
Hector: *That is different from the rectangle in the top right. That one has 10 square units. So the 2 sections on the left are 2 out of 10 units or two-tenths of the whole rectangle.*
Polly: *So are the fractions for the sections similar?*
Kim: *No. In the left rectangle those shapes are two-eighths. In the right rectangle those shapes are two-tenths. The sizes of the two large rectangles are different, so even though the sections are the same, the fractions can't be the same.*

The dynamic representations provided by the virtual Geoboard allowed students to explore various ways to partition a rectangular space and make the connections between the area of their sections and fractions. By using the technology, the representations could easily be generated and manipulated.

Conjecture Testing

Dynamic representations are indispensible tools for conjecture testing because of the ease with which they allow changes to be made and understood. For example, in one of our mathematics curriculum courses, students were exploring a particular task from the *Interactive Mathematics Program* (Fendel, Resek, Alper, & Fraser, 2011) high school mathematics series. The task asked students to explore situations in which a particular game would be fair or would favor one of two players. The purpose was to introduce a critical aspect of the Pythagorean Theorem—that the squares created by the sides lengths of the triangle have a particular relationship when the triangle formed between them is a right triangle. After working on the task as suggested in the book—using poster paper and exploration with paper squares—we introduced a dynamic sketch of the situation that had been created in *Geometer's SketchPad®* (GSP; Key Curriculum Press, 2010, See Figure 3). When we looked at the relationships create by dragging the vertices of the triangle created between the three squares, one of the students noticed that not only did a right triangle result in the sum of the areas of the two smaller squares being equal to the area of the larger square ($a^2 + b^2 = c^2$), but also that the right triangles were formed as point k moved along an arc. We were able to hypothesize the size of the arc as it related to other elements in the sketch (See arc jg in Figure 3), construct it, and test the conjecture within a matter of moments. The students were then able to discuss what they saw happening in the diagram and connect it to what they already knew about the Pythagorean Theorem.

By using the dynamic environment to explore the relationship, the students in the course were able to make conjectures about what relationships resulted in a fair game. Further, we were able to explore those conjectures immediately by making relatively small changes to the original dynamic representation. The paper-based investigation of the relationship had not made the relationships as

Figure 3. Dynamic geometry sketch of a game for understanding the Pythagorean theorem

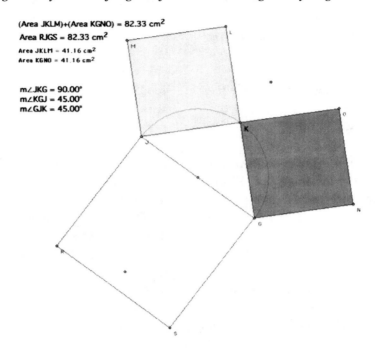

readily apparent as the digital representations. Further, the digital version allowed easy conjecture testing that was not possible with the paper version both because of the limited number of side combinations that could be created with the paper and because of the relative difficulty of testing any emergent conjectures within the limitations of the paper-based medium.

Social Negotiation of Content

Because they are visual and manipulable, dynamic representations form the basis for discussions that allow social negotiation of understanding. In a second grade classroom, students were working with properties of geometric shapes. As part of their state standards, students must examine various ways to cover a two-dimensional region with smaller geometric shapes. On the interactive whiteboard, the teacher opened up a virtual pattern blocks applet (http://ejad.best.vwh.net/java/patterns/patterns_j.shtml) to engage students in a series of tasks designed to meet the curricula goal

of students solving shape puzzles with various constraints. For example, students were first asked to cover two adjacent hexagons using only one geometric shape that was not a hexagon. Figure 4 shows the examples that they came up with.

Next, students were challenged to fill the same template using two different types of pattern blocks. Students struggled to find an organized way to do this; rather than using their solution from the first part (covering with one type of shape), every student took all of the blocks off and started over by randomly placing pattern blocks on the template. Hoping that students would see the concept of trading shapes to find new solutions, we decided to ask students about their mathematical thinking. The next excerpt comes

Figure 4. Using pattern blocks to solve shape puzzles

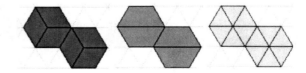

from conversation with a student who had just completed the first task by covering the puzzle with 12 triangles. She was standing at the interactive whiteboard figuring out how to cover the puzzle with two different types of shapes:

Teacher: *Tell me about how you covered the puzzle the first time.*
Lucy: *I have twelve triangles.*
Teacher: *What is part two asking you to do?*
Lucy: *Fill it with two different shapes (She begins to remove all 12 triangles).*
Mitch: *Wait, Lucy. There has to be a way to solve it without having to start all over.*
Lucy: *I don't know. What do you think?*
Mitch: *I know that two triangles is the same as a blue rhombus.*
Keisha: *If we put blue rhombuses on top of the triangles we could still cover the hexagon, couldn't we?*
Lucy: *I don't know. (She puts a blue rhombus on top of two triangles. Figure 5a).*
Mitch: *It works! The puzzle is covered and we used two different shapes.*
Teacher: *Are there other solutions with triangles and rhombuses?*
Keisha: *We still have triangles in our puzzle. What if we put one more blue rhombus on top of two more triangles? (Lucy puts another rhombus on top of two more triangles, Figure 5b).*
Lucy: *I think that we can keep adding rhombuses, can't we?*
Mitch: *We should be able to.*

Figure 5. The class' first (a) and second (b) solution

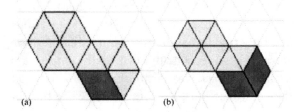

(a)   (b)

Teacher: *How can we organize all of our solutions involving triangles and rhombuses?*
Lucy: *Let's make a chart (Lucy draws a two-column chart on the whiteboard with the headers triangles and rhombuses).*
Teacher: *Who can help Lucy fill out this chart?*
Kendall: *The first solution had 10 triangles and 1 rhombus.*
Mitch: *The second one had 8 triangles and 2 rhombuses.*
Teacher: *What do you think the third one would be?*
Lucy: *Each time we replace two triangles with 1 rhombus. So I think it would be (pauses).*
Mitch: *Lucy, we have 8 triangles so if we replace 2 we would have (He pauses and looks at Lucy).*
Lucy: *6 'cause 8 minus 2 equals 6. We have 6 triangles. And we had 2 rhombuses before adding another, so we have 3. The next solution is 6 triangles and 3 rhombuses.*
Teacher: *Do the rest of you agree? (class nods). What would the next solution be?*
Kendall: *We would replace 2 more triangles and 6 minus 2 is 4 so we would have 4 triangles. We are adding one rhombus so we would now have 4. We have 4 of each.*

This conversation continued with the class finding the remaining solution, 2 triangles with 5 rhombuses. After the table was created, the teacher asked the class, "What patterns do you notice in the table?"

Students shared a variety of observations, including the teachers' main mathematical idea, "when the number of triangles goes down by 2, the number of rhombuses goes up by 1." The teacher followed-up by asking, "How can we make sense of that pattern?" Lucy, who was struggling earlier in the lesson responded, "The rhombus is double the size of the triangle. That means that every time we add a rhombus we have to take two triangles off." The teacher then posed the following task to the class to work with concrete pattern blocks: what are the solutions you could have to cover the puzzle with triangles and trapezoids?

In this vignette, the dynamic nature of the virtual manipulatives allowed the second grade students to create mathematical representations and talk about the mathematics while exploring a cognitively-demanding task. It is unlikely that the students would have been able to do this task without input from their peers. And, it is unlikely that the input would have been as helpful had Lucy not had access to the dynamic representation. The classroom culture of mathematical discourse had been previously established, which allowed the teacher to effectively step out of the conversation and have students socially negotiate both problem solving strategies and mathematical ideas.

Uncovering Limitations in Understanding

A final way dynamic representations can support learning is through engaging learners in conversations that allow limitations in understanding to emerge. For example, in a recent effort, both teachers in PD and students in a 7th grade class were faced with new challenges when they were asked to *construct* shapes rather than draw them. In mathematics, constructions are unique in that they rely on the relationships between basic elements that can be created with a compass and straightedge to create accurate geometric drawings. Dynamic geometry software such as GSP supports the creation of these constructions in ways that allow them to be tested for "breakage." If a person cannot produce a construction for a given shape (e.g., a rectangle or an angle bisector) it suggests that they do not yet fully understand the attributes of that shape and how they work together. For example, there are many ways to create a rectangle, one simple way would be to draw a line segment, create two perpendiculars to that segment that are some distance apart, then draw a second line segment parallel to the first line that ends on the perpendiculars (See Figure 6). In this way, the constructor is assured two pairs of parallel lines that are perpendicular to each other, thus producing the requisite 90-degree angles.

Figure 6. Construction of a rectangle using perpendicular lines

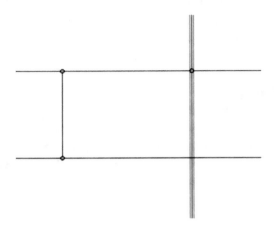

In the PD session, talking through the construction of an angle bisector using GSP, we uncovered that the teachers did not understand the difference between a construction and a drawing. Because they had asked to see how to use GSP, thus making the session technology-focused, the teachers were able to see mathematics they thought they knew in a different way. This allowed us to engage them in a conversation about how constructions differ from drawings and the mathematics needed for each. Without the technology, the teachers would not have been faced with their knowledge limitation, thus leading to an ongoing misperception about an important mathematics topic. The dynamic software prompted a conversation that would otherwise not have happened.

Later in the day, we challenged a class of 7th grade students to construct a rectangle using GSP. To motivate the students and emphasize the mathematics, we noted that they had to create a rectangle that we could not "break" (e.g., force to lose its shape) by dragging the vertices or sides. Despite being in a poor achieving school, having no previous experience with GSP or constructions and only traditional instruction in geometry, the students engaged with this task for the entire class period. Our task was to circulate, trying to break their constructions. By doing this, we had the opportunity to see whether the students understood the attributes of rectangles as well as how to construct them. As we circulated, breaking many rectangles that were not properly constructed, we were able to use questioning to support students in thinking about how they could use the attributes of a rectangle to construct one. Without the GSP activity, we would not have been able to determine whether the rectangles were properly constructed because a simple drawing of a rectangle cannot be tested for appropriate construction.

These two short vignettes highlight the affordances of digital representations, paired with questioning, in uncovering problematic understandings that learners may not realize they have. For example, the 7th grade students were able to define a rectangle, but they were unable to create one with their definition-oriented understanding. Similarly, the technology provided a catalyst, as well as a safe environment, for discussions with the 7th grade teachers that uncovered a significant issue with their understanding of the mathematics that they teach.

DISCUSSION AND CONCLUSION

Theories of learning grounded in socio-cultural perspectives argue that communication is a necessary component of learning. Similarly, research on the use of visual representations suggests that learning is enhanced through students' use of these tools. Yet, standards, textbooks, and professional development too often treat communication and representations as separate aspects of pedagogy. In this chapter, we have highlighted the synergistic opportunities that arise from combining digital representations and communication. Because there is an artifact, discussions about what it is showing and how it was made can be had. Further, new conjectures can be tested as they arise supporting reasoning through the representations not just with them.

We assert that building a culture of communication around dynamic representations and discussion can facilitate learning in a few key ways. First, the use of dynamic representations

removes the ambiguity and potential confusion too often pervasive in mathematics classrooms. In our Fraction Bars example, prior, for example, Claire talked about her mathematical decisions as she moved the pieces of her model around, thus making her description very clear. There were illustrations of her thinking to which she could point, thus eliminating the use of indefinite pronouns. Second, dynamic representations allow immediate conjecture testing and facilitate pattern development because they provide an easy-to-manipulate world in which limitless possibilities exist. This was highlighted particularly in the *conjecture testing* section before. Third, communication about representations allows a safe environment in which learners can be challenged to think more about mathematics. For example, in the *uncovering limitations in understanding* section we saw learners struggling with basic ideas that should have been apparent. However, the representational environment (in this case GSP) was new, which allowed the participants to learn more about the mathematics by interrogating the potential of the tool. Finally, representations and communication marry to create opportunities for the construction of shared meanings. In the vignette from second grade, students collaboratively explored a geometric shape puzzle by discussing approaches, solutions, and the mathematical ideas that were embedded in the task. The teacher, in that vignette, had created a classroom culture where students felt comfortable helping, questioning, and working with each other.

While not evident in the vignettes, cognitive demand played a critical role in supporting learning in each of these examples. Maintaining high cognitive demand ensures that the underlying mathematics of a task is worth discussing. Further, to compel learners to reason about mathematics through representations, the task needs to provide a context that warrants such modeling. A simple, low cognitive demand task that asks a learner to solve an algorithm or engage with a routine task does not warrant engagement in the activity of exploring the mathematics. For example, a routine task such as finding the amount of carpeting needed for a 10 ft x 13 ft room does not require or suggest the use of dynamic representations. If it is represented at all, chances are a static rectangle with 10 ft marked on one side and 13 ft marked on the other would suffice. However, if we engage students with more meaningful tasks, there are more reasons to interact with the mathematics (and other people) using a digital representation. For example, if instead of carpeting a room, we considered the largest possible pen that could be created for a pet using 48 feet of fencing, the use of representations becomes more meaningful. Clearly, cognitive demand is a critical aspect of the synergistic interplay between representation and communication.

IMPLICATIONS, CHALLENGES, FUTURE DIRECTIONS

Digital representations clearly have potential to support mathematics teaching and learning processes when coupled with cognitively demanding tasks and opportunities for learners to engage in conversations about tasks, approaches, and mathematical ideas. As shown in our examples here, an experienced facilitator can use this synergistic relationship to meet a number of mathematical goals. However, these kinds of examples are still difficult to find in everyday classrooms. To foster effective implementation of the digital representation and discussion synergy in classrooms, we need to examine how to best prepare and support teachers who have not developed the skills for implementing mathematics lessons in these ways. As shown in our examples, supporting learning through high cognitive demand tasks that benefit from discussion focused on dynamic representations requires strong facilitation.

To be a strong facilitator in these environments, teachers need to have well-developed knowledge for teaching (e.g., Ball, Thames, & Phelps, 2008; Manizade & Mason, 2011; Shulman, 1986; Silverman & Thompson, 2008) as well as Technological

Pedagogical and Content Knowledge (TPACK). Mathematical knowledge for teaching includes the particular knowledge about mathematics teachers have that other adults do not need. For example, how to multiple whole numbers four different ways. It also extends to include the pedagogical approaches a teacher needs to develop in order to support student learning of mathematics—such as using representations and asking questions that promote connection making (e.g., Manizade & Mason, 2011; Shulman, 1986). It is clear that teaching high cognitive demand tasks requires that the teacher be able to support learners through a variety of solution paths.

TPACK provides a frame for considering the teacher knowledge needed to achieve high-level implementation of these pedagogies. TPACK helps to explain the intersection of knowledge necessary for effective technology integration. Knowledge of technology, pedagogy and content, at the point of intersection of all three knowledge components (Mishra & Koehler, 2006; Neiss, 2005), is necessary to achieve the high leverage practices such as those presented here. Specifically, the effective use of digital mathematical representations and mathematical conversations requires teachers to have a deep understanding of the mathematical concepts, the creation and manipulation of digital representations, and pedagogies related to leveraging digital representations in a conversation about mathematical ideas. Both educational technologists and mathematics educators should examine ways to support teachers in developing TPACK for the enactment of digital representations and mathematical conversations.

Thus, to support teachers and prospective teachers in developing rich learning environments that capitalize on dynamic representations and communication, teacher educators and professional developers need to consider how to support the development of specialized knowledge that teachers need as well as TPACK. We suggest that a starting place for this development is through the engagement of teachers in learning opportunities like those described previously.

CONCLUSION

In this chapter, we presented a case for the value of combining dynamic representations and classroom discussion to support mathematics learning. We provided four diverse examples of classrooms in which this happened to illustrate four different ways that dynamic representations can support communication in the mathematics classroom. We concluded with a suggestion for teacher knowledge development that would support teaching and learning in these environments.

ACKNOWLEDGMENT

The work reported here was funded in part by a series of grants from organizations including the North Carolina Mathematics and Science Partnership (MSP) Program, the National Science Foundation, and Georgia's Teacher Quality Higher Education Program. The opinions expressed here are those of the authors and do not necessarily reflect those of the granting agencies. We thank the students and teachers who have participated in our learning environments for allowing us to learn from them.

REFERENCES

Ares, N., Stroup, W. M., & Schademan, A. R. (2009). The power of mediating artifacts in group-level development of mathematical discourses. *Cognition and Instruction, 27*(1), 1–24. doi:10.1080/07370000802584497.

Ball, D. L., Thames, M. H., & Phelps, G. (2008). Content knowledge for teaching: What makes it special? *Journal of Teacher Education, 59*(5), 389–407. doi:10.1177/0022487108324554.

Battista, M. T., & Clements, D. H. (2007). *Constructing geometric concepts in logo.* Retrieved from http://investigations.terc.edu/library/book-papers/constructing_geo_concepts.cfm

Bitter, G. G., & Hatfield, M. M. (1994). The calculator project: Assessing school-wide impact of calculator implementation. In Bright, G. W., Waxman, H. C., & Williams, S. E. (Eds.), *Impact of calculators on mathematics instruction* (pp. 49–66). Lanham, MD: University Press of America.

Brown, R. E. (2009). *Community building in mathematics professional development.* (Doctoral dissertation). University of Georgia, Athens, GA.

Clements, D. H., & Battista, M. T. (1989). Learning of geometric concepts in a logo environment. *Journal for Research in Mathematics Education, 20*, 450–467. doi:10.2307/749420.

Clements, D. H., & Battista, M. T. (2001). Logo and geometry. *Journal for Research in Mathematics Education,* 10.

Cobb, P. (1994). *Learning mathematics: Constructivist and interactionist theories of mathematical development.* New York: Springer.

Cobb, P., Wood, T., & Yackel, E. (1993). Discourse, mathematical thinking, and classroom practice. In Forman, E., & Stone, A. (Eds.), *Contexts for learning: Sociocultural dynamics in children's development* (pp. 91–119). New York: Oxford University Press.

Cobb, P., Yackel, E., & McClain, K. (2000). *Symbolizing and communicating in mathematics classrooms: Perspectives on discourse, tools, and instructional design.* Mahwah, NJ: Lawrence Erlbaum Associates.

Fendel, D. M., Resek, D., Alper, L., & Fraser, S. (2011). *Interactive mathematics program: Integrated high school mathematics.* Key Curriculum Press.

Franke, M. L., Kazemi, E., & Battey, D. (2007). Mathematics teaching and classroom practice. In Lester, F. K. (Ed.), *Second handbook of research on mathematics teaching and learning.* Charlotte, NC: Information Age Publishing.

Friedlander, A., & Tabach, M. (2001). Promoting multiple representations in algebra. In Cuoco, A. A. (Ed.), *The roles of representations in school mathematics: 2001 yearbook of the national council of teachers of mathematics (NCTM)* (pp. 173–185). Reston, VA: NCTM.

Hegedus, S. J., & Penuel, W. R. (2008). Studying new forms of participation and identity in mathematics classrooms with integrated communication and representational infrastructures. *Educational Studies in Mathematics, 68*(2), 171–183. doi:10.1007/s10649-008-9120-x.

Henningsen, M., & Stein, M. K. (1997). Mathematical tasks and student cognition: Classroom-based factors that support and inhibit high-level mathematical thinking and reasoning. *Journal for Research in Mathematics Education, 28*(5), 524–549. doi:10.2307/749690.

Hiebert, J., Carpenter, T. P., Fennema, E., Fuson, K., Human, P., & Murray, H. et al. (1996). Problem solving as the basis for reform in curriculum and instruction: The case of mathematics. *Educational Researcher, 25*(4), 12–21. doi:10.3102/0013189X025004012.

Hufferd-Ackles, K., Fuson, K. C., & Sherin, M. G. (2004). Describing levels and components of a math-talk learning community. *Journal for Research in Mathematics Education, 35*(2), 81–116. doi:10.2307/30034933.

Johnson, C. D. (2002). The effects of the geometer's sketchpad on the van Hiele levels and academic achievement of high school students. *ETD Collection for Wayne State University.* Retrieved from http://digitalcommons.wayne.edu/dissertations/AAI3071795

Kazemi, E., & Stipek. (2001). Promoting conceptual thinking in four mathematics classrooms. *The Elementary School Journal, 102*(1), 59–80. doi:10.1086/499693.

Key Curriculum Press. (2001). *The geometer's sketchpad: Dynamic geometry software for exploring mathematics.* Berkeley, CA: Key Curriculum Press.

Kilpatrick, J., Swafford, J., & Findell, B. (2001). *Adding it up.* Washington, DC: National Research Council.

Leong, Y. W., & Lim-Teo, S. K. (2003). Effects of geometer's sketchpad on spatial ability and achievement in transformation geometry among secondary two students in Singapore. *The Mathematics Educator, 7*(1), 32–48.

Manizade, A. G., & Mason, M. M. (2011). Using Delphi methodology to design assessments of teachers' pedagogical content knowledge. *Educational Studies in Mathematics, 76*(2), 183–207. doi:10.1007/s10649-010-9276-z.

Mishra, P., & Koehler, M. J. (2006). Technological pedagogical content knowledge: A new framework for teacher knowledge. *Teachers College Record, 108*(6), 1017–1054. doi:10.1111/j.1467-9620.2006.00684.x.

National Council of Teachers of Mathematics. (2000). *Principles and standards for school mathematics.* Reston, VA: NCTM.

National Governor's Association/Chief Council of State School Officers. (2010). *Common core state standards for mathematics.* Retrieved from http://corestandards.org/assets/CCSSI_Math%20Standards.pdf

Niess, M. L. (2005). Preparing teachers to teach science and mathematics with technology: Developing a technology pedagogical content knowledge. *Teaching and Teacher Education, 21*, 509–523. doi:10.1016/j.tate.2005.03.006.

Olive, J., & Lobato, J. (2008). The learning of rational number concepts using technology. In M. K. Heid & G. W. Blume (Eds.), Research on technology and the teaching and learning of mathematics: Volume 1 – Research syntheses. Charlotte, NC: Information Age Publishing.

Orrill, J. (2003). *Fraction bars.* [software]. Retrieved from http://www.transparentmedia.com/software.php

Preston, R. V., & Garner, A. S. (2003). Representation as a vehicle for solving and communication. *Mathematics Teaching in the Middle School, 9*(1), 38–43.

Rasmussen, C., & Marrongelle, K. (2006). Pedagogical content tools: Integrating student reasoning and mathematics instruction. *Journal for Research in Mathematics Education, 37*(5), 388–420.

Roberts, D. M. (1980). The impact of electronic calculators on educational performance. *Review of Educational Research, 50*(1), 71–98. doi:10.3102/00346543050001071.

Schoenfeld, A. H. (2002). Making mathematics work for all children: Issues of standards, testing, and equity. *Educational Researcher, 31*(1), 13–25. doi:10.3102/0013189X031001013.

Shulman, L. S. (1986). Those who understand: Knowledge growth in teaching. *Educational Researcher, 15*(2), 4–14. doi:10.3102/0013189X015002004.

Silverman, J., & Thompson, P. W. (2008). Toward a framework for the development of mathematical knowledge for teaching. *Journal of Mathematics Teacher Education, 11*, 499-511. DOI: 0857-008-9089-5

Steen, K., Brooks, D., & Lyon, T. (2006). The impact of virtual manipulatives on first grade geometry instruction and learning. *Journal of Computers in Mathematics and Science Teaching, 25*(4), 373–391.

Stein, M. K., Engle, R. A., Smith, M. S., & Hughes, E. K. (2008). Orchestrating productive mathematical discussions: Five practices for helping teachers move beyond show and tell. *Mathematical Thinking and Learning, 10*(4), 313–340. doi:10.1080/10986060802229675.

Stein, M. K., Grover, B. W., & Henningsen, M. (1996). Building student capacity for mathematical thinking and reasoning: An analysis of tasks used in reform curriculum. *American Educational Research Journal, 33*(2), 455–488. doi:10.3102/00028312033002455.

U. S. Department of Education. (2008). *Foundations for success: The final report of the national mathematics advisory panel.* Retrieved from http://www.ed.gov/about/bdscomm/list/mathpanel/report/final-report.pdf

van Es, E. A., & Sherin, M. G. (2008). Mathematics teachers' learning to notice in the context of a video club. *Teaching and Teacher Education, 24*, 244–276. doi:10.1016/j.tate.2006.11.005.

Wenglinsky, H. (1998). Does it compute? The relationship between educational technology and student achievement in mathematics. *Educational Testing Service Policy Information Center.* Retrieved from http://www.mff.org/pubs/ME161.pdf

Wood, T., Williams, G., & McNeal, B. (2006). Children's mathematical thinking in different classroom cultures. *Journal for Research in Mathematics Education, 37*(3), 222–255.

Zbiek, R. M., Heid, M. K., Blume, G. W., & Dick, T. (2007). Research on technology in mathematics education: A perspective of constructs. In Lester, F. (Ed.), *Second handbook of research on mathematics teaching and learning* (pp. 1169–1207). Charlotte, NC: Information Age.

KEY TERMS AND DEFINITIONS

Dynamic Representation: Any representation that is created using technology and that can be manipulated in some way. These include, but are not limited to, constructions in dynamic geometry software, virtual manipulatives such as tangrams, and number-based representations such as spreadsheets.

Chapter 3
Implementing Common Core State Standards using Digital Curriculum

Michelle Rutherford
Apex Learning, USA

ABSTRACT

Teachers and educators transitioning to the Common Core State Standards face a significant challenge of creating new lessons and resources, as well as formative assessments that match the increased rigor required. Teachers must ensure that each student achieves and demonstrates higher levels of understanding. Many aspects of this transition can be mitigated, supported, and enhanced through blended learning. Blended learning leverages digital curriculum to assist teachers in creating a student-centered learning experience while providing a curriculum that meets the new standards. Students receive individualized instruction at their own pace, achieve mastery, and experience success in high school. They are equipped with a deeper level of understanding and the critical thinking and problem solving skills needed to succeed in college and work.

INTRODUCTION

The new Common Core State Standards require all students to achieve at higher levels, with more challenging content and new assessments. Public schools implementing the Common Core State Standards face a significant challenge in providing a curriculum with lessons and activities that teach students to apply mathematical thinking to real-world situations, and specifically increase their skills in problem solving, reasoning, and modeling. In addition to requiring a new curriculum, new formative assessments are needed to evaluate student progress toward competency in each Standard.

Educators and teachers are charged with overcoming these implementation challenges. The new Common Core State Standards for

DOI: 10.4018/978-1-4666-4086-3.ch003

Mathematics change the grade level at which certain content is introduced and are more rigorous than many current state Standards. Although they reduce the breadth of Standards coverage, they require students to demonstrate and apply conceptual understanding in greater depth. Educators implementing the Common Core State Standards for Mathematics must create new lessons and resources to address the Standards, as well as assessments to match the increased rigor required. In addition, teachers must ensure that each student achieves and demonstrates higher levels of understanding. While implementation may seem daunting, districts leveraging digital curriculum specifically developed for the Common Core State Standards for Mathematics are well positioned for a smooth transition.

THE CHALLENGE OF TEACHING IN TODAY'S CLASSROOM

In the traditional classroom, teachers are tasked with a multitude of duties: lesson planning, presentation of course content, creation, delivery and scoring of assessments, classroom management, and communicating with parents, all while ensuring that each student achieves to his or her highest level. Traditional classroom teachers receive a set of Standards for each course they teach, and are often required to follow a common district pacing guide that governs the scope and sequence for the delivery of lessons that address the Standards throughout the course.

Even before the adoption of the Common Core State Standards, educators faced the challenge of how best to address the diverse learning needs of all students and ensure that each one achieves to his or her potential. The typical classroom teacher teaches 180 students per day, in 5 or 6 classes with an average of 30 students in each class. Teachers are held accountable for ensuring that every student masters the content Standards on the same schedule. This is an enormous task for even the best teachers.

At the same time, students come to school with distinct learning styles, different strengths and weaknesses, and varied levels of competency in prerequisite skills needed for grade-level success. Traditional classroom pacing assumes all students will achieve mastery of course content at the same time, using the same lessons and activities. Traditional assessments are summative in nature and are used to deliver a grade, not as significant formative data points a teacher can use to direct and differentiate instruction to ensure the greatest learning outcomes. The traditional approach to instruction does not account for the differing abilities of students and the individualized support teachers must provide to address each student's needs.

For example, consider that 70% of American high school students currently read below grade level and that 15-year-olds in the United States rank 25th out of 30 countries in math performance (National Center for Education Statistics, 2011). These students already require special intervention and support, so it will be necessary to develop new learner-centered strategies to assist struggling students in meeting the new Standards and bridging the knowledge gap between current state Standards and the Common Core State Standards. Every student does not learn in the same way or on the same day (Costa & Callick, 2008). On average, a handful of students are capable of accelerating, yet they are held to the same pace as the average student. Consequently, those accelerating students often lose interest, get bored, and perform poorly. With the higher expectations of the Common Core State Standards, teachers will face even greater challenges in supporting an entire classroom of students. Blended learning, combining face-to-face instruction with digital curriculum is a method for making it possible.

NEW STANDARDS, NEW CURRICULUM, DIFFERENT INSTRUCTIONAL METHOD

Implementing the Common Core State Standards requires a new curriculum. Teachers are learning to adopt Standards that emphasize problem-solving and other higher-order skills. Educators are developing a new curriculum to meet the Standards. To support the transition, districts are providing professional development to inform teachers not only about changes in the Standards and how to rewrite lessons and assessment items but also how best to deliver the new instruction to students. Using digital curriculum in a blended delivery method of instruction can accelerate and ease this transition.

Digital curriculum provides teachers with high-quality lessons, activities, and assessments specifically designed to meet the intent of the Common Core State Standards for Mathematics. This enhances the learning process for students by creating active learning experiences that keep them attentive and engaged. The purposeful use of media throughout instruction provides students with opportunities to explore and understand new concepts, allowing each student to move at his or her own pace. Students can have frequent opportunities to check their understanding and apply what they have learned, thereby deepening their mastery of difficult concepts.

In addition, digital curriculum provides the tools and capacity to individualize the learning experience for each student. Teachers using a digital curriculum and the data provided by the learning management system can differentiate instruction to personalize learning. Data specifically shows teachers where each student needs further instruction, and teachers can target instruction to fill the gaps in a student's knowledge and skills. Teachers can also group students together by skill and provide targeted small-group face-to-face instruction. This differentiated instructional approach leads to greater student learning outcomes by personalizing learning for each student.

A myriad of challenges exist with the implementation of the new Standards, and among the top priorities is the need to increase student performance and rise to meet the higher expectations set forth by the Common Core State Standards for Mathematics. Educators must determine how best to address the needs of individual students and prepare them for success in college and work. That said there is also great need for professional development, teacher resources, and materials that meet the expectations and intent of the Common Core State Standards.

TEACHING AND LEARNING COMMON CORE WITH DIGITAL CURRICULUM

Teachers using digital curriculum will be ahead of their more traditional counterparts because lessons, activities, and assessments designed for the Standards are available for immediate use. Instead of spending time creating lessons to adapt to the new Standards, teachers can focus on working with students and analyzing student performance data. In turn, students benefit from a more student-centered, interactive learning experience. Students in courses or programs that use a digital curriculum have the opportunity to achieve at higher levels than students participating in those that rely solely on traditional methods of instruction and assessment (US Department of Education, 2010).

There are several benefits to teaching and learning with digital curriculum. First, each teacher adopts a common, approved curriculum, using the same scope and sequence. This provides districts the assurance that each student has access to high-quality lessons and activities that address and assess the Standards. Second, students can work through the course content at their own pace, with the benefit of scaffolding and opt-in supports matched to their unique learning needs. Third, the teacher has access to real-time data revealing what students know and what they have yet to learn. The data can be used to identify and group students by skill mastery and to develop targeted instructional strategies for whole-group, small-group, and individual instructional sessions. Last, the teacher is no longer responsible for all whole-group direct instruction; therefore, the teacher has more time to work with individual and small groups of students to provide individualized instruction.

Digital curriculum changes the model of the classroom and uniquely addresses the daily challenges teachers face in a multitude of ways. In many cases teachers can adopt digital content specifically designed to address the Common Core State Standards for Mathematics as the core curriculum, whether the implementation is in a blended learning environment where students access online courses in a brick and mortar classroom with a teacher present, or in a virtual environment where content and instruction are delivered with the teacher and student separated by distance. In other cases, teachers use digital curriculum as a resource to enhance instruction, pulling lessons and interactive activities into whole-group instruction with the aid of an interactive whiteboard. Digital lessons can be leveraged to provide individual and small- group differentiated instruction in a computer lab or with a one-to-one initiative. Students take diagnostic assessments and receive individualized study plans based on assessment results. In each case, digital curriculum delivers a comprehensive, Standards-based scope and sequence that enables students to access rigorous content to develop mathematical "habit of mind" and problem-solving skills.

Students and teachers are empowered because digital curriculum allows students to learn at their own pace — they can spend as little or as much time as needed on concepts and have multiple opportunities to model and apply that knowledge. Students receive formative feedback several times throughout a unit, and assessments can be used to improve their learning outcomes. In this way, assessment is not the end of learning, but rather a checkpoint that reveals areas of weakness to both the student and the teacher. As students feel supported and empowered, they experience success, learn, stay in school, and progress toward graduation. Teachers often say they find their role more rewarding because digital curriculum allows them the opportunity to get to know students and build relationships, while better meeting each individual's academic needs. Because the teacher is freed from the expectation that each student must hear the same lesson on the same day, he or she can be more flexible and meet each student where he or she is academically. By decreasing the burden placed on teachers to prepare and deliver lessons and assessments to a whole group, digital curriculum enables teachers to work in more effective ways to ensure that each student experiences successful learning outcomes.

Much of that burden is mitigated by the availability of data. For example, teachers using Apex Learning Courses and Tutorials have immediate access to data delivered at every point throughout a math Course and Tutorial. By using these data, teachers have a unique view into what students know and can do. Teachers can review an individual student's progress or get an aggregate view of the class. This real-time access to data allows teachers to identify each student's learning needs and provide strategic targeted intervention, re-teaching, and remediation before the summative assessment. Teachers can group students by mastery and deliver small-group instruction or individual mini-lessons to help them learn difficult subject matter. In addition, students have access to individualized learning plans that are generated from diagnostic and prescriptive assessments. Students who progress are free to continue learning at their own pace.

COMMON CORE STATE STANDARDS FOR MATHEMATICS EMBEDDED IN DIGITAL CURRICULUM

Apex Learning Common Core Courses and Tutorials provide schools with a solution to meet the expectations of the standards.

The Common Core raised the bar in terms of rigor, higher order skills, and expectations for assessment. In doing so, it also raised the need for greater instructional supports to ensure students at all academic levels can meet the expectations of the standards.

Apex Learning Common Core mathematics courses were designed specifically to address those needs. They focus on providing rigorous content, the development of higher order skills, preparation for the assessments, and an instructional model that ensures all students can reach the expectations of the Common Core.

Content publishers have long been focused on developing content and then aligning it to national and state Standards. Apex Learning has always started with the Standards and developed courses based on those Standards. After a thorough evaluation of the Common Core State Standards, we are developing new Courses and Tutorials to fully meet the learning expectations that are established.

The instructional design of each Apex Learning Common Core mathematics course guides students through the use and development of the higher order skills necessary to apply their knowledge to complex, unfamiliar problems. The skills emphasized throughout the curriculum are those

identified by the Common Core's 8 Standards for Mathematical Practice, which include modeling, using tools, reasoning, solving problems, constructing arguments, and attending to precision. Through active learning opportunities embedded into the direct instruction, students constantly hone these skills as they move through the course. Students further deepen their comprehension and build their skills in journaling, modeling, and performance task activities designed specifically for the Common Core.

The new math curriculum supports true mathematical proficiency via a balanced instructional approach that targets two key outcomes:

- Deepening Conceptual Understanding
  - Comfort and ability to work with math concepts in concrete, abstract, and generalized scenarios.
  - Ability to recognize the big picture behind a given math problem or real-world application.
  - Development of problem-solving skills that empower students to apply and extend their solution strategies across a variety of contexts.
- Developing Computational Proficiency
  - Fluency in calculations involving numbers and operations.
  - Ability to solve equations that are presented in a variety of forms.

The Apex Learning mathematics Course instructional philosophy is based on a discovery-confirmation-practice model.

- **Discovery:** Each lesson begins by engaging students with real-world problems, guiding students as they discover new principles and build the higher order skills they need to solve them. Students then deepen their conceptual understanding of new topics by using on-page tools and exercises that let them explore the impact of changing parameters on models, formulas and other mathematical representations.

- **Confirmation:** Students confirm their grasp of lesson topics through interactive, feedback-rich instruction. This active learning approach lets students apply their skills and check their comprehension in real-time, telling them whether they're on track page by page as they progress through the course.
- **Practice:** Students build mastery by taking on a range of complex problems designed to hone computational fluency and a combination of skills that includes using tools, modeling information, writing, and solving real-world problems.

Apex Learning Common Core mathematics Tutorials is another solution that provides an innovative instructional approach to build knowledge, develop critical thinking skills, and deepen understanding. Tutorials personalize learning with prescriptive pretests and grade-level content modules focused on Common Core State Standards-aligned learning objectives.

- **Learn It:** Provides direct instruction that engages students in active learning.
- **Try It:** Develops skills and knowledge with interactive practice and application.
- **Review It:** Reinforces concepts through high impact videos.
- **Test It:** Assesses student knowledge through randomized assessment.

Apex Learning digital curriculum is developed according to research-based design principles, contain a high standard of rigor, and provide solid Standards-based coverage of topics. Mathematics

courses and Tutorials support conceptual understanding and computational proficiency, promote active learning, implement a purposeful use of technology, provide a student-centered, interactive learning experience, and offer students frequent practice in applying mathematical ways of thinking to real-world problems and situations.

CONCLUSION

Teachers and educators transitioning to the Common Core State Standards face significant challenges. Blended learning, however, enables teachers to create a student-centered learning experience while providing a digital curriculum that meets the new Standards. Additionally, Apex Learning digital curriculum address the Standards in mathematics by focusing on developing students' skills to demonstrate conceptual understanding, show and explain their reasoning, and apply this knowledge to everyday life. Students learn at their own pace, achieve mastery, and experience success. With Apex Learning digital curriculum, teachers have comprehensive Courses and Tutorials at the ready that include lessons, interactive activities, formative, diagnostic, and summative assessments, practice activities, study guides, and other Standards-based resources to support instruction. Using the blended model of instruction, teachers are better able to meet a wide range of student learning needs.

Not every provider of digital curriculum adheres to the same high standards; therefore, districts need to evaluate digital curriculum providers carefully. High-quality digital curriculum is developed using evidence-based instructional practices important to student learning and designed using a balanced body of research. Research shows that to foster successful learning, the curriculum must motivate the desire to learn, engage students in deep understanding of concepts, and build adaptive expertise and application of knowledge in new situations (Moore & Baer, 2010). A quality digital curriculum also offers direct instruction, constructive practice, and formative feedback. All content should integrate critical thinking, problem solving, and questioning to support engagement and active learning. Flexible implementation options such as blended learning and virtual learning allow every student to observe, inquire, confirm, connect, and create as they build knowledge in lessons. Teachers using digital curriculum can be more effective, meet diverse learning needs, and increase student learning outcomes. This is all the more important with the introduction of the Common Core State Standards for Mathematics.

REFERENCES

Costa, A., & Kallick, B. (2008). *Learning and leading with habits of mind*. Alexandria, VA: Association for Supervision and Curriculum Development.

Moore, A. M., & Baer, T. (2010). *Research put into practice*. Apex Learning Curriculum & Pedagogy.

National Center for Education Statistics. (2011). *The nation's report card*. Reading: National Center for Education Statistics.

US Department of Education. (2010). *Evaluation of evidence-based practices in online learning*. Retrieved June 15, 2012, from http://www2.ed.gov/rschstat/eval/tech/evidence-based-practices/finalreport.pdf

KEY TERMS AND DEFINITIONS

Active Learning: Active learning occurs when students are engaged in activities, such as reading, writing, discussion, and problem solving that promote analysis, synthesis, and evaluation of course content.

Blended Learning: According to the Innosight Institute, blended learning is a formal education program in which a student learns at least in part through online delivery of content and instruction with some element of student control over time, place, path, and pace, and at least in part at a supervised brick-and-mortar location away from home.

Digital Curriculum: A digital curriculum provides Standards-based courses that can be accessed online. The courses contain interactive direct instruction, guided practice, and integrated formative, diagnostic, and summative assessment.

Differentiated Instruction: Teachers meet each student where they are by providing different methods of instruction and activities based on each student's unique learning pace, needs, and preferences.

Learning Management System: A learning management system, or LMS, is a software application that delivers course content, communication, assessment, and feedback online. The LMS includes a teacher Grade Book as well as data collection and reporting tools used by teachers to track student progress and group students to provide instructional intervention.

Traditional Instruction: The focus of traditional instruction is on the teacher. Students are taught and assessed in a monolithic, synchronous manner.

Chapter 4
A Framework for TPACK Action Research

P. Mark Taylor
Carson-Newman University, USA

ABSTRACT

In the implementation of the Common Core State Standards, teacher educators have an unprecedented opportunity. Both preservice and inservice teachers are aware that they have much to learn about the effective implementation of the standards. This is especially true in light of the standards inclusion of technology on the list of tools, which students should be selecting and properly using. Action research can be an effective pedagogical tool for teacher educators to employ as we support teachers' learning about these technology tools for learning mathematics. Four levels of TPACK action research are suggested as a framework for teacher educators to use as they take advantage of this opportunity.

INTRODUCTION

It has now been well established that there is a need to further develop the Technological Pedagogical Content Knowledge (TPACK) of both inservice and preservice teachers (Mishra & Koehler, 2006; Niess et al., 2009). The vast majority of the research on TPACK consists of learning opportunities presented in preservice teacher education programs and or professional development opportunities. While these experiences provide great opportuni-

ties for learning, much of what the typical teacher learns is done in their daily work. These "on the job" learning opportunities to learn often occur without the awareness of the teacher. If the teacher is not expecting to learn any new, then they are not preparing to learn by asking themselves key questions; even if they have questions, they may not be thinking about answering the questions in an organized, evidence-based manner. Moreover, without the teachers' awareness of the opportunity to learn there is a good chance that metacognition

DOI: 10.4018/978-1-4666-4086-3.ch004

will not occur. Perhaps even more dangerous is the situation when the teacher learning is based on outcomes without analysis of the variables and how they may have affected those outcomes. For these reasons and more, teacher educators have advocated for decades that a mindset of reflective practitioner for teachers at all stages of their career.

In the era of data-driven decisions, it is only natural that we extend this reflective practitioner model into the model of ongoing action research. Many preservice teacher education programs across the country have some form of data-driven action research as a component of their course-work. When teachers move on to complete their masters degree, an overwhelming majority end up completing an action research project as a culminating capstone experience. The goal of including action research, whether for preservice or inservice teachers is the same: to encourage a mindset of reflective practitioner through an ongoing cycle of data-driven decision-making. What is the end goal of such an ongoing cycle? The goal is ongoing learning of pedagogical knowledge in context. When the teachers turn their attention towards the effective use of technology their students' learning of specific mathematics, then the goal of action research is the teachers' learning of specific Technological Pedagogical Content Knowledge (TPACK).

Certain conditions increase the likelihood that teachers will engage in such a cycle of action research. These conditions serve as catalysts that encourage the teacher to engage in the learning process. A perceived need to learn is always a prerequisite to any purposeful learning experience. Without motivation, there is no reason to put in the effort. Whether you can call it cognitive disso-nance, a perturbation, or disequilibrium, it simply means that teachers believe they have a problem to solve. If they believe they have a problem, then they will begin to look for a solution. Another prerequisite is a means of learning. Despite the plethora of professional literature and professional meetings that they could attend, teachers often feel

like they don't know how to begin the learning process, especially if they are entering unfamiliar ground with new math topics or new technolo-gies. In many cases, they simply refuse to try to learn until someone comes to present them with that knowledge. Simply put, a teacher that does not know where to start learning will not start learning. Finally, many teachers are much more comfortable entering into a learning situation with someone that they consider their peer. They want to learn along with someone from their context (school, grade-level, etc.) or a similar context that has a similar need to learn.

THE NEED FOR TEACHERS TO LEARN: THE ROLE OF TECHNOLOGY IN THE COMMON CORE

The current environment of high stakes testing and the move to the Common Core State Standards (CCSS) has created a perceived need to learn for the vast majority of teachers, especially for those that teach mathematics. Since most teacher evaluation systems are now incorporating student achievement scores as a major component of the annual review process, many teachers are scram-bling to find anything that will give their students a little more of an advantage. CCSS outlines not only specific content standards, but also defines mathematical processes. In the Standards for Mathematical Practice, the CCSS outlines how students are to operate as they learn and apply the content standards.

- **CCSS.Math.Practice.MP1:** Make sense of problems and persevere in solving them. Older students might, depending on the context of the problem, transform algebra-ic expressions or change the viewing win-dow on their graphing calculator to get the information they need (p. 6).

- **CCSS.Math.Practice.MP5:** Use appropriate tools strategically. Mathematically proficient students consider the available tools when solving a mathematical problem. These tools might include pencil and paper, concrete models, a ruler, a protractor, a calculator, a spreadsheet, a computer algebra system, a statistical package, or dynamic geometry software. Proficient students are sufficiently familiar with tools appropriate for their grade or course to make sound decisions about when each of these tools might be helpful, recognizing both the insight to be gained and their limitations. Mathematically proficient students at various grade levels are able to identify relevant external mathematical resources, such as digital content located on a Website, and use them to pose or solve problems. . They are able to use technological tools to explore and deepen their understanding of concepts (p. 7).

Since the standards for mathematical practice apply to every grade level, it is important for mathematics teachers at all grade levels teach with these tools. They must be prepared to assist students not only in learning the technologies, but also in making decisions about how, when and why to use them. Here are two specific references to technology tools from the content standards:

- **Mathematics:** High School, number and quantity (introduction) calculators, spreadsheets, and computer algebra systems can provide a way for students to become better acquainted with these new number systems and their notation. They can be used to generate data for numerical experiments, to help understand the workings of matrix, vector, & complex number algebra, and to experiment with non-integer exponents (p. 58).

- **CCSS.Math.Content.HSS-ID.A.4:** Use the mean and standard deviation of a data set to fit it to a normal distribution and to estimate population percentages. Recognize that there are data sets for which such a procedure is not appropriate. Use calculators, spreadsheets, and tables to estimate areas under the normal curve (p. 81).

In these two cases, the technology to be used in teaching the content has been listed. In most of the content standards, however, specific technology tools are not specified. As a result, teachers are left to make their own decisions as to how Mathematics Process Standard 5 should play out in their classroom. Teachers must be prepared to make informed decisions about which technologies to employ for the teaching and learning of any particular content standard.

Teachers in these states already have a perceived need to help their students to adjust to the CCSS and to do well on the corresponding state assessments. Combined with the important role of technology in achieving those standards, this provides us as teacher educators with an unprecedented open door. Teachers know that they have much to learn and they most understand that this includes TPACK.

A MEANS OF LEARNING: CYCLE OF TPACK ACTION RESEARCH

"How do you know?" This is the key questions to ask a teacher that says that a teaching idea or method worked or did not work. All too often, teachers struggle to give specific answers to this question. If they have an answer, it is often a vague generalization like "they just didn't get it, so I changed the lesson." If teachers really want to improve their TPACK with the goal of implementing the CCSS effectively, then they must purposefully set up the implementation of the lesson to include specific means of generating student data of various forms. If not, then they will remain in the cloudy haze of general notions of whether the lesson "worked" or not.

A personal note: When offering action research as a method of examining their teaching, I often have to reframe it to make it more comfortable for the teachers. Many get overwhelmed by the idea of research, believing it is too technical. When I reframe it as "collecting carefully constructed forms of student-generated work" at each stage of the lesson, teachers find it a much more friendly process.

The action research process has been well documented in various formats since its introduction in 1934 (Mills, 2011). For the purposes of this chapter, we will go with the model outlined next. The model is specifically designed to assess the impact of implementing a pedagogical idea and evaluating its effectiveness across a lesson, cluster of lessons, or a full unit of instruction.

1. Carefully define the problem to be solved and/or method to be tried. If you can't describe this in the form of one or two succinct question, then you may be attempting too much for an action research.
2. Explore professional literature to find what methods have shown to be successful with regards to the specific problem – OR – what techniques support the effective implementation of the method to be tested.
3. Plan the lesson or series of lesson based on the literature:
    a. Carefully constructing assessments at each stage of each lesson that will provide student-generated evidence of understanding and ability to successfully meet the objectives.
    b. Thinking ahead about how those assessments will combine to inform the answer to your question.
4. Implement the lessons and assessments as designed, or at least as close to the original plan as possible. Tweaks may be necessary due

to the surprises that teaching often brings, but adhering to main ideas and methods will allow you to answer your questions.
5. Gather all of the forms of data and analyze them to find exactly what each can add to your understanding of the question. Summarize what you learn from each data source, but also examine how they work together to inform you.
6. Draw a conclusion and share your findings.

How does the focus on TPACK for effective implementation of CCSS impact that process? From the first step of the process, there is a potential for TPACK to affect the process. A lack of TPACK will often lead to overlooking technology-based methods to investigate. Focusing the teachers attention on technology and its impact of student learning of CCSS objectives means that technology will be written into the questions being researched. This focus would then follow through at every stage of the process. The review of professional literature would necessarily include a look at general technology strategies, technology specific literature, & strategies for implementing technologies that support the specific content being taught. This obviously impacts decisions at stage 3 in terms of the lessons. Just as important, the teacher-researcher must make informed decisions as to the interaction of the assessment methods and the technologies. Should technologies be used by the student while the assessment is occurring? Should you do some with the technology and some without? After the design and implementation, the teachers will analyze the data and come to some conclusions. One of the natural questions will be "How much of the effect of the lesson was technology-enhanced?" In other words, could the factors that really improved instruction be done without the technology? How did the technology enable or enhance the lesson?

A COLLEAGUE WITH WHOM TO LEARN IT: TEACHER EDUCATORS AS CATALYSTS

Teacher educators, whether college instructors, district personnel, math coaches, or other teacher educator roles, play an important role in the process of getting teaching to engage in action research. Whether requiring action research as a part of a course or encouraging action research as an interested and supportive colleague, teachers often needs that extra push that teacher educators provide. Along with an encouraging nudge, however, teachers need other forms of ongoing support.

Another way to be a catalyst is by actively seeking research partners for teachers. As with most things in life, teachers are much more likely to participate with someone that they consider to be a colleague. Specifically, teachers tend to seek out those that they believe has with similar roles and responsibilities. If you want an algebra 1 teacher to engage in action research, for example, then find another algebra 1 teacher that has some of the same questions. With similar questions to answer and similar responsibilities, it is much more likely that the teachers will see the input of the other as relevant and applicable to their own situation.

TPACK ACTION RESEARCH QUESTIONS

Once teachers are convinced that engaging in action research is doable and helpful, what questions will they have? Specifically, what are some of the technology-related questions that teachers are likely to have when seeking to effectively implement CCSS? In my experience, there are four levels of questions:

Level 1 - Role/Interpretation: What is the Role of Technology in the Common Core?

Level 2 - Efficacy: Does this technology really help students learn? How?

Level 3 - Local Best Practice: What are the best ways to use this technology?

Level 4 - Tweaking for Maximum Effect: What small changes in my lesson can provide even more of a positive effect?

Table 1 provides examples for each of these levels.

Although we as teacher educators would like to start at levels three and four, we often find that we must give the teachers time to struggle though

Table 1. Examples of TPACK action research questions

Level	Example Questions
Level 1: Role/ Interpretation	• Which technology tools might be helpful as I prepare to teach a lesson on representing data to my 3rd graders? • For which standards do I use dynamic geometry software? • Is there a Web-based tool that will help me teach concept of function at a 7th grade level?
Level 2: Efficacy	• When is it counterproductive to use calculators in learning number concepts? • In what ways does the use of interactive Web applets have on students understanding of rates of change and slope? • Is this software package intended to support the learning of the concept or is it more about practicing after they have learned?
Level 3: Local Best Practice	• What are the most effective ways to use dynamic geometry software with this content? • Should I create a separate lesson just on how to use spreadsheets or should those skills be learned while focusing on math content? • How do I effectively manage/supervise the students' use of Web-based data sources for this lesson?
Level 4: Tweaking for Maximum Effect	• Should I have them study this pattern on their own using spreadsheets or should I give them a step-by-step guide? What learning outcomes change when I make that change? • For my lesson on even numbers, will it be more effective to start with the calculator activity first and then move to the basketball shoot-off? Should I switch the order and do the basketball activity first? • Should I model the use of this Web applet first or allow the students to explore on their own first? How will this change affect students' ability to stay on task?

levels one and two before they are willing to tackle questions at levels three and four. In fact, from the perspective of a great many teachers, the questions at levels three and four may not make sense and/or may seem irrelevant until they have struggled through the first two levels. In short, the teacher must believe that technology both can and should support students learning of the mathematics outlined in the standard before they are willing to explore the nest practices for using such technologies in their teaching. In their concern for students learning of "real math" as they understand it, the teachers may feel unable to accept the word of one or two teacher educators in good conscience.

In the case of a teacher who remains at level one or two, the role of the teacher educator must include that of playing referee regarding the process of exploring what the "research" has to say. Specifically, we must constantly remind the teachers of the standards by which the education community operates regarding evidence and peer review. If a teacher wants to find publications that stand firm against the use of technology, they will find plenty. If, however, you set a standard of a peer-reviewed journal article and require that there be real data from real classrooms supporting their conclusions, then they have precious little that will support their position. Our role is a tough one. We MUST allow it to be their journey, but we must also make sure they stay within those constraints. If they do, they will eventually be willing to begin the process of "trying out" the technologies.

The role of the teacher educator changes once the teacher is ready to engage in action research in their classroom using a technology-based lesson. We are still playing referee, but now we are ensuring that:

- The technology is being implemented in ways consistent with the best practices outlined in the research.
- Assessment data is being collected at all stages that is useful and informative towards the specific questions being asked.
- The teacher examines the evidence in an objective, coordinated, and useful fashion.

In over a decade of guiding action research of preservice and inservice teachers, I have found that if I can get them to play by this set of rules, one good action research project can move a teacher past levels one and two. Moreover, it can pique their interest enough to motivate a stage three study into using the technology more effectively.

REFERENCES

Common Core Standards Initiative. (2010). *The common core state standards for mathematics*. Retrieved from http://www.corestandards.org/assets/CCSSI_Math%20Standards.pdf

Mills, G. E. (2011). *Action research: A guide for the teacher researcher* (4th ed.). Boston, MA: Pearson.

Mishra, P., & Koehler, M. J. (2006). Technological pedagogical content knowledge: A framework for teacher knowledge. *Teachers College Record*, *108*(6), 1017–1054. doi:10.1111/j.1467-9620.2006.00684.x.

Niess, M. L., Ronau, R. N., Shafer, K. G., Driskell, S. O., Harper, S. R., & Johnston, C. et al. (2009). Mathematics teacher TPACK standards and development model. *Contemporary Issues in Technology & Teacher Education*, *9*(1), 4–24.

ADDITIONAL READING

American Association of Colleges of Teacher Education (AACTE). (2007). *Handbook of technological pedagogical content knowledge*. New York: Taylor and Francis.

Common Core Standards Initiative. (2010). *The common core state standards for mathematics*. Retrieved from http://www.corestandards.org/assets/CCSSI_Math%20Standards.pdf

Mills, G. E. (2011). *Action research: A guide for the teacher researcher* (4th ed.). Boston, MA: Pearson.

Mishra, P., & Koehler, M. J. (2006). Technological pedagogical content knowledge: A framework for teacher knowledge. *Teachers College Record*, *108*(6), 1017–1054. doi:10.1111/j.1467-9620.2006.00684.x.

Niess, M. L., Ronau, R. N., Shafer, K. G., Driskell, S. O., Harper, S. R., & Johnston, C. et al. (2009). Mathematics teacher TPACK standards and development model. *Contemporary Issues in Technology & Teacher Education*, *9*(1), 4–24.

Section 2
Content and Context

Chapter 5
Fostering Mathematical Competence through Technology–Enhanced Interactive Environments

Azita Manouchehriazi
The Ohio State University, USA

Yating Liu
Old Dominion University, USA

Jennifer Czocher
Texas State University-San Marcos, USA

Pingping Zhang
The Ohio State University, USA

Ravi Somayajulu
Eastern Illinois University, USA

Jenna Tague
The Ohio State University, USA

ABSTRACT

In this longitudinal research project, the authors traced the impact of a mathematics enrichment program on a group of approximately 80 middle and high school students as they worked on mathematical explorations using interactive computer software for three years. The results indicate that learning environments designed for children supported their development of mathematical practices emphasized by the CCSMP while increasing their exposure to and understanding of content standards.

INTRODUCTION

Common Core Standards of Mathematical Practices (CCSSMP) propose that all students of mathematics must be nurtured so to:

1. Make sense of problems and persevere in solving them.
2. Reason abstractly and quantitatively.
3. Construct viable arguments and critique the reasoning of others.
4. Model with mathematics.
5. Use appropriate tools strategically.
6. Attend to precision.
7. Look for and make use of structure.
8. Look for and express regularity in repeated reasoning (CCSS, p. 5).

DOI: 10.4018/978-1-4666-4086-3.ch005

The central idea embodied in the CCSSMP is the view that mathematical competence entails not just acquisition of factual information about various concepts covered in the curriculum, but also the attainment of dispositions and the reasoning tools crucial both to authentic mathematical thinking and the mathematizing (Schoenfeld, 1994) process. Inherently, the ultimate vision of CCSSMP is for all children to develop a mathematical point of view (Schoenfeld, 2005); build an inclination to view and interpret what is encountered using mathematical tools and using those tools in the service of finding/describing structurally important features and/or relationships in and among phenomena observed or experienced. The particular emphasis that CCSS place on using mathematics to model phenomenon capitalizes the need to increase the children's capacity to think and engage in practices common among mathematicians: search for patterns and generalities, use patterns to predict the behavior of the phenomenon under study, and test and validate results systemically. Therefore, the mathematical practices provide a platform for considering mathematics as a mode of thinking and a particular type of intellectual disposition that needs to be supported throughout all mathematical experiences designed for children. As such, these practices and content standards cannot and should not be treated as mutually exclusive, but as deeply intertwined and reflexive domains. Mathematical content provides a context for development of desired mathematical practices. Inversely, mathematical practices provide a structure for designing curriculum and instruction around the content. Therefore, the design of instructional tasks as well the media used to engage children in those tasks serve as two vital instructional ingredients since they provide the means for the type of mathematical thinking and dispositions children learn to develop. The presence of interactive technologies (mathematical software), and its use as an instructional medium, further punctuates the need for careful selection of instructional tasks since together they can form

venues for engaging children in mathematics and mathematical thinking that are not accessible in traditional static environments of the past. We will elaborate on this point more fully later. Lastly, the primary postulate in our work is the notion that the development of mathematical dispositions desired by the CCSS is less likely to be achieved through episodic exposure to quality resources and is instead fostered through deliberate, regular, and continuing interactions with quality interrelated resources and tasks. Therefore, in our work we aimed to go beyond illustrating or examining children's practices on isolated tasks,[1] and instead trace the students' growth overtime.

GENERATIVE TASKS

In mathematics education literature and professional journals, a number of terms have been coined to describe quality tasks conducive to advancing mathematical cognition of learners. Among many include: rich, authentic, open-ended, cognitively demanding, exploratory and investigative. Despite some minor differences in structure, these labels share several common characteristics: they allow rooms for multiplicity of entries and responses, provide opportunities for practice of communication, reasoning, and problem solving, and engage students in understanding of mathematical concepts while eliciting justifying and explaining of answers. We fully endorse the importance of these characteristics and believe they are necessary conditions for nurturing mathematical abilities of learners and strengthening their conceptual understandings. However, we argue that these attributes are not sufficient to characterize the types of tasks that foster the mathematical practices described in the common core standards. We view mathematics as a structure-finding activity and so we propose the construct *Generative*, to suggest three additional features of tasks that aim to move students towards generalizing: extendibility, coherence, and significance. These three features focus sharply on the mathematical destination of the task, as a cumulative activity, towards the goal of advancing the learners' mathematical thinking and dispositions. Extendibility implies that the task affords the learners the opportunity to consider classes of mathematical objects, for example, through searching for unique and common features of mathematical objects in a systemic way. Coherence means that the experience of doing the task allows for development of generalizations regarding relationships among mathematical objects and structures. Significance suggests that the task addresses important mathematics central to the subject and the topic under investigation.

These features become particularly important when used in technologically rich environment where individuals gain immediate access to numerical, visual, and graphical feedback on their mathematical actions. The use of technology in solving generative tasks neither reduces the integrity of the mathematics involved, nor leads students to immediate answers. Instead, it facilitates the students' engagement in mathematical explorations geared towards finding and describing structures, by allowing them a conjecturing space, immediate access to representations and data they could use to test ideas and answers. These features have been identified as central to conducting productive inquiry, leading to generative discourse among learners.

CONTEXT

Our longitudinal study traced the growth of mathematical practices of approximately 80 middle and high school children (3 cohorts) as the result of their involvement in an enrichment program designed around the use of technological resources, inquiry based instructional methods, and generative tasks. The students (30 in 8th grade, 25 in 9th grade, and 25 in 10th grade) were drawn from multiple urban schools. The program brought the children together two Saturdays a month, for approximately two hours, throughout the entire academic year (approximately 20 sessions per year). The children's participation in the program was voluntary and they did not receive any monitory compensation for doing so.

The students were referred as participants in our program through the office of Diversity and Inclusion at the institution where the mathematics enrichment program resided. All students were drawn from urban communities. Collectively, the cohorts comprised 85% African-American and recent immigrants from African countries, 10% Latino, and 5% Caucasian students. We augmented their respective curricular experiences with generative tasks, and traced the development of the children's mathematical thinking as they progressed from 8th to 10th grade by focusing on the evolution of their problem solving skills, development of reasoning techniques, and execution of those reasoning techniques as they explored of a variety of mathematical topics.

Our work was guided by 5 key principles, which highlighted not only our beliefs about mathematics and its spirit as a discipline, but also in establishing the culture of inquiry and mathematical dispositions we hoped to foster among learners. The program instructors shared and reinforced these principles and their content throughout the range of their interactions with children.

- **Explore:** Look, search, and experiment!
- **Extract:** What do you notice? Is there a pattern? What stays the same? What changes? What new mathematics do you see?
- **Explain:** How do you explain this result? Why does this happen? What do we already know that can help us explain this result?
- **Extend:** What if we now consider the same relationship but among a different class of objects?

- **Elaborate:** How can we justify accuracy of these results and findings? How can we convince others?

All students at all grade levels were introduced to three specific dynamic interactive software programs including: Geometer's Sketchpad (CCP, 2012), spreadsheets (Microsoft excel, 2012), and Graphing Calculators (aka. Nucalc) (Pacific, 2000). They used the software as they worked on mathematical explorations and modeling tasks we assigned them during the sessions.

CURRICULUM

The problems selected and used with each cohort came exclusively from two sources: Intermath Project (Wilson, 2012a) and Jim Wilson's Technology in Secondary Mathematics Education course Webpage (Wilson, 2012b, 2005). Our choice of these particular resources was deliberate since their activities met the criteria of generative task we wished to use. Additionally, the sites offer pre-constructed interactive media for exploring specific mathematical contexts that the students could easily manipulate.

Rather than differentiating the content that different aged children experience according to grade level or subject area, as it is done traditionally in schools, we focused instead on exposing all children to the same content topics but at different levels of sophistication in a manner that matched their development and background knowledge. Four main topics included: Geometric transformations (isometries), functions and their behaviors under different transformations and operations, numerical analysis, and mathematical modeling. Appendix A includes two illustrative examples of the types of tasks used, levels of task sophistication, and content standards addressed by them.

The majority of tasks (approximately 70%) we used with children are exclusively computer-based explorations. All other activities endorsed autonomy to children allowing them to recruit the tools they wished to use and procedures they selected to employ when solving them. Choice and autonomy granted them opportunities to draw on and apply knowledge and techniques that they deemed fitting or appropriate to each problem. Computers were made available; graphing calculators were also present during all sessions. Children could choose to move from one media to another when solving problems.

During each session, children were presented with a multi-part activity. They worked either individually or in small groups on tasks using computers and graphing calculators. Whole group sharing of observations and discussion of results were ongoing as students were encouraged to communicate their spontaneous findings with the entire group as a means to provide contexts for examination of ideas and extension of tasks. The teacher facilitated the group work and inquiry by asking questions, responding to questions, or challenging children's ideas when under and over-generalization is shared.

In our work, we used exclusive use of three specific interactive computer programs: Graphing Calculator (NuCalc); Geometer's sketchpad, and Mircosoft Excel. The capabilities of each of these software environments matched the type of desired activities suggested by the CCSS of content. A description of each of these environments is provided next.

TECHNOLOGY

- **Graphing Calculator (a.k.a NuCalc) Software:** (Pacific Tec, 2000) Is an interactive computer based relation-grapher that affords the user symbolic and numeric methods for visualizing two and three dimensional mathematical objects. The user needs only to type any mathematical relation (not limited to functional relationship) and view the graph of the relationship immediately and simultaneously. Explorations with conic sections, parametric, and polar relationships become easily accessible to young users permitting them to seek regularities among different mathematical relationships graphically and so provides means for building intuition and visualization skills. The software also allows for creating dynamic animations of mathematical object. For instance, given the input y=sinπx+nsin2πx, the software treats n as the changing parameter in the equation and produces graphs of functions for different values of n, creating an animated movie of y for various instances of n. By adjusting the range of n, the user has control over the range of functions examined in sequence. This particular capability provides fertile ground for the user to seek regularities and examine structural features of parent functions or relations (See Figure 1).

Figure 1. Example

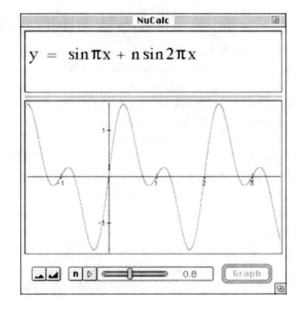

- **Geometer Sketchpad:** (Key Curriculum press, 2012) Is an interactive, dynamic geometry software widely used at both pre and college levels. The user can manipulate dynamic models of fractions, number lines, and geometric patterns; explore ratio and proportion, rate of change, and functional relationships through numeric, tabular, and graphical representations; construct and transform geometric shapes and functions from linear to trigonometric. This tool gives a tangible and visual way to explore mathematics, making it more meaningful and promoting deep understanding.

- **Excel Spreadsheets:** (Microsoft, 2012) The spreadsheet is a utility tool that can be used in a variety of types of explorations, and simulations in mathematics. It is an easy media to use and manipulate for exploring number structures. The environment makes available opportunities for users to create recursive sequences and generating functions. It provides a conjecturing space where students can quickly examine patterns and structures among large data sets, both numerically and graphically, test for best-fit functions, and seek generalization.

BEHAVIORAL INDICATORS: MATHEMATICAL PRACTICES

In documenting potential shifts in students' dispositions and their mathematical practices, we considered 18 behavioral indicators as representatives of the 8 standards of mathematical practices based on either the suggestions of literature in mathematics education or commonly agreed upon norms of practice within the mathematics community[2] (NRC, 2011, Hadlock, 2007) A description of indicators conceived as relevant to each proposed standard are listed and described as followed.

MP1: Make sense of problems and persevere in solving them.
  1.1. Amount of time spend on the task without teacher intervention.
  1.2. Requests for further explaining (from each other or the teacher).

MP 1 most accentuates the need for children to engage and invest in tasks. That is, for the learners to personalize mathematics, attempt to make sense of what they are asked and to navigate solution processes accordingly. Thus, we considered the amount of time they spent on tasks, and whether they asked for explanations regarding the conditions and assumptions of problems as evidence of their engagement in exploring mathematics. Of particular concern was whether these actions were self/group initiated or reinforced by the teachers. Therefore, we considered self initiated episodes as indicators of personalization and attempts at internalization of mathematics under study.

MP2: Reason abstractly and quantitatively.
  2.1. Episodes of unsupported assertions.
  2.2. Simple reasons for justifying observed mathematical behaviors.
  2.3. Elaborated reasons for justifying observed mathematical behaviors.

Explaining and justifying are two crucial epistemic actions central to mathematical thinking. We interpreted the MP2 to imply that the learners would rely on data when posing arguments and justifying conjectures. We differentiated among the levels of reasoning used in their discourse and whether they adopted more conventional modes of mathematical argumentation. For the purpose of our work, we considered "Unsupported assertions" to include instances when statements were made without any supporting explanation. This type of assertion could easily lead to either an over-generalization or an under-generalization. Simple reasoning relied on calculations and instances of solutions to explain and justify. In contrast, when multiple, interrelated arguments were made to support a certain assertion, it was marked as elaborated reasoning. Relative to each of the previous items, we also determined whether group members objected to the unsupported assertions their peers made. In this way we measured the participants' responsiveness to mathematical explanations offered in the whole group. These same indicators became relevant when seeking evidence of actions pertaining to the third standard, as described next.

MP3: Construct viable arguments and critique the reasoning of others.
  3.1. Objections to unsupported assertions.
  3.2. Number of times the students challenged conjectures proposed.

Third mathematical practice expects that the individual will learn to critically examine arguments, analyze, and respond to mathematical statements and propositions they encounter. In determining individuals' growth, we considered both verbal and non-verbal clues. For instance we considered a return to technology or paper and pencil for further exploration as a non-verbal clue indicating the influence of a peer on extending the mathematical activity of the group. When students asked "what if" questions, challenged an argument, or made statements such as "I see," "Is that right? Could this be correct?" "Let me try it," we characterized them as verbal clues including engagement in mathematical thinking.

MP4: Model with mathematics.
  4.1. Episodes of representing the problem with mathematical tools.
  4.2. Episodes of explaining results using mathematics.

Modeling with mathematics is perhaps one of the broadest standard of practice among the list provided by CCSS since its content can easily vary from learners describing a simple sequence to numbers using a formula, using a particular algorithm for solving problems, or finding best fit functions for given data sets. Without the loss of generality, we considered episodes of reliance on mathematical tools as evidence of individuals' work pertaining to this particular standard.

MP5: Use appropriate tools strategically
> 5.1. Episodes of shifts in the choice of representations used.
> 5.2. Episodes of shifts in the choice of problem solving heuristic used.

Successful mathematical problem solving depends largely on the individuals' ability to assess their own progress, be flexible in their thinking and make necessary shifts in approaches if those previously used prove ineffective in launching mathematical insight. Two major areas in which such flexible decision making become evident is in individuals' choices of heuristics, and representations when solving problems. The ability to recognize the need to shift from one representational mode to another, or to change the problem solving strategy when appropriate and needed is key to effective mathematical thinking. As such we considered the two indicators of growth along this standard to include episodes of presence of each of these two specific actions in their work.

MP6: Attention to precision
> 6.1. Episodes of testing and verifying answers.
> 6.2. Search for counter examples.
> 6.3. Consideration of the impact of assumption on behaviors of objects.
> 6.4. Episodes of under and over generalization.

Although measuring individuals' attention to precision, as a general dispositional attribute, might be difficult to do since its nature depends largely on the context posed, we perceive this standard to imply greater commitment to mathematical rigor in formulating assertions and arguments by students. From this perspective, we considered episodes of testing and verifying answers, searches for counter examples to general assertions, re-evaluations of assumptions held when examining the answers as evidence of the children's development in this area.

Attention to structure and regularity:

MP7: Look for and make use of structure.
> 7.1. Number of extensions pursued/explored.
> 7.2. Number of informed generalizations made.

MP8: Look for and express regularity in repeated reasoning

We acknowledge that depending on mathematical context under study, the qualities of MP7 and MP8 might be different. However, for the purpose of our coding and in light of the qualities of our preferred tasks, we believed it more useful to cluster the behaviors that surfaced along these two standards.

PROCEDURE

In detecting shifts in the participants' mathematical dispositions as described by the MP standards, we relied on two different types of analysis. First, we reviewed and coded the videotapes of the sessions for each of the grade-based cohorts during the first two sessions (Phase I) and the last two sessions (Phase II) of the first year of their involvement in the program (approximately 8 hours of video footage per cohort, total of 24 hours of video data). For each of the practices described in the previous section, we calculated the total

Table 1. Children's performance after one year of exposure to the program

	Beginning of the year N=80		End of the year N=76		
	Mean	SD	Mean	SD	t
MP1: make sense of problems and persevere in solving them					
1.1. Amount of time spend on the task without teacher intervention	4.67	2.05	22.00	1.41	12.04 **
1.2. Episodes of requests for further explaining (from each other or the teacher)	2.33	2.05	12.33	2.36	5.54 **
MP2: Reason abstractly and quantitatively					
2.1. Episodes of unsupported assertions	25.33	4.99	18.33	4.03	-1.89
2.2. Simple reasons justifying or explaining results	24.33	3.30	34.33	6.65	2.33
2.3. Elaborated reasons justifying or explaining results	3.33	1.70	9.33	3.30	2.80 *
MP3: Construct viable arguments and critique the reasoning of others					
3.1. Objections to unsupported assertions	2.67	1.89	8.33	1.70	3.87 *
3.2. Number of times the students challenged conjectures proposed	3.00	2.16	6.00	0.82	2.25
MP4: Model with mathematics					
4.1. Episodes of representing the problem with mathematical tools	5.33	1.70	11.33	3.09	2.95 *
4.2. Episodes of explaining results without carrying calculations	3.00	0.82	9.33	2.05	4.96 **
MP5: Use appropriate tools strategically					
5.1. Shifts in choice of representations (suggested or initiated)	0.67	0.94	4.67	1.89	3.29 *
5.2. Shifts in choice of heuristics (suggested or initiated)	0.00	0.00	5.00	3.27	2.65
MP6: Attention to precision					
6.1. Episodes of testing and verifying answers	1.67	1.70	34.33	1.70	23.54 **
6.2. Search for counter examples	0.00	0.00	12.33	0.47	45.32 **
6.3. Consideration of the impact of specific assumptions on behaviors of objects	2.00	0.82	13.00	2.16	8.25 **
6.4. Episodes of under and over generalization	18.33	1.89	12.00	1.41	-4.65 **
MPs 7 & 8: Look for and express regularity in repeated reasoning Look for and make use of structure					
7.1. Number of Extensions initiated by students	0.00	0.00	18.00	3.56	8.76 **
7.2. Number of informed generalizations made	1.00	0.82	13.00	2.16	9.00 **

Numbers represent the mean and standard deviations during the first and last two sessions at the end of the first year. Time is measured in minutes.

* significance at alpha = 0.05 (. t > 2.78) **significance at alpha = 0.01 (t > 4.60)

number of times each target behavior occurred at each phase and for each of the groups during the whole class discussions and interactions[3]. We then computed descriptive statistics (mean and standard deviation) for each of the measures. We compared the data on quantitative measures of the group actions to explore how the presence of technology influenced the mathematical practices of the participants. Pair-wise comparisons were conducted on all target measures using t-tests maintaining an experiment-wise alpha at .05. The results are summarized in Table 1.

For the second level of analysis, we chose to consider the practices of the only cohort that had 3 consecutive years of exposure to the program as a means to trace long term impact of their involvement with mathematical experiences we provided them. These were the students that had joined the enrichment program when in the 8th grade and maintained involvement though 9th and 10th grades while in their respective schools. For this cohort, we selected the last two sessions at the end of each of the three years to view and analyze in detail. We then followed the evolution of their mathematical practices. The results are summarized in Table 3.

FINDINGS

Table 1 summarizes the entire group's mathematical practices at the beginning and the end of one full year of exposure to our technology-enhanced inquiry-based enrichment program.

Figure 2 offers a comparison of means along each performance indicator.

Data indicated significant changes in the participants' mathematical practices, as exhibited during the sessions we reviewed, along 13 of the 18 targeted measures, with the level of significance at 0.01 level for 9 of such measures. These changes were the result of exposure to only 20 hours of enrichment activities they had encountered. A closer inspection of the data revealed interesting results. Significant increase in the amount of time students spent on task without teacher intervention (1.1), coupled with the significant increase in the number of extensions of tasks they pursued and mature generalizations they made (7.1, 7.2) during the sessions suggest not only engagement in autonomous mathematical work but also informed and focused attempts at finding and generalizing results. Data indicate that not only the average amount of time the students spent explaining ideas increased but also the amount of time they stayed focused on mathematical work. Positive changes also occurred in the number of times students requested further

Figure 2. The heights denote the value of the mean; while 1.1-7.2 denotes the index # of the items (See Table 1 for details)

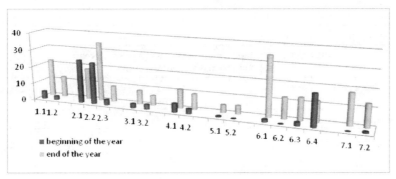

Table 2. Children's performance after three years of exposure to the program. The number represent the total number of times each behavior was exhibited during the sessions used for analysis.

	Beginning of Yr I (8th grade) N= 25	End of Yr I (8th grade) N= 25	End of the Yr II (9th grade) N=22	End of Yr III (10th grade) N=20
	Total	Total	Total	Total
MP1: Make sense of problems and persevere in solving them				
1.1. Amount of time spend on the task without teacher intervention	2	20	45	92
1.2. Requests for further explaining (from each other or the teacher)	5	14	22	23
MP2: Reason abstractly and quantitatively				
2.1. Episodes of unsupported assertions	32	24	22	12
2.2. Simple reasons justifying or explaining results	20	25	30	12
2.3. Elaborated reasons justifying or explaining results	1	5	18	34
MP3: Construct viable arguments and critique the reasoning of others				
3.1. Objections to unsupported assertions	0	6	15	34
3.2. Number of times the students challenged conjectures proposed	0	5	28	23
MP4: Model with mathematics				
4.1. Episodes of representing the problem with mathematical tools	3	7	43	58
4.2. Episodes of explaining results without carrying calculations (relying on theoretical reasoning)	4	12	25	41
MP5: Use appropriate tools strategically				
5.1. Shifts in choice of representations (suggested or initiated)	0	2	11	18
5.2. Shifts in choice of heuristics (suggested or initiated)	0	1	7	15
MP6: Attention to precision				
6.1. Episodes of testing and verifying answers or suggestions	4	32	56	95
6.2. Search for counter examples	0	13	29	42
6.3. Consideration of the impact of specific parameters on behaviors of objects	1	10	28	45
6.4. Episodes of under and over generalization	21	13	10	15
MPs 7 & 8: Look for and express regularity in repeated reasoning Look for and make use of structure				
7.1. Number of Extensions initiated by students pursued/explored	0	13	28	45
7.2. Number of informed generalizations made	1	15	22	36

Table 3. Comparison of performance of children according to grade level

	Experimental group at the end of the 9th grade	Control group at the end of the 9th grade	Experimental group at the end of the 10th grade	Control group at the end of the 10th grade
	Total	Total	Total	Total
MP1: Make sense of problems and persevere in solving them				
1.1. Amount of time spend on the task without teacher intervention	45	21	92	23
1.2. Requests for further explaining (from each other or the teacher)	22	9	23	14
MP2: Reason abstractly and quantitatively				
2.1. Episodes of unsupported assertions	22	15	12	38
2.2. Simple reasons justifying or explaining results	30	40	12	16
2.3. Elaborated reasons justifying or explaining results	18	13	34	10
MP3: Construct viable arguments and critique the reasoning of others				
3.1. Objections to unsupported assertions	15	9	34	10
3.2. Number of times the students challenged conjectures proposed	28	7	23	6
MP4: Model with mathematics				
4.1. Episodes of representing the problem with mathematical tools	43	14	58	13
4.2. Episodes of explaining results without carrying calculations (relying on theoretical reasoning)	25	7	41	9
MP5: Use appropriate tools strategically				
5.1. Shifts in choice of representations (suggested or initiated)	11	6	18	16
5.2. Shifts in choice of heuristics (suggested or initiated)	7	5	15	19
MP6: Attention to precision				
6.1. Episodes of testing and verifying answers or suggestions	56	35	95	36
6.2. Search for counter examples	29	12	42	12
6.3. Consideration of the impact of specific parameters on behaviors of objects	28	15	45	14
6.4. Episodes of under and over generalization	10	10	15	13
MPs 7 & 8: Look for and express regularity in repeated reasoning Look for and make use of structure				
7.1. Number of Extensions initiated by students pursued/explored	28	21	45	20
7.2. Number of mature generalizations made	22	10	36	14

explanation and elaborations from one another on problems they explored. This point is further supported by the significant decrease in the number of rushed conjecturing episodes (6.4) prominent during the first two sessions.

Note also that although the number of unsupported assertions posed during the session appear to have remained stable, when we consider, in tandem, this result with the significant gains in the area of tending to precision (6.1 and 6.2) it would only mean that the children developed regulatory skills for monitoring their own conjectures. Similarly, although the number of times the participants objected to irrelevant explanations or unsupported conjectures of peers (3.2) did not change significantly, but evidence of reflective analysis and testing by asking for further explaining (1.2), increased occasions of objecting to unsupported assertions (3.1) evidences a higher degree of sensitivity to mathematical accuracy on their part. This occurred both in terms of their interactions with peers and with mathematics content.

An important observation concerns positive shift in the level of sophistication of mathematical arguments students formed and the quantity of mathematical explanations they presented in class. The results also indicate a significant increase in the number of instances of reflective behavior students exhibited.

Lastly, significant shifts in the participants' choice of representations (5.1) suggest positive impact of exposure to the technological environments. It appears that by moving from one representational media to another in the context of the same task they learned how to extract needed information from the variety that could be used as resources.

GROUP PERFORMANCE: AFTER THREE YEARS OF EXPOSURE

Previous analysis concerned the performance of children after one full year of exposure to the program. Of particular interest to us was detecting the impact of these learning experiences on children who had experienced the program for three consecutive years. In examining this issue we coded the videotapes of sessions at four phases of children's involvement: First two session of year I (Phase I), last two sessions of year I (Phase II), last two sessions of their second year (Phase III) and last two sessions of their third year (Phase III) of participation. This analysis would provide a trajectory of growth of participants[4] over time. Table 2 summaries the results of the group performance on selected targeted measures. Figure 3 summarizes the same data graphically. Visual inspection of the graph suggests that children

Figure 3. Note: The heights denote the value of the total; while 1.1 – 7.2 denotes the index # of the items, See Table 1 for details

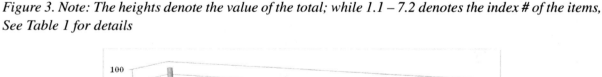
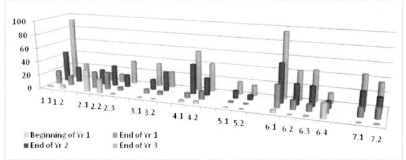

showed growth in all domains, most prominently along standards 1, 4, 6, and 7. Less notable growth patterns seem to have occurred along standards 2, 3 and 5. Analysis of data by standard reveals a compelling explanation of growth, described in Table 2.

INDIVIDUAL ANALYSIS

Figures 3-9 offer accounts of children's performance on each individual standard of MP.

Figure 4 shows steady gains on the two indicators chosen to capturing growth in MP1. However, substantially larger rate of growth was achieved on 1.1 (time spent on tasks without teacher intervention) during the third year of involvement. In comparison, requests for further explaining from each other seemed to reach a plateau towards the end of the second year. This could mean that as children gained greater facility with both technology and task expectations they became more autonomous in mathematizing. Such an interpretation is further supported with results are augmented with descriptive data on significant gains in the area of attention to precision.

Figure 5 shows the children's overtime performance on the three indicators used to document

practices pertaining to MP2. Data shows that although episodes of elaborated reasoning when justifying answers increased steadily throughout the three years, the decline in the number of unsupported assertions experienced less rapid decline. This result however, merit further analysis. On the one hand, when comparing the percentage of episodes of unsupported assertions to the total number of the episodes of explaining and justifying during coded sessions at each year, significant decreases become most visible. The decline in the number of simple explanations during the third year could be attributed to one of two things. On the one hand, the tendency to offer elaborated explanations replaced the practice of providing simple explanations. On the other hand, the types of activities used during the third year demands far more detailed descriptions from children (See Figure 6).

Figure 7 offers a remarkable view of children's work regarding children's practice of modeling with mathematics. While the habit of producing theoretical explanations seems to have followed steady growth during all three years, the facility with using mathematical tools when representing mathematics gained substantially during the second year. This could be attributed to the symbolic tools children had developed in school since

Figure 4. Children's performance on MP1 over the course of three years

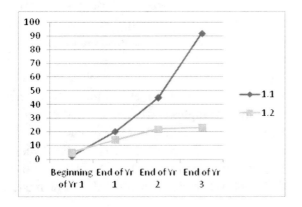

Figure 5. Children's performance on MP2 over the course of three years

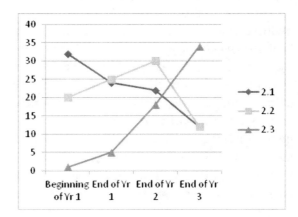

Figure 6. Children's performance on MP4 over the course of three years

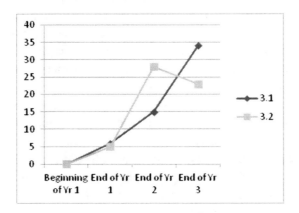

Figure 8. Children's performance on MP5 over the course of three years

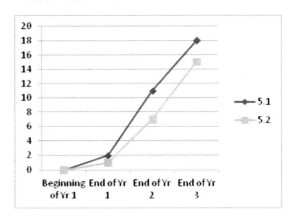

Figure 7. Children's performance on MP4 over the course of three years

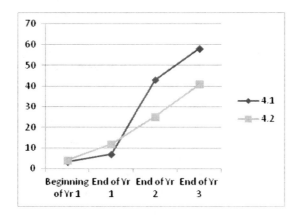

Figure 9. Children's performance on MP6 over the course of three years

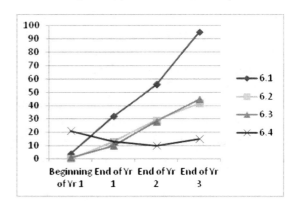

a majority of the participants were enrolled in an Algebra course during that year.

Figure 8 captions children's flexible use of multiple representations and problem solving heuristics when engaged in tasks. Although lines show growth in both areas we are concerned that children seem less inclined to shift their choice of problem solving heuristics. Considerable growth in the area of flexible use of representations is understandable due to access provided for them through technology. Drawing on this result we are inclined to believe that since no direct instruction on problem solving heuristics was

given to children during the sessions then opportunities for their development in this area was limited. This signals the need to make deliberate efforts towards not only designing tasks that elicit multiple heuristics, but making explicit the utility of each heuristic in different mathematical contexts.

Figure 9 illustrates constant increase in the number of times children tested ideas, searched for counter examples and examined assumptions that could influence answers to problems, with greatest variance occurring during the third year. The phenomenon of the low rate of decline in the number of over-and-under generalizations made

Figure 10. Children's performance on MP7 over the course of three years

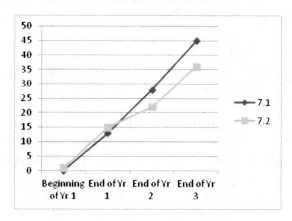

by children can be explained in a manner similar to the compatible results revealed in case of their use of unsupported assertions. That is, while the rate of decline is low the overall percentage of comments evident during the session show significant decrease.

Figure 10 proposes that the habit of extending mathematical investigations was most significantly supported during the second and third years of exposure to the program.

DOES THREE YEARS MATTER?

A major issue for our research team was accuracy of claims that we could make regarding the influence of the length of time of involvement in the program and the children's development. That is, we were concerned whether participation in the program beyond a first year could have significantly influenced children's mathematical work as depicted in the results. Additionally, questions were raised whether certain patterns of behaviors were a natural consequence of maturation (age) and their school mathematical experiences. In investigating these issues we decided to compare data on the performance of the experimental sample with those obtained from 9th and 10th graders with only one year of experience in the program. We

compared the data from the sample of 8th graders (experimental samples) with the grade-based compatible groups (control samples) at the end of each year. We use the labels of experimental and control only to differentiate between the children's years of exposure to program. Table 3 offers a summary of data obtained from each group at the end of each year.

Results indicate that at the end of end of 9th and 10th grades, the experimental group demonstrated significantly higher facility with the standards of mathematical practice than their peers with only one year of experience in the program. Considerable gains in areas concerning persistence on tasks and pursuing larger number of extensions, mature generalization made, modeling with mathematics and attention to precision and use of theoretical knowledge are of particular importance to us since these attributes are central to success in advanced mathematical work. Although growth appear to follow at a linear rate greatest degrees of maturity in 9 of the 18 targeted measure (1.1, 2.3, 3.1, 4.1, 4.2, 6.1, 6.3, 7.1, 7.2) seem to have become evident in the third year of involvement.

DISCUSSION

Our research findings and observations of children's sustained work on technology-enhanced mathematical explorations suggest that the type of partnership, which supports students' capacity for pursuing understanding of mathematical content and shapes the relationship between their content knowledge and the dispositions that engender productive mathematical practices, lies in consistent and coherent use of technology within the classroom. As our task examples suggest quality of mathematics that our students experienced are significantly more sophisticated than those expected of them by the content standards. The presence of technology did not reduce the mathematical rigor expected of children's work but instead increased it.

Results indicate that technology can accommodate successful implementation of CCSS by: (1) allowing students entry into mathematical tasks and granting them immediate access to multiple representations and feedback; (2) affording learners opportunities for abstracting and generalizing hence, shifting their mathematical work from examination of isolated cases to finding and describing patterns; (3) providing a communication tool for engagement in sustained mathematical inquiry. We further highlight the role of technology as vital cultural and mathematical scaffolding mechanism when implementing CCSS for both content and mathematical practices (Wilensky, 2006). Although technology can be used to serve a variety of functions in mathematics classrooms (i.e. as an information provider [Internet search] or presentation media [smart-board]), of particular concern in our work is its utility for fostering mathematical thinking and productive dispositions that enhance children's mathematical cognition. Consequently, we emphasize the power of interactive software, coupled with generative tasks, for allowing students access to mathematics, serving as a problem solving assistant and a structure finding aid.

Whilst the CCSS themselves do not dictate curriculum pedagogy or delivery of content (CCSM, p. 84), research over the past two decades sheds light on the type of curriculum, teaching practices, and classroom environments that can assist in development of the skills and dispositions advocated by them. Balance between cultivating student achievement through striving for conceptual understanding (Star, 2010) and building a learning environment that is receptive to effective teacher scaffolding (e.g., multiple representations, discourse, peer collaboration) must be sought. In our classrooms, the teachers supported individual explorations and stressed the importance of inquiry along with collaborative construction of knowledge with peers. The activities used were geared fundamentally towards providing opportunities for children to consider important mathematical ideas, push their thinking towards describing patterns and regularities, and using mathematics in its multiple forms.

Although the results of our study suggest significant gains among the participants in our program, we do resist the temptation to claim exclusive rights to their progress as the result of their exposure to learning environments provided for them. Certainly, the mathematical experiences of the participants were embedded in and certainly derived from their school experiences as well. As mentioned earlier, our work was an augmentation to their existing school lives, though students' own reports position us well in our understanding that their school experiences were drastically different from those they encountered while with us. The children also acknowledged that the type of mathematical and instructional expectations that they had come to recognize as cultural norms of practice during the enrichment sessions were not present in their schools. That is, how they interacted with mathematics and ways in which they were expected to do mathematics in their classrooms was incompatible with practices we reinforced. Assuming these reports to be accurate description of their daily educational experiences in mathematics classrooms, we interpret our findings to have at least two serious implications for curriculum and instructional planning that aim to meet the demands of CCSM.

First, considering that the children's enrichment experiences consisted only of 120 hours over the course of three academic years (40 hours per year)—an insignificant amount of time when compared to their school based mathematical experiences—we are compelled to believe that extensive changes in their practices may have had more to do with the culture of inquiry and norms of mathematical practice embedded in our design and nurtured among children through deeply personal and mathematical interactions by the program staff. Children's understanding of and trust in the consistency of the expectations may have directly influenced the types of actions and practices they exhibited in our setting. In light of this possibility, we posit that influencing substantially positive and long-term change in children's dispositions towards mathematics, as envisioned by CCSS, may have less to do with tools and activities used and more dependent upon the climate and culture of learning environment in which such activities and tools are used.

Second, our program was not designed to focus on reinforcing mastery of procedural knowledge, but to foster intellectual explorations of mathematics as a domain worthy of study for its own sake, within an environment where taking intellectual risks was safe. Data provide support that children grew to recognize and take part in, if not to endorse, such an intellectual journey. Although we are not in a position to make claims about what and how children might have transferred from our setting to their own school based environments, it is logical to suggest creating a balance of inquiry and skills development is not only achievable but also necessary for children's development in ways that both content and practice standards are realized.

REFERENCES

Geometer's Sketchpad Resource Center. (n.d.). Retrieved May 10, 2012 from http://www.dynamicgeometry.com/General_Resources.html

Graphing Calculator (NuCalc). (n.d.). Retrieved June 13, 2012 from http://www.nucalc.com/WhatsNew.html

Hadlock, C. R. (2007). Practicing mathematics in the public arena: Challenges and outcomes in some prominent case studies. *The American Mathematical Monthly*, *114*(10), 849–870.

Kilpatrick, J., Swafford, J., & Findell, B. (2001). *Adding it up: Helping children learn mathematics*. Washington, DC: National Academy Press.

Microsoft Excel Features and Benefits. (n.d.). Retrieved June 1, 2012 from http://office.microsoft.com/en-us/excel/excel-2010-features-and-benefits-HA101806958.aspx

National Research Council. (2011). *Successful k-12 stem education: Identifying effective approaches in science, technology, engineering, and mathematics*. Washington, DC: The National Academies Press.

Schoenfeld, A. (1994). Reflections on doing and teaching mathematics. In Schoenfeld, A. (Ed.), *Mathematical Thinking and Problem Solving* (pp. 53–69). Hillsdale, NJ: Lawrence Erlbaum Associates.

Schoenfeld, A. H. (2005). On learning environments that foster subject-matter competence. I L. Verschaffel, E. De Corte, G. Kanselaar, & M. Valcke (Eds.), Powerful environments for promoting deep conceptual and strategic learning, (pp. 29-44). Leuven, Belgium: Studia Paedagogica.

Schoenfeld, A. H. (2007). What is mathematical proficiency (and how can it be assessed)? In Schoenfeld, A. H. (Ed.), *Assessing Mathematical proficiency* (pp. 59–73). Cambridge, UK: Cambridge University Press. doi:10.1017/CBO9780511755378.008.

Star, J. (2010). Reconceptualzing procedural knowledge in mathematics. *Journal for Research in Mathematics Education*.

Wilson, J. W. (2005). *Technology in mathematics teaching and learning*. Retrieved June 13, 2012 from http://jwilson.coe.uga.edu/texts.folder/tech/technology.Paper.html

Wilson, J. W. (2012a). *Intermath project*. Retrieved from http://intermath.coe.uga.edu/

Wilson, J. W. (2012b). *Technology and secondary school mathematics*. Retrieved from http://jwilson.coe.uga.edu/emt668/emt668.html

ENDNOTES

[1]   We do acknowledge that such reports are valuable as they provide insight into the types of tasks that can motivate children's engagement in desired mathematical practices. However, any conclusions drawn about their long-term impact is only conjectural.

[2]   We agree that these standards are deeply intertwined and could not be measured independently. We also agree that the range of behavior indicators we used for coding purposes should not be assumed as exhaustive OR unique to a particular Mathematical Practice Standard.

[3]   Our decision to consider only the whole group discussion episodes was motivated, in part, by convenience since whole group discussions were videotaped in their entirely with the camera at a convenient location which captured both the sound and individual students' gestures and interactions with others. However, from a conceptual standpoint we were interested in the activities of the cohorts as a unit of analysis rather than their small group interactions.

[4]   Among the 25 8th graders that started the program only 20 of them completed the three years. Three children relocated to other states. Two children opted to not participate in the sessions during the third year. Twenty of the original 25 students completed the program and currently in 11th grade.

[5]   These problems are used with permission from James W. Wilson at the University of Georgia.

APPENDIX

Activity 1

Standards of transformations are shown in Table 4.

Table 4. Standards of transformations

Standards of transformations for 8ᵗʰ grade
8.G.1. Verify experimentally the properties of rotations, reflections, and translations:
8.G.2. Understand that a two-dimensional figure is congruent to another if the second can be obtained from the first by a sequence of rotations, reflections, and translations; given two congruent figures, describe a sequence that exhibits the congruence between them.
8.G.3. Describe the effect of dilations, translations, rotations, and reflections on two-dimensional figures using coordinates.
8.G.4. Understand that a two-dimensional figure is similar to another if the second can be obtained from the first by a sequence of rotations, reflections, translations, and dilations; given two similar two-dimensional figures, describe a sequence that exhibits the similarity between them.
Standards of Transformations for High school
Experiment with transformations in the plane
G.CO.1. Know precise definitions of angle, circle, perpendicular line, parallel line, and line segment, based on the undefined notions of point, line, distance along a line, and distance around a circular arc.
G-CO.2.. Compare transformations that preserve distance and angle to those that do not (e.g., translation versus horizontal stretch).
G-CO.3. Given a rectangle, parallelogram, trapezoid, or regular polygon, describe the rotations and reflections that carry it onto itself.
G-CO.4. Develop definitions of rotations, reflections, and translations in terms of angles, circles, perpendicular lines, parallel lines, and line segments.

Level 1: Transformations and Isometries

Transformations in geometry are the tools for moving figures around the plane. There are five types of transformations: Rotation, reflection, translation, dilation, and glide reflection.

- **Rotation:** A transformation that turns a figure about a fixed point at a given angle and a given direction.
- **Reflection:** A transformation that "flips" a figure over a mirror or reflection line. A reflection leaves all the points of L unchanged.
- **Translation:** A transformation that "slides" each point of a figure the same distance in the same direction.
- **Dilation:** A transformation that changes the size of an object, but not its shape. This is also referred to as a Scaling.
- **Glide Reflection:** A translation followed by a reflection.

A *fixed point* of a transformation is a point A that remains in its original location after tranformation is completed. In mathematics we use the term *Isometry* to refer to a rigid motion, a transformation that preserves distance.

Open a GSP sketch and draw a triangle ABC (label its vertices). Let us explore the transformations listed previously using GSP.

Note that to perform a particular transformation you need to begin first with the defining data. That is, to reflect, you need to identify a mirror first. To do this, draw a line anywhere on the screen. From the transform menu select "Mark Mirror." Select then your triangle (be sure to select all points and segments) and choose "reflect" from the transform menu.

Similarly, to rotate your triangle, you need to first identify your center of rotation. To do this, draw a point on your screen. From the transform menu select "mark center." Select your triangle and rotate it using some angle of rotation.

Try translating your triangle by selecting 'translate' from the transform menu. First translate by "polar" vector. What do you notice? Try changing the measure of fixed angle. Trace the movement of image after each translation. Can you explain how the image is being translated? What does the fixed distance determine? What does the angle determine?

Repeat the previous activity by choosing the rectangular vector. Consider a translation of your object by a fixed distance of 1 and an angle of translation of 180. How might you emulate this transformation using rectangular translation vector?

To translate an object we need to define a vector that determines both the direction of slide and its magnitude. To emulate this, draw a segment on the screen. From the transform menu select "mark vector." Then select your object and choose 'translate" from the transform menu. You will be asked to determine the vector of translation. You can select "by marked vector."

In a dilated image, a particular ratio is used to move every point of the original closer to or farther away from the center point. If the ratio is greater than 1, the image points are farther away from the center than the originals and the image is larger than the original image. If the ratio is less than 1, the image points are nearer the center and the image is smaller.

To dilate objects, select a point to act as the center for dilation and choose Mark Center from the Transform menu. You can also double-click the desired center point with the Selection Arrow tool.

The animation indicates that the point has been marked as a center for subsequent rotations and dilations. If you dilate without first making a center, GSP will mark one for you. Select the object(s) you wish to dilate. Choose Dilate from the Transform menu.

The Dilate dialog box appears, and a dilated image of your selection(s) appears in the sketch. Choose either Fixed Ratio or Marked Ratio, as described next.

You can click a point in the sketch to change the marked center, you can click a measurement with no units to set the marked scale factor, or you can click two segments to set the marked segment ratio.

When you have chosen the options you want and entered any required values, click on Dilate.

The dilated image appears.

- Experiment with different ratios and decide what happens as the scale factor is larger than 1 or smaller than one. Write a summer of your findings.
- How might we do a glide reflection? (Remember that we need to translate the object first and then reflect it about the same vector or one parallel to it).

In the previous activity you considered a triangle as your parent object. Which of the properties you identified prior may also be true for other polygons. Choose a polygon of your liking and examine accuracy of statements you made in previous case.

Let us consider the following question:

- Which of the five transformations listed previously is an isometry? Explain your reasoning.
- Consider the orientation of the object after the transformation. In which case is the orientation of the object preserved? Which isometry changes the orientation of the object?
- Which of the five transformations listed previously is orientation preserving?
- Which of the five transformations listed previously is orientation reversing? Explain your reasoning.
- Which of the five transformations listed previously has a fixed point? No fixed point? Infinitely many fixed points?

Make a list of observations/conjectures regarding the properties of each of the isometries you explored. For instance, Table 5 was generated a group of students regarding reflections.

Table 5.

Type	Properties
Reflection	
Rotation	
Translation	
Glide reflection	
Dilation	

Isometries and Tessellations

Using only reflection, what patterns can you generate? What are the properties of these patterns? Which shapes would lead to a pattern? Are there specific conditions that must be true about the location of mirror of reflection?

Using only rotation, what patterns can you generate? What are the properties of these patterns? Which shapes would lead to a pattern? Are there specific conditions that must be true about the location of the center of rotation?

Now, using both the rotation and reflection, what patterns can you generate? What are the properties of these patterns? Which shapes would lead to a pattern? Are there specific relationships between the location of mirror and the center of rotation?

Level 2: Product of Isometries

- Can we emulate the result of a rotation with two reflections?
- Can we emulate the result of a reflection with two rotations? How about with a combination of rotation and reflection?

- What is the result of a translation followed by a rotation?

Consider the table of the product of isometries in Table 6.

- Fill in each cell of the matrix with products of corresponding isometries in each row and column.
- Is the set of isometries closed under product? That is, is the result of the product of isometries is an isometry? Explain your reasoning.

Table 6. Product of isometries

	Identity	Translation	Rotation	Reflection	Glide Reflection
Identity					
Translation					
Rotation					
Reflection					
Glide Reflection					

- Is composition of isometries commutative? (Consider for example, a reflection followed by a rotation first. Compare the result with a rotation followed by a reflection).
- Is composition of isometries associative?
- Does each isometry have an inverse? List the inverse of each type of isometry.

Level 3: Lines of Symmetry

When we ask about lines (or axes of) symmetry we are basically asking "How many lines can a polygon be reflected about and still be self-coincident (i.e., fall back onto itself)?"

In case of a circle there are infinitely many lines of symmetry. Can you explain why?

Take any diameter of the circle and reflect the circle about that diameter and it will be self-coincident. There are an infinite number of diameters of a circle, so there is an infinite number of such lines. Since the circle is also self-coincident under any rotation. So there are an infinite number of symmetry rotations of the circle. But how about polygons?

Let us begin by considering an example you examined in your MATH 261 last semester, a square shown in Figure 11.

When we flip the square about a line of symmetry or rotate the square, we get a rigid motion, because the square maintains its shape.

You learned last semester that a square has 4 lines of symmetry: the horizontal line, the vertical line, and the two diagonals. It also has 4 rotations: the 90 degree turn, the 180^0 turn, the 270^0 turn and the 360 degree turn.

The horizontal line flip switches 1 and 3, and switches 2 and 4. The vertical line flip switches 1 and 2, and switches 3 and 4. The 1,4-diagonal line flip switches 3 and 2 and leaves both 1 and 4 fixed.

The 3,2-diagonal line flip switches 1 and 4 and leaves both 3 and 2 fixed.

Figure 11. Square showing lines of symmetry

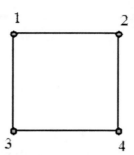

The 360 degree (or 0 degree, however you look at it) rotation leaves everything fixed.
The 90 degree rotation moves 1 to 2, 2 to 4, 4 to 3, and 3 to 1.
The 180 degree rotation moves 1 to 4, and 2 to 3.
The 270 degree rotation moves 1 to 3, 3 to 4, 4 to 2, and 2 to 1.
Recall from our work on the Isometries that any composition of two rigid motions produces another rigid motion. For example: The horizontal flip, followed by the 90 degree rotation switches 3 and 2 and leaves 1 and 4 fixed, which is the same as the 1,4-diagonal flip.
How might we find the lines of symmetries of other regular polygons?

Activity 2[5]

Standards for functions are shown in Table 7

Level 1: Mathematical Relations

1.   Open a new sketch in the Graphing Calculator and type: y=nx.

Table 7. Standards for functions

Standards of functions for 8th grade
8.F.1. Understand that a function is a rule that assigns to each input exactly one output.
8.F.3. Interpret the equation $y = mx + b$ as defining a linear function, whose graph is a straight line; give examples of functions that are not linear.
Use functions to model relationships between quantities.
8.F.4. Construct a function to model a linear relationship between two quantities.
8.F.5. Describe qualitatively the functional relationship between two quantities by analyzing a graph (e.g., where the function is increasing or decreasing, linear or nonlinear).

continued on following page

Table 7. Continued

Standards of functions for high school
F-BF.3. Identify the effect on the graph of replacing f(x) by f(x) + k, k f(x), f(kx), and f(x + k) for specific values of k (both positive and negative); find the value of k given the graphs.
F-BF.4. Find inverse functions.
F-BF.5. (+) Understand the inverse relationship between exponents and logarithms and use this relationship to solve problems involving logarithms and exponents.

Hit return and consider the graph of the function for different value of n. You can increase or decrease the range of n by changing the initial and final values on the scaler. What patterns do you see?

- Examine special cases when the range of n include both positive and negative values? What is the impact of n on the behavior of the graph?
- Let n be exclusive of values between 0 and 1. How do you describe the behavior of the functions? How does n influence the slope?
- Consider now: $y=x^n$. Repeat the investigation for this case by changing n and considering behaviors of the corresponding graphs. Write a summary of your observations.

2. Construct a graph of any function $y = f(x)$ by generating a table of values with the x values in one column and the y values in another.

Level 2: Search for Patterns

1. Make up *linear* functions **f(x)** and **g(x)**. Explore, with different pairs of f(x) and g(x) the graphs for
    a. $h(x) = f(x) + g(x)$
    b. $h(x) = f(x).g(x)$
    c. $h(x) = f(x)/g(x)$
    d. $h(x) = f(g(x))$

Report observations and conjectures.

- Consider the case when f(x) and g(x) are both quadratic functions? Cubic functions?

2. Can you generate the equations that produce the graphs in Figure 12? Test your ideas first.

3.   Let **f(x) = a sin(bx + c)** and **g(x) = a cos(bx + c)**. For selected values of a, b, and c, graph and

Figure 12. Graphs

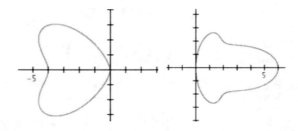

explore:

a.   h(x) = f(x) + g(x)
b.   h(x) = f(x).g(x)
c.   h(x) = f(x)/g(x)
d.   h(x) = f(g(x))

Summarize, explain, and illustrate.

Level 3: Data Analysis

1.   A function in the form $y = a + \dfrac{b}{x - c}$ will level off as the x-values get very large. What y-value
will this level occur near? Examine this same question for functions in the form $y = a + \dfrac{bx}{x^2 - c}$.
What generalizations can you form?

2.   Given a quadratic function, $y = Ax^2 + Bx + C$, how many times can a linear function, $y = Ax + B$, intersect the parabola? Consider all cases.

3.   Generate a Fibonnaci sequence in the first column using f(0) = 1, f(1) = 1, f(n) = f(n-1) + f(n-2)

a.   Construct the ratio of each pair of adjacent terms in the Fibonnaci sequence. What happens as n increases? What about the ratio of every second term? etc.

b.   Explore sequences where f(0) and f(1) are some arbitrary integers other than 1. If f(0)=1 and f(1) = 3, then your sequence is a Lucas Sequence. All such sequences, however, have the same limit of the ratio of successive terms.

Chapter 6
Using Technology to Engage Students with the Standards for Mathematical Practice:
The Case of DGS

Milan Sherman
Drake University, USA

ABSTRACT

This chapter discusses how the use of Dynamic Geometry Software (DGS) can be used to support students' engagement with the Standards for Mathematical Practice as outlined in Common Core State Standards for Mathematics (CCSS-M). In particular, the aim of this chapter is to (1) describe what students' strategic use of appropriate tools might entail in a DGS environment, and (2) argue that for students to engage in these practices in a DGS environment, they must construct meaning for and with these tools in the process of instrumental genesis. Illustrative examples are provided from three secondary mathematics classrooms, and the chapter concludes with recommendations for future research and teacher education in this area.

INTRODUCTION

Research on the use of technological tools for mathematics instruction and learning has proliferated over the last twenty years (e.g., Burrill et al., 2002; Heid & Blume, 2008; Kaput, 1992; Zbiek, Heid, Blume, & Dick, 2007), and has demonstrated that the use of technological tools can be effective in supporting students' learning of important mathematical concepts and procedures. Concurrently there has been increasing emphasis on developing students' ability to engage in

DOI: 10.4018/978-1-4666-4086-3.ch006

mathematical thinking and reasoning (e.g., Cuoco, Goldenberg, & Mark, 1996; Hiebert et al., 1997; National Council of Teachers of Mathematics, 2000, 2009; Stein, Smith, Henningsen, & Silver, 2009). The release and adoption of the Common Core State Standards by the majority of U.S. states, and in particular the Standards for Mathematical Practice, has resulted in increased attention on how to engage students in these practices. For the first time in the history of mathematics education in the United States, students' mathematical thinking and behaviors, and not just content, may be specifically assessed on a large scale as part of binding policy.

However, most research on the use of technology for mathematics instruction and learning has focused on how technological tools support students' learning of content. More research is needed that focuses on how technological tools may be used to support students' mathematical thinking and behaviors, such as those outlined in the Standards for Mathematical Practice. In particular, both researchers and practitioners need a deeper understanding of what using appropriate tools strategically consists of, how teachers can foster this behavior in their students, and how it is related to the other mathematical practices outlined in the Standards.

The purpose of this chapter is to present examples that illustrate (1) what using appropriate tools strategically may consist of in a classroom learning environment integrating Dynamic Geometry Software (DGS), and (2) the role of instrumental genesis in supporting or hindering students' ability to engage in this practice. The aim is not to advocate for the use of DGS, or technology in general, as a magic pill for promoting students engagement with the mathematical practices. Indeed, the non-examples described in this chapter are poignant counterexamples of such a notion. Rather, by unpacking the ways in which students use, or fail to use, appropriate tools strategically, the reader may gain insight into what this practice

consists of in a DGS environment. In addition, the importance of students having opportunities to construct mathematical meaning for the tools that they use, and the role of this process in supporting students' engagement with this practice when using DGS, is highlighted in these examples.

The Case of Dynamic Geometry Software (DGS)

Dynamic geometry software (DGS) such as Cabri Geometry, Geometer's Sketchpad, and GeoGebra are a specific case of a more general learning context that has been referred to as Dynamic and Interactive Mathematics Learning Environments (DIMLE) (Karadag, Martinovic, & Frieman, 2011). In addition to DGS, these refer to any learning environment in which digital technologies are used to engage students in explorative learning. Dynamic geometry software in particular has become increasingly common in secondary schools, and provides a means of making mathematics instruction more student-centered by having students learn new content through guided exploration rather than lecture and applications. Both the ubiquity of this technology, and the ability to integrate it into classroom instruction for the learning of new content, make it important to understand how this tool can also support students' engagement in mathematical practices.

THEORETICAL BACKGROUND

An intended contribution of this chapter is to connect the practice of *using appropriate tools strategically* to theoretical lenses developed in the mathematics education literature. In particular, the use of DGS to engage students in *transformational reasoning* (Simon, 1996) is proposed as an important element of strategic use of this tool. The notion of *instrumental genesis* (Drijvers & Trouche, 2008; Guin & Trouche, 1999) as a way to describe how learners construct meaning with and for tools, and is used to describe a necessary condition for students to engage in this practice.

Using Appropriate Tools Strategically

Of the Standards for Mathematical Practice in the Common Core, the ability to *use appropriate tools strategically* is most directly related to the use of technological tools for mathematics learning and instruction: "These tools might include pencil and paper, concrete models, a ruler, a protractor, a calculator, a spreadsheet, a computer algebra system, a statistical package, or dynamic geometry software" (Common Core State Standards Initiative, 2010). This practice is both prerequisite and often inseparable from students' ability to use technological tools to engage in the other practices described in these Standards. That is, when one uses a tool, he or she presumably does so for some purpose that transcends the tool; they use it to accomplish some task or goal. For example, a student might use DGS to explore the properties of the angle bisectors of a triangle, including the properties of the intersection of the angle bisector, the incenter. Some properties students might discover are that the incenter always remains inside a given triangle regardless of whether that triangle is acute, obtuse, or right, and the that the incenter is always equidistant from each side of the triangle. By looking for invariant properties of the incenter, and making and testing conjectures about them, students are engaging in the mathematical practices of *looking for and making use of structure* and *constructing viable arguments*. The point is that one does not use a tool for its own sake, and thus using appropriate tools strategically will always involve being focused on something besides the tool, and quite often will involve the other practices described in these Standards.

Ultimately, *using appropriate tools strategically* requires knowing which tools to use when, including when *not* to use a particular tool.

Students must connect the affordances of various tools to the requirements of a specific task. "Mathematically proficient students consider the available tools when solving a mathematical problem" (Common Core State Standards Initiative, 2010). For example, students might use DGS to investigate the Triangle Inequality Theorem, i.e., the sum of the lengths of two sides of a triangle is always longer than the length of the third. If students are asked to make a conjecture about the relationship between the sum of the lengths of two sides of a triangle and the length of the third side of a triangle, they must first recognize that one basis for a conjecture is the examination of numerous examples. If a student perceives this as a requirement of the task, they must then understand how the tools within a particular DGS might meet that need by providing a means of generating numerous examples via dragging, and by dynamically measuring these triangles in order to examine the relationships in question. Note that this behavior requires more than knowing which buttons to push; students must understand when and why they might push those buttons.

According to the standard for *using appropriate tools strategically*, mathematically proficient student, "are able to use technological tools to explore and deepen their understanding of concepts" (Common Core State Standards Initiative, 2010). In this regard, another important affordance of DGS is the potential to engage students in *transformational reasoning* (Simon, 1996). Transformational reasoning is defined by Simon to overlap with inductive and deductive reasoning, but to be distinct from both. Inductive reasoning seeks to generalize a particular pattern, and deductive reasoning moves from established general principles to demonstrating how those principles govern a particular case. Transformational reasoning is the manipulation of an object or system mentally or physically in order to understand how or why it works. Transformational reasoning can be a bridge between making a conjecture and generating a proof, but it need not be. By providing students with virtual objects or systems that they can manipulate, DGS can be an effective means of supporting students' transformational reasoning. For example, students investigating the relationship between the lengths of sides of a triangle may make the conjecture that the sum of the lengths of two sides must always be greater than third. Students might conjecture this relationship without understanding why it must be true; they simply notice a pattern in the side lengths. At this point students have engaged in inductive reasoning. However, students might investigate a triangle created in DGS to gain insight into why it must be true. Namely, if the sum of two side lengths of a triangle equals the third side length, then the three sides of the triangle would be collinear, i.e., it would not be a triangle. Students who explore why a claim might be true, even if they are not completely successful in coming to a conclusion, are engaging in transformational reasoning. Although understanding why something is true in this sense falls short of a formal proof, it is nonetheless an important insight that goes beyond merely generalizing a pattern. I propose that using DGS to engage students in transformational reasoning is an important aspect of developing students' ability to use appropriate tools strategically in a DGS environment. However, before students can choose the most appropriate tool for a task, or use it strategically to solve a problem or explore a concept, they must first construct meaning for the tools at their disposal in a process that has been referred to as *instrumental genesis* (Drijvers & Trouche, 2008; Guin & Trouche, 1999).

Instrumental Genesis

Instrumental genesis is the process by which an artifact, such as a calculator or computer, becomes a tool, or instrument, for students' mathematical thinking and learning, and in a certain sense becomes an extension of his or her thinking. Meaning is not inherent in a tool, but rather students

construct meaning for and with it by using it. The process by which students construct meaning for tools, and how teachers support that process in a classroom environment, is an important question, and hypotheses are discussed at the end of this chapter.

Guin and Trouche (1999) distinguish between an *artifact* and a *tool*, and instrumental genesis describes the process by which an artifact becomes a tool for a user. According to Vygotsky (1978), all human thought is mediated by tools, including oral and written language, as well as material artifacts. The transition from an artifact to a tool takes place within the user; the artifact in itself is unchanged, but the perceived affordances of the artifact in relation to some goal change as the user constructs meaning for and with the tool. When an artifact, such as a pencil, compass, protractor, or piece of software is introduced into a mathematical learning environment, it does not have mathematical meaning for students; there is little or no sense of the affordances of the artifact in relation to mathematical activity. To begin with, a student needs to use the tool in the context of some mathematical activity in order to begin to perceive its affordances in that context.

For example, if one wants to examine the effects of the parameters a, b, and c, of a general quadratic function, on its graph, one could create a slider in a dynamic geometry environment. A slider allows the user to control one parameter, represented by a point on a segment, and "slide" the point along the segment (representing an interval), in order to examine the effect of varying that single parameter on the shape of the graph. For a student who has never used dynamic geometry software, or who has never used sliders, the existence or affordances of such a tool may be completely unanticipated. A user cannot begin to connect the capabilities of a tool to mathematical goals or behaviors if they have no sense of those capabilities. On the other hand, knowing the capabilities of a tool does necessarily mean that students will connect them to a mathematical goal or activity. That is,

I may know that I can use DGS to create a slider, but if I have not used it or observed it being used in the context of some meaningful mathematical activity, it may hold no meaning for me. The questions may remain, "when, why, or how, would I use this?" However, if a student is guided to construct and use sliders to examine the effect of the individual parameters of a quadratic on its graph, they have some context for how this tool can be used for mathematical activity. Ideally, in another situation in which it may be useful to vary a single parameter while holding other parameters constant, students may understand and utilize the affordances of a slider.

This example highlights the need for students to construct meaning for a tool by constructing mathematical meaning with the tool. The affordances of a tool are perceived in the context of meaningful mathematical activity. Returning to the example previously, if students are asked to consider the effects of the parameters of a general quadratic on its graph prior to using sliders, the affordances of a slider may be more readily perceived by students insofar as they have considered how they might achieve the task in question. Perhaps by sketching the graphs of multiple quadratic equations with different values for the leading coefficient by hand, students may perceive the need for a means to vary that parameter more quickly, efficiently, and precisely even before knowing that DGS can provide such a means.

The process of instrumental genesis is a complex dialectic in which students construct greater meaning for tools by actively using them in the context of meaningful mathematical activity, and in turn are able to construct deeper or different mathematical meanings with the tool. As Hiebert et al. (1997) noted:

Meaning developed for tools and meaning developed with tools both result from actively using tools. Teachers do not need to provide long demonstrations before allowing students to use tools; teachers just need to be aware that when students

are using tools they are working on two fronts simultaneously: what the tool means and how it can be used effectively to understand something else (p. 55).

A primary thesis of this chapter is that this construction of meaning for and with tools by students is a necessary condition for using appropriate tools strategically. The purpose of this chapter is not to explicate a microgenetic account of this process, but rather to consider what it means for students to use DGS strategically, and the role of instrumental genesis in supporting that practice. Data collected from three secondary mathematics classrooms is used to discuss the ways in which teachers may support students in developing the ability to use DGS strategically by facilitating their engagement with the other mathematical practices. Examples and non-examples from this data are used to describe this process in practice, and to suggest how teachers may support the instrumental genesis of their students.

Data Context

Table 1 provides a brief summary of the classrooms in which the following data examples were observed. Each teacher was observed for a unit of instruction consisting of 12 to 17 lessons, and detailed lesson observation field notes were recorded, student work collected, and post-lesson interviews were conducted after each lesson. All three teachers taught Geometry and integrated the use of DGS for investigations by their students for some of the topics in their unit. In general, Ms. Lowe[1] was more successful in engaging her students in mathematical practices using DGS than either Ms. Jones or Ms. Young, and differences in the ways in which these teachers supported their students' mathematical thinking while using DGS have been discussed elsewhere (Sherman, 2012). However, it is important to address the temptation to attribute the differences in students' engagement with the mathematical practices in these

Table 1. Classroom contexts for data collection

	Grade/Class Level	Topics
Ms. Jones	9th grade Integrated Math	• Angle relations • Triangle Inequality • Similarity
Ms. Young	11th grade Inclusion	• Angle relations • Triangle Inequality
Ms. Lowe	10th grade Honors	• Points of concurrency in a triangle • Triangle Inequality

examples to the fact that Ms. Lowe taught an Honors Geometry class, while the other teachers did not. Research has shown that to the degree that academic tracking in mathematics education is inequitable, much of the inequity stems from the differing expectations that teachers have for their students (Boaler & Staples, 2008; Boaler, Wiliam, & Brown, 2000), and this may have been the case with these teachers as well. However, the focus of these examples is to explicate how DGS can support students' engagement in using appropriate tools strategically, and the necessity of constructing meaning for these tools in that process, regardless of factors that shaped what students did or did not do.

The examples discussed next are used to unpack what *using appropriate tools strategically* might consist of when students are using DGS for guided exploration, and are organized into three categories: using tools strategically in a DGS environment, choosing appropriate tools, and the role of instrumental genesis. There is certainly overlap among these three categories, as all are dimensions of the practice of using appropriate tools strategically. However, the episodes described in each category lend themselves to analysis along the particular dimension of this practice. Each section describes two episodes, with a separate discussion of how that particular example illustrates that dimension of this practice. While students may engage in other mathematical practices in the episodes described, the focus of

the analysis is on how students use tools strategically, as this practice is seen as a necessary condition for engaging in the others.

USING TOOLS STRATEGICALLY IN A DGS ENVIRONMENT

One element of *using appropriate tools strategically* is the *strategic* aspect. This element is not completely independent of the choice of the tool, as a tool ill-suited for a particular task is not likely to be used strategically. However, there are many ways in which a given tool might be used strategically to accomplish a particular task, and these examples are not meant to be exhaustive. Rather, these examples illustrate how some of the tools in DGS may be used strategically, how that strategic use depends on the meaning students have constructed for the tools, and how this practice supports engagement with other practices outlined the Standards.

Dragging as Strategic Use

The ability to dynamically drag an object by manipulating its graphical representation directly is a fundamental affordance of DGS, and the thinking involved in dynamically dragging an object in DGS has been described elsewhere (Hollebrands, Laborde, & StraBer, 2008). In this example students used GeoGebra to investigate the properties of the centroid of a triangle, which is the intersection of the medians of a triangle, where a median is a segment connecting the midpoint of a side of a triangle to the opposite vertex.

This particular lesson was the fourth in a five-day span of instruction in which students were using GeoGebra to investigate the properties of points of concurrency in a triangle, e.g., incenter, circumcenter, orthocenter, and centroid. Students were provided with a worksheet that guided them in constructing a triangle, its medians, and the centroid, measuring the segments from each vertex to the centroid, and from the centroid to the midpoint of the opposite side, and recorded these measurements in a table in order to look for a pattern or relationship and make a conjecture. A relationship that students were intended to discover is that the segment from the midpoint to the centroid is 1/3 the length of the median, and the segment from the centroid to the opposite vertex is 2/3 the length of the median (See Figure 1).

The following conversation between two students was observed as they worked on the task. At this point in the task, they had constructed a triangle, the medians, and the centroid, and had recorded the measurements from each of the midpoints to the centroid, and from the centroid to each of the vertices in a table. This episode takes place while these two students are examining their tables and their figures in order to look for patterns and make a conjecture.

Nick and Brian are dragging their figures and discussing what it is that they're supposed to be noticing.

Nick: *There are lots of things to notice.*

Brian: *Yeah, but most of them are obvious.*
Nick: *I'm going to make it a right triangle. What would that do? It would stay at the center of the triangle, right?*
Brian: *Look at this.*

Brian shows Nick his table, pointing out the 6.17 and the 3.08 (See Figure 2).

Brian: *This one is almost exactly double that one.*
Nick: *You can't make assumptions from one triangle*

Both start dragging their triangles.

Nick: *I see something like that, but if you stretch it far enough...*

They continue dragging their triangles and looking at the measurements.

Nick: *One is always half of the other*
Brian: *The distance from the vertex is always double the distance to the midpoint.*

Figure 1. A student's construction of a centroid in GeoGebra

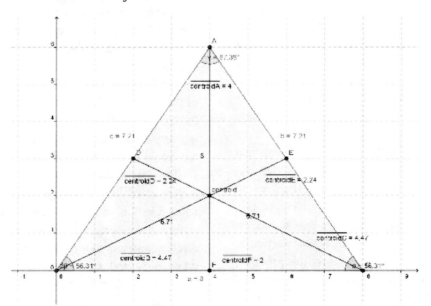

Figure 2. Student work on the centroid task

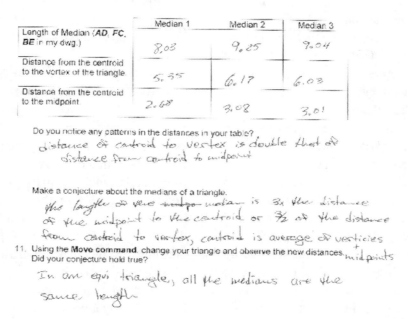

Teacher: *Change it, see if you can disprove it.*

Starting over with a new triangle, Brian begins to measure the distances from the centroid to the vertex and from the centroid to the midpoint for each median.

Brian: *(As he measures each segment) That is double that, and that is double that, and that is double that.*

Nick drags his figure.

Nick: *Yes, it does stand true. (Field note, 2/7/11)*

Discussion

This example illustrates how dragging is instrumental in supporting students in making and testing of conjectures, and how that dragging becomes more strategic as the conjecture is refined and tested. Students must consider the purpose of dragging in terms of an overarching goal, in this case making a conjecture about the medians of a triangle. Brian and Nick had noticed a pattern in their table that they used as a candidate for making a conjecture. Nick's statement that one "can't make assumptions from one triangle," and the subsequent dragging of his triangle indicates that he understands that one instance is not a sufficient basis for a general claim, and both students return to the figures that they have constructed. Implicit in their work is an understanding that the goal of this task is a relationship that can be generalized, and the affordances of dragging the figure in relation to that goal. This is further confirmed after Brian points out the relationship in the median segments while helping Nick to measure those segments, and Nick drags the triangle to test the claim before agreeing with it.

In general, students using dragging in DGS must consider what information would be helpful in achieving a goal, and what sort of dragging might provide that information. Once that move is made, students must assess if the object behaved in the anticipated manner, and if not, why, and what the next move should be in light of this information. If the object does behave in the anticipated manner, students may still consider if and how dragging the figure in a different way may produce a case that violates the general relationship that is proposed.

The ability to use DGS to interact directly and dynamically with representations is an important part of using DGS strategically. "One very important aspect of mathematical thinking is the abstraction of invariance. But, of course, to recognize invariance – to see what stays the same – one must have variation" (Kaput, 1992, p. 525). Although dragging is one of the most fundamental actions that students can perform in DGS, its strategic use in support of making and testing conjectures, and investigating why an object behaves as it does, is not necessarily apparent to a novice user. During their first investigation in this series, most students had constructed figures but did not drag them. Indeed, this sort of behavior was observed in all three classrooms at the beginning of the unit. Rather, they used the figure they had constructed as a static example that they could refer to while answering the questions posed in the worksheet they were given.

Through the support and guidance that Ms. Lowe offered during these investigations, including the use of dragging to check the accuracy of a construction, her students had constructed meaning for the dragging tool in GeoGebra, as evidenced by how Brian and Nick drag their figures in order to test their conjecture. In addition, the previous investigations allowed students to notice that the location of some points of concurrency, such as the circumcenter, vary depending on whether it is an acute, obtuse, or right triangle, while others, such as the incenter, always remain inside the triangle regardless of whether the triangle is acute, obtuse, or right. Having examined these points of concurrency with DGS previously, they have become more attuned to the structure and regularity that is characteristic of these objects, and the need to examine numerous cases before making a generalization. Thus, this example demonstrates the meaning that Brian and Nick had constructed for the dragging tool in GeoGebra,

i.e., the affordance of dragging in making and testing conjectures about invariant properties or relationships within geometric figures.

Posing and Investigating "What if...?" Questions

In this example, one of Ms. Lowe's students extends the guided investigation of the points of concurrency in a triangle to a special case of an equilateral triangle. Both the posing of this question, as well as his investigation of it, demonstrate his engagement in numerous mathematical practices and provide evidence of the mathematical meaning this student had constructed for this tool.

This episode occurred toward the end of the second investigation in Ms. Lowe's class. Students had previously investigated the circumcenter of a triangle, and determined that it is equidistant to the vertices of the triangle. During the present lesson, students had been exploring the properties of the incenter, including the idea that it is equidistant to each of the sides of the triangle. Toward the end of the class period Paul asked the Ms. Lowe, "if the triangle is an equilateral triangle, will the incenter be the same distance to the sides as the vertices?" Ms. Lowe responded by telling him that that is an interesting question, and encouraged him to use GeoGebra to investigate it.

Paul started trying to answer his question right away, but struggled with making a "free hand" equilateral triangle. In DGS there is a difference between resizing a given triangle to make the side lengths equal separately, and constructing a triangle in which the side lengths are defined to be equal. In the former case, creating an equilateral triangle can be very difficult, since dragging a vertex always changes the lengths of two of the sides. In addition, if one is successful in making an equilateral triangle in this manner, any dragging of such a triangle would result in a triangle that is not equilateral. Paul continued to investigate his question after the bell had rung (this class was the last period of the day), and after having worked for an additional 10 minutes, he expressed his inability to create an equilateral triangle that remains equilateral when dragged. After being shown how to construct an equilateral triangle in GeoGebra, he goes on to construct the figure displayed in Figure 3, where the circumcenter is the center of the circle through the vertices (since it is equidistant from the vertices), and the incenter is the center of the circle inscribed in the triangle (as it is equidistant from the sides of the triangle). He reported to Ms. Lowe that in an equilateral triangle the circumcenter and incenter are the same (concurrent), and that the perpendicular distance from the incenter to the sides of the triangle is exactly half the distance to the vertices. Ms. Lowe asked him to show her, and he explained that although it doesn't look like it, the distance to the sides is exactly half the distance to the vertices, because the program is rounding. As Ms. Lowe's students had yet to study special right triangles, Paul did not recognize the triangle formed as a 30-60-90 triangle, but Ms. Lowe worked with him to use the Pythagorean Theorem to determine the relationship between the side lengths of the triangle.

Discussion

The posing and investigating of this question reveals Paul's strategic use of the tools in GeoGebra. In this case, the strategic use consisted in using DGS to engage in other mathematical practices. The habit of making and testing conjectures is considered an important part of *constructing viable arguments*: "[mathematically proficient students] make conjectures and build a logical progression of statements to explore the truth of their conjectures. They are able to analyze situations by breaking them into cases, and can recognize and use counterexamples" (Common Core State Standards Initiative, 2010). Paul's wondering if there is a relationship between these points of concurrency in special triangles, such as an equilateral triangle, is evidence of considering a special case of these points of concurrency. This question also demonstrates his search for an underlying structure or relationship that may be contingent on certain conditions, and that he is clearly trying to make sense of the individual points of concurrency by considering a relationship among them, i.e., *making sense of problems*. Furthermore, he *attends to*

Figure 3. Paul's construction of an equilateral triangle

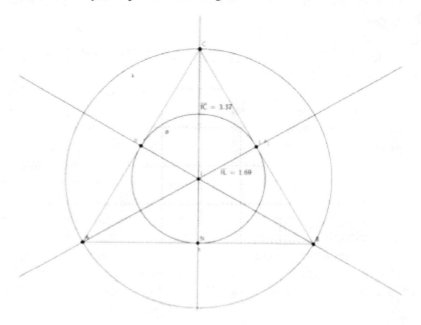

precision by identifying a potential relationship between the segments despite the fact that some the measurements generated while dragging are not an exact example of it. He understands that these measurements are limited in their precision, and thus cases generated in which the relationship is not exact (as in Figure 3) should not be considered a counterexample to the general relationship he has identified.

The fact that he posed this question in the context of using DGS demonstrates how *using appropriate tools strategically* may consist of using tools to engage in other practices, and also depends on it. This is not to say that he could not pose or investigate this question without the use of DGS. But the fact remains that it was in the context of using DGS to investigate the properties of the circumcenter and incenter that this episode took place. While it certainly depends on a student's background, prior knowledge, and disposition, for many students the time and effort involved pursuing this conjecture with paper and pencil may not support or encourage this type of thinking to the same degree as DGS.

This example also demonstrates the meaning that Paul had constructed for this tool, i.e., evidence of instrumental genesis. His use of GeoGebra had resulted in the construction of mathematical meaning that makes this question possible, but also an understanding that the tools in GeoGebra provide a means to answer the question. The affordances of the tools that were utilized in investigating the incenter and the circumcenter suggested a way for him to investigate this new question that arises from the results of those previous investigations. His resulting construction demonstrates that he was able to connect the affordances of the technology to the question he had posed. In addition to constructing an equilateral triangle and measuring the distance from the incenter to the vertices and sides of the triangle, he dragged the triangle in order to test his conjecture, and when he found that it was false, looked for a pattern or invariant relationship. Insofar as he constructed,

measured, and dragged a figure with a particular question in mind, he connected the affordances of these tools to a mathematical goal, which is an essential aspect of using appropriate tools strategically, and evidence of the meaning he had constructed for these tools.

This episode also suggests that the best way to foster instrumental genesis is in the context of using tools purposefully. When he posed his question initially, he did not know how to create an equilateral triangle in GeoGebra, i.e. a triangle that always remains equilateral no matter how it is dragged. However, he understood that this is what he needed to answer his question, even before he knew how to use GeoGebra to do it. Thus, when he was shown how to create an equilateral triangle, he already understood the mathematical significance of this affordance of GeoGebra. Another way to describe the process of instrumental genesis is the perception and connection of affordances of a tool to a specific goal or activity. Paul needed to create, measure, and drag a figure that could test his conjecture. He connected the affordances of these tools to that mathematical activity and was able to interpret mathematically the result of his work in order to gain deeper mathematical insights. Thus, this episode is an example of the result of instrumental genesis, as well as its deepening.

CHOOSING APPROPRIATE TOOLS

The phrase "use appropriate tools strategically" implies that students are given some freedom to choose the tools that they will use in relation to the goal of their mathematical activity. Indeed, evidence of this practice may include knowing when to use a particular tool as well as when *not* to. "Proficient students are sufficiently familiar with tools appropriate for their grade or course to make sound decisions about when each of these tools might be helpful, recognizing both the insight to be gained and their limitations" (Common Core State Standards Initiative, 2010).

The first choice students may make in this regard is whether to choose a technological tool or not. Further considerations may consist of choices such as whether or not to use a graphing calculator or DGS, or one DGS versus another. Providing students with such choices may be an important element of developing this practice among students, but I suggest that in practice, students' decision making actually proceeds in the opposite direction. One may think of a DGS as an environment that provides the user a set of tools, such as a line tool, a dragging tool, a measuring tool, or a slider. Thinking of tools at this grain size corresponds more accurately with the way that a user chooses a tool. From this perspective DGS, or a graphing calculator, or a set of physical tools (such as a compass and straightedge) would be a "tool shop." A user generally considers the particular tool that they may need to accomplish a task, such as a slider, and then goes to the "tool shop" where it is "stored". In most of the examples described in this chapter the choice of which "tool shop" to go to is not left students, but is made by the teacher in designing the task. However, it is important to note that this does not mean that students have no choices to make regarding the tools that they use. Even in an exploration in which students are guided to use particular tools to construct a figure, there may be opportunities for students to make some choices about using particular tools while investigating the properties of the figure that they have constructed.

Although students in the next example were not initially given the autonomy to choose the tools they used for the investigation they engaged in, they realized the limitations of the tools chosen by the teacher for the given task and completed their investigation using GeoGebra. The second example described in this section demonstrates the necessity of allowing students some freedom with respect to using tools in DGS in order to engage students in transformational reasoning.

Issues of Precision when Choosing Tools

Ms. Lowe's class investigated the Triangle Inequality Theorem using uncooked spaghetti by breaking it into pieces, constructing triangles, and measuring and recording the lengths of the sides. Although her students had a good deal of experience using GeoGebra, she chose to use spaghetti for this exploration because, due to the rounding error in GeoGebra, she worried that students would be able to construct a triangle in which the sum of two sides equaled the third, thus contradicting the Triangle Inequality Theorem. As students worked on the task they quickly determined that the sum of two side lengths of a triangle could not be less than the length of the third, but had difficulty determining if they could be equal. In fact, due to limitations in students' ability to measure and break spaghetti precisely, some students claimed they had constructed triangles out of spaghetti for which the sum of two side lengths of the triangle was equal to third.

As Ms. Lowe was discussing the case of equality with one of the groups, one student, Bruce, thought that it was not possible to create a triangle in which the sum of two sides lengths is equal to the third, but the rest of his group was unsure. Ms. Lowe asked Bruce to try to convince the rest of his group of his conjecture, and left the group to discuss the matter while she worked with other groups of students.

Ms. Lowe returns to Bruce's group, and he announces that he was wrong. Ms. Lowe asks him who convinced him he was wrong, and he said that he saw the other students in his group make a triangle. Ms. Lowe asks what the measurements of the sides are, and Jennifer says that the long side is 1 inch, and the other two sides are a ½ inch, and she shows her the triangle made with spaghetti on Grace's desk. Laura asks, "did we do it wrong?" and Ms. Lowe says, "I didn't say that." She asks Grace what she's doing, and Grace says that she's trying to draw it, but it doesn't work out. Laura says something about a triangle with sides 6, 4, and 2 cm, and then she says, "I need GeoGebra!" (Field note, 2/21/11).

Ms. Lowe's students had previously used Geo-Gebra for a number of investigations during this unit, and thus were familiar with how it might be useful for the present task. Since students did not have access to GeoGebra during the lesson (they generally went to a computer lab to use GeoGebra), the lesson ended with students debating in their small groups whether the sum of two side lengths could equal the third, and many students continued the investigation at home using GeoGebra. Ultimately, some of the students concluded that the sum of two side lengths is always greater than the length of the third side by changing the default accuracy within GeoGebra and measuring the side lengths to 15 places of decimal accuracy.

Discussion

This episode is a clear example of the importance of choosing appropriate tools. Some of Ms. Lowe's students recognized the limitations of breaking and measuring spaghetti for this task, and seemed to believe that the tools in GeoGebra were better suited to this task. For these students, the difficulty and potential error in making precise measurements with spaghetti and rulers was greater than in GeoGebra. Furthermore, changing the default precision in GeoGebra in order to investigate the problem is an example using the measurement tools in GeoGebra strategically.

This example also suggests that students may need to have a variety of tools at their disposal in order to develop their ability to determine which one is most appropriate. Students who are not provided the opportunity to choose the tools they use in relation to a particular purpose or problem will not consider which tool is most appropriate, or critically examine the advantages or disadvantages of using a particular tool. While Ms. Lowe did

not anticipate the issues her students had while working on this task, purposefully designing a similar task in which students are provided with both spaghetti and rulers as well as DGS may be an effective way to develop the habit of critically examining the appropriateness of the tools they use in relation to a given task.

Although technology was not originally used as part of this investigation, this example illustrates the idea of tool-mediated thought that is the result of instrumental genesis. Laura seemed to understand how the tools in GeoGebra might help her to investigate the question at hand, and how it might support her thinking and reasoning regarding this particular question. While measurement tools cannot provide a proof of the Triangle Inequality Theorem, and the appropriateness of investigating this theorem empirically might be questioned, DGS can certainly be used to form and test an accurate conjecture, and to support students' engagement in transformational reasoning (Simon, 1996). If the goal of transformational reasoning is to understand why a system behaves in a particular manner, students needed a tool that could support making such a conjecture, and could allow students to investigate why it is true. In this case, students needed a tool that would represent the triangle as a straight line when the sum of two of the side lengths is equal to the third, something students were unable to accomplish using spaghetti and rulers.

Applets vs. Constructions

Students in Ms. Young's Geometry class investigated properties of parallel lines cut by a transversal using a pre-constructed GeoGebra applet instead of constructing the figure using tools in a DGS environment. Using an applet relieves students of the necessity of constructing mathematically accurate figures with which to investigate the properties of an object, which was an issue for a number of students in Ms. Jones' class described next. However, such an approach to guided exploration has important implications for students' ability to be strategic in their use of tools, and in particular their ability to engage in transformational reasoning (Simon, 1996). Furthermore, constraining students' freedom with regard to the tools they have available does not guarantee that students will attend to mathematically meaningful aspects of the task, as this episode illustrates.

The applet these students manipulated was constructed properly, including the measurements of the angles formed by parallel lines cut by a transversal, and even displayed angles with certain relationships, such as corresponding, vertical, or alternate interior, in the same color, as shown in Figure 4.

Using an interactive whiteboard, Ms. Young demonstrated how the points can be dragged on the applet, and how to put the figure back to its beginning state by refreshing the page. She pointed out that there was a table for them to complete on their worksheet and that there were some directions before the table about what to do.

She explained to the class that on the worksheet she gave them a pair of angles with a certain relationship, and asked them to find another pair with the same relationship. She explained that they needed to make an observation about each type of angle relationship, and that *observation* means, "what do you see, notice, what's true?" As student began to work on the task, almost immediately they started asking each other what they were supposed to be doing. In response to a question on their worksheet that asked them to make an observation about corresponding angles, some students asked the teacher, "what's an observation?" Others wrote that both the angles were blue, or that both the angles were 141 degrees. After the lesson she commented:

They don't understand the word 'observations,' and neither did my Honors kids, because they had that same worksheet only they didn't have the conjecture as fill-in-the-blank. They don't know what to write for observations. They're like "they're both blue" or "one is blue and one is

Figure 4. Parallel lines cut by a transversal applet used by Ms. Young's students

Properties of Parallel Lines

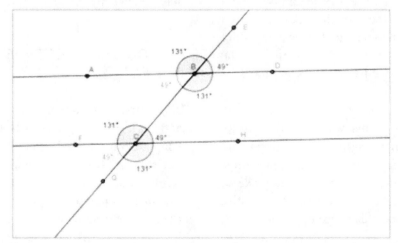

Lines AB and FC are parallel. Line BC is a transversal of the two parallel lines AB and FC.

Use points A, B, and C to change the angle values. When a transversal intersects two parallel lines, what angle relationships are formed? Make as many observations as you can.

green." These kids were like, "they are both 141 degrees," which, they were on the right track, but that doesn't help when you move A, and now that angle is 107, so now your observation is not right (Interview, 9/29/10).

Discussion

These students failed to make conjectures about generalizable relationships between the angles in their figure, in spite of the fact that they had been provided with a tool that would support that activity. That is, they failed to use the tool that they had been provided with strategically to accomplish this goal. However, this episode illustrates that using tools strategically does not lie entirely on the side of the tool, but that it also involves understanding the type of activity that the tool makes possible. Making mathematically meaningful observations in a DGS environment can be an open-ended and difficult endeavor for students, as they may have trouble knowing what types of things to pay attention to. In the first example prior, Nick and Brian began by acknowledging that there were many observations that they could have made. Unlike Nick and Brian, however, Ms. Young's students did not understand the goal of the task to be the formulation of a generalizable relationship that could be the basis for a conjecture, or understand the affordances of the tool that they had been provided in relation to that goal. This contrasting case in Ms. Young's class further underscores the meaning that Nick and Brian had constructed for the dragging tool.

Ms. Young seemed to underestimate the support that her students would need to make mathematically meaningful observations that could provide a basis for making conjectures. As her students had never been asked to make an observation or a conjecture, providing them with a tool that could support that activity did not result in their ability to do so. As teachers use DGS to create opportunities for students to engage in mathematical practices, they must support not only

their students' use of the tool, but the behaviors they want students to engage in while using it.

This example also demonstrates that making tools simpler to use does not guarantee that they will be used strategically, and in fact, can obscure the complexity of the underlying structure, thereby preventing students from engaging in transformational reasoning (Simon, 1996). Constructing the system using tools in DGS, even if they are guided in doing so, can provide insight into the rules that govern the system for students, and may be a prerequisite to any further investigation of how the system operates.

In addition, the process of constructing objects in DGS, versus merely manipulating pre-constructed figures, is an important opportunity for students to construct meaning for the tools in DGS. While pre-constructed applets constrain students' investigations in ways that may appear beneficial for their ability to achieve a specific learning goal while participating in mathematical activity, they do not allow students the freedom extend their thinking or their investigation beyond those specific goals or examples, such as the "what if" question posed by Paul in the special case of an equilateral triangle prior. Ultimately, developing students' ability to assess the appropriateness of a tool in relation to the goals of task will require that students are given such freedom.

THE ROLE OF INSTRUMENTAL GENESIS

In the first two examples described previously, students used appropriate tools strategically while using DGS for guided exploration. The meaning that students had constructed for DGS and the various tools available in that environment, and how that supported this practice was discussed. The episode described next is an example of what can happen when students use tools that they have not constructed mathematical meaning for. A second contrasting example is included that suggests that teaching students to assess their constructions in DGS is an important element of using tools strategically.

Drawing vs. Construction

Ms. Jones' students were given a worksheet that guided them to use Geometer's Sketchpad (GSP) to create parallel lines cut by a transversal, and to make conjectures about the relationship between the angles formed by such a figure. A primary goal of the task was for students to identify and reason about which pairs of angles are congruent and which pairs are supplementary. However, while working on the task, seven students were observed to connect a collection of line segments that looked like parallel lines cut by a transversal, but when dragged deformed into a figure like that shown in Figure 5.

In addition, these students were not observed to make any corrections to their construction after dragging the figure, but simply adjusted their figure until it *looked like* parallel lines cut by a transversal again, and continued working through the handout. Thus, when these students used GSP to measure the eight angles formed by this figure,

Figure 5. Dragging reveals that the figure is not a representation of parallel lines cut by a transversal

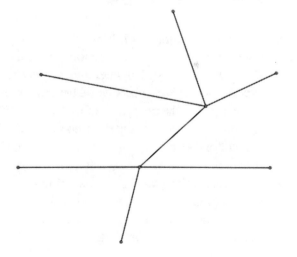

most of them were not congruent or supplementary even though the lines looked parallel, as in the student work shown in Figure 6.

Without the properties built into the construction that students were intended to investigate, exploration, observations, or generalization of the properties of parallel lines cut by a transversal was a futile endeavor.

Discussion

This particular episode exemplifies the idea that instrumental genesis involves more than knowing which buttons to push. These students were given directions for how to make this construction in a handout provided by the teacher, and Ms. Jones told students that if their lines were not parallel, "this won't work," and gave no further explanation of what parallel meant, indicating she believed that her students understood of this term. Furthermore, students always adjusted their figures back to something that looked parallel, which further suggests that they knew what parallel meant, at least visually. The directions in the handout were explicit in directing students to create a line, and a point not on the line, and a line parallel to the original line through the point, including precisely how to do this in GSP.

Although this behavior was noticed in only seven of the students in this class, the fact that any student would engage with this task in such an unanticipated manner is noteworthy. At least part of the explanation for this behavior may lie in the mathematical meaning, or lack thereof, that these students had constructed for this tool. These students did not understand what *parallel* meant in a dynamic geometry environment, which may also reveal a deficiency in their understanding of the concept of parallel in general. That is, they did not understand that when parallel lines are *constructed* in a dynamic geometry environment, the parallel property will be maintained; moving one line will result in the line parallel to it automatically mirroring the same movement in order

Figure 6. Student work in GSP on the parallel lines cut by a transversal task

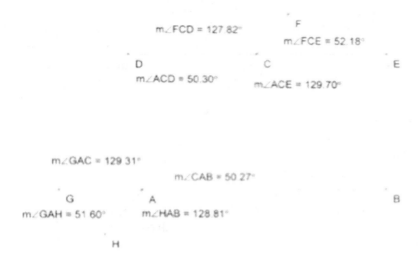

to maintain the "parallel-ness" of the two lines. These students seemed to consider "parallel" to be a contingent rather than necessary property of the lines displayed on their screen. Thus, the lines were parallel when they looked parallel, which would explain why they simply adjusted their figure back to something that appeared to be parallel.

Furthermore, these students did not verify that the two lines were indeed parallel, perhaps because they did not understand how to verify this property mathematically, did not know how to use the tools in GSP to do this, or did not perceive a need to verify it. Indeed, this episode also reveals these students' lack of engagement with another mathematical practice described in the Standards: the need to attend to precision. "Looking" parallel was not precise enough to reveal the relationships among the angles formed when the parallel lines were cut by a transversal, and they were unable strategically use the tools at their disposal to ensure the construction possessed the necessary precision.

This episode illustrates how mathematics is built into DGS tools, how the use of these tools requires a certain amount of prior knowledge on the part of students, and thus demonstrates that the process of instrumental genesis with DGS involves constructing *mathematical* meaning for, and with, these tools. For example, in GSP, and in mathematics, there is a definite difference between lines constructed to be parallel and lines that are made to look parallel. Students' inability to understand this difference, and how it is represented in GSP, prevented them from using the tools in GSP strategically, and ultimately from participating in other mathematical practices, such as making sense of the mathematics, or investigating the structure inherent in the representation of this object.

Self-Monitoring as Evidence of Instrumental Genesis

A contrasting example of how constructing meaning for the tools in DGS supports students' use of it for meaningful mathematical activity occurred in Ms. Lowe's class while her students were investigating the properties of midsegments of a triangle, i.e., a segment that connects the midpoint of one side of a triangle to the midpoint of another side. One of her students, Will, asked her for another activity worksheet, explaining that when he dragged his figure, he realized that he had not created a midpoint because it did not stay on the segment representing the side of the triangle.

After re-starting the investigation, he created the construction shown in Figure 7.

Discussion

Will generated two correct conjectures after correcting the error that he discovered in his original construction, as shown in Figure 8. Unlike the students in Ms. Jones' class who did not understand the difference between two lines that look parallel and two lines that are constructed to be parallel in GSP, Will understood the mathematical difference between a point that looks like it is the midpoint of a segment and one that is constructed to be, and how this is represented in GeoGebra. Perhaps more importantly, he understood the need to assess his construction, and how dragging can be used to do this. In a DGS environment, this is a crucial habit for students to develop in order to use appropriate tools strategically. Using the dragging tool in DGS in this manner may be considered strategic, since if the object to be investigated is constructed incorrectly, students will not have access to information that will guide their subsequent investigation. Students' ability to use DGS to engage in any of the mathematical practices described in the Standards hinges on their ability to monitor their own work in DGS in this manner. In addition, this example demonstrates how students who assess their constructions are already beginning to engage in transformational reasoning, by understanding how the system should behave if constructed correctly.

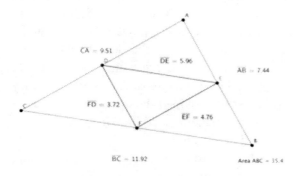

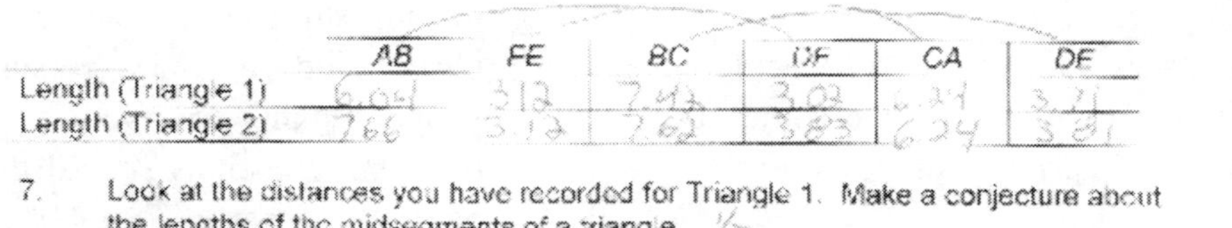

These contrasting examples also provide some insight into the role of dragging in the process of instrumental genesis with DGS. When students in Ms. Jones' class dragged their figures and they deformed, they simply adjusted them until they looked parallel again. The mathematical meanings of their actions in DGS were not apparent to them. Will, on the other hand, recognized that dragging was a way to test a figure and assess whether or not it had been constructed appropriately. He understood the mathematical significance of creating the midpoint of a segment, that when such an object is constructed it is a property inherent in the figure. According to the standard for using appropriate tools strategically, "[mathematically proficient students] detect possible errors by strategically using estimation and other mathematical knowledge" (Common Core State Standards Initiative, 2010). In a DGS environment, fostering students' ability to test the accuracy of their constructions using tools such as dragging

Figure 7. Will's corrected construction on the midsegments task

Figure 8. Will's conjecture on the midsegments task

	AB	FE	BC	DF	CA	DF
Length (Triangle 1)	6.04	3.12	7.43	3.02	6.24	3.21
Length (Triangle 2)	7.66	3.12	7.62	3.83	6.24	3.81

7. Look at the distances you have recorded for Triangle 1. Make a conjecture about the lengths of the midsegments of a triangle.

midsegment is ½ the length of the segment opposite on the triangle. They are also parallel

is an important element of teaching students to use tools strategically.

IMPLICATIONS, CHALLENGES, FUTURE DIRECTIONS

The previous analysis demonstrates that there is a strong connection between the practice of using tools strategically and the meaning that students construct for the tools that are available to them. Building on the work of Trouche and his colleagues (Drijvers & Trouche, 2008; Guin & Trouche, 1999), researchers have identified the development of students' instrumental genesis as crucial to the integration of technology in the classroom: "A key challenge, then, for the integration of technology into classrooms and curricula is to understand and to devise ways to foster the process of instrumental genesis" (Hoyles, Noss, & Kent, 2004, p. 314). Doerr and Zangor (2000) examined the practice of a teacher experienced in the use of a graphing calculator for mathematics instruction in order to investigate the meaning that her students had constructed with and for this tool, and how those meanings were shaped by the teacher. More research of this nature is needed regarding students' use of DGS, and connected to the idea of using appropriate tools strategically. I claim that the process of instrumental genesis is at the heart of using appropriate tools strategically, and make hypotheses regarding the factors that support this process in a classroom learning environment.

Factors Supporting Instrumental Genesis

Certain classroom-based factors seem particularly important in supporting students' development of the ability to use appropriate tools strategically:

- **Time:** Students need time to develop meaning for tools. It is not a process that can

be rushed. By making *use of appropriate tools strategically* a specific mathematical practice that will be assessed, there is hope that teachers will find more support and justification for using instructional time for this goal.

- **Support:** Students need support in developing mathematical meaning for their actions in a DGS environment. Teachers can support students by helping them learn to assess their own progress and interpret feedback provided by DGS tools, a habit that Ms. Lowe had instilled in her students. In the version of the parallel lines cut by a transversal activity implemented in Ms. Jones' class, proper support by the teacher might have resulted in a rich discussion about what it means for two lines to be parallel, and how the representation of parallel lines in GSP is related to that meaning.

- **Accountability:** Often students are not held accountable for their thinking and reasoning using technological tools, but only for the products of these investigations. Teachers may be more focused on content goals when students use DGS, looking for correct conclusions but disregarding the reasoning process that lead to those conclusions. In order for students to learn to engage in mathematical practices, they must be provided the opportunity to share their mathematical thinking, both orally and in writing.

- **Questioning:** While good questioning by teachers is crucial to effective mathematics instruction in general, the types of questions that teachers ask are key to supporting students in making sense of their observations in DGS, versus stopping at simply making observations. In particular, teachers' questions should direct students back to their work in DGS to reflect and interpret that work mathematically, and to encourage students to engage in transformational reasoning by prompting them to understand why a conjecture might be true.

These factors and others are discussed in greater detail elsewhere (author, blinded for review). However, more work aimed at understanding how teachers can support students' progression through a trajectory of instrumental genesis using DGS is needed. In particular, there is a need to identify specific behaviors that would provide evidence of students' instrumental genesis via tasks that require that students use tools strategically, and to develop and test strategies that teachers could use to help students achieve those goals. The results of an iterative process of designing, testing, and refining instructional strategies for fostering students' instrumental genesis could help teachers to be more intentional in developing students' ability to use appropriate tools strategically.

Using Narrative Cases to Support Teacher Learning

An understanding of the importance of instrumental genesis as foundational for students' strategic use of appropriate tools, and knowledge of strategies for fostering students' instrumental genesis might be considered an important component of mathematics teachers' Technological Pedagogical Content Knowledge (TPACK) (Mishra & Koehler, 2006; Niess et al., 2009). Ultimately, in order to impact classroom instruction, the results of the type of research discussed and proposed in this chapter must impact teacher education and professional development. One way to do this is to incorporate examples such as those described previously into materials for teacher education so that teachers can learn from them and apply that knowledge to their own practice.

An important tool in mathematics teacher education is the use of narrative case studies in which teachers examine a written narrative of a classroom episode to identify elements of the classroom context, especially those shaped by the

teacher, and to reflect on the relationship between the pedagogical moves of the teacher and student thinking and learning (Lundeberg, Levin, & Harrington, 1999; Markovits & Smith, 2008; Smith & Friel, 2008; Tirosh & Wood, 2008). The strength of narrative cases in mathematics teacher education is that teaching becomes the object of study, providing teachers with opportunities to carefully examine many elements that make up the complex environment of a K-12 mathematics classroom in a way that is not possible during live observations or even video of classroom episodes (Stein et al., 2009). Narrative case materials of both *exemplars* and *problem situations* have been found to be an effective tool in mathematics teacher education (Markovits & Smith, 2008), but none currently exist in the area of using technology for mathematics instruction. For example, teachers could engage in using DGS to investigate the properties of parallel lines cut by a transversal, and be provided with more in-depth descriptions of Ms. Young's and Ms. Jones' implementations of this task, including excerpts from the post-lesson interviews. Teachers could then be guided to conduct their own analyses of these episodes in terms of the opportunities for and impediments to using tools strategically, and the role of instrumental genesis in this practice. A carefully planned discussion around teachers' analyses can help teachers to identify important classroom practices necessary to supporting students' strategic use of tools. Similar cases could be developed around exemplars of practice, such as some of the episodes that occurred in Ms. Lowe's classroom. Developing case materials that exemplify the issues discussed in this chapter, could provide teacher educators with a tool to support teachers in developing their students' ability to use appropriate tools strategically while using DGS.

CONCLUSION

The ability to use appropriate tools strategically is certainly an important skill for students to develop in order to be college and career ready in today's society. Furthermore, if students are to use technological tools to engage in the other mathematical practices outlined in the Standards, this ability is a necessary prerequisite. The issues discussed in this chapter provide insight into what this ability may consist of in a DGS environment and suggest ways that teachers may help their students to develop it; and also how research and teacher education may contribute to a more effective preparation of mathematics teachers in this area.

Although the use of technological tools for mathematics learning and instruction has been a growing area of research in mathematics education for the last 40 years, (c.f., Heid, 1997; Kaput, 1992; Zbiek et al., 2007), the articulation of this mathematical practice in the CCSSM, and in particular the forthcoming assessments, may provide the necessary impetus for K-12 teachers and administrators to place a greater emphasis on developing this skill in their students. Mathematics education researchers and teacher educators must be prepared to assist teachers in meeting this important challenge.

REFERENCES

Bliss, J., & Ogborn, J. (1989). Tools for exploratory learning. *Journal of Computer Assisted Learning*, 5, 37–50. doi:10.1111/j.1365-2729.1989.tb00196.x.

Boaler, J., & Staples, M. (2008). Creating mathematical futures through an equitable teaching approach: The case of railside school. *Teachers College Record*, *110*(3), 608–645.

Boaler, J., Wiliam, D., & Brown, M. (2000). Students' experiences of ability grouping - Disaffection, polarisation and the construction of failure. *British Educational Research Journal*, *26*(5), 631–648. doi:10.1080/713651583.

Burrill, G., Allison, J., Breaux, G., Kastberg, S., Leatham, K., & Sanchez, W. (2002). *Handheld graphing technology in secondary mathematics*. Retrieved from http://education.ti.com/sites/UK/downloads/pdf/References/Done/Burrill,G.%20(2002).pdf

Common Core State Standards Initiative. (2010). *Common core state standards (mathematics standards)*. Retrieved from http://www.corestandards.org/the-standards/mathematics

Cuoco, A., Goldenberg, E. P., & Mark, J. (1996). Habits of mind: An organizing principle for mathematics curricula. *The Journal of Mathematical Behavior*, *15*(4), 375–402. doi:10.1016/S0732-3123(96)90023-1.

Doerr, H. M., & Pratt, D. (2008). The learning of mathematics and mathematical modeling. In Heid, M. K., & Blume, G. W. (Eds.), *Research on technology in the teaching and learning of mathematics: Research syntheses* (Vol. 1, pp. 259–286). Charlotte, NC: Information Age Publishing.

Doerr, H. M., & Zangor, R. (2000). Creating meaning for and with the graphing calculator. *Educational Studies in Mathematics*, *41*(2), 143–163. doi:10.1023/A:1003905929557.

Drijvers, P., & Trouche, L. (2008). From artifacts to instruments: A theoretical framework behind the orchestra metaphor. In Heid & G. W. Blume (Eds.), Research on technology and the teaching and learning of mathematics (Vol. 2, pp. 363–392). Academic Press.

Guin, D., & Trouche, L. (1999). The complex process of converting tools into mathematical instruments: The case of calculators. *International Journal of Computers for Mathematical Learning*, *3*, 195–227. doi:10.1023/A:1009892720043.

Heid, M. K. (1997). The technological revolution and reform of school mathematics. *American Journal of Education*, *106*, 5–61. doi:10.1086/444175.

Heid, M. K., & Blume, G. W. (Eds.). (2008). *Research on technology in the teaching and learning of mathematics: Research syntheses (Vol. 1)*. Charlotte, NC: Information Age Publishing.

Hiebert, J., Carpenter, T. P., Fennema, E., Fuson, K., Wearne, D., & Murray, H. et al. (1997). *Making sense: Teaching and learning mathematics with understanding*. Portsmouth, NH: Heinemann.

Hollebrands, K. F., Laborde, C., & StraBer, R. (2008). Technology and the learning of geometry at the secondary level. In M. K. Heid & G. W. Blume (Eds.), *Research on technology in the teaching and learning of mathematics: Research syntheses* (Vol. 1, pp. 155–205). Charlotte, NC: Information Age Publishing.

Hoyles, C., Noss, R., & Kent, P. (2004). On the integration of digital technologies into mathematics classrooms. *International Journal of Computers for Mathematical Learning*, *9*(3), 309–326. doi:10.1007/s10758-004-3469-4.

Kaput, J. J. (1992). Technology and mathematics education. In Grouws, D. A. (Ed.), *Handbook of research on mathematics teaching and learning* (pp. 515–556). New York, NY: Macmillan.

Karadag, Z., Martinovic, D., & Frieman, V. (2011). Dynamic and interactive mathematics learning environments. In L. R. Wiest & T. Lamberg (Eds.), *Proceedings of the thirty-third annual conference of the North American Chapter of the International Group for the Psychology of Mathematics Education*. Reno, NV: PME-NA.

Lundeberg, M. A., Levin, B. B., & Harrington, H. L. (Eds.). (1999). *Who learns what from cases and how? The research base for teaching and learning with cases*. Hoboken, NJ: Lawrence Erlbaum.

Markovits, Z., & Smith, M. S. (2008). Cases as tools in mathematics teacher education. In Tirosh, D., & Wood, T. (Eds.), *The international handbook of mathematics teacher education: Tools and processes in mathematics teacher education* (*Vol. 2*, pp. 39–64). Rotterdam, The Netherlands: Sense Publishers.

Mishra, P., & Koehler, M. J. (2006). Technological pedagogical content knowledge: A framework for teacher knowledge. *Teachers College Record*, *108*(6), 1017–1054. doi:10.1111/j.1467-9620.2006.00684.x.

National Council of Teachers of Mathematics. (2000). *Principles and standards for school mathematics*. Reston, VA: National Council of Teachers of Mathematics.

National Council of Teachers of Mathematics. (2009). *Focus in high school mathematics: Reasoning and sense making*. Reston, VA: National Council of Teachers of Mathematics.

Niess, M. L., Ronau, R. N., Shafer, K. G., Driskell, S. O., Harper, S. R., & Johnston, C. et al. (2009). Mathematics teacher TPACK standards and developmental model. *Contemporary Issues in Technology & Teacher Education*, *9*(1), 4–24.

Sherman, M. F. (2012). Supporting students' mathematical thinking during technology-enhanced investigations using DGS. In Martinovic, D., McDougall, D., & Karadag, Z. (Eds.), *Mathematics education and technology: Contemporary issues*, (pp. 147–182). Santa Rosa, CA: Informing Science Press.

Simon, M. A. (1996). Beyond inductive and deductive reasoning: The search for a sense of knowing. *Educational Studies in Mathematics*, *30*(2), 197–210. doi:10.1007/BF00302630.

Smith, M. S., & Friel, S. (Eds.). (2008). *Cases in mathematics teacher education: Tools for developing knowledge needed for teaching*. Association of Mathematics Teacher Educators.

Stein, M. K., Smith, M. S., Henningsen, M. A., & Silver, E. A. (2009). *Implementing standards-based mathematics instruction: A casebook for professional development* (2nd ed.). New York: Teachers College Press.

Tirosh, D., & Wood, T. (Eds.). (2008). *Tools and processes in mathematics teacher education.* Rotterdam, The Netherlands: Sense Publishers.

Vygotsky, L. (1978). *Mind in society: The development of higher psychological processes.* Boston: Harvard University Press.

Zbiek, R. M., Heid, M. K., Blume, G. W., & Dick, T. P. (2007). Research on technology in mathematics education: The perspective of constructs. In Lester, F. K. (Ed.), *Second handbook of research in mathematics teaching and learning* (pp. 1169–1207). Charlotte, NC: Information Age Publishing.

ADDITIONAL READING

Ball, L., & Stacey, K. C. (2005). Teaching strategies for developing judicious technology use. In Masalski, W. J., & Elliott, P. C. (Eds.), *Technology-supported mathematics learning environments, 2005 yearbook of the national council of teachers of mathematics* (pp. 3–15). Reston, VA: National Council of Teachers of Mathematics.

Dick, T. P. (2008). Keeping the faith: Fidelity in technological tools for mathematics education. In Blume, G. W., & Heid, M. K. (Eds.), *Research on technology in the teaching and learning of mathematics: Syntheses, cases, and perspectives* (*Vol. 2*, pp. 333–339). Charlotte, NC: Information Age Publishing.

Goos, M., Galbraith, P., Renshaw, P., & Geiger, V. (2003). Perspectives on technology mediated learning in secondary school mathematics classrooms. *The Journal of Mathematical Behavior*, 22(1), 73–89. doi:10.1016/S0732-3123(03)00005-1.

Scher, D. (2005). Square or not? Assessing constructions in an interactive geometry software environment. In Masalski, W. J., & Elliott, P. C. (Eds.), *Technology-supported mathematics learning environments, 2005 yearbook of the national council of teachers of mathematics* (pp. 113–124). Reston, VA: National Council of Teachers of Mathematics.

Suh, J. (2010). Leveraging cognitive technology tools to expand opportunities for critical thinking in elementary mathematics. *Journal of Computers in Mathematics and Science Teaching*, 29(3), 14.

Zbiek, R. M., & Hollebrands, K. F. (2008). A research-informed view of the process of incorporating mathematics technology into classroom practice by in-service and prospective teachers. In Heid, M. K., & Blume, G. W. (Eds.), *Research on technology in the teaching and learning of mathematics: Research syntheses* (*Vol. 1*, pp. 287–344). Charlotte, NC: Information Age Publishing.

KEY TERMS AND DEFINITIONS

Dynamic and Interactive Mathematics Learning Environments (DIMLE): Refers to any learning environment in which digital technologies are used to engage students in explorative learning.

Dynamic Geometry Software (DGS): Any software program that allows users to construct representations of mathematical objects, and to interact with them in real time through a graphical interface.

Instrumental Genesis: The process by which a learner constructs meaning for and with a tool.

Mathematical Practices: Ways of thinking or behaving that are characteristically mathematical in nature.

Technological Pedagogical Content Knowledge (TPACK): The essentially integrated and highly contextual knowledge needed by teachers to determine effective strategies for teaching particular concepts using technological tools.

Transformational Reasoning: Distinct but overlapping with inductive and deductive reasoning, transformational reasoning is the process of examining a system in order to understand how it works, or why it behaves in a particular manner.

ENDNOTES

[1]   Pseudonyms.

Chapter 7
The Incorporation of *Geometer's Sketchpad* in a High School Geometry Curriculum

Lisa Ames
Wood-Ridge High School, USA

Heejung An
William Paterson University, USA

Sandra Alon
William Paterson University, USA

ABSTRACT

The Common Core State Mathematics Standards (CCSSM) recommend that technology should be integrated into teaching and learning Mathematics. This chapter addresses how the Geometer's Sketchpad computer program can support students' thinking skills and learning outcomes in a high school geometry class, in particular for more effectively addressing the High School Geometry Standards (CCSSM: G.CO.10, G.CO. 11, and G.CO. 12). The findings from the study presented in this chapter indicate that this tool can help high school students increase their learning of geometry in terms of inductive reasoning and conceptual knowledge, but may not help improve students' motivation to learn geometry.

INTRODUCTION

Geometry is a "network of concepts, ways of reasoning and representation systems, used to explore and analyze shape and space" (Battista, 2007, p. 843). This critical area of mathematics appears in both the physical and virtual world that students encounter every day. Yet, according to the Learning Principle from National Council of Teachers of Mathematics (NCTM) (2000), middle and high school standardized test results in mathematics from the past 10 years indicate that many U.S. students lack conceptual understanding and reasoning skills in geometry. At the current time, mathematics education in U.S. schools places an emphasis on learning procedural and basic skills,

DOI: 10.4018/978-1-4666-4086-3.ch007

before applying them to concepts. As a result, there has been a lack of understanding of the "big ideas" in mathematics and how they relate to other disciplines. When students lack conceptual understanding in mathematics, they also tend to lose interest and motivation to continue their learning because it comes across as the study of isolated facts and procedures rather than a process of reasoning and critical thinking (Acker, 1999; Anderman & Maehr, 1994; Teoh, Koo, & Singh, 2010). The Learning Principle from NCTM (2000) therefore indicates that there is a need to focus on conceptual learning in order for students to be able to apply their knowledge to a variety of mathematical situations. NCTM (2008) has also stressed in its position statement on technology that it is an essential tool for mathematical success in the 21st century.

As a proposed solution, many reformers have suggested that technology can play a role in improving learning outcomes in mathematics (Bos, 2007; Isikasal & Askar, 2005; Myers, 2009; Ploger & Hecht, 2009; Santos-Trigo & Cristobal-Escalante, 2008). Within the area of geometry, technology has been cited as being particularly useful in enhancing visualization (Kimmins, 1995; Mayes, 1995; Myers, 2009). Furthermore, while the Common Core State Mathematics Standards (CCSSM) focus on mathematics content, they also emphasize integrating technology as a way to learn mathematical knowledge and skills. The Standards for Mathematical Practice (http://www. corestandards.org/the-standards/mathematics/introduction/standards-for-mathematical-practice/) expect that mathematically proficient students should know which tools would help them perform various tasks more effectively and use the appropriate tools strategically. One of these tools includes a highly visual discovery-based, interactive dynamic geometry computer program called *Geometer's Sketchpad* that can target key understandings identified in the CCSSM. When developing mathematical models, this rich, hands-on learning tool can help students visual-

ize the results of various assumptions, to explore consequences and compare predictions. This tool is uniquely positioned to transform learning geometry through critical thinking and active exploration, thus empowering students to discover new relationships (See Figure 1).

Moreover, in recent years, mathematics teachers have been faced with a strong push towards using technological tools in their classrooms to supplement their print resources and to gain the interest of our ever-growing millennial student population, who are surrounded by and use technology on a constant basis. Current educational research is also stressing the need to

Figure 1. Using the measurement and construction tools in Geometer's sketchpad to determine properties of quadrilaterals

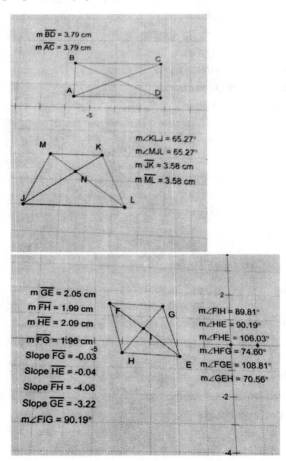

tap into students' reasoning skills through the use of technology, in order to improve mathematical achievement as well as students' interest in mathematics (Isikasal & Askar, 2005).

BACKGROUND AND LITERATURE REVIEW

The CCSSM recommends that technology should be integrated into academics. The standards call for not only basic technology skills, but also ways to integrate various technologies into mathematics classrooms. In particular, technology supports key components of the Standards for Mathematical Practice. These standards expect students to make sense of problems and persevere in solving them, to use appropriate tools strategically, to reason abstractly and quantitatively, and to construct viable arguments and models with mathematics. The technology can be used to support these thinking skills. Furthermore, technology allows teachers to help transform the way they teach mathematics classes: from being teacher-centered to more students centered.

Within the literature examining the effects of various technologies on teaching and learning mathematics, there have been mixed results in terms of learning outcomes to generate conceptual understanding and inductive reasoning. For instance, Ploger and Hecht (2009) found that *Chartworld*, an interactive technology program, was an effective method of instruction for improving conceptual knowledge. Similarly, Myers (2009) found that *Geometer's Sketchpad* had a significant effect on conceptual knowledge through achievement scores on standardized mathematical tests and for mathematical skills in a high school classroom. Bos (2007) studied the effect of using Texas Instruments calculators in a mathematics classroom and found significant gains in conceptual knowledge when the calculators were fully utilized. Santos-Trigo and Cristobal-Escalante (2008) also conducted a study to analyze the problem solving approaches of high school students when using the Cabri-Geometry software. The results showed that the students who used this software to explore dynamic representations of each task gained higher-level thinking about each task. The software allowed students to explore additional questions not initially considered by the original task and therefore increased their inductive reasoning. Lastly, Isikasal and Askar (2005) studied the effect of *Autograph*, a software program that incorporates the dynamic, interactive, and visual aspects and found that students who used it outperformed those who did not in terms of inductive reasoning, while also having more enjoyment in their learning.

As for the effects of infusing technology on motivation toward the mathematics in the K-12 classrooms, past research also revealed conflicting results. Kebritchi, Hirumi, and Bai (2010) studied the effects of a mathematical computer game on student achievement and motivation and found no significance gain in the students' motivation for those using the game, even though there was a gain in achievement. On the other hand, Nguyen, Hsieh, and Allen (2006) looked at the effect of a mathematics Web-based program and found gains in student interest because of the immediate feedback they received when using the program. Additionally, Hannafin, Burruss, and Little (2005) found that Grade 7 students who used the *Geometer's Sketchpad* program showed greater enthusiasm in the subject area.

As previously mentioned, the effects of various technologies on students' conceptual understanding, reasoning, and motivation in mathematics classrooms has been mixed. Consequently, it appears that the type of technology and how it is implemented can greatly affect how students' interest in mathematics and understanding may increase.

STUDY

This study was conducted in order to examine the effects of *Geometer's Sketchpad* in two -high school mathematics classes, one using *Geometer's Sketchpad* and one completing the same activities using paper and pencil and various geometry tools such as protractors, rulers, and compasses. The following research questions guided this study.

1. Would high school students show greater conceptual understanding of quadrilaterals when using *Geometer's Sketchpad* than using paper and pencil materials tools to determine the properties of quadrilaterals?
2. Would high school students increase their inductive reasoning of quadrilaterals more when using *Geometer's Sketchpad* than using paper and pencil based tools?
3. Would students' motivation to learn geometry be greater when using *Geometer's Sketchpad* than without it?

Participants and Settings

The participants in this study were thirty-eight 10th and 11th grade students enrolled in two geometry classes in a northern New Jersey high school during the Spring, 2012 semester. These two classes were taught by the first author of this chapter and the intervention lasted for 6 weeks. Table 1 shows the demographic information of the two classes. The Geometer's Sketchpad group (GSP group) was the first period geometry class with eighteen students and the paper and pencil group (PP group) was the fifth period geometry class with twenty students. The mean Rasch Unit (RIT) scales based on national grade level percentiles were reported in order to gauge each student's mathematical academic ability. As shown in Table 1, there was not any significant RIT scale difference between the two groups.

Table 1. Demographics of the participants

	GSP Group	PP Group
Total	18	20
Gender	9 male, 9 female	12 male, 8 female
Ethnicity	12 Caucasian, 6 Hispanic	12 Caucasian, 6 Hispanic, 2 Asian
Grade level	16 10th grade and 2 11th grade	16 10th grade and 4 11th grade
Mean RIT scale	233.8	238.3

Data Collection and Analyses

Overall, three types of data were collected and analyzed. First, conceptual knowledge was measured with a 10 question open-ended pre-and post-assessment, scored as 0 to 3 points for each question based on a teacher-made rubric, leading to the maximum of 30 points. The scores from these pre- and post-assessments were compared by using an Analysis of Covariance (ANCOVA) test, in order to examine whether the difference in students' conceptual understanding on the triangle and quadrilateral properties was significant between the GSP and PP groups.

Over the six-week intervention period, students in the GSP group completed 2 problem sets per week for 45 minutes using *Geometer's Sketchpad* to discover various properties of quadrilaterals. The PP group completed the same problem sets twice a week for 45 minutes with a paper and pencil and geometric tools such as compasses, protractors, and rulers. The student responses on the problem sets as well as the sketches they constructed were used in order to assess their inductive reasoning of quadrilateral properties. Each problem set was scored as 0 to 3 possible points based on a rubric from the State of NJ Department of Education (http://www.state.nj.us/education/assessment/hs/hspa_mathhb.pdf). A T-test was conducted to compare the total mean scores of these groups.

The students in both groups also completed a motivation pre-and post Likert-scale survey, with 5 options, ranging from 1 – 5, made up of 20 questions, leading to a maximum score of 100. (1: Strongly disagree, 2: disagree, 3: neutral, 4: agree, 5: Strongly agree). The teacher also used informal observation notes to assess the student's motivation towards learning the geometric concepts. The ANCOVA test was used to analyze the pre and post survey data between these GSP and PP groups.

Results

Table 2 showed that for conceptual understanding, there was a significant difference in the post assessment mean scores for the open-ended assessments in the GSP group, as compared to the PP group ($F(1) = 7.940, p = .008$).

The results shown in Table 3 indicated that students in the GSP group significantly increased their inductive reasoning of quadrilaterals when using the *Geometer's Sketchpad* program as compared to students in the PP group ($T(36) = 2.371, p = .021$). When looking at each week's scores in Figure 2, for all weeks, the mean scores in GSP group were higher than the mean scores in the PP group.

Table 2. Total mean scores on open-ended conceptual knowledge pre- and post-tests

		GSP Group	PP Group	F score	p value
Pre-test	Mean (SD)	14.28 (4.01)	11.95 (4.99)	7.940	.008
Post-test	Mean (SD)	26.28 (2.37)	23.05 (3.49)		

Table 3. Mean score on problem sets by total

	GSP Group	PP Group	T score	p value
Total mean	30.06 (2.94)	27.05 (4.59)	2.371	.021

As for motivation, there was no significant increase in the motivation of the GSP group when compared with the PP group, as shown in Table 4 ($F(1) = .208, p = .651$). Rather, the motivation survey scores decreased in both groups after the intervention period, which was an unexpected finding.

DISCUSSIONS, IMPLICATIONS, AND RECOMMENDATIONS

This study demonstrated that using *Geometer's Sketchpad* can effectively help students to learn geometry in terms of both inductive reasoning and conceptual knowledge. It also appears that the extent of its effects on inductive reasoning depends on the geometric topic that it is being used for. For instance, when looking at inductive reasoning through the weekly problem sets, the largest difference in mean scores between the two groups was during the week in which quadrilaterals were discussed. As such, *Geometer's Sketchpad* may be most helpful to students when used with topics that require constructing and measuring more complex figures accurately (e.g., kites, trapezoids, and regular polygons).

Unlike the study conducted by Hannafin, Burruss, and Little (2001), usage of *Geometer's Sketchpad* didn't appear to improve students' motivation toward learning mathematics. This is perhaps because *Geometer's Sketchpad* is not a multimedia based program that tends to elicit "enjoyment." It also requires a time commitment in order to gain familiarity, even though students who participated in this study were exposed for a short-time period to the program before the study. Yet, it is important to note that through informal observations, higher achieving students seemed to exhibit more motivation when using GSP as compared to students in the PP group. This latter issue needs to be researched further.

Inclusion of *Geometer's Sketchpad* into the classroom also affected the way teacher taught the math classes. It affected the amount of discovery

Figure 2. Mean scores on problem sets by week

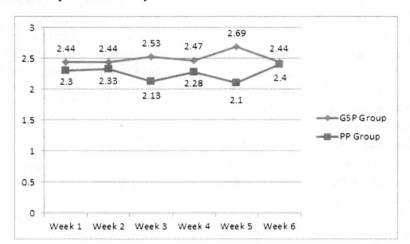

Table 4. Mean scores on pre- and post-motivation surveys

		GSP Group	PP Group	F score	*p* value
Pre-survey	Mean (SD)	63.83 (13.96)	66.00 (12.15)	.208	.651
Post-survey	Mean (SD)	59.11 (15.55)	62.05 (11.07)		

based instruction the teacher used, compared with direct instruction. *Geometer's Sketchpad* allowed the teacher to have students discover geometric properties rather than providing them with the properties without any means of exploration.

On a broader level, *Geometer's Sketchpad* can be used to explore geometry concepts related to the CCSSM through usage of a rich, hands-on learning tool. Technology, if used effectively, can deepen and enhance the learning process of Geometry in K-12 classrooms. Since the CCSSM emphasize learning of Geometry concepts, rather than just mathematical/computational skills, integrating technology into classroom instruction can be an instructional vehicle to achieve this. *Geometer Sketchpad* is a tool that offers visualizing, modeling and experimenting to observe a

phenomenon and view the results graphically, to aid in understanding and forming conclusions all relevant to the CCSSM.

Finally, there are some recommendations that teachers should take into account when using *Geometer's Sketchpad,* to bring about the maximum positive learning outcomes of this program. First, a hands-on training session with *Geometer's Sketchpad* needs to be provided for students beforehand, to make them feel comfortable and confident using this program, so that their cognitive load can be used fully for learning mathematics, rather than being bogged down in learning the computer program, itself. Second, teachers should still provide the necessary scaffolding for students. This computer program cannot be considered as a substitute teacher. Rather, it is a tool that teachers and students can use to teach and learn the geometry more effectively. Teachers need to determine on an individual basis the detail and depth of scaffolding their students require to excel when using *Geometer's Sketchpad*. Third, effective technology integration should happen across the Geometry curriculum in ways that research shows deepen and enhance the learning process. The positive effects of this program would not occur if it is used haphazardly.

CONCLUSION

When used effectively, technology tools such as *Geometer's Sketchpad* can be an effective support tool for implementation of the CCSSM. Furthermore, this tool has the potential to affect the way in which teachers teach mathematics in a more student-centered and active hands-on manner. Technology offers effective ways to reach learners and assess their understanding. When technology is used to support the curricula it helps make learning more meaningful. In this chapter, we addressed how *Geometer's Sketchpad* can play a role in this regard. *Geometer's Sketchpad* helped high school students understand the concepts by providing them with the ability to explore different geometric properties by constructing and measuring them. *Geometer's Sketchpad* also allowed them to determine patterns with the geometric measurements as well as make conclusions about the data they constructed when using the program.

REFERENCES

Acker, S. (1999). *The realities of teachers' work: Never a dull moment.* New York: Cassell & Continuum.

Anderman, E. M., & Maehr, M. L. (1994). Motivation and schooling in the middle grades. *Review of Educational Research, 64*(2), 287–310. doi:10.3102/00346543064002287.

Battista, M. T. (2007). The development of geometric and spatial thinking. In Lester, F. (Ed.), *Second Handbook of Research on Mathematics Teaching and Learning* (pp. 843–908). Reston, VA: NCTM.

Berthold, K., & Renkl, A. (2009). Instructional aids to support a conceptual understanding of multiple representations. *Journal of Educational Psychology, 101*(1), 70–87. doi:10.1037/a0013247.

Biesinger, K., Crippen, K., & Muis, K. (2008). The impact of block scheduling on student motivation and classroom practice in mathematics. *NASSP Bulletin, 92*(3), 191–208. doi:10.1177/0192636508323925.

Bos, B. (2007). The effect of the Texas instrument interactive instructional environment on the mathematical achievement of eleventh grade low achieving students. *Journal of Educational Computing Research, 37*(4), 351–368. doi:10.2190/EC.37.4.b.

Hannafin, R., Truxaw, M., Vermillion, J., & Liu, Y. (2008). Effects of spatial ability and instructional program on geometry achievement. *The Journal of Educational Research, 101*(3), 148–157. doi:10.3200/JOER.101.3.148-157.

Hannafin, R. D., Burruss, J. D., & Little, C. (2001). Learning with dynamic geometry programs: Perspectives of teachers and learners. *The Journal of Educational Research, 94*(3), 132–144. doi:10.1080/00220670109599911.

Isiksal, M., & Askar, P. (2005). The effect of spreadsheet and dynamic geometry software on the achievement and self-efficacy of 7th-grade students. *Educational Research, 47*(3), 333–350. doi:10.1080/00131880500287815.

Kebritchi, M., Hirumi, A., & Bai, H. (2010). The effects of modern mathematics computer games on mathematics achievement and class motivation. *Computers & Education, 55*(2), 427–443. doi:10.1016/j.compedu.2010.02.007.

Kimmins, D. (1995). *Technology in school mathematics: A course for prospective secondary school mathematics teachers.* Paper presented at the Eighth Annual International Conference on Technology in Collegiate Mathematics. Houston, TX.

Mayes, R. L. (1995). The application of a computer algebra system as a tool in college algebra. *School Science and Mathematics, 95*(2), 61–67. doi:10.1111/j.1949-8594.1995.tb15729.x.

Myers, R. Y. (2009). The effects of the use of technology in mathematics instruction on student achievement. *FIU Electronic Theses and Dissertations*. Retrieved from http://digitalcommons.fiu.edu/etd/136

National Council of Teachers of Mathematics. (2008). *The role of technology in the teaching and learning of mathematics.* Retrieved from http://www.nctm.org/standards/content.aspx?id=26809

Nguyen, D., Hsieh, Y., & Allen, G. (2006). The impact of web-based assessment and practice on students' mathematics learning attitudes. *Journal of Computers in Mathematics and Science Teaching, 25*(3), 251–279.

Ploger, D., & Hecht, S. (2009). Enhancing children's conceptual understanding of mathematics through chartworld software. *Journal of Research in Childhood Education, 23*(3), 267–278. doi:10.1080/02568540909594660.

Porter, M., & Masingila, J. (2000). Examining the effects of writing on conceptual and procedural knowledge in calculus. *Educational Studies in Mathematics, 42*(2), 165–177. doi:10.1023/A:1004166811047.

Teoh, S. H., Koo, A. C., & Singh, P. (2010). Extracting factors for students' motivation in studying mathematics. *International Journal of Mathematical Education in Science and Technology, 41*(6), 711–724. doi:10.1080/00207391003675190.

The Learning Principle. (2000). Retrieved from http://www.nctm.org/standards/content.aspx?id=26807

KEY TERMS AND DEFINITIONS

Conceptual Understanding: Knowledge about the relationships or foundational ideas of a specific topic.

Geometer's Sketchpad: Geometer's Sketchpad is a type of interactive dynamic geometry software program that gives students a hands-on and visual approach to learning mathematics. Students are able to construct geometric diagrams and measure parts of them to discover geometric properties about them.

Inductive Reasoning: A reasoning method and a process involved in creating generalizations from an observed phenomenon.

Technology Integration: Technology is integrated into classrooms so that students use technology to learn content with it, not just their expertise with a tool, or not as a separate class.

Chapter 8
Integrating Digital Technologies for Spatial Reasoning:
Using Google SketchUp to Model the Real World

D. Craig Schroeder
Fayette County Public Schools, USA

Carl W. Lee
University of Kentucky, USA

ABSTRACT

The Common Core State Standards for Mathematics include mathematical practices for modeling and also references to the appropriate use of technology. Several new dynamic programs can be leveraged using Technological Pedagogical Content Knowledge (TPACK) to enhance the conceptual and practical knowledge of students. The authors used Google SketchUp to develop understandings of 3-dimensional shapes and models. In the successful project, middle school students were introduced to the program, given small challenges, and then, as a culminating project, asked to model rooms within their school. The result was an exact replica of the schoolrooms and a project that could be used for virtual tours. This type of project-based learning can be implemented in most classrooms, even those in which the instructor has limited knowledge of SketchUp. Students were actively engaged throughout the instruction and were able to work with their peers and develop practical mathematical skills.

INTRODUCTION

As we move into the Common Core State Standards for Mathematics (CCSSM) era teachers are being asked to review and revise their instructional approaches to many common mathematical topics.

Simultaneously the last two decades have seen a rapid advance in accessible technology for the masses. Technological Pedagogical Content Knowledge (TPACK) is an essential construct for teachers to successfully implement technology into their classrooms. Not only will today's students

DOI: 10.4018/978-1-4666-4086-3.ch008

emerge into careers that use technology, they will be required to assimilate creative thoughts and develop new technologies of their own.

Teachers often use new technology devices in the same pedagogical way they used the old technology devices—for instance, a document camera used in the same way as a chalkboard, or an iPad used to read a text rather than a hard copy. These uses result in no difference in the way students are pedagogically instructed and thus the same achievement levels in student learning result. Moving beyond these typical instructional styles requires creativity and the leveraging of technology to present "old" topics in a new, more pedagogically sound way.

The purpose of this book chapter is to provide a rich example of developing spatial reasoning in middle school students, especially the 2- and 3-dimensional relationship, through the use of Google SketchUp (http://sketchup.google.com/) in a real world context.

BACKGROUND

Spatial Reasoning

Spatial reasoning is essential to everyday life; we use it on a regular basis by positioning and orientating ourselves in everyday environments. While we are born with a certain amount of innate spatial reasoning, it is essential this spatial reasoning become further developed, especially when visualizing a 3-dimensional object from a 2-dimensional drawing, and conversely creating a 2-dimensional representation of a 3-dimensional object.

Transforming mental images is a spatial skill that engineers and designers depend on. When a hiker pauses with a map and compass, it is the spatial intelligence that conceptualizes the path. Through the spatial sense, a painter "feels" the tension, balance, and composition of a painting. Spatial ability is also the more abstract intelligence of a chess master, a battle commander, or a theoretical physicist, as well as the familiar ability to recognize objects, faces, and details (Grow, 1990, para. 2).

The CCSSM emphasizes its importance by introducing the notion of spatial reasoning as early as kindergarten. Throughout the CCSSM, there is less explicit use of the term "spatial", and more of an emphasis on "modeling", "decomposing", and "applying" concepts to real world situations (e.g., G.MG.1-3, G.GMD.4). Perhaps more important, though, is the focus on the *processes* of mathematics through the intentional use and structure of the eight Standards for Mathematical Practice. For geometry, especially in the area of spatial reasoning, the most important of these practices is the modeling of mathematics within everyday life.

The ability to develop mental models and reason spatially can begin at a young age (Piaget & Inhelder, 1973). In the development of problem solving skills students need spatial reasoning to make sense of real-world problems. The development of spatial reasoning allows for the mental manipulation of abstract mental imagery (La Pierre & Fellenz, 1988). Educators must actively develop this cognitive skill through targeted activities and projects. As pointed out in the *Principles and Standards for School Mathematics* (NCTM, 2000):

Some students may have difficulty finding the surface area of three-dimensional shapes and their two-dimensional representations because they cannot visualize the unseen faces of the shapes. Experience with models of three-dimensional shapes and their two-dimensional "nets" is useful in such visualization...Students should build three-dimensional objects from two-dimensional representations (p. 237).

To help develop children's spatial reasoning Clements (1998) suggests using manipulatives, pictures, and computer manipulatives to develop the visual language of children. While differences between genders exist in regards to spatial reasoning (La Pierre, 1993), recent research has shown success in working with elementary and middle school populations (Brinkman, 1997; Obara, 2009) that incorporated student-centered models and constructivist techniques. Using real-life activities requiring problem solving skills and spatial reasoning allows students to develop their ability to visualize, create, and construct spatial arrangements in 2-dimensional drawings (Lowrie & Logan, 2006). Moving the activity to a virtual software environment does not decrease the effectiveness of the manipulation, but rather, it creates multiple interactions (reflections, rotations, translations) which can significantly affect and improve performance of spatial reasoning processes (Liang & Sedig, 2010).

Early research in using 3-dimensional software shows a statistically significant difference in using a Teacher with Module approach to instruction as opposed to a Module only or Existing Materials approach (Basham & Kotrlik, 2008). Within real-world situations, spatial ability is directly linked to the formation of causal models and problem solving in the field of astronomy (Reddman, 2002). Not only are these skills important, but the development of practical skills is necessary to effectively translate to future careers. For instance, when given a problem in a typical classroom students use cognitive phases (paper and pencil techniques) to find solutions. However, for an experienced plumber, for example, the problem takes on a real-world meaning in which models are constructed and tested to verify their usefulness in solving the problem. This leads to more creative ideas and models that work when the task is "real" (Jurdak & Shahin, 2001). Moving spatial tasks from pencil and paper problem solving to real-world tasks using 3-dimensional software can increase spatial reasoning and transition students toward careers.

Modeling

Modeling is a focus of the CCSSM with an entire strand devoted to it in the high school standards. With new innovations in technology and software development it is becoming easier for students to work with 3-dimensional models. Transferring from 2-dimensional to 3-dimensional figures and back is a skill students need to be successful in this burgeoning field. With the free public offering of SketchUp from Google, students and citizens alike have access to Computer-Aided Design (CAD) software that can create models to be used in a plethora of fields.

In the classroom, SketchUp can be used as a tool to visualize, manipulate, and think with a variety of shapes (Coulter, 2007). Rotating views and objects can provide virtual manipulatives to tap into the students' spatial reasoning. Creating or mimicking provided objects can lead to connections between the viewed objects and their underlying geometric constructs (Gow, 2008). Many different techniques have been used to create 3-dimensional models of real-life objects starting with simple shapes like cones and cylinders (Zhou & Li, 2010) and progressing to models of more complicated objects like unfoliaged trees (Lopez, Ding, & Yu, 2010). Students do not necessarily need to understand the underlying algorithms, but they must have an understanding of the transfer from 3-dimensional to 2-dimensional and vice versa to effectively create a model of a real-world object.

Beyond the classroom many job fields are using these tools (or similar software) to develop products. Thinglas and Kaushal (2008) outline a technique used to optimize an inverted trap for sewer solids management based on 3-dimensional CAD modeling and experimental measurements to find the most efficient trap configuration. In designing highways in Canada, 3-dimensional models were used in a driving simulator to determine driver visual demand and effectively design the safest highway possible (Easa & He, 2006). A new trileaflet aortic valve was designed and produced using CAD software. The software allowed the team to determine functional dimensions for the components of the valve (Kumar & Mathew, 2010). Through the use of time lapse and 3-dimensional software, 4D city models can be used to teach students about sustainability in urban systems in much the same way as Sim City (Weber et. al., 2008).

Transformations

Transformations are firmly established as a basic topic in secondary geometry; CCSSM (2011) emphasizes their instruction in grade eight. Students often struggle with the procedural aspect of computing transformations and even more so their conceptual understanding (Ada & Kurtulus, 2009). Modules from previous instructional eras show a rudimentary, procedural approach to instruction with very few realistic applications (Brotherton, et al., 1975; Olson, 1969). Today's educational environment lends itself to more advanced approaches, especially ones utilizing technology. Using literacy to develop transformational concepts (Harris, 1998) and dynamic software such as Geometer's Sketchpad (Burke et al., 2006) are some of the research-based approaches being implemented today.

Transformations provide a great opportunity to develop real-world applications and experiences for students. The gap in student understanding between formal and concrete mathematical learners is exacerbated by traditional instructional approaches. By developing concrete activities that lead to conceptual and formal understandings teachers can increase achievement among all learners (Rowell & Mansfield, 1980). Project-based learning experiences have begun to be accepted as the preferred method of learning for undergraduate students in mathematical fields such as computer graphics (Marti, Gil, & Julia,

2005). Project-based learning allows for students to interact with each other and explore and develop ideas in a non-structured way. This leads to greater conceptual learning and higher self-efficacy. Situating the topic in the appropriate engaging activity, such as through the use of technology, improves the students' conceptual understanding of transformations (Sedig, 2008).

Real-World Applications

Mathematics is contained in the world around us but students often only view it as a formalized course they must complete. With the abundance of new technology, teachers have the ability to engage students in real-world problems and activities with viable products. Today's students are adept at using technology and can quickly learn software and programming. Fields like Automotive Design are looking for employees who have 3-dimensional experiences (Deusing, 2006). Urban developers use satellite views and mathematical calculations to create 3-dimensional models of urban areas based solely on the understanding of 2-dimensional views (Croitoru & Doytsher, 2004). Recently, software has been used to design bus routes that automatically adjust to provide shorter wait times (Treiguts, 2012). Traffic engineers are using virtual 4-dimensional models to simulate traffic patterns on intersections and roadways that are in design phase (Sewall et al., 2010). For more student-centered/project-based learning activities students could be asked to design their own park given constraints such as money, time, and space (Tepper, 1999). The use of technology has opened up the possibilities and made real-world applications possible in every classroom.

Technological Pedagogical Content Knowledge (TPACK)

Recent research in mathematics education has focused on teachers' mathematics knowledge for teaching (MKT) and its relation to student achievement (Hill, Rowan, & Ball, 2005). As we have moved into the 21st century it has become apparent that students will need to be successful in applying technologies in their daily lives. Educators are being pushed to develop more technology-rich lessons to meet the need for 21st century skills.

An emerging area of study has been Technological Pedagogical Content Knowledge (TPACK) in the mathematics classroom. Building on Shulman's (1986) view of pedagogical content knowledge (PKT), Koehler & Mischra (2008) use TPACK "…to describe how teachers' understanding of technologies and pedagogical content knowledge interact with one another to produce effective teaching with technology" (p. 12). This interaction is a melding of technology knowledge, content knowledge, and pedagogical knowledge that produces effective teaching and student achievement (Guerrero, 2010) (See Figure 1). Koehler & Mishra describe this intersection as

…an understanding of the representation of concepts using technologies in constructive ways to teach content; knowledge of what makes concepts difficult or easy to learn and how technology can help redress some of the problems that students face; knowledge of students' prior knowledge and theories of epistemology; and knowledge of how technologies can be used to build on existing knowledge and develop new epistemologies or strengthen old ones (pp. 17-18).

Figure 1. Technological pedagogical content knowledge (Guerrero, 2010)

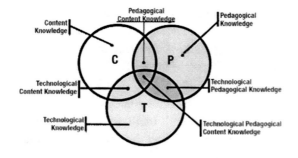

The theory is still being composed with many questions to be answered regarding its usefulness and clarity (Graham, 2011). Archambault and Barnett (2011) found only the factor of technology to be statistically significant in an analysis of the TPACK framework. Much of this is due to the overlapping and intertwined nature of the constructs and mirrors researched issues in PKT. In summary, through the use of current mathematics knowledge for teaching, pedagogical content knowledge, and the addition of technological pedagogical knowledge, instructors can more effectively engage students and address difficulty areas through a use of technological resources.

TPACK has a profound connection with the release of the CCSSM. The Mathematical Practice Standards specifically call for students to model mathematics and to use appropriate tools strategically.

Mathematically proficient students consider the available tools when solving a mathematical problem. These tools might include pencil and paper, concrete models, a ruler, a protractor, a calculator, a spreadsheet, a computer algebra system, a statistical package, or dynamic geometry software…When making mathematical models, they know that technology can enable them to visualize the results of varying consequences, and compare predictions with the data. Mathematically proficient students at various grade levels are able to identify relevant external mathematical resources, such as digital content located on a Website, and use them to pose or solve problems. They are able to use technological tools to explore and deepen their understanding of concepts (p. 7).

These practices are also interwoven throughout the standards. In addition, specific standards are written using technology as an instructional tool. Some middle school examples are:

- Compute (using technology) and interpret the correlation coefficient of a linear fit (p. 81).

- Draw (freehand, with ruler and protractor, and with technology) geometric shapes with given conditions. Focus on constructing triangles from three measures of angles or sides, noticing when the conditions determine a unique triangle, more than one triangle, or no triangle (p. 50).

- Perform operations with numbers expressed in scientific notation, including problems where both decimal and scientific notation are used. Use scientific notation and choose units of appropriate size for measurements of very large or very small quantities (e.g., use millimeters per year for seafloor spreading). Interpret scientific notation that has been generated by technology (p. 54).

As the standards move toward conceptual understanding, rather than procedural skill-based mathematics, teachers will need to utilize technology in teaching and learning mathematics. Utilizing TPACK toward this aim, teachers must go beyond knowledge of how the technological tool works, to understanding how the tool can be leveraged as a pedagogical instrument that effectively increases student understanding (Guerrero, 2010). Guerrero posits there are four distinct components of TPACK: conception and use of technology, technology-based mathematics instruction, management, and depth and breadth of mathematics content (See Figure 2).

First, the teacher must have a working knowledge of how best to use technology, if at all, in addressing mathematical content (Guerrero, 2010). This use is grounded in pedagogical approaches and not simply on using the technology as a "show". The teacher must have an understanding of mathematics that appreciates the capabilities of technology in developing mathematical concepts. Secondly, the instructor must accurately determine which technology is appropriate for a given topic (Guerrero, 2010). The instructor must be comfortable with the technology and

Figure 2. Components of TPACK (Guerrero, 2010)

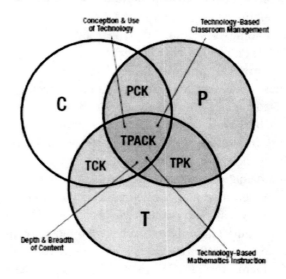

understand its relationship to the desired outcomes. Third, the teacher needs to understand management issues related to the use of technology that is not present in "typical" instructional situations (Guerrero, 2010). Teachers need to be able to engage students with technology and manage their use. Through engaging activities, teachers can instruct students even when the novelty of the technology has worn off. Finally, teachers need to have an in-depth understanding of mathematics to be successful (Guerrero, 2010). Giving the students powerful tools allows them to explore numerous mathematical concepts in-depth. Instructors must have this knowledge or be willing to explore their own mathematical knowledge openly with the students. This ability opens up the doors for students and models that mathematical knowledge is not static, but ever increasing as we make new discoveries.

Technology can be a powerful tool in fostering conceptual understanding of mathematical concepts. Interventions using technology have been successful in teaching, for example straight-line equations (Lawrence, 2002). Special education students with disabilities also benefit from the effective use of technology in the mathematics classroom (Obudo, 2008). Teaching fractions, algebra applications, quadratic equations, and graphing can all be enhanced through the use of technology (Arnold, 2004; Garafalo & Sharp, 2003; Palmer, 1994; Wander & Pierce, 2009).

However, pragmatic knowledge reveals that these successes are linked to a small percentage of teachers who have a strong TPACK. Pre-service teachers need more experiences with technology (Stahlhut, 1992) in order to effectively use it in their instruction. Once in the classroom, mathematics teachers receive little technology-based professional development specific to their needs. Classroom coaches can be instrumental in providing this bridge. Coaches who model technology are effective in creating an environment for increasing TPACK among practicing teachers (Becker, 2001). Professional development aimed at increasing TPACK development has also led to teachers' selection and use of learning activities being more conscious, more student-centered lessons, and more thoughtful technology use (Harris & Hofer, 2011).

GOOGLE SKETCHUP MODELING PROJECT

The project details were conceived by the authors, a middle school mathematics and science teacher and a university mathematics professor, through a joint-discussion around the mathematical implications of dynamic mathematics software and its impact on spatial reasoning. The authors had prior experience in using Google SketchUp to develop 3-dimensional models for demonstration but had not used the software with students below the college level. Google SketchUp is a free computer-aided design (CAD) software program that facilitates 3-dimensional modeling. Prior to the project, the researchers developed a set of examples and exercises to introduce students to the numerous features and tools in Google SketchUp.

The activities described took place in an urban middle school (population ~ 900) in the South. The 21 students who participated were part of an Eighth Grade Advanced Geometry course. The students had been a "cohort" for three years and all students successfully completed the course for advancement to Advanced Algebra II in the traditional sequence. The course's scope and sequence is a formalized, proof-based discovery of Euclidean Geometry. The activities described took place in the final two months of the academic year when the students had completed all of the traditional requirements (approximately eight weeks of instruction). The class met each day for 52 minutes during the morning. The students had been exposed to traditional manipulatives and group activities throughout the year. While the students were advanced in their coursework, they lacked any formal instruction in transformations or 3-dimensional manipulations and structures prior to the course. The students were instructed on solids and the surrounding constructs immediately prior to this activity.

The instruction relied on documents that were distributed through the district Moodle site. This site had been utilized by the class throughout the year and all students were familiar with its navigation. All project files were uploaded through this site and the end of project survey was also distributed in this manner.

SketchUp

SketchUp is a 3-dimensional modeling program that was offered by Google, but is now becoming a product of Trimble. Free and "Pro" versions are available from the Website http://sketchup.google.com. From here one can download the program and find links to an impressive array of resources, such as written and video tutorials, a gallery of examples, detailed case studies, resources for developers, and resources for K-12 and higher education instructors and students. The free version is sufficiently powerful and available to be a valuable teaching and learning tool both inside and outside the classroom.

SketchUp is a versatile 3-dimensional computer aided design software, suitable for applications in architecture, product design, and to some extent video game design. In particular, structures and components created in SketchUp can be contributed to a virtual warehouse, and buildings can be exported to Google Earth. It is well suited to model and manipulate mathematical solids, though it does not offer the option of graphing functions of two variables or of displaying curves described by parametric equations.

The set of tools is well designed for both relative ease of initial access and use, as well as sophisticated manipulation of objects. A comprehensive description is beyond the scope of this article, but a new user, regardless of age, can begin constructing appealing structures within just a few minutes—sketch a polygon in the plane, pull it up into a prism, draw regions on the prism, push or pull these regions out and in, grab and move individual points, lines, faces, and entire objects, apply some texture, and the results are immediately compelling. Students find SketchUp very attractive.

The SketchUp scene comes equipped with a set of three colored-coded axes, which can be repositioned and referenced for the purpose of orientation and coordinates during the sketching process. The basic toolbox includes tools for:

- **Viewing:** Positioning, rotating, translating, and zooming the camera view, walking through a scene, making cross-sections.
- **Drawing:** Making line segments, rectangles, polygons, circles, arcs, and freehand curves, erasing.
- **Moving and Modifying Elements (Points, Lines, Faces, Solids):** pushing and pulling (extrusion of two dimensional regions into three dimensions), translating, rotating, scaling (in one, two, or three directions), offsetting, intersecting, subdividing, grouping.
- **Measuring:** Measuring and labeling lengths, measuring angles, creating guide lines.
- **Labeling:** Inserting 2-dimensional and 3-dimensional text.
- **Decorating:** Adding materials, textures, colors, and transparencies; displaying with shadows and fog.
- **Animating:** Creating layers within scenes and sequenced sets of scenes.
- **Sharing:** Exporting to the online warehouse.

With experience (which is rapidly gained) comes greater sophistication in wielding the tools, and mathematics instructors at all levels will find themselves posing modeling and visualization challenges to themselves and their students, many directly motivated by the CCSSM: How can you make sets of two-dimensional shapes (or three dimensional solids) for students to categorize, reason with, manipulate to model properties of fractions, derive and understand area formulas, and illustrate symmetries? How can SketchUp be used to model and solve real-world and mathematical problems involving distance, angle, area, surface area, and volume? How can you make nets of solids? What sketches can be created to understand the role of translations, rotations, reflections, and dilations in defining and testing similarity and congruence of two- and three-dimensional figures? How can various solids be created by rotating two-dimensional figures?

Outline of SketchUp Sessions: Content and Assessments

Work began with the students in March 2010. During the SketchUp sessions the class gathered in a computer lab in the school's library. Each student had a computer, and the lab was equipped with a projector and computer for the presenters. The university faculty member met with the class and taught with the class teacher seven times over a period of five weeks, each session lasting about 45 minutes. A typical session began with the demonstration of a set of tools, examples of their applications, and recommendations for constructions to attempt. Certain specific constructions called "challenges" were assigned as homework. In addition, the class teacher worked with the students for an additional 3 weeks, providing some additional challenges and giving students time to complete some of the projects.

One important consideration was to deliberately introduce a collection of the SketchUp tools in an appropriate sequence to gradually unfold its capabilities. The facilitators provided written notes, which they updated throughout the project. The latest version is posted at the Website https://sites.google.com/site/jessieclarksketchup.

We summarize here the sequence of activities, which will also provide an overview of some of SketchUp's capabilities. (Note that the numbering is for convenience, and the numbers do not correspond precisely to specific sessions.)

1. After a brief introduction to the nature of SketchUp the students began experimenting with a basic working set of tools.

    a. **Orbit:** This tool enables the student to change the direction of view, and seeing this in action for the first time immediately drew the students into the program. Mathematically this corresponds to a rotation of the camera.

    b. **Zoom, Zoom Extents, and Pan:** These provide other convenient means to modify the point of view of a scene. Panning corresponds to translating the camera.

    c. **Select:** With this the student can select an element or collection of elements of the current construction for manipulation.

    d. **Rectangle:** This provides a quick way to create rectangles of desired dimensions.

    e. **Line:** This tool constructs line segments, and thus the student can also, for example, draw polygonal regions.

    f. **Push/Pull:** This powerful tool provides the capability to "extrude" regions into three-dimensional shapes, and is one of the most powerful elements of SketchUp. Its demonstration is immediately enticing and attractive. Pulling a base polygon results in a prism, but any region can be extruded outward or inward.

    g. **Circle:** Circles in SketchUp are actually many-sided polygons. Of course, students can extrude circles into cylinders.

    h. **Polygon:** With this students can easily draw regular polygons with specified numbers of sides.

    i. **Paint Bucket:** By now students were creating a wide variety of shapes, and they used this tool to adorn them with textures and colors.

    j. **Shadows:** This is designed to illuminate the scene and cast shadows. Students can even select lighting corresponding to particular locations and times of day.

    k. **Move:** Once students have constructed a collection of scene elements, they may wish to move (translate) or duplicate them.

The facilitators took special care to use appropriate geometric vocabulary throughout. Student progress during the initial session was rapid and impressive, and by the end of this session most students had made substantial progress on, or completed, the first challenge problem:

Challenge #1: Make your own "still life" with a cube, a rectangular prism, a pentagonal prism, a prism with a base that is not a regular polygon, and a cylinder.

This became a class assignment, submitted by students into the course Website for grading. An example of student work appears in Figure 3.

2. The second challenge problem, which highlighted the ability to extrude regions "inwards" into solids to create holes through objects, became the second homework assignment:

Challenge #2: Construct a 4' x 4' cube with a cylindrical hole having radius 1.5'. What is its volume?

3. The third challenge problem, making reference to the Giant's Causeway in Ireland—a impressive array of massive basalt columns in the shape of hexagonal prisms—provided an opportunity for students to see how SketchUp might be used to model real-life objects.

Figure 3. Student example of "still life" challenge

By now it was clear to the facilitators that students were gaining skill and comfort with the program at such a pace to suggest a more challenging and longer project. The teacher assigned two rooms in the middle school building to each student. The task entailed carefully inspecting and measuring each room, and then creating an accurate virtual model of the room. To assist this process the facilitators introduced a new round of tools over the next few sessions.

a.   **Warehouse:** The SketchUp project has established a virtual warehouse of objects, now populated by an overwhelming searchable collection of creations submitted by users around the world. Students found this resource invaluable in their modeling, drawing upon instances of desks, chairs, doors, windows, bookcases, etc., to furnish their rooms. Students in turn submitted some of their own constructs to the warehouse for others to use, including a wad of gum to be placed beneath a desk.

b.   **Arc:** Students use this to draw arcs of circles.

c.   **Freehand:** This tool draws general freehand curves.

d.   **Copy:** This is a modification of the move tool with which students can make a copy or array of copies of a given object. For one homework assignment students started by creating arrays of open-top boxes, and then strategically deleted sides of certain cubes to create mazes that they could then walk through virtually.

e.   **Rotate:** Students can select an object, specify an axis and angle, and then rotate the object about that axis. There is also the option to create a rotated copy or array of copies of the original object.

f. **Scale:** Students can easily scale objects in different ways: uniformly (dilation), uni-directionally, and bi-directionally. Negative scaling factors are allowable, which can be used to create reflections of objects through points and planes.

g. **Follow Me:** There is no specific tool in SketchUp to make a sphere. But to make one it suffices to draw a circle and sweep out a sphere by having it follow the path of a certain perpendicular circle. The Follow Me tool is useful this way, and in general students can make any two-dimensional region follow any curve and thereby sweep out an unlimited family of three dimensional shapes.

h. **Tape Measure:** This virtual tape measures lengths in the model, and can also set up guide lines for the placement of objects. There is also a protractor for measuring angles.

i. The facilitators introduced various other tools as well, such as those used for creating cross-sections of objects, animations of scenes, and virtual walk-throughs of scenes.

4. To demonstrate the power of the Copy and Move tools, the teacher assigned Challenge #5, which was to create a Sierpinski pyramid (See Figure 4). Starting with a single tetrahedron, students applied iterations of the copying and moving operations to create a multilevel pyramid that approximates its limiting fractal form.

5. The facilitators dedicated most the time during the final set of sessions to completing the room modeling project. Lab time was characterized by active student collaboration and mutual assistance. Typical conversations were similar to:

a. "How do I put a door in?" "Draw a rectangle on the wall according to the measurements of the door and then

Figure 4. Student example of Sierpinski pyramid challenge

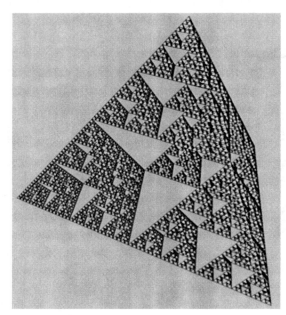

delete it to make the hole. Get a door from the Warehouse that looks like the one you want. Use Move to translate it into position. Now rescale it until it fits the doorway." "How do I make it part way open?" "You need to use the Rotate tool to rotate the door on its vertical side".

b. "How did you get your tile floor?" "Click on the Paintbucket to select the Tile pattern that you want, and edit the colors. Now place it on the floor. You can rescale to match size of the actual pattern".

In the end the students produced models of more than 30 rooms. One example is pictured in Figure 5. Note some of the details: this student designed the filing cabinet from scratch, down to the labels on the individual drawers. She imported the rug on the wall from the Warehouse but recolored it to match the actual rug in the classroom. She found a chair in the Warehouse and used the Copy and Move tools to make duplicates and posi-

Figure 5. Student example of a complete room project

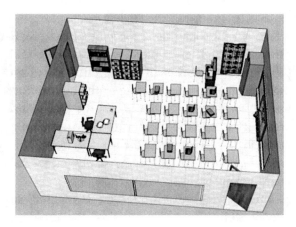

tion them. She used the Move, Scale, and Rotate tools to construct the doors. Even the door to the tall storage cabinet is slightly ajar.

Throughout the project, most of the students demonstrated a high level of persistence and ingenuity, even in the face of typical problems associated with trying to become familiar with a new piece of software. The entry into SketchUp is sufficiently accessible to yield initial successes that then inspire a certain degree of confidence and willingness to persevere.

IMPLICATIONS, CHALLENGES, FUTURE DIRECTIONS

Student Reflections

At the conclusion of the project, the teacher asked the students to reflect on the project by responding to questions about their participation. Their answers generally indicated that, though tasks were not necessarily easy, the project was engaging and they recognized the connections to concepts in geometry. On a scale from 1 (lowest) to 5 (highest), the average enjoyment level was 4.1. When asked to "describe ways in which you used at least three different geometry concepts and skills as part of this project" some responses were:

- I used area to size up my room. I also used volume for the cylindrical objects in my room. Then I used conversion to change measurements from inches to centimeters.
- Planes/Coordinates: SketchUp has a red axis, blue axis and green axis and we have to build our object on the certain axis, sometimes using points and coordinates.
- I had to know how the angles of different objects connect and fit together.
- I used my knowledge of area to determine length and width of an object. I use my knowledge of volume to determine length, width, and heighth (sic) of an object. I also used my knowledge of sliding, reflecting, and tessellating (sic) to move my object in the right spot.
- We had to scale different objects to fit the scaled room. We also had to use angle measurements to rotate the objects and create 3-dimensional objects on the program.

The next question asked students to describe problems they encountered when building their room model. One repeated answer was the slowness of the model in the 3-D Warehouse. The 3-D Warehouse is a public repository for models. Students could download chairs and other office items that had already been constructed rather than building it themselves. The slowness was undoubtedly due to two factors. One was that for the majority of the project the students were using netbooks with slow processors. This increased the time to download models and also hampered their movement within SketchUp. The second factor was the wireless connection. With limited access points, the students were all vying for a limited amount of bandwidth from a single room. The students complained that the computers would often freeze up, especially at the end of a model when there were numerous objects created.

Another identified issue was that of scaling objects. The program can be cumbersome in this area and no detailed instruction was given on scaling. Students had difficulties determining which node to choose to scale an object and how to get it to be the exact dimensions they needed. Students also had difficulty placing objects in exact spots. The 2-dimensional view of a 3-dimensional model makes this nearly impossible without the use of guide points. Students often were not zoomed in close enough to find the exact location on their model as they complained it wouldn't put it in the exact measurement.

Finally the students were asked to elaborate on uses of Google SketchUp outside of the classroom. They had many ideas including designing a room or house, art projects at art camp, designing buildings, viewing places without actually visiting them in person, architectural career, designing my future home, creating a design for a bookshelf, verifying you have enough carpet to cover a room, engineering design, reorganizing rooms without physically moving furniture to view different designs, and remodeling a bathroom. One student even replied that their family was currently using SketchUp to design and place their garden to maximize sunlight using the location features. There are numerous uses for 3-dimensional software and all of these students had ideas and the experience to use it in other real-world context outside the school environment. In conclusion, 81% responded they would freely take an elective course on SketchUp if it were offered next year in high school.

Student Impact

This student project was unlike any other the researchers had been a part of previously. The extended timeframe and the open-endedness of it led to unimagined outcomes. The most outwardly obvious result was the increase in student attitudes toward mathematics. Students were fervently engrossed in the project during the class time and also readily worked on the project before and after school and at home despite no requirements for completion during these times. This excitement showed the students valued the end product (a model of their school) and viewed it as something they could accomplish as a group.

In addition, the students gained knowledge of real-world applications of mathematical principles. One group reported that in determining the diameter of a round table top they pivoted their measuring stick on a fixed point and recorded the largest measurement. This action relied on the conceptual understanding of the diameter as the largest chord of a circle and the real-world creativity to use the measuring stick pivot on a point on the table to make the measurement. This type of synthesis is lacking in traditional formal learning approaches.

Finally, the most important mathematical impact stems from the basis of the projects. Students were able to take a 3-dimensional room and create an identical model in a 3-dimensional software environment. Successful completion in turn demonstrates the students' ability to construct an abstract 3-dimensional model and then recreate that mental image in the software program, in essence translating from a viewed image, to a mental model, to a 3-dimensional model constructed from many different 2-dimensional views. This construction is a high-level process that is in demand for numerous career fields including engineering, architecture, and construction. Through their survey responses students were able to indicate a way they could leverage this newly constructed knowledge in their own lives to their benefit. Undoubtedly, there were many more intangible benefits or unseen results, but those mentioned were far above the anticipated results and any previous successes the researchers encountered.

As a result of the project, the researchers and one of the middle school students participated in a district professional development activity in which other teachers were taught how to use Google SketchUp. The student was able to instruct the teachers on how to use the program, showing both poise and confidence as the expert in the field.

Facilitator Reflections and Future Directions

The purpose of this project was to "test the waters" to gauge the possibilities and viability of using SketchUp in a middle school geometry classroom. Would the steepness of the learning curve negate the potential benefits of the modeling experience? Would students learn, recognize, and retain geometry concepts that are actively at play in the assignments?

With respect to the first question, this experiment suggests there are some challenges to gaining facility with the software. Nevertheless, the user interface is accessible and inviting, and students adapt and learn quickly—recall how students could produce their first "still life" within the first 52 minutes of being introduced to SketchUp. Indeed, some suggest the learning curve for teachers might be a greater challenge.

With respect to the second question, we have just begun to test the potential of SketchUp to provide meaningful and motivating contexts for a wide variety of geometrical concepts and skills. Student reflections suggest they are explicitly aware of the deployment of geometry concepts and skills, as well as the process of geometric modeling. More formal research studies and assessments could offer insight into the impact on student learning and retention.

Taking these questions together, it would be fruitful to carefully design a sequence of SketchUp activities that unfold a set of tools of increasing complexity and versatility, while simultaneously moving appropriately through a progression of geometric concepts and skills of the CCSSM with the Mathematical Practices of the CCSSM firmly in the foreground.

CONCLUSION

We hope the prior details along with the dedicated Website have provided the reader with the tools necessary to move forward with instruction using Google SketchUp. The sharing of successful projects such as this is pivotal to TPACK growth among teachers. As we move forward in the 21st century, the CCSSM Mathematical Practices must be modeled for students. We must look for ways to develop their creativity in practical applications of their formalized mathematical knowledge.

REFERENCES

Ada, T., & Kurtlus, A. (2010). Students' misconceptions and errors in transformation geometry. *International Journal of Mathematical Education in Science and Technology, 41*(7), 901–909. doi:10.1080/0020739X.2010.486451.

Archambault, L. M., & Barnett, J. H. (2010). Revisiting technological pedagogical content knowledge: Exploring the TPACK framework. *Computers & Education, 55*, 1656–1662. doi:10.1016/j.compedu.2010.07.009.

Arnold, S. (2004). Integrating technology in the middles school: Years 5-9. *Australian Primary Mathematics Classroom, 9*(3), 15–19.

Basham, K. L., & Katrlik, J. W. (2008). The effects of 3-dimensional CADD modeling on the development of the spatial ability of technology education students. *Journal of Technology Education, 20*(1), 32–47.

Becker, J. R. (2001). Classroom coaching: An emerging method of professional development. In *Proceedings of the Annual Meeting of the North American Chapter of the International Group for the Psychology of Mathematics Education.* Snowbird, UT: PME.

Brinkman, P. (1997). Students build math skills by visualizing problems. *Christian Science Monitor, 89*(251).

Brotherton, S., Bruckhart, G., & Reed, J. (1975). *Transformations: Geometry module for use in a mathematics laboratory setting.* Denver, CO: Regional Center for Pre-College Mathematics, University of Denver.

Burke, J., Cowen, S., Fernandez, S., & Wesslen, M. (2006). Dynamic gliding. *Mathematics Teacher, 195*, 12–14.

Chief Council of State School Officers. (2011). *Common core state standards for mathematics.* Retrieved from http://www.corestandards.org

Clements, D. H. (1998). *Geometric and spatial thinking in young children* (White paper). Washington, DC: National Science Foundation.

Coulter, B. (2007, March-April). Sketching a path into geometry. *Connect*, 16-17.

Croitoru, A., & Doytsher, Y. (2004). Right-angle rooftop polygon extraction in regularized urban areas: Cutting the corners. *The Photogrammetric Record, 19*(108), 311–341. doi:10.1111/j.0031-868X.2004.00289.x.

Deusing, B. (2006, April). Automotive design program inspires creative students. *Tech Directions*, 12–14.

Easa, S. M., & He, W. (2006). Modeling driver visual demand on three-dimensional highway alignments. *Journal of Transportation Engineering, 132*(5), 357–365. doi:10.1061/(ASCE)0733-947X(2006)132:5(357).

Garafalo, J., & Sharp, B. D. (2003). Teaching fractions using a simulated sharing activity. *Learning and Leading with Technology, 30*(7), 36–39, 41.

Gow, G. (2008, February). Tips on creating complex geometry using solid modeling software. *Tech Directions*, 18–20.

Graham, C. R. (2011). Theoretical considerations for understanding technological pedagogical content knowledge (TPACK). *Computers & Education, 57*, 1953–1960. doi:10.1016/j.compedu.2011.04.010.

Grow, G. (1990). *Writing and multiple intelligences.* Paper presented at the Annual Meeting of the Association for Educators in Journalism and Mass Communication. Retrieved from http://www.longleaf.net/ggrow

Guerrero, S. (2010). Technological pedagogical content knowledge in the mathematics classroom. *Journal of Digital Learning in Teacher Education, 26*(4), 132–139.

Harris, J. (1998). Using literature to investigate transformations. *Teaching Children Mathematics, 4*(9), 510–513.

Harris, J. B., & Hofer, M. J. (2011). Technological pedagogical content knowledge (TPACK) in action: A descriptive study of secondary teachers' curriculum-based, technology-related instructional planning. *Journal of Research on Technology in Education, 43*(3), 211–229.

Hill, H. C., Rowan, B., & Ball, D. (2005). Effects of teachers' mathematical knowledge for teaching on student achievement. *American Educational Research Journal, 42*(2), 371–406. doi:10.3102/00028312042002371.

Jurdak, M., & Shahin, I. (2001). Problem solving activity in the workplace and the school: The case of constructing solids. *Educational Studies in Mathematics, 47*(3), 297–315. doi:10.1023/A:1015106804646.

Koehler, M. J., & Mischra, P. (2008). Introducing technological and pedagogical knowledge. In AACTE Committee on Innovation and Technology (Eds.), The handbook of technological pedagogical content knowledge for educators. New York: Routledge/Taylor & Francis Group for the American Association of Colleges of Teacher Education.

Kumar, G. P., & Mathew, L. (2010). Three-dimensional computer-aided design-based geometric modeling of a new trileaflet aortic valve. *Artificial Organs, 34*(12), 1121–1124. doi:10.1111/j.1525-1594.2009.00973.x PMID:20545658.

La Pierre, S. D. (1993). *Issues of gender in spatial reasoning.* Paper presented at the Annual Conference of the National Art Education Association. Chicago, IL.

La Pierre, S. D., & Fellenz, R. A. (1988). *Spatial reasoning and adults.* Bozeman, MT: Center for Adult Learning Research, Montana State University.

Lawrence, V. (2002). Teacher-designed software for interactive linear equations: Concepts, interpretive skills, applications & word-problem solving. In *Proceedings from ED-MEDIA 2002 World Conference on Educational Multimedia, Hypermedia & Telecommunications.* Denver, CO.

Liang, H., & Sedig, K. (2010). Role of interaction in enhancing the epistemic utility of 3D mathematical visualizations. *International Journal of Computers for Mathematical Learning, 15,* 91–224. doi:10.1007/s10758-010-9165-7.

Lopez, L. D., Ding, Y., & Yu, J. (2010). Modeling complex unfoliaged trees from a sparse set of images. *Computer Graphics Forum, 29*(7), 2075–2082. doi:10.1111/j.1467-8659.2010.01794.x.

Lowrie, T., & Logan, T. (2006). Using spatial skills to interpret maps: Problem solving in realistic contexts. *Australian Primary Mathematics Classroom, 12*(4), 14–19.

Marti, E., Gil, D., & Julia, C. (2006). A PBL experience in the teaching of computer graphics. *Computer Graphics Forum, 25*(1), 95–103. doi:10.1111/j.1467-8659.2006.00920.x.

National Council of Teachers of Mathematics. (2000). *Principles and standards for school mathematics.* Reston, VA: NCTM.

Obara, S. (2009). Where does the formula come from? *Australian Mathematics Teacher, 65*(1), 25–33.

Obudo, F. (2008). *Teaching mathematics to students with learning disabilities: A review of literature.* Retrieved from http://www.eric.ed.gov/ERICWebPortal/contentdelivery/servlet/ERICServlet?accno=ED500500

Olson, A. T. (1969). *High school plane geometry through transformations: An exploratory study.* Whitewater, WI: The Wisconsin State Universities Consortium of Research Development, Wisconsin State University-Whitewater.

Palmer, L. (1994). *It's a wonderful life: Using public domain cinema clips to teach affective objectives and illustrate real-world algebra applications.* Paper presented at the Annual Conference of the International Society for Exploring Teaching Alternatives. Salt Lake City, UT.

Piaget, J., & Inhelder, B. (1973). *Memory and intelligence.* London: Routledge and Kegan Paul.

Rowell, J., & Mansfield, H. (1980). The teaching of transformation geometry in grade eight: A search for aptitude-treatment interactions. *The Journal of Educational Research, 74*(1), 55–59.

Rudmann, D. S. (2002). *Solving astronomy problems can be limited by intuited knowledge, spatial ability, or both.* Paper presented at the Annual Meeting of the American Educational Research Association. New Orleans, LA.

Sedig, K. (2008). From play to thoughtful learning: A design strategy to engage children with mathematical representations.

Sewall, J., Wilkie, D., Merrell, P., & Lin, M. C. (2010). Continuum traffic simulation. *Computer Graphics Forum, 29*(2), 439–448. doi:10.1111/j.1467-8659.2009.01613.x.

Shulman, L. S. (1986). Those who understand: A conception of teacher knowledge. *American Educator, 10*, 9–15, 43.

Stahlhut, R. G. (1992). *Math student teachers: How well prepared are they?* Paper presented at the Annual Conference of the National Council of Teachers of Mathematics. Nashville, TN.

Tepper, A. B. (1999). A journey through geometry: Designing a city park. *Teaching Children Mathematics, 5*(6), 348–352.

Thinglas, T., & Kaushal, D. R. (2008). Three-dimensional CFD modeling for optimization of invert trap configuration to be used in sewer solids management. *Particulate Science and Technology, 26*, 507–519. doi:10.1080/02726350802367951.

Treiguts, E. (2012, May 17). *Waiting for a bus? Math may help.* Retrieved from www.lightyears.blogs.cnn.com

Wander, R., & Pierce, R. (2009). Marina's fish shop: A mathematically- and technology-rich lesson. *Australian Mathematics Teacher, 65*(2), 6–12.

Weber, B., Muller, P., Wonka, P., & Gross, M. (2009). Interactive geometric simulation of 4D cities. *Computer Graphics Forum, 28*(2), 481–492. doi:10.1111/j.1467-8659.2009.01387.x.

Zhou, J., & Li, B. (2011). Rapid modeling of cones and cylinders from a single calibrated image using minimum 2D control points. *Machine Vision and Applications, 22*, 303–321. doi:10.1007/s00138-009-0241-8.

ADDITIONAL READING

Build Google SketchUp Skills. (n.d.). Retrieved from http://sketchup.google.com/support/bin/answer.py?answer=116359&cbid=18706mcj9x6za&src=cb&lev=index

Clements, D. H. (1998). *Geometric and spatial thinking in young children* (White paper). Washington, DC: National Science Foundation.

3DVinci. (n.d.). Retrieved from http://www.3dvinci.net/ccp0-display/forteachers.html

Google SketchUp for Educators. (n.d.). Retrieved from http://sitescontent.google.com/google-sketchup-for-educators/Home

Google SketchUp Student Showcase. (n.d.). Retrieved from http://sitescontent.google.com/google-sketchup-for-educators/Home/student-created-showcase

Introduction to Google SketchUp. (n.d.). Retrieved from http://www.assortedstuff.com/stuff/?p=298

Kumar, G. P., & Mathew, L. (2010). Three-dimensional computer-aided design-based geometric modeling of a new trileaflet aortic valve. *Artificial Organs, 34*(12), 1121–1124. doi:10.1111/j.1525-1594.2009.00973.x PMID:20545658.

Liang, H., & Sedig, K. (2010). Role of interaction in enhancing the epistemic utility of 3D mathematical visualizations. *International Journal of Computers for Mathematical Learning, 15*, 91–224. doi:10.1007/s10758-010-9165-7.

Weber, B., Muller, P., Wonka, P., & Gross, M. (2009). Interactive geometric simulation of 4D cities. *Computer Graphics Forum, 28*(2), 481–492. doi:10.1111/j.1467-8659.2009.01387.x.

Zhou, J., & Li, B. (2011). Rapid modeling of cones and cylinders from a single calibrated image using minimum 2D control points. *Machine Vision and Applications, 22*, 303–321. doi:10.1007/s00138-009-0241-8.

KEY TERMS AND DEFINITIONS

Computer-Aided Design: The use of computer software to create virtual representations of objects in 2- or 3-dimensional space.

Dynamic Geometry Software: Interactive software in which the user can create and manipulate geometric constructions.

Geometry: The school study of Euclidean plane and solid geometry, both with and without coordinates.

Modeling: "Modeling is the process of choosing and using appropriate mathematics and statistics to analyze empirical situations, to understand them better, and to improve decisions" (CCSSO, 2011).

SketchUp: A software package for three-dimensional modeling and computer aided design currently available through Google and Trimble.

Spatial Visualization: The process of constructing and manipulating mental models of 2- and 3-dimensional objects and locations.

TPACK: Technological Pedagogical and Content Knowledge – "to describe how teachers' understanding of technologies and pedagogical content knowledge interact with one another to produce effective teaching with technology" (Koehler & Mischra, 2008, p. 12).

Chapter 9
Design and Implementation of Computational Modeling for Learning Mathematical Concepts

Shelby P. Morge
University of North Carolina Wilmington, USA

Chris Gordon
University of North Carolina Wilmington, USA

Mahnaz Moallem
University of North Carolina Wilmington, USA

Gene Tagliarini
University of North Carolina Wilmington, USA

Sridhar Narayan
University of North Carolina Wilmington, USA

ABSTRACT

The Common Core State Standards (CCSS) call for a change in the way mathematics is taught. The mathematical practices outlined by the CCSS call for mathematics as a problem-solving endeavor, rather than routine exercises and practice. A quick Web search can provide mathematics teachers with an abundance of workshops and courses, examples, and videos of the different mathematical practices to help them understand what they mean and look like in practice. However, those examples do not go far in changing the current culture of mathematics instruction. In this chapter, the authors discuss current US mathematics instructional practices and how the CCSS are asking for distinctly different teaching practices. In addition, the authors share how the innovative Using Squeak to Infuse Information Technology Project (USeIT) sidestepped traditional mathematics instructional approaches and utilized problem-solving activities and the development of computational models to support students' learning of STEM concepts. The authors illustrate how the design, development, and implementation of a Squeak Etoys and Problem-Based Learning (PBL) activity addresses the CCSS expectations for mathematics content, practice for learning, and assessment, and discuss what this means for mathematics teacher education and professional development.

DOI: 10.4018/978-1-4666-4086-3.ch009

BACKGROUND

Mathematics Teaching

Traditionally, teaching mathematics has focused on procedural knowledge or what Davis (1984) called "rote mathematics" (p. 8), in which learning information and facts and applying formulas rather than learning relational or conceptual knowledge ("meaningful mathematics") have been emphasized (Davis, 1984; Skemp, 1976). In rote mathematics or routine processes the successful and automatic use of rules, algorithms or procedures have often been perceived to be necessary and sufficient for conceptual knowledge, thus, factual knowledge is augmented with demonstrations of how to solve a problem and then students are asked to solve similar problems by identifying the right formula, plugging data into it, and accepting whatever answer is reported by their calculator. However, modern cognitive science and approaches in learning mathematics demonstrate that procedural knowledge usually involves automatic and unconscious steps whereas conceptual knowledge typically requires conscious thinking. Using only procedural knowledge, a learner may skillfully combine two rules without knowing why they work. Furthermore, rote mathematics does not show how mathematics is used in the real world, which by no means is routine, thus making it difficult to understand and not motivational. Teaching mathematics as a complex thinking and problem solving skill, on the other hand, is interesting and motivating (Zimmerman, Fritzla, Haapasalo, & Rehlich, 2011).

Unfortunately, emphasis on problem solving and conceptual understanding in mathematics teaching has not made its way in the classroom. Stigler and Hiebert (2004) suggest that mathematics teaching has not changed much in the last 100 years. Their review of videos from the Trends International Mathematics and Science Study (TIMSS) provided little evidence that classroom practices reflect the goals of teaching reform. Stigler and

Hiebert (2004) found that eighth-graders in the United States spend little time in the classroom engaged in understanding mathematics concepts instead most of their time is devoted to practicing routine procedures. They claim, "even when the curriculum includes potentially rich problems, U.S. teachers use their traditional cultural teaching routines to transform the problems and reduce their instructional potential" (2004, p. 17). This finding is discouraging given the expectations of the newly adopted Common Core State Standards.

Common Core State Standards: A New Reform

The Common Core State Standards (CCSS) for mathematics, organized by the National Governors Association Center for Best Practices and the Council of Chief State School Officers (CCSSO), emphasize the connectedness of each of the areas of mathematics and shift away from disparate content guidelines in mathematics (Porter, McMahen, Hwang, & Yang, 2011). The CCSS further underline the relationship of each area of mathematics to science and technology. More importantly, one of the main messages embedded in the CCSS is that students' mathematical thinking and reasoning should be nurtured in the classroom. This can be seen in the mathematical content described by the standards, guidelines provided for expected pedagogy and practice for learning, and a new set of expectations for what is to be assessed. Mathematical content refers to the mathematics that is addressed by the standards and meant to be learned by students. Porter, McMaken, Hwang, and Yang (2011) claim that "the Common Core standards represent considerable change from what states currently call for in their standards and in what they assess" (p. 114). In their analysis of the standards, they found a low alignment correlation (0.25) between the CCSS and previously used state standards in mathematics. The low correlation is attributed to differences in topics that are addressed as well as the CCSS focus on student development of cognitive skills. Expected pedagogy and practice for learning refers to the type of instruction that happens in the mathematics classroom. Teachers and students are expected to spend less time on memorization and procedures and more time understanding and analyzing, as seen in the CCSS's eight mathematical practices (e.g., construct viable arguments, critique the reasoning of others, and model with mathematics [Common Core State Standards Initiative, 2012]) (Porter et al., 2011). In other words, approaches to mathematics instruction must be significantly different than they are now, with less of a focus on memorizing procedures and more focus on deeply investigating fewer, interesting problems. There is a large gap between existing mathematics pedagogy and practice and the CCSS expectations.

Along with teaching practices, CCSS represent considerable changes in the assessment of mathematics content. Van de Walle, Karp, and Bay-Williams (2013), contend that "truly understanding mathematics is more than just content knowledge" (p. 80). Assessments, therefore, should provide evidence of understanding mathematical concepts and procedures, mathematical processes and practices, and students' disposition to mathematics. This suggestion moves beyond the traditional right or wrong assessment approach and supports measuring thinking processes and performance within the context of solving problems and developing or creating solutions.

Simulations and Problem/Project-Based Learning in Mathematics

Problem solving is "a process that takes a problem description, a goal, and a knowledge base as input, and derives a solution that satisfies the goal" (Aamodt, 1990, p. 4). The goal contains a specification of the requirements that must be fulfilled in order for a result to be a solution to the problem. A problem may be "structured as sub-problems and the problem solving process correspondingly split into sub-processes" (Aamodt,

1990, p. 4). Therefore, a student who is solving a real world problem should be able to dynamically change the scope and goals of a problem during problem solving, and deal with the contradictions and inconsistencies that are introduced in this process. During the process of problem solving, the student can engage in generating hypotheses, test the hypotheses, and formulate and justify a plausible and meaningful explanation for the results (problem-solving processes). Such complex Problem-Based Learning (PBL) processes, as they relate to Science, Technology, Engineering and Mathematics (STEM), immerse learners in realistic situations while allowing them to use technology and engineering as a cognitive or instrumental tool. Teaching STEM in the context of PBL, therefore, combines scientific study, technology design, engineering technology, and mathematical analysis.

Problem solving has been a focus in mathematics education for decades (e.g., Schoenfeld, 1992; Silver, 1985). Nevertheless, the implementation of effective teaching of problem solving into the classroom has not been easy (e.g., Lester & Kehle, 2003; Zimmerman, et al, 2011). Zimmerman and his colleagues argue that one reason is the fact that "teaching mathematical problem solving is very difficult and itself a very complex problem" (p. 13). One alternative to traditional—simple procedure-based—problem solving perspectives that has emerged from research is a simulation and modeling approach on mathematics problem solving. Simulation and modeling approaches to teaching problem solving emerged from research on conceptual development. In mathematics and science, conceptual systems that humans develop to make sense of their experiences generally are referred to as models (Lesh & Sriraman, 2005). Aamodt (1990) argues that a computational model—a framework-for knowledge-intensive problem solving and learning from experience is a viable solution for teaching scientific and mathematical problem solving and conceptual understanding. Simulation modeling allows learners to test and analyze different scenarios to understand their impact on a broader 'system' or provide 'proof of concept' evidence before moving forward with implementation plans (Aamodt, 1990). With simulation modeling, the learners collect data or create assumptions about a process or system, and then use computer software to build the model. The model is then run to simulate a real event or a projection of assumptions made, over a period of time. Hence, it is safe to assume that such learning processes have a high potential for enhancing scientific and mathematical knowledge and problem solving.

Squeak Etoys: A Simulation Tool

Squeak Etoys (www.squeakland.org) was inspired by LOGO, PARC Smalltalk, Hypercard, and star-LOGO. It is a media-rich, authoring environment with a simple powerful scripted object model for many kinds of objects created by end-users that runs on many platforms and is free and open source (Kay, 2007). Squeak Etoys is based on programmable objects behaving on a computer screen. Users may create simulations by scripting 2D and 3D objects to move, interact, make

sound, and save them to share with others. On the opening screen seen in the screenshot shown in Figure 1, a script for the red car (Car script1) shows instructions for the car that were created using drag-and-drop tiles.

Squeak Etoys, as a computer simulation tool, motivates students by keeping them actively engaged in the learning process through requiring that problem-solving and decision-making skills be used to make the simulation run (Ludwigs, 2009). As the simulation runs, it is modeling a dynamic system in which the learner plays a role and engages in systems thinking and enhances understanding of systems as well as of science and mathematics concepts. Developing computer models and running simulations expedites the process of problem solving and shifts the learner's focus from acquisition of facts to "cognitive processes like manipulation and understanding which then encourage curiosity and creativity" (Ludwigs, 2009, p. 33).

In the USeIT project, a project funded by the National Science Foundation in 2007, Squeak Etoys was used with middle and high school students and their teachers to expand their information technology experiences and to deepen

Figure 1. Screenshot of Squeak Etoys

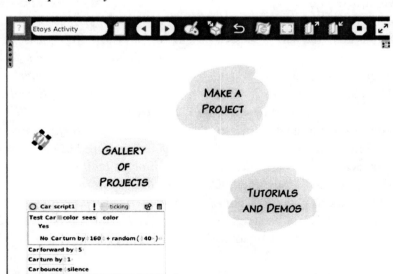

their scientific and mathematical knowledge. Specifically, the project aimed to assist students and their teachers to exploit the Squeak Etoys modeling and simulation tool to improve problem solving and critical thinking skills as well as enhance STEM conceptual knowledge in a hands-on, problem-based, meaningful learning setting. As with the CCSS, the USeIT project focus was not on memorization and procedures, but on applying mathematical and scientific knowledge using Squeak Etoys technology, as a cognitive tool and engineering environment. In collaboration with the project team, the teachers developed and posed a series of complex, real world problem statements to students. The purpose of the challenge was to allow the students to implement what they had learned from their mathematics and/or science courses and deepen their conceptual and procedural understanding in a challenging but fun setting in which they used technology to test their assumptions and develop a solution. The design of Squeak Etoys simulation and modeling process was assumed to provide the avenue or engineering environment for this challenge. Middle and high school students worked in small teams and were mentored by their teachers in a four-day summer enrichment program to complete their projects or simulations. The given problem statements were open-ended, but were structured as sub-problems, and the problem solving process for each problem was correspondingly divided into sub-processes so as students were able to plan, re-plan, monitor and assess their progress and problem solving approaches and solutions.

Four PBL activities were developed in which students were required to use Squeak Etoys to design a solution in form of a simulation. The problem statement for each activity was centered on a scientific topic for several reasons. First, it allowed students to think like a scientist by conducting inquiry and formulating hypotheses before solving the problem. Second, the scientific topic made the task relevant and real-world and allowed the students to see how mathematical concepts and procedures are inseparable from science and integrated in everyday life. The selected topics for the activities were forces, motion, natural disasters, and ecosystems. The diversity of the topics for each activity also allowed teachers and students to focus on different areas of the curriculum.

The remainder this chapter will focus on one of the activities—the motion activity—to address the following research questions:

- How did teacher mentors' pedagogical approaches impact student learning?
- What do teacher mentors report about students' understanding of mathematics content?
- What mathematics content do students learn in the context of problem-solving activities as assessed through their learning processes and products?

MAIN FOCUS OF THE CHAPTER

Student Learning of Mathematical Content

The motion activity provided the following problem statement.

Assume that you are hired by the Advanced Research Center (ARC)—one of the U.S. Army Space and Missile Defense Command's major research and development facilities for Missile Defense research. As a scientist, you are asked to develop the next generation of ground-based missile defense systems, much like the Patriot missile defense system (surface-to-air missile system). Before investing billions of dollars, ARC wants a prototype built using software. This prototype will allow you to simulate various flight paths and intercept capabilities of your system. You will need to develop a prototype using Squeak Etoys. With your prototype, you should prepare a final report for ARC in which you explain how your prototype establishes the feasibility of a particular interceptor for certain threats.

Teachers worked in teams throughout the Spring 2010 semester to design the Squeak Etoys and PBL activities and plan the daily enrichment program objectives. The teams were intentionally composed of cross-curricular teachers from various grade levels to help meet the needs of all students participating in the program. The teachers started planning by brainstorming ideas based on the Squeak Etoys activities they had completed with their students throughout the academic year, their understanding of the state curriculum expectations, and examples provided by the project team. During one Saturday meeting, the teachers developed their initial problem statements. With specific guidance from the USeIT Project team members and teacher leaders, the problem statements were revised to be more complex and ill-defined and to better meet state standards, and project goals. After developing the problem statement, the teachers were asked to identify underlying mathematical concepts, procedures and principles that they thought students would have to apply in order to be able to solve the problem. The purpose of this task was to help teachers be prepared to ask guiding questions and scaffold students during the activity to focus on applying targeted mathematical concepts, principles and procedures. It also allowed them to assess students' prior knowledge when forming teams. The following are specific mathematical concepts, principles and procedures that were targeted for the motion activity (See Table 1).

In addition, to provide initial guidance without directing students to a specific solution, the motion problem statement was broken into sub-problems. This approach also helped teachers to guide rather than direct and created proper structure for continuation of the activity for several days. Ten students divided into five teams of two worked on the motion project. Each team worked closely with the same teacher mentor for each day of the workshop. The following is the break-down of the problem statement and student learning for the first day (See Table 2).

Table 1. Mathematical concepts, principles, and procedures targeted for the motion activity

Concepts	Principles	Procedures
Acceleration	Relationship	Calculating slope
Angles	between launch	Scaling the
Circular Motion	orientation and	displacement
Displacement ratio	speed	Calculating
Functions	Relationship	angular velocity
Gravity	between	Calculating
Horizontal speed	displacement ratio	acceleration
Intersecting Lines	and orbital radius	Calculating
Launch orientation	Relationship	speed
Linearity	between speed and	
Motion	time	
Projectile Motion	Relationship	
Slope	between launch	
Velocity	angle and speed	
Vertical speed		

Teacher Mentors' Reports of Day 1 Student Learning

The sub-problems and processes were supported with guidance and questioning from the teacher mentors. The teacher mentors asked questions as the students were working on their projects to assess their understanding of the mathematics content and to encourage their thinking in areas that they may not have considered. The questions that were asked varied depending on the mentor teacher and the group's needs. After the each day of the workshop, a reflective session was held during which mentor teachers and the project team discussed the day and teachers completed individual surveys. On the first day, teacher mentors made the following statements related to their assessment students' prior knowledge about the mathematics content:

Had limited knowledge about motion.

Basic understanding of STEM content. Had knowledge of motion and what happens when two objects in Squeak react with one another.

The teacher mentors also reported that students had learned the following topics by the end of the first day.

Table 2. Breakdown of problem statement and sub-problems for day 1

Day	Instructions
Day 1 of the enrichment program	Goal: Investigate, form idea, and plan your prototype Step 1: Create and instrument two objects that undergo linear motion by which one can intercept the other To accomplish step 1, you should investigate linear motion by planning a linear trajectory by which one object traveling with constant linear motion can intercept another. For this step it is very likely that you would need to use the following Squeak Etoys features and functions. a) Create an object and controls that allow one to vary its speed, direction and acceleration b) Create instruments to record and display the speed, direction, and acceleration of this object over time c) Create a second object and controls that will enable it to intercept the first object subject to: 1. The first object traveling in a linear path at constant velocity 2. Only the initial speed and direction of the second object may be altered and its subsequent trajectory must be linear Once you have created a, b, and c, check your prototype to make sure that it includes the following features recommended by ARC 1. Two objects capable of linear motion 2. Controls allowing the velocity and direction of each object to be varied 3. Visual displays of the speed, direction, and acceleration of both objects over time 4. A "fire" capability that allows object two to begin its travel toward object one from a fixed launch position

They learned how to design a Squeak model that represented the two missiles interacting. They wrote scripts that controled [sic] the two missiles and allowed for variable speed, and direction. They also learned how to use the motion detection probe.

They learned more about linear motion they controlled missiles using it and had to figure out how to in order to complete the project.

Student Reports from Day 1

Throughout the enrichment, student understanding of the mathematics content was assessed using formative and summative methods. At the end of each day, students used the flap feature within Squeak Etoys to explain their progress on completing the project. At the end of the first day, one group claimed:

We made an Anit-missile [sic] Defense system for our project. We used forward motion, scripts, pause script, reset script, hide, and show scripts. We also used buttons, headings, and sliders. One challenge that we faced was finding a way to make the anti-missile to move after the first missile was already launched. Everything else was pretty much a success.*

Students were also asked to respond to a series of questions both individually and as a team at the end of each day of the enrichment. The questions were meant to improve students' critical thinking skills, help them think strategically about their projects, evaluate their work for the day, and make plans for the next day. Daily individual questions included: what did I learn today as a result of working with my team?; what role did I play as a team member?; how do I feel about working with a team?; and what do I need to work on to be more effective in my team? In our analysis, we will focus on student responses related to understanding of the mathematics concepts.

Students and teams responses to the daily enrichment program questions were coded using an open coding strategy. Students narrative responses to daily questions were first organized by the PBL tasks and then grouped using open coding system (identifying, naming, categorizing and describing phenomena found in the text) (Strauss and Corbin, 1990). At the end of the first day, students claimed that they learned:

...about making missiles move and all the feautres [sic] they have.

...how to make the offensive missle [sic] become more life-like as it approached the defensive missle [sic] in an arc shaped flight.

...what missiles were, how they were used, and what they did.

...how to make the missile curve the right way and I learned how to get pictures into Squeak.

Daily team questions included: what did we learn today (what did we accomplish today)?; what scientific and mathematical concepts did we learn today?; how do we feel about today's work as a team?; and what do we plan to do next? To respond to the team questions, students were asked to talk about the questions as a team, and, then, one member of the team was responsible for posting team's responses to each question. At the end of the first day of work on the motion project, students reported learning:

Adding together numbers to reach a different variable, times by negative numbers to get positives to change the direction.

We used mathematical signs and learned what happens when missiles crash.

We used different equations to make the missles [sic] become more life-like as gravity effected [sic] it.

We learnded [sic] about speed and angles.

Speed and multiple varibles [sic] affecting an object.

The sub-problems from the first day encouraged students to focus on the research and development of their motion projects. When reporting what they learned individually, students focused on more superficial understandings such as what missiles are and how they are used. After talking with their team members, their reflections showed that they learned how to incorporate mathematics concepts such as speed and angles into their Squeak Etoys projects. In the project flaps, they described their progress and challenges they encountered. However, their project scripts show little correlation to the intended mathematical understandings. Students used Squeak features such as "forward by" to move an object forward, rather than applying the concepts of linear motion and constant velocity. In the following script, the anti-missile already has a heading, which designates its angle. By assigning the forward motion the value of the slider, students are able to vary the speed of the object without connections to the mathematics. They merely have to move the slider up and down to adjust the speed. They are not using a linear equation and finding an intersection point with another object traveling in a linear path. Students were having a difficult time translating the real world situation into mathematics, or reasoning abstractly and quantitatively and modeling with mathematics (Common Core State Standards Initiative, 2012) (See Figure 2).

Teacher Mentors' Reports of Day 2 Student Learning

The breakdown of the problem statement and sub-problems given to students on day 2 can be found in Table 3. At the end of the second day, in the reflective session the teacher mentors reported asking several questions related to the mathematics concepts students were expected to learn. Those questions included:

Figure 2. Student script for anti-missile movement

Table 3. Breakdown of problem statement and sub-problems for day 2

Day	Instructions
Day 2 of the enrichment program	Goal: Continue expanding your ground-based interceptors and begin testing your prototype Step 2: Extend the prototype to investigate angular velocity and circular motion To accomplish step 2 you should investigate circular motion by creating an object in a circular orbit around a fixed point from which a second object is launched to intercept it. Check your prototype to make sure that you have included the following: a) Create an object with a circular trajectory, with constant, but changeable, angular velocity about a fixed, but movable, point. b) Create controls that allow an object at the orbit center to be launched upon a linear path with constant velocity to intercept the orbiting object. c) Introduce a control that enables the radius of the orbit to be varied. d) Enable a mechanism that allows the size of the interceptor to vary. e) Automate the process of determining the launch orientation for a given interceptor speed. Step 3: If your prototype has the above features, investigate the following questions and document your responses • How are the launch orientation and speed related? • How could you use your laboratory to model an electronic transmission from earth to a planet?

How does an object move horizontally? How does an object move vertically? Does it slow down, speed up, or go the same speed? What happens to the distance the projectile moves vertically each second? What does the shape of a projectile look like? If your rocket was fired from here, what would its path look like? Why would the path look that way? What do we need to control in the squeak program to make the missile move that way?

How could you change that so your missile goes in the opposite direction? Is there a way for you to write a different script for that?

What affects the flight of a missile? What direction does gravity affect it?

What does gravity do? Which direction does it affect? What letter on the coordinate plane does that stand for? How can you make you object do what you are trying to do? Is there any other ways [sic] to make that work? Is your missile doing what you want it to do?

Through their observations and work with student groups on day 2, teacher mentors reported that students learned some of the intended mathematics concepts. Those included:

…how to modify their existing Squeak projects to include how velocity, direction, and angle influence a moving object. They also learned how to use the motion probe to control one of those factors.

They better understood gravity, they all applied it to their projects in some capacity they learned how to control something with a probe, they applied it to their projects as well.

More about projectile motion and the x and y velocity components. I know this because I questioned them and lead them in a discussion about the effect of constant horizontal velocity and vertical acceleration on the path of a projectile.

Student Reports from Day 2

Within their Squeak Etoys projects, students recorded their day 2 progress by writing:

We still have our general idea of the project but we expanded on it to include another aspect. We added a missile and made it air to surface and included gravity and velocity as a factor…which was not easy, it involved a lot of math…

…we used scripts that were a lot harder and complicated and our newer project is more mathematically realistic because we used objects x and y-axis.

On the individual surveys taken at the end of day 2, students focused more on the mathematics concepts that they learned and incorporated in their projects than they did on day 1. They claimed they learned:

…the fundamental with moving things in motion and using velocity and gravity.

That gravity is a major factor in objects.

…how to make gravity play a role in the missiles course.

…a new equation having to do with gravity.

…how to make an object follow another, specifically, heading.

The team surveys also reflected the development of mathematical understandings. Teams reported:

We used gravity and velocity in our Squeak model.

We learned about quadratic equations.

We learned how to incorporate gravity into the missiles flight.

About angles and gravity. And distance on a prone [sic] that a person can control speed.

The day 2 results show that the teacher mentor involvement increased and the students were making connections between the features of Squeak Etoys and the mathematics concepts, principles, and procedures involved in the motion project. Students were able to apply the mathematics

in the scripts they created for their missiles and to run the scripts to test the results. These new understandings may be attributed to teachers' use of guiding, directed questions to support students in the development of their models. However, the questions teachers asked did not require students to use high-level thinking skills. The questions only required one correct answer. This lack of critical thinking was evident in students' reflections on what they learned. The students mentioned topics such as velocity and gravity, but not what those topics meant or how they related to the real world problem statement.

Teacher Mentors' Reports of Day 3 Student Learning

The breakdown of the problem statement and sub-problems given to students on day 3 can be found in Table 4. After the third day of the enrichment, the teachers reported asking questions that were more focused on the mathematics content and less focused on the use of Squeak Etoys. For example:

What do you use in Squeak to cause an object to move? Why did you set up the equation that way? What could you change about that equation to show how gravity would affect your star?

What axis will gravity affect? Does the motion look correct? What should happen? What are all of the variables in your problem?

What happens when you drop an object? What does the motion of the object look like as it falls down? How does the object move horizontally? What do you know about horizontal motion? What do you know about vertical motion? Why do objects move at a constant velocity horizontally? Are there any forces other than air resistance that would act on an object as it moved horizontally? How far does the object move during the next second horizontally? vertically? What is the equation we

Table 4. Breakdown of the problem statement and sub-problems for day 3

Day	Instructions

Day 3 of the enrichment program	Goals: Continue expanding your ground-based interceptors and test your prototype by comparing and contrasting various systems using your Squeak model and document your findings
	Step 4: Extend the prototype to investigate other types of two-dimension motion
	To accomplish step 4 task you should investigate the two-dimensional motion of a projectile.
	For this step, it is very likely that you would need to use Squeak Etoys to create the following features and functions.
	a) Extend the previous labs by enabling horizontal and vertical components of velocity.
	b) Create a circularly orbiting object and plot its scaled vertical and horizontal displacements over time subject to:
	1. Scale each displacement by dividing the displacement by the orbital radius
	2. Rescale the ratios as needed for display purposes
	3. Questions:
	    i. What is the range of the ratios?
	    ii. Are there any patterns in their variations?
	    iii. At what orbital positions do they acquire their extreme values?
	    iv. How are the ratios affected by changes in the orbital radius?
	4. The ratios are called the sine and cosine. Note that Squeak Etoys provides built methods for calculating these ratios for any angle and the ratios can be scaled to problem specific information such as the magnitude of a velocity.
	c) Simulate the launch of a projectile, like an arrow, and mark its flight path by asking the following questions:
	1. How can you use the observations from the first exercise to determine the horizontal and vertical components of the projectile's motion?
	2. The projectile must be launched from some position on the ground.
	3. The launch orientation must be variable.
	4. The launch speed must be variable.
	5. The trajectory must be subject to gravity.
	6. The projectile must stop on impact with the ground.
	7. Plot the height, horizontal speed, and vertical speed of the projectile over time.
	To test your prototype, address the following questions and document your responses:
	• How does the horizontal speed change with time?
	• When is the vertical speed of the projectile largest?
	• When is the vertical speed of the projectile smallest?
	• When is the projectile at its highest point?
	• How is the maximum elevation of the projectile affected by the launch angle and speed?
	• How is the range of the projectile affected by the launch angle and speed?

are using? How can we represent it in Squeak? What variables are in the equation?

In our analysis of the questions asked on day 3, we noticed the teacher mentors' new focus on real world connections. They encouraged students to consider whether or not their simulation projects matched what they see in the real world. This correlates to the CCSS Mathematical Practices, which call for students to "model with mathematics" (Common Core State Standards Initiative, 2012, p. 7). In standard 4, students are expected "to apply the mathematics they know to solve problems arising in everyday life, society, and the workplace" (Common Core State Standards Initiative, 2012, p. 7).

In their reports of what students learned, teacher mentors noticed that students were more focused and able to apply the mathematics concepts, principles, and procedures to their Squeak Etoys projects. Teacher mentors claimed that students learned:

There are two components to projectile motion based upon velocity, angle and time.

How to use variables in Squeak, all students created variables and used equations to make objects move according to the laws of physics.

Differences between velocity and acceleration how the x and y components of motion are independent of each other.

They learned how to use variables in Squeak so they could set up mathematical [sic] formulas to control objects instead of using forward by and turn by.

Student Reports from Day 3

Student teams did not record anything in their project flaps on day 3, but their responses to the individual and team survey questions reflect the teacher mentors' focus on mathematics content and real world connections. Individual students reported learning:

…how to use gravitational formulas into my project to make it more life-like.

…That Projectiles move differently according to Velocity and gravity.

Student teams also highlighted the connection to the real world in their responses. They claimed:

We learned how to add mathmatical [sic] equations to out projects such as Free Fall, Trajectory motion, Gradual Constants, Horazontal [sic] Motion with gravity.

We combined ideas of trigonomatry [sic] and variables into equations to perform functions in the squeak program.

Today we worked on incuding [sic] gravitational formulas to make things move more life-like.

We made used scripts to make projectile shapes.

After reviewing the day 3 results, it is clear that the teacher mentors' intentional focus on the mathematics concepts and real world connection had a direct impact on what students learned and incorporated in their projects. Students were able to connect their projects to mathematics concepts and the real world, demonstrating deeper understandings. This ability to move between and among different representations of mathematics improves student understanding and retention (Van de Walle, Karp, and Bay-Williams, 2013).

Teacher Mentors' Reports of Overall Student Learning

The breakdown of the problem statement and sub-problems given to students on day 4 can be found in Table 5. At the end of Day 4, teacher mentors were asked to reflect on their experiences over the week and students' achievement of the targeted objectives. Teachers' responses reflected a range in students' understandings. For example:

They completed them by implementing equations related to projectile motion and creating variability between each scenario.

I think students improved their Squeak skills but did not increase their knowledge of physics content knowledge that much. I feel that students still have misconceptions about scientific concepts such as gravity, forces, mass, and acceleration. I feel that most students did a great job achieving each day's targeted objectives. I think students have a better understanding of acceleration due to gravity and projectile motion, but they are not completely comfortable or correct with it. My evidence is the Squeak projects they created and the review of their answers to day three questions. When reviewing the questions posed in day 3 my group had a lot of misconceptions and wrong answers, but we worked through those.

Table 5. Breakdown of the problem statement and sub-problems for day 4

Day	Instructions
Day 4 (final day of enrich-ment program)	Goals: Test your prototype by comparing and contrasting various systems using your Squeak model and document your findings and write a report summarizing the results of your investigation and your test of the systems that you created. Step 5: Extend prototype to determine the launch angle needed to hit a target at a given range with a projectile whose initial speed is known. To accomplish step 5, you should investigate the following. 1. Simulate a target object at a known, but variable range having the same elevation as the launch point. 2. Implement controls to allow one to determine the launch angle needed to hit the target. 3. Automate the process of determining the launch angle. 4. Extend the project to allow one projectile to intercept a second projectile given that both are subject to gravity and experience parabolic trajectories. a) Assume that the initial velocity and launch location of the second projectile are known
Final Project and Reflection	Now use your findings to write your report for ARC. Your report should include: 1. A brief summary of the results of your investigation and your testing of the system 2. A brief description of your Squeak model (e.g., how the model allows the user the test the hypotheses) 3. A list of recommendations based on your findings using the Squeak model and a list of future studies and factors to consider. Add a brief reflection based on what you learned from the experience. 1. What did you learn by building software models of real phenomena? 2. What did you learn about principles of mathematics and science? 3. What did you learn about programming with Squeak Etoys?

Students' Final Reports

Students' final project flaps included brief overall reflections on their work. This provided evidence of their lack of previous experiences with justifying and explaining their thinking related to mathematics. One group claimed

We made a missile simulation, from air to land, using variables. Using a forward-by and added randomness to its direction. Using a slider to control its speed and a joystick to control "USA" missile. We made them intersect and disappear.

Although there was no explanation of why they did these things, they were able to connect the features of Squeak Etoys to mathematics concepts. Another group mentioned some mathematics concepts, but did not mention the features of Squeak Etoys that allowed them to model those concepts. Their statement in the flap was, "We added a missile and made it air to surface and included gravity and velocity as a factor. Yes it

is, we added gravity to it which was not easy, it involved a lot of math."

In addition to the daily questions, individuals and teams were also asked to reflect on their own learning at the end of the last day and upon completion of their projects. Students were asked: (1) After four days of working on a specific project, what do you think you have learned about science, math and technology? What do you think you learned about math, science and technology that you did not know before? (2) Throughout the week you had a chance to work with a partner (or two partners) to complete your project; how do you feel about your accomplishments as a team? What strategies did you use (as a team) that you think were effective? What strategies did you use that you think were not effective and you would change if you would have to work with a team again? (3) Assess your overall experience of participating in the summer enrichment program? What do you think about various events and activities that you participated and which one do you think had major impact on your thinking about what you would do in the future?

The mathematics content that the students who worked on the motion activity reported learning included:

- Trigonometry and laws for motion.
- I learned a lot about trajectory and more equations.
- I have learned that you are able to use those formulas and incorporate them into a project to make objects move more life-like.
- A lot that I really can't just remember. . . definitely the free fall and velocity formulas, and how to read programming better.

They also reported related to the application of math and science, that:

- I learned that math and science take a huge part into real life things. I did not know that math & science was [were] the most important things to use and that math from what you learned was included.
- I've learned that many of these subjects are needed in order to accomplish primarily anything.
- I learned that math and science can be applied to a lot more things than I thought before.

Students' final projects and thinking processes were evaluated using a set of criteria developed by the project team. The criteria allowed the mentor teachers and the project team to score students products on the basis of whether or not what students developed could be considered a simulation and, if it could, what characteristics defined the product as a model. The criteria also evaluated whether or not the targeted STEM concepts, principles and procedures were used in the model to allow the student to use it as a test bed for determining the solutions.

Analysis of the five student projects demonstrated a range of fluency in the use of Squeak Etoys. For example, one team's project, scoring the lowest on the simulation/model criteria, showed no evidence of a connection to the underlying mathematical and scientific concepts, principles and procedures. Another team's project received the highest score in this category because it showed clarity of thought by virtue of the way they wrote the program (see an example script in Figure 4). Not only was this team's project tied to the important mathematics and scientific concepts, principles and procedures, but their programming skills (writing scripts, calling scripts, etc.) made their understanding of the targeted concepts very clear and easy to evaluate.

The students' levels of understanding of the mathematics concepts, principles and procedures also varied. All five teams demonstrated some level of understanding of the concepts of gravity, time, motion, and velocity. Because they developed analytic expressions for their calculations, most demonstrated a level of understanding of the principles of scaling and vertical speed. In addition, all five teams that worked on this project understood the procedure of calculating a parabolic trajectory.

The screen shot in Figure 3 is an example of a completed motion project in which the student team created an offensive missile to fly toward a defensive missile. They used scripts to move the missiles and determine when they crossed paths.

The script shown in Figure 4, taken from the offensive missile (AMG) in the previous project, highlights some of the mathematics content and student understanding involved in this project. The students working on this project created variables for time, gravity, and velocity and incorporated those into equations for horizontal and vertical components of projectile motion.

Throughout the week as students worked on their projects, they engaged in various CCSS

Figure 3. Screenshot of students' motion project

Reset all reset
Defensive Missile firedefensebutton
1
USeIT Go!
Start Stop On
redduster[1]2 enemyAim
Attacking Missile Ground enemyfire

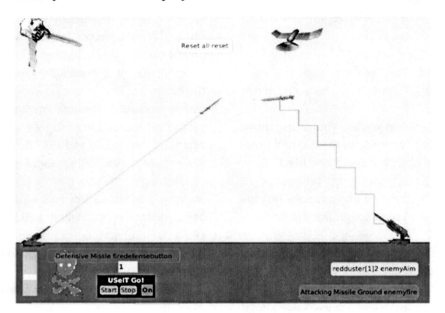

Figure 4. Attacking missile ground (AMG) launch script from students' motion project

AMG groundLaunch
normal
AMG's x ← 100 - (AMG's vel * AMG's time * degreeCos (AMG's angle1))
AMG's y ← AMG's vel * AMG's time * degreeSin (AMG's angle1) - 0.5 * AMG's grav * square (AMG's time) + 217
AMG pause script heading
AMG's time increase by 1
AMG's heading decrease by 5

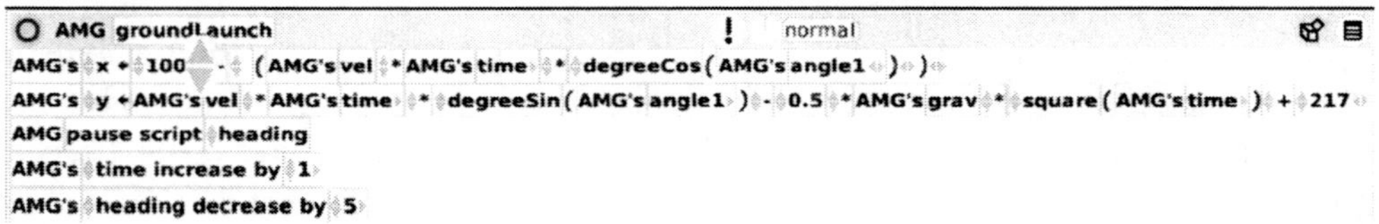

Mathematical Practices such as make sense of problems and persevere in solving them, reason abstractly and quantitatively, construct viable arguments and critique the reasoning of others, use appropriate tools strategically, and model with mathematics (Common Core State Standards Initiative, 2012). However, the specific mathematics content that they learned can also be linked to the CCSS mathematics content standards. Some of the CCSS addressed in the previous script include:

- 7th Grade:
    - **Standard 7.EE.2:** Understand that rewriting an expression in different forms in a problem context can shed light on the problem and how the quantities in it are related.
    - **Standard 7.EE.4:** Use variables to represent quantities in a real-world or mathematical problem, and construct simple equations and inequalities to solve problems by reasoning about the quantities.
- 8th Grade:
    - **Standard 8.F.5:** Describe qualitatively the functional relationship between two quantities by analyzing a graph. Sketch a graph that exhibits the qualitative features of a function that has been described verbally.
- High school:

- ○ **Standard A-CED.2:** Create equations in two or more variables to represent relationships between quantities; graph equations on coordinate axes with labels and scales.
- ○ **Standard F-BF.1:** Write a function that describes a relationship between two quantities.
- ○ **Standard F-LE.5:** Interpret the parameters in a linear or exponential function in terms of a context.

IMPLICATIONS FOR PRACTICE AND RESEARCH

Teachers' Influence on Student Learning

The results of this enrichment program demonstrate the influence that teachers have on student learning of mathematics concepts, principles, and procedures. The results of our analysis suggest that in order to engage students in the mathematical problem solving that the CCSS require, teachers need sound mathematical knowledge. Teachers' abilities to ask just-in-time mathematical questions allow students to re-examine their work and apply mathematical concepts more strategically rather than using trial and error. In addition, teachers' sound mathematical knowledge allows them to assess students' thinking processes by examining their work or by listening to their conversation and identifying the type of support they need. Thus, while teachers can develop general guiding questions for the problem statement, the power of scaffolding is when differentiated guiding questions are asked. The guiding questions posed to students should not be superficial or they will lead to shallow understanding of mathematics content.

This result suggests that teacher education programs should focus on helping teachers learn how to guide and scaffold and ask progressively more complex and content specific questions. Our experience suggests that teachers are often more comfortable directing and telling students what to do or not to do rather than asking just-in-time, good guiding questions that assist students to think more about the problem. In addition, our experience suggests that while teachers often think they can formulate an open-ended problem statement they have a difficult time formulating problem statements that are complex enough to require students to apply critical thinking skills and problem solving. This result also has implications for research. As Zimmermann and his colleagues (2011) argue, solving complex problems has been a domain of cognitive psychology for more than three decades. Thus, research in mathematics education has to test some of these strategies for their applications in mathematical problem solving. On Day 1, the teachers and students had not done much research and were less comfortable with the content they were teaching and learning. As the days of the enrichment program progressed, students and teachers both reported that their focus on content made it easier to apply mathematics to their projects. Student mathematical thinking and understanding was nurtured.

In addition, teachers should be able to support students to think critically. Having students plan a solution strategy, reflect on their planning, and revise their plan develops critical thinking skills. Mentor teachers participating in the enrichment program had to be guided to lead students through this problem solving process during the reflective sessions held at the end of each day. Our experiences reflect research findings that teaching problem solving is difficult for teachers (Zimmerman et al., 2011). Future research focusing on the behaviors of teachers who are successful in developing critical thinking skills in their students will inform classroom practice and support mathematics teachers' abilities to engage students in the CCSS mathematical practices.

Students' Understanding of Mathematics Content

Our analysis also suggests that some level of preparation is required for students to be able to engage in problem solving. Students need prior knowledge to build upon in problem solving situations. Traditional assessments such as quizzes or tests at the end of pre-planned instructional units are not necessarily built upon students' prior knowledge. Teachers' abilities to assess student prior knowledge will help students acquire some basic understandings of the mathematical concepts before attempting to solve the problem. Teachers who start with a pre-assessment then develop and use sub-problems and guiding questions throughout the problem solving experience are activating students' prior knowledge, helping them make connections and build upon that knowledge while they are completing the activity.

Thus, pre-service and in-service mathematics teachers need experiences that will help them develop strong content and pedagogical knowledge related to problem-based teaching of mathematics. There is more to teaching mathematics than the content knowledge acquired in mathematics courses. Ball and Phelps (2008) reported that teachers also need knowledge that will help them make sense of student understanding and be able to find methods of representing mathematics so that it makes sense to students. The results of this enrichment program show that the more teachers can support students in making connections between prior knowledge, real world experiences, and the mathematics concepts, the more likely students are to demonstrate understanding.

CONCLUSION

Students attending the summer enrichment program who engaged in the motion problem-solving activity did not only demonstrate understanding of CCSS mathematics content in their final projects, but they researched, discussed, and reflected on the content throughout their problem solving processes. Their engagement in the problem solving started with the challenging problem correlated to the mathematics expectations of the CCSS that they were given to solve. The lack of a routines and procedures in the motion problem statement promoted activation of students' minds and engagement in conscious thinking (Zimmerman, Fritzla, Haapasalo, & Rehlich, 2011).

The motion problem statement was open-ended, but was structured as sub-problems by the teachers, and the problem solving process was correspondingly divided into sub-processes. So over the four days of the enrichment program, students were able to plan, re-plan, monitor and assess their progress and problem solving approaches and solutions. Thus, they "made sense of problems and persevered in solving them" (Common Core Standards State Initiative, 2012, p. 6). In addition, teacher mentors' guidance and questions pushed students to apply appropriate mathematical and scientific concepts in their project and continually evaluate their progress. These teaching practices were unlike the common practices of rote instruction in which the teacher demonstrates how to solve a problem and the students are asked to solve similar problems. However, they were highly correlated the expectations of the CCSS mathematical practices.

As a result of this focus on CCSS for mathematics and appropriate mathematics teaching practices, students showed interest and high engagement in their own learning and constructed deeper understandings of the mathematics concepts. Assessments of student engagement and understanding focused on measuring thinking processes (teacher questions, daily reflection questions, and flaps) and performances (Squeak Etoys projects) within the context of solving problems and developing or creating solutions. The process of developing Squeak Etoys projects showed that when students are guided and receive proper scaffolds, they show improvement in their thinking and problem solving skills. The analysis of students Squeak Etoys projects further show that they are able to develop complex Squeak Etoys projects and demonstrate higher level thinking skills and mathematical content knowledge. These students also demonstrate advanced technology skills in using Squeak Etoys and a higher level of engagement in problem solving.

ACKNOWLEDGMENT

This chapter is based upon work supported by the National Science Foundation under Grant No. ESI-0624615. Any opinions, findings, and conclusions or recommendations expressed in this material are those of the authors and do not necessarily reflect the views of the National Science Foundation.

REFERENCES

Aamodt, A. (2005). A computational model of knowledge-intensive learning and problem solving. WBC, 90, 1-20.

Ball, D. L., Thames, M. H., & Phelps, G. (2008). Content knowledge for teaching what makes it special? *Journal of Teacher Education, 59*(5), 389–407. doi:10.1177/0022487108324554.

Common Core State Standards Initiative. (2012). *Mathematics: Standards for mathematical practice*. Retrieved from http://www.corestandards. org/Math/Practice

Davis, R. B. (1984). *Learning mathematics: The cognitive science approach to mathematics education*. Praeger Pub Text.

Kay, A. (2007). *Children learn by doing: Squeak Etoys on the OLPC XO*. Glendale, CA: Viewpoints Research Institute.

Lesh, R., & Sriraman, B. (2005). John Dewey revisited—Pragmatism and the models-modeling perspective on mathematical learning. In A. Beckmann, C. Michelsen, & B. Sriraman (Eds.), *Proceedings of the 1st International Symposium on Mathematics and its Connections to the Arts and Sciences* (pp. 32–51). Berlin: Franzbecker Verlag.

Lester, F. K., & Kehle, P. E. (2003). From problem solving to modeling: The evolution of thinking about research on complex mathematical activity. *Beyond constructivism: Models and modeling perspectives on mathematics problem solving, learning, and teaching*, 501-517.

Ludwigs, A. (2009). Mental models and problem solving: Technological solutions for measurement and assessment of the development of expertise. In Blumschein, P., Hung, W., Jonassen, D., & Strobel, J. (Eds.), *Model-Based Approaches to Learning: Using Systems Models and Simulations to Improve Understanding and Problem Solving in Complex Domains* (pp. 17–40). Boston: Sense Pub..

Porter, A., McMaken, J., Hwang, J., & Yang, R. (2011). Common core standards: The new U.S. intended curriculum. *Educational Researcher, 40*(3), 103–116. doi:10.3102/0013189X11405038.

Schoenfeld, A. H. (1992). Learning to think mathematically: Problem solving, metacognition, and sense making in mathematics. In *Handbook of research on mathematics teaching and learning* (pp. 334–370). Academic Press.

Silver, E. A. (1985). Research on teaching mathematical problem solving: Some under-represented themes and needed directions. In Silver, E. A. (Ed.), *Teaching and learning mathematical problem solving: Multiple research perspectives* (pp. 247–266). Hillsdale, NJ: Lawrence Erlbaum Associates.

Skemp, R. (1976). Instrumental understanding and relational understanding. *Mathematics Teacher*, 77, 20–26.

Sriraman, B., & English, L. (2010). *Theories of mathematics education: Seeking new frontiers.* Belrin. Springer-Verlag. doi:10.1007/978-3-642-00742-2.

Stigler, J. W., & Heibert, J. (2004). Improving mathematics teaching. *Educational Leadership*, 61(5), 12–17.

Van De Walle, J. A., Karp, K. S., & Bay-Williams, J. M. (2013). *Elementary and middle school mathematics: Teaching developmentally* (8th ed.). Boston: Pearson.

Zimmerman, B., Fritzla, T., Haapasalo, L., & Rehlich, H. (2011). Possible gain of IT in problem oriented learning environments from the viewpoint of history of mathematics and modern learning theories. *The Electronic Journal of Mathematics and Technology*, 5(2).

ADDITIONAL READING

Jimoyiannis, A., & Komis, V. (2001). Computer simulations in physics teaching and learning: A case study on students' understanding of trajectory motion. *Computers & Education*, 36(2), 183–204. doi:10.1016/S0360-1315(00)00059-2.

Schoenfeld, A. H. (1992). Learning to think mathematically: Problem solving, metacognition, and sense making in mathematics. In *Handbook of research on mathematics teaching and learning* (pp. 334–370). Academic Press.

KEY TERMS AND DEFINITIONS

Common Core Mathematical Practices: Describe varieties of expertise that mathematics educators at all levels should seek to develop in their students.

Common Core State Standards: Describe the knowledge and skills in English Language Arts and Mathematics that students will need.

Computer Model: A computer simulation, a computer model, or a computational model is a computer program that attempts to simulate an abstract model of a particular system.

Problem-Based Learning: A student-centered pedagogy in which students learn thinking skills and content knowledge about a subject through the experience of problem solving.

Problem Solving: A process that takes a problem description, a goal, and a knowledge base as input, and derives a solution that satisfies the goal.

Squeak Etoys: A media-rich, authoring environment with a simple powerful scripted object model for many kinds of objects created by end-users that runs on many platforms and is free and open source.

Chapter 10
PhET Interactive Simulations:
New Tools to Achieve Common Core Mathematics Standards

Karina K. R. Hensberry
University of Colorado Boulder, USA

Emily B. Moore
University of Colorado Boulder, USA

Ariel J. Paul
University of Colorado Boulder, USA

Noah S. Podolefsky
University of Colorado Boulder, USA

Katherine K. Perkins
University of Colorado Boulder, USA

ABSTRACT

This chapter focuses on the design and use of interactive simulations as a powerful tool for learning mathematics. Since 2002, the PhET Interactive Simulations project at the University of Colorado Boulder (http://phet.colorado.edu) has been developing and studying the use of interactive simulations in teaching and learning STEM. While the project's initial work focused on science learning, the project now includes a significant effort in mathematics learning. In this chapter, the authors describe the PhET project, including theoretical perspective, design goals, and research-based simulation design principles. They demonstrate how these design principles are applied to simulations, describe how they support achievement of the Common Core State Standards for Mathematics (CCSSM), and provide supporting evidence from individual student interviews. Finally, the authors discuss various approaches to using these simulations in class and provide guidance on leveraging their capabilities to support knowledge construction in mathematics in a uniquely engaging and effective way.

INTRODUCTION

The use of tools—concrete manipulatives, calculators, measurement devices, computers, etc.—has long been recognized as important in mathematics education, and advances in Computer Technology (CT) position virtual manipulatives and interactive simulations as powerful new tools for teaching and learning mathematics. National Council of Teachers of Mathematics ((NCTM), 2000) Technology Principal asserts that students can learn more mathematics more deeply with the appropriate

DOI: 10.4018/978-1-4666-4086-3.ch010

use of technology because it allows students to shift their focus from computation to reflection, decision making, reasoning, and problem solving. Educational research adds support to NCTM's call for the use of technology for teaching and learning mathematics. In a meta-analysis of relevant literature, Li and Ma (2010) concluded that CT can positively impact mathematics achievement.

Lei (2010) argues that the *quality* of educational technology—what and how it is used—is more predictive of student outcomes than the *quantity* of technology students interact with. Research supports Lei's notion that the first aspect of the quality of instruction—the what—is important. Characteristics of CT that impact student achievement include allowing students to experiment and test hypotheses, scaffolding students to avoid common error patterns (Suh, Moyer, & Heo, 2005), providing immediate feedback (Reimer & Moyer, 2005), and presenting information in multiple representational forms (Li & Ma, 2010; Roschelle et al., 2010; Vahey, Lara-Meloy, Moschkovich, & Velazquez, 2010). For example, in a large-scale study examining the impact of an interactive representational technology, Roschelle et al. (2010) found that students in the treatment classes performed equally well on standardized measures of basic mathematical knowledge and significantly better on measures of advanced mathematics than control group students who received "business as usual" instruction.

Regarding the second aspect of the quality of technology—how it is used (Lei, 2010)—Li and Ma (2010) found in their meta-analysis that effect sizes of CT were greatest when combined with instruction that aligned with mathematics reform. Other studies also suggest that instruction aligned with constructivist principles rather than drill and practice is necessary for CT to be effective (e.g., Vahey et al. 2010; Wenglinsky, 2005). For instance, problem solving is a key component of mathematics reform, and the use of CT in a problem-based learning environment was found to support students in developing computation and problem-solving skills (Bottge, Grant, Stephens, & Rueda, 2010). Reform instruction also stresses the use of manipulatives, and virtual manipulatives have been found to be as effective as, and sometimes more than, concrete manipulatives for improving student learning (Burns & Hamm, 2011; Lee & Chen, 2010; Moyer-Packenham & Westenskow, 2012; Moyer-Packenham & Suh, 2011; Reimer & Moyer, 2005; Suh et al., 2005; Yuan, Lee, & Wang, 2010). The immediate feedback provided by virtual manipulatives is important for helping students monitor their own understanding and learning of concepts, and they are easier and faster to use than concrete models or paper and pencil tools (Reimer & Moyer, 2005). Other aspects of reform mathematics teaching found to support students of various backgrounds and ability levels in learning from CT include: ample opportunities for discussion with peers (Vahey et al., 2010; Zahner, Velazquez, Moschkovich, Vahey, & Lara-Meloy, 2012); a focus on meaning and student construction of informal rules before formal introduction of rules and vocabulary (Suh et al., 2005; Vahey et al., 2010; Zahner et al., 2012); and addressing incorrect answers using higher-level moves (Zahner et al., 2012).

In this chapter, we introduce the PhET Interactive Simulations project at University of Colorado Boulder and explore in detail *what* aspects of the design make PhET simulations unique and effective, and *how* teachers can effectively integrate the simulations into their instruction. Since 2002, the PhET project has focused on understanding and leveraging the educational potential of interactive simulations through a combined effort of research and development. Here, we aim to provide a basis of knowledge about the design and use of PhET simulations that will support educators in (1) recognizing the multiple affordances provided by simulations, (2) better understanding how these affordances influence learning, and (3) effectively designing and implementing instruction that leverages these affordances to address the new Common Core State Standards for Mathematics (CCSSM).

We begin with some background information on the PhET project, including our theoretical perspective on learning, our design goals, and our research-based simulation design principles. Through examples, we demonstrate how these design principles are applied to simulations for teaching and learning mathematics and how they support achievement of the CCSSM. Excerpts from an interview of a student using a simulation provide an examples of how the simulation design supports student engagement in practices and content learning aligned with the CCSSM. Finally, we present various ways in which PhET simulations can be integrated into courses, and some effective strategies for designing and implementing lessons that leverage their capabilities.

PROJECT BACKGROUND

To date, the PhET Interactive Simulations project has developed over 125 interactive simulations to support STEM education, all accessible for free from our Website or downloadable for offline use. The overall mission of the project is to advance STEM literacy and education worldwide, and currently our Website has recorded over 90 million simulation runs to date with over 35 million simulations run in 2012. Broadly, the goals for each simulation are to engage students in exploration, to promote student conceptual understanding, and to increase student interest in and engagement with mathematics and science. To this end, the simulations are designed to be fun and interactive, to connect to the real world, to make the invisible visible, to provide multiple representations, and to allow rapid inquiry cycles.

The PhET project began with a focus on simulations for learning introductory physics concepts, and has since expanded to include simulations covering a range of topics across the science and mathematics subjects. Recently, with support from the Hewlett Foundation and the O'Donnell Foundation, the PhET project launched a significant new effort focused on the design and study of simulations for mathematics learning in upper-elementary and middle school.

A core component of the PhET project is that it is strongly grounded in research, drawing from research findings in the literature and the results of our own research (PhET Interactive Simulations, 2012a). Next, we describe our simulation design goals and principles along with some of the theory and research that inform them. Thus, while the project's focused effort on simulations for teaching and learning mathematics is relatively young, we have been able to inform our work in mathematics by combining our foundation of research and experience in simulation design and use in science with input from (1) new mathematics education researchers on our team, (2) published research on student learning, curriculum design, and education technology from the mathematics education community, (3) practicing mathematics teachers, and (4) the CCSSM.

Theory and Research Base

PhET's goals and design philosophy are influenced by a number of sources. Most fundamentally, we ground our work in the theoretical perspectives of Piaget, who argued that people "construct their own understanding" by actively engaging with content, and Vygotsky, who highlighted the importance of tools (e.g. sims) and the active role they play in mediating the learner's engagement with the content (Piaget, 1926; Vygotsky, 1978). Thus, we design sims to encourage and support the active process of knowledge construction – an interactive exchange between the student(s) and the content – rather than knowledge transmission.

Knowing that the design of the simulation will influence how students engage with the content and their process of construction, we seek additional guidance for our designs by drawing on the cognitive science and education research community findings on developing expertise and how people learn (Bransford, Brown, & Cocking, 2000; Duschl, Schweingruber, & Shouse, 2007; National Research Council, 2005). This research, for example, points to the importance of developing an underlying structure to organize knowledge that allows for efficient retrieval and application of ideas (Chi, Feltovich, & Glaser, 1981) and to monitoring and reflecting on one's own understanding (Schoenfeld, 1987). In interactive simulation design, feedback becomes a critical design tool that can be honed to aid learners in forming effective mental models and organizational structures, and to provide cues to refine their understanding. Research also shows that motivation and perspective towards learning significantly impacts learning choices, approaches, and outcomes (Dweck, 2000). We tailor the simulation design to promote sense-making and growth of understanding, as opposed to knowledge demonstration and answer-making, and redesign if our testing shows otherwise. Finally, research on

cognitive load (Sweller, 1988) and education technology design (e.g. Clark & Mayer, 2007) points to the need to attend to moderating and guiding student's cognitive attention through the choice and placement of controls, the visual representations and animations, and the feedback design.

Simulation Design Goals

With this perspective on how people learn, the PhET project has articulated a set of broad goals for students that underpin our simulation design work (PhET Interactive Simulations, 2012b). The goals were originally crafted for science learning, and have been modified slightly for application to mathematics. The results are PhET's goals for students, which are listed in Figure 1 and are well aligned with the many of the standards for mathematical practices outlined in the CCSSM as well as the literature on reform-based mathemat-

Figure 1. PhET's goals for students (© 2012, PhET Interactive Simulations, Used with permission)

Students will …
- See mathematics as accessible, understandable, and enjoyable
  - o Identify themselves as capable of understanding and "doing" mathematics
  - o Develop further interest in mathematics
  - o Experience the joy of and persist in problem solving
  - o View mathematics as more than a set of rules and procedures
- Make connections to everyday life (e.g. mathematics to the real world)
- Achieve conceptual learning
  - o Identify relationships and generalize patterns
  - o Engage in flexible thinking
  - o Make meaning of and translate between pictorial and mental models, and use them to make sense of mathematical concepts
  - o Develop facility with commonly-used representations and measurement tools (e.g. visual models, equations, number lines, tables, graphs, formulas, rulers, vectors, …)
  - o Coordinate across representations, models, and real world situations
- Engage in mathematical exploration with multiple, positive learning outcomes
  - o Formulate and ask questions, make conjectures, and justify conclusions
  - o Plan their solution pathway and reflect on the reasonableness of their results
  - o Test emerging ideas
  - o Engage in mathematical reasoning and argumentation
  - o Monitor and reflect on their own understanding (e.g. through self-assessment with simulation feedback, discussion with a partner, or teacher-led checks for understanding).
- Take and sense ownership of their learning experience
  - o Direct their own learning through exploration
  - o Persist through intellectual challenges
  - o Feel a sense of accomplishment

ics instruction. PhET's mathematics simulations are designed to support students in achieving these goals.

Simulation Design Principles

To be aligned with these perspectives and goals, interactive sims would be designed to allow and attract students to actively engage with the material—that is to explore and discover new ideas; to practice applying the ideas being learned; and to receive feedback on their thinking that would allow them to monitor and correct their own understanding. The sims would include features that tie to students' prior knowledge (e.g. real world connections) and include a structure that allows students to progressively refine and build upon prior understanding (e.g. scaffolding through simulation structure, multiple panels, and activity design). Sims would convey and promote expert-like skills, models, and organizational structures. Sims would encourage students to engage in questioning and sense making.

We achieve this type of environment by applying our design principles—a set of design strategies that have emerged from our work over the past 10 years and are informed by the research literature and over 400 individual interviews with students using PhET simulations (Adams et al., 2008a, 2008b; Podolefsky, Perkins, & Adams, 2010; Lancaster, Moore, Parson, & Perkins, 2013). Perhaps the most significant tool in PhET's design toolbox is our use of *implicit scaffolding* within interactive sims – an approach which allows the students to perceive the simulation as an engaging, open exploration space, while the implicit scaffolding provides cuing and guidance so students are inclined to interact with the simulation in productive ways. This scaffolding is built-in (e.g. through choice of controls, dynamic feedback, visual representations, sequence of challenges, etc.) and can focus students' attention on the most important aspects of the mathematics, illuminate causal relationships, cue interactions,

and reduce cognitive load; while simultaneously providing the freedom to take different pathways in exploring the content as their understanding evolves. Implicit scaffolding builds on prior work in tool and education technology design (Norman, 2002; Clark & Mayer, 2007), and is described in more detail elsewhere (Podolefsky, Paul, Moore, & Perkins, 2013).

PhET's design principles include:

- **Use Implicit Scaffolding:** Make careful design choices to naturally focus students' attention on important aspects of the content and enable construction of knowledge. Guide students without them feeling guided (Podolefsky, Paul, Moore, & Perkins, 2013).

- **Make Sims Highly Interactive:** Allow users to directly manipulate or control key parameters, tools, or settings in the simulation environment.

- **Provide Dynamic Feedback:** Provide real-time, visual feedback in response to user interactions, allowing testing of ideas, identification of patterns, and development of conceptual understanding.

- **Use Multiple, Linked Representations:** Provide multiple representations that are dynamically linked, to support development of a more robust and flexible understanding of a concept by allowing users to coordinate across these representations.

- **Allow Pedagogically Powerful Actions, Even if Difficult or Impossible in Real Life:** Allow direct access to actions that are not normally accessible, but pedagogically powerful for learning, such as slowing down time, continuously changing parameters, or instantaneously dividing objects into equal-sized pieces.

- **Provide an Intuitive Interface:** Create a highly intuitive and inviting user interface – one useable without explicit instruction – to engage users in learning the content, not the interface. Use minimal text, chosen to have clear meaning for the student or to be a technical term for which the student can develop an operational definition through exploration.

- **Emphasize Real World Connections:** Connect to everyday life experiences, and through that approach, build off prior knowledge and increase motivation by making the context relevant.

- **Create a Game-Like Environment that is Engaging, Fun, and Open:** Recognize that learning requires significant cognitive work and create a fun, engaging environment which triggers curiosity and a sense of challenge, motivating students to interact and explore at length.

Figure 2 provides an example of these simulation design principles in action, in tab 2 of the *Moving Man* simulation and tab 1 of the *Fractions*

Figure 2. PhET's Moving Man simulation (tab 2) and Fractions Intro simulation (tab 1) illustrate use of the simulation design principles (© 2012, PhET Interactive Simulations, Used with permission)

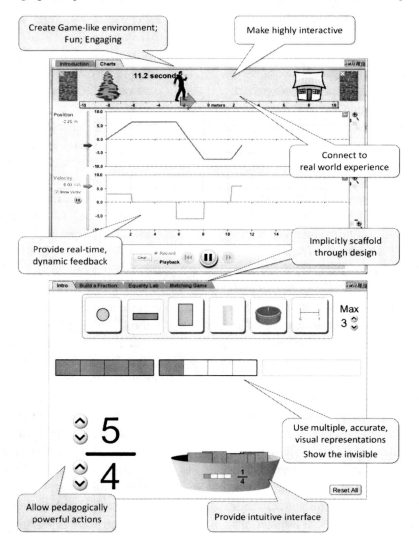

Intro simulation. The combination of interactivity and feedback can be particularly powerful for developing relationships, and can often include allowing actions that are difficult in real life. In the *Moving Man*, for instance, students can control the man's velocity directly, with the position slider or with the man himself, and through investigation can correlate negative velocities with motion to the left. In the *Fractions Intro* simulation, students can independently change the numerator and denominator and see immediate dynamic responses, helping students to build connections to number of pieces and piece size. Both simulations include multiple representations – such as values, graphs, vectors, shapes (including partitioning), and number lines – and allow coordination with a change in one representation dynamically coupled to the other representation.

For students to explore and discover the deep conceptual ideas embedded these simulations, they must actively engage with the simulation in productive ways. The intuitive interface, real-world connections, and game-like environment are critical to engaging students and making their interaction productive. The *Moving Man* simulation and the *Fractions Intro* use familiar, easy-to-use controls (e.g. buttons, sliders, play/pause) and everyday objects to cue productive interactions (e.g. buckets hold things that I can take out). Both simulations include a series of tabs across the top, which allow scaffolding of complexity as students explore the simulation. For instance, in tab 1 (Intro) of *Fractions Intro* students can freely explore the meaning of the numerator and denominator, while in tab 2 (Build a Fraction) they can test their understanding with different challenges, in tab 3 (Equality Lab) they can explore equivalent fractions, and in tab 4 (Matching Game) they can test their understanding of matching different representations of fractions.

Overall, our interviews with students have demonstrated that well-designed interactive simulations typically engage students in a cycle of self-generated questions where the dynamic, visual feedback of the simulation allows them to progressively build, monitor, and correct their understanding as they make sense of the content and construct their own mental models. We call this mode of learning Engaged Exploration (Adams et al., 2008a, 2008b;Podolefsky et al., 2010), and we have observed it with both our mathematics and science simulations.

PHET SIMULATIONS FOR MATHEMATICS EDUCATION

PhET simulations can be used to support student engagement in content learning and mathematical practices aligned with the CCSSM. In this section, we explore this notion and provide an excerpt of a student interview as an example of the ways in which these simulations can support standards-based mathematics learning.

Addressing the Content Standards

Aligning simulations with the Common Core State Standards is an overarching goal of the simulation design process. To this end, the first phase of this process involves outlining learning goals and identifying which standards will be addressed. For example, consider the *Fractions Intro* simulation shown in Figure 2. This simulation explicitly addresses third and fourth grade CCSSM that fall under the Number and Operations – Fractions and Geometry domains (Table 1).

There are several mathematics simulations currently available on the PhET Website that are designed to address a range of content standards (Table 2). There are additionally several simulations currently in development that cover a range of K-12 topics such as, fraction operations, graphing inequalities, functions, number lines and number sense.

Throughout the design process, we frequently return to the standards we identified to ensure they are being addressed. For instance, we conduct

Table 1. Example of common core state standards addressed in Fractions Intro simulation

Standard	Description
3.NF – Develop understanding of fractions as numbers	1. Understand a fraction 1/b as the quantity formed by 1 part when a whole is partitioned into b equal parts; understand a fraction a/b as the quantity formed by a parts of size 1/b. 3. Explain equivalence of fractions in special cases, and compare fractions by reasoning about their size. a. Understand two fractions as equivalent (equal) if they are the same size, or the same point on a number line. b. Recognize and generate simple equivalent fractions, e.g., 1/2 = 2/4, 4/6 = 2/3). Explain why the fractions are equivalent, e.g., by using a visual fraction model. c. Express whole numbers as fractions, and recognize fractions that are equivalent to whole numbers. *Examples: Express 3 in the form 3 = 3/1; recognize that 6/1 = 6; locate 4/4 and 1 at the same point of a number line diagram.*
3.G – Reason with shapes and their attributes	2. Partition shapes into parts with equal areas. Express the area of each part as a unit fraction of the whole. For example, partition a shape into 4 parts with equal area, and describe the area of each part as 1/4 of the area of the shape.
4.NF – Build fractions from unit fractions by applying and extending previous understandings of operations on whole numbers.	3. Understand a fraction a/b with a > 1 as a sum of fractions 1/b. b. Decompose a fraction into a sum of fractions with the same denominator in more than one way, recording each decomposition by an equation. Justify decompositions, e.g., by using a visual fraction model. Examples: 3/8 = 1/8 + 1/8 + 1/8; 3/8 = 1/8 + 2/8; 2 1/8 = 1 + 1 + 1/8 = 8/8 + 8/8 + 1/8

Table 2. Examples of mathematics topics addressed in PhET simulations

Topic	Example Simulation(s)
Graphing linear equations	Graphing: Lines
Graphing quadratic equations	Equation Grapher; Projectile Motion
Graphing derivatives and integrals	Calculus Grapher; Moving Man
Estimation	Estimation
Probability	Plinko Probability; Radioactive Dating Game
Data analysis	Curve Fitting
Modeling with Functions	Build an Atom; Balancing Act; Under Pressure; Gas Properties
Arithmetic	Arithmetic
Equivalent Fractions	Fractions Intro; Build a Fraction; Fraction Matcher
Vectors	Vector Addition; Forces and Motion
Trigonometry	Ladybug Revolution; Pendulum

student interviews before publishing a simulation to not only determine whether the interface is user-friendly and engaging, but also to ensure students are able to interpret and learn the content we target with the simulation.

In addition to mathematics-specific simulations, there are many PhET simulations that focus on science topics. These can and are being used in mathematics instruction to address the CCSSM—for instance, by providing exploratory real-world contexts in which to investigate and apply mathematical concepts (see Sokolowski & Rackley, 2011). Figure 3 provides two examples of such simulations. The first, *Balancing Act*, addresses science topics such as force, torque, and rotation, but can also be used to support students in learning about proportional reasoning—an important topic for middle school mathematics—and two-variable functions (distance and mass) (Hallinen et al., 2012). The second, *Build an Atom*, is a chemistry simulation that students can explore with the goal of writing simple functions for an atom's mass or charge and choosing the appropriate independent variables, thus addressing the high school mathematics standards on modeling. Therefore, while some simulations are explicitly designed to address mathematics content standards, others can be leveraged for this purpose.

Figure 3. PhET's Balancing Act simulation (tab 2) and Build an Atom simulation (tab 1) illustrate science simulations that provide real-world applications of mathematics topics (© 2012, PhET Interactive Simulations, Used with permission)

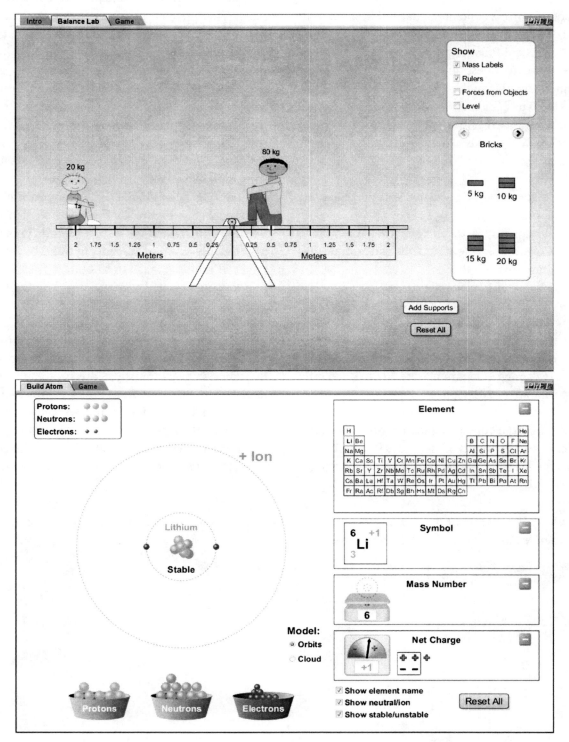

Addressing the Standards for Mathematical Practice

In addition to the content standards, PhET simulations can help teachers address the Standards for Mathematical Practices outlined in the CCSSM. These practices describe the type of expertise in mathematics that students should be encouraged to develop. The Standards for Mathematical Practice, which are based on the NCTM (2000) process standards and strands of mathematical proficiency (Kilpatrick, Swafford, & Findell, 2001), are:

1. Make sense of problems and persevere in solving them.
2. Reason abstractly and quantitatively.
3. Construct viable arguments and critique the reasoning of others.
4. Model with mathematics.
5. Use appropriate tools strategically.
6. Attend to precision.
7. Look for and make use of structure.
8. Look for and express regularity in repeated reasoning (Common Core State Standards Initiative, 2010, pp. 6-8).

As with the content standards, many of these practices are explicitly addressed in PhET simulations but teachers can support students to engage in all of them by the ways in which they choose to structure activities. Consider the first practice, *make sense of problems and persevere in solving them.* This practice requires students to plan a solution path rather than beginning immediately on the solution, monitor and evaluate their own progress, alter their solution path if necessary, and understand the correspondence between multiple representations. Recently, the second tab of *Fractions Intro* was expanded upon and now exists as a stand-alone simulation, *Build a Fraction.* In *Build a Fraction*, students are given target fractions that they must build with a finite number of cards, and the targets and cards are either pictorial or numerical (See Figure 4). For these challenges, we have constrained the available cards in order to implicitly scaffold students to build the same target in multiple ways or to build a fraction in a more sophisticated way (such as building 1½ with two half pieces and two quarter pieces rather than one whole piece and one half piece). This simulation, therefore, pushes students to think ahead about how they will build their targets – if they stick to less sophisticated ways to build the target fractions they will run out of cards before completing the challenge. It also allows them to monitor their progress and understanding by providing instantaneous feedback about the correctness of their answers. Finally, *Build a Frac-*

Figure 4. Illustration of two types of challenges in PhET's Build a Fraction simulation (© 2012, PhET Interactive Simulations, Used with permission)

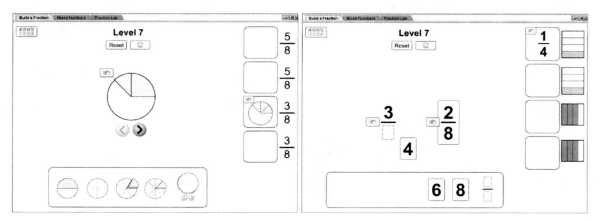

tion requires students to correctly interpret both written/numerical and pictorial representations of fractions and understand the relationship between the two types of representations to successfully complete the challenges in the simulation.

As another example, consider the *Graphing: Lines* simulation, in which students can manipulate parameters (e.g., (x_1, y_1), m, or b) of a linear equation and notice how the graph of the line is changed. Conversely, they can manipulate the graph and notice how the equation is changed. This symmetry not only supports students to translate between written symbols (the equation) and pictorial (graphical) representations of a line (Lesh, 1979), but it provides them with an opportunity to notice patterns, make conjectures about the purpose of each parameter in the point-slope and slope-intercept forms of a line, and then test their understanding by setting up different cases. Furthermore, teachers may choose to employ such a simulation in class to provide a common experience for students upon which to base classroom discussions. Thus, *Graphing: Lines* can be used to address the third and seventh Standards for Mathematical Practice (i.e., *construct viable arguments and critique the reasoning of others*, and *look for and make use of structure*).

Example from a Student Interview

To further illustrate the ways in which PhET simulations can support the implementation of the Common Core State Standards for Mathematics, we provide an excerpt from a student interview. In general, our approach to interviewing students involves very little interaction between the interviewer and interviewee. Our goal is to observe how students naturally engage with the simulation with minimal influences – that is, to observe the exploration patterns they follow, the questions they ask themselves, and their interpretation of the representations and feedback displayed by the simulation. Thus, the student is first asked to think aloud as he or she explores the simulation

and is given no further instructions or feedback as to the correctness of actions and statements. After the student has fully finished their exploration, the interviewer may ask some follow-up questions to probe the students' understanding – as seen in the following excerpt. Interviews are video recorded, and the student's onscreen activity is also captured using Camtasia screen recording software, allowing us to include student actions in the interview transcripts.

Figure 5 is a screenshot from an interview with a female fourth grade student. Here, about 37 minutes into the interview and after the student had finished exploring, the interviewer asked her to explain what the numerator and denominator are. The interviewer specifically did not use the terms "numerator" and "denominator," however, in an attempt to avoid cueing a rote definition. The student provided an explanation while gesturing with the mouse to different representations on the screen.

I: So I'm curious how would you explain the, the difference between the top number and the bottom number in a fraction? How would you describe those?

S: [Hovers cursor over one of the numerators in the Equality Lab tab] *Well I think the top number is like* [clicks on the Intro tab] *how much of something there is.* [Cursor points at the numerator] *Like there are 47* [moves cursor across the six cake representations] *pieces of cake within all of these shapes.*

I: Okay. And how about the bottom number?

S: I think that's... [begins clicking the down spinner for the numerator. Eighth-sized pieces of cake move back to the bucket one at a time; stops clicking the spinner when the numerator reaches 40, leaving the sixth circular outline of a cake empty] *how many shapes fit – well, how many shapes* [clicks on one eighth piece of cake

Figure 5. Screenshot of an early version of PhET's Fractions Intro simulation (tab 1) illustrates one student's use of the simulation (© 2012, PhET Interactive Simulations, Used with permission)

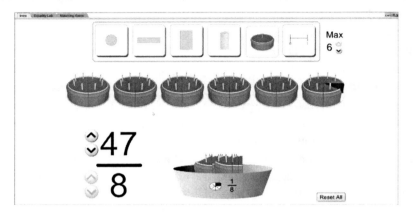

and moves it around inside the bucket] *can fit in this shape* [gestures with the cursor to the empty circular outline of the cake. Clicks the denominator spinner down one so it changes from 8 to 7] *Or, how many little pieces can fit.*

There are several points worth noting regarding this student's answer to the interviewer's questions. First, the student clearly knew how to navigate and use the simulation without any guidance from the interviewer, supporting the suggestion for open exploration time outlined in the following section on designing and facilitating lesson. Second, she used the simulation as a tool for communication. The student switched tabs from the "Equality Lab" to the "Intro", and then described the numerator while gesturing toward the numerical and pictorial representations. She also gestured toward the one-eighth-sized pieces of cake and then toward the empty outline of the whole cake when describing the denominator as being the number of smaller pieces that "fit" in the larger whole.

Third, several of the CCSSM Practices suggest that students need to learn the multiple ways of representing a mathematical concept, know when each of those representations is useful, and understand the correspondence between multiple representations. *Fractions Intro* includes several different representations of fractions—number line, symbolic/numerical, virtual manipulatives/pictorial (e.g., rectangle, circle), real-world (e.g., cake, beaker)—and as any one is modified, the other representations change to reflect that modification, thereby supporting students to draw connections between each of the representations. In this excerpt, the student clicked on spinners to modify the value of the numerator and denominator, and then pointed her mouse toward the cake representation in the center of the screen or clicked and moved the fractional pieces in the bucket as she spoke, indicating an understanding of the relationship between the symbolic/numerical, pictorial, and real-world representations.

Fourth, it appears that this student used the simulation to investigate and test her understanding. For example, *before* she changed the denominator from eight to seven, she *predicted* that by changing the value of the denominator, the number of cake pieces that fit in the whole cake would change. And then she made the change, and received the feedback from the simulation that she her prediction was correct.

Finally, the simulation supported the student to understand the meaning of the parts of a fraction rather than just teaching her a definition to be memorized. She did not use the formal terms of numerator and denominator (nor did the interviewer), but she was able to communicate her understanding of these concepts. In a classroom setting, the teacher, as a facilitator, can introduce the formal mathematical vocabulary after the concept is understood. This approach is consistent with educational research and standards-based instruction (National Council of Teachers of Mathematics, 2000; Zahner et al., 2012), which suggests students should use familiar/informal language when discussing new ideas and the teacher can later introduce formal vocabulary terms.

Thus, this episode highlights that in using the simulation, this student was able to communicate mathematically, draw connections between representations, make predictions, and use a tool (the simulation) to confirm those predictions and to communicate her ideas, and focus on concepts in a manner consistent with the Standards for Mathematical Practice.

IMPLEMENTING PHET SIMULATIONS IN CLASS

While the PhET simulations are honed—through their design and user-testing—to provide students with new possibilities for engaging with and making sense of the mathematics, students' overall learning experience and their achievement of the practices and content standards outlined in the CCSSM will be influenced by how the simulations are integrated into instruction. One goal for the PhET project is to provide highly flexible tools, allowing the teacher to customize which simulations they use and how they integrate them into their teaching. The teacher best knows their students' needs, the technology resources available to them, and the particular goals they most need to achieve on any given school day.

Some ways that PhET simulations can be used in teaching include:

- **In-Class, as a Demonstration:** With the simulation projected onto a screen or interactive whiteboard, the teacher uses it to provide a dynamic visualization to better communicate ideas to the students.

- **In-Class, with Clicker Questions or Other Interactive Discussion:** The teacher, for example, poses a question where students must predict what will happen when the teacher makes a change in the simulation. Or the teacher challenges students with how to accomplish something in the simulation, followed by a think-pair-share, and then invites a student up to try out their suggestion with the simulation projected onto a screen or interactive whiteboard. A key characteristic of this use strategy is that students are actively processing the ideas in the simulation—by discussing with their peers, sharing ideas and reasoning with the class, or using the simulation in front of the class to help demonstrate, communicate, or test an idea.

- **In-Class, as Part or all of an Inquiry-Based Classroom Activity:** With enough in-class computers or a computer lab, students can work in small groups to explore the simulation paired with an activity sheet provided by the teacher. While the simulations can be used in many ways, they are specifically designed to support inquiry-based learning. Strategies for activity design and facilitation are discussed in more detail in the following section.

- **As Homework:** Simulations can play many different roles within homework assignments. Teachers can have students openly explore and investigate a simulation—recording patterns they see, ideas they learn, or questions they have—to seed ideas and help prime students before covering the topic in class. Or teachers can design homework questions around the simulations that help deepen, reinforce, or extend ideas after they have been addressed in class.

- **As Individual Remediation or Advancement Resource:** Teachers have used simulations to enable differentiated learning opportunities within the classroom. Since demands on teachers' time often forms a significant constraint to supporting differentiated learning, the feedback built into the simulation can help students who are working on their own while reviewing a topic not previously mastered, or support students who have already mastered the topic at the level expected, but who want to go further or to learn other topics independently.

The last bullet speaks to the ability of PhET simulations to be used across a broad range of populations—from lower performing students to accelerated students. The design naturally accommodates individual student differences by allowing students to take a learning path that matches their needs—taking more time to investigate some aspects they find confusing and taking less time on aspects they are comfortable with—and by allowing teachers to hone the plan of their simulation-based activity to match their learning goals. In the *Graphing: Lines* simulation, for instance, younger or lower performing students might limit their focus to determining the slope of an individual line whereas teachers could challenge advanced students to find and explain patterns for the slopes of perpendicular lines.

This use of simulations across populations is also supported by technology research in mathematics education. While some teachers may be hesitant to use computer technology with their lower performing students (Roschelle et al., 2010), some evidence suggests that computer technology may be an important strategy for supporting struggling students. Li and Ma (2010) found in their meta-analysis that effect sizes were largest for special needs students, and other studies (e.g., Roschelle et al., 2010; Vahey et al., 2010; Zahner et al., 2012) demonstrate that computer technology can be effective with culturally and linguistically diverse students. To further support use with diverse populations, the PhET simulations are easily translatable and are available in 70 languages—including native languages of many English language learners.

As we highlighted in the design section, the PhET simulations provide students with an open, yet implicitly-scaffolded, environment in which they can engage in exploring and making sense of core concepts in mathematics. In this way, PhET simulations are well designed to support student-centered, inquiry-based teaching. While our work in designing lessons and observing simulation use in the K-12 classroom has largely revolved around science content, many of the recommendations emerging from that work are not content-specific and will likely to translate well to teaching mathematical ideas.

Designing and Facilitating Student-Centered, Inquiry-Based Lessons

The activity design and facilitation strategies described here support student-centered lessons – that is, lessons where students engage in inquiry around mathematical content, discuss their thoughts, and share ideas. Goals are to emphasize sense-making rather than answer-making, and for learning through interaction with the simulation to be the central focus. We have observed simulation-based lessons that provide powerful opportunities to promote student agency where students actively drive their learning, to hear and value student ideas, and to build on students' prior knowledge. We have observed teachers leveraging the design of the simulation to practice responsive teaching, flexibly adapting to emergent student ideas.

Typically, an inquiry-based lesson includes an activity sheet; however, how the activity sheet is structured and how the question prompts are written can significantly influence students' experiences. When activity sheets are too structured or include simulation-related procedural instructions, students' natural tendencies for sense-making and question-asking with the simulation can be undermined. We recommend designing more open, modular activities that allow teachers to take advantage of teachable moments as they arise, to respond to students' discoveries, to allow for student collaboration, and to facilitate discussions.

Based on our work with middle school science teachers and students, we compiled some teacher resources (Perkins, Moore, Podolefsky, Lancaster, & Denison, 2012; PhET Interactive Simulations, 2012b) and summarize some key recommendations here:

- **Begin with 5-10 Minutes of Open Exploration Time:** During this time, students explore the simulation without any specific instructions. We have found that this approach helps teachers create a more student-centered learning experience (Podolefsky, Rehn, & Perkins, 2013). It can: develop students' ownership of the simulation as their tool for learning; decrease the need for simulation-related procedural instructions; help establish a sense-making mode of student learning rather than answer-making; reduce later off-task exploration; and engage students.

- **Avoid Explicit Direction on how to Manipulate the Simulation:** When students are told explicitly in the activity sheet which controls to use or not use, we see students focusing on following the directions, sometimes blindly. Thus, we recommend avoiding explicit instructions (e.g. "What is the effect of changing the numerator spinner?" or "Fill 1 cake with 4 pieces, now increase the denominator by 1, explain what happens?"), and instead asking more open questions (e.g. "Explore the simulation and record your ideas about what determines how much cake you have.")

- **Keep Activity Sheet Short and use Minimal Wording:** Shorter activity sheets (1-2 pages) allow opportunities for stu-

dents and teachers to engage in meaningful simulation exploration and responsive discussions, as opposed to trying to "get through" the entire activity. In addition, keeping each written prompt short also helps frame the activity sheet as a helpful tool for students to guide and organize their progress towards the learning objectives.

- **Seize Opportunities for Games or Challenges:** From interviews, we see that students make and enjoy games and challenges within the sims. Thus, designing sections of the activity sheet to leverage games or challenges within the simulation that relate to the activity's learning objectives can be effective – engaging students to use the simulations to explore a concept, increasing classroom discussion and stimulating student questions. While some simulations have built-in games, we have also found the following sorts of prompts useful in designing activities:
  ○ **Find all the ways to...** make 3/4. *(Build a Fraction – Fraction Lab Tab)*
  ○ **What's the largest...** slope you can make? *(Graphing: Lines)*
  ○ **How many...** levels can you complete in 5 minutes? *(Build a Fraction)*
  ○ **List the minimum required information...** to know the man is moving to the right. *(Moving Man)*
  ○ **What are two ways to...** increase the quantity of cake displayed? *(Fractions Intro)*
  ○ **How can you make...** The cake pieces ...**smaller?** *(Fractions Intro)*
  ○ **Develop a rule/equation for...** determining the charge of an atom. *(Build an Atom)*
  ○ **Develop a strategy for...** improving your estimations. *(Estimation)*

Any of these can be followed by the phrase "and explain why that makes sense" or "and explain your reasoning" or similar.

- **Scaffold with Tables:** Tables can provide a framework for productive exploration without being overly prescriptive, and offer a well-defined place for students to record responses to open-ended questions. Figure 6 illustrates an example table structure that orients students to cue in on patterns that underlie key conceptual aspects of the learning objectives. Providing simulation representations like the blank balance in Figure 6 also focuses students on balancing objects and recording results, rather than drawing unnecessary pictures of the simulation.

- **Solicit Student Ideas:** Provide opportunities for students to practice mathematical sense-making and argumentation. Teachers can seize opportunities to facilitate rich, student-centered class discussions by asking students to share their ideas and inviting students to demonstrate their findings or test their ideas using the classroom-projected simulation. In addition, encouraging and listening to student-student conversations can also provide additional practice as well as ideas for productive class discussions.

Overall, PhET simulations provide an opportunity for teachers to design a student-centered classroom environment where students can feel a sense of ownership over the learning tool (the simulation) and can engage in authentic sense-making around rich mathematical concepts.

CONCLUSION

The purpose of this chapter has been to introduce the PhET Interactive Simulations project and provide a depiction of the qualities of this technology (Lei, 2010) that can support the implementation of the Common Core State Standards for Mathematics. We began by addressing the *what* of this technology by describing the theory and research base underlying simulation development and outlined our design principles. Next we discussed in detail the ways in which PhET simulations can address the CCSSM and provided support for this argument with an excerpt from a student interview. Finally, we provided suggestions to teachers on how to use simulations in class and to write student-centered, inquiry-based activities, thereby describing the quality of *how* this technology is and can be used to engage students and support learning.

Getting Started: Resources for Teachers

Today, teachers are asked to address many standards. PhET simulations provide an opportunity

Figure 6. Example of using a table-structured prompt with the Balancing Act simulation, Intro tab. The prompt cues student exploration towards discovery of important patterns, but avoids providing explicit procedures for how to manipulate the simulation (© 2012, PhET Interactive Simulations, Used with permission).

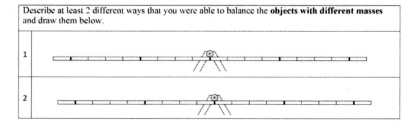

for teachers to simultaneously address both the *content* standards and the *mathematical practice* standards, as well as help students make connections between mathematics and real-world applications. Several resources on the PhET Website can help teachers to get started using PhET simulations. In addition to the resources described here, the PhET Website archives teacher workshop and Webinar handouts and, when available, provides links to videos (https://phet.colorado.edu/en/for-teachers/workshops).

To find simulations on a particular topic, teachers can either browse the simulations by using the left-hand navigation panel, which organizes simulations by subject or by grade, or use the search feature by typing a keyword into the search box. Each simulation has a dedicated Webpage that includes links to run the simulation online, download the simulation for offline use, or embed the simulation into their own Webpage. In addition, the simulation page includes resources for teachers. For instance, each page lists the main topics, provides examples of learning goals, and links to a "Teacher Guide" document specific to that simulation. These "Teacher Guide" documents include tips about the controls, describe any important modeling assumptions or approaches, summarize some of the interesting insights into student thinking and use from our student interviews, and provide suggestions for using the simulation in class.

PhET's activity database allows teachers to upload and share any simulation-based teaching materials—clicker questions, in-class activities, homework, lecture notes, etc.—with each other. Teachers can either search or browse the activity database directly, or view the activities associated with a particular simulation from that simulation's dedicated Webpage (in the "Teaching Ideas" section). While PhET's focused effort in mathematics is relatively new, there are some posted activities written for mathematics classes. We encourage readers to share any activities they create and grow this library.

Looking Forward

In the past, most of our research on simulation design and use has focused on science topics. While some of what we have learned from these studies will translate to mathematics, every discipline is unique with unique goals, practices, and content learning challenges for students. Thus, we are currently building on the work in the mathematics education community and focusing our research efforts on simulation design and implementation toward student achievement in mathematics.

Contingent on funding, PhET plans to continue to expand our mathematics simulation offerings, and we encourage readers to provide suggestions for additional PhET simulations by contacting phethelp@colorado.edu. In addition, by 2014, the PhET Website will include significantly more teacher resources, available through an all-new "Teach" side of the Website. Planned resources include curriculum alignment, activity design and facilitation, example videos of PhET use, annotated activities, searchable standards alignment, and individual teacher accounts allowing teachers to build collections of simulations or activities.

Based on what we have learned from existing literature on teaching with technology as well as our own student interviews and classroom observations, we believe PhET simulations can serve as a powerful new tool for mathematics educators, especially when paired with instruction that draws on reform-based teaching practices and the recommendations for designing and facilitating lessons outlined in this chapter.

ACKNOWLEDGMENT

We thank the entire PhET team for their contributions and dedication to this work with special thanks to the software development team of Sam Reid, Chris Malley, John Blanco, Jon Olson, and Mike Dubson. We also thank all of our teacher partners and their students for their participation in these efforts. This work was supported by grants from the O'Donnell Foundation, the Hewlett Foundation, and the National Science Foundation (DRK12-1020362).

REFERENCES

Adams, W. K., Reid, S., LeMaster, R., McKagan, S. B., Perkins, K. K., Dubson, M., & Wieman, C. E. (2008a). A study of educational simulations part I - Engagement and learning. *Journal of Interactive Learning Research*, *19*(3), 397–419.

Adams, W. K., Reid, S., LeMaster, R., McKagan, S. B., Perkins, K. K., Dubson, M., & Wieman, C. E. (2008b). A study of educational simulations part II – Interface design. *Journal of Interactive Learning Research*, *19*(4), 551–577.

Bottge, B. A., Grant, T. S., Stephens, A. C., & Rueda, E. (2010). Advancing the math skills of middle school students in technology education classrooms. *NASSP Bulletin*, *94*(2), 81–106. doi:10.1177/0192636510379902.

Bransford, J., Brown, A. L., & Cocking, R. R. (Eds.). (2000). *How people learn: Brain, mind, experience, and school.* Washington, DC: National Academy Press.

Burns, B. A., & Hamm, E. M. (2011). A comparison of concrete and virtual manipulative use in third- and fourth-grade mathematics. *School Science and Mathematics*, *111*(6), 256–261. doi:10.1111/j.1949-8594.2011.00086.x.

Chi, M., Feltovich, P., & Glaser, R. (1981). Categorization and representation of physics problems by experts and novices. *Cognitive Science, 5*(2), 152, 121.

Clark, R. C., & Mayer, R. E. (2007). *e-Learning and the science of instruction: Proven guidelines for consumers and designers of multimedia learning* (2nd ed.). San Francisco: Pfeiffer.

Common Core State Standards Initiative. (2010). *Common core state standards for mathematics.* CCSSI.

Duschl, R. A., Schweingruber, H. A., & Shouse, A. W. (Eds.). (2007). *Taking science to school: Learning and teaching science in grades K-8.* Washington, DC: National Academies Press.

Dweck, C. S. (2000). *Self-theories: Their role in motivation, personality, and development.* Philadelphia, PA: Psychology Press.

Hallinen, N. R., Chi, M., Chin, D. B., Prempeh, J., Blair, K. P., & Schwartz, D. L. (2013). Applying cognitive developmental psychology to middle school physics learning: The rule assessment method. In *Proceedings of 2012 Physics Education Research Conference.* Academic Press.

Kilpatrick, J., Swafford, J., & Findell, B. (Eds.). (2001). *Adding it up: Helping children learn mathematics.* Washington, DC: The National Academies Press.

Lancaster, K., Moore, E., Parson, R., & Perkins, K. (2013). Insights from using PhET's design principles for interactive chemistry simulations. In *Proceedings of Pedagogic Roles of Animations and Simulations.* ACS.

Lee, C.-Y., & Chen, M.-P. (2010). Taiwanese junior high school students' mathematics attitudes and perceptions towards virtual manipulatives. *British Journal of Educational Technology, 41*(2), E17–E21. doi:10.1111/j.1467-8535.2008.00877.x.

Lei, J. (2010). Quantity versus quality: A new approach to examine the relationship between technology use and student outcomes. *British Journal of Educational Technology*, *41*(3), 455–472. doi:10.1111/j.1467-8535.2009.00961.x.

Lesh, R. (1979). Mathematical learning disabilities: Considerations for identification, diagnosis, and remediation. In Lesh, R., Mierkiewicz, B., & Kantowski, M. G. (Eds.), *Applied Mathematical Problem Solving* (pp. 111–180). Columbus, OH: ERIC/SMEAC.

Li, Q., & Ma, X. (2010). A meta-analysis of the effects of computer technology on school students' mathematics learning. *Educational Psychology Review*, *22*(3), 215–243. doi:10.1007/s10648-010-9125-8.

Moyer-Packenham, P. S., & Suh, J. (2011). Learning mathematics with technology: The influence of virtual manipulatives on different achievement groups. *Journal of Computers in Mathematics and Science Teaching*.

Moyer-Packenham, P. S., & Westenskow, A. (2012). *Effects of virtual manipulatives on student achievement and mathematics learning.* Paper presented at the Annual Meeting of the American Educational Research Association (AERA). Vancouver, Canada.

National Council of Teachers of Mathematics. (2000). *Principles and standards for school mathematics.* Reston, VA: NCTM.

National Research Council. (2005). *How students learn: History, mathematics, and science in the classroom.* Washington, DC: National Academies Press.

Norman, D. A. (2002). *The design of everyday things.* New York: Basic Books.

Perkins, K., Moore, E., Podolefsky, N., Lancaster, K., & Denison, C. (2012). Towards research-based strategies for using PhET simulations in middle school physical science classes. *AIP Conference Proceedings*, *1413*(1), 295–298. doi:10.1063/1.3680053.

PhET Interactive Simulations. (2012a). *PhET publications.* Retrieved from http://phet.colorado.edu/en/research

PhET Interactive Simulations. (2012b). *PhET's teacher resources: Goals, facilitation, and activity design.* Retrieved from https://phet.colorado.edu/en/contributions/view/3610

Piaget, J. (1926). *The language and thought of the child.* New York: Harcourt, Brace, Jovanovich.

Podolefsky, N. S., Paul, A., Moore, E., & Perkins, K. K. (2013). *Implicit scaffolding as a design approach for interactive simulations: Theoretical foundations and empirical evidence.* Academic Press.

Podolefsky, N. S., Perkins, K. K., & Adams, W. K. (2010). Factors promoting engaged exploration with computer simulations. *Physical Review Special Topics - Physics. Education Research*, *6*(2), 020117.

Podolefsky, N. S., Rehn, D., & Perkins, K. (2013). Affordances of play for student agency and student-centered pedagogy. In *Proceedings of the 2012 Physics Education Research Conference.* Academic Press.

Reimer, K., & Moyer, P. S. (2005). Third-graders learn about fractions using virtual manipulatives: A classroom study. *Journal of Computers in Mathematics and Science Teaching*, *24*(1), 5–25.

Roschelle, J., Shechtman, N., Tatar, D., Hegedus, S., Hopkins, B., & Empson, S. et al. (2010). Integration of technology, curriculum, and professional development for advancing middle school mathematics three large-scale studies. *American Educational Research Journal*, *47*(4), 833–878. doi:10.3102/0002831210367426.

Schoenfeld, A. H. (1987). What's all the fuss about meta-cognition. In Schoenfeld, A. H. (Ed.), *Cognitive Science and Mathematics Education* (pp. 189–215). Hillsdale, NJ: Lawrence Erlbaum Associates.

Sokolowski, A., & Rackley, R. (2011). Teaching harmonic motion in trigonometry: Inductive inquiry supported by physics simulations. *Australian Senior Mathematics Journal*, *25*(1), 45–53.

Suh, J., Moyer, P. S., & Heo, H.-J. (2005). Examining technology uses in the classroom: Developing fraction sense using virtual manipulative concept tutorials. *Journal of Interactive Online Learning*, *3*(4), 1–21.

Sweller, J. (1988). Cognitive load during problem solving: Effects on learning. *Cognitive Science*, *12*, 257–285. doi:10.1207/s15516709cog1202_4.

Vahey, P., Lara-Meloy, T., Moschkovich, J., & Velazquez, G. (2010). Representational technology for learning mathematics: An investigation of teaching practices in Latino/a Classrooms. In *Proceedings of the 9th International Conference of the Learning Sciences*. Chicago, IL: Academic Press.

Vygotsky, L. S. (1978). *Mind in society: The development of higher psychological processes* (Cole, M., John-Steiner, V., Scribner, S., & Souberman, E., Eds.). 14th ed.). Boston: Harvard University Press.

Wenglinsky, H. (2005). *Using technology wisely: The keys to success in schools*. New York: Teachers College Press.

Yuan, Y., Lee, C.-Y., & Wang, C.-H. (2010). A comparison study of polyominoes explorations in a physical and virtual manipulative environment. *Journal of Computer Assisted Learning*, *26*(4), 307–316. doi:10.1111/j.1365-2729.2010.00352.x.

Zahner, W., Velazquez, G., Moschkovich, J., Vahey, P., & Lara-Meloy, T. (2012). Mathematics teaching practices with technology that support conceptual understanding for Latino/a students. *The Journal of Mathematical Behavior*, *31*(4), 431–446. doi:10.1016/j.jmathb.2012.06.002.

ADDITIONAL READING

Adams, W. K., Reid, S., LeMaster, R., McKagan, S. B., Perkins, K. K., Dubson, M., & Wieman, C. E. (2008). A study of educational simulations part I - Engagement and learning. *Journal of Interactive Learning Research*, *19*(3), 397–419.

Finkelstein, N. D., Adams, W. K., Keller, C. J., Perkins, K. K., & Wieman, C. E. (2006). HighTech tools for teaching physics: The physics education technology project. *Journal of Online Teaching and Learning*, *2*(3), 110–121.

Perkins, K. K., Loeblein, P. J., & Dessau, K. L. (2010). Sims for science: Powerful tools to support inquiry-based teaching. *Science Teacher (Normal, Ill.)*, *77*(7), 46–51.

Sokolowski, A., & Rackley, R. (2011). Teaching harmonic motion in trigonometry: Inductive inquiry supported by physics simulations. *Australian Senior Mathematics Journal*, *25*(1), 45–53.

Sokolowski, A., Yalvac, B., & Loving, C. (2011). Science modelling in pre-calculus: How to make mathematics problems contextually meaningful. *International Journal of Mathematical Education in Science and Technology, 42*(3), 283–297. doi :10.1080/0020739X.2010.526255.

Wieman, C. E., Adams, W. K., & Perkins, K. K. (2008). PhET: Simulations that enhance learning. *Science, 322*(5902), 682–683. doi:10.1126/science.1161948 PMID:18974334.

Zahner, W., Velazquez, G., Moschkovich, J., Vahey, P., & Lara-Meloy, T. (2012). Mathematics teaching practices with technology that support conceptual understanding for Latino/a students. *The Journal of Mathematical Behavior, 31*(4), 431–446. doi:10.1016/j.jmathb.2012.06.002.

KEY TERMS AND DEFINITIONS

Inquiry-Based Instruction: Instruction that aligns with a constructivist approach to teaching and emphasizes student-centered classrooms, discourse, sense-making, and conceptual understanding. The teacher's role is that of a facilitator, and students are active agents in the learning process.

Interactive Simulation: A computer-based environment that models a system and allows user interaction with the system, including, but not necessarily limited to, parameters of the model. Feedback, showing how the system changes in response to user interaction, is a defining feature of interactive simulations.

Virtual Manipulatives: Interactive, computer-based representations of concrete manipulatives that students use to explore mathematical content. May or may not include feedback.

Chapter 11
Do Technologies Support the Implementation of the Common Core State Standards in Mathematics of High School Probability and Statistics?

Woong Lim
Kennesaw State University, USA

Dong-Gook Kim
Dalton State College, USA

ABSTRACT

This chapter reviews the roles of technology in statistics education and introduces technologies available for classroom use. A few concrete examples of how select technologies support the teaching of probability and statistics guided by the Common Core State Standards in Mathematics of high school Probability and Statistics (CCSSM-PS) are presented. The reality of the implementation of the CCSSM poses a rather exciting opportunity for all of us in mathematics education. It presents an opportunity to plan and create mathematics lessons based on good teaching strongly tied with technology. As the efficacy of the CCSSM-PS hinges on how teachers draw upon their content knowledge to facilitate student learning through technology, it is significant to provide professional development programs that help teachers infuse technology with the teaching of probability and statistics.

INTRODUCTION

The Common Core State Standards in Mathematics of high school Probability and Statistics (CCSSM-PS) present an overarching conception of statistics. The standards have domains orga-

nized sequentially so that students can develop an understanding of statistics as the subject area that provides tools for explaining variability in data that enables students to make informed decisions or predictions. The four domains are as follows: (1) interpreting data, (2) making infer-

DOI: 10.4018/978-1-4666-4086-3.ch011

ences and justifying conclusions, (3) conditional probability, and (4) making probability-based decisions. The CCSSM-PS go beyond addressing descriptive statistics and introduce key ideas for understanding inferential statistics. The standards introduce the conditional probability, the rules of probability, and using probabilities to make informed decisions.

Statistics is a powerful tool in scientific methods to turn data into a cohesive unit of findings, interpretations, and informed decisions. For example, based on the sample data, one computes numbers to represent the sample and uses the numbers to better grasp the larger group called population (i.e., parameters). One can also make predictions about the likelihood of an event of interest by computing a probability based on mathematical representations of the population (or sample) distributions. The CCSSM-PS introduce discrete probability distributions or probability density functions as such representation. The discussion of the probability density functions of the normal distribution, however, does not appear in the standards, presumably because the topic involves the use of calculus.

The CCSSM-PS are closely related to statistical thinking that highlights several key components including process thinking; understanding variation; and using data to guide decision-making (Snee, 1990). Statistical thinking acknowledges that all processes in a system of input and output exhibit variation. It manages uncertainty by quantifying the variation, and the language of uncertainty is probability. That is, through statistical thinking researchers examine a system of process consisting of input and output; perform data collection and analysis to identify variation to address uncertainty; and technology enhances the ability of practitioners of statistics to solve many problems in the analysis of data (Rubin & Hammerman, 2006). In this way, statistical thinking, a major

philosophy of the CCSSM in framing statistical education, is related to learning to think critically facilitated with technology, and each domain in the CCSSM-PS is not left out as a stand-alone area but remain a part of interconnected body of knowledge.

A brief summary of the new directions in CCSSM-PS is as follows:

- Presenting a comprehensive view of statistics as a tool for data analysis and decision making.
- Promoting statistical thinking, which can be as essential as reading and writing for efficient citizenship (Wallman, 1993).
- Providing a sequential structure of key topics.
- Emphasizing building practical (rather than theoretical) knowledge of probability, such as calculating probabilities of compound events for inferential statistics.
- Proposing the probability distributions and the expected value of random variables as topics in order to be college and career ready.

This chapter aims to explain the role of technology in these new directions. In an effort to do so, this chapter demonstrates multiple roles of technology in statistics education and introduces technologies available for classroom use. A few concrete examples of how select technologies support the teaching of probability and statistics guided by CCSSM-PS are presented. The chapter demonstrates how good teaching can integrate technology in order to address specific standards and calls for more supports for designing and implementing effective teacher development programs that help teachers infuse technology with the teaching of probability and statistics.

IMPLICATIONS OF THE CCSSM-PS

Implications for Students

The CCSSM-PS call on high school students to practice applying statistical ways of thinking to real world issues and challenges. In the past, students were taught statistics by doing tedious computations driven by formulas far from reflecting the actual practice of statistics (Hogg, 1991). Learning probability was similar with learning statistics in that students were presented with definitions, rules, and examples with little experience with simulations as well as with little explanation of how probability relates to statistics.

The CCSSM-PS address the development of statistical thinking in all students and offer different learning experiences that is more cohesive, connected, and relevant to the work of statisticians and mathematicians. In the CCSSM, the developing understanding of statistical thinking is first introduced in Grade 6. In middle grades, students learn to investigate data and specific ways to summarize them. Randomization in data collection is introduced and serves as the basis of statistical inferences. More specifically, students in Grade 6 build on the knowledge and experiences in data analysis developed in earlier grades and use histograms and box-and-whisker diagrams to represent data. Seventh graders experience collecting data and develop some knowledge of probability as the basis of statistical inference. In Grade 8, students begin to think possible associations between two variables typically represented by scatter plots.

High school students are expected to deepen their understanding of categorical and bivariate data. Students experience modeling categorical associations of bivariate data and quantifying the associations in terms of correlation coefficients. With large-scale data, students learn the probability distributions, which contribute to an empirical understanding of the normal distribution, explaining variability in data, leading to the ability to make appropriate inferences.

In this way, the CCSSM-PS promote students' experience with data in the real world (problem solving) and result in a meaningful growth in their capacity in the mathematics of inference procedures. Use of technology, in conjunction with the learning of concepts and problem solving, offers students new ways of learning statistics and probability in a more authentic context of the real world. For example, students can work in groups, plan and perform data collection, and use technology to perform the mathematics of data analysis. As a result, technology can allow students to focus more on "what is not automated" (Ben-Zvi, 2000), such as statistical reasoning and analysis and interpretation of real life datasets (Broers, 2008). Such an approach allows students to model quantitative data and experience how probability plays out in making informed decisions based on probability models and statistical thinking.

Implications for Teachers

There has been a shift in how to teach statistics (Huck, 2007). In the early 1990s, recommendations of professional organizations of statisticians and mathematicians, such as the American Statistical Association (ASA) and the Mathematical Association of America (MAA) focused on developing statistical thinking with more emphasis on concepts than computations driven by formulas and providing more authentic learning experience with data. This change has led to a movement to reform the teaching of statistics to address content, pedagogy, and technology (Moore, 1997). Overtime, a cumulating body of literature did lend more credence to the view that teachers should teach statistics conceptually along with the empirical view of statistical inference. Most recently, the CCSSM-PS elucidate the structure of the subject so that teachers have a clear understanding of (1) what constitutes conceptual understanding of statistics and (2) what our students are expected to know and be able to do. With a clear vision of what defines and forms appropriate learning of statistics and probability in high school, effective teaching of probability and statistics hinges on how to teach and the nature of learning environments (pedagogy and technology).

The CCSSM-PS mention *technology*: "technology plays an important role in statistics and probability by making it possible to generate plots, regression functions, and correlation coefficients, and to simulate many possible outcomes in a short amount of time." (p.79) Despite the reference to technology as an important tool in the standards, researchers and mathematics educators involved in NCTM (2010) asserted that the CCSSM minimally recognized how technology supports students' mathematical growth.

There is little doubt that the CCSSM-PS do not address pedagogy and technology in much detail. However, this does not necessarily mean for teachers that the CCSSM-PS discourage the use of technology. Certainly, the standards do not offer specific ways to use technology as a learning tool. In fact, framing the appropriate curriculum content and proposing a structure in statistics education may take precedence over the task of providing teachers with some specifics on technology. Therefore, it is important for teachers to recognize the progressions in the standards and develop lessons that deliver the sequential body of content instead of broken pieces of the standards taken out of context. Equally important is to recognize the powerful role of technology in statistics education and understand that technology does afford teachers with a variety of strategies for the very ideal teaching of probability and statistics the CCSSM-PS envisage.

Implications for Teacher Educators

The efforts to change statistics education include supporting collaboration among researchers, teacher educators, and teachers; and developing resources and professional development programs to help prepare teachers as they implement the new standards. The changing nature of technology, however, is an ongoing challenge for statistics educators, and research efforts about the role of technology in teaching and learning statistics have increased (Friel, 2007). In the 1997 Round Table Conference of the International Association for Statistical Education (IASE) addressed important questions (Garfield & Burrill, 1997):

- What constitutes educational technology?
- What use, and in some cases misuse, is being made of technology in statistical education?
- What has research shown us about the role of technology?

The NCTM Principles and Standards (NCTM, 2000) include a content standard that emphasizes statistical thinking in all grades. The CCSSM-PS add the standards of progressions in statistical thinking appropriate in high school. Our teachers, in turn, present the standards to students. Understanding this dynamics lends credence to a view that the efficacy of the CCSSM (or any national and state standards) lies in how teachers draw upon their content knowledge to create effective activities, including the use of technology to address the standards.

With the introduction of the CCSSM-PS, mathematics teacher educators need to reflect on the process of disseminating the results of cumulative research on using technology in statistics education and influencing teachers to implement educational practices strongly tied to technology. There is a growing body of research supporting a framework for understanding technology integration in education in order to prepare our teachers to implement technology in teaching (Ives, Lee, & Starling, 2009). More recently, researchers proposed a model of the various components of Technological Pedagogical Content Knowledge (TPACK) that connects mathematics, technology, and pedagogy (Lee & Hollenbrands, 2008). What has emerged overtime is a theme that in addition to mastering the specifics of current technology tools, teachers need to reflect on appropriate uses of technology and to prepare for pedagogical issues by incorporating technology in teaching. For this reason, as teachers start using the CCSSM-PS, teacher educators should provide comprehensive professional development programs in which teachers map out their lesson plans following the CCSSM-PS with feedback from a group of experts and peers, experience various instructional technologies at a deeper level, discuss specific ways in which technologies improve student thinking and learning, and have multiple opportunities to practice the delivery of the lessons with strong ties to technology.

SURVEY OF TECHNOLOGY FOR STATISTICS AND PROBABILITY INSTRUCTION

We provide a survey of contemporary technologies of statistics and probability (mostly instructional software) and then discuss how they can support teachers in designing learning activities with technology in adherence to CCSSM-PS.

Data Collection Devices

- **Google Forms:** Can help streamline data collection by sharing information online and allows hassle-free online publication. Teachers may visit http://sites.google. com/site/colettecassinelli/spreadsheet and participate in the online community in which teachers share experiences with the software and see how other teachers and students use the technology in their classroom. Currently, students need to be at age 13 or older to be able to use the service.

- **SurveyMonkey:** (www.surveymonkey. com) Simplifies the survey process and allows teachers and students to publish online surveys by creating a virtual link. It also enables users to produce graphic summaries and export the survey data into

more advanced analysis software, such as SAS or SPSS. Just like Google Forms, it is particularly helpful in providing students with a powerful learning experience with data collection, which is a key process in addressing the CCSSM-PS cluster, S-IC.3, S-IC.4, S-IC.5, and S-IC.6. Students can create their own research questions and survey instruments as well.

- **Texas Instruments:** Offers a variety of textbooks and products for data collection in math and science. Teachers may visit http://education.ti.com and search data collection devices. The company also offers teaching materials, including model lessons and sample activities from which teachers can assess technology or select appropriate lessons with the use of technology.

Interactive Statistical Software

- **Fathom:** Easy-to-use software by Key Curriculum Press that illustrates concrete and abstract statistical concepts by letting students manipulate data in a clear graphic form, including bar charts, scatter plots, function plots, and histograms. It also runs probability simulations and calculates regression lines.

- **GeoGebra:** Free mathematics software application that creates dynamic graphics and tables. Currently GeogebraTube is available, and teachers can upload and share free materials related to the use of technology in teaching. It is particularly powerful when teachers and students can use animation to illustrate changes in graphical representations as variables or parameters change. The software program is available for download at http://www.geogebra.org.

- **TinkerPlots:** Exploratory data visualization and modeling tool designed for middle school students. It was developed by

Clifford Konold and Craig Miller at the University of Massachusetts Amherst and is published by Key Curriculum Press. It has some similarities with Fathom and allows users to enter their own data. TinkerPlots is especially useful for teachers who align their teaching with recommendations of the NCTM's Curriculum Standards and the Common Core State Standards for Probability and Statistics. To help illustrate variability in data, it offers stimulating visual formats, which helps students discover covariation. The Sampler Engine does probability simulations to incorporate probability in learning of statistics. The software program is available for download at http://www.keycurriculum. com/products/tinkerplots.

- **Probability Explorer:** Research-based software application that enables users to design a simple event of probability, simulate, and analyze the outcomes. The software can be used for activities from elementary grades through high school. Probability Explorer provides an open-ended learning environment with multiple ways to represent data that engage students in developing strong probabilistic thinking. It is available for download at http://www. probexplorer.com.

- **Internet-Based Tools:** Can be used as teacher-led computer demonstrations to the whole class; the teacher will need a projector that displays the computer screen. For example, National Library of Virtual Manipulatives (NLVM) is a collection of interactive math tools for all students available free online at www.nlvm.usu.edu. It covers multiple strands of mathematics, including measurement, data analysis, and probability. Additionally, using the eNLVM website, teachers can browse through various learning units and sample activities for individual teachers' needs.

Other Technology Resources

- **Illuminations by The National Council of Teachers of Mathematics:** Like NLVM, the Illuminations website by the National Council of Teachers of Mathematics is available free online at http://illuminations. nctm.org and offers rich resources. It provides online activities and model lessons; it also shows how the activities reflect the NCTM standards and shares other online resources identified by their editorial panel. It can actually serve a role model for the CCSSM to clarify their standards.

- **Learner.org:** Offers instructional resources in data analysis, statistics, and probability and introduces statistics as a problem-solving process. In this course, teachers can build pedagogical content knowledge and skills through investigations of different ways to organize and represent data and describe and analyze variation in data. Through practical examples, teachers can come to understand the key concepts in statistics, such as association between two variables, probability, random sampling, and estimation and the teaching of the key ideas. The case studies, divided into grade bands, demonstrate how to prepare for pedagogical issues in the classroom.

- **Graphing Calculators:** Are a common hand-held tool widely available in classrooms. An option for the teacher to demonstrate calculator use to the whole class is a document camera or a graphing calculator emulator, such as TI-SmartView emulator software. The random number generator is built into a graphing calculator like a TI-84+. A number of random number generators are also available on the Internet. For example, some can be found at http://www. random.org/integers.

- **Excel:** Is perhaps the mostly extensively used spreadsheet application and serves as a tool that increases the efficiency of various processes in statistics. Most businesses use Excel every day in turning data into reports and charts. Students collect data, analyze and develop a mathematical model to represent their data and make predictions. Excel is a great way of introducing the idea of variables (e.g. "cells") in mathematical thinking and reasoning. In statistics, students use Excel to create a spreadsheet, make a scatter plot, and generate a linear regression with the equation of the best fit. Meanwhile, Excel helps students and teachers focus on selecting appropriate representations of the data, discussing the statistical output, and drawing conclusions. This illustrates the role of technology as an efficient computational tool in light of integrating technology to support the CCSSM. Since Excel is a commercial software, students and teachers may consider using Gnumeric, known as an Excel clone, which functions with the same features of Excel. Gnumeric is available at http://statpages. org/javasta2.html. This website also offers a plethora of free statistics packages.

- **Preparing to Teach Mathematics with Technology (PTMT):** A project dedicated to increasing pre-service teachers' development of TPACK. The website resources include teacher education curricula on teaching and learning data analysis and probability. The group is supported by the National Science Foundation (NSF) and led by Karen Hollebrands and Hollylynne Stohl Lee at North Carolina State University. Reviewing the website may help teachers gain insight on research-based practices with a focus on integrated teaching with technology and the current efforts by mathematics teacher educators to develop effective professional development programs to aid teachers in increasing technological pedagogical content knowledge, the very knowledge in high demand for implementing the CCSSM-PS.

BENEFITS OF USING TECHNOLOGY IN CLASSROOM IN WAYS THAT SUPPORT THE CCSSM-PS

Using Technology to Develop Statistical Thinking

The CCSSM-PS promote statistical thinking and create learning opportunities with increased relevancy of statistical thinking in careers in which one uses data to recognize variability and make data-driven decisions. Statistics instruction in light of the CCSSM-PS may present two instructional stages. First is to get the numerical results by following certain procedures based on data and calculating statistics. Second is to interpret the results, reflect on the context, and make informed decisions.

The first stage typically involves calculating various descriptive statistics, such as mean, variance, and standard deviation; and running various procedures, such as regression and analysis of variance. However, the calculations involved in the first stage are often tedious and complex, so completing the first stage by hand can require a lot of practice and time.

In the first stage, one chooses appropriate statistical methods. To illustrate this, let's consider a situation in which a shop initially decided to order 200 widgets for the coming month. The shop can evaluate this decision about the order quantity based on data. To do so, appropriate numerical, graphical, or tabular summaries of the data should be produced first or percentiles can be computed. The next step is to interpret this summary and make a decision. If the 95th percentile of the monthly demand turns out to be 100, the demand exceeds 100 only in 5% of the time. As a result, the order quantity of 200 can be too high and lowered. One can further discuss the cost of ordering 100 instead of 200 using the probabilities from the distribution of the data.

As the quality of the second stage depends on the accurate analyses of data in the first stage, traditionally teachers emphasize accurate mathematical calculations of statistics in classrooms. This results in little time for practicing interpreting and making decisions based on statistics in classrooms. Computers, however, can automate many calculations and procedures in the first stage (Ben-Zvi, 2000). When computers were not readily available, students of statistics had no choice but to do the first stage by hand, and real-life datasets at large-scale could not be used. For example, the median is a simple concept: a middle number of a sorted data. However, calculating a median from a large dataset by hand is not a simple task as sorting many numbers in the dataset is tedious and time consuming. Computers can do such complex computations quickly and accurately.

The CCSSM-PS promote statistics as the science of analysis and inductive reasoning from numerical observations and call for conveying statistics in the broader context in which students learn to interact with skills and tools for reasoning from evidence. This is an essential part of completing the second stage of learning statistics. When teachers integrate technology in the teaching of statistics, students can spend more time on analysis and critical thinking about the data. In this way, when teachers teach statistics in alignment with CCSSM-PS, they can benefit a great deal from using technologies in classrooms. With limited class time, technologies enable teachers and students to focus more on statistical thinking using real-life datasets and decision making based on the analysis the data.

Three Major Benefits of Using Technology

In this section, we introduce three major benefits of using technology to support statistical thinking in light of the CCSSM-PS: (1) computational tools, (2) learning tools for simulations and visualizations, and (3) tools for building professional skills. Technology can help students experience how to applying statistical procedures and knowledge to real-world data. Without help of technologies,

students and teachers alike may have to spend most of their class time in learning and teaching the mathematical procedures of statistical methods. Even if students have a good understanding of statistical procedures, such as linear regression, applying their understanding to real-world data manually can be tedious. A lot of these tedious steps can be automated through technologies. Technologies for automation include commercial software such as MS-Excel, SPSS, and Minitab and free software, such as Gnumeric and PSPP. A list of more free statistical software can be found on the following website: http://statpages. org/javasta2.html. Most free software can carry out statistical procedures necessary to illustrate statistical concepts and thinking as recommended in the CCSSM-PS.

Besides being efficient computations tools, through visualization and simulation, technology can help students better grasp statistical concepts, statements and procedures about which mathematical justifications are often too complicated or sophisticated for students to understand (Gordon & Gordon, 2009). For example, an appropriate graphical simulation can help students enhance their understanding of the Central Limit Theorem (CLT), by which a sample mean can be assumed to follow a normal distribution if the sample is sufficiently large. The way the same concept is illustrated in the CCSSM-PS is as follows: "Use data from a sample survey to estimate a population mean or proportion; develop a margin of error through the use of simulation models for random sampling (S-IC.4)." Gordon and Gordon (2009) used Excel simulation to visualize the effect of sample size and the population distribution on the distribution of sample means. Simulation can aid students in discovering the CLT by themselves when they try different population distributions and different sample sizes.

Using technology can also help students prepare for future careers that draw upon statistical thinking and knowledge. Better understanding of statistics through technology can help students do well in college statistics courses and increase students' interest in professions that use statistical knowledge including actuary, manufacturing technician, industrial engineer, statistician, or production manager. More career choices can be found on the website of the American Statistical Association (www.amstat.org/careers/index.cfm). Further, some technologies, such as Excel, are commonly used in workforces. Learning how to use such technologies in handling data can certainly be beneficial to one's career and related endeavors. In the following, we explore the aspect of technology as a learning tool more in detail using examples to illustrate the standards in the CCSSM-PS.

Visualization

The CCSSM promote students' learning to display data graphically through technology. For example, one standard states that students use technology to compute correlation coefficients of a linear fit and interpret the correlation coefficient (S-ID.8). Technology can satisfy this goal by calculating correlation coefficients. More importantly, it can help students understand the meaning of the correlation coefficient: a degree and direction of *linear* relationship. The following screenshots (Figure 1) were generated by Gnumeric. The first screenshot is a graph of data having a correlation coefficient of zero. With the number alone, students may think there is no relationship at all. However, the graph clearly shows a relationship, albeit non-linear. Therefore, students can learn through visualiza-

tion that small correlation coefficients mean weak *straight* line relationship. The correlation coefficients of the second and third screenshots are 0.444 and 0.924, respectively. The data points in the second screenshot are more dispersed from the regression line than those in the last screenshot. That is, the higher the correlation coefficient, the closer the data points are clustered along the straight line. Further, these two screenshots illustrate the effect of outliers ($x=9$; $x=9.6$) on the correlation coefficients, which change from 0.444 with outliers to 0.924 without ones. An applet titled Scatterplot available on www.nlvm.usu.edu can do the same task in more interactive ways. The use of a simple digital technology allows students to have the opportunity to think about how the two data points affect the correlation coefficients and the regression line in the context of the data. Furthermore, students can be more receptive to learning the intricate mathematics of correlation coefficients and how mathematics plays an essential role in statistical thinking in college. Technology can help facilitate time-consuming computational tasks, and teachers can focus on discussing the linear relationship, measuring the strength of the linear relationship, modeling, and goodness of fit. This learning experience can help address specific standards of CCSSM-PS, such as S-ID.6.b, S-ID.6.c, S-ID.7, and S-ID.8.

Other possible areas in which visualization enhances understanding include investigating effects of the mean and standard deviation on a normal distribution. The following are illustrations created with GeoGebra. The first pair of screen-

Figure 1. Three cases where the correlation coefficient values change as the data change

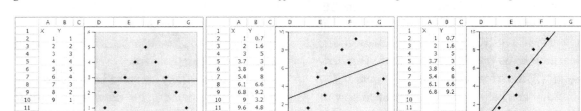

shots (Figure 2) shows the effect of a mean change on a normal distribution, and the second pair of screenshots (Figure 3) shows the effect of a standard deviation change on a normal distribution. This type of activity using technology can help address the CCSSM-PS, such as S-ID.3 and S-ID.4.

Simulation

Simulation can play an important role in teaching probabilities and randomness in light of the CCSSM. One example is the Law of Large Numbers, which states that the mean of the results of a large number of identical experiments should be close to the expected value. This relates to standards, such as S-MD.2, S-MD.3, and S-MD.4. Students, however, do not grasp this law easily (Watson & Moritz, 2000). For example, students think

there should be 5 heads based on the expected value calculation if a fair coin is tossed 10 times. Such misconceptions can be rectified through a graphical simulation shown in Gordon and Gordon (2009) in which researchers used an Excel simulation to visualize the Law of Large Numbers. Using the simulation, students can understand that the expected value may not occur in a short run, and that an expected value is not a value that one can expect to see from experiments; rather it is a long-run relative frequency. Similarly, teachers can design simulations in which students can compare theoretical and experimental probability and perform decision making as they make statistical inferences from the data to estimate the probability of an event. The following diagram (Figure 4) illustrates two simulations, run by Probability Explorer, of throwing a fair die 4 times and 96 times respectively. The use of technology

Figure 2. The effect of a mean change on a normal distribution, created with GeoGebra

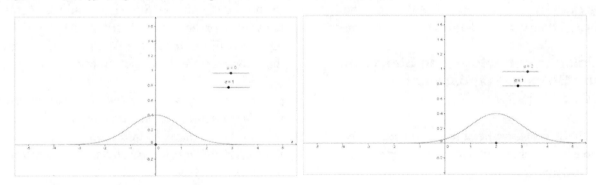

Figure 3. The effect of a standard deviation change on a normal distribution, created with GeoGebra

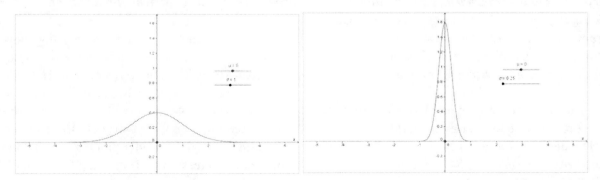

Figure 4. Illustration of throwing a fair die 4 times and 96 times respectively and a summary table of the outcomes in various numerical representations (© 1999-2005, Hollylynne Stohl Lee, Used with permission)

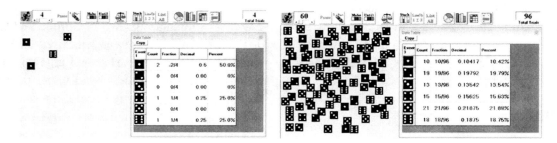

enables students to experience randomness in the short run (4 times) and the asymptotic nature of experimental probability in the long run (96 times). That is, experimental probability does not coincide with theoretical probability in the short run; experimental probability approaches to theoretical probability in the long run. From this simulation, teachers can discuss the relationship between theoretical probability and experimental probability and how probability can be estimated by experiments (i.e., the probability distribution for a random variable defined for a sample space).

Linking Technologies in Statistics and Specific Standards of the CCSSM-PS

In this section, we list a few standards for which the use of technology can play a significant role in students' learning.

(S-ID.4) Use the mean and standard deviation of a data set to fit it to a normal distribution and to estimate population percentages. Use calculators, spreadsheets, and tables to estimate areas under the normal curve. Note that there are data sets for which such a procedure is not appropriate.

The following sample problem can provide an opportunity to address this standard effectively: "The lifetime of a light bulb is normally distributed with a mean life of 540 hours and a standard deviation of 28 hours. Find the probability that a randomly selected light bulb lasts longer than 500 hours." This problem can be rewritten as $P(X > 500)$, where X is normally distributed with a mean of 540 and a standard deviation of 28. This probability can easily be calculated using Gnumeric. Gnumeric provides a function *normdist*, which calculates a probability that a normally distributed random variable is less than a certain value, that is, $P(X < a)$. The following screenshot (Figure 5) shows the answer to the question using the normdist function. Students should apply the knowledge of the normal distribution to build the equations illustrated in the first screenshot, and the second picture shows the numerical outcomes.

(S-ID.6.b) Represent data on two quantitative variables on a scatter plot, and describe how the variables are related by informally assessing the fit of a function by plotting and analyzing residuals.

(S-ID.8) Compute (using technology) and interpret the correlation coefficient of a linear fit.

The screenshots in Figure 6 demonstrate how Gnumeric adds a trend line, a regression equation, and a coefficient of determination. The final outputs are illustrated in the second screenshot. The applet available on www.nlvm.usu.edu can be also used to support these two goals. Excel can do the same through its scatter plot command. One may run a regression analysis using Excel, SPSS or other technologies.

Figure 5. Illustration of calculating the probability P(X > 500) using Gnumeric, where X is normally distributed with a mean of 540 and a standard deviation of 28

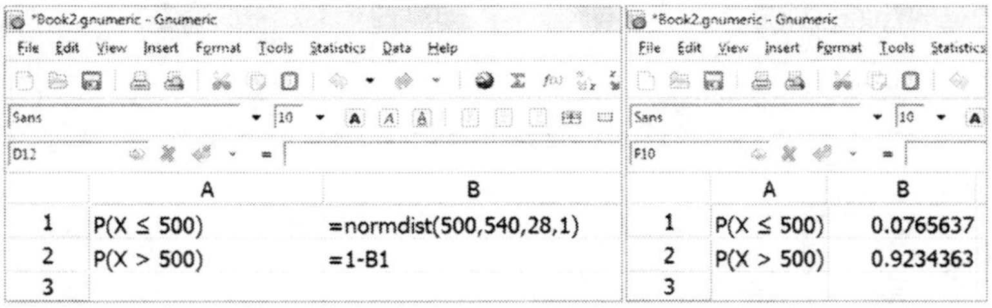

Figure 6. The output generated by Gnumeric with a trend line, a regression equation, and a coefficient of determination

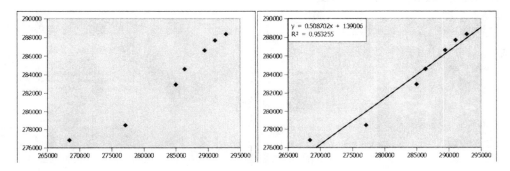

(S-IC.2) Decide if a specified model is consistent with results from a given data-generating process, e.g., using simulation. For example, a model says a spinning coin falls heads up with probability 0.5. Would a result of 5 tails in a row cause you to question the model?

Probability Explorer can support this goal as shown in the simulation examples mentioned previously. In Gnumeric (or Excel), the command, *randbetween* can be also used to generate random outcomes, either 0 or 1 for this coin example. However, the results could be less intuitive than those, for example, by Probability Explorer that presents a more dynamic illustration than Gnumeric. The screenshots in Figure 7 are the simulation in which tossing the coin occurred 5 times from which the head appeared 4 times and the tail appeared once. Gnumeric allows students to try the simulation at a large scale and reflect on

how long run behaviors of a random event can be different from short run behaviors as the number of tossing increases.

(S-IC.4) Use data from a sample survey to estimate a population mean or proportion; develop a margin of error through the use of simulation models for random sampling.

(S-IC.5) Use data from a randomized experiment to compare two treatments; use simulations to decide if differences between parameters are significant.

The web applet on http://onlinestatbook.com/stat_sim/conf_interval/index.html is developed by the Rice Virtual Lab in Statistics (Figure 8) and simulates the 95% and 99% confidence intervals for the population mean. Through this simulation, students can learn that the term *confidence* is not the probability that the confidence interval

Figure 7. Illustration of a random tossing of a coin five times by using Gnumeric

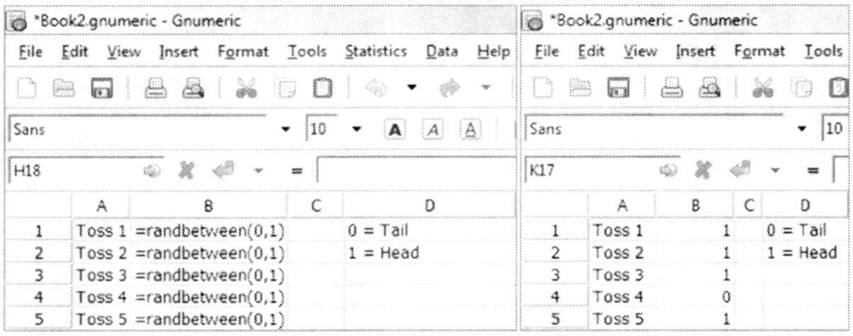

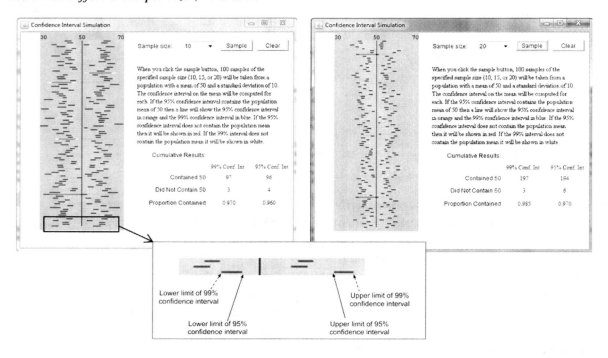

Figure 8. Illustration of two simulations of the 95% and 99% confidence intervals for the population mean with different sample sizes, 10 and 20

they calculate from a sample will contain the true value of a parameter. Rather, it is the percentage of confidence intervals that would contain the true value of the parameter among all confidence intervals constructed from all possible samples of the same size. Students can also learn the effect of the sample sizes on the margin of error (i.e., half the width of a confidence interval) by changing the sample sizes. This applet simulates sampling from a population with a mean of 50 and a standard deviation of 10. The intervals for the various

samples are displayed by horizontal lines as shown in Figure 8. Each line shows both 95% and 99% confidence intervals. From the figures, students can learn that 99% confidence intervals are wider than 95% confidence intervals, and that the former intervals contain the true value of the mean more often than the latter intervals. The screenshots also illustrate the effect of sample sizes on the width of confidence intervals: the larger the sample is, the narrower the confidence interval becomes. It is apparent that the confidence intervals with the sample size 20 (i.e., right screenshot) are narrower on average than those with the sample size 10 (i.e., left screenshot). Thus, students can learn that to improve the precision of confidence intervals, one can increase the samples sizes.

CONCLUSION

The CCSSM's vision on teaching and learning of probability and statistics is to provide the new content standards with progression so that students develop appropriate content knowledge in statistics and acquire the specific thinking and reasoning capability commonly used in careers that draw on the knowledge of statistics. The progression in the standards includes what knowledge students bring to the class, what knowledge students need to acquire with the teacher, and how new knowledge extends to future learning of statistics and probability.

The CCSSM-PS have yet to provide specifics on the pedagogy and technology of statistics, and currently, no assessments aligned with the standards are available. Developing and publishing assessment instruments that evaluate the mastery of the standards effectively can aid teachers in structuring lessons in line with appropriate skills and the levels of complexity (Chance, 2002). This in turn should help achieve a successful implementation of CCSSM.

The reality of the implementation stage poses a rather exciting opportunity for all of us in mathematics education—-the opportunity to create mathematics lessons based on the progressions specified in the standards and to deliver the lessons based on good teaching strongly tied with technology. Students' understanding of statistics and probability can deepen and become richer through good curriculum designs based on the standards, and the latter's potential can be strengthened greatly through the use of technology. This chapter presented multiple roles of technology in statistics education and introduced technologies available for classroom use. The chapter also demonstrated how good teaching could integrate technology in order to address specific standards.

The reality of the implementation of the CCSSM integrated with technology also presents us with a need to formulate professional development programs specifically designed to aid teachers in building the pedagogical and technological capacity to facilitate student learning through technology. In addition, the CCSSM-PS envision students equipped with strong statistical literacy, and there is no doubt statistical thinking should be an integral part of statistics instruction. However, the reality of our classrooms in which (1) teachers have little experience in data analysis activities or applied statistics (Ben-Zvi & Garfield, 2004) and (2) students might be accustomed to calculating a numerical answer using memorized formulas (Chance, 2002) may not change unless (1) more teachers benefit from effective professional development programs and (2) the assessments are designed in a way that values statistical thinking and allows students to focus on analysis and critical thinking facilitated by technology. Indeed, it is about time that stakeholders in statistics education support both teachers and teacher educators in their efforts to shape good teaching of statistics with strong ties to technology in light of the CCSSM-PS.

REFERENCES

Ben-Zvi, D. (2000). Toward understanding the role of technological tools in statistical learning. *Mathematical Thinking and Learning, 2*, 127–155. doi:10.1207/S15327833MTL0202_6.

Ben-Zvi, D., & Garfield, J. (2004). Statistical literacy, reasoning, and thinking: Goals, definitions, and challenges. In Ben-Zvi, D., & Garfield, J. (Eds.), *The challenge of developing statistical literacy, reasoning and thinking* (pp. 3–16). Springer.

Broers, N. J. (2008). Helping students to build a conceptual understanding of elementary statistics. *The American Statistician, 62*(2), 161–166. doi:10.1198/000313008X302091_a.

Chance, B. (2002). Components of statistical thinking and implications for instruction and assessment. *Journal of Statistics Education, 10*(3). Retrieved from http://www.amstat.org/publications/jse/v10n3/chance.html.

Common Core State Standards Initiative. (2010). *Common core standards for mathematics.* Retrieved from http://http://www.corestandards.org/the-standards/mathematics/hs-statistics-and-probability/introduction/

Friel, S. (2007). The research frontier: Where technology interacts with the teaching and learning of data analysis and statistics. In Blume, G. W., & Heid, M. K. (Eds.), *Research on technology and the teaching and learning of mathematics: Case and Perspectives* (Vol. 2, pp. 279–331). Greenwich, CT: Information Age Publishing, Inc..

Garfield, J., & Burrill, G. (Eds.). (1997). *Research on the role of technology – Teaching and learning statistics.* Voorburg, The Netherlands: International Statistical Institute.

Gordon, S. P., & Gordon, F. S. (2009). Visualizing and understanding probability and statistics: Graphical simulations using Excel. *PRIMUS (Terre Haute, Ind.), 19*(4), 346–369. doi:10.1080/10511970701882891.

Hogg, R. (1991). Statistical education: Improvements are badly needed. *The American Statistician, 45*(4), 342–343.

Huck, S. W. (2007). Reform in statistical education. *Psychology in the Schools, 44*(5). Retrieved from http://onlinelibrary.wiley.com/doi/10.1002/pits.20244/pdf doi:10.1002/pits.20244.

Ives, S. E., Lee, H. S., & Starling, T. (2009). Preparing to teach mathematics with technology: Lesson planning decisions for implementing new curriculum. In *Proceedings of Research in Undergraduate Mathematics Education.* Raleigh, NC: Academic Press. Retrieved from http://mathed.asu.edu/crume2009/Ives_LONG2.pdf

Lee, H., & Hollebrands, K. (2008). Preparing to teach mathematics with technology: An integrated approach to developing technological pedagogical content knowledge. *Contemporary Issues in Technology & Teacher Education, 8*(4). Retrieved from http://www.citejournal.org/vol8/iss4/mathematics/article1.cfm.

Moore, D. S. (1997). New pedagogy and new content: The case of statistics. *International Statistical Review, 65,* 123–137.

National Council of Teachers of Mathematics. (2010). *NCTM public comments on the common core standards for mathematics.* Retrieved from http://www.nctm.org/about/content.aspx?id=25186

National Council Teachers of Mathematics. (2000). *Principles and standards for school mathematics.* Reston, VA: NCTM.

Rubin, A., & Hammerman, J. K. (2006). Understanding data through new software representations. In Burrill, G. (Ed.), *Thinking and reasoning with data and chance: Sixty-eighth yearbook* (pp. 241–256). Reston, VA: NCTM.

Snee, R. D. (1990). Statistical thinking and its contribution to total quality. *The American Statistician, 44*(2), 116–121. doi:10.2307/2684144.

Stohl, H. (2005). *Probability explorer*. Retrieved from http://www.probexplorer.com

Wallman, K. K. (1993). Enhancing statistical literacy: Enriching our society. *Journal of the American Statistical Association, 88*(421), 1–8.

Watson, J. M., & Moritz, J. B. (2000). Developing concepts of sampling. *Journal for Research in Mathematics Education, 31*, 44–70. doi:10.2307/749819.

Chapter 12
Sketchpad®, TinkerPlots®, and Fathom®:
Using Dynamic Geometry® Software Tools Strategically

Karen Greenhaus
Consultant, Edtech Professional Development, USA

ABSTRACT

The Common Core State Standards for Mathematics (CCSSM) include overarching Standards for Mathematical Practice that cite dynamic geometry® software as one of the tools mathematically proficient students should know how to use strategically. Dynamic geometry software or more generally, dynamic mathematics software, provides visible and tangible representations of mathematical concepts that can be dragged and manipulated to discover underlying properties, investigate patterns and relationships, and develop deeper understandings of the concepts. The Geometer's Sketchpad®, TinkerPlots®, and Fathom® are examples of dynamic mathematics software. This chapter outlines how dynamic mathematics software supports the CCSSM. Specific mathematic content examples are described using these three resources to model the use of dynamic mathematics software for learning mathematics. Challenges for successfully integrating dynamic mathematics software are described with suggestions for training and support.

INTRODUCTION

The Common Core Standards for Mathematics (CCSSM) (National Governors Association Center for Best Practices (NGA Center) and Council of State School Officers (CCSSO), 2010) include both content standards and pedagogical practices to support teachers in developing mathematical proficiency in their students. Dynamic geometry®

software is one of several tools that are referenced to help support the standards. This chapter outlines three specific dynamic geometry tools, or more generally, dynamic mathematics tools that are well known in mathematics education: *The Geometer's Sketchpad® [Sketchpad]* (KCP Technologies, 2011b), *TinkerPlots® Dynamic Data Exploration (TinkerPlots)* (University of Massachusetts, 2005–2012), and *Fathom® Dynamic Data (KCP*

DOI: 10.4018/978-1-4666-4086-3.ch012

Technologies, 2011a), discusses their overall design, and gives specific examples of how they can be used strategically in elementary, middle, and high school mathematics. I also provide suggestions for implementation and teacher training, because the success of any new resource or strategy requires planning and support.

Common Core State Standards for Mathematics

The Standards for Mathematical Practice (SMP) within the CCSSM (NGA Center and CCSSO, 2010) are processes and proficiencies that mathematics educators should foster in their students. The Standard for Mathematic Practice *Use Appropriate Tools Strategically* states:

Mathematically proficient students consider the available tools when solving a mathematical problem. These tools might include pencil and paper, concrete models, a ruler, a protractor, a calculator, a spreadsheet, a computer algebra system, a statistical package or dynamic geometry software. Proficient students are sufficiently familiar with tools appropriate for their grade or course to make sound decisions about when each of these tools might be helpful, recognizing both the insight to be gained and their limitations (NGA Center and CCSSO, 2010, p. 7).

In the classroom, when a student is given a simple calculation, paper and pencil may be the most appropriate tool. However, if multiple calculations are required to arrive at a solution, a calculator might be a more appropriate tool. For demonstrating the effect of a specific coefficient on an equation and its graph, dynamic geometry software is the most appropriate tool because of its ability to plot functions with dynamic parameters for the coefficients. These dynamic parameters can easily be increased or decreased one at a time, or they can be used to create a visual representation

of a family of functions. They allow students to quickly see multiple examples of how a specific coefficient affects the behavior of the function, thus allowing them to "visualize the results of varying assumptions" (NGA Center and CCSSO, 2010, p. 7) (Figure 1).

The term "dynamic geometry software" was originally used in 1990 (Jackiw, 2009, p. 5) by the designer, Nick Jackiw, and publisher, Steve Rasmussen, of *The Geometer's Sketchpad* (KCP Technologies, 2011). Dynamic geometry describes the ability of *Sketchpad* to drag "mathematical images through an infinite number of continuously related examples all sharing the same mathematical definition used to construct them" (Jackiw, 2009, p. 4). Since that time, the term has come to represent "rapid expression, continuous and interactive direct manipulation, and the tangible experience of the consequences of variation" (Jackiw, 2009, p. 5). Dynamic geometry software is important for mathematical visualization for all grade levels and for all mathematical concepts because of its ability to "infuse that mathematics with life, movement, and mathematical behavior" (Jackiw, 2009, p. 5). The ability to dynamically drag objects to compare and discover relationships is what makes dynamic geometry software a powerful mathematical learning tool, since, according to Finzer and Erickson (1998), "the learning takes place during the drag".

Dynamic Mathematics Software from Key Curriculum

The Geometer's Sketchpad (KCP Technologies, 2011) is dynamic geometry software that allows for the construction of interactive mathematical models for math concepts from elementary to higher levels past calculus. *Sketchpad* provides the ability to manipulate dynamic models for fractions, number lines, and geometric patterns, to build understanding of algebraic properties and functional relationships, and to construct

Figure 1. Family of functions with Sketchpad

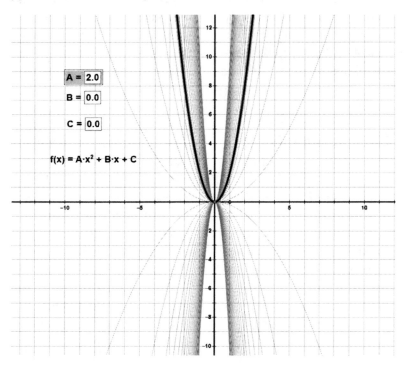

and transform geometric shapes and functions. The dynamic, moving environment of *Sketchpad* helps users explore the behaviors of mathematical systems.

Sketchpad (KCP Technologies, 2011b) is a software tool that supports all of the SMP (NGA Center and CCSSO, 2010). The ability to quickly construct and manipulate visual representations of mathematic concepts in *Sketchpad* enables users to explore concepts dynamically in a continuous and interactive way, allowing them to test their conjectures and collect evidence to support or reject these conjectures (Jackiw, 2009). Visualizing mathematical concepts and manipulating models provides the opportunity to explore properties, recognize patterns, and formalize repeated reasoning. An example of this would be constructing an isosceles triangle using a circle and two radii, measuring the sides and angles of the triangle, and then dragging the vertices to explore the properties of the triangle. Through dragging and changing

the side and angle measures, students investigate not just one isosceles triangle, but rather the set of (almost) all isosceles triangles, and thus can conjecture that every isosceles triangle has two angles that are always congruent (Figure 2). *Sketchpad's* dynamic environment provides a way to focus on the underlying constructs of mathematic concepts and exploring these concepts and constructs to develop clear and precise definitions and deepen understanding.

TinkerPlots (University of Massachusetts, 2005–2012) is dynamic mathematics software that supports the visualization and simulation of data (Konold, 2005). With *TinkerPlots*, students drag data attributes into plots that can then be manipulated into a variety of graphical representations as students explore the data. *TinkerPlots* is designed to develop students' understanding of data, numbers, probability, and graphs at the upper elementary through ninth grade level. In *TinkerPlots*, students can decide what relation-

Figure 2. Dragging isosceles triangles with Sketchpad

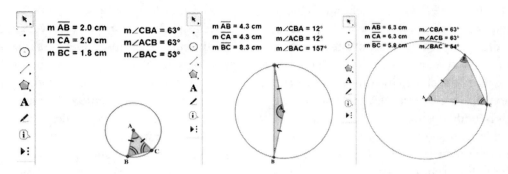

ships to investigate, and then explore the relationships by creating their own graphs. For example, students looking at Presidential data may investigate the relationship between birth state and political party using a bar graph and color gradient for political party to discover that New York had the only Whig party candidate (University of Massachusetts, 2005–2012). Or, when looking at Olympic data, and comparing high-jump distance to Olympic year using a scatter plot, students may discover that distance has increased in a linear pattern over 26 Olympics (University of Massachusetts, 2005–2012). The focus is on creating visual representations of data and dynamically exploring relationships, analyzing data, and reasoning about mathematical systems. Like *Sketchpad, TinkerPlots* gives students the ability to drag objects, in this case data, and create a variety of graphs in order to explore relationships and patterns.

The ability to make conjectures about patterns and relationships when exploring data and probability and to quickly test those conjectures is at the heart of *TinkerPlots* (University of Massachusetts, 2005–2012), making it an appropriate dynamic mathematics software tool to address both the CCSSM (NGA Center and CCSSO, 2010) content standards and the SMP. *TinkerPlots* lets users explore, visualize, model real-world, cross-curricular data. Students can use these explorations to reason both abstractly and quantitatively about the data, construct viable arguments, and

make sense out of problems and relationships by asking questions of interest and very quickly dragging the data to explore those questions. The dynamic, easily manipulated environment within *Tinkerplots* allows students to work with data, probability, tables, and graphs in an engaging way that provides opportunities to explore, reason, make conjectures, and deepen understanding of probability and statistics concepts.

Fathom® Dynamic Data (KCP Technologies, 2011a) is dynamic mathematics software that helps students visualize data and statistical models, with a deeper focus on statistical analysis capabilities that address the high school statistics and probability concepts of the CCSSM (NGA Center and CCSSO, 2010). Like *Sketchpad* and *TinkerPlots, Fathom* allows users to manipulate mathematical objects directly (Finzer, 2000). In *Fathom,* data values, lines, parameter sliders, and axes can be dragged and manipulated to see the effects of different scales, model fitting curves, and observe how data values influence statistical measures. *Fathom* also allows users to build probability simulations, and vary their assumptions to deepen their understanding of probability. For example, students can simulate the flip of a fair coin and a weighted coin and then simulate 10, 100, or 1000 flips of each coin and observe the distributions.

Fathom (KCP Technologies, 2011a) allows for "visualization of statistical concepts, dynamically shows how concepts work and reveals the meaning of underlying mathematical symbols" (Finzer

& Erickson, 1998, p. 3); it is a powerful tool to support the CCSSM (NGA Center and CCSSO, 2010) and the SMP for high school statistics. Through dragging and dynamic changes to data, students can observe, ask questions, and explain behaviors. They are able to look for structure and connections, be precise in their understandings, and reason both abstractly and quantitatively because they can see the visual representation as well as the numeric and algebraic representations. Through its sampling capabilities, *Fathom* makes the study of inferential statistics accessible, allowing for modeling of hypothesis and conjectures quickly and dynamically. Users are able to explore, analyze, and model data through a variety of graphs, and demonstrate standard statistical analyses.

Sketchpad (KCP Technologies, 2011b), *TinkerPlots* (University of Massachusetts, 2005–2012), and *Fathom* (KCP Technologies, 2011a) allow students to construct, manipulate and visualize mathematical concepts in order to make connections and discover relationships. These dynamic mathematics tools help students develop conceptual understanding of mathematics and the underlying relationships. The CCSSM (NGA Center and CCSSO, 2010) for all grade levels can be better understood through the use of these dynamic tools.

CCSSM ELEMENTARY CONTENT APPLICATIONS

The CCSSM (NGA Center and CCSSO, 2010) "stress conceptual understanding of key ideas" and "continually return to organizing principles" (p. 4). The elementary content standards center on number and operations, including counting, algebraic thinking, measurement and data, and then geometry, with each successive grade building upon the ideas and concepts from earlier grades. "What students can learn at any particular grade

level depends upon what they have learned before" (p. 5). Embedded throughout this progression of learning are the SMP, because "developing student practitioners of the discipline of mathematics increasingly ought to engage with the subject matter as they grow" (p. 8). While the content standards are designed to balance procedural knowledge with conceptual understanding, students with a shallow, procedural approach to mathematics "... may be less likely to consider analogous problems, represent problems coherently, justify conclusions...." So attending only to the procedural components of mathematics does not meet the demands of the SMP. The use of dynamic mathematics software can help elementary students make connections between math concepts and math processes and procedures.

Grade 3 Geometry Example with *Sketchpad*

The *Reason with shapes and their attributes* content standard 3.G.1 under the Geometry domain for grade 3 in the CCSSM (NGA Center and CCSSO, 2010), states that students will:

Understand that shapes in different categories (e.g., rhombuses, rectangles, and others) may share attributes (e.g., having four sides) and that the shared attributes can define a larger category (e.g., quadrilaterals). Recognize rhombuses, rectangles, and squares as examples of quadrilaterals, and draw examples of quadrilaterals that do not belong to any of these subcategories (p. 26).

Constructing a virtual geoboard and using the polygon tool in *Sketchpad* (KCP Technologies, 2011b) is one method of using dynamic geometry that allows for the drawing of several examples of quadrilaterals, which can then be dragged, measured, and manipulated to help discover the attributes of quadrilaterals. Students can quickly change the size, shape, and orientation of their examples in order to find patterns, identify common and unique attributes, explore relationships, and identify subcategories (Figure 3).

Another option is to use a premade sketch, such as *Square or Not: Properties of Squares* (Key Curriculum Press, 2012a, p. 107), which provides the opportunity for students to take ready-made examples of quadrilaterals that appear to be squares, measure their lengths and angles, and drag vertices to test whether the quadrilaterals are in fact squares. If the quadrilaterals do not stay squares as their vertices are dragged, students identify which attributes are changing, categorize the types of quadrilaterals that are actually represented, and explain and justify their categorizations.

Both examples allow students to dynamically manipulate shapes and immediately see the results of those manipulations on measures, shape, and orientation. The ability to drag vertices to create an infinite variety of quadrilateral examples helps students identify shared attributes and categorize quadrilaterals. Students are more likely to discover patterns and relationships and have a better grasp of the hierarchical organization because of the ability to dynamically move from one type of quadrilateral into another, thus establishing for example, which shape properties are common to all rhombuses and which shape properties are only true for square rhombuses

Figure 3. Identifying attributes with Sketchpad

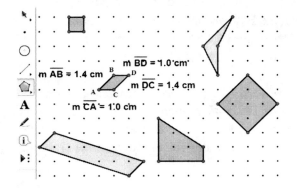

Grade 4 Data Example with *TinkerPlots*

Under the Measurement and Data domain for Grade 4, the *Represent and interpret data* content standard 4.MD.4 states that students will be able to:

Make a line plot to display a data set of measurements in fractions of a unit (1/2, 1/4, 1/8). Solve problems involving addition and subtraction of fractions by using information presented in line plots. For example, from a line plot find and interpret the difference in length between the longest and shortest specimens in an insect collection (p. 31).

This standard can easily be addressed using *TinkerPlots* (University of Massachusetts, 2005–2012) using one of the data sets that come with the software. In the Science data category, there is a data set on cicadas (University of Massachusetts, 2005–2012) that fits this standard perfectly. The data set provides information on 104 cicadas, including attributes such as body weight, body length, and wing length and wing width. Students can view information on each cicada separately by browsing a set of data cards, they can view the data in tabular format, and they can also drag attributes into a plot to begin comparing and sorting the data to discover patterns and relationships.

Dragging and dropping the attribute of body length into the plot immediately separates the 104 data points into two bins, or categories. Grabbing any data point and dragging it creates more bins by length, subdividing the data into smaller and smaller groupings. Continuing to drag eventually separates the data completely and the data can then be stacked on the axis to create a line plot (Figure 4).

Students can add additional attributes to the graph to investigate relationships among attributes. For example, students can add wing length to the vertical axis to investigate whether cicadas with

Figure 4. Separating data in TinkerPlots

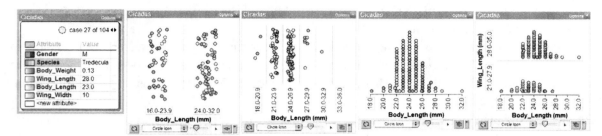

longer bodies have longer wings. Because graphs in *TinkerPlots* incorporate color, students can layer a third attribute onto the graph, such as the species, to determine if certain cicada species have longer bodies or longer wings than others.

According to Konold (2005) the design of *TinkerPlots* (University of Massachusetts, 2005–2012) encourages students to change and add attributes as they explore relationships and trends. The graphs emerge from students' interests and questions about the data. As students delve deeper, they can add measures of central tendency, box plots, or lines of fit to describe and model data. Students can drag, hide, or add data points to see how outliers impact the shape of graphs and measures of center, fostering a deeper and more nuanced understanding of data analysis. TinkerPlots allows students to make small changes in the graphs and see the immediate impact of those changes, helping them to discover patterns and relationships (Konold, 2006).

CCSSM MIDDLE SCHOOL CONTENT APPLICATIONS

There are several critical areas of mathematical content focus as students progress through the CCSSM (NGA Center and CCSSO, 2010) in grades 6, 7, and 8. Students work with ratio and rate and progress into proportional reasoning. They extend their understanding of fractions to rational numbers and work with expressions and linear

equations. In the middle grades, students begin to develop their understanding of functional relationships and use functions to model linear relationships. The standards emphasize the development of statistical thinking, leading to informal work with sampling and conjectures about populations based on random samples. In geometry, middle school concepts involve working with scale and basic geometric constructions and delving more deeply into two- and three-dimensional shapes, including solving problems involving area and volume. Dynamic mathematics software can be an instrumental tool for middle school mathematics as concepts become more abstract.

Grade 7 Algebra Example with *Sketchpad*

Solving real-world problems and applying mathematical concepts to real-world situations is an important focus of the CCSSM (NGA Center and CCSSO, 2010) and SMP. The *Solve real-life and mathematical problems using numerical and algebraic expressions* and equations standard 7.EE.4 in the Expressions and Equations domain of the 7th grade CCSSM (NGA Center and CCSSO, 2010) states that students will:

Use variables to represent quantities in a real-world or mathematical problem, and construct simple equations and inequalities to solve problems by reasoning about the quantities (p. 49).

Sketchpad (KCP Technologies, 2011b) can be used to model real-world problems, allowing for multiple representations of the situation through tables, graphs, and equations. Students can visualize the quantities in the problem in multiple ways and use a variety of approaches to understand the quantities, work with the variables, and reach conclusions and solve the problem.

An activity that exemplifies *Sketchpad's* (KCP Technologies, 2011b) capabilities to dynamically represent and solve real-world problems involving equations is *Hikers: Solving through Multiple Representations* (Key Curriculum Press, 2012b, p. 135–141). Students are given a scenario with two hikers, one at a campsite, and one at a lake, who are walking on a trailhead towards each other at different rates of speed. The problem is to determine at what time and at what distance from the trailhead they will meet. Using *Sketchpad*, students first work to understand the problem and get an estimate of the time and distance of the meeting through an animated simulation of the two hikers walking towards each other on the trailhead path. Through questioning and reasoning, students then determine how to get a more precise answer by using the quantities given in the problem to create algebraic expressions that represent each hiker and create a table of values for specific time increments.

From the table, students move to a visual representation of the data, plotting the table values and using the algebraic expressions to create dynamic points that trace the path of each hiker.

These dynamic paths help students recognize the need for a linear equation to give an exact answer to the problem. From the table, expressions and graphs, students reason about the quantities represented, connecting the different start values and rates of speed to the *y*-intercepts and slopes of the graphs, and determine the linear equations that represent the hikers. Students are then able to plot the linear functions and determine an exact point of intersection. (Figure 5) Thus *Sketchpad* facilitates students in modeling and solving real-world problem with multiple representations of tables, graphs, and equations.

Grade 8 Statistics Example with *TinkerPlots*

The focus on statistics in the middle school content standards extends elementary concepts to exploring and analyzing bivariate data. This "requires students to express a relationship between two quantities in question and to interpret components of the relationship in terms of the situation" (NGA Center and CCSSO, 2010, p. 52). In the Statistics and Probability domain of the 8th grade CCSSM standards, students are expected to *Investigate patterns of association in bivariate data*, where they will:

Construct and interpret scatter plots for bivariate measurement data to investigate patterns of association between two quantities. Describe the patterns of association between two quantities.

Figure 5. Multiple representations with Sketchpad

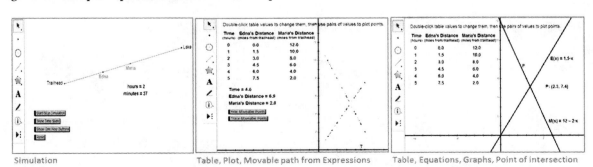

Simulation   Table, Plot, Movable path from Expressions   Table, Equations, Graphs, Point of intersection

Describe patterns such as clustering, outliers, positive or negative association, linear association, and nonlinear association (p. 56).

Often times, students work with paper and pencil or calculators to explore these concepts. *TinkerPlots* (University of Massachusetts, 2005–2012) allows for more creative and in-depth exploration because students can drag bivariate data into a plot, drag and separate the data to create a scatter plot, explore patterns quickly, and look for linear and non-linear associations. Students can analyze the data to determine relationships, investigate outliers, and compare many variables from the same data set to investigate multiple bivariate measurements quickly.

TinkerPlots (University of Massachusetts, 2005–2012) comes with many data sets that offer a cross-curricular, real-world perspective and contain suggestions for exploratory questions. Students can also collect their own data or find data on the Internet and enter them into *TinkerPlots*. The data set called *Body Measurements,* which can be found under the Health category in Data and Demos, has data for 507 adults, 247 men and 260 women, with 23 different attributes collected on each person. The attributes, or variables, include height, weight, wrist diameter, and bicep girth. Students can choose two attributes they think might have a relationship, such as height and weight, and drag one to the horizontal axis and one to the vertical axis. This initially creates a graph with four sections, but by dragging data

points both right and up, students can separate the data until the graph becomes a scatter plot. From the scatter plot, it is evident that there is a positive association between height and weight. By adding a diagonal reference line, students can begin to investigate whether a linear model is appropriate and explore the meaning of the slope and *y*-intercept in the original context. Students can layer the attribute of gender on top of the bivariate graph to explore the difference between males and females. (Figure 6) This is just one example of infinitely many bivariate data comparisons and relationships that students can investigate using *TinkerPlots*, allowing them to model real-world data, make conjectures, and immediately test and justify their conclusions.

CCSSM HIGH SCHOOL CONTENT APPLICATIONS

The high school CCSSM (NGA Center and CC-SSO, 2010) are focused on content that students need to be college- and career-ready and prepared for advanced concepts such as calculus and discrete mathematics. The high school standards are organized around conceptual categories and these categories are not bounded by specific courses of study, but may span several courses of study. For example, the conceptual category of functions contains standards which might be studied in several courses such as algebra, geometry, and precalculus. The high school standards "portray a coherent

Figure 6. Bivariate data with TinkerPlots

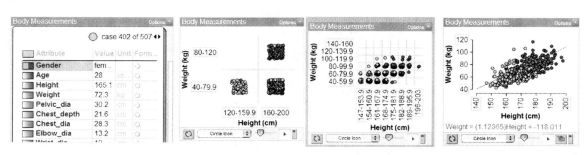

view of high school mathematics" (p. 57), with the conceptual category of modeling interwoven throughout the high school standards. The use of dynamic mathematics software is a particularly important tool for high school mathematics standards because the concepts are increasingly more abstract. Being able to manipulate visual models of mathematical concepts makes abstract concepts more accessible for all students.

Geometry Example with *Sketchpad*

Congruence is a concept traditionally covered in geometry courses. The CCSSM (NGA Center and CCSSO, 2010) takes an approach to congruence not previously emphasized in standards, which is to focus on describing congruence in the context of rigid transformations, such as translations, reflections, and rotations. The CCSSM uses the principle of superposition, which defines two objects as congruent "if there is a sequence of rigid transformations that carries one onto another" (p. 74). Under the Congruence domain, the *Understand congruence in terms of rigid motion* standard G-CO.6 states students will:

Use geometric descriptions of rigid motions to transform figures and to predict the effect of a given rigid motion on a given figure; given two figures, use the definition of congruence in terms of rigid motions to decide if they are congruent (p. 76).

This approach to teaching congruence may be new for many teachers. Dynamic mathematics software like *Sketchpad* (KCP Technologies, 2011b) gives students the ability to drag, manipulate, and animate shapes using rigid transformations so that they can see the sequence of transformations that maps one shape onto another.

Using *Sketchpad* (KCP Technologies, 2011b), students can construct or draw a polygon, or pre-image, and then use different rigid transformations to create one or more images of the original. Measuring corresponding sides and angles and exploring the figures as they are dragged helps to identify properties of the rigid transformations. In this example (Figure 7), the pre-image, triangle ABC, has been rotated about the origin and transformed into image A'B'C'. Using an angle of transformation, traces of the image as it is rotated by degrees are captured to show the sequence of movements that map ABC onto A'B'C'. Corresponding angles and measures show that the two shapes are congruent. Student can drag the vertices to create different triangles and explore the transformation, test their conjectures about the properties, and justify their conclusions.

Statistics Example with *Fathom*

The high school Statistics and Probability standards in the CCSSM (NGA Center and CCSSO, 2010) focus on examining and interpreting data

Figure 7. Rigid motion with Sketchpad

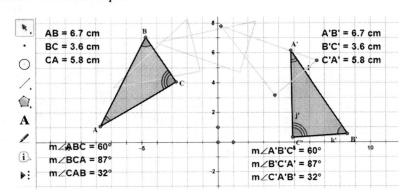

to find patterns and describe characteristics. Students learn about measures of shape, center, and spread and are expected to compare distributions numerically, using statistical measures, and visually, using various plots. Students' questions and the dynamic actions they take to examine and explore data distributions determine the statistics and plots they use. In the Interpreting Categorical and Quantitative Data domain, standard S-ID.6 from *Summarize, represent, and interpret data on two categorical and quantitative variables* states that students will:

Represent data on two quantitative variables on a scatter plot, and describe how the variables are related; a) Fit a function to the data; use functions fitted to data to solve problems in the context of the data (p. 81).

Fathom (KCP Technologies, 2011b) allows students to take quantitative variables and display them in a variety of different plots, including scatter plots. Students can add a moveable line, which displays its equation using the variable descriptors, modeling the function within the context of the data. Visually, as they manipulate the line, students can see how the equation and the plot reflect the context. The ability to use the variables that relate to the real-world context helps students model the mathematics and make sense of the problem and understand how the statistics describe the situation.

There are built-in data sets within *Fathom* (KCP Technologies, 2011a) that cover both mathematical topics and cross-curricular topics such as health, science, and social studies. These data sets provide real-world data for students to explore and analyze, making statistical and probability concepts relevant. An example data set is in the United States data category within the Social Studies files in the Sample Demos of *Fathom*. The data set, *U.S. Cities,* provides students with information on population size, land area, labor percentage, crime rate, median house rate, and many other attributes drawn from U.S. Census data. Students can explore many questions simply by choosing variables they think might have a correlation, creating plots, and using either moveable lines or function plots to model the data. One possible question to explore is whether the percentage of the labor force that is female is related to the percentage of the labor force with college degrees (Figure 8). Students drag and drop the female labor attribute onto the horizontal axis of the plot and the education level attribute onto the vertical axis and can immediately see that there is a positive correlation between the two. The data seem to indicate that the more educated people in a city, the higher the percentage of female workers. Students can add a moveable line to the graph and immediately see a function, whose variables are the attributes of educated and female labor. They can adjust to get a line of best fit and discuss the meaning of the

Figure 8. Correlations and modeling data with Fathom

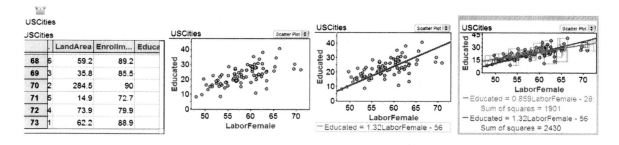

function in relation to the context. Students can add a least-squares line and compare it to their line of fit, and then show the sum of the squares and talk about what the distances from the data points to the line of fit means in this context. With *Fathom* (KCP Technologies, 2011a), questions and conjectures can be investigated immediately. The data, statistics, functions, and graphs all work together to help make connections between the context, visual representation, and symbolic representation.

IMPLICATIONS, CHALLENGES, FUTURE DIRECTIONS

Helping teachers integrate dynamic mathematics software like *Sketchpad* (KCP Technologies, 2011b), *TinkerPlots* (University of Massachusetts, 2005–2012), and *Fathom* (KCP Technologies, 2011a) is important for effecting change in both teacher practice and student achievement. The ultimate goal is that these tools will help students master math content and become mathematically proficient, as described in the CCSSM (NGA Center and CCSSO, 2010). The challenge is in choosing the right tools and using those tools effectively. "Learning a few good tools well enough to use them knowledgeably, intelligently, mathematically, confidently, and appropriately in solving otherwise difficult problems makes a genuine contribution to a student's mathematical education" (Goldenberg, 2000, p. 7).

There are many different options for dynamic mathematics software, of which *Sketchpad* (KCP Technologies, 2011b), *TinkerPlots* (University of Massachusetts, 2005–2012), and *Fathom* (KCP Technologies, 2011a) are among the leaders. Choosing the best fit for schools, teachers, and students is a challenge and should be done with a clear plan to ensure that the tools ultimately chosen match the goals of the school, including plans for

training and support. According to Goldenberg (2000), it is important to make sure the technology that is ultimately chosen matches the goals of the classroom and the needs of the student.

Teachers will need training on not only the skills, or the how-to's of the dynamic mathematics software, but more importantly, the pedagogy, or how to integrate these tools into instruction and mathematical lessons appropriately, where it will have the intended outcome of improving student understanding and achievement (National Staff Development Council, 2012). Helping teachers focus on the purpose of the lesson and what tools are most important to achieve the lesson goals should be part of lesson planning and training. Additionally, time is a key component. Changing teacher practice and integrating new tools takes time, and teachers need time to implement, practice, and reflect. It is important to offer continued support and time for collaboration on a long-term basis, including helping teachers focus on the goals of the curriculum and specific lessons, determining when dynamic mathematics is an appropriate tool, and considering how to use the tool efficiently to help students learn and construct meaning.

I have worked with several different models that show long-term success in supporting teacher's integration of dynamic mathematics software. Blended professional development, combining periodic face-to-face meetings with follow-up online components, works because it allows teachers to focus on specific math content and learn how to use dynamic mathematics software to teach those concepts over time. During the online portions, teachers explore the content standards, practice dynamic mathematics skills, and collaborate to create lesson plans that they try in their classrooms. Through discussion forums and reflections online, teachers get feedback, support, and ideas as they implement the use of dynamic mathematics instruction. Face-to-face meetings provide time for sharing of student artifacts and lessons, collaborative feedback, and learning and modeling of more specific dynamic mathematics and instructional strategies.

Online courses by themselves, such as those offered by Key Curriculum (2012), also provide a longer-term learning model that allows for learning skills and content, trying lessons in the classroom, and then using the collaborative online community to provide feedback and support. Another model that works well is the development of a collaborative school team that meets together on a regular basis to plan lessons together. With the goal of integrating dynamic mathematics on a regular basis, the team plans a lesson that everyone will try that addresses content standards and fits in with pacing and instructional goals. Each person on the team implements the lesson and the team then shares and debriefs each experience. This includes looking at student artifacts from the lesson, a video of the actual lesson, or reflective notes each teacher keeps. The team debriefs, makes adjustments, and discusses instructional strategies that worked and did not work, and then uses those analyses to plan the next set of lessons. This approach involved learning the necessary skills together, focusing on specific teaching strategies, modeling, and coaching (Meng & Sam, 2011). This lesson-study model ensures a long-term, sustained, consistent use of dynamic mathematics in a supportive, collaborative environment over time

CONCLUSION

Dynamic mathematics software is a tool that helps students become mathematically proficient because of its ability to make mathematics visible and tangible. It promotes reasoning and problem solving because of the ease with which students can make a conjecture and drag and manipulate the mathematics on the screen to test and verify their conclusions. Having the capability to see

many iterations of mathematical concepts, create simulations and a multitude of examples, and observe specific characteristics and variables and their impact on mathematical constructs provides a deeper understanding of mathematical concepts.

According to Goldenberg (2000), technology provides a different set of mathematics problems that can be presented to students because it allows for visual representations that "respond to students' questions, answers, or commands" (p. 1). Technologies, such as dynamic mathematics software, that are "well designed and well used, can increase the variety of problems that students can think about and solve" (p. 1). How the tool is used is as important as what tool is used. Used appropriately, dynamic mathematics software can "help students develop new and powerful ways of looking at problems" (p. 2). *Sketchpad* (KCP Technologies, 2011b), *TinkerPlots* (University of Massachusetts, 2005–2012), and *Fathom* (KCP Technologies, 2011a) are examples of dynamic mathematics software that can support the CCSSM (NGA Center and CCSSO, 2010). Through their use, students learn specific math content but are also able to pose questions, test conjectures, and see immediate results from their own dragging and manipulations, supporting the Standards for Mathematical Practice. To have a true impact on the math proficiency and understanding of students, dynamic mathematics software must be used appropriately and strategically. This requires evaluating which tools are the most appropriate for school, teacher, and student learning goals and outcomes and choosing tools that will meet school goals and student needs. Teachers need training in both skills and pedagogy surrounding the use of dynamic mathematics software and long-term support for implementation if sustained, effective use is expected. Dynamic mathematics software can be a powerful learning tool for mathematics if carefully chosen, with clear goals and expectations for teachers and students in mind.

REFERENCES

Finzer, W. (2000). *Design of Fathom™, a dynamic statistics environment for the teaching of mathematics.* Paper presented at the International Congress on Mathematical Education (ICME). Tokyo, Japan.

Finzer, W., & Erickson, T. (1998). Dataspace: A computer learning environment for data analysis and statistics based on dynamic dragging, visualization, simulation and networked collaboration. In *Proceedings of the Fifth International Conference on Teaching Statistics.* Voorburg, The Netherlands: International Statistical Institute.

Goldenberg, E. (2000). *Thinking (and talking) about technology in math classrooms.* Newton, MA: Education Development Center, Inc..

Jackiw, N. (2009). *Dynamic geometry® Sketchpad's big idea. Spark! Teaching Mathematics with The Geometer's Sketchpad.* Emeryville, CA: Key Curriculum Press.

KCP Technologies Inc. (2011a). *Fathom® dynamic data software (version 2.11).* [Software]. Retrieved from http://www.keycurriculum.com/fathom/download

KCP Technologies Inc. (2011b). *The geometer's Sketchpad® dynamic geometry® software for exploring mathematics (version 5.04).* [Software]. Retrieved from http://www.keycurriculum.com/sketchpad/download

Key Curriculum. (2012). *Online courses.* Retrieved from www.keycurriculum.com/online-courses

Key Curriculum Press. (2012a). *Exploring expressions and equations with the geometer's Sketchpad® version 5: Addressing the common core state standards for mathematics.* Emeryville, CA: Steven Rasmussen.

Key Curriculum Press. (2012b). *Exploring geometry and measurement with the geometer's Sketchpad® version 5: Addressing the common core state standards for mathematics.* Emeryville, CA: Steven Rasmussen.

Konold, C. (2005). *Exploring data with TinkerPlots.* Emeryville, CA: Key Curriculum Press.

Konold, C. (2006). Designing a data tool for learners. In M. Lovett & P. Shah (Eds.), *Thinking with data: The 33rd Annual Carnegie Symposium on Cognition,* (pp. 267-292). Hillside, NJ: Lawrence Erlbaum Associates.

Meng, C., & Sam, L. (2011). Enhancing pre-service secondary mathematics teacher's skills of using the geometer's Sketchpad through lesson study. *Journal of Science and Mathematics Education in Southeast Asia, 34*(1), 90–110.

National Governors Association Center for Best Practices, Council of Chief State School Officers. (2010). *Common core state standards for mathematics.* Washington, DC: National Governors Association Center for Best Practices, Council of Chief State School Officers. Retrieved from http://www.corestandards.org/assets/CCSSI_Math%20Standards.pdf

National Staff Development Council. (2012). *Standards for professional learning.* Retrieved from http://www.learningforward.org/standards/standards.cfm

University of Massachusetts. (2012). *Tinkerplots® dynamic data exploration (version 2.0).* [Software]. Retrieved from http://www.keycurriculum. com/tinkerplots/download

ADDITIONAL READING

Edwards, M., & Phelps, S. (2008). Can you fathom this? Connecting data analysis, algebra, and geometry with probability simulation. *Mathematics Teacher, 102*(3), 210–216.

Fitzallen, N. (2007). Evaluating data analysis software: The case of TinkerPlots®. *Australian Primary Mathematics Classroom, 12*(1), 23–28.

Hohenwarter, J., Hohenwarter, M., & Lavicza, Z. (2010). Evaluation difficulty levels of dynamic geometry software tools to enhance teacher's professional development. *The International Journal for Technology in Mathematics Education, 17*(3), 127–134.

Konold, C., Harradine, A., & Kazak, S. (2007). Understanding distributions and modeling them. *International Journal of Computers for Mathematical Learning, 12*(3), 217–230. doi:10.1007/s10758-007-9123-1.

Lehrer, R., Kim, M., & Schauble, L. (2007). Supporting the development of conceptions of statistics by engaging students in measuring and modeling variability. *International Journal of Computers for Mathematical Learning, 12*(3), 195–216. doi:10.1007/s10758-007-9122-2.

Martin, T., Cullen, C., & Day, R. (2011). What's 2 got to do with it? Using dynamic geometry environments to find surprising results and motivate proof. *New England Mathematics Journal, 43,* 49–62.

Paparistodeumou, E., & Meletious-Mavrotheris, M. (2008). Developing young student's informal inference skills in data analysis. *Statistics Education Research Journal, 7*(2), 83–106.

Sinclair, N., & Moss, J. (2012). The more it changes, the more it becomes the same: The development of the routine of shape identification in dynamic geometry environment. *International Journal of Educational Research, 51-52*(3), 28–44. doi:10.1016/j.ijer.2011.12.009.

Steketee, S., & Scher, D. (2011). A geometric path to the concept of function. *Mathematics Teaching in the Middle School, 17*(1), 48–55.

Walsh, J., Fitzallen, N., Wilson, K., & Creed, J. (2008). The representational value of hats. *Mathematics Teaching in the Middle School, 14*(1), 4–10.

Walsh, J., & Wright, S. (2008). Building informal inference with TinkerPlots® in a measurement context. *Australian Mathematics Teacher, 64*(4), 31–40.

Walsh, T. (2011). Implementing project-based survey research skills to grade six ELP students with the survey toolkit and TinkerPlots®. *Journal of Statistics Education, 19*(1).

KEY TERMS AND DEFINITIONS

Drag: The ability to grab something on the screen (vertex, side, measure, data point, attribute, etc.) and move it to another location.

Dynamic Geometry Software: Software that allows for mathematical concepts to be shown visually, then dragged and manipulated to show multiple examples that show changes in measures, data, shape, and other characteristics.

Dynamic Mathematics Software: A more general term for dynamic geometry software that includes any software that allows for mathematical concepts to be shown visually, then dragged and manipulated to show multiple examples that show changes in measures, data, shape, and other characteristics.

Implementation: The integration of a specific tool or strategy into instructional practice on a regular basis.

Manipulate: The ability to change constructs on the screen (the size, shape, measures, location, direction, grouping, etc.) in order to explore and investigate.

Mathematically Proficient: Able to solve mathematical problems using available tools and the understanding of mathematical concepts and justify conclusions using age-appropriate and mathematically correct language and resources.

Real-World Problems: Problems arising from everyday situations that require the application of mathematical concepts and relationships to reach a solution.

Strategically: Knowing what tools best fit the mathematical problem or situation and knowing how to use the tools to help solve, explain, and justify conclusions.

Section 3
Vignettes and Cases

Chapter 13

Solving Equations is All about Balance:
Using Virtual Manipulatives in the Middle School Classroom

Robin Magruder
University of Kentucky, USA

Margaret Mohr-Schroeder
University of Kentucky, USA

ABSTRACT

Virtual manipulatives provide benefits to students as they encounter the Common Core State Standards for Mathematics content and practice standards. The National Library of Virtual Manipulatives provides an abundant supply of virtual manipulatives for all K-12 grades and mathematics content areas. Specifically, in this chapter, the authors explore the use of Algebra Balance Scale manipulatives in a middle school mathematics classroom. Using virtual manipulatives increases understanding of the equal sign, algebraic symbols, and increases procedural and conceptual knowledge. In this chapter, the authors demonstrate how using virtual manipulatives helped middle school students to meet grade level content standards for solving equations in one variable. Additionally, practice standards, such as making sense of problems and persevering to solve them, modeling with mathematics, and using tools strategically through the use of virtual manipulatives are addressed. They conclude by considering practical issues related to incorporating virtual manipulatives in mathematics classrooms.

INTRODUCTION

With the release of the Common Core State Standards for Mathematics (CCSSM; CCSSO, 2011), teachers have been searching for unique ways to engage their students in the rigorous content. Central to the implementation of the new standards are the eight mathematical practices. The use of virtual manipulatives is one way for teachers to actively engage all students in their classroom. Through the strategic use of virtual manipulatives, students can utilize the mathematical practices in order to gain a better understanding of the content found in the standards.

DOI: 10.4018/978-1-4666-4086-3.ch013

The purpose of this chapter is to describe the successful use of virtual manipulatives for solving equations in a middle school classroom and to discuss how this learning experience helps students meet the Common Core State Standards for Mathematics. This chapter includes a discussion of related common core standards and common challenges students face meeting these standards, a brief review of literature discussing research-based arguments for using virtual manipulatives, and evidence and vignettes from a qualitative study conducted in a middle school classroom using virtual manipulatives to solve equations.

BACKGROUND

The Common Core State Standards for Mathematics (CCSSM) include grade-specific content standards and over-arching mathematical practice standards. An important theme of the algebra strand of the CCSSM is that middle school students are expected to reason about and solve one-variable equations (CCSSO, 2011). For example, a sixth grade-specific standard (6.EE.7) states students should solve real-world and mathematical problems by writing and solving equations of the form $x + p = q$ and $px = q$ for cases in which p, q, and x are all nonnegative rational numbers. A similar example at the eighth grade level (8.EE.7) states students should solve linear equations in one variable. Additionally, according to the sixth-grade standard 6.NS.5, students should understand that positive and negative numbers are used together to describe quantities having opposite directions and values.

Students often face challenges in mathematics content, especially when trying to make sense of abstract concepts such as solving one-variable equations. Specifically, researchers have identified three common challenges that students often face when attempting to solve equations:

1. Lack of understanding of the equal sign (Knuth, Stephens, McNeil, & Alibali, 2006).
2. Lack of symbolic understanding within an equation (Kilpatrick & Izsak, 2008; Poon & Leung, 2010).
3. Reliance on procedural knowledge without conceptual understanding (Capraro & Joffrion, 2006; Siegler, 2003; Star, 2005).

Students can increase their understanding of solving equations in one-variable by interacting with representations found in virtual manipulatives (Durmus & Karakirik, 2006; Sarama & Clements, 2009).

Meaning of the Equal Sign

Research dating as far back as the 1970s indicates that many students have an incomplete understanding of the meaning of the equal sign (Kieran, 1992; Knuth et al., 2006; Rojano, 2002). Although the equal sign is a ubiquitous element in mathematics classrooms, little time is devoted to its meaning (Knuth et al., 2006). In their seminal work on student understanding of mathematics, Kilpatrick, Swafford, and Findell (2001) described student misconceptions related to the equal sign. Many students described the equal sign as a separation of the question and answer. Other students described a directional symbol, stating that they should work from left to right to solve problems.

Knuth et al. (2006) revealed student misconceptions of the equal sign as they conducted a quantitative study of middle school students (n=177). A majority of students described the equal sign as operational, expecting or announcing an answer. Students had difficulty solving equations with variables on both sides because they were unsure how to proceed based on their limited understanding of the equal sign. A limitation of this study was a lack of exploration of teaching methods, which led students to their understandings of the equal sign.

Symbolic Understanding

Students often have difficulties understanding various symbols while learning algebra. For example, students are often unable to differentiate between *4* and *4x*. Students also have difficulty with symbols with multiple meanings such as the minus sign. Poon and Leung (2010) conducted a quantitative study investigating symbolic understanding of grade nine equivalent students (n=815) from Hong Kong. They described a weakness in the algebra curriculum citing students whom simply accept formal rules and techniques of algebra without understanding concepts. Results of their study indicated students did not understand the different roles of constants and coefficients within an equation. For example, students treated *3x* and *3* in the same way, combining them as like terms.

Vlassis (2008) conducted a qualitative study of eighth grade students (n=17) investigating their understanding of the minus sign in various algebraic contexts. Vlassis noted students had difficulty solving equations with negative coefficients and equations, which produced a negative solution. Although Vlassis' study provided insight into student performance, generalizability is difficult because of a small number of participants.

Conceptual and Procedural Knowledge

In order to solve equations successfully, students must have conceptual and procedural understanding. Star (2005) provided a definition of *procedural knowledge,* focusing on understanding symbols and rules. Star additionally defined *conceptual knowledge* as making connections and creating networks within information. According to the CCSSO:

The standards stress not only procedural skill but also conceptual understanding, to make sure students are learning and absorbing the critical information they need to succeed at higher lev-

els - rather than the current practices by which many students learn enough to get by on the next test, but forget it shortly thereafter, only to review again the following year. ("Key Points in Mathematics," 2011)

Since US textbooks tend to emphasize rules and procedures to a greater degree than concept development (Kilpatrick et al., 2001), it is important that students have exposure to activities and lessons that will help them to develop conceptual knowledge of a particular standard.

Siegler (2003) discussed problems that arise when students depend on procedural knowledge without conceptual understanding, describing this type of learning as "Exercises in symbol manipulation, without any connection to real-world contexts" (p. 222). Capraro and Joffrion (2006) investigated seventh and eighth grade students (n=668) who were translating written words into algebraic equations. The results indicated that students with stronger conceptual understanding were more successful because of greater flexibility than students relying more on procedural understanding.

Virtual Manipulatives

Although there are several interpretations of what a virtual manipulative is, Moyer, Bolyard, and Spikell (2002) defined a virtual manipulative to be "an *interactive,* Web-based visual representation of a dynamic object that presents opportunities for constructing mathematical knowledge" (p. 371, emphasis added). A group at Utah State University, sponsored by the National Science Foundation, created the *National Library of Virtual Manipulatives* (NLVM) providing free access to teachers, parents, and students of many Web-based Java™ applets (2010). According to NLVM designers, using virtual manipulatives provides students the opportunity to become active participants in learning (2010). The NLVM endorses an active role for students, stating that students should be engaged at all grade levels. They additionally provide interactive online learning units and classroom management tools to support teachers as they integrate virtual manipulatives in their classrooms.

The Algebra Balance Scale virtual manipulative, available on the NLVM Website (http://nlvm.usu.edu/), uses a balance scale and two different sized blocks – the smaller cube representing one unit and the larger rectangular prism, or "*x*-blocks", representing variables. This applet allows students to model solving an equation in one variable by generating random problems to solve, or students can input their own equations. As students place the appropriate items on the scale, it is shown to be out of balance until the problem is represented completely and correctly (Figure 1). This visual representation helps students see the importance of equality in an equation. Next, students select the operations they need to use (add, subtract, multiply, or divide) in order to successfully solve the equation. Each step is represented on the balance scale, and the corresponding new equation is recorded in the equation window. These visual cues help students see the connection between the representation and the written equation. As students work with the equation, the applet pro-

vides feedback indicating a correct solution, or an incorrect attempt. The Algebra Balance Scale Negatives applet works similarly but introduces negative constants and variables with balloons and allows students to solve equations with negative values.

Using virtual manipulatives to solve equations also helps students to utilize several of the mathematical practices emphasized in the standards including: making sense of problems and persevering in solving them, modeling with mathematics, and using tools strategically (CCSSO, 2011). These CCSSM practice standards were derived from NCTM process standards and proficiency goals presented by the National Research Council. According to the CCSSI Website (www.corestandards.org), to be successful mathematical thinkers, students must process information well and have positive habits of mind (2011). Students must understand the types of problems they are solving and the relationships between various models within problems. Students are expected to engage in metacognitive processes and use concrete or pictorial models of problems. Students using virtual manipulatives have the opportunity to meet these practice standards as well as the specific grade-level standards previously mentioned.

USING VIRTUAL MANIPULATIVES TO SOLVE ONE-VARIABLE EQUATIONS

Seventh grade mathematics students (n=22) in a public school in rural Southeast United States spent a week using the *Algebra Balance Scale* applet (NLVM, 2010) to strengthen their understanding of solving equations. The researcher developed materials for students to complete at their own pace. The materials included: one-step equations in the form of $x + p = q$ or $px = q$ where p, q, and x were all nonnegative rational numbers; multi-step equations with nonnegative rational numbers; and equations with negative constants and coefficients.

Figure 1. An equation modeled using algebra balance scales, which emphasizes balance between two sides (© 2010 MATTI Assoc. and Utah State University. Used with permission)

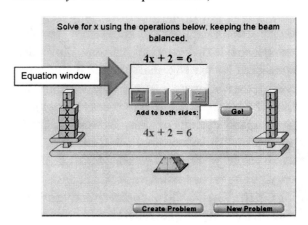

Finally, a mixed review of all types of one-variable equations completed the materials, for a total of forty equations for students to solve within the week. Students were asked to record the steps of solving the equation within the materials provided.

The teacher of record began the week with investigations with the virtual manipulative, *Algebra Balance Scale*, by modeling an equation on a SMART® Board in the classroom. The teacher demonstrated how to enter the equation into the applet and to drag items to both sides of the equation. Next, she showed the possible operations necessary for solving the equation. She reminded students that the goal of solving equations is to isolate the variable, and find its value. The teacher pointed out unique features of the applet such as the balance scale, the equation window, and feedback provided for correct and incorrect actions. Students expressed enthusiasm as the equation was demonstrated, some saying, "That's cool", or "I get it." Many students had "ah-ha moments" when the equation became balanced.

Next, students were dismissed to the computer lab to solve equations at their own pace. After learning how to set up equations properly, students worked through the materials independently with occasional assistance from other students or the teacher as needed. Students reacted positively to working with virtual manipulatives and remained actively engaged throughout the lessons.

Data Collection Procedures

The researcher utilized qualitative research methods including interviews and observations of students and the teacher. At the onset of the study, the researcher interviewed the teacher discussing prior teaching experience, challenges students face solving equations, and the teacher's experience using manipulatives in the classroom. The researcher observed all lessons in which the students used virtual manipulatives. During the first two class periods, the researcher merely ob-

served classroom activity, student-teacher interaction, and other student activities. The researcher took a more active role through the remainder of the study, interacting with students, asking them to explain their steps and reasoning as they used virtual manipulatives. Students discussed their understanding of the equal sign and other symbols. A focus group interview of four randomly selected students (three boys and one girl) took place after all classwork was completed. Finally, the researcher interviewed the teacher to discuss perceived benefits and challenges of using virtual manipulatives. All classroom observations and interviews were transcribed and coded.

Meaning of the Equal Sign

The Algebra Balance Scale virtual manipulatives increased students' understanding of the equal sign by providing a visual representation. As students place boxes representing variables and constants on one side of the equation, the heavier side of the scale drops (Figure 2). Once the correct boxes are placed on the other side, the scale is balanced once again. Although Sarama and Clements (2009)

Figure 2. An equation that is not complete and unbalanced, which emphasizes the role of the equal sign within an equation (© 2010 MATTI Assoc. and Utah State University. Used with permission)

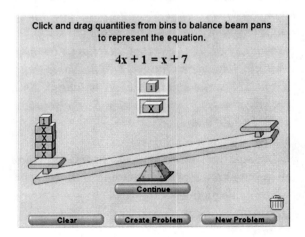

were not specifically referencing the Algebra Balance Scale, they discussed benefits of virtual manipulatives, stating:

Computer manipulatives can also serve as symbols for mathematical ideas, often better than physical manipulatives can. For example, the computer manipulative can have just the mathematical features that developers wish it to have and just the actions on it that they wish to promote- not additional properties that may be distracting. (p. 148)

The notion of balance as it relates to the equal sign on the Algebra Balance Scale is a good example. Each time students correctly model the equation, the scale becomes balanced, emphasizing the equality between the sides.

Melanie (all student names were changed) input the equation, $2x + 4 = x + 5$, and began to solve. When asked by the researcher to verbalize how she was thinking about the equation, she stated, "I know that since there are four on the left side and five on the right side, I can take four away from both sides." With that statement, Melanie input *subtract 4* and the new equation,

$2x = x + 1$, was displayed within the equation window and as boxes on the balance scale. She continued:

Before using the virtual manipulatives, I would not know what to do. I did not know that I could take an x away from both sides because I did not know the value of x. Now I realize that it doesn't matter what x is, because as long as I do the same thing to both sides, the equation stays balanced. So I can take x away from both sides. So the solution is x = 1 (field notes).

Melanie and other students benefitted from the representation of the equal sign as the balance point of an equation.

Eli was solving the equation, $2x + 4 = x + 6$. When asked by the researcher why the equation was balanced, he stated:

I have 2x and four on that (left) side and one x and six on that (right) side and it balances out. So I subtract four ones from both sides because this side has four and this side has more than four, and they cancel out. This one has a two (x) and this one has a one (x), so you can subtract x from both sides. (field notes)

He concluded, "The virtual manipulatives help me understand that both sides have to be equal. All of the things on one side have to be equal to the things on the other side." The Algebra Balance Scale explicitly demonstrates that all student actions affect *both* sides of equations equally. The strength of the virtual manipulative is that it does not allow students to manipulate just one side of the equation. This realization helps students broaden their conceptual knowledge of the equal sign from one as merely a computational symbol to a symbol of equality.

Symbolic Understanding

The virtual manipulative Algebra Balance Scale helped the students strengthen their symbolic understanding; it provided distinct representations for various algebraic objects. Poon and Leung (2010) indicated that students often do not distinguish between the roles of constants and coefficients. Using virtual manipulatives helps students make this distinction. For example, Michael solved the equation, $2x + 2 = x + 4$, and incorrectly input subtract 2x from both sides, and the virtual manipulative displayed the feedback, "You can't subtract 2x unless there is at least 2x's on each side." This feedback helped Michael realize that subtracting 2 and 2x are not equivalent actions. With the clue provided by the feedback, Michael changed course and subtracted *2* from both sides. Michael's error is common for middle school students; many have difficulty recognizing the difference between constants and coefficients (Poon & Leung, 2010). Without feedback provided by the Algebra Balance Scale, this error often leads to incorrect simplification of equations and combining like terms incorrectly.

As students set up equations to be solved constants and coefficients are represented by different objects – letters, numbers, and/or symbols. The difference between algebraic objects becomes even more distinct as students solve equations with the Algebra Balance Scales Negatives Applet, in which negative variables and constants are represented by red balloons while the positive values remain blue boxes. Another student, Sadie noticed there were no similar elements on both sides of the equation, *2x - 3 = -2x + 1* (Figure 3). In a discussion about this equation with her teacher, she stated, "I can't just remove the same thing from both sides because nothing is on both sides." Sadie's teacher encouraged her to use trial and error and reminded her that the goal of solving equations is to get the variable isolated on one side of the equation in order to discover its value. Sadie continued, "Well, the *x* is positive on this side (the left side), so I am going to add three to both sides to get it by itself." The resulting *2x = -2x + 4* was displayed in the equation window as boxes and balloons on the balance scale. Sadie continued, "The *x* is by itself, but there are other *x*'s on the other side so I need to put them all together on one side. Since they are *-2x*, I think I need to add *2x*." Sadie added *2x* to the equation and *4x = 4* was the result, Sadie immediately recognized that *x = 1*. Without the benefit of the representation provided by the virtual manipulatives, students often have difficulties distinguishing the difference between positive and negative variables, which results in errors.

Conceptual and Procedural Knowledge

Sarama and Clements (2009) praised the strong connection between virtual manipulatives and the mathematics they represent. The record of steps allows students the opportunity to reflect on their thinking process, which increases conceptual understanding. Teachers and students overwhelmingly agree that using virtual manipulatives increased conceptual knowledge. After using the Algebra Balance Scales, students seemed to have a deeper understanding of the purpose of solving one-step equations. Additionally, students developed a clearer understanding of constraints while solving equations. The teacher attributed student gains in conceptual knowledge to the feedback and the ability to explore with virtual manipulatives. She stated:

Students gained conceptual understanding because if they messed up; they could see what happened, and fix it, or explore more of 'what if I do this', or trying out other things. Students could always look back at the equations and figure out what caused the results they obtained. (field notes)

Figure 3. An equation modeled with algebra balance scales negatives, which distinguishes between positive and negative variables and exponents (© 2010 MATTI Assoc. and Utah State University. Used with permission)

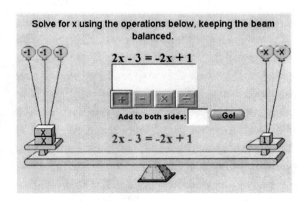

207

Virtual manipulatives helped the students improve their conceptual knowledge of one-step equations and the concepts associated with them because of the flexibility that is allowed in student work. For example, to solve the equation, $2x + 6 = 4x + 4$, there is not a set order of procedures that must be followed. This equation could be solved by first subtracting $2x$ from both sides, subtracting 4 from both sides, or dividing both sides of the equation by 2. By using the Algebra Balance Scale, the concepts of equality and symbols are emphasized over rigid rules such as steps for solving equations.

Not all students gained conceptual knowledge by using virtual manipulatives alone. One student, Mary was solving the equation, $2x + 3 = x + 4$, and the following exchange took place:

Mary: I am subtracting 3 from both sides.
Researcher: Why?
Mary: Because.... Um...You just do. So you can solve the problem (Mary laughs nervously). The goal is to get the answer (Mary laughs again and seems unsure of how to explain solving equations).

While she is talking, Mary works the problem out completely to get the solution, x=1, yet she is unable to explain what she is doing or why she is doing it, so the researcher suggests that she start the equation again.

Mary: I will subtract 3 from both sides.
Researcher: Let's look at the way this equation is set up, why would you subtract 3 from both sides?
Mary: ...Because... Because there is three that you can subtract from both sides.
Researcher: Right, because if there is the same thing on both sides, you can take it away, and the equation will remain balanced, that is how a scale works.
Mary: Now I can subtract x from both sides for the same reason and x=1 (field notes).

This exchange between the researcher and Mary indicates reliance upon procedural skills likely obtained from prior experiences solving equations while focusing on procedural knowledge. The feedback and visual representation may be adequate for many students to develop a deeper conceptual understanding, but the teacher still plays an important role in the classroom. Because students are able to work independently while using virtual manipulatives, teachers have the opportunity to spend time with individual students, such as Mary, to provide assistance or probe conceptual understanding. Students benefit from these exchanges because they are communicating as well as actively participating in solving equations.

IMPLICATIONS, CHALLENGES, FUTURE DIRECTIONS

Common Core State Standards Grade Level Standards

As students use the Algebra Balance Scale and Algebra Balance Scale Negatives, they are engaging in a hands-on approach to learn about solving one-step equations, an important foundational algebraic concept. Several grade level standards specifically address solving equations. For example, standard 6.EE.7 states that students should solve real-world and mathematical problems by writing and solving equations of the form $x + p = q$ and $px = q$ for cases in which p, q, and x are all nonnegative rational numbers (CCSSO, 2011). While using the Algebra Balance Scale, students meet and exceed this expectation by solving expected forms of equations, as well as more complicated equations, such as the form $ax + b = cx + d$. Another grade level standard (8.EE.7) states that students should solve linear equations in one variable. Additionally, according to standard 6.NS.5, students should understand that positive and negative numbers are used together to describe quantities having opposite directions and values. Students make this realization as they work with the Algebra Balance Scales Negatives.

Common Core Practice Standards

Active learning, which allows students to build their own understanding of concepts and procedures, is a salient feature of Constructivism, the primary paradigm of mathematics education (Ernest, 1996). Many Constructivists advocate the use of manipulatives because students model mathematics, which increases perseverance and understanding at a deeper level. "It is clear that learning is not about accumulating random information, memorizing it, and then repeating it on some exam; learning is about understanding and applying concepts, constructing meaning, and thinking about ideas" (Gordon, 2009, p. 743). The eight practice standards advocated by the CCSSM seem to line up with Constructivist philosophy. Three of these practice standards, making sense of problems and persevering in solving them, modeling with mathematics, and using tools strategically are reflected in the use of virtual manipulatives.

Making Sense of Problems and Persevering in Solving Problems

Students must develop a clear understanding of a problem in order for to meet the practice standard of making sense of a problem and persevering in solving it. According to NLVM creators, "Learning and understanding mathematics, at every level, requires student engagement. Mathematics is not, as has been said, a spectator sport" ("Project Information," 2010). As described later, active engagement afforded by virtual manipulatives may lead to increased student understanding. In the focus group interview, students reported that while using the Algebra Balance Scale, they were able to learn from their successes and their mistakes. Students described the feedback as a key to their success.

Solving equations with virtual manipulatives requires multiple steps; as students attempt to solve equations, they sometimes make mistakes. Feedback provided by virtual manipulatives helps students realize their errors and persevere in correcting them. For example, as Karen solved the equation, $2x - 3 = -2x + 1$, her first step was to subtract three from both sides of the equation which resulted in the new equation, $2x - 6 = -2x - 2$. When the resulting equation was displayed, it was not what Karen expected. Soon, Karen realized that she should have added three to both sides to simplify. Her next step was to add 6, and she was well on her way to solving the equation correctly. This experience helped Karen make sense of solving equations because she realized that in order to simplify the equation, she had to perform the opposite operation.

Another student, Sean persevered through a unique experience as he solved the equation, $2x - 4 = -2x + 4$. Initially, in a conversation with his teacher, he stated, "I know I need to add four on this (the left) side, but I don't know what to do after that." His teacher encouraged him to try this approach and to consider the equation as a whole. At this point, Sean was troubled because he was not sure how to simplify the equation to eliminate the $-2x$ on the right side of the equation, and he did not understand how it related to the left side of the equation. He became frustrated, but with assistance from his teacher, he realized that all of the constants and coefficients were multiples of two, so he divided the equation by two, with the resulting equation, $x = -x + 4$. Although this action simplified the equation, Sean was still puzzled. His next step was to subtract x from both sides of the equation. Upon seeing the result on the balance scale and in the equation window (Figure 4), which displayed $0 = -2x + 4$, he responded, "Now I can't do anything." His teacher encouraged him to keep thinking, and he realized that in order to get the variable by itself, he could move it to the left side (by adding $2x$). Finally, Sean divided by 2 to solve the equation. It is unlikely that Sean would have been successful

209

Figure 4. An equation modeled with algebra balance scales negatives showing intermediate equations as a student attempted to solve, as well as an equation with 0 on the left side (© 2010 MATTI Assoc. and Utah State University. Used with permission)

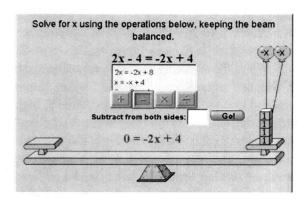

in solving this equation without the feedback and support provided by the virtual manipulatives and his teacher. Even though he could have solved the equation more efficiently, he persevered.

Modeling with Mathematics

Virtual manipulatives provide a model of mathematics that can be interacted with, changed, and which provides valuable feedback to students (Moyer et al., 2002; NLVM, 2010). In a study comparing concrete and virtual manipulatives in elementary mathematics classrooms, Martin (2008) stated, "If children's work with the virtual manipulative is recorded, children can play their actions back, providing greater opportunities for reflection" (p. 270). He described the processing as *representational redescription*. According to Martin, students benefit from working with manipulatives because they allow time for reflection.

During this study, students modeled equations with virtual manipulatives, and they were also asked to draw the corresponding steps in the materials they were given. Drawing the steps provided students with one more opportunity to model the equations. Students took two ap-

proaches to this task. About half of the students completely solved the equation with the virtual manipulatives and then drew each step that was taken. This approach allowed students to reflect on the equation solving process as a whole. One student reported that he would sometimes forget how he solved the equation, so drawing the steps allowed him to rethink the entire equation, which strengthened his understanding.

Other students in the study drew each step immediately after completing the step using the virtual manipulatives. This approach allowed students a clearer picture of how each step caused the equation to change. A student stated that this approach helped him make the connection between the actions he took and the results of the actions, which he believes strengthened his understanding. Regardless of which approach they chose, students overwhelmingly agreed that drawing the steps helped to increase their understanding. The teacher noted that in general, students enjoy drawing and often use drawings to understand and solve problems. She concluded, "Students love drawing; writing helps them, drawing helps, it helps the math stick, they have seen it, done it on the virtual manipulatives, and drawn it." Drawing steps allows students one more opportunity to reflect on and interact with each equation.

Using Tools Strategically

Students should have access to a variety of tools as they learn mathematics (Van de Walle & Lovin, 2006). These tools may include concrete manipulatives, virtual manipulatives, calculators, and other devices. Teachers often design lessons around tools they expect students to use. Other times, students should have the opportunity to self-select tools (Van de Walle & Lovin, 2006). With time and reflection afforded by representations such as virtual manipulatives, students may learn more advanced mathematical concepts and move away from needing manipulatives. Gradually, as understanding increases, students should rely less on manipulatives, and move toward abstract thinking and processing. The time students spend learning with manipulatives becomes prior knowledge that can be transferred to abstract concepts in the future. Although they disagreed about specifics, iconic Constructivists Jerome Bruner, Seymour Papert, and Jean Piaget discussed the importance of concrete representations and their role in preparing students for abstract concepts (Kafai, 2002; McLeod, 2008; Wadsworth, 1996; Wood, Smith, & Grossnicklaus, 2001).

Practical Considerations

Although using virtual manipulates for solving equations provided many benefits, practical considerations need to be addressed. Practical benefits of using virtual manipulatives include free, unlimited access for students, teachers, and families. Students can access virtual manipulatives from their home at their convenience, or in enrichment programs after school. There is no clean-up required after using virtual manipulatives; students can clean up with the touch of a button or a click of the mouse. Teachers can set up courses for their classes, which record assessment results and student progress.

One limitation of virtual manipulatives is software constraints. For example, the Algebra Balance Scale currently does not accept variables larger than nine or fractional variables or constants. This limitation prohibits students from solving equations in the form of $(a/b)x = c$. Other concerns include adequate Internet accessibility and availability of quality computers. Although most schools have adequate Internet access, not all schools do.

The computer lab used in this study was not state-of-the-art; the average computer was approximately eight years old. Using older, slower computers meant lost class time as students had to wait for NLVM Webpages to load. It took an average of ten minutes for all students to log in and work on the virtual manipulatives, wasting valuable class time. Although little can be done to improve computer or Internet quality, teachers

could load Webpages prior to the beginning of class, which would reduce waiting time for students. However, this is not always possible. In the school district where this study was conducted, each student must log in with a distinct user name and password. Because of these constraints, the teacher was unable to prepare the computers prior to class time. NLVM virtual manipulatives may be purchased by schools and downloaded directly onto computers, which would reduce lost class time; however, it would cost the school some money.

Future Directions

There are several future directions for studies related to virtual manipulatives. The preponderance of research related to manipulatives, including virtual manipulatives, occurs at the elementary school level. More research needs to take place at middle school and secondary levels to study the effectiveness of manipulatives with older students. Several studies have been published in which researchers compared the effectiveness of concrete and virtual manipulatives. However, most of these studies took place in the elementary level. In addition to studies that compare the effectiveness of concrete and virtual manipulatives, researchers may study the effectiveness of lessons including multiple representations, blending both types of materials together. Little research exists related to student attitudes toward virtual manipulatives. Finally, longitudinal studies could explore the effectiveness of virtual manipulatives over time.

CONCLUSION

Virtual manipulatives provide benefits to students as they meet Common Core State Standards for Mathematics content and practice standards. The National Library of Virtual Manipulatives is just one source of virtual manipulatives for K-12 grades and content areas. In this study, the Algebra Balance Scale increased understanding of the equal sign, algebraic symbols, and increased procedural and conceptual knowledge. Unique features of virtual manipulatives such as the visual representation, recording of results, and feedback are essential elements which help to increase student understanding of mathematics.

REFERENCES

Capraro, M. M., & Joffrion, H. (2006). Algebraic equations: Can middle-school students meaningfully translate from words to mathematical symbols? *Reading Psychology*, *27*, 147–164. doi:10.1080/02702710600642467.

Common Core State Standards Initiative. (2011). *Common core state standards for mathematics.* Retrieved October 30, 2011, from http://www.corestandards.org/

Durmus, S., & Karakirik, E. (2006). Virtual manipulatives in mathematics education: A theoretical framework. *The Turkish Online Journal of Educational Technology, 5*(1).

Ernest, P. (1996). Varieties of constructivism: A framework for comparison. In Steffe, L. P., Nesher, P., Cobb, P., Goldin, G. A., & Greer, B. (Eds.), *Theories of mathematical learning* (pp. 389–398). Hillsdale, NJ: Erlbaum.

Gordon, M. (2009). The misuses and effective uses of constructivist teaching. *Teachers and Teaching: Theory and Practice*, *15*, 737–746. doi:10.1080/13540600903357058.

Kafai, Y. B. (2002). Constructionism. In Sawyer, R. K. (Ed.), *Cambridge handbook of the learning sciences*. West Nyack, NY: Cambridge University Press.

Kieran, C. (1992). The learning and teaching of school algebra. In Grouws, D. (Ed.), *Handbook of research on mathematics teaching and learning* (pp. 390–419). New York: Macmillan Library Reference.

Kilpatrick, J., & Izsak, A. (2008). A history of algebra in the school curriculum. In Greenes, C. E. (Ed.), *Algebra and algebraic thinking in school mathematics* (pp. 3–18). Reston, VA: National Council of Teachers of Mathematics.

Kilpatrick, J., Swafford, J., & Findell, B. (2001). *Adding it up: Helping children learn mathematics.* Washington, DC: National Academy Press.

Knuth, E. J., Stephens, A. C., McNeil, N. M., & Alibali, M. W. (2006). Does understanding the equal sign matter? Evidence from solving equations. *Journal for Research in Mathematics Education, 37*(4), 297–312.

Martin, T. (2008). Physically distributed learning with virtual manipulatives for elementary mathematics. In Robinson, D. H., & Schraw, G. (Eds.), *Recent innovations in educational technology that facilitate student learning* (pp. 253–275). Charlotte, NC: Information Age Publishing.

McLeod, S. A. (2008). *Simple psychology.* Retrieved from http://www.simplypsychology.org/bruner.html

McNeil, N. M., & Uttal, D. H. (2009). Rethinking the use of concrete materials in learning: Perspectives from development and education. *Child Development Perspectives*, *3*(3), 137–139. doi:10.1111/j.1750-8606.2009.00093.x.

Moyer, P., Bolyard, J. J., & Spikell, M. A. (2002). What are virtual manipulatives? *Teaching Children Mathematics, 8*, 372–377.

National Library of Virtual Manipulatives. (2010). *National library of virtual manipulatives.* Retrieved January 2, 2011, from http://nlvm.usu.edu/en/nav/vlibrary.html

Polly, D. (2011). Technology to develop algebraic reasoning. *Teaching Children Mathematics, 17*(8), 472–478.

Poon, K., & Leung, C. (2010). Pilot study on algebra learning among junior secondary students. *International Journal of Mathematical Education in Science and Technology*, *41*(1), 49–62. doi:10.1080/00207390903236434.

Rojano, T. (2002). Mathematics learning in the junior secondary school: Students' access to significant mathematical ideas. In English, L. (Ed.), *Handbook of international research in mathematics education*. Mahwah, NJ: Lawrence Erlbaum Associates.

Sarama, J., & Clements, D. H. (2009). Concrete computer manipulatives in mathematics education. *Child Development Perspectives*, *3*(3), 145–150. doi:10.1111/j.1750-8606.2009.00095.x.

Siegler, R. S. (2003). Implications of cognitive science research for mathematics education. In Kilpatrick, W. B. Martin, & D. E. Schifter (Eds.), A research companion to principles and standards for school mathematics (pp. 219-233). Reston, VA: National Council of Teachers of Mathematics.

Star, J. (2005). Research Commentary: Reconceptualizing procedural knowledge. *Journal for Research in Mathematics Education*, *36*, 404–411.

Van de Walle, J. A., & Lovin, L. H. (2006). Teaching student-centered mathematics grades 5-8. Boston: Pearson.

Vlassis, J. (2008). The role of mathematical symbols in the development of number conceptualization: The case of the minus sign. *Philosophical Psychology*, *21*, 555–570. doi:10.1080/09515080802285552.

Wadsworth, B. (1996). *Piaget's theory of cognitive and affective development*. New York: Longman Publishers.

Wood, K. C., Smith, H., & Grossnicklaus, D. (2001). Piaget's stages of cognitive development. In M. Orey (Ed.), *Emerging perspectives on learning, teaching, and technology*. Retrieved from http://projects.coe.uga.edu/epltt/

ADDITIONAL READING

McGraw-Hill Higher Education. (2010). *Virtual manipulative kit*. Retrieved from http://highered.mcgraw-hill.com/sites/0073519456/student_view0/virtual_manipulative_kit.html

Moyer, P. S., Niezgoda, D., & Stanley, J. (2005). Young children's use of virtual manipulatives and other forms of mathematical representations. In Masalaski, W. J., & Elliot, P. C. (Eds.), *Technology-Supported Mathematics Learning Environments* (pp. 17–34). Reston, VA: National Council of Teachers of Mathematics.

National Council of Teachers of Mathematics. (2012a). *Core math tools home*. Retrieved from http://www.nctm.org/resources/content.aspx?id=32702

National Council of Teachers of Mathematics. (2012b). *Illuminations*. Retrieved from http://illuminations.nctm.org/

Office for Mathematics, Science, and Technology Education (MSTE). (n.d.a). *Applets*. Retrieved from http://mste.illinois.edu/m2t2/appletslist.html

Office for Mathematics, Science, and Technology Education (MSTE). (n.d.b). *Internet links and resources*. Retrieved from http://mste.illinois.edu/m2t2/resources.html

Polly, D. (2011). Technology to develop algebraic reasoning. *Teaching Children Mathematics*, *17*(8), 472–478.

Robinson, D. H., & Schraw, G. (Eds.). (2008). *Recent innovations in educational technology that facilitate student learning*. Information Age Publishing.

Shodor. (2012). Inter*activate*. Retrieved from http://www.shodor.org/interactivate/

KEY TERMS AND DEFINITIONS

Algebra: A branch of mathematics concerning the study of rules of operations and relations, the constructions and the constructions and concepts arising from them. Often cited as the "gateway" to mathematics.

Conceptual Knowledge: Making connections and creating networks within information (Star, 2005).

Equal Sign: The mathematical symbol used to denote equality.

Middle School Mathematics: Mathematics taken in grades 6 – 8.

Procedural Knowledge: Ability to execute action sequences to solve problems (Star, 2005).

Solving Equations: Manipulating an equation to find a value or set of values that fulfills the stated condition.

Virtual Manipulatives: "An interactive, Web-based visual representation of a dynamic object that presents opportunities for constructing mathematical knowledge" (Moyer, Bolyard, and Spikell, 2002, p. 371).

Chapter 14
Two Classroom Portraits Demonstrating the Interplay of Secondary Mathematics Teachers' TPACK on their Integration of the Mathematical Practices

Jessica Taylor Ivy
Mississippi State University, USA

Dana Pomykal Franz
Mississippi State University, USA

ABSTRACT

This chapter examines the practices and beliefs of two secondary mathematics teachers with similar demographic backgrounds. The influence of their practices and beliefs on teaching and student learning is considered through the lens of the TPACK Development Model and through evidence of student engagement in the Mathematical Practices. Even though they face common barriers to instructional technology integration, both teachers speak to their successes and positive impacts on student learning. Rich descriptions of conversations, classroom observations, and self-report survey data highlight critical contrasts between the practices of the two teachers. These differences represent the unique challenges faced by instructional technology researchers and other educational stakeholders. The purpose of this chapter is to highlight these subtle, yet far-reaching, areas of distinction in which the teachers unknowingly provide different levels of opportunity for teaching and learning in the mathematics classroom.

DOI: 10.4018/978-1-4666-4086-3.ch014

INTRODUCTION

Instructional technologies such as graphing calculators offer invaluable opportunities for teaching and learning in mathematics classrooms. According to the National Council of Teachers of Mathematics (NCTM) Technology Principle, technology has the potential to offer access to multiple representations and deeper mathematics by allowing students to explore mathematical patterns, make conjectures, and test those conjectures in ways that would not be feasible without technology (NCTM, 2000). Instructional technology is constantly evolving, and it is becoming more available for use in classrooms. Unfortunately, this increase in availability often does not translate to an increase in the actual use of instructional technology in the classroom (Dunham & Hennessy, 2008). The abundance of possibilities for enhancing student learning is promising; however it is up to teachers to use technology in ways that most benefit students.

With the recent introduction of the Common Core State Standards for Mathematics (CCSS-M), the issue of appropriate instructional technology use has gained more visibility. Among the Standards for Mathematical Practice described in the Common Core document is that students should "use appropriate tools strategically" (Common Core State Standards for Mathematics, 2010, p. 7). Through engagement in this standard, students should use technology in ways which allow them to gather information, analyze information, make and test conjectures, and develop generalizations. This type of engagement is markedly different than practices which involve the use of calculator programs solely for checking computations or completing procedures previously learned with paper and pencil. Yet, at first glance, these differences may not be obvious.

This chapter presents a comparative case study analysis of two teachers who both have access to graphing calculators in secondary-level mathematics classrooms. These data were obtained as part of a larger project, which examined seven secondary mathematics teachers' perceptions of their integration of instructional technology. At face value, both teachers appeared to integrate instructional technologies in ways which exemplify strategic use of graphing calculators. Through conversations, observations, and classroom artifacts, we gain a better understanding of the vast differences between two teachers' perceptions and integrations of instructional technology.

BACKGROUND

TPACK and the Standards for Mathematical Practice

Data obtained through this study was examined through the lens of an established development model, described briefly in this paragraph. The knowledge needed to teach mathematics with technology is known as Technology, Pedagogy, And Content Knowledge (TPACK; Niess et al., 2009). This construct grew out of an identification of the types of knowledge necessary for teaching. This unique type of knowledge, known as TPACK, encompasses the intersection of content knowledge, pedagogical knowledge, and technological knowledge. This chapter assumes a familiarity with the themes and levels described in the TPACK Development Model (e.g., Niess et al., 2009).

The ability to foster students' engagement in the Standards for Mathematical Practice (SMP) is connected to a teachers' own understanding of each of the standards. Further, the teacher must have a developed understanding of TPACK with a given technology to be able to apply it to the SMPs. Clearly if students in a classroom are going to use technology to "make sense of problems", "model with mathematics", or "use appropriate tools strategically", the teacher must understand the interplay of the relevant technology, pedagogy, and content. Moreover, teachers must reconcile the challenges they face when using technology with their beliefs and practices. Many teachers integrate technology in their classrooms in ways which do not engage students in the aforementioned Mathematical Practices – and the authors propose that these practices correspond to low levels of the teaching and learning themes of the TPACK Development Model.

Barriers to Integrating Instructional Technologies

As previously mentioned, availability of instructional technologies does not always imply integration of instructional technologies (Dunham & Hennessy, 2008). Research provides insight into the barriers that prevent instructional technology integration, which inherently impact opportunities for integrating instructional technologies in ways which enhance the teaching and learning of mathematics. These barriers can be either extrinsic or intrinsic to the teacher, and are referred to as *first-order barriers* and *second-order barriers*, respectively (Ertmer, 1999).

First-order barriers to instructional technology are often related to existing school structure and norms such as a lack of planning time, inadequate access to technology support, misalignment between the existing curriculum and the technology, and the general structure of the classroom not being conducive to the integration of a particular technology (Honey & Moeller, 1990). These barriers may be the most obvious and perhaps lead to the clearest solution. It is certainly feasible to envision a school addressing each of these issues in hopes of reducing or eliminating obstacles to the integration of instructional technologies.

It is naïve, however, to expect that such actions would automate technology integration, because there are barriers that exist which are intrinsic to teachers. Intrinsic (second-order) barriers to instructional technology integration include teachers' knowledge, beliefs, skills, and practice (Ertmer, 1999). Certainly these constructs are more difficult to approach and reform than first-order barriers.

In considering teachers' knowledge, Hokanson and Hooper (2004) identified five stages through which a teacher progresses as their knowledge gap related to their understanding of technology integration is narrowed. This model proposed that teachers must first take time to become familiar and comfortable with a technology, and then they progress to a level where they are able to use the technology. Next, the teacher becomes capable of integrating the technology into existing practices. Finally, the teacher begins to develop and implement tasks that are dependent on technology. Over time, and with success at each preceding stage, the teacher is able to teach using technology seamlessly to enhance student learning in the classroom. The greatest determination of success at each stage is an internal motivation, or overcoming the second-order barriers. These stages illustrate the complexity of the second-order barriers. Unlike first-order barriers, they are not material in nature, nor are they easily assessed or described.

Technology Lessons

With the previously described barriers clearly noted through research, Ertmer and Ottenbreit-Leftwich (2009), explored ways in which technology was integrated during mathematics lessons in order to shed light on where efforts to facilitate change in instructional technology should focus. Though they did note significant use of instructional technologies in mathematics classrooms, most of the integration of technology was focused on drill, typing assignments, or completing practice work in ways which were not considered student-centered. Certainly the integration observed during the aforementioned study did not exemplify the capacity of technology to enhance opportunities for student learning as described in the NCTM Technology Principle (NCTM, 2000) nor were teachers engaging students in the Mathematical Practices by using technology to foster development of conceptual foundations related to mathematical ideas.

TWO CLASSROOM PORTRAITS

This project explored the perceptions of instructional technology integration in seven secondary classrooms, two of which are highlighted in this chapter for the sake of comparison. The similarities between the demographic backgrounds of the two teachers portrayed in this chapter are extensive. The two teachers use some similar phrases, and, perhaps if they engaged in a friendly conversation, they might expect that their classrooms offered comparable opportunities for student learning of mathematics. Data collected from each participating teacher included personal interviews, classroom observations, self-reported surveys, and lesson samples. Data from the first three sources will be used to describe and compare the two cases.

Ms. James[1] and Ms. Thomas had both been teaching high school mathematics for more than twenty years in communities with similar socio-economic demographics, within the same southeastern state in the U.S. They were faced with similar challenges of teaching in districts with graduation rates less than seventy percent, budget shortfalls, and significant achievement gaps between minority and nonminority student groups. Ms. James and Ms. Thomas both wholeheartedly believed that they integrated technology in ways which enhanced student learning. They perceived themselves to have similar goals and both communicated that they used technology in their classrooms to introduce and explore new topics, foster students' development of mathematical ideas, and access mathematics that would not otherwise be reachable. But further exploration of their classroom practices highlighted stark differences in the

TPACK of these two teachers. These differences also aligned with differences in the engagement of students in the SMPs, such as making sense of mathematics, modeling with mathematics, and using appropriate tools strategically.

Ms. James

Initial interview

During an initial conversation with Ms. James she recounted her teaching experiences before the availability of graphing calculators, "I just think about how I taught before we got technology. . . . I think a lot of concepts were probably lost with kids that needed a visual to see why things work and how they're connected." This statement indicated that Ms. James was very cognizant of the learners' experiences and the ways in which technology enhanced those experiences. She often envisioned herself as the learner when making instructional decisions. For example, she referenced the pre-technology era and stated, "[m]ath wouldn't have made sense to me if I were in those classes because now I don't see how math makes sense without seeing a picture of it and using graphing calculators or technology". Her statements indicate that she values mathematical modeling and strategic use of appropriate tools, as defined in the Standards for Mathematical Practice (Common Core State Standards for Mathematics, 2010).

In describing her first experiences with graphing calculators, Ms. James recounted collaborating with a colleague and persuading local businesses to donate the funds necessary to purchase classroom graphing calculators. At that point they realized that they needed to better understand the functionality of the calculators and ways in which they could be used in the classroom. Ms. James described ways in which she actively sought out professional opportunities through conferences, workshops, and collaboration with others. Ultimately, though, she described her most successful strategy for learning more about new technologies – letting students explore the technology on their own and bring ideas back to the classroom. "My students, they can teach me a lot. . . . Like with the [TI-89] graphing calculator. . . . They take one home, and they have one with them all the time. They come back, and they show me what it does," she recounted. These statements indicated that Ms. James was at the exploring level for the teaching theme of TPACK (Niess et al., 2009).

Through conversation, it became apparent that Ms. James envisioned her journey as a teacher and a learner with technology to be an ongoing process, "I have the [dynamic geometry software], but I haven't taught myself enough. . . . I haven't gotten to the part of calculus that I know that I want to use it for. I haven't taken the time to sit down and learn it yet, but I do have it. . . . During [winter break], I can get down to that, and figure it all out." Ms. James's internal motivation to continue to grow and explore new technological opportunities for her classroom was profound. She reflected, "You just have to dig your heels in and say, 'I'm going to use it' because too much good comes out of it. For example, the kids are all engaged when you're using the Navigator system." She further recognized the challenges associated with the introduction of instructional technologies, "It's hard to keep them all on task when they realize that technology does so much. . . . You have to take the good with the bad". This vision of technology as having advantages and challenges was mentioned in nearly all of the interviews, though different participants expressed the concepts in different ways.

Ms. James viewed technology as an integral component of her classroom. She stated, "I don't ever think about not using it. It's an everyday thing." Her integration of technologies was apparent to her colleagues and she reported often reaching out to help them integrate technology in their classrooms.

Classroom Observation

During the observed pre-calculus lesson, Ms. James began by making connections to the previous class session. They procedurally worked through an item from the homework assignment which required students to consider the graphs of two equations – a circle and a line – and determine the intersections of their graphs. This item facilitated a discussion which began with her asking students to consider why the circle did not "look like a circle" when graphed in the calculator with the default window setting. Following this discussion, Ms. James introduced the daily activity.

To begin the daily activity, Ms. James polled the class by asking, "how many of you have iPods?" Then she introduced a summary of the history of recorded audio formats. Using the data, students entered information into *lists* in the calculator. One student was selected to operate SmartView software and allow other students to confirm their steps as they worked through the task. Ms. James reacted quickly to anticipated technical difficulties that students had. Students were instructed to display the data using a scatterplot. Ms. James asked students to make a variety of predictions about the appearance of the graphs and expectations if the graphs were continued for future years.

Next, Ms. James challenged students to find a line that fit a specific set of data points and facilitated a discussion of whether or not a linear model was appropriate. Many of Ms. James questions were divergent questions, requiring students to discuss what they noticed about the data and make further generalizations. One observation students made was that the number of individual songs purchased increased while compact disc sales decreased. A subsequent discussion focused on how students could predict when the sale of digital albums would exceed the sale of compact discs. Though the lesson was led by Ms. James, she required active student participation. The nature of the task allowed some opportunities for students to make decisions on how to proceed. The focus on the use of technology during the lesson was to enhance and assess student understanding of previously learned concepts. The observation data suggested that Ms. James was at the adapting level for the teaching theme of TPACK.

Certainly this observation provided evidence of students using graphing calculator technology as a tool for learning and exploring mathematics. Further students were encouraged to consider each other's rationale, thus "constructing viable arguments and critiquing the reasoning of their peers". Finally, the students learned about "persevering in solving problems" as they began to understand the work from the previous day and how this work modeled data in real problems (Common Core State Standards for Mathematics, 2010).

Follow-Up Interview

Following the classroom observation, an additional conversation with Ms. James ensued. In this interview Ms. James described how she valued student-centered instruction, though she admitted that she likely only initiated this environment once or twice each week. She reflected on the observed lesson as being more teacher-directed than she would have liked, accounting this to the presence of a visitor in the classroom. She described how she would change the lesson in the future, "I can see that activity being easily student-led or at least be done in small groups first and then do a whole group discussion on it. Then students lead that as presentations or carousels or something like that." Ms. James consistently demonstrated a reflective nature and a desire to continually improve. She further described how her students used technology to engage in projects and decision making tasks. Ms. James described a challenge she had assigned in a previous class based on a student's suggestion. Students were challenged to find piece-wise graphs that made a Christmas tree shape. This task was not planned, but rather it was an extension task used to further explore

the concept from the daily lesson. The follow-up interview data indicated that Ms. James was at the exploring level for the teaching and learning themes of TPACK.

Self-Report Survey

Responses to the TPACK Development Model Self-Report Survey indicated Ms. James perceived her TPACK levels to be slightly higher for the teaching and learning themes than the levels suggested by other data obtained by the researcher. Ms. James classified herself to be primarily at the advancing and exploring levels for the teaching and learning themes, respectively. Analysis by the researcher, however, indicated that Ms. James was at the exploring level for the learning theme and transitioning from the adapting level to the exploring level for the teaching theme of TPACK (Niess et al., 2009).

Ms. Thomas

Initial Interview

In an initial conversation with Ms. Thomas, she described instructional technology as "a great way for the kids to explore concepts and really use their critical thinking skills." She quickly followed up with a caveat that, "it's important for [students] to learn basic skills before they get loose on the calculator because they get really dependent." She elaborated, "the way I do it in my classroom is that I will teach a concept. Sometimes I use the calculator to introduce a concept and then we'll use pen and just work them out by hand." She continued with an example, "if you were writing an equation for a line that's parallel to another line and passes through a point. . . . if you took the calculators, you could show them how to graph first to introduce parallel lines – that they have the same slope. And they could explore by graphing those two lines on a calculator and seeing what they look like, then what's in common, what's different. . . . And then when they got through and they understand the concept that they have the same slope, then, they could take the problem and work it out. And then they could check it with the calculators to see that they're parallel." On the surface Ms. Thomas's statement suggests that she is using instructional technology to build conceptual understanding and facilitate student exploration of the concept of slope; however, a deeper consideration reveals that this is not the case.

During the conversation with Ms. Thomas, she repeatedly expressed concerns that students would become dependent on graphing calculators and her statements implied that her view of the technology tool was more of a "time saver" or "short cut" than as a tool with the potential to enhance opportunities for student learning. She was also insistent that students should learn concepts prior to being allowed to freely use instructional technology, indicating that she was at the recognizing level for the teaching theme of TPACK (Niess et al., 2009). Although Ms. Thomas described how graphing calculators could be used to display parallel lines, thus offering a representation to students, her explanation implied that she viewed the technology as a teaching tool, but not as a learning tool. That is, she did not describe how students could explore concepts or make any strategic decisions that would influence the flow of the lesson, indicating that she was at the recognizing level for the learning theme of TPACK (Niess et al., 2009).

Ms. Thomas discussed her reasoning for integrating technology was out of a fear of "getting left behind" rather than a desire to improve learning opportunities. Like Ms. James, she described professional opportunities that she sought out to improve her integration of instructional technology. She described modeling her lessons after some of these experiences. Further, she too envisioned technology as a daily part of her classroom instruction, but she was limited in her expectations of the capacity of technology to enhance the learning environment. She described the role technology

played in her classroom, ". . . a concept or objective that I'm teaching they can use the calculator on because that's not a tested objective for that area. . . . I'm not testing them on whether they can multiply or add or subtract or whatever. So I do that mostly until January or so, and then once they've learned some of the concepts I want them to know. . . . I use it a lot in Algebra I and Transitions [during the] spring semester to do a lot of things." Her statement indicates that she used the calculators for computations and occasional graphing. She also expressed that she limited the availability of the technology during the formative phase of concept development. Many of her statements indicate that she is at the recognizing level for the teaching and learning themes of TPACK; however, the researcher rated her at the accepting level for these themes due to occasional technology use for concept development and exploration as well as involvement in professional growth experiences (Niess et al., 2009).

Like Ms. James, Ms. Thomas expressed that technology had marked advantages and challenges. She noted that technology offered access to representations that would not otherwise be accessible to students, but this advantage was overshadowed by her feeling that technology posed a threat to the learning of mathematics. Given her limited use of technology, she is not really using technology in ways that will impact any of the SMPs.

Classroom Observation

The researcher observed an Algebra I lesson in Ms. Thomas's room. As students entered the room, they each selected a graphing calculator from a wall caddy and took it to their desks. After distributing graded exams and reviewing solutions, Ms. Thomas began the lesson by displaying a linear equation on the white board and asking students to graph the equation in their graphing calculators. Ms. Thomas used the SmartView program to display the graph on the electronic whiteboard. Ms. Thomas verbally stated the slope and y-intercepts of the line, then asked the students to graph a second linear equation, which was parallel to the first line. Ms. Thomas asked, "What do you notice about their slopes? What do you notice about their y-intercepts? Why are they parallel?" She allowed minimal time for students to consider the questions and moved quickly to a second example in which two lines intersected but were not perpendicular to each other. She verbally provided instructions for using the calculators to find the point of intersection, with a focus on the necessary keystrokes.

The lesson continued with six additional examples and counterexamples of parallel lines. The final example asked students to consider two linear equations, and students noted that these two equations represented the same line. Ms. Thomas instructed students to record the following in their notes, "if they share the same line, they have infinitely many solutions. If they intersect, they have one solution, and if they're parallel, they have no solutions." Without answering additional questions, Ms. Thomas told the class they would further consider this topic the following day.

During the observed lesson Ms. Thomas limited students' use of graphing calculators to graphing linear equations and using an application to find the point of intersection. The use of technology did not allow students to learn or access mathematics in ways that would not have been possible without the graphing calculators, nor did students use calculators to explore new concepts or develop conceptual understanding. Observation data indicated that Ms. Thomas was at the recognizing level for the teaching and learning themes of TPACK (Niess et al., 2009) and she did not engage in the SMPs.

Follow-Up Interview

The initial interview and the classroom observation indicated conflicting levels for the teaching and learning themes of TPACK, so the researcher sought to reconcile this disagreement during the follow-up interview. In this conversation, Ms. Thomas stated that she often used technology to build connections to the real world; however, she was unable able to provide any examples of tasks she had used that offered students this experience. Further, Ms. Thomas was not able to provide any details of situations in which she fostered explorations using graphing calculators or other instructional technologies.

Ms. Thomas stated that time limitations kept her from using instructional technology for student projects, specifically time restraints related to standardized testing. In general her responses suggested that she did not view technology as a tool that was useful or efficient for exploring new mathematical topics. Analysis of the follow-up interview data indicated that Ms. Thomas was at the recognizing level for the teaching and learning themes of TPACK (Niess et al., 2009). It might be assumed she will make similar statements in regards to the SMP.

Self-Report Survey

Responses to the TPACK Development Model Self-Report Survey indicate that Ms. Thomas perceived herself to be at a higher TPACK level than that suggested by other data collected during the study. Ms. Thomas identified herself most often with exploring level descriptors for the teaching and learning themes, while other data suggested she was at the recognizing level for these themes.

CONNECTIONS AND FUTURE DIRECTIONS

The commonalities and differences between the beliefs regarding the integration of instructional technologies of Ms. James and Ms. Thomas have been established. The differences have profound effects on the level at which students engage in the Common Core Standards for Mathematical Practice. Although the classroom expectations were established prior to the initiation of this study, the effects are evident through the snapshot provided by the interview and observation data. Samples of these differences for each of the eight Mathematical Practices are provided in the following paragraphs.

Connections to Mathematical Practices

Make Sense of Problems and Persevere in Solving Them

In Ms. James's classroom students were introduced to new concepts through a problem. She established a classroom environment in which students were expected to devise strategies for approaching and solving problems, learning from the frustration and experience. The graphing calculators provided the students with a tool as they struggled to make sense of the problem. Ms. Thomas's classroom was void of such opportunities. Instead, the teacher demonstrated a strategy to solving a problem that was presented, without allowing time for students to struggle with the mathematics or make any decisions regarding the flow of the lesson.

Reason Abstractly and Quantitatively

Ms. James and Ms. Thomas both attempted to foster connections between abstract concepts. Ms. Thomas asked for students to recognize commonalities and differences between linear equations which were parallel and tried to build on these ideas. Unfortunately, it was Ms. Thomas, rather than the students, who was reasoning abstractly. Ms. James fostered this reasoning by requiring students to consider whether a line or some other graph would be appropriate for representing the relationship from the data (during the observed lesson). She also asked for elaboration and explanation for students' predictions, requiring quantitative reasoning to substantiate their arguments.

The graphing calculators gave the students a tool to help them quickly visualize the data and make comparisons between sets of data and parameters presented in the problem.

Construct Viable Arguments and Critique the Reasoning of Others

The establishment of an environment conducive to mathematical arguing was outside of the scope of this study; however, there was evidence that this had occurred in Ms. James's class. She required students to reflect on each other's statements without verbally assessing the correctness of their statements. Ms. Thomas had not established such an environment. Instead she quickly followed up student responses with affirming or corrective statements – essentially repeating pieces of her didactic-style lesson. During the observed lesson Ms. Thomas did not encourage students to communicate with each other or to reason through each other's arguments.

Model with Mathematics

In Ms. James's class students were required to create multiple representations of data and interpret the data to make inferences and predictions. Although Ms. Thomas required students to represent data in multiple ways (graphs and equations), the connections between the representations were made primarily by Ms. Thomas and were focused solely on identifying the slopes and y-intercepts of the equations.

Use Appropriate Tools Strategically

Both Ms. James and Ms. Thomas required students to use graphing calculators during the observed lessons. Ms. James, however, saw value in allowing students to make decisions about how to proceed. Further, Ms. James, at times, allowed students to determine which strategy they would use to approach problems. Due to a desire to have closely managed her classroom, Ms. Thomas did not allow opportunities for students to decide which tools to use, nor how to use the tools, to solve mathematical problems.

Attend to Precision

The expectations for discussion provided in Ms. James's classroom allowed the researcher to observe students attending to precision through their mathematical arguments. In these explanations, students referenced mathematical vocabulary and concepts and used these ideas to construct arguments and proofs. Graphing calculators were used in Ms. James's class to find "precise solutions" with value given to multiple strategies. Due to a lack of student dialogue in Ms. Thomas's room, this was not evident.

Look For and Make Use of Structure

The students in Ms. James's class were expected to examine their representations and draw conclusions from patterns that became apparent through the representations. Though Ms. Thomas verbally stated some generalizations that could be drawn from the structure of the linear equations and their graphs, she did not facilitate her students' engagement in this practice.

Look For and Express Regularity in Repeated Reasoning

The differences in how this practice was observed in the two classrooms is particularly interesting, as both teachers offered opportunities for repetition with a goal of leading to generalizations that strengthen students' understanding of mathematical concepts. Ms. James asked students multiple, connected questions about a single set of data. The questions varied in complexity, with some questions requiring students to make assumptions and others asking for predictions. Ms. Thomas, on the other hand, posed several unrelated ex-

amples of pairs of linear equations. Her goal was for students to find similarities and differences among these examples and apply them to future problems involving parallel and non-parallel pairs of lines. The disconnect, though, is that students were essentially starting over with each new pair of lines – making the generalizations difficult to recognize. Further, Ms. Thomas did not allow the students to draw the conclusions. Instead, she highlighted what she felt was most important, allowing for minimal student input and interaction.

Future Directions

Details of these two classrooms have been shared through conversations, classroom observations, and survey data. Examples and nonexamples of students' engagement in the Mathematical Practices through the use of graphing calculators reflect or demonstrate how subtle differences in teachers' beliefs can have profound impacts on their pedagogical practices. It has been noted that teachers' perceptions of their integration of instructional technologies is inflated (McCrory, 2010; Ivy, 2011). This presents challenges to researchers, teachers, and other educational stakeholders that deem further exploration. Notably, the following questions arise:

1. How can stakeholders help teachers to view technology as a tool for learning mathematics, as described in the NCTM Technology Principle?
2. How can stakeholders reconcile lack of connection between teachers' perceptions of their integration of technology with their actual practice?
3. What types of professional opportunities best highlight the differences between the perceived student engagement in mathematical practices, as exemplified by Ms. Thomas, and the actual student engagement in mathematical practices, as exemplified by Ms. James?

4. How do these disparities in teachers' perceptions and practices regarding TPACK and student engagement in mathematical practices influence the design of technology-based research?

IMPLICATIONS AND CONCLUDING REMARKS

By definition TPACK encompasses the interaction of Pedagogical Content Knowledge (PCK) and the knowledge of instructional technologies. In essence, a lack of PCK is inevitably a barrier to advancing a teacher's TPACK of an instructional technology, such as a graphing calculator. That is to say, that until a teacher is able to integrate appropriate instructional techniques *without* technology, the teacher will be unsuccessful at integrating appropriate instructional techniques *with* technology.

This PCK-deficiency is evident upon consideration of the lack of student discourse in Ms. Thomas's room. Ms. Thomas taught through didactic teacher-led instruction that was not reactive to student input. In contrast, Ms. James's instruction was dependent upon student ideas and input. Ms. James viewed her role as that of a facilitator of learning, while Ms. Thomas viewed her role as a dispenser of mathematical ideas.

As researchers and providers of experiences directed toward improving teachers' PCK and TPACK, coupled with larger goals of helping teachers to effectively integrate the Mathematical Practices, we must not ignore these dynamic interactions of the knowledge domains. Mathematics teacher educators must provide teachers with opportunities to understand these seemingly small, yet vital differences in beliefs and their effects on student learning and engagement in the Mathematical Practices.

Through the examination of two case studies in secondary mathematics classrooms, this chapter explored the implications of TPACK levels within the teaching and learning themes on teachers' capacity to engage students in the Mathematical Practices. In addition to considering the interplays of beliefs and knowledge, the implications for mathematics educators involved in conducting research related to instructional technologies and professional experiences for teachers is also a critical issue. Though both of these teachers had overcome first-order (extrinsic) barriers to technology integration, the second-order (intrinsic) barriers regarding practices and beliefs inhibited integration of instructional technology for one of the teachers. Both Ms. James and Ms. Thomas had decades of teaching experience, sought out professional support, and viewed their classrooms as technologically rich. Yet, opportunities for student learning were vastly different and student expectations were not equitable.

REFERENCES

Dunham, P., & Hennessy, S. (2008). Equity and use of educational technology in mathematics. In Heid, M. K., & Blume, G. (Eds.), *Research on technology and the teaching and learning of mathematics* (Vol. 1, pp. 345–418). Charlotte, NC: Information Age Publishing.

Ertmer, P., & Ottenbreit-Leftwich, A. (2009). *Teacher technology change: How knowledge, beliefs and culture intersect.* Paper presented at the Annual Meeting of the American Educational Research Association. Denver, CO.

Ertmer, P. A. (1999). Addressing first- and second-order barriers to change: Strategies for technology integration. *Educational Technology Research and Development, 47*(4), 47–61. doi:10.1007/BF02299597.

Hokanson, B., & Hooper, S. (2004). *Integrating technology in classrooms: We have met the enemy and he is us*. Paper presented at the convention of the Annual Meeting of the Association for Educational Communication and Technology. Chicago, IL.

Honey, M., & Moeller, B. (1990). *Teachers' beliefs and technology integration: Different values, different understandings*. New York, NY: Center for Technology in Education.

Ivy, J. T. (2011). *Secondary mathematics teachers perceptions of their integration of instructional technologies*. (Doctoral dissertation). University of Mississippi, Starkville, MS.

McCrory, M. R. (2010). *An exploration of intial certification candidates' TPACK and mathematics-based applications using touch device technology*. (Unpublished doctoral dissertation) University of Mississippi, Oxford, MS.

National Council of Teachers of Mathematics. (2000). *Principles and standards for school mathematics*. Reston, VA: NCTM.

National Governors Association Center for Best Practices. (2010). *Common core state standards (mathematics)*. Washington, DC: Council of Chief State School Officers.

Niess, M. L., Ronau, R. N., Shafer, K. G., Driskell, S. O., Harper, S. R., & Johnston, C. et al. (2009). Mathematics teacher TPACK standards and development model. *Contemporary Issues in Technology & Teacher Education*, *9*(1), 4–24.

ADDITIONAL READING

Cuban, L., Kirkpatrick, H., & Peck, C. (2001). High access and low use of technologies in high school classrooms: Explaining an apparent paradox. *American Educational Research Journal*, *38*, 813–834. doi:10.3102/00028312038004813.

Ertmer, P. A., Ottenbreit-Leftwich, A., & York, C. S. (2007). Exemplary technology use: Teachers' perceptions of critical factors. *Journal of Computing in Teacher Education*, *23*(2), 55–61.

Ertmer, P. A., Ross, E. M., & Gopalakrishnan, S. (2000). Technology-using teachers: How powerful visions and student-centered beliefs fuel exemplary practice. In *Proceedings of Society for Information Technology & Teacher Education International Conference* (pp. 1519–1524). San Diego, CA: Academic Press.

Groth, R., Spickler, D., Bergner, J., & Bardzell, M. (2009). A qualitative approach to assessing technological pedagogical content knowledge. *Contemporary Issues in Technology & Teacher Education*, *9*, 392–411.

Kastbert, S., & Leatham, K. (2005). Research on graphing calculators at the secondary level: Implications for mathematics teacher education. *Contemporary Issues in Technology & Teacher Education*, *5*, 25–37.

Li, Q. (2007). Student and teacher views about technology: A tale of two cities? *Journal of Research on Technology in Education*, *39*, 377–397.

McGraw, R., & Grant, M. (2005). Investigating mathematics with technology: Lesson structures that encourage a range of methods and solutions. In Masalski, W. J., & Elliott, P. C. (Eds.), *Technology-supported mathematics learning environments* (pp. 303–317). Reston, VA: The National Council of Teachers of Mathematics, Inc..

Mishra, P., & Koehler, M. J. (2006). Technological pedagogical content knowledge: A framework for teacher knowledge. *Teachers College Record*, *108*, 1017–1054. doi:10.1111/j.1467-9620.2006.00684.x.

Norton, S., McRobbie, C. J., & Cooper, T. J. (2000). Exploring secondary mathematics teachers' reasons for not using computers in their teaching: Five case studies. *Journal of Research on Computing in Education*, *33*(1), 87–109.

Shulman, L. S. (1986). Those who understand: Knowledge growth in teaching. *Educational Researcher*, *15*, 4–14. doi:10.3102/0013189X015002004.

KEY TERMS AND DEFINITIONS

Barrier: A construct, either intrinsic or extrinsic to the teacher, which prevents sufficient integration of instructional technologies.

Content Knowledge: The mathematical knowledge possessed by the teacher.

First-Order Barrier: A barrier which is extrinsic to the teacher.

Instructional Technology: Technology used for the purpose of fostering student learning of mathematics.

Pedagogical Content Knowledge (PCK): Knowledge which integrates appropriate mathematical content and methods for teaching the content.

Second Order Barrier: A barrier which is intrinsic to the teacher.

Technology Integration: Consistent use of instructional technology for the purposes of engaging students in learning.

Technology, Pedagogy, and Content Knowledge (TPACK): The knowledge that encompasses the intersections of technological knowledge, pedagogical knowledge, and content knowledge.

ENDNOTES

[1]   Pseudonyms are used for this and all other names presented.

Chapter 15
Supporting Pattern Exploration and Algebraic Reasoning through the Use of Spreadsheets

Ayhan Kursat Erbas
Middle East Technical University, Turkey

Chandra Hawley Orrill
University of Massachusetts Dartmouth, USA

Sarah Ledford
Kennesaw State University, USA

Drew Polly
University of North Carolina at Charlotte, USA

ABSTRACT

As teachers prepare to teach the Common Core State Standards for Mathematics (CCSSM), students' exploration of patterns and relationships between numbers has gained more importance. Specifically, students' conceptual understanding of numerical patterns is critical in middle school, as it lays a ground-work for fostering mathematical thinking at all levels. Educational technologies can enhance student's explorations of patterns by providing opportunities to represent patterns, test conjectures, and make generalizations. In this chapter, the authors illustrate how spreadsheets can support students' explorations of both arithmetic and geometric patterns in the middle grades.

INTRODUCTION

According to Mason (1996), "at the heart of teaching mathematics is the awakening of pupil sensitivity to the nature of mathematical gener-alisation" (p. 65). We consider identifying and describing patterns, whether numerical, geometric or algebraic, as a foundation for mathematical generalizations. School mathematics standards throughout the world (e.g., National Curriculum Board, 2009; National Council of Teachers of Mathematics, 2000; National Governor's Associa-tion/Chief Council State School Officers, 2011; Qualifications and Curriculum Authority, 2007; Singapore Ministry of Education, 2007) require students to recognize, generate, and understand a

DOI: 10.4018/978-1-4666-4086-3.ch015

variety of patterns that are not immediately apparent. These include linear and nonlinear patterns that can be represented numerically, graphically, and symbolically. Educational technologies have the power to enhance students' explorations of patterns by offering opportunities for extending patterns, providing easy-to-use tools for conjecture-testing and allowing students to consider enough number of iterations of patterns in order to generalize mathematical ideas. From supporting students in understanding the equation for a simple linear pattern to allowing students to see the dynamic manipulation of variables in ways that allow them students to see and understand patterns of change in the moment, technology can become a valuable tool for supporting students in engaging in higher-order thinking. In this article, we present two examples of pattern problems (one arithmetic and one geometric) to demonstrate how spreadsheets may support students as they investigate, generate, and understand various patterns and develop specific Standards for Mathematical Practice in the Common Core Standards.

USING PATTERNS TO EXPLORE ARITHMETIC SEQUENCES

Investigating arithmetic patterns can support students in making connections among mathematical concepts as well as connecting classroom mathematics to the world around them. Since arithmetic patterns change by a fixed amount, arithmetic sequences are fairly simple to observe and study. However, they are also robust enough to support students as they make sophisticated conjectures and generalizations. Mathematical software can facilitate the analysis and interpretation of arithmetic patterns. For example, spreadsheets allow students to extend arithmetic patterns by working numerous, rote calculations freeing students to focus on developing generalizations based on the patterns in the spreadsheet. Spreadsheets also allow students to perform manipulations on a pattern

and quickly view the effect of the manipulations on the rest of the numbers in the pattern. Clearly, this is beneficial in allowing students to test conjectures. Below is one example of an investigation that exemplifies the value of using technology for solving patterns:

A cruise line has 3-day, 4-day, and 7-day cruises. After each cruise, a ship returns for one day and repeats the pattern. If one cruise of each type leaves today, when will all three cruises leave again on the same day? Generalize your solution for x-day, y-day, and z-day cruises.

The day that each cruise line leaves can be represented as an arithmetic pattern. One possible method of exploring this pattern includes the teacher leading a whole-class discussion in which students are challenged to see the relationships for each cruise line which lasts 3, 4, and 7 days. Another pathway for exploration could be to engage students in a "think-pair-share" strategy in which the students analyze the problem for relevant information and calculate an answer to the first question on their own, then discuss their answer in a pair. In this pair, they could also extend this exploration by generating strategies for solving the problem for *x, y* and *z* days. The goal before the technology is used is for the students to develop an initial conjecture that they will be able to test and refine with the technology.

Technology can support learners in thinking mathematically. In the case of the 3-day cruise, the ship will be at sea for three days, return for a day and leave every fourth day. The 4-day cruise will leave port every five days. Further, the 7-day cruise line will leave port every eight days. Using spreadsheet software, students can produce a table (Figure 1). The spreadsheet formula in Figure 1 uses the Integer (INT) function to identify values that yield integers when divided by a given number of days. In this way, the spreadsheet can quickly show students all the days a ship will leave from port for a given schedule and to compare those

Figure 1. Microsoft Excel spreadsheet setup for various cruises and times they are in port

	A	B	C	D	E
1	Days		CL1 returns	CL2 returns	CL3 returns
2	0		=IF(INT($A2/4)=$A2/4,"Y","")	Y	Y
3	1				
4	2				
5	3				
6	4		Y		
7	5			Y	
8	6				
9	7				
10	8		Y		Y
11	9				
12	10			Y	

schedules against one another across columns. For example, the 3-day cruise schedule has a "Y" placed in the column for each day that is evenly divisible by four, since the ship leaves port every four days. The same formula is used for the 4-day cruise and the 7-day cruise. The solution to the first part of the problem occurs when a "Y" is in all three columns on the spreadsheet, which is day 40[1].

The patterns in the spreadsheet can be manipulated rapidly, which allows generalizations to be made for cruises that last x, y and z days. Table 1 features a table of various cruise lines and the first day the cruise lines leave port simultane-

ously. Using a representation such as Table 1, students can observe that the next day the ships will simultaneously leave port is always the least common multiple of the frequency of the ships. For example, for cruises that last 1, 2, and 3 days, the ships would leave the port every 2, 3, and 4 days respectively. All three ships will leave again simultaneously on day 12, which is the least common multiple of 2, 3, and 4.

This generalization that the next day all three ships are in port is the least common multiple of the 3 numbers can be seen clearly on a spreadsheet, as the spreadsheet allows patterns to be extended and manipulated rapidly and provides a visual display of the data that is readily accessible. It should be noted that the technology is a tool that adds to the investigation, and does not replace the student's need for understanding arithmetic patterns. Prior to use of spreadsheets, students had to identify the expected patterns for the three-day, four-day and seven-day cruises. Once students recognize the pattern, the spreadsheet can be used to extend the pattern and explore the pattern for different variable, allowing students to not only observe the patterns but also analyze the data produced, and form conjectures based on the data. Technology facilitates the exploration of the task, allowing learners to focus on the analysis of numbers in the pattern rather than taking time to generate all of the terms of the pattern.

Table 1. Examples of cruises with different frequencies and their common leave days

What day will three ships leave at the same time?			
Frequency of Cruise x	Frequency of Cruise y	Frequency of Cruise z	Day
2	4	5	20
3	5	7	105
3	7	8	168
3	7	11	231
4	6	8	24
4	6	10	60
4	3	6	12
4	10	12	60

This task has many connections to Common Core Grade Level Standards. The Common Core requires students to explore mathematical patterns beginning in Grade 5, which leads into evaluating expressions and solving equations in Grades 6 and 7. This task also has relevance in Grade 4 as students look at the various multiples and factors of numbers within 100.

USING PATTERNS TO DEVELOP GEOMETRIC SEQUENCES AND SERIES

In mathematics, geometric sequences and series are usually learned after arithmetic sequences. As with arithmetic patterns, geometric sequences can be explored with technologies and classroom discourse to yield a definition or rule. Depending on the situation, students may work on problems such as the following:

A hot-air balloon moves up 200 feet during its first minute of flight. Then it will continue to rise each minute thereafter for a distance of 80% of the distance traveled the previous minute. If you ignore air pressure, will the balloon fly out into space (in other words, will it rise indefinitely)? Explain why or why not.

This task could be initially explored with some discussion about what students think will happen based solely on intuition. In such a discussion, the teacher could ask questions to help them develop their thought processes about this task. Through such questioning, the teacher can help foster student curiosity in the problem and help students think about how technology can support their further work on the task. As with the arithmetic sequences, this geometric sequence can be explored in a spreadsheet. Column one can denote the time in minutes, column two can show each rise at each minute and column three can show the total rise of the hot air balloon (Figure 2). As a pedagogical strategy to isolate the pattern, column

Figure 2. Excerpt from spreadsheet on the rise of the balloon

	A	B	C
1	Time (min)	Rise (ft)	Total Rise (ft)
2	minute	"=0.8*B2"	"=C2+B3"
3	1	200	200
4	2	160	360
5	3	128	488
6	4	102.4	590.4
7	5	81.92	672.32
8	6	65.536	737.856
9	7	52.4288	790.2848
10	8	41.94304	832.22784
11	9	33.554432	865.782272
12	10	26.8435456	892.6258176
13	11	21.47483648	914.1006541
14	12	17.17986918	931.2305233
15	13	13.74389535	945.0244186
16	14	10.99511628	956.0195349
17	15	8.796093022	964.8156279
18	16	7.036874418	971.8525023
19	17	5.629499534	977.4820019
20	18	4.503599627	981.9356015
21	19	3.602879702	985.5384812
22	20	2.882303762	988.470785
23	21	2.305843009	990.776528
24	22	1.844674407	992.6213024
25	23	1.475739526	994.0970419
26	24	1.180591621	995.2776335
27	25	0.944473297	996.2221063
28	26	0.755578637	996.9776855
29	27	0.60446291	997.5821484
30	28	0.483570328	998.0057187
31	29	0.386856262	998.452575

three should not be entered into the spreadsheet until students have studied the second column and identified a pattern.

In this task, technology allows students to quickly generate the heights of the balloon at different times, which allows students to see a more developed pattern than would be possible if they had arbitrarily chosen four or five values to compute. Further, spreadsheet software further enhances the problem-solving process by creating graphs from the tabular data. This process greatly simplifies a process that would be time-consuming for the student, thus allowing more time for focusing on higher-order thinking activities such as predicting, making and testing conjectures, and interpreting the graphs. In the graphs for this example (Figures 3 and 4), it is clear that the balloon will not rise above 1000 feet. This provides a good opportunity to link to the mathematical

Figure 3. Graphical representation of rise of balloon

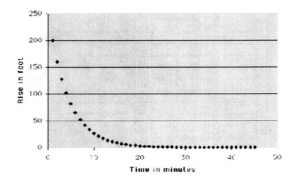

Figure 4. Graphical representation of height of balloon

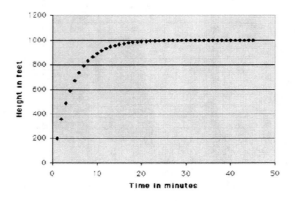

definitions of the *n*th term of a geometric sequence, the sum of *n* terms of a geometric sequence, and the infinite geometric series.

The Common Core Grade Level Standards include Geometric Patterns and Series in Grade 8 when students explore non-linear functions by examining equations, creating and analyzing graphs of the functions, and by connecting real-world situations to the values of the equation. In earlier grades (Grades 5, 6, and 7) students work with and explore mathematical patterns and equations, but do not formally work with non-linear functions.

STANDARDS FOR MATHEMATICAL PRACTICE

Both tasks presented above provide opportunities for students to explore mathematical patterns in the context of real-world situations. Both tasks provide multiple ways for learners to begin or enter the problem, and include a level of complexity that requires students to make sense and also persevere during problem exploration (Mathematical Practice 1). As students explore tasks with mathematical patterns there are numerous opportunities to look for and use repeated reasoning as they extend and analyze patterns (MP 8). In each of these tasks learners had opportunities to use spreadsheets as tools (MP 5) to model the mathematical situations by connecting the real-life situation to numerical values and equations (MP 4). Further, learners are encouraged to reason abstractly and quantitatively (MP 2) as they generalize the patterns. Other Mathematical Practices, such as constructing viable arguments (MP 3) and attending to precision (MP 6) could also be incorporated as students communicate orally or in writing about the task.

CONCLUSION

The power of technology, specifically spreadsheets, allows teachers to support students' development of mathematical understanding as well as their work with specific mathematical practices while exploring tasks incorporating patterns. As illustrated in our examples, spreadsheets afford students with opportunities to make predictions and easily test them, to study patterns and generate descriptions of them, and to engage in conceptual mathematical thinking. These processes lead to a deeper understanding of mathematical concepts.

REFERENCES

Mason, J. (1996). Expressing generality and routes of algebra. In N. Bednarz, C. Kieran, & L. Lee (Eds.), *Approaches to algebra: Perspectives for research and teaching* (pp. 65-86). Dordrecht, The Netherlands: Kluwer Academic.

National Council of Teachers of Mathematics. (2000). *Principles and standards for school mathematics*. Reston, VA: NCTM.

National Curriculum Board. (2009). *Shape of the Australian curriculum: Mathematics*. Retrieved from http://www.acara.edu.au/verve/_resources/Australian_Curriculum_-_Maths.pdf

Qualifications and Curriculum Authority (QCA). (2007). *Mathematics: Programme of study for key stage 4*. London: Qualifications and Curriculum Authority. Retrieved from http://orderline.qcda.gov.uk/gempdf/1847215408.PDF

Singapore Ministry of Education. (2007). *Singapore mathematics syllabus*. Retrieved from http://www.moe.sg/education/syllabuses/sciences/files/maths-primary-2007.pdf

ENDNOTES

[1] "Y" denotes days that the ship is in port.

Chapter 16
Common Core Standards for Mathematical Practice and TPACK:
An Integrated Approach to Instruction

Jayme Linton
Lenior-Rhyne University, USA

David Stegall
Newton-Connover City Schools, USA

ABSTRACT

This chapter seeks to answer the guiding question: How does the TPACK (Technological Pedagogical Content Knowledge) framework influence how technology can support the implementation of the Common Core Standards for Mathematical Practice? The authors provide an overview of the Standards for Mathematical Practice and an application of the TPACK framework to the Common Core State Standards for Mathematics. Classroom scenarios describe how teachers can use the TPACK framework to integrate technology into the Standards for Mathematical Practice from kindergarten to eighth grade. The authors conclude with implications for professional developers, teacher educators, and administrators as they work to develop teachers' TPACK and prepare teachers for implementing the Common Core State Standards for Mathematics.

INTRODUCTION

Mathematics teachers across the nation are charged with implementing the Common Core State Standards for Mathematics (CCSSM), which comprise the Standards for Mathematical Content and the Standards for Mathematical Practice. Many teach-

ers, schools, and districts are taking advantage of professional development offerings focused on the grade level content standards. However, many teachers have noticed a lack of support and resources for integrating the Standards for Mathematical Practice, which were designed to be taught across all grade level standards from

DOI: 10.4018/978-1-4666-4086-3.ch016

Kindergarten through twelfth grade. Along with changes in mathematics curriculum and teaching practices, teachers are expected to integrate more technology into their classrooms to meet the needs of today's learners and prepare students for college and careers in the 21st century. Technology integration is a complex task that requires not only knowledge about technological tools but also training and support in how to use them appropriately.

This chapter describes one vision for technology integration within the CCSSM, introducing the TPACK (technological pedagogical content knowledge) framework (Mishra & Koehler, 2006) as a tool to support technology integration and effective teaching of the Standards for Mathematical Practice. The goal of this chapter is to provide a framework for integrating technology into the teaching and learning of mathematics as specified by the Standards for Mathematical Practice. To this end, this chapter includes a brief description of the Standards for Mathematical Practice, a thorough analysis of how the CCSSM can be situated within the TPACK framework and classroom scenarios to guide educators in integrating technology within the Standards for Mathematical Practice. It is our hope that this chapter will serve as a resource for teachers, administrators, professional developers, and teacher educators striving to increase effective use of technology in teaching and learning about mathematics.

BACKGROUND

Integrating technology into the curriculum has been a recent shift occurring in the past ten years (Niess, 2005). Although staff developers, and therefore teachers, have tended to focus on technology itself rather than on how it can be used in the classroom, we agree with Mishra and Koehler (2006) that simply "knowing how to use technology is not the same as knowing how to teach with it" (p. 1033). Technology integra-

tion is complex, requiring teachers to possess not only technological knowledge and skills but also an awareness of how to facilitate learning with technology. According to the National Council for Teachers of Mathematics (NCTM), technology has the potential to empower mathematics teachers and students. However, there is very little mention of technology in the Common Core State Standards for Mathematics. NCTM commented on the newly-released standards:

Unless technology is woven throughout these standards, the credibility of any claim that they will better prepare students in the 21st century is diminished. Moreover, without ties to technology, many of these standards read like school expectations from the last century rather than expectations intended to equip students for a mathematical future in the 21st century (National Council for Teachers of Mathematics, 2010, n.d.).

The TPACK framework can provide the missing support that teachers need to effectively integrate technology within the Common Core State Standards for Mathematics. Technological pedagogical and content knowledge (TPACK) is a framework for technology integration developed by Mishra and Koehler (2006), extending Shulman's work on pedagogical content knowledge. Shulman (1986) defined pedagogical content knowledge as the blending of content and pedagogy into an understanding of how to organize and represent subject matter to enhance the learning of it. The TPACK framework adds a third dimension—technology—to the knowledge needed for effective instruction. TPACK is the foundation of good teaching with technology that requires teachers to understand not only their content knowledge and effective pedagogical strategies but also how technology can be utilized to strengthen teaching and improve student learning (Mishra & Koehler, 2006). While technological knowledge has typically been viewed as a separate set of skills isolated from knowledge of content and pedagogy, the TPACK model emphasizes the interaction of these three types of knowledge. TPACK helps teachers find answers to questions that guide instructional planning:

- How can I represent important concepts with technology?
- Which pedagogical techniques use technology in constructive ways to teach those concepts?
- How can I use technology to build on students' prior knowledge of those concepts?
- How can technology help students increase their understanding of those concepts?
- How can students use technology to represent their understanding of those concepts?

TPACK AND THE COMMON CORE STATE STANDARDS FOR MATHEMATICS

Common Core Standards for Mathematical Practice

The Common Core State Standards for Mathematics seem to have burst onto the scene in many states overnight. In fact, they have evolved through a multitude of report findings, recommendations from national leaders, and research. Many of these research reports were conducted by the National Council of Teacher of Mathematics. However, the focus on a set of standards for college and career readiness in Mathematics and English Language Arts became a priority when the National Governors Association and the Council of Chief State School Officers came together to create a set of voluntary national standards. They enlisted the help of three lead writers who would focus on the Mathematic standards. These lead writers worked through a vetting process with writing and review teams and created a set of Common Core State Standards for Mathematics. These standards are

available for adoption by states, with the stipulation that adoption must be verbatim as they were written. In June, 2010, a public joint statement was issued by NCTM, the Association of Mathematics Teacher Educators, the National Council of Supervisors of Mathematics, and the Association of State Supervisors of Mathematics welcoming the Common Core State Standards for Mathematics. In particular, the standards were praised for their two types of standards: the Content Standards and the Standards for Mathematical Practice.

The writers of the CCSSM identified eight Standards for Mathematical Practice for mathematically proficient students called processes and proficiencies. These processes and proficiencies are based heavily on two previous documents that describe mathematical processes. The first of these is the Principles and Standards for School Mathematics (National Council of Teachers of Mathematics, 2000). This document describes five overarching process standards of mathematics: problem solving; reasoning and proof; communication; connections; and representations. The second document guiding the development of these mathematical processes is *Adding It Up* by the National Research Council (2001). This research document grew out of a concern for the scarcity of research or directives to guide instruction in early mathematics.

The mathematics students need to learn today is not the same mathematics that their parents and grandparents needed to learn. When today's students become adults, they will face new demands for mathematical proficiency that school mathematics should attempt to anticipate (NRC, 2001, p. 1).

The *Adding It Up* report outlines five strands of mathematical proficiencies similar to the process standards described by NCTM in 2000, even going beyond those described by NCTM. These proficiencies are:

- **Conceptual Understanding:** Comprehension of mathematical concepts, operations, and relations.
- **Procedural Fluency:** Skill in carrying out procedures flexibly, accurately, efficiently, and appropriately.
- **Strategic Competence:** Ability to formulate, represent, and solve mathematical problems.
- **Adaptive Reasoning:** Capacity for logical thought, reflection, explanation, and justification.
- **Productive Disposition:** Habitual inclination to see mathematics as sensible, useful, and worthwhile, coupled with a belief in diligence and one's own efficacy.

Based on these two guiding documents, the eight Common Core State Standards for Mathematical Practice are:

1. **Make Sense of Problems and Persevere in Solving Them:** This practice focuses on students explaining the meaning of a problem by analyzing the givens, the constraints, as well as the relationships and goals of the problem. Students should develop a solution pathway and then monitor their progress towards the solution. If needed, students should re-chart their plan to find a new solution pathway to determine if the solution makes sense.
2. **Reason Abstractly and Quantitatively:** This practice outlines how students should use givens to justify their arguments. They can do this by decontextualizing (theorizing a symbolic representation of a problem and manipulating the symbols to begin to solve a problem) and contextualizing (reviewing the original problem during the manipulation process to consider the units involved and the meaning of the symbols used).
3. **Construct Viable Arguments and Critique the Reasoning of Others:** Students are encouraged to utilize givens to construct and justify arguments. This may be done using concrete illustrations as well as logical cases using definitions, assumptions, and previously established outcomes.
4. **Model With Mathematics:** Students should apply the mathematics they know to real world examples in order to analyze and draw conclusions.
5. **Use Appropriate Tools Strategically:** This practice expresses that students should understand and be familiar with mathematical tools necessary to solve problems, including technological and digital content located on a Website. Students should be able to analyze a given problem, consider possible tools for solving the problem, and select an appropriate tool to resolve the problem.
6. **Attend to Precision:** Students should be precise with their communication including labeling various parts of a problem and its solution. Labels should specify units of measurement.
7. **Look for and Make Use of Structure:** This practice encourages students to look for patterns and structure to problems. Students can also periodically reexamine a problem and solution to shift their perspective.
8. **Look for and Express Regularity in Repeated Reasoning:** Mathematically proficient students should look for shortcuts based upon repeated calculations, keeping a constant eye on evaluating the reasonableness of their incremental results.

These eight Standards for Mathematical Practice are procedures and understandings that are based upon previous research about varieties of expertise that students should develop.

Integrating the TPACK Framework within the CCSSM

Teachers must develop an understanding of each piece of the TPACK model before they can design instruction that represents the nuanced interaction between content, pedagogical, and technological knowledge. In order to build a strong case for the TPACK framework as a model for integrating technology into the Common Core Standards for Mathematical Practice, we provide a thorough description later of each component of the framework and how it relates to the CCSSM. We use the TPACK framework to represent the intersection of the Standards for Mathematical Content, the Standards for Mathematical Practice, and technological knowledge (See Figure 1).

Content Knowledge (CK)

According to Mishra and Koehler (2006), content knowledge can be defined as knowledge of key facts, concepts, and procedures within a discipline as well as knowledge of frameworks that can be used to organize and connect ideas within the discipline. Within our model for integrating TPACK into the CCSSM, the content knowledge teachers need to possess is represented by the Common Core Standards for Mathematical Content. These grade

Figure 1. Integrating TPACK within the CCSSM (adapted with permission from www.tpack.org)

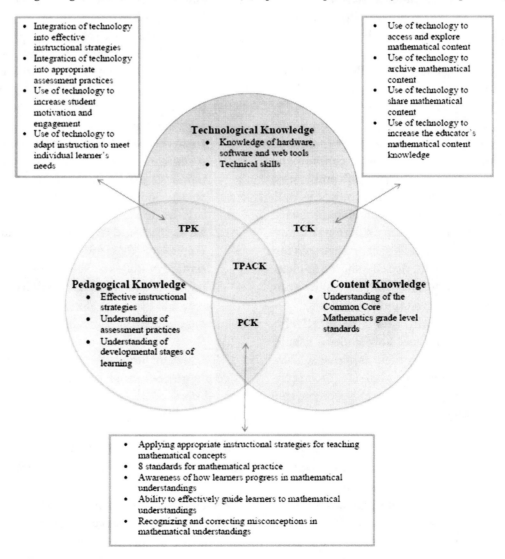

level standards provide descriptors of the necessary mathematical concepts and skills students should master at each grade level. CCSSM grade level standards represent mathematical content knowledge "not only by stressing conceptual understanding of key ideas, but also by continually returning to organizing principles such as place value or the properties of operations to structure those ideas" (Common Core State Standards Initiative, 2010, p. 4). While the eight Standards for Mathematical Practice do not represent content knowledge, they were designed to be embedded into these grade level standards.

Pedagogical Knowledge (PK)

Knowledge of instructional strategies for teaching content is identified by Shulman (1986) and Mishra and Koehler (2006) as pedagogical knowledge. However, acquiring pedagogical knowledge is not quite as simple as mastering a few instructional techniques. Pedagogical knowledge also encompasses an understanding of the processes involved in teaching and learning and knowledge of strategies for assessing student understanding of content (Mishra & Koehler, 2006). Pedagogical knowledge itself is not directly tied to content knowledge; rather, it represents a necessary set of knowledge and skills required for effective instruction. Quantitative studies have identified pedagogical knowledge has having the largest impact on development of teachers' TPACK (Chai, Koh, & Tsai, 2010).

Technological Knowledge (TK)

Within the TPACK framework, technological knowledge is a key component of quality teaching. It is as central to effective teaching as content and pedagogical knowledge (Mishra & Koehler, 2006). Technological knowledge is not a static set of concepts teachers need to master; it changes as technology evolves. Therefore, it is imperative that teachers remain current with technological tools and their applications for education. The International Society for Technology in Education (ISTE) identified key technological concept and skills for teachers and students, referred to as the National Educational Technology Standards (NETS). These standards are recognized worldwide as the important technological knowledge and skills teachers and students should master across content areas and grade levels (ISTE, 2011).

Pedagogical Content Knowledge (PCK)

Pedagogical Content Knowledge (PCK) represents the intersection of content and pedagogy. Shulman (1986) defined PCK as the heart of teaching. Developing PCK involves selecting instructional approaches based on their fit for teaching and learning specific content. Teachers who possess PCK recognize how the different components of a discipline can be arranged so that students can more easily understand it. This includes knowledge of the most powerful illustrations, examples, analogies, and demonstrations within the subject area. In addition, these teachers are able to identify and address misconceptions and potential misapplications of students' prior knowledge (Mishra & Koehler, 2006).

Teachers implementing the Common Core State Standards for Mathematics (CCSSM) must apply appropriate instructional strategies for teaching the grade level standards. Additionally, teachers must develop an awareness of how learners progress in mathematical understandings and be able to effectively guide students toward those understandings. Our model for integrating TPACK into the CCSSM locates the Standards for Mathematical Practice within PCK. These standards focus on key mathematical processes that are to be developed across mathematical concepts. Effective integration of the Standards for Mathematical Practice makes it necessary for teachers to not only possess a strong understanding of their grade level standards but also the ability to help students learn to think mathematically. This development of mathematical processes within different domains of mathematical content exemplifies the PCK needed for teaching the CCSSM.

Technological Content Knowledge (TCK)

While PCK represents the complex relationship between content and pedagogy, Technological Content Knowledge (TCK) is used to describe the interaction between knowledge of content and knowledge of technological applications. TCK encompasses an awareness of applications of technology that can be used to represent, organize, or change content knowledge (Mishra & Koehler, 2006). When applied to the CCSSM, TCK involves the use of technology to access, explore, archive, and share mathematical content related to the grade level standards. Teachers must rely on TCK to increase students' understanding of mathematics as well as their own.

Technological Pedagogical Knowledge (TPK)

The use of technology to increase the effectiveness of instruction or enhance students' learning is captured by Technological Pedagogical Knowledge (TPK), which is defined as "knowledge of the existence, components, and capabilities of various technologies as they are used in teaching and learning settings" (Mishra & Koehler, 2006, p. 1028). TPK advocates for teachers to recognize that a variety of tools exist for a particular instructional task and develop the ability to choose a tool based on how well it matches the task at hand. Technology should not be an additional component of classroom instruction; its purpose should be to support learning (Polly, McGee, & Martin, 2010). Although many teachers use technology to learn about their content, Niess (2005) argues that learning content with technology is much different from learning to teach that content with technology. Results from a study by Chai, Koh, and Tsai

(2010) suggest that teachers increase their TK in tandem with raising their PK so that technology has a positive impact on teaching practice. Teachers who possess strong TPK incorporate technology into their assessment practices, use technology to increase student motivation, and adapt instruction to meet the needs of individual learners.

Technological Pedagogical Content Knowledge (TPACK)

At the center of the diagram designed by Mishra and Koehler (2006) and adapted by the authors of this chapter lies TPACK – the intersection of content, pedagogy, and technology. According to the developers of ISTE's NETS for students and teachers, technology must become "an integral component or tool for learning and communications within the context of academic subject areas" (ISTE, 2000, p. 17). This is the aim of TPACK - technology integration aligned with effective instructional strategies appropriate for specific content. The relationships between content, pedagogy, and technology are complex and nuanced. No single technology tool or technological strategy applies to every classroom, every subject area, or every student (Mishra & Koehler, 2006). Teachers who develop strong TPACK have the knowledge and skills necessary to use the right tool for the right purpose at the right time with the right content.

Application of the TPACK Framework to the Standards for Mathematical Practice

In an effort to bring TPACK and the CCSSM to the classroom level, in this section we provide teachers with practical examples for applying the TPACK framework to the Standards for Mathematical Practice. Next, we describe how technology can influence teaching of the Common Core State Standards for Mathematics. A classroom scenario is provided for each of the eight standards, showcasing an example of how TPACK can support mathematics teaching and learning. Sample grade level standards from Kindergarten through eighth grade are included later to illustrate connections between the Standards for Mathematical Content and Standards for Mathematical Practice. The Standards for Mathematical Practice were designed to be integrated across all grade level standards. However, we feel that providing sample grade level standards helps to ground the classroom scenarios in mathematical content as well as mathematical practices.

Make Sense of Problems and Persevere in Solving Them

Description of Standard for Mathematical Practice

Students are proficient with a variety of tools and know when and why to use them. Students choose a specific tool to solve a specific problem. Students check their solutions using a different method and ask "Does my answer make sense?" and "Can I solve the problem a different way?"

- Facilitation Questions:
  - What are you trying to solve?
  - What information do you have?
  - What strategies that you've learned could you utilize?
  - Do you need to step back and consider other options?

Sample Technology Tools

- Problem of the Day Websites:
  - Virtual Manipulatives
  - Online Calculators
  - Problem Solving Apps

Grade Level Standard for Mathematical Content

1.OA.8: Determine the unknown whole number in an addition or subtraction equation relating three whole numbers. For example, determine

the unknown number that makes the equation true in each of the equations $8 + ? = 11$, $5 = | | - 3$, $6 + 6 = | |$.

Sample Classroom Scenario

The teacher poses a problem while students use a variety of learned strategies to solve it. Students share the methods they used with partners, in small groups, or with the whole class and discuss different approaches to the same problem. Students discuss the most efficient method to solve the problem based on procedures attempted by the class. Students and teacher create a digital database of methods that are the best fit for certain kinds of problems. They can refer to this database in the future when they encounter similar problems. Web tools for creating a digital toolbox include Wikispaces and Livebinders.

Reason Abstractly and Quantitatively

Description of Standard for Mathematical Practice

This standard involves two processes: contextualizing and decontextualizing. Contextualizing refers to the process of providing or creating a context for mathematical processes while giving meaning to the quantities involved, while decontextualizing involves removing a problem from context in order to work with the mathematical operations and reasoning through the mathematical process involved to solve the problem..

Sample Technology Tools

- Virtual Manipulatives:
  - Blog as Math Journal
  - Equation Generators
  - Probability Simulation Tools
  - Dice Probability Generator (http://www.vrtisworks.com/kiki/fun/cdice.htm)

Grade Level Standard for Mathematical Content

7.SP.6: Approximate the probability of a chance event by collecting data on the chance process that produces it and observing its long-run relative frequency, and predict the approximate relative frequency given the probability. For example, when rolling a number cube 600 times, predict that a 3 or 6 would be rolled roughly 200 times, but probably not exactly 200 times.

Sample Classroom Scenario

Students decontextualize the probability scenario presented in 7.SP.6 by breaking apart the problem and constructing a mathematical expression to represent the scenario and then solving it. Students then contextualize the expression by visualizing, designing and implementing an investigation which involves rolling dice a set number of times in order to predict what would happen with a higher number of rolls. Students use online probability tools such as http://stattrek.com/online-calculator/probability-calculator.aspx to recreate the experiment 500 times, 1000 times, and 10,000 times to demonstrate what happens as the number of rolls increases.

Construct Viable Arguments and Critique the Reasoning of Others

Description of Standard for Mathematical Practice

Students respond to questions such as "How did you get that?", "Why is that true?", and "Does that always work?" Students construct arguments using verbal or written explanations accompanied by expressions, equations, inequalities, models, graphs, tables, etc.

Sample Technology Tools

- Blog as Math Journal
- Presentation Tools to Demonstrate Student Learning (VoiceThread, Prezi, Keynote, Glogster EDU, etc.)
- BrainPop
- Khan Academy
- Mind Mapping Software (Bubbl.us, Inspiration, Popplet)

Grade Level Standard for Mathematical Content

4.NF.1: Explain why a fraction a/b is equivalent to a fraction (n × a)/(n × b) by using visual fraction models, with attention to how the number and size of the parts differ even though the two fractions themselves are the same size. Use this principle to recognize and generate equivalent fractions.

Sample Classroom Scenario

Teacher presents a given fraction to the class and asks students to construct an equivalent fraction. To develop arguments and critique the reasoning of others, students work collaboratively to create a multimedia slideshow using a tool such as VoiceThread. Each student creates one slide to represent his/her equivalent fraction. Each slide should include a written, verbal, and symbolic explanation of why the fraction generated by the student is equivalent to the given fraction. Students comment on each other's slides, critiquing, responding to, and extending each other's thinking. (VoiceThread allows students to leave text, voice, or Webcam comments on their own and each other's slides.)

Model with Mathematics

Description of Standard for Mathematical Practice

Modeling with mathematics involves the use of concrete, pictorial, and verbal representations. Students also model by creating an appropriate problem situation from an equation and using multiple representations appropriate to a problem's context.

Sample Technology Tools

- Virtual Manipulatives:
  - Blog as Math Journal
  - Online Animation Tools (Xtranormal, Go Animate)
  - Software and Web Tools for Creating Graphs, Tables, and Charts

Grade Level Standard for Mathematical Content

5.NF.7: Apply and extend previous understandings of division to divide unit fractions by whole numbers and whole numbers by unit fractions.

- Interpret division of a unit fraction by a non-zero whole number, and compute such quotients. For example, create a story context for $(1/3) \div 4$, and use a visual fraction model to show the quotient. Use the relationship between multiplication and division to explain that $(1/3) \div 4 = 1/12$ because $(1/12) \times 4 = 1/3$.
- Interpret division of a whole number by a unit fraction, and compute such quotients. For example, create a story context for $4 \div (1/5)$, and use a visual fraction model to show the quotient. Use the relationship between multiplication and division to explain that $4 \div (1/5) = 20$ because $20 \times (1/5) = 4$.

Solve real world problems involving division of unit fractions by non-zero whole numbers and division of whole numbers by unit fractions, e.g., by using visual fraction models and equations to represent the problem. For example, how much chocolate will each person get if 3 people share 1/2 lb of chocolate equally? How many 1/3-cup servings are in 2 cups of raisins?

Sample Classroom Scenario

Teacher provides a mathematical expression, and students generate a real-world situation from the expression. Students create an online skit using a tool such as Go Animate or Xtranormal to act out the scenario that contextualizes the mathematical expression. Students create the characters and setting and develop a script for the scene. Characters in the online skits must use mathematical terminology to explain the student's approach to solving the problem. Students can accompany the video representation with an additional model that is appropriate for the context of the problem (using numbers, words, objects, etc.).

Use Appropriate Tools Strategically

Description of Standard for Mathematical Practice

Students choose appropriate tools for solving specific types of problems and use them strategically. Students are fluent with a variety of mathematical tools and can apply them in appropriate contexts.

Sample Technology Tools

- Calculators
- Protractors
- Compasses
- Rulers
- Base Ten Blocks
- Clocks
- Virtual Manipulatives

Grade Level Standard for Mathematical Content

2.NBT.6: Add up to four two-digit numbers using strategies based on place value and properties of operations.

Sample Classroom Scenario

Students are presented with an addition problem including up to four two-digit numbers and are given a variety of tools for solving it (base ten blocks, virtual manipulatives, calculators, etc.). Students identify the most appropriate tool for solving the problem, explain the tool they chose, and give a rationale for why they selected it. Students then solve the same problem using a different tool and construct a comparison of both tools applied to the specific problem. Students can create a two-column chart, Venn diagram, or other graphic organizer to compare and contrast the use of both tools for the specific problem. Students share their comparisons with the class and discuss which tools are most effective for solving addition problems. The class can create a digital collection of students' graphic organizers throughout the year and use them as a reference "tool box" for choosing the most appropriate representation or tool for a given problem.

Attend to Precision

Description of Standard for Mathematical Practice

Should present their mathematical thinking precisely and accurately and include appropriate units of measurement.

Sample Technology Tools

- Blog or Online Graphic Organizers as Math Vocabulary Journal
- Online Math Glossary
- Digital Word Wall (Wallwisher)
- Presentation Tools (VoiceThread, Prezi, Keynote, Glogster EDU, etc.)

Grade Level Standard for Mathematical Content

6.EE.2: Write, read, and evaluate expressions in which letters stand for numbers.

- Write expressions that record operations with numbers and with letters standing for numbers. *For example, express the calculation "Subtract y from 5" as $5 - y$.*
- Identify parts of an expression using mathematical terms (sum, term, product, factor, quotient, coefficient); view one or more parts of an expression as a single entity. *For example, describe the expression $2 (8 + 7)$ as a product of two factors; view $(8 + 7)$ as both a single entity and a sum of two terms.*

Evaluate expressions at specific values of their variables. Include expressions that arise from formulas used in real-world problems. Perform arithmetic operations, including those involving whole-number exponents, in the conventional order when there are no parentheses to specify a particular order (Order of Operations). *For example, use the formulas $V = s3$ and $A = 6 s2$ to find the volume and surface area of a cube with sides of length $s = 1/2$.*

Sample Classroom Scenario

Students collaboratively create an interactive math glossary of key terminology related to the CCSSM grade level standards. A tool such as Wikispaces would be a good fit for an interactive glossary. Students should include a technical definition and a description of each term in the students' own words as well as pictorial, symbolic, and expressive representations. As students encounter new vocabulary during math instruction, they create a new entry in the glossary. Students refer to the math glossary wiki throughout the year and use it at home to help with homework. Multiple classes could partner collaboratively on this project by contributing to a glossary shared by more than one class or by commenting on each other's class glossaries.

Look for and Make Use of Structure

Description of Standard for Mathematical Practice

Students examine problems to determine patterns and structure within and across mathematical problems. Students are able to examine problems from various perspectives and recognize similar structures across a variety of problems.

Sample Technology Tools

- Online Math Glossary
- Equation Generator
- Virtual Manipulatives
- Blog as Math Journal
- Computer Algebra System (CAS)
- Scientific Notation Generator (www.edin-formatics.com/math_science/scinot6.htm)

Grade Level Standard for Mathematical Content

8.EE.4 Perform operations with numbers expressed in scientific notation, including problems where both decimal and scientific notation are used. Use scientific notation and choose units of appropriate size for measurements of very large or very small quantities (e.g., use millimeters per year for seafloor spreading). Interpret scientific notation that has been generated by technology.

Sample Classroom Scenario

Students examine these questions:

- How does changing an equation in decimal form lead to changes in scientific notation for the same equation?
- How are these two equation forms (decimal and scientific notation) related?

- How does a change in one form relate to a change in the other?

Students use an online scientific notation generator to practice and develop an understanding of this relationship. Students document their understanding of the relationship between these two forms using a math journal blog. Students can comment on each other's blogs to challenge and extend their thinking.

Look for and Express Regularity in Repeated Reasoning

Description of Standard for Mathematical Practice

Students recognize similarities across different types of problems and look for shortcuts. Students examine whether the results they see are reasonable and make adjustments or try different approaches when necessary.

Sample Technology Tools

- Online Math Glossary
- Blog as Math Journal
- Online Function Machines (http://www.mathplayground.com/functionmachine.html)

Grade Level Standard for Mathematical Content

4.NF.4b: Understand a multiple of a/b as a multiple of 1/b, and use this understanding to multiply a fraction by a whole number. For example, use a visual fraction model to express $3 \times (2/5)$ as $6 \times (1/5)$, recognizing this product as 6/5. (In general, $n \times (a/b) = (n \times a)/b$.)

Sample Classroom Scenario

Students use repetitive action models to make generalizations about the algorithms that are at work. Students utilize models to investigate patterns and then create algorithms to explain the patterns. An example would be for students to use visual fraction models such as the ones found at http://www.conceptuamath.com/fractions/equivalent-fractions.html to compare equivalent fractions and explain their relationships. Students can use this model of repeated reasoning to write further equivalent fractions.

IMPLICATIONS

In order to develop TPACK, teachers need to be explicitly aware of their current knowledge and areas for improvement in each component of the TPACK model. Professional development can assist teachers in developing this awareness. One failure of some professional development efforts is a focus on isolated knowledge (i.e. TK, CK, or PK) rather than an integrated approach. Technology professional development tends to treat technological knowledge as an isolated set of skills, while it should take an integrated approach to developing teachers' content, pedagogical, and technological knowledge. Kadijevich (2012) argues that professional development for technology integration should focus mainly on pedagogy, and Chai, Koh, and Tsia (2010) agree that increasing pedagogical knowledge is key to developing teachers' TPACK. However, we argue that appropriate pedagogy and technology should be embedded in specific content given that content area requires unique learning processes and proficiencies.

Those who are responsible for designing and delivering professional development must rethink the knowledge teachers need and view professional development as an opportunity to bring content, pedagogical, and technological knowledge together (Doering, Veletsianos, Scharber, & Miller, 2009). However, not every approach to professional development will work for every teacher because each teacher's knowledge within the TPACK framework varies. Instead, teachers

need multiple and varied opportunities to actively engage in learning new tools and teaching techniques in order for them to transfer to teaching practice. In addition, teacher knowledge is increased when connections are made between professional development and the everyday work of teachers and students. As such, professional development should be ongoing, differentiated, and embedded with the context of the classroom (Garet, Porter, Desimone, Birman, & Yoon, 2001; Polly et al., 2010). The scenarios described within this chapter can serve as a starting point for planning and delivering effective professional development for increasing teachers' TPACK in implementing the Common Core State Standards for Math.

Likewise, teacher educators charged with preparing pre-service teachers for teaching the Common Core State Standards for Mathematics and integrating technology into their classrooms can use the TPACK framework as a model for their coursework. A TPACK-driven teacher education program should provide pre-service teachers with a coherent and meaningful learning experience and model effective technology integration in all content areas. This could involve moving away from isolated coursework—separate courses for content, methods, and technology integration, for example—toward a more integrated design.

Administrators working to support the development of teachers' TPACK and effective implementation of the CCSSM are encouraged to provide support following professional development opportunities. It is key that administrators create a structure and culture that fosters successful implementation of curricular, instructional, and professional development initiatives. This support should be ongoing and occur in real-time as teachers work to integrate technology into their mathematics instruction. Such a structure might include professional learning community team meetings, peer observations, collaborative lesson planning, constructive feedback, peer coaching, and mentoring. One essential and often missing component of effective implementation of any school initiative is fidelity monitoring. To ensure that processes, procedures, and practices are being implemented effectively, administrators are charged with understanding key components of TPACK and CCSSM in order to continuously monitor with a focus on outcomes of the initiative.

CONCLUSION

Increasingly, educators are faced with learning how to teach with technology as a tool for developing deeper understanding for students. The TPACK model provides a framework for educators to apply the use of sound pedagogical approaches, effective technological strategies, and research-based standards for mathematical practice to deepen understanding of the Common Core State Standards of Mathematical Content. By positioning the Standards for Mathematical Practice within the TPACK model, educators can strategically develop approaches to learning that interrelate technology and the eight Standards for Mathematical Practice as supportive, interdependent tools for the content.

REFERENCES

Chai, C., Koh, J., & Tsai, C. (2010). Facilitating preservice teachers' development of technological, pedagogical, and content knowledge (TPACK). *Journal of Educational Technology & Society*, *13*(4), 63–73.

Common Core State Standards Initiative. (2010). *Common core standards for mathmatics*. Retrieved from http://corestandards.org/assets/CCSSI_Math%20Standards.pdf

Doering, A., Veletsianos, G., Scharber, C., & Miller, C. (2009). Using the technological, pedagogical, and content knowledge framework to design online learning environments and professional development. *Educational Computing Research*, *41*(3), 319–346. doi:10.2190/EC.41.3.d.

Garet, M. S., Porter, A. C., Desimone, L., Birman, B. F., & Kwang Suk, Y. (2001). What makes professional development effective? Results from a national sample of teachers. *American Educational Research Journal*, *38*(4), 915–945. doi:10.3102/00028312038004915.

International Society for Technology in Education. (2000). *National educational technology standards for students: Connecting curriculum and technology*. Eugene, OR: ISTE.

International Society for Technology in Education. (2011). *ISTE NETS*. Retrieved from http://www.iste.org/standards.aspx

Kadijevich, D. M. (2012). TPACK framework: Assessing teachers' knowledge and designing courses for their professional development. *British Journal of Educational Technology*, *43*(1), E28–E30. doi:10.1111/j.1467-8535.2011.01246.x.

Mishra, P., & Koehler, M. J. (2006). Technological pedagogical content knowledge: A framework for teacher knowledge. *Teachers College Record*, *108*(6), 1017–1054. doi:10.1111/j.1467-9620.2006.00684.x.

National Council for Teachers of Mathematics. (2010). *NCTM public comments on the common core standards for mathematics*. Retrieved from http://www.nctm.org/about/content.aspx?id=25186

National Council of Teachers of Mathematics. (2000). *Principles and standards for school mathematics*. Reston, VA: NCTM.

National Research Council. (2001). *Adding it up*. Washington, DC: National Academic Press.

Niess, M. L. (2005). Preparing teachers to teach science and mathematics with technology: Developing a technology pedagogical content knowledge. *Teaching and Teacher Education, 21*(5), 509–523. doi:10.1016/j.tate.2005.03.006.

Polly, D., McGee, J. R., & Martin, C. S. (2010). Employing technology-rich mathematical tasks in professional development to develop teachers' technological, pedagogical, and content knowledge (TPACK). *Journal of Computers in Mathematics and Science Teaching, 29*(4), 455–472.

Rosenthal, I. G. (1999). New teachers and technology. *Technology & Learning, 19*(8), 22–27.

Shulman, L. S. (1986). Those who understand: Knowledge growth in teaching. *Educational Researcher, 15*(2), 4–11. doi:10.3102/0013189X015002004.

ADDITIONAL READING

Common Core Standards for Mathematical Practice. (2012). Retrieved from http://www.insidemathematics.org/index.php/common-core-standards

Common Core State Standards. (2012). Retrieved from http://www.explorelearning.com/index.cfm?method=cResource.dspBrowseCorrelations&v=s&id=CC Loyola University Chicago School of Education. (n.d.). *Using Quicktime movies to develop math skills*. Retrieved from http://mathflix.luc.edu/

McGraw Hill Education. (2011). *Keys to the common core*. Retrieved from http://www.commoncoresolutions.com/mathematical_practice.php

NC State University. (2012). *Turn-on common core math*. Retrieved from http://turnonccmath.com/

NCSM. (2012a). *Illustrating the standards for mathematical practice*. Retrieved from http://www.mathedleadership.org/ccss/itp/index.html

NCTM. (2012b). *Activities*. Retrieved from http://illuminations.nctm.org/ActivitySearch.aspx

NCTM. (2012c). *Core math tools home*. Retrieved from http://www.nctm.org/resources/content.aspx?id=32702

NCTM. (2012d). *E-examples from principles and standards for school mathematics*. Retrieved from http://www.nctm.org/standards/content.aspx?id=24600

Polly, D. (2011). Examining how the enactment of TPACK varies across grade levels in mathematics. *Journal of Computers in Mathematics and Science Teaching, 30*(1), 37–59.

Read Tennessee. (2012). *Mathematical practices*. Retrieved from http://www.readtennessee.org/math/teachers/teachers_mathematics_toolkit/mathematical_practices.aspx

U.S. Coalition for World Class Math. (2010). *Comments on the common core standards for mathematics*. Retrieved from http://usworldclassmath.Webs.com/U.S.%20Coalition%20for%20World%20Class%20Math%20Comments%20on%20June%202010%20CCSSI%20Math%20Standards.pdf

KEY TERMS AND DEFINITIONS

Common Core Standards for Mathematical Content: Grade level standards which define the mathematical knowledge and skills students should know and be able to do.

Common Core Standards for Mathematical Practice: Mathematical processes and ways of thinking that were designed to be integrated across all mathematics content standards in all grade levels.

Content Knowledge: Knowledge of key facts, concepts, and procedures within a discipline.

ISTE NETS: National Educational Technology Standards for students and teachers developed by the International Society for Technology in Education.

National Council for Teachers of Mathematics (NCTM): National organization for mathematics educators which supports quality instruction as well as support and professional development for teachers of mathematics.

Pedagogical Knowledge: Knowledge of how to teach, including strategies for instruction and assessment, as well as knowledge of how learners develop.

Technological Knowledge: Knowledge of technological tools and their applications for teaching and learning.

Technological Pedagogical Content Knowledge (TPACK): The effective use of technologies aligned with effective instruction for teaching specific content.

Chapter 17
Supporting the Common Core State Standards in Mathematics through Mathematics Journals

Christie Martin
University of North Carolina at Charlotte, USA

Drew Polly
University of North Carolina at Charlotte, USA

ABSTRACT

The Common Core State Standards in Mathematics and English/Language Arts necessitate that teachers provide opportunities for their students to write about mathematical concepts in ways that extend beyond simply a summary of how students solve mathematical tasks. This study examined how mathematics journals in a fourth grade classroom supported students' mathematical experiences and reflected their understanding of concepts. Implications for the use of technology to support mathematics journals are also discussed.

INTRODUCTION

As part of the Common Core State Standards in both English Language Arts and Mathematics (CCSSI, 2011), teachers have been asked to provide opportunities for students to write about mathematical concepts. However, this can be a difficult task given that most teachers have had

little experience using writing as a tool to learn and communicate their understanding of mathematics (Totten, 2005). Literacy and writing skills need to be utilized by teachers in their own mathematical work to model for students how to competently write and communicate mathematically. Competent communication of mathematics includes using the symbols of the content along with definitions

DOI: 10.4018/978-1-4666-4086-3.ch017

and/or vocabulary effectively (Franz & Hopper, 2007). To communicate numeric facts and patterns effectively, students should be taught to draw upon concepts and skills from each of the major academic disciplines and develop quantitative literacy (Miller, 2010). Teachers seeking to use writing in their mathematics lessons to develop quantitative literacy may question which type of writing to employ. Many teachers struggle to link writing and mathematics and honor the integrity of both disciplines at the same time (Wilcox & Monroe, 2011). Teachers find the integration of writing easier in the science or social studies classroom, where there is more factual knowledge (Varelas, Pappas, Kokkino & Ortiz, 2008). In mathematics, writing tends to be limited to merely the summary of steps taken to solve a problem, often lacking depth and opportunities for higher-level thinking (Pugalee, 2009).

Writing across the curriculum is a research-based strategy for supporting students' conceptual understanding (CCSSI, 2011; Pugalee, 2009). Still, writing in mathematics is an area of writing across the curriculum with very little research. With the beginning of implementation of the Common Core State Standards, teachers are called to provide opportunities for students to write about what they are learning in mathematics, science and social studies. It is important for research to examine the influence of mathematics journals on students' understanding as well as how to best support students' experiences writing about mathematics concepts.

PURPOSE OF THE STUDY

The purpose of our study is to gain a greater understanding of how the implementation of writing in the mathematics classroom influences student learning. This study plans to answer the following research questions (1) How does the teacher perceive the value of the instructional approach (journal writing in mathematics) and what are the expectations? (2) How do teachers support students' writing in a mathematics journal? (3) How does writing in a mathematics journal influence students' understanding of mathematics?

THEORETICAL FRAMEWORK AND LITERATURE REVIEW

Theoretical Framework

The research study conducted here is based in a social constructivist framework. Constructivism is a learning theory that suggests an individual constructs meaning and knowledge through their social environment and interaction (Beck & Kosnik, 2006). Constructivist theory stresses the importance of learning being of value for the learner. Writing should be meaningful for children arousing an intrinsic need. Further, writing should be incorporated into a task that is necessary and relevant for life (Vygotsky, 1978). Mathematics lessons are occurring in classrooms each day in the forms of direct instruction, group work, pair activities, and individual work. Each individual learner is constructing meaning from these lessons and assigning their own value and understanding to the concepts presented. Journals will serve to identify the individual's constructed meanings.

Literature Review

The use of mathematical discourse, both in the spoken and written forms are pivotal to the construction of mathematical concepts and the development of mathematical thinking (D'Ambrosio, Johnson & Hobbs, 1995). Mathematical discourse means the communication of mathematical concepts through speech and writing (Jingzi & Normandia, 2009). The combination of literacy strategies in the mathematics content area, including all types of writing, is becoming an important focus in the classroom. The National Council of Teachers of Mathematics, 2000 has created an objective centered on the ability to communicate mathematical concepts clearly and coherently. Schuster and Anderson (2005) pointed out that teachers of mathematics need to focus on getting students to communicate how they came to understand a concept just as much as the underpinnings of the concept itself. Teachers play an important role in introducing mathematics discourse and literacy strategies that will benefit students in their theoretical understanding of mathematics concepts. This literature review will focus on defining mathematics discourse, exploring teacher roles in mathematics communication, explaining the power of writing, and indicating its use in mathematics. Specifically, it will address journaling, shared writing, expository writing, and mathematics writing workshop. It is then the intention of this review to show the importance of writing in inquiry based mathematics curriculum.

Student Mathematics Discourse

Mathematics discourse is the communication that is either verbalized or written and contains the language and vocabulary conducive to understanding mathematical concepts. Jingzi and Normandia (2009) and Jingzi, Normandia and Greer (2005) conduct classroom observations to analyze mathematical discourse of both students and teachers. The analysis focused on discerning the level of theoretical understanding presented by students. Their discourse analysis revealed students were able to express mathematics concepts at the level of describing actions and sequence of steps. This type of discourse is less cognitively demanding, however difficulties arose as students tried to express conceptual knowledge, reasons behind actions and defending their choices. Teacher discourse and interactions with the difficulty faced by students is an important aspect of mathematics instruction.

The observations before mentioned indicate that teacher discourse is rich in expressing a variety of knowledge structures associated with various aspects of mathematics content. Students discourse remained on the procedural level and when pushed by teachers to explain further the concepts, principles, or methods employed in their solution there was hesitation. The hesitation and failure to articulate the next level of understanding led teachers to jump in and finish the task.

Power of Writing

Newkirk and Atwell (1982) emphasize that writing is thinking and students are active in the role of producing a written work. Students make choices about words, structure, and voice in order to convey meaning, which enhances their own meaning-making. Individual choice in topic and expression are important for fostering a passion for writing and engagement in the recursive nature of writing (Calkins, 1983; Graves, 1983; Murray, 2004).

Written communication helps students become active learners and improves their academic achievement because students use language to facilitate their understanding and writing provides students with opportunities to communicate what they know and don't know (Kostos & Shin, 2010 p.225).

Burns (1995) suggests the key components of the writing process, gathering, organizing, revising and clarifying are skills that can be readily applied to mathematical problems. The opportunity to write in the mathematics classroom provides learners and outlet to clarify, refine, and consolidate their thinking.

Writing in Mathematics

Writing, another traditional comprehension enhancing strategy, has demonstrated utility in mathematics classrooms by adding a dimension of literacy; however writing is not utilized frequently in mathematics classrooms (Baxter, Woodward & Olson, 2005). And although frequent discussion is given to reading being emphasized across the curriculum, mathematics is often left out of this equation (Ediger, 2005). Studies in the area of teaching and learning mathematics reveal that reflection and communication are the key processes in building understanding (Hiebert et al., 1996; MacGregor & Price, 1999; Manouchehri & Enderson, 1999; Monroe, 1996). Jingzi and Normandia (2009) interviewed students who expressed that writing in mathematics was different from doing mathematics in that it was cognitively and linguistically more demanding. They also felt that writing in mathematics was different from writing in English or other social sciences. Even though the students expressed a dislike for writing in mathematics due to its demanding nature the majority of the students felt that writing in mathematics has benefited them. Numerous and varied opportunities for this integration support students as they learn to think their way into mathematics and make it their own (Zinsser, 1988). Different forms of writing can be implemented to strengthen mathematics discourse and comprehension.

Journals

A journal is a form of writing that offers a personal space that is a free flowing record of experiences, observations, thoughts, questions, and responses. In this form of writing there need not be specific form or revision. Goldsby and Cozza (2002) assert that mathematics journals provide a window in the mind of the student engaged in mathematical activities, providing an opportunity to see the thinking behind the process. As students are engaged in journal writing to explain their process they develop a greater understanding of concepts and correctly use mathematical vocabulary (Tuttle, 2005). Kostos and Shin (2010) used a mixed method action research design with second graders to evaluate the effect of mathematics journals on mathematical thinking and communication. The results showed an increased use of mathematical vocabulary supported by interviews, students'

journal, interviews, and teacher reflection. The pre-post tests produced statistically significant results which indicated an increase in mathematical thinking. Adams (1998) emphasize journals as a tool for assessing children's communication skills along with providing an avenue for assessing children's reflections of their own capabilities, attitudes and dispositions, and for evaluating their ability to communicate mathematically, through writing.

The teacher involved in the research from Kostos and Shin (2010) also found the journals to be an excellent source of assessment information and well worth the time spent collecting and reading. McIntosh and Draper (2001) coined the term learning logs which serve for students to reflect on what they are learning and learn while they are reflecting on what they are learning. Similar to journals, learning logs provide an opportunity for students to experience metacognition, which will enhance their understanding of their own learning process.

Adding writing in reflective journals to my daily routine in mathematics class extended my students' thinking about the strategies they use to problem solve in mathematics class (Carter, 2009). Journals are effective because they increase metacognition, provide space for vocabulary development, and allow students to explain their process.

Expository Writing

Expository writing can be defined as structured writing on one particular topic. Mathematical concepts in the form of data, ratio, and relationships are becoming a prevalent part of testing in areas outside of mathematics. Science and social studies are two areas in the humanities that are requiring explained data in response to assessment questions. Miller (2010) advocates using the expository structure used of essay writing in language arts classes and transferring the organization and techniques into quantitative writing. Vocabulary, analogies, and metaphors can be infused in quantitative writing to explain relationships and direction indicated by the data. The strongest descriptions of numeric patterns combine vocabulary or analogies with numeric information because those approaches reinforce one another and tap into different ways of explaining and visualizing patterns that will appeal to students with varied academic strengths and learning styles (Miller, 2010).

METHODS

Research Design

This is a basic or generic qualitative study used to identify recurrent patterns in the form of themes through a social constuctivist lens. Data was collected through interviews, observations, or document analysis and findings will be a mix of description and analysis using the theoretical framework of the study (Merriam, 1997). This study was seeking an understanding of the journal process and the perspective of those involved which make a basic qualitative study most applicable (Merriam, 1997).

Participant and Site Selection

Participants were recruited in person. The responsible faculty has an ongoing relationship with that school due to other research and service projects. Teachers were recruited in February, 2012 via a face-to-face meeting after school. During the meeting, the study was explained to them, and teachers were given the opportunity to participate or opt out of the study. During the meeting, teachers were given information on mathematics journals and advice on writing good prompts. Teachers nominated students for interviews and parent permission was attained. This entire study occurred at Shady Brook Elementary School in Kannapolis City Schools. The participants included 120 students, 7 teachers Students: 60% female, 40% male, Teachers: 100% female Stu-

dents: 55% Latino, 30% African American, 15% Caucasian; Teachers: 100% Caucasian Students: 4th Grade- Age 8-10. Students in third and fourth grade classrooms at an elementary school in Kannapolis City were included in this study. Also, their classroom teachers were included in this study.

Data Collection and Analysis

Data were analyzed by one researcher using an inductive approach; the analysis began with a tentative theory that was revised based on findings. During classroom instruction, teachers provided at least two writing prompts to their students each week for the next two months. Students had between three-ten minutes to complete prompts each time in their mathematics journals. Journals, were already de-identified when collected by the researchers and photo copies were made. Every two weeks, the researchers conducted a 10-15 minute meeting with teacher-participants to answer questions and collect feedback. At the end of the two month project, the researchers conducted audio-recorded interviews with all seven teachers as well as selected students. From each classroom, two low-achieving and two high-achieving students, that were nominated by the teachers, were selected to participate in a five minute interview about their experiences with mathematics journals. Teacher interviews took approximately 15 minutes to complete.

Journal entries were entered into an Excel spreadsheet, read, coded and organized according to themes. The thematic analysis began with open coding to allow categories to emerge (Ezzy, 2002), data was futher analyzed with a constant comparison thematic analysis. A constant comparison thematic analysis was employed because in the constant-comparison method, comparisons allow data to be grouped and differentiated as categories are identified (Ezzy, 2002). By taking each piece of data and comparing it with all others the possible relationships between the data were revealed. After forming themes, researchers revisited the data to confirm their themes, or adjust themes based on reanalyzing the data. Interviews were transcribed and coded for themes and revisited for further analysis.

QUALITY CONTROL STRATEGIES

Several strategies were used for quality control of the data analysis. First I utilized peer debriefing at crucial junctures of the research analysis. Peer debriefing is a process of exposing oneself to a disinterested party and will help me become aware of the influence of my personal values and theoretical orientations on the collection and interpretation of the data (Ezzy, 2002). Another strategy for ensuring trustworthiness of my data is to practice both confessional and theoretical reflexivity. Confessional requires the researcher to turn in on oneself in a critical manner producing the awareness of our own subjectivity and quiets the notion of absolute truth, whereas theoretical reflexivity goes back and forth between the concrete experience and the abstract theoretical explanation of that experience (Foley, 2002). Utilizing these methods of reflexivity during my analysis strengthened the interpretation. Analyzing the data while the study is ongoing allowed the point of saturation to become evident. Having a point of saturation strengthens the analysis because the themes begin to reappear over and over.

FINDINGS

Research Question #1: How Does the Teacher Perceive the Value of the Instructional Approach (Journal Writing in Mathematics) and What are the Expectations?

The teacher perceptions of the value of the instructional approach were identified through the expression of her pre-journal thoughts, emotions, ideas, and expectations surrounding the project before its implementation. She exuded excitement and positive expectations and noted that this particular group of teachers is very open to trying new things. Her feelings were evident in the comments "I am excited to try the journal and see how it works with them as their morning work… we are willing to try just about anything with this group". Overall positive effects were expected to result from the practice of journals in mathematics. She expressed that the journals would enhance understanding of mathematics concepts which would further solidify concepts. She presented the idea that knowing a concept is at one level and being able to write clearly about that area is at a higher level. She expressed these ideas throughout the interview "We'll get a better idea of that they're actually understanding and where they are mis-stepping… I think if they can explain it in writing then they really have a concrete understanding of what they are doing." When asked about sharing journal responses she responded"… sharing how they solve the problems I think, I think it will help them A) to see how their writing is, but I also think that um it will, what they say may help someone else who is struggling with it, or to look at it a different way." She expects the sharing of the journals will foster collaboration, offer classmates insights from one another, and broaden ideas about writing in mathematics. The journal will be a place to strengthen their use of mathematics vocabulary. She also feels the journals will serve as a springboard for discussion.

Research Question #2: How Do Teachers Support Students' Writing in a Mathematics Journal?

The implementation procedures were decided by the teacher and in their plan for implementation the strategies for support became clear. She explained the journals would be used for two weeks for a total of nine days. Although the prompts have been provided, she felt discussion and modeling would be essential to the students understanding the expectation. Her feelings about the structure of journal writing were apparent in this excerpt from the interview "I think the questioning or the question or the prompt would have to be something that's very specific that they would hit those different things whether it was the patterns or the place value or the breaking apart of numbers or… I think it would have to be somewhere in the prompt very specific in the prompt of what you would want from them." The fourth grade classes are grouped by ability and her class is considered a lower ability level for mathematics. The amount of support and modeling were increased due to the ability grouping. She mentioned focused prompts were a vital part of the project. Similar to the writer's workshop format already in place, the students will also share responses from their journal. She felt the journals would provide a window into the level of understanding attained by each student. In particular, the journal of the student who seems to have an understanding or "flies under the radar" would present evidence of their actual level. The journal can be used for EOG (End-of-grade test) review. This teacher will use the window of information provided by the journal to adjust her lesson planning and provide more support.

Research Question #3: How Does Writing in a Mathematics Journal Influence Students' Understanding of Mathematics?

Originally, I planned to examine the journals of the students from each of the fourth grade classrooms, due to time constraints I examined five journals from the classroom of the teacher I interviewed. This allowed me to continue with the constant-comparison analysis plan I included in my method section. The rest of the materials will be analyzed in the near future. The themes that emerged from the journals were the role of modeling, comprehension and strategy, and reflection. It became evident that the first two journal prompts were completed with modeling and scaffolding from the teacher. The five journals analyzed had the same distinct explanations for the operations of carrying, borrowing, perimeter, and area. Example 1 illustrates the distinct responses that show the modeling effect.

Example 1

Josh: *Area is the inside surface of an object. For example you would use area to decide how much carpet to buy, or grass seed to buy, our how much flooring to buy.*

Matt: *Area is the inside surface of an object. For example you would use are to dicide how much carpet to buy, or grass seed to buy, or how much flooring to buy to find area you would multiple the length times the width.*

Sarah: *Area is the inside surface of an object. For example you would use area to decide how much carpet to buy, or grass seeds to buy, or how much flooring to buy.*

The responses were lengthy and well expressed, but failed to reveal the true thought process of the individual student. However, the modeling may have provided the example that enhanced future entries. The rest of the entries presented more data for the individual student. The third entry asked for an explanation of the relationship between multiplication and division and why learning these inverse operations together would be helpful. This entry varied drastically between the five students. The depth of their knowledge of these operations was apparent in their entries. Example 2 demonstrates the individual responses and depth of knowledge.

Example 2

Sarah: *Even though when you multiply your numbers get bigger and when you divide they get smaller, using your multiplication facts can help you in division. I (f) you have a division problem like 24÷6, if you know*

6 X 4=24 you know it has to be 4 or if you have a big one like 240÷12 you could use a multiplication fact to start: 12 x 10 = 120, 12 x10 = 120, 12 x20 = 240 It's soooo easy!

Josh: *Multiplication and divided are oppos thing but they are almost the same. Like 10 x ? = 50 and divided is 50 ÷ ? = 5 they are like the same but a little different it is oppsit.*

Nick: *In a division problem to get the quotient you would multiply to get the division problem like 22 x 12 = 244, 244 ÷ 12= 12 we these operations because we can teach other people it.*

In nearly all of the entries strategies were explained and examples of how these strategies could be implemented were provided. The last theme of reflection was represented in several entries. In particular the fifth entry was a multi-step problem that required full description for solving the problem; it also included a sample of a wrong response and asked for advice for the fictional student with the wrong answer. Each one of these entries indicated a precise reflection of the processes used to solve the problem, followed by sound advice for the fictional student. The advice included reading carefully and doing one step at a time or follow step by step to avoid getting mixed up. Example 3 is of the fifth entry and the responses illustrate the use of strategy and reflection.

Example 3

The prompt asks, Marley ran 5 miles a day for 5 days on the sixth day he ran 4 miles and on the seventh day he ran 6 miles. How many total miles did he run in seven days? Marley needs to complete 30 miles a week for his training, did he complete the needed miles? If so, did he go over and by how much? If not, how many miles did he miss in his training?

Nick: *5 x 5 = 25 + 4 + 6 = 35 She ran the miles she wanted to run, she ran extra 5 miles. I multiplied 5 times 5 and the answer was 25. I added 4 miles equals 29 miles. I added 6 miles equals 35 miles cause I added. Yes, she ran 35 but she only needed to run 30 miles. She ran 5 miles more. I can do 35 subtract 30 = 5 miles. He (Bert) should have added 5 extra but before that he should have 25 + 4+ 29 and 29 + 6 = 35.*

Sarah: *I timed 5 x5 = 25 miles because she ran 5 miles a day for 5 days. I added 4 +6 = 10 miles because she ran those miles. (on the last two days). I added to get my total 25 + 10 +35. 35 – 30 = 5. Marley ran 5 miles over so she complete the needed miles. I would tell him (Bert) to read the question very carefully then I would tell him to do 5 x5 =25 because she ran 5 miles for 5 days. Then add 4 +6=10 because she ran 4 miles and 6 miles on the last 2 days. Then add it together 25 +10=35 and so Marley is 5 miles over. (** Sarah also wrote notes to herself next to the problem. The notes included an arrow pointing to a section and writing multiplication and addition, on the last 2 days they had different amounts, and another arrow explaining follow then step by step you might get mixed up)*

DISCUSSION

This pilot study examined the implementation of journal writing in the mathematics classroom to gain a greater understanding its influence student learning. The results of this study support the belief that mathematics journals provide a window into the mind of the student engaged in mathematical activities, providing an opportunity to see the thinking behind the process (Goldsby and Cozza, 2002; Carter,2009). The results also support the idea of students reflect on what they are learning and learn while they are reflecting on what they are learning (McIntosh and Draper, 2001). The findings relate to the literature which emphasizes journals as a tool for assessing children's communication skills along with providing an avenue for assessing children's reflections of their own capabilities, attitudes and dispositions, and for evaluating their ability to communicate mathematically, through writing (Adams, 1998). The teacher in this analysis illustrated the focus in the literature of getting students to communicate how they came to understand a concept just as much as the underpinnings of the concept itself and the important role of introducing mathematics discourse and literacy strategies that will benefit students in their theoretical understanding of mathematics concepts (Schuster and Anderson, 2005).

This pilot study produced findings that were aligned closely with the existing literature, there were however areas of divergence. One of the main tenants of the research for teaching and using writing in the classroom is individual choice. Individual choice in topic and expression are important for fostering a passion for writing and engagement in the recursive nature of writing (Calkins,1983; Graves,1983; Murray, 2004). The literature advocating for individual choice asserts it is essential and Calkins (1983) describes the transaction of teacher provided topic as writer's welfare, which creates a belief in the student that they have no writing territory of their own. Their ideas seem unworthy to write about and given the chance to choose a topic they are stymied. In this study, per request of the teacher and discussion with STEM professors, mathematics centered journal prompts were provided. The results failed to address the issues described in the literacy writing research. Writing in the content areas may require a different set of strategies to encourage students.

The area of divergence between this study and the literature on writing in literacy should be further examined in future research. The difference in writing in mathematics with a particular prompt versus individual choice may produce results that will highlight the best strategy for mathematics content writing. Another area for future research is to include different grade levels and types of writing. Many teachers struggle to link writing and mathematics while honoring the integrity of both disciplines (Wilcox & Monroe, 2011), therefore it will be important for research to offer strategies for teachers.

FUTURE DIRECTIONS AND CHALLENGES

There is a need to consider how teachers can utilize the wealth of Web 2.0 tools and emerging technologies to support the writing process. The classroom in which this study took place had limited computer access but was getting iPads in the near future. Various Web-based writing tools and iPad applications have the potential to support students' work in mathematics journals during class time. In this section we highlight two of them, Story Jumper (Story Jumper, 2012), a free Web-based program, and Show Me (Show Me, 2012), an iPad application that allows students to write on a whiteboard and orally talk about their work simultaneously.

In a Kindergarten classroom, Story Jumper was used when students were working on solving and explaining how they solved an addition word problem. Prior to starting, the teacher had typed the problem and put it on the top of the working mat. In order to show their work, students moved clip art onto the working mat. Finally, they typed text in order to explain their process and rationale for their process. As students worked, they spent time working on *Mathematical Practice 1: Making Sense and Persevere while Solving Problems*, as they made sense of the story problem and created a digital representation. Students also worked on *Mathematical Practice 6: Attend to Precision*, as they communicated their process and rationale for their problem solving process.

Show Me, provides opportunities for students to write on a workspace on the iPad with their finger or stylus. As students write, it records a movie which contains all of the writing on the iPad as well as any information spoken into the microphone on the iPad. As students are working on *Show Me*, there is more of an opportunity for students to orally share and demonstrate their processes. Teachers need to be very explicit about writing expectations.

Other technological tools that could support the use of mathematics journals include Weblogs (a.k.a. blogs) on Websites such as WordPress (WordPress, n.d.) and Blogger (Blogger, n.d.). Students could create blogs in which they provide their rationale and explanation about how they solved a particular problem, or respond to a prompt or question about mathematical concepts. While a lot of educational blogs are for teachers, there is a great deal of potential for K-12 students to either contribute to a class blog or write their own blog about mathematical problems and concepts. As technologies continue to be more readily accessible in K-12 schools, there will be countless opportunities for teachers to leverage these technologies to support students' writing about mathematics.

REFERENCES

Baxter, J. A., Woodward, J., & Olson, D. (2005). Writing in mathematics: An alternative form of communication for academically low-achieving students. *Learning Disabilities Research & Practice, 20*(2), 119–135. doi:10.1111/j.1540-5826.2005.00127.x.

Beck, C., & Kosnik, C. (2006). *Innovations in teacher education: a social constructivist approach.* Albany, NY: State University of New York Press.

Calkins, L. (1983). *Lessons from a child: On the teaching and learning of writing.* Portsmouth, NH: Heinemann.

Carter, S. (2009). Connecting mathematics and writing workshop: It's kinda like ice skating. *The Reading Teacher, 62*(7), 606–610. doi:10.1598/RT.62.7.7.

Common Core State Standards Initiative (CCSSI). (2011). *Common core state standards.* Retrieved from http://corestandards.org

D'Ambrosio, B., Johnson, H., & Hobbs, L. (1995). Strategies for increasing achievement in mathematics. In Cole, R. W. (Ed.), *Educating everybody's children: Diverse teaching strategies for diverse learners: What research and practice say about improving achievement* (pp. 121–137). Alexandria, VA: Association of Supervision and Curriculum Development.

Ediger, M. (2005). Struggling readers in high school. *Reading Improvement, 42,* 34–39.

Franz, D., & Hopper, P. F. (2007). Is there room in mathematics reform for pre-service teachers to use reading strategies? National implications. *National FORUM of Teacher Education Journal, 17*(3).

Graves, D. H. (1983). *Writing: Teachers and children at work.* Portsmouth, NH: Heineman.

Hiebert, J., Carpenter, T. P., Fennema, E., Fuson, K. C., Wearne, D., Murray, H., & Human, P. (1996). *Making sense: Teaching and learning mathematics with understanding.* Portsmouth, NH: Heinemann.

Jingzi, H., & Normandia, B. (2009). Students' perceptions on communicating mathematically: A case study of a secondary mathematics classroom. *International Journal of Learning, 16*(5), 1–21.

Jingzi, H., Normandia, B., & Greer, S. (2005). Communicating mathematically: Comparison of knowledge structures in teacher and student discourse in a secondary mathematics classroom. *Communication Education, 54*(1), 34–51. doi:10.1080/14613190500077002.

Kostos, K., & Shin, E. (2010). Using mathematics journals to enhance second graders' communication of mathematical thinking. *Early Childhood Education Journal, 38*(3), 223–231. doi:10.1007/s10643-010-0390-4.

MacGregor, M., & Price, E. (1999). An exploration of aspects of language proficiency and algebra learning. *Journal for Research in Mathematics Education, 30*, 449–467. doi:10.2307/749709.

Manouchehri, A., & Enderson, M. C. (1999). Promoting mathematical discourse: Learning from classroom examples. *Mathematics Teaching in the Middle School, 4*, 216–222.

McIntosh, M. E., & Draper, R. J. (2001). Using learning logs in mathematics: Writing to learn. *Mathematics Teacher, 94*(7), 554–557.

Miller, J. E. (2010). Quantitative literacy across the curriculum: Integrating skills from English composition, mathematics, and the substantive disciplines. *The Educational Forum, 74*(4), 334–346. doi:10.1080/00131725.2010.507100.

Murray, D. (1968). *A writer teaches writing: A practical method of teaching composition.* Boston: Houghton Mifflin.

Newkirk, T., Atwell, N., & Northeast Regional Exchange, I. A. (1982). *Understanding writing: Ways of observing, learning & teaching.*

Schuster, L., & Anderson, N. C. (2005). *Good questions for mathematics teaching: Why ask them and what to ask.* Sausalito, CA: Mathematics Solutions.

Show Me. (2012). *ShowMe.* Retrieved from http://www.showme.com

Story Jumper. (2012). *Story jumper.* Retrieved from http://www.storyjumper.com

Telese, J. A. (1999). *The role of social constructivist philosophy in the teaching of school algebra and in the preparation of mathematics teachers.*

Totten, S. (2005). Writing to learn for pre-service teachers. *The Quarterly of the National Writing Project, 27*, 17-20, 28.

Varelas, M., Pappas, C. C., Kokkino, S., & Ortiz, I. (2008). Methods and strategies: Students as authors. *Science and Children, 45*(7), 58–62.

Vygotsky, L. (1978). *Mind in society: The development of higher psychological processes.* Cambridge, MA: Harvard University Press.

Wilcox, B., & Monroe, E. (2011). Integrating writing and mathematics. *The Reading Teacher, 64*(7), 521–529. doi:10.1598/RT.64.7.6.

Zinsser, W. K. (1988). *Writing to learn.* New York: Harper & Row.

ADDITIONAL READING

Baxter, J. A., Woodward, J., & Olson, D. (2005). Writing in mathematics: An alternative form of communication for academically low-achieving students. *Learning Disabilities Research & Practice, 20*(2), 119–135. doi:10.1111/j.1540-5826.2005.00127.x.

Calkins, L. (1983). *Lessons from a child: On the teaching and learning of writing.* Portsmouth, NH: Heinemann.

Carter, S. (2009). Connecting mathematics and writing workshop: It's kinda like ice skating. *The Reading Teacher, 62*(7), 606–610. doi:10.1598/RT.62.7.7.

Franz, D., & Hopper, P. F. (2007). Is there room in mathematics reform for pre-service teachers to use reading strategies? National implications. *National FORUM of Teacher Education Journal, 17*(3).

Kostos, K., & Shin, E. (2010). Using mathematics journals to enhance second graders' communication of mathematical thinking. *Early Childhood Education Journal, 38*(3), 223–231. doi:10.1007/s10643-010-0390-4.

Totten, S. (2005). Writing to learn for pre-service teachers. *The Quarterly of the National Writing Project, 27,* 17-20, 28.

Varelas, M., Pappas, C. C., Kokkino, S., & Ortiz, I. (2008). Methods and strategies: Students as authors. *Science and Children, 45*(7), 58–62.

Wilcox, B., & Monroe, E. (2011). Integrating writing and mathematics. *The Reading Teacher, 64*(7), 521–529. doi:10.1598/RT.64.7.6.

Zinsser, W. K. (1988). *Writing to learn.* New York: Harper & Row.

APPENDIX

Student Interview

Semi-Structured Format

Please tell me what you write in your mathematics journal.
Do you use it to show your work?
Do you explain how you solved your problems?
Do you defend your strategies?
Please tell me about what you like about writing in your mathematics journal.
Please tell me about what you do not like about writing in your mathematics journal.
Do you think mathematics journals help you learn?
Why or why not?

Teacher Interview

Please tell me about your students' experiences with mathematics journals this year.
Please tell me about the types of things that your students wrote about.
Please tell me about how frequently students wrote in their mathematics journal.
Please tell me about the use of prompts for journal entries.
How did they help? How did they hinder writing?
Do you think mathematics journals help your students learn?
Why or why not?
Do you think mathematics journals help you to better assess your students?
Why or why not?
Please tell me how you would use mathematics journals differently in future years.

Chapter 18
The Impact of *Investigations and the Interactive Whiteboard* on Students' Mathematical Practice in *Investigations* Classrooms

Linda Boland
Pearson Education Inc., USA

ABSTRACT

This chapter relates the classroom experiences of 44 teachers across the United States, implementing Investigations in Number, Data, and Space, an elementary school mathematics curriculum. These teachers participated in a "tryout" of Investigations for the Interactive Whiteboard with their students. Investigations for the Interactive Whiteboard was developed in collaboration by Pearson, TERC, and SMART Board. The teachers' reactions showcase how the use of this technology enhanced the teaching and learning of mathematics. These vignettes illuminate the essence of Common Core Standards for Mathematical Practice (CCSSI, 2010), which describe how students should engage with the mathematical skills and concepts of the Common Core Content. The use of the interactive whiteboard engaged all students, motivated them to participate beyond their norm, allowed modeling of the mathematics which opened access to all students, and encouraged students to explain, argue, and defend their ideas while listening to and critiquing others, the essences of the Standards for Mathematical Practice.

DOI: 10.4018/978-1-4666-4086-3.ch018

INTRODUCTION

This chapter shares the "story" of teachers using interactive whiteboard software in their classrooms to support, enhance and extend their teaching of mathematics using *Investigations in Number, Data, and Space, 2nd edition*, and the students' engagement, interactions and strategic thinking in learning mathematics. This chapter will also showcase the history and development of the *Investigations* program and the *Investigations and the Interactive Whiteboard* technology, relate the teachers' experiences using the software in their classrooms through anecdotes, and highlight the impact it makes on students' motivation, participation and achievement of Common Core Mathematical Practice.

INVESTIGATIONS IN NUMBER, DATA, AND SPACE CURRICULUM

In 1989, the National Council of Teachers of Mathematics (NCTM) produced the *Curriculum and Evaluation Standards for School Mathematics*. At the time, this document was controversial because they called for drastic change in mathematics teaching. And in education, making a change is often controversial! These Standards called for more emphasis on conceptual understanding and problem solving informed by a constructivist understanding of how children learn. The National Science Foundation (NSF) issued a call for the development of curricula based on the NCTM *Curriculum and Evaluation Standards for School Mathematics*. In 1990, TERC, a non-profit research and development organization whose mission is to improve mathematics, science, and technology teaching and learning, was awarded a grant to develop a K-5 elementary mathematics curriculum.

Led by Susan Jo Russell, the project's Principal Investigator, the first edition of *Investigations in Number, Date, and Space* was created and

implemented in classrooms. The intention in developing the curriculum was to ensure that all students are included in significant mathematics learning through these aspects (Economopoulos, Mokros, & Russell, 1998):

- Students spend time exploring problems in depth.
- Students find more than one solution to many problems they work on.
- Students develop their own strategies and approaches, rather than relying on memorized procedures.
- Students choose from a variety of materials and appropriate technology as a natural part of their everyday mathematical work.
- Students work in a variety of groupings - whole class, individually, in pairs, and in small groups.
- Students move around the classroom as they explore the mathematics in their environment and talk with their peers.

These goals from 1998 align closely to the CCSSM Standards for Mathematical Practice. In fact the authors of the CCSSM (CCSSI, 2010) wrote:

The Standards for Mathematical Practice describe varieties of expertise that mathematics educators at all levels should seek to develop in their students. These practices rest on important "processes and proficiencies" with longstanding importance in mathematics education. The first of these are the NCTM process standards of problem solving, reasoning and proof, communication, representation, and connections. The second are the strands of mathematical proficiency specified in the National Research Council's report Adding It Up: adaptive reasoning, strategic competence, conceptual understanding (comprehension of mathematical concepts, operations and relations), procedural fluency (skill in carrying out procedures flexibly, accurately, efficiently and appropriately), and productive disposition (habitual inclination to see mathematics as sensible, useful, and worthwhile, coupled with a belief in diligence and one's own efficacy).

At the time *Investigations* was also the only elementary mathematics program that had student software specifically written along with the curriculum to support student learning of the curriculum. The curriculum went through a major revision in the early-to-mid-2000s and a second edition, ©2008 was created. The software also went through major revisions, which resulted in two student-centered pieces of computer software, *Shapes* for K-2, and *LogoPaths* for grades 3 to 5. The *Investigations* curriculum incorporated the use of two forms of technology in the classroom: calculators and computers. Calculators were assumed to be standard classroom materials, available for student use in any unit. Computers were explicitly linked to one or more units in each grade level, utilizing *Shapes* and *LogoPaths*.

But the world of technology in the classroom had been changing over the years and with only computers and calculators *Investigations* was no longer on the cutting edge. So Pearson decided to enhance the next copyright update of *Investigations* with technology. Pearson saw great potential in SMART Board technology. Teachers were using SMART Boards in their *Investigations* classrooms with great success. Pearson's hope for the new component was that it would be a tool for enhancing what is already in the *Investigations* curriculum. Pearson could foresee that in the elementary classroom, especially in the primary grades the SMART Board could help students see ideas and strategies more easily and clearly. It could highlight and showcase how a student used manipulatives or strategies, and demonstrate it for their classmates. Interactive whiteboards were becoming more prevalent in elementary classrooms, so it seemed to be a likely candidate for developing

an enhancement. Interactive whiteboard lessons would help facilitate group instruction, add an interactive element, and look really cool!

When Pearson first approached the TERC authors about this idea for an interactive whiteboard product, the first thing TERC requested was to be shown the technology, and any samples of the use of the technology. They agreed that the technology could be a powerful instructional tool - it could make some activities easier to use both in terms of materials (like cards) and students' ability to see the whole class demonstration or explanation. They could see its potential in improving instruction. But they needed to be assured that the content and pedagogy of the program was maintained. The authors then went through every Session in the curriculum and made recommendations for at least one activity (it might only be the Classroom Routine or Ten-Minute Math) per Session. They also recommended which Sessions to absolutely not use because students actually needed to be touching the manipulatives, or creating their own representations, etc.

INVESTIGATIONS FOR THE INTERACTIVE WHITEBOARD

The purpose for developing this Pearson product was to provide teachers with visual support for Session activities, discussions, workshops, routines, and/or games in the *Investigations* program. The interactive whiteboard gave Pearson the opportunity to create a completely custom technology product that supported daily *Investigations* instruction, rather than supplement or supplant it. This is the incredible thing about classroom use of the Interactive Whiteboards... the seamless integration into the daily instruction of students.

In 2009, Pearson's editorial group developed a structure for this product:

- A whiteboard teaching tool based on the most appropriate and effective use in a part of the session, or the routine associated with the session, with the goal of maximizing the number of sessions that utilize a whiteboard teaching tool.
- A whiteboard teaching tool to provide a visual representation, formatted for attractive and clear display, that enhances the interaction between teacher and students, or among students, but not replace any writing, recording, or representing that should be done actively by teachers and students.
- A whiteboard teaching tool to support introducing games, as appropriate.
- The majority of the whiteboard teaching tools to be dynamic - have more interactivity, such as tapping to highlight, hide, reveal, clone, etc.
- The product to be provided through one download package per grade, accessed through the interface by Session.

The collaborative development process moved forward. TERC authors wrote all the storyboards. A storyboard consisted of a word document that contained one page for one interactive whiteboard slide. The TERC authors explained what content they wanted on the screen and gave a description of how the content should be used. Pearson editorial personnel edited all the storyboards and sent them on to NETS, an educational product developer (providing quality educational materials for teachers and students) for pouring into the SMART platform. The screens went through a Pearson editorial and design review. Then, comments were sent back to NETS.

As this was progressing... In June, 2010 the National Governors Association Center for Best Practices and the Council of Chief State School Officers released a set of state led education standards, the *Common Core State Standards*. It was announced that "the standards established clear and consistent goals for learning that will prepare America's children for success in college and work." (NGACBP, CCSSO, 2010) The release of these standards signaled the start of the adoption and implementation process by the states. By October, 2010, 37 states and the District of Columbia had voluntarily adopted the standards. Textbook publishers took note, and began publishing updated or new versions of their mathematics programs to encompass these Common Core State Standards. *Investigations for the Common Core* program was ready for classroom use at the start of the 2011-2012 school year. As of May, 2012 all but five states, Alaska, Minnesota, Nebraska, Texas, and Virginia, have voluntarily adopted the *Common Core State Standards for Mathematics*.

Even though *Investigations and the Interactive Whiteboard* was developing prior to the release of the *Common Core State Standards*, its purpose and goals supported the instruction of mathematics through Mathematical Practice as defined in the *Common Core* document (NGACBP, CCSSO, 2010):

All of these practices come to life in classrooms using *Investigations in the Interactive Whiteboard*. As noted in the *Common Core* document: "The Standards for Mathematical Practice describe ways in which developing student practitioners of the discipline of mathematics increasingly ought to engage with the subject matter as they grow in mathematical maturity and expertise throughout the elementary, middle and high school years." (NGACBP, CCSSO, 2010) It describes "points of intersection" between the Content and the Practice that "most merit the time, resources, innovative energies, and focus necessary to qualitatively improve the curriculum, instruction, assessment, professional development, and student achievement in mathematics." (NGACBP, CCSSO, 2010) These "points of intersection" have been part of the foundation of the *Investigations'* curriculum, and the development of *Investigations and the Interactive Whiteboard* was given the time, resources, innovative energies, and focus necessary to qualitatively make these improvements (See Figure 1).

TEACHERS TRYING OUT THE SOFTWARE

Because this was such a radically different product being added to the *Investigations* curriculum, Pearson wanted to know what was happening in those classrooms where *Investigations and the Interactive Whiteboard* was being used, so a Teacher Tryout was designed. The software was just being released for school year 2010-2011. The tryout ran from August of 2010 through February of 2011, so as not to impose on the teachers' time during state testing.

Teachers were recruited to participate in this teacher tryout through personal contacts, sales reports, sales representatives' suggestions, and recommendations from the TERC authors. They would need to have an interactive whiteboard in their classroom, and would be provided with their grade-specific interactive whiteboard software.

Their level of comfort with technology did not matter; we were looking for a range of teachers from beginning teacher to experienced teacher, from a digital native to a pioneer to an immigrant... but no avoiders! A total of 44 teachers, at 31 school sites, from 22 school districts, in 15 states across the U.S. were assembled. All were volunteers or were "volunteered" to participate by their district CAPS – coach, administrator, principal, or supervisor. All communication to the tryout teachers was also copied to their CAPS, so all were openly informed of all responsibilities, timelines, and benefits.

During the recruitment time, which ran from March through June of 2010, the Pearson Academic Research team worked to develop a demographic survey. The survey would capture a "picture" of the range of teachers in the Tryout. We wanted to know about their: grade, gender, years of teaching experience, level of education, hours of professional development in the last three years, experience teaching the *Investigations* curriculum, and their experience using an interactive whiteboard in the classroom.

At the same time pre-and post-tryout surveys were developed.

Figure 1. Common core states

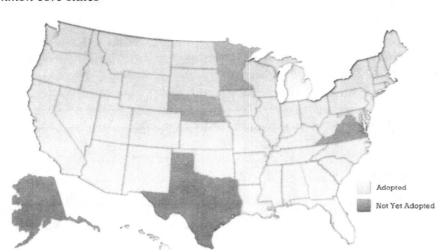

The pre-tryout survey was focused on technology attitudes. It included 12 statements for them to rate on a range from 4 being definitely true, to 1 being definitely untrue. Statements included:

- Using technology is something I enjoy.
- My coworkers say I'm good at using technology.
- I get excited about learning something new from technology.
- I think it's important to use technology in class everyday.

For fun… but also to inform, teachers placed themselves on the spectrum in Figure 2.

There were eight additional multiple-choice statements to complete, such as:

- I (never, sometimes, often, nearly always) worry that I am falling behind when it comes to learning technology.
- I tell other teachers about different ways I'm using technology in my classroom (never, almost never, sometimes, a lot).

The post-survey would glean information about their User Experience, teaching with *Investigations and the Interactive Whiteboard*, their students' experiences analyzed against their per-survey responses. Their first responsibility was completing the demographic survey and the pre-tryout survey, and returning them.

The *Teacher Access Package* for *Investigations and the Interactive Whiteboard* was sent to them in late August as it came off press. They needed to register the software through *SuccessNet*, the Pearson portal by September 28, 2010, become familiar with the mechanics of the software, and be able to access it online by October 4. They also were informed that the software would be "rolled out" in a series of uploads. Tryouts began in August – accessing, experimenting, planning, then using Units 1-3. Units 4-6 would be available in October; all Units available by the end of January, 2011. They did not have the benefit of the *Investigations and the Interactive Whiteboard Implementing Guide*, because it was not yet written… that came later! But the teachers were troopers, and worked through the issues they had using their own expertise, their district technology experts and our Pearson editorial technology expert… who later wrote *Implementing Guide for the Interactive Whiteboard*! Even our Pearson tech helpline personnel had only a two-page document to support the software on day one!

During recruitment, we found that most teachers in the tryout had SMART Boards, but some had Prometheans. The software was developed in collaboration with SMART Board. We were not sure if teachers with Promethean boards would have the same experience as teachers with SMART Boards. Then we found another group with Mimeo boards who also wanted to participate. And again, we extended the tryout to include them also but stating up front they would be "guinea pigs", because we were not sure what their experience would be.

Tryout teachers were sent *Research into Application: How Scientifically-based Research Findings Apply to Investigations and the Interactive Whiteboard*. It introduced the research in this way: "Interactive Whiteboards significantly affect teaching and learning in positive ways. For example, interactive whiteboards have shown to

Figure 2. Spectrum of digital users

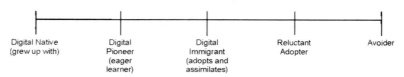

enable teachers to reduce two other major causes of stress - heavy workloads and the inability to meet the needs of all students. Research indicates the following findings as a result of the use of interactive whiteboards in the classroom. Applications specific to the *Investigations and the Interactive Whiteboard* product are provided." (Pearson, 2010) This was sent to the teachers in September 2010. Beyond the surveys, their responsibilities included participating in five monthly WebEx sessions, scheduled in September, October, and November 2010 and in January and February 2011.

Their next endeavor was participating in the introductory WebEx to clearly understand the purpose and goals of the Tryout, their responsibilities, timelines, and benefits. They realized that this software was a radical departure for *Investigations*, and they were all very excited to try it! During that WebEx, a Pearson editorial technology expert answered any questions the teachers had about loading the software, accessing it and any other technology issue they may have had. Some of the issues they brought up were technology and hardware related, some questions dealt with functionalities of the software, and some questions were specific to a session or activity.

Reaction e-mails would be the main vehicle for gathering information about their experiences with the software in their classrooms. Their email reaction might be a response to a prompt provided, their reaction to ease-of-use, new ways they found to use the product, anecdotes that happened with their students, parents' reactions, other teachers' curiosity, or a suggestion for an improvement or enhancement for the product. They could share questions they had, student work, and photographs, if they had permission.

While the tryout was getting underway, the *Common Core State Standards and Mathematical Practice* was filtering through and gaining traction at the state, district, school, and classroom levels. Math Coordinators were offering teachers Professional Development regarding *Common Core State*

Standards in states that had already signed on. And two Assessment Consortia, *Smarter Balanced Assessment Consortium* led by the Washington State Department of Education, and *Partnership for Assessment of Readiness for College and Careers (PARCC)* led by the Florida Department of Education and coordinated by Achieve Inc. began developing assessments for *Common Core State Standards*. Both consortia are working with their member states to develop next-generation assessments that align to the new *Common Core State Standards* to accurately measure student progress toward college and career readiness. A characteristic of these developing state assessments is that students will take them online, because of its added benefits. Online testing offers opportunity for more rigorous, computer-based tasks, enhanced and expanded test-item types, measures students' abilities in ways that a paper/pencil test cannot, and timely feedback to inform instruction. In a press release (Partnership for Assessment of Readiness for College and Careers (PARCC), 2012) in January, 2012 these two Consortia announced that they awarded a contract to Pearson to develop a new Technology Readiness Tool which will help states facilitate the evaluation of current technology and infrastructure for online testing. With all logistics, surveys, and uploads completed... the fun began... with the arrival of the first set of reaction emails from the Tryout Teachers! In the first round, the reactions (teacher's first name, grade and state) were focused on the features that were "teacher" benefits.

I can bring a math program to life visually for the students and allow them to interact with the content. I also like being able to save or print the lesson for future reference. Things written on a whiteboard with regular dry erase pens just have to be erased. The ease with which you can navigate from lesson to lesson is great. It takes away from time consuming transitions (Michelle, K, FL).

The program's ease of use was also mentioned by teachers. Anna, a 1ˢᵗ grade teacher in North Carolina said: "My instructional life is easier with *Investigations and the Interactive Whiteboard* because it organizes my lessons. I am able to follow the *Investigations* program with more fidelity because the lessons are in order."

Zak agreed:

The product is exceptionally easy to use. It is one click away from ready-to-go, with exceptional mathematics prompts that align directly with the teacher materials. It just doesn't get much better than that. It allows me to free up my time to work on important mathematical ideas and conversations (Zak, 4ᵗʰ-5ᵗʰ, FL).

Teachers also mentioned how much support the materials provided them. Deb, a 4ᵗʰ Grade teacher in Ohio mentioned: "For a teacher new to *Investigations* this would be an incredible resource and would also further insure that the entire program (especially Ten-Minute Math) is being taught."

By the end of October, 2011 Tryout Teachers were sent *Investigation Interactive Whiteboard Help* an 8-page pdf to help guide their implementation, but most had already worked out any challenges they encountered and were sailing ahead. However, several teachers with ELL students shared how *Investigations and the Interactive Whiteboard* helped students overcome their challenge.

Interestingly enough, even children who are in different needs-categories are more willing to pay attention, and attempt to participate. My ADD/ADHD students, along with my academically at-risk students and above grade-level students are all able to focus, participate in some manner, and then move along to the work assigned/games to be played. I have children who have NEVER willingly volunteered in math to demonstrate or to partici-

pate in class doing this now. In fact, now when I ask, "Who would be willing to (volunteer/show us/be next) on Investigations and the Interactive Whiteboard?", and all the hands go up almost every time. Now I have had to say everyday for over a week, "If you have had a chance to (lead/show us/share) please remember to put your hand down and let your friends have a chance too!" (Kim, 1ˢᵗ, MN).

Investigations promotes materials that are used repeatedly as math tools. While Investigations is engaging, it also uses the same tools over and over letting students see the math in the hands-on activities rather than distracted by the materials. For some reason ELL students have a more difficult time in my classroom making transitions between materials, so I have come to appreciate the straightforward approach to the activities and with Investigations and the Interactive Whiteboard (Val, K, WA).

I have NO Spanish children. All of mine are Somali speakers. BUT, with the SIOP model of ESL support, Investigations and the Interactive Whiteboard allows you to isolate vocabulary (because you can obviously write on each chart) and then save and return to charts previously made, as well as flip between charts in the current lesson. All this aids the ESL student because it allows them to connect the learning to prior learning. Also, it allows you to isolate the words or language objectives by highlighting it within each slide (Kaylen, 4ᵗʰ, MN).

The interactivity and visuals have enhanced the way my students learn and acquire new knowledge. I teach in a Bilingual classroom and having the vivid colors and geometric images has facilitated my students' ability to make connections to their schema and perform at competitive levels parallel to their monolingual classmates (Ricardo, 5ᵗʰ, NM).

I have students in my classroom that speak all sorts of languages from Burmese to Korean, Spanish, Kurdish... I also have some Bosnian. Anything that I can use on the SMART board that is interactive and has words with the pictures is helpful. If I have pictures and images of the math games and activities, it is very helpful for these students. Their vocabulary is limited in English and they have become very good at just smiling and nodding, so you don't always know what they understand and what they don't. The more visual things are, the better, and Investigations and the Interactive Whiteboard helped a lot (Sara, 4th MO).

Along with praise for *Investigations and the Interactive Whiteboard* from the tryout teachers, came challenges, questions, and suggestions. From their experiences, they were full of ideas for changes, improvements, and enhancements. Getting files unzipped, frustration using the pen tools, manipulating charts... these glitches were rectified, questions answered, and requests for assistance supported. Their great ideas, such as more options for building arrays, including 300 or 10,000 charts, and providing multiple copies of number puzzles, are filed away in a safe place for future development!

By February 2011 all Units for *Investigations and the Interactive Whiteboard* were uploaded and available through Pearson *SuccessNet*. A new, more detailed *Implementing Guide for the Interactive Whiteboard* (Pearson, 2011) was also available online that helped support implementation.

ILLUSTRATIVE MODELING: COMMON CORE MATHEMATICAL PRACTICE

Many of the reactions over the winter months appeared to be rich illuminations of *Common Core Mathematical Practice* in these classrooms. The teachers, through their anecdotes were ex-

emplifying the "points of intersection" between the content of the *Investigations for the Common Core* program and Common Core Mathematical Practice that is foundational to the *Investigations* curriculum. After we analyzed the post-surveys, we found the 8 Mathematical Practices were repeatedly mentioned or illuminated in classroom scenarios, as noted next.

1. Make Sense of Problems and Persevere in Solving Them

"Approaching the mathematics content through investigations helps students develop flexibility and confidence in approaching problems..." (Economopoulos, Mokros, & Russell, 1998) as the tryout teachers reveal in these narratives.

Investigations and the Interactive Whiteboard has motivated my students to be more active learners. The graphics are exactly like the materials they have in front of them, so they have become more engaged. Demonstrations of the games and activities have been much more successful with the Interactive Whiteboard - students no longer have to guess or imagine what it would be like using the real cards and game pieces because it looks exactly the same! (Judy, 3rd, OH).

Investigations and the Interactive Whiteboard has motivated my students... by challenging their desire to only do what they are "comfortable" with to be over-powered by their desire to try using the board—even if it is something new—therefore defeating the fear of the unknown/new with the desire to "just do it" because of the board itself... by making math interesting, and challenging, even though the time allotted to the 6 year-olds is the last 90 minutes of the day, all students are participating, and working hard until the end of class... by motivating the "try harder frame of mind" (e.g. perseverance) versus the "I give up" or "I don't care" attitude... by being better at their sportsmanship in the regular classroom (instead of just in the PE class or at recess)... by focusing longer and harder on the task at hand, needing less "breaks" They ask to keep "playing" the math games all the time (Kim, 1ˢᵗ, MN).

2. Reason Abstractly and Quantitatively

The teachers' stories illustrate that, "Each *Investigations* Unit on counting, numbers, and operations includes a focus on reasoning and generalizing about numbers and operations" (Russell & Economopoulos, 2012, 60).

Playing "Build it" in Investigations and the Interactive Whiteboard made it so everyone could see the cards (as opposed to huddling around a desk or carpet area) and we had incredible discussions around the use of a ten frame to build numbers. Students were not only able to explain their thinking to their classmates, they could show them in a way that classmates could follow their thinking process and have dialogue about their thinking. The power of this tool to increase participation and engage students can be directly linked to increased achievement. With the addition of Investigations and the Interactive Whiteboard to my classroom, my students are more accountable for showing and explaining their thinking. It has raised the level of conversation in my classroom, and the ability for students to share their thinking on the format of Investigations and the Interactive Whiteboard, has created a culture of conversation and attributed to a stronger mathematical community. My students talk to each other more because of the visual component of Investigations and the Interactive Whiteboard and they consistently engage in dialogue about mathematics in a way that astounds me (Claire, K, FL).

I'm really enjoying using the Morning Routine stuff! It makes planning for deep discussions so much easier when the materials are already

"pulled" for me. I have more time to think about deep questions rather than keeping track of, finding and organizing materials! (Monica, 1ˢᵗ, CO).

3. Construct Viable Arguments and Critique the Reasoning of Others

"Whole class discussion time is precious class time; it should serve to consolidate or move ahead the math thinking of all students", (Russell & Economopoulos 2012, 66) as these tryout teachers articulate (See Figure 3).

Investigations and the Interactive Whiteboard has motivated my students to share their thinking, explore new ideas, and present collective efforts. Investigations and the Interactive Whiteboard provides them with the opportunity to enrich every new experience (Emma, 3ʳᵈ, AZ).

After using Investigations and the Interactive Whiteboard only for a few days, I realize that I will now have time to work on my conversation with the students which is the heart of Investigations (Anna, 1ˢᵗ, NC).

Figure 3. Student using the interactive whiteboard to share her strategy

4. Model with Mathematics

The insights from these tryout teachers prove that "Thinking with representations and contexts allows students to express and further develop their ideas and enables students to engage with each other's ideas." (Russell & Economopoulos, 2012, 55) (See Figure 4).

By far, my favorite, and I believe the most effective part of the Investigations and the Interactive Whiteboard sessions were the Ten Minute Math activities. The Quick Images were set to the perfect time and allowed for my students to begin to see different combinations that they may not have seen in paper versions. For example when flashing the arrangement on the document camera in previous years, my timing may not have been as accurate. The accuracy in timing ensured that the students were focusing on the arrangements and "forcing" them to see the distributive property (Zak, 4th-5th, FL)

Figure 4. Student sharing her solution using the interactive whiteboard

I incorporate Investigations and the Interactive Whiteboard several times each week during workshop time and small groups of students can use the SMART Board This allows for ongoing modeling to the rest of the students constantly going on in the 'background' and also allows me to assess at a glance the understanding of the group working at the SMART Board. I love the integration of the technology into the curriculum! (Val, K, WA).

5. Use Appropriate Tools Strategically

As illuminated in these anecdotes, in the *Investigations* program, "Students develop the habit of making drawings, building models, and using representations to think with and to explain their thinking to others" (Russell & Economopoulos, 2012, 55):

When I did the problem-solving with my class, it was nice to have various tools to solve present in the screens for this lesson. On the problem solving screens, it is useful that there is a number line provided as one tool, however I find I don't use it so much as a blank screen, because I am trying to train my students to create their own open number lines and mark on what they need. The number line was very helpful to model counting back or counting up. It would be helpful to be able to move the number line higher since student heads were in the way for people at the back of the room. Coming to think of it, I didn't try moving the number line, so perhaps it is movable! The 100 chart was another useful tool. I also use an interactive 100 chart with my class, and wondered if the 100 chart in this session could be made interactive? I think it would be great for students to see us "turn over" the numbers in the problem, like 19 and 30, to be able to count from one to another (Sujata, 2nd, AZ).

The way Investigations and the Interactive Whiteboard has enhanced my teaching in the classroom is that it allows me to teach with tools and ma-

nipulatives that the students can actually see on the whiteboard and visualize what I am trying to explain. Students are given the opportunity to interact as well as get an opportunity to manipulate with tools as they learn, rather than trying to visual through oral instruction. Both student learning and achievement has shown growth in my class. My students have a clear understanding of what is expected and they have tools to help with the process (Monique, 2nd, MD).

6. Attend to Precision

The tryout teachers show how "Every session requires students to communicate with precision. Many of the sessions' focal points stress the use of "clear and concise" notation. Students are expected to solve problems efficiently and accurately" (Russell & Economopoulos, 2012, xii) (See Figure 5).

I know my students are improving because I have students who could not accurately count to 7. They would get a different answer each time. Now, they are finding 8 different ways to make seven and most of them know how to make sure they found each possibility because they model and draw them in order. Without modeling this in Investigations and the Interactive Whiteboard everyday, they would have not been able to achieve this in the time they have (Anna, 1st, NC).

My students are willing to take the "risk" to demonstrate their skills, their numeracy, their geometric thinking, just for a chance to use Investigations and the Interactive Whiteboard and demonstrate. I have students who never speak out loud, or never participate in class, who are raising their hand, answering questions, and/or being a leader in class--- just for the chance to go to the board. Vocabulary is increasing: rotate was one of those things that they just never mastered. But now, they are coaching each other: "Hey, tap it

Figure 5. Many students' solutions recorded on the interactive whiteboard

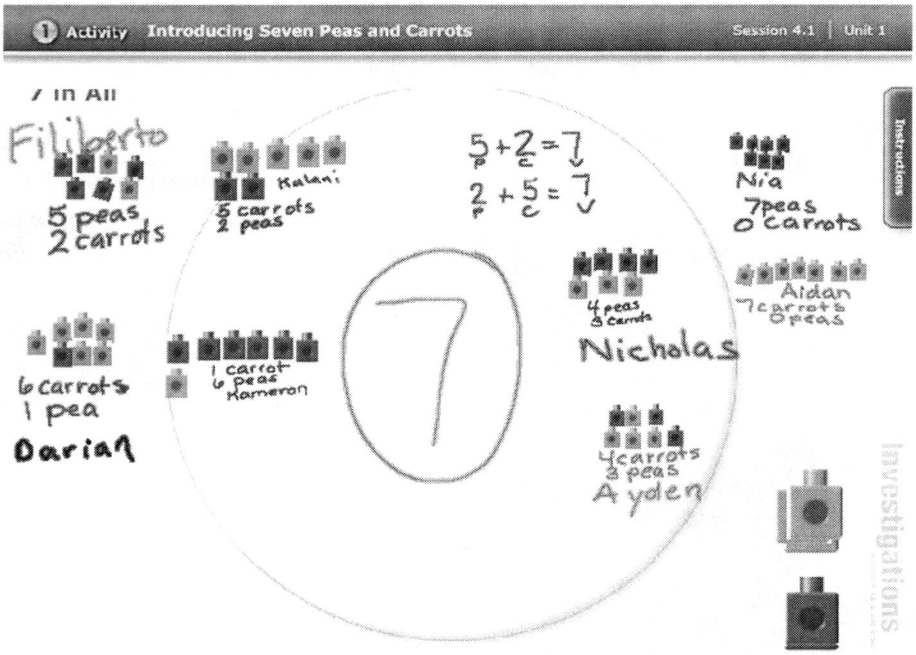

and get the green handle bar! I think that you can rotate it and make it fit!" A hexagon is not just the "yellow thing-y," a trapezoid is not the "red one" any longer. They talk more concisely, in mathematical verbiage (Kim, 1ˢᵗ, MN).

7. Look For and Make Use of Structure

"Classroom Routines and Ten-Minute Math activities afford more situations in which students discover and use the various structures of mathematics" (Russell & Economopoulos 2012, xiii), as these vignettes from their classrooms confirm.

I am convinced that Investigations and the Interactive Whiteboard is key to model, conceptualize, and experience - how the power polygons can form other polygons by simply manipulating or interacting with the images. As students and I interacted with these images, there were several occasions where I could just see "the light in their eyes." Being able to superimpose the images on top of the others and see the corresponding angles match, as well as the sides, provided the needed experience to understand similarities between these images (Ricardo, 4ᵗʰ-5ᵗʰ, NM).

I have used Investigations and the Interactive Whiteboard every day since we had access. I really like how the Classroom Routines are included in each lesson. The best part is the time when doing Quick Images. Also, the way they are set up leads to good discussions. What I mean is the numbers or shapes that are picked to be used have connections and this had led to really good mathematical connections (Cindy, 1ˢᵗ, DE).

8. Look For and Express Regularity in Repeated Reasoning

The study of number and operations extends beyond efficient computation to the excitement of making and proving conjectures about mathematical relationships that apply to an infinite class of numbers (Russell & Economopoulos 2012, 64).

See Figure 6.

I used the Close to 1,000 activity with the students. I moved the slides so that I had two games going on side by side, and projected them this way to the students. I had two students come up to the white board competing against each other. I divided the class and had one side work with Student A's cards and one side with Student B's cards. Great discussion ensued.

Figure 6. A student demonstrating strategic game moves using the interactive whiteboard

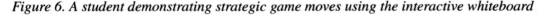

I know my students understood the Close to 1,000 game after this activity, because we played the game the next day and the students were coming close to the 1,000 mark. There was good mathematical discussion as well. For those who had a challenge with 1,000, we played close to 100 but they understood the concept because of presenting the game using the SMART Board (Nicole, 5th, CT).

As far as my Investigations and the Interactive Whiteboard reflections... it has been a bit difficult because we are currently implementing Unit 6 on decimals and that Unit isn't up yet. But I have been creating some of my own questions based on the games that are in that unit. For example, I have made the decimals in-between game with cards already placed and asked the students to choose their best next play and why they would make that move. It has been really great to watch them come up and move the cards and then show why it would be best to move it there.

As far as the fraction unit...which we just finished...the fraction track game was exceptional! The kids loved playing it on the SMART Board and it definitely increased their motivation to play the game and they were much more willing to do it in front of their classmates because it was on the smart board. And this increased our class discussions because more students were willing to come up and share and talk about best moves! (Zak, 4th-5th, FL).

These anecdotes from the Tryout Teachers were reflections on their transitions from one activity to another, program organization, the decrease of their prep time leading to increased instructional time, and the support of Mathematical Practices. They were reactions from their students, about *Investigations and the Interactive Whiteboard* as a support for motivation to learn, persistence in their efforts to solve problems, and engagement in their participation. But there were others who were also intrigued by this new classroom technology... their parents! And when we intrigue parents, we gain opportunities to educate them also. The *Common Core State Standards and Mathematical Practice* becomes familiar to them as they hear about them more and more from their children and the teachers.

Parents have been intrigued with Investigations and the Interactive Whiteboard and...Their children tell them what they get to do with the whiteboard (and parents ask questions of the teacher as a result). They are "happening by" for a visit, in the hopes of seeing their child working on the whiteboard in math. They are asking their children "what did you do in math" type questions more often. They are more willing to let me (the Webpage administrator for the class and the whole school) to use their child's picture on the Webpage(s) (Kim, 1st, MN).

I even have parents who come and peek through the window to see what we are doing; some who come just at math time with the "Oh, I need to pick so-and-so up a little early, but we don't need to leave yet. I'll just stay here and watch."---but then they stay until after the buses leave so they can see their child do things with the program, and so that they can try it out too! (Nicole, 5th, CT).

Parents have been intrigued with Investigations and the Interactive Whiteboard because we were able to use it at Curriculum Night and demonstrate the games we play and explain the reasoning behind them (Anna, 1st, NC).

Parents have been intrigued with Investigations and the Interactive Whiteboard because they have observed students take control over their learning in a more 21st century-themed learning environment (Emma, 3rd, AZ).

IMPLICATIONS, CHALLENGES, FUTURE DIRECTIONS

Today's students are digital natives! They are comfortable with technology; it is often a big part of their daily lives. *Investigations and the Interactive Whiteboard* showcases and proves how digital technology can support and enhance students' processes and proficiencies with the Standards for Mathematical Practice in these ways:

- Using *Investigations and the Interactive Whiteboard* motivates students to keep struggling with a problem, and work through it until they successfully find a solution.
- *Investigations and the Interactive Whiteboard* provides a dynamic, visual, and interactive "slate" upon which students can expose their reasoning of complex, abstract ideas for themselves, and for others; making difficult math ideas more accessible to students in a concrete and visual way.
- The visual aspect of *Investigations and the Interactive Whiteboard* allows students to communally demonstrate, prove, defend, discuss and critique their work, and the work of others.
- *Investigations and the Interactive Whiteboard* provides students opportunities to confidently demonstrate their ability to use technology in a collaborative learning environment, and digital opportunities to visually model their mathematics.
- *Investigations and the Interactive Whiteboard* provides students a multitude of electronic, digital tools from which to strategically choose and use to solve problems.

- By providing the Classroom Routines and Ten-Minute Math activities through *Investigations and the Interactive Whiteboard,* students intently practice and increase their set of mental math strategies which increases their precision using math facts.
- Because of the varied presentations offered through *Investigations and the Interactive Whiteboard,* more students have access to the mathematics through multi-sensory dimensions, and all students can focus on key mathematical ideas to deepen their understanding of the structure of the mathematics.
- *Investigations and the Interactive Whiteboard* offers opportunities for teachers demonstrating the Close to... "games to point out regularities, strategies, methods and even shortcuts about numbers and operations".

The lessons learned throughout this Teacher Tryout of *Investigations and the Interactive Whiteboard* will inform our future development of this software. The teachers' practical suggestions for improvements and enhancements are valuable resources to be considered. A publisher's challenge is always "staying ahead in the game" as states' decisions, educational research findings, and technological advancements forge ahead into the future. But...

Tomorrow's students will still be digital natives! However, we cannot even imagine what their world will present for them through technological advances. But, if they continue to develop their thinking through Common Core Mathematical Practice, they will have the processes and proficiencies needed to be successful in their future endeavors.

CONCLUSION

The TERC authors of *Investigations* intentionally developed a curriculum that connected "Mathematical Practice" to the mathematical content as a foundational goal. Pearson, as a designer of curricula, assessments, and professional development believes we are "Always Learning". Together, we learned in developing this software to use the power of the technology to further students' learning and ease teachers' challenges; we learned from the tryout teachers using this software what the power of this technology can draw out in students' thinking and sharing and, their suggestions for further enhancements. This will inform our development of future technologies to support the *Common Core State Standards*. *Investigations and the Interactive Whiteboard* illuminates the "points of intersection" between the *Common Core Standards for Mathematical Content* and the *Common Core Standards for Mathematical Practice*, so that students with a "flexible" base, develop understanding to "consider analogous problems, represent problems coherently, justify conclusions, apply the mathematics to practical situations, use technology mindfully to work with the mathematics, explain the mathematics accurately to other students, step back for an overview, or deviate from a known procedure to find a shortcut." (NGACBP, CCSSO, 2010) In essence, students develop understanding of mathematical content and engage in mathematical practice because *Investigations and the Interactive Whiteboard* facilitates Common Core Mathematical Practices enacted in the context of the Common Core Content Standards. Today's engaged students are tomorrow's strategic leaders!

REFERENCES

Economopoulos, K., Mokros, J., & Russell, S. J. (1998). *From paces to feet*. Glenview, IL: Scott Foresman.

National Governors Association Center for Best Practices, Council of Chief State School Officers. (2010). *Common core state standards: Mathematical practice*. Washington, DC: National Governors Association Center for Best Practices, Council of Chief State School Officers.

Partnership for Assessment of Readiness for College and Careers (PARCC). (2012). *Press release: New technology readiness tool*. Retrieved May 15, 2012, from http://www.parcconline.org/press-release-new-technology-readiness-tool

Pearson. (2010). *Research into application: How scientifically-based research findings apply to investigations and the interactive whiteboard*. Glenview, IL: Pearson Education, Inc. Retrieved May 15, 2012, from http://www.pearsonschool.com/index.cfm?locator=PS1cHy

Pearson. (2011). *Implementing guide for the interactive whiteboard*. Glenview, IL: Pearson Education, Inc. Retrieved May 15, 2012, from http://rebekahvictoria.com/resume.pdf

Russell, S. J., & Economopoulos, K. (2012a). *Implementing investigations in grade 3*. Glenview, IL: Pearson Education, Inc..

Russell, S. J., & Economopoulos, K. (2012b). *Investigations and the common core state standards*. Glenview, IL: Pearson Education, Inc..

ADDITIONAL READING

Manzo, K. K. (2010, January 8). Whiteboards' impact on teaching seen as uneven. *Education Week.*

Marzano, R. J. (2009). Teaching with interactive whiteboards. *Educational Leadership*, *67*(3), 80–82.

McCrummen, S. (2010, June 11). Some educators question if whiteboards, other high-tech tools raise achievement. *Washington Post.* SMART Technologies Inc. (200). *Interactive whiteboards and learning.* Retrieved May 15, 2012, from http:// downloads01.smarttech.com/media/research/ whitepaper/int_whiteboard_research_whitepaper_update.pdf

Thomas, M., & Cutrim, S. E. (Eds.). (2010). *Interactive whiteboards for education: Theory, research and practice.* Hershey, PA: IGI Global. doi:10.4018/978-1-61520-715-2.

Section 4
Innovative Approaches to Teacher Education and Professional Development

Chapter 19
Lesson*Sketch*:
An Environment for Teachers to Examine Mathematical Practice and Learn about its Standards

Patricio Herbst
University of Michigan, USA

Wendy Aaron
Oregon State University, USA

Vu Minh Chieu
University of Michigan, USA

ABSTRACT

This chapter describes how the authors have utilized digital graphics and Web 2.0 technologies to design an information technology environment, LessonSketch. In LessonSketch teachers can learn about mathematical practice in instruction through the transaction of representations of practice. The authors describe the main features of LessonSketch, its collection of lessons, and its authoring tools, and illustrate what teacher educators have done with them.

INTRODUCTION AND BACKGROUND

The development and wide adoption of the Common Core State Standards for Mathematics (National Governors Association Center for Best Practices and Council of Chief State School Officers, 2010) has brought unprecedented attention to the importance of mathematical practice in classrooms. The eight Standards for Mathematical Practice (SMP) set expectations for what that mathematical practice needs to be like. As with the content standards but perhaps even more considering the novelty of the SMP, it is critical for policy makers and teacher developers to help teachers support students' engagement in mathematical practice and recognize when the standards

DOI: 10.4018/978-1-4666-4086-3.ch019

for mathematical practice are met. To facilitate this, the educational community needs a way to communicate about mathematical practice and in particular to illustrate what the SMP mean, what mathematical practice looks like, and what are the circumstances in which a particular Standard for Mathematical Practice could be met. In the following pages we suggest that technological tools, such as those we have developed in Lesson*Sketch* (https://www.lessonsketch.org/login.php), can be useful in the communication and learning of mathematical practice and its Standards.

Lesson*Sketch* is an online environment where teachers and teacher educators can create, share, and discuss classroom scenarios. At the center of Lesson*Sketch* is a graphic language for representing classroom interaction, and software tools that allow users to create comic strips displaying instructional scenarios. This graphic language is comprised of two-dimensional images of people and objects that populate classrooms (e.g., teachers, students, whiteboards, desks, textbooks), and tools for representing their interaction (e.g., speech bubbles, facial expressions, and arm positions). This graphic language provides an alternative to written or spoken language for communicating about classroom interaction. Inside Lesson*Sketch*, users can use this language to create comic strips displaying instructional scenarios that can then be shared and discussed.

Lesson*Sketch* is a useful tool that can help solve the challenge of how to make mathematical practice and its standards into a theme for discussion and learning. While the content Standards describe knowledge and skills that students should learn in school, the Standards for Mathematical Practice describe characteristics of the activities involved in creating and handling mathematical knowledge. Thus, while Mathematical Content Standards can be represented with lists of mathematical topics or problem types that students should be able to solve (e.g., The Geometry-Congruence 1 Standard says that high school geometry students should "Know precise definitions of angle, circle, perpendicular

line, parallel line, and line segment, based on the undefined notions of point, line, distance along a line, and distance around a circular arc," National Governors Association Center for Best Practices and Council of Chief State School Officers, 2010, p. 76), a richer representation may be needed to communicate what meeting the Standards for Mathematical Practice means. For example SMP 6 "Attend to precision", is described in the Common Core State Standards as follows:

6 Attend to precision. Mathematically proficient students try to communicate precisely to others. They try to use clear definitions in discussion with others and in their own reasoning. They state the meaning of the symbols they choose, including using the equal sign consistently and appropriately. They are careful about specifying units of measure, and labeling axes to clarify the correspondence with quantities in a problem. They calculate accurately and efficiently, express numerical answers with a degree of precision appropriate for the problem context. In the elementary grades, students give carefully formulated explanations to each other. By the time they reach high school they have learned to examine claims and make explicit use of definitions. (National Governors Association Center for Best Practices and Council of Chief State School Officers, 2010, p. 7)

The description of SMP 6 provides a list of circumstances in which attention to precision could be apparent. But to understand how that attention to precision might matter as students engage in mathematical practice, how attention to precision could be manifest in students' action, and how a teacher could help students attend to precision in practice, a representation of practice that goes beyond that description might be more helpful. Representations of mathematical practice in instruction can provide contexts for understanding when and how the standards for mathematical practice apply.

REPRESENTATIONS OF MATHEMATICAL PRACTICE IN INSTRUCTION

As a provisional elaboration we could say that mathematical practice refers to what people do when they do mathematics. Like other practices, mathematical practice happens over time and involves not only people but also the tools of the practice, particularly language, symbols, diagrams, and often also technological devices. Mathematical practice involves what has, at other times, been referred as mathematical processes (e.g., communication, making connections, problem solving, reasoning and proof, representation; NCTM, 2000). The mathematical processes of individual mathematicians have been documented in textual representations like Polya's (1945) *How to Solve It*, which outlines the process through which one could make sense of and solve mathematical problems. But mathematical practice involves not only ways of thinking and habits of mind (Cuoco, Goldenberg, and Mark, 1996). It also involves ways of doing and being in the world, including the world of work (Hoyles, Morgan, and Woodhouse, 1999). To represent mathematical practice requires not only illustrating how people think mathematically but also what they do with mathematical objects and apparatuses and other people, over time. Representations of this work are important reference objects for discussing and learning mathematical practice.

As regards to communicating and discussing the Standards for Mathematical Practice and their application in classrooms, it is also important to note that representations of mathematical practice need to be situated inside instruction, inside the interactions among teacher, students, and content (Cohen, Raudenbush, and Ball, 2003). Representing mathematical practice in instruction requires we give special consideration to the unique characteristics of classroom interactions and the features a representation would need so as to sufficiently allow for the visualization of these interactions.

Doyle (1979) describes classroom interaction as characterized by *multidimensionality, simultaneity, immediacy, unpredictability*, and *history*:

These classroom realities give rise to several distinctive and persistent features of this environment such as multidimensionality, simultaneity, immediacy, unpredictability, and history (see Doyle, 1977a). These terms simply mean that classrooms are crowded with people, activity, and interruptions; many events take place at the same time; and there is little time available for a teacher to reflect before acting or even anticipate the course of events. In addition, classroom groups meet regularly over an extended period of time so that rules evolve for the behavior of teachers and students and decisions at one point have consequences for action in the future. It would also seem that these features are indigenous to classrooms. If teachers met their students one at a time and at the students' initiative, the setting for teaching would contain few of these elements (p. 139).

This quote from Doyle highlights the dynamic and complex nature of classroom interactions. To represent mathematical practice in a manner that is faithful to this dynamism and complexity the representation must allow for the communication of these features. That is, the language of the representation must allow for the communication of several events that are taking place at the same time and involve many people who express their emotions or reactions in different ways (e.g., gestures, voices). It must also allow for the communication of the unfolding of events over time and bring to the viewers' mind the history and customs that are common to classrooms.

Therefore, representing mathematical practice inside instruction is very different from representing the mathematical practice of individuals. Textual representations (e.g., Pólya, 1945) can be powerful in their ability to capture the invisible thought process of individuals. However, textual representations are not very effective at capturing the immediacy, multivocality, or multidimensionality of instruction. Video has been used to capture the mathematical practice of classrooms because they can display some of that complexity, but they cannot be the only resource—video is particularly ill suited to represent events that have not happened or that happened at a different spot than where the camera was recording. While we recognize the value of continuing to use video to record and represent mathematical practice in instruction, we note that Lesson*Sketch,* through its *Depict* software (Herbst & Chieu, 2011), allows the *creation* of representations of mathematical practice inside classrooms. These representations can take into account the multidimensionality, simultaneity, immediacy, unpredictability, and history of classroom interaction.

Furthermore, the creation of representations of mathematical practice inside instruction can help develop a shared language for practice. Ball and Forzani (2009) have also called for a shared language for the work of teaching. They argue that as a community we are lacking the vocabulary to name and discuss the critical features of teaching practice. While we, as a community of teachers and teacher educators, still need to develop a shared verbal language to discuss teaching, Lesson*Sketch* provides an important step in this direction through the contribution of graphic resources for creating and sharing instructional scenarios. These scenarios may involve objects or practices that could later be named and discussed—being able to represent them graphically, as sequences of actions in context, can help to identify them and make them themes of conversation. Furthermore, Lesson*Sketch* can help mitigate some of the important limitations of conceptual language in representing practice (Dreyfus, 2007).

Stories as Containers of Knowledge

Professional knowledge, such as knowledge of teaching, can effectively be conveyed through stories (Brown & Duguid, 1991; Bruner, 1991).

Stories not only allow the representation of professional practices as they deploy over time, with people, and with tools and resources, but they can also incorporate important complexities such as the stuff of life that ordinarily accompanies and interferes with practice even if it is not essential to the practice—enacting a practice also includes some amount of coping with ineffable stuff (Dreyfus, 2007). Stories also provide a container for communicating both strategic and tactical knowledge that is situated in the particulars of the classroom.

Because practice is embodied in the particulars of the context, stories are well suited for communicating it. Furthermore, since those stories happen in classrooms, with their simultaneity and multimodality, comics can be a particularly useful medium to narrate those stories. Instead of encoding practice into propositions, such as, "assigning open-ended problems to students can support students in persevering and making sense of problems," a story can provide an example of how that proposition about practice can be embodied in interactions between a teacher and her students. This way of representing practice affords itself to communicating the types of dynamism and complexity described before by Doyle (1979). In a comic strip, for example, multiple events can be unfolding in the same frame and each event can span one or several frames (McCloud, 1994). Each event, instead of being described in words that the reader must then translate into imagined action, can be shown directly through a series of images that depict action, while the viewer can infer other actions as they pass from one frame to the next.

The *Depict* software in Lesson*Sketch* provides a canvas for laying out stories of classroom interaction as sequences of frames using elements of a graphic language for the communication of mathematical practices. Through the creation and sharing of instructional stories of mathematical practice, teachers and teacher educator can develop and share their knowledge of how to support their students in meeting the Standards for

Mathematical Practice. The graphic language and the *Depict* software used to create comic strips facilitate the creation and examination of scenarios of mathematical practice in classrooms. Users of Lesson*Sketch* can also share and discuss these and other classroom scenarios with other users. But to provide a more comprehensive idea of what is available and possible to do in Lesson*Sketch* we describe the platform in more general terms.

THE LESSON*SKETCH* ENVIRONMENT AND ITS COMPONENTS

In what follows, we describe Lesson*Sketch*'s main components. These include a Collection of Lessons, software Tools, and Experiences for users to navigate the collection and use the tools.

The Collection of Lessons

Lesson*Sketch* houses a collection of lessons: Animated stories that feature mathematical practice in classrooms and can promote discussions of the Standards for Mathematical Practice. Most of these animated episodes of high school geometry and

algebra instruction were originally developed for Herbst & Chazan's (2004) Thought Experiments in Mathematics Teaching project. These animated episodes display scenarios that are familiar to experienced high school mathematics teachers' though they often display breaches to normal classroom interaction (Herbst, Nachlieli, & Chazan, 2011). Each animated episode is enacted by a cast of two-dimensional cartoon characters and their speech is conveyed through a voice track. Various character sets called ThExpians (Thexpians B, C, M, N, and P, See Figure 1) have been used in various animations. Each of those casts of characters has different graphic resources to represent different degrees of individuality (Herbst, Chazan, Chen, Chieu, & Weiss, 2011) and have varying capabilities for facial expressions and body positions.

These animated episodes display mathematical practice in instruction and can support discussions of it. We have enabled these discussions in Lesson*Sketch* in two different ways. On the one hand, each lesson has an associated Forum, open to everybody, where participants can express their opinions about the practice shown in the animation. On the other hand, teacher developers can create Experiences for their clients (inservice or preservice teachers) in which they can navigate

Figure 1. ThExpians (ThExpians B, C, N, and P are copyright by The Regents of the University of Michigan. ThExpians M are copyright by The University of Maryland)

ThExpians B

ThExpians C

ThExpians M

ThExpians N

ThExpians P

an animation and share their comments with other participants of the same experience. For example, in response to the animated lesson called The Square, a teacher candidate who had seen this animation in an online experience that was part of his methods class made comments in a forum that involved his classmates and instructors to discuss *actions* concerning the mathematics:

The first thing I noticed was that the teacher links the material to the information that they just learned about the angle bisectors of a triangle. As we know prior knowledge is important and student's (sic) use this knowledge in order to work on new things. I liked how the teacher allowed the students to discuss with each other at first without much guidance on her part. **Once she brought the class together I thought it was a good move that she asked for conjectures and had students come to the board in order to draw exactly what they were trying to explain. From the different student's (sic) responses and discussions it seemed that the question needed clarification on the part of the teacher.** *This question could lead in multiple directions and that is why I think the students were getting confused in the end as to what exactly they were trying to show. One particular thing that I noticed was the responses that the teacher was giving to some of the students. The way that she would respond when some students gave answers gave the impression that the student was wrong and could lead to the student not wanting to participate in future discussions. Overall, allowing the students to explore on their own is important, but the teacher needed to do a better job of making sure everyone understood what was being said by the different students (emphasis added).*

The quoted comment attests to how well the animation helped teacher candidates notice the simultaneity and multidimensionality of classroom interaction. A feature of the technology, that the animated instructional story (The Square) was

embedded directly into the forum discussion space in Lesson*Sketch*, might have helped preservice teachers notice critical and simultaneous events implicating the teacher's moves and different students' responses. The teacher candidate was able to make an important comment (see the italic emphases before) on how to support students in constructing viable arguments and critiquing others' reasoning (i.e., the Standard for Mathematical Practice #3).

In another methods class, in which both preservice and beginning teachers used a similar online forum (Chieu, Kosko, & Herbst, in review) to discuss the animated episode, A Proof about Rectangles, which supported teachers in talking about another crucial Standard for Mathematical Practice: attending to precision (SMP #6). Here are comments by a novice teacher:

It was irritating that **throughout this lesson there was a lack of correct mathematical sentences.** *In addition to this, there was a lack of objectification when the teacher first put the example on the board. I understand that the teacher wanted the students to make assumptions and try to think through possible proofs. At the same time, without any objectification, a student can easily make many misconceptions and may lead the student to repeat the same mistakes in the future.* **In regards to the lack of correct mathematical sentences, the statements of 3,4 = 45; 1+2 = 90; 1=2=901 show that the teacher lacked common content knowledge. The teacher should use terms and notation properly and there was a chance for him to make this adjustment when another student brought it up to the class. Instead the teacher said that they would fix it later and this in turn caused other students to be confused by the notation which could have been avoided** *(emphasis added).*

And here is a response to the previous posting by another novice teacher:

*I agree that **the incorrect mathematical notation was very distracting to me and to the class of students. I don't understand why the teacher would not correct this when a student brought it up. It was a great teaching moment and he just ignored it instead of taking advantage of it. Students were left confused and may have gotten the wrong idea from the teacher that it wasn't that important (emphasis added).***

As it can now be noted, the fact that the animations displayed some times desirable mathematical practice and other times questionable practices enabled the participants to respond to those stories in ways that can be seen as relevant to the Standards for Mathematical Practice. The possibility for participants to interact in Lesson*Sketch* forums and the capacity to embed the animation in the forum space (as opposed to having video player and forum in separate screens) were also useful for participants to make these observations.

Depict: A Tool for Creating Representations of Mathematical Practice

As noted prior, Lesson*Sketch*'s *Depict* tool can facilitate the understanding of mathematical practice and its related standards in instruction by enabling users to create representations of instruction that they can later annotate and share. *Depict* (Figure 2) allows users to create comic strips by dragging graphic elements and dropping them on a canvas, then manipulating them individually. Thus after the user has laid out seats and desks and placed individual students, the user can select individual students and manipulate their facial expressions or their body position (they can turn each character 90 or 180 degrees). Once these comic strips have been saved and published they can be posted in discussion forms where they can be shared, discussed, and edited by other users. The user may also add speech bubbles to represent students' dialogue.

Figure 2. Creating an instructional episode with the Depict tool ("© [2012] [The Regents of The University of Michigan] Used with permission.")

Depict is a powerful tool for teacher education due to the way that it makes visible some of the characteristics of instruction that Doyle (1979) points out. For example, by showing a classroom full of students the user is reminded of the diversity of student thinking and personalities that might be present in a classroom and the possibility that students may be simultaneously engaged in multiple activities, both highlighting multidimensional and multivocal aspects of instruction, as well as its simultaneity and immediacy characteristics. By allowing the option of several different facial expressions for the teacher and students, the user is prompted to thinking about students' emotional responses and about the multimodality of classroom communication (how students can communicate nonverbally). When creating a new character or selecting an existing one the user can easily customize the character at a fine-grained level with different options of facial expressions, hand positions, shirt colors, and front or back or side views (See the popup window on the right hand side in Figure 2). In addition, the explicit layout of the instructional story in a series of slides (See the navigation component on the left hand side of Figure 2) can help the user attend to the temporality of instructional practice.

Teachers can use the *Depict* tool to represent events that happened in their classroom or to anticipate how planned lessons might unfold in their classroom (Chen, 2012). In a professional development Experience, for example, teachers could be asked to illustrate how they have supported their students in meeting a particular Standard for Mathematical Practice. Or teachers could be provided with a mathematical task and a Standard for Mathematical Practice and then asked to use *Depict* to illustrate how that task could provide an opportunity for students to meet that practice standard. Furthermore, a teacher educator can use some advanced features of Depict to teach about practice by depicting not only the classroom episode but also a play-by-play commentary. *Depict* users can enable an outside layer

of characters (Figure 3) to represent observers of a classroom, and they can add speech bubbles to those characters. In those speech bubbles they can include commentary of the classroom action seen.

The first author has used *Depict* and its commentary layer to illustrate two Standards for Mathematical Practice from the Common Core State Standards for the Illustrative Mathematics Project (http://illustrativemathematics.org/). In the first illustration, "Which angles are congruent? (http://www.slideshare.net/pgherbst/which-angles-are-congruent; See Figure 4) we portrayed a teacher educator and prospective teacher observing a class that was grappling with issues of mathematical precision when referring to angles in the context of doing a proof in high school geometry. The outside observers comment on the classroom events, relating these to SMP6, "Attend to precision." The students in the classroom scenario run into difficulties when using only one letter to note angles and the teacher slowly pushes them to recognize the need to increase precision by notating angles using three letters. In the meantime, the teacher educator and prospective teacher discuss how those actions support students in meeting the "attend to precision" Standard for Mathematical Practice, including when it is appropriate to press for precision.

A second example of a scenario illustrating a Standard for Mathematical Practice is the story "Making Bags of Apples" (http://www.slideshare.net/pgherbst/making-bags-of-apples; See Figure 3) and deals with the Standard for Mathematical Practice 8, "Looking for and expressing regularity in repeated reasoning." In this illustration a second grade class is putting groups of apples into paper bags as part of a lesson preliminary to multiplication, where they are developing ways of expressing the operations involved in counting by 2s or by 5s. In this illustration the teacher educator and prospective teacher discuss the developmental and mathematical reasons for engaging students in this activity and the way the

Figure 3. A frame in Making Bags of Apples. (The characters are copyright by The Regents of the University of Michigan. The screen and story content are CC-BY).

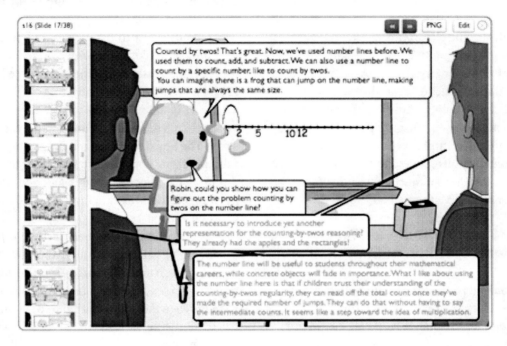

Figure 4. A frame in Which Angles are Congruent. (The characters are copyright by The Regents of the University of Michigan. The screen and story content are CC-BY).

teacher supports students' use of repeated reasoning.

This format of overlaying a conversation over a comic illustrating classroom instruction is useful for providing prospective teachers with viewing focus and commentary. In the case of helping teachers unpack and discuss the Standards for Mathematical Practice, these representations allow for both concrete illustrations of what mathematical practice might look like in instruction and commentary on the specific parts of the action that are related to the enactment and support of the Standards for Mathematical Practice.

Lesson*Sketch's* Tools for Teacher Educators' Creation of Experiences

In addition to its collection of animations and the *Depict* tool, Lesson*Sketch* offers Experiences that teachers and teacher candidates can join in order to explore some issues in depth. *Experience* is a general term that includes course modules, assessments, and research instruments. Teacher educators who have advanced user accounts have access to special tools and more resources with which to create those Experiences. In particular, teacher educators can use *Plan*, an authoring tool, which allows users to create *Agendas* for Experiences. An agenda is basically the sequence of activities and actions that end users will do when they join the Experience—in Lesson*Sketch* those screens may involve heavy use of media and *Plan* helps teacher educators set up how they want their clients to use the media. Teacher educators create agendas by "dragging and dropping" elements into a list-like canvas (Figure 5). Those elements enable decisions such as showing a message or text on the screen, showing a representation of instruction, asking teachers to mark important moments in a video or animation, asking teachers to create a comic showing classroom interaction, asking teachers to respond to open- or close-ended questions, or asking teachers to discuss a classroom scenario in a forum. Figure 5 shows how a simple agenda

is organized and created, in this case the experience was created by the first author for his class on secondary methods: (1) the author dragged the Message function to the canvas and customized it to show a welcome message where the instructors explain to users what the experience is about; (2) then he dragged the Media Show function to set a media show up that would allow teachers to watch and annotate an animated instructional story, The Square; (3) he then dragged the Forum function to set up an online forum for teachers to discuss what they have annotated; and finally (4) he dragged the Message function again to make a last comment.

Once agendas have been designed, they are broadcast to teachers through Experiences that are set up with an *Experience Manager* tool (Figure 6). An experience contains one or more agendas (See the area 1 in Figure 6) along with a list of participants (See the area 2 in Figure 6 where names have been replaced with pseudonyms) who will have access to the agenda(s), a time period during which the experience is active (See the area 3 in Figure 6), and optional prerequisites for the experience (See the area 4 in Figure 6).

By making agendas teacher educators can design sets of activities for teachers that allow for exploration of Standards for Mathematical Practice. Next we describe an experience designed by members of our team and aimed for practicing teachers. The experience is part of a professional development program currently in preparation.

The example we describe next is the introductory experience in a three-part professional development module for in-service teachers. This experience introduces teachers to the Standard for Mathematical Practice #1, "Make sense of mathematical problems and preserve in solving them." After teachers read the description of the Standard from the Common Core State Standards they are asked to watch an animation and identify moments in the story where students can be seen to be meeting the Standard. To mark those

Figure 5. Creating an agenda with the Plan authoring tool ("© [2010] [The Regents of The University of Michigan] Used with permission.")

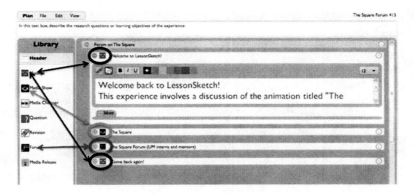

Figure 6. Setting up an experience with the Experience Manager tool ("© [2010] [The Regents of The University of Michigan] Used with permission.")

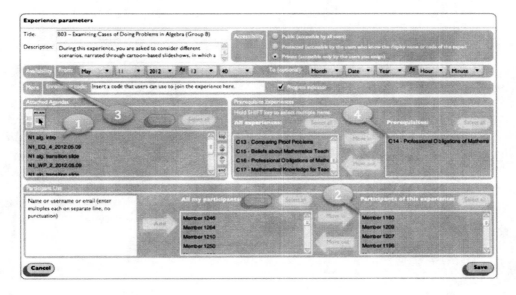

moments, the participant places colored pins on the timeline of the animation. Each teacher then compares the moments that he or she marked to moments that had been marked in advance by the author of the experience.

This experience utilizes several of the advanced features of Lesson*Sketch* but is simple to construct. To configure the screen where participants examine the video, the author needs to choose an animation from the Lesson*Sketch* collection of instructional stories described earlier or insert a YouTube video link (See the area 1 in Figure 8 where the author selects an animation: The Tangent Circle). The author sets the beginning and end points for the clip they want to show (See the area 2 in Figure 8), and chooses the labels for the pins (See the area 3 in Figure 8). To set up the comparison between the moments marked by the teacher and those marked by the author, the author needs to place the pins at the appropriate points on

Figure 7. An agenda for a professional development experience based on SMP-1 ("© [2010] [The Regents of The University of Michigan] Used with permission.")

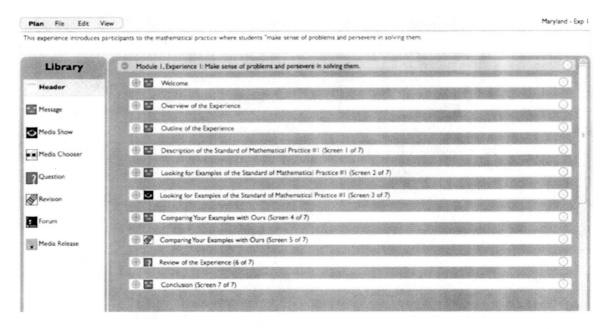

Figure 8. Configuring a media show in Plan ("© [2010] [The Regents of The University of Michigan] Used with permission.")

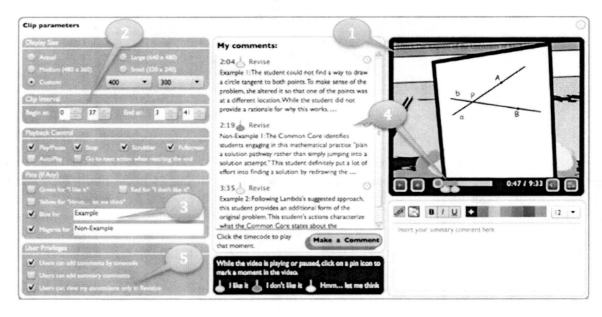

the video timeline and optionally provide justification for these marks (See the area 4 in Figure 8). The author may check the option that allows end users to add comments or the option that enables end users to see the author's marked moments and comments only in the following Revision action (See the area 5 in Figure 8). These tools allow the author to construct complex agendas through the use of a straightforward user interface (See Figure 7).

In a subsequent experience of the same professional development module, participating teachers are asked to use *Depict* to show how they engaged their own class in making sense of mathematical problems and persevere in solving them. Their depictions are uploaded to a forum and discussed among colleagues.

CONCLUSION

The CCSSM have brought attention to mathematical practice through the establishment of eight Standards for Mathematical Practice. These Standards for Mathematical Practice focus on the type and quality of students' mathematical activity in addition to the mathematical content that they are expected to learn. As these practice standards are established in school district across the country, teachers will need to be able to recognize and assess students' work toward these standards as well as support and teach their enactment. This chapter discusses how media and information technologies can be useful in representing mathematical practices, so as to support teachers' learning about them and teachers' support of those practices in their classroom work.

Of course, while technology does offer a hopeful panorama for supporting teachers in enacting the Standards for Mathematical Practice, many questions remain that need to be addressed. Among them are whether and how more learning about practice ensues from creating and using representations of practice in these online forums.

ACKNOWLEDGMENT

The work reported here has been supported by National Science Foundation grants ESI-0353285 and DRL- 0918425 to P. Herbst. All opinions are those of the authors and do not necessarily represent the views of the Foundation. The cartoon characters pictured and the software screens shown in this chapter are © The Regents of the University of Michigan, except where otherwise indicated.

REFERENCES

Ball, D., & Forzani, F. (2009). The work of teaching and the challenge for teacher education. *Journal of Teacher Education*, *60*(5), 497–511. doi:10.1177/0022487109348479.

Brown, J. S., & Duguid, P. (1991). Organizational learning and communities-of-practice: Toward a unified view of working, learning, and innovation. *Organization Science*, *2*(1), 40–57. doi:10.1287/orsc.2.1.40.

Bruner, J. (1991). The narrative construction of reality. *Critical Inquiry*, *18*(1), 1–21. doi:10.1086/448619.

Chen, C. L. (2012). *Learning to teach from anticipating lessons through comics-based approximations of practice*. (Unpublished doctoral dissertation). University of Michigan, Ann Arbor, MI.

Chieu, V. M., Kosko, K. W., & Herbst, P. (2013). Enhancing mathematics teachers' online discussions with animated classroom stories as reference objects. *International Journal of Computer-Supported Collaborative Learning*.

Cohen, D., Raudenbush, S., & Ball, D. (2003). Resources, instruction, and research. *Educational Evaluation and Policy Analysis*, *25*(2), 119–142. doi:10.3102/01623737025002119.

Cuoco, A., Goldenberg, E. P., & Mark, J. (1996). Habits of mind: An organizing principle for mathematics curricula. *The Journal of Mathematical Behavior, 15*, 375–402. doi:10.1016/S0732-3123(96)90023-1.

Doyle, W. (1977). Learning the classroom environment: An ecological analysis. *Journal of Teacher Education, 28*(6), 51–55. doi:10.1177/002248717702800616.

Doyle, W. (1979). Classroom effects. *Theory into Practice, 18*(3), 138–144. doi:10.1080/00405847909542823.

Dreyfus, H. L. (2007). The return of the myth of the mental. *Inquiry: An Interdisciplinary Journal of Philosophy, 50*(4), 352–365. doi:10.1080/00201740701489245.

Herbst, P., & Chazan, D. (2004). *Thought experiments in mathematics teaching.* Grant proposal to the National Science Foundation, funded 2004-2011.

Herbst, P., Chazan, D., Chen, C., Chieu, V.M., & Weiss, M. (2011). Using comics-based representations of teaching, and technology, to bring practice to teacher education courses. *ZDM—The International Journal of Mathematics Education, 43*(1), 91-103.

Herbst, P., & Chieu, V. M. (2011). *Depict: A tool to represent classroom scenarios.* Technical report. Retrieved from http://hdl.handle.net/2027.42/87949

Herbst, P., Nachlieli, T., & Chazan, D. (2011). Studying the practical rationality of mathematics teaching: What goes into installing a theorem in geometry? *Cognition and Instruction, 29*(2), 1–38. doi:10.1080/07370008.2011.556833.

Hoyles, C., Morgan, C., & Woodhouse, G. (1999). *Rethinking the mathematics curriculum.* Philadelphia, PA: Falmer. doi:10.4324/9780203234730.

McCloud, S. (1994). *Understanding comics.* New York: Harper.

National Council of Teachers of Mathematics. (2000). *Principles and standards for school mathematics.* Reston, VA: NCTM.

National Governors Association Center for Best Practices and Council of Chief State School Officers. (2010). *Common core state standards mathematics.* Washington, DC: National Governors Association Center for Best Practices, Council of Chief State School Officers.

Polya, G. (1945). *How to solve it: A new aspect of mathematical method.* Princeton, NJ: Princeton University Press.

ENDNOTES

[1] In the animation, while writing a proof students had written those statements in the way cited, while they would be more appropriately written as $m\angle 3 = m\angle 4 = 45°$, $m\angle 1 + m\angle 2 = 90°$, and $m\angle 1 = m\angle 2 = 90°$.

Chapter 20
Supporting Teachers' Instrumental Genesis with Dynamic Mathematical Software

Sandra Madden
University of Massachusetts Amherst, USA

ABSTRACT

This chapter addresses the need to prepare and support teachers of mathematics in order that they will be able to co-construct with their students classroom environments in which the Standards for Mathematical Practice as well as the content standards (CCSSM, 2010) are implemented fruitfully. Specifically, the chapter describes and illustrates design elements of learning environments with potential to positively impact pre- and in-service teachers' knowledge of mathematics, facility with technology, and beliefs about how mathematics may be learned. The practice of using appropriate tools strategically is highlighted; however, each of the practice standards is integral to a classroom environment which supports mathematical proficiency (National Research Council, 2001). This chapter examines and illustrates the explicit and intentional instructional design features of using provocative tasks, dynamic technology scaffolding, and sustained intellectual press, which together interact in classrooms to promote the mathematical practices and habits of mind explicated in the CCSSM.

INTRODUCTION

Common Core State Standards for Mathematics (2010) lays out a vision for students to be mathematically proficient as discussed in Adding It Up, with the strands of mathematical proficiency including conceptual understanding, procedural fluency, strategic competence, adaptive reasoning, productive disposition (National Research Council, 2001). Students are encouraged to develop productive mathematical habits of mind (Cuoco, Goldenberg, & Mark, 1996). Students

DOI: 10.4018/978-1-4666-4086-3.ch020

in schools are expected to practice and exhibit standards of mathematical practice and knowledge of mathematical content. To achieve these kinds of goals, students benefit from feeling invited into the powerful world of mathematical thinking and reasoning when they come to recognize that these goals are not deterministic and achievable as entities. Rather, successful mathematical learners will be those who develop dispositions to see their progress in mathematics as a process of *coming to know,* rather than knowing or somehow being done. As learners come to know mathematics in ways that are sensible to them, myriad ways of thinking, representing, computing, exploring, connecting, and communicating are beneficial. The use of digital tools to support learners *coming to know* affords possibilities that otherwise may not exist.

Through repeated studies with pre-service and in-service teachers, my research has suggested that under the conditions that will be discussed in this paper, teachers may come to see the use of *digital* dynamic cognitive tools (DCT) (e.g., *Fathom, TinkerPlots, Cabri II Geometry, Geometer's Sketchpad, CPMP-Tools, GeoGebra, TI-Nspire*) as well as other tools as increasingly valuable for supporting the mathematical learning of a wide range of learners. In light of CCSSM, if students are expected to use tools strategically and become mathematically proficient, it is imperative that their teachers are given an opportunity to do so as well.

The reality of living in the 21st century is that digital technology is rapidly evolving and will likely continue to do so. Research literature suggests that many mathematics teachers do not use technology with students or allow students to use technology in their classrooms for a host of reasonably predictable reasons such as personal concerns related to their role as teacher, management concerns related to managing the classroom as well as student learning, and technology concerns related mostly to personal facility with tools (Zbiek & Hollebrands, 2008). I make a distinction

about digital technology in this chapter to mean DCT as opposed to digital tools like social media, smartboards, document cameras, and the like. Like Zbiek, Heid, Blume, and Dick (2007), I assume a potentially synergistic relationship between technical and conceptual mathematical activity in a technology-rich environment.

According to Pea (1985), "A cognitive technology is provided by any medium that helps transcend the limitations of the mind, such as memory, in activities of thinking, learning, and problem solving" (p. 168). DCTs may include rudimentary technologies such as pipe cleaners and straws, geostrips and other physical tools used to explore mathematical relationships as well as computer- or calculator-based dynamic tools such as *TI-NSpire, Fathom 2, TinkerPlots, Cabri II Geometry, Cabri 3D, Geometers' Sketchpad, GeoGebra, Core Math Tools*, and online applets, to name a few. I see all of these as DCT with potential to support learners' technical and conceptual mathematical activity (Zbiek, et al., 2007). Furthermore, the non-digital DCT can serve as important scaffolding devices for the digital DCT. This will become more apparent in later sections.

Over the past 15 years of my career, I have had the honor of working closely with pre- and in-service teachers in rural and urban settings as well as undergraduate and graduate students pursuing mathematics education-related careers. Through this work and associated research, I have come to more fully understand some of the complexities of supporting the work of mathematics teachers. In the mix of considerations, and perhaps at the heart of the work presented in this paper, lies the big question of, "What does it mean to learn mathematics?" Related questions include: Who gets to learn mathematics? How do they get to engage with mathematical ideas? How will someone determine whether another person has learned something? I summarize these questions frequently by: Who is learning? What are they learning? and, How do you know? These questions transcend learning environments and have had a profound impact on my practice, my students' practices, and the nature of the activity in which we collectively engage. My intention in this chapter is to share some of this work.

Because teachers are not likely to use digital technologies with students until they have developed some facility with the technology themselves, the main research question guiding the studies discussed in this paper is: What characteristics of a learning environment may support teachers progressing toward instrumental genesis with respect to the use of digital DCT for learning (instrumental genesis will be discussed in the next section)?

Several challenges for supporting teachers will be explored:

1. In what ways may we productively attend to teachers' views of what it means to learn mathematics under new conditions of CCSSM and in the presence of technology?
2. How may teachers' dispositions toward the use of technology be supported?
3. What kinds of tasks and tool combinations may encourage teachers to expand their mathematical and technological repertoire?

Next I will discuss some theoretical commitments and some design characteristics that are at the heart of the work. Then I will take on these challenges through the explication of what appears to be productive instructional design elements augmented with examples of task sequences and samples of teachers' work, classroom discourse, and teacher narratives.

PRODUCTIVE DESIGN ELEMENTS FOR INSTRUCTIONAL SPACES

It is important for me to begin this section by acknowledging the work of researchers, some outside of mathematics education, whose scholarship has tremendously impacted the work of my

own. This paper is not meant to be a theoretical exploration of understanding, meaning, sense making, instrumental genesis, flow, shame, or self-determination, yet the roots of theories associated with these concepts are acknowledged as they have influenced the work (e.g., Brown, 2007, 2010; Csikszentmihalyi, 1990; Csikszentmihalyi & Csiksentmihalyi, 2006; Guin & Trouche, 1998; Leont'ev, 1978; Leontyev [or Leont'ev], 2009; Radford, Schubring, & Seeger, 2011; Ryan & Deci, 2000; Vygotsky, 1962, 1978). This chapter will attempt to weave among mathematics education issues threads from the collective work of the afore-mentioned scholars through the embodiment in practices, while highlighting CCSSM and digital technologies. Experimental conditions that may have contributed to learners developing instrumental genesis with an array of DCTs are documented. The word "tool" is used to indicate an object or artifact utilized by a learner for the purpose of accomplishing some goal.

I will briefly introduce some ideas from Flow Theory, Self-Determination Theory, and Shame Theory as related to my research and then introduce three design principles that I suggest support instrumental genesis with digital DCT. The next section of the chapter will illustrate, through examples from research, the ways in which I justify my claims.

Self-Determination Theory

Ryan and Deci (2000) relate self-determination theory to three innate psychological needs of competence, autonomy, and relatedness. Their claim is that for people to exhibit the characteristic of self-determination, these psychological needs must be met. I see self-determination as a powerful construct related to learning and aspire to co-create, with learners, environments where individuals are engaged, motivated, self-directed, curious, and persistent—and these goals are consistent with those of CCSSM. This theory resounds strongly with my work as a curriculum designer.

Flow Theory

Csikszentmihalyi's Flow Theory (1990) asserts that people are happiest when in flow, that is, in a state in which they are entirely immersed in an activity such that nothing else seems to matter. To experience flow, the task at hand must be sufficiently challenging and matched to skill level of the performer or learner. Mismatches between level of challenge and skill level otherwise may result in states of arousal, anxiety, worry, apathy, boredom, relaxation, and control. As a task designer and researcher, this theory suggests attention to the learner and the importance of the design of tasks that reasonably match learners' skill level. My particular interpretation of Flow Theory results in the design of tasks, which tend to be on the high challenge end, thus emotional states other than flow tend to occasionally emerge for learners in my laboratory, I mean, classroom. It is not a surprise, however, that as a mindful practitioner, instruction and classroom dynamics can intervene in ways that support productive learning environments. Learning is not always experienced as a happy thing in every moment, but recognizing educative discomfort (Frykholm, 2004) and learning to perturb it in productive ways is somewhat of an art and a worthwhile endeavor.

Shame Theory

The shame and whole-hearted research of Brené Brown (2007, 2010) was introduced to me through a TED Talk (see http://www.ted.com/talks/brene_brown_on_vulnerability.html). This may seem a strange theory to draw upon when exploring the support of CCSSM and digital technologies. Brown talks of courage, compassion, connection, and vulnerability as essential for experiencing love and belonging. Now, consider classroom environments as the origins of extreme vulnerability for learners and the breeding ground for shame in the case of far too many students. Regrettably, many students in mathematics accrue scars and wounds from mathematics "learning" that often cut deeply and last a lifetime. Being authentically known as a mathematical learner is scary in some environments and yet being vulnerable is part of being a learner. Co-creating, with students the conditions for everyone to be known, to be vulnerable, and to be supported as human beings and learners of mathematics is a mission for me and influences all aspects of my work.

Together, theories of self-determination, flow, and shame impact my ways of being with students, my perspectives for designing curriculum, how I listen and respond to students, and ultimately for how I care for the amazing and often fragile lives I have been given the opportunity to influence. I could not tell the stories I am about to tell without recognizing this influential work for it has profoundly influenced mine. I will now briefly describe instrumental genesis as an influential construct because it connects learning with new technologies and provides a lens for viewing evidence of learning.

Instrumental Genesis

Instrumental genesis (Guin & Trouche, 1998) is a construct that may be used to explain why the use of technology may differ from person to person. "The core of instrumental genesis in mathematics education is understanding the mathematics of the technology and being able to use it for one's own purposes" (Zbiek, et al., 2007, p. 1179). I like to think of instrumental genesis as the process of "becoming one with the tool" and find this construct useful to consider when designing learning environments in which new technologies are being explored with the purpose of investigating some kind of mathematical phenomenon. Instrumental genesis is described in the literature as the process of the artifact becoming an instrument for the user.

But it is important to stress the difference between two concepts: the artifact, as a manmade material object, and the instrument, as a psychological construct. The point is that no instrument exists by itself. A machine or a technical system does not immediately constitute a tool for the subject. Even explicitly constructed as a tool, it is not, as such, an instrument for the subject. It becomes so when the subject has been able to appropriate it for himself—has been able to subordinate it as a means to his ends—and, in this respect, has integrated it with his activity. Thus, an instrument results from the establishment, by the subject, or an instrumental relation with an artifact, whether material or not, whether produced by other or by himself (Verillon & Rabardel, 1995, pp. 84-85).

As I will explore further in following sections, through my research with mathematics education graduate students who are mainly pre- and in-service mathematics teachers, I have experienced learners with little and often no facility with DCT come to appreciate the use of these tools and to take them up in their own classrooms as teachers with their students. From both past experiences as well as research literature, the kinds of transformation in belief and practice that I think I am witnessing appears profound and robust. My students begin as novices and yet they develop the courage and willingness to go live with these technologies with their students, both during and following a specially designed one-semester course. The process of instrumental genesis unfolds somewhat predictably in our communal environment. It is for these reasons I seek to better understand the mechanisms through which this transformation occurs and why it may be useful to others.

Using methods of design research (Cobb, Confrey, DiSessa, Lehrer, & Schauble, 2003), and through retrospective analyses of multiple iterations of a learning environment, three particularly useful instructional design elements have consistently contributed to teachers' mathematical learning, facility with a range of DCT, and pedagogical practices consistent with sharing authority for knowledge among students and teacher. These design tools include: (1) the

use of provocative tasks, (2) implementation of task sequences utilizing dynamic technology scaffolding, and (3) sustained intellectual press. My claim is that, collectively, these elements support teachers' development of technological pedagogical content knowledge (TPACK) (Mishra & Koehler, 2006; Niess, 2005), but there appears to be a delicate interplay between TPACK and instrumental genesis. Next, I will describe each of these design tools before illustrating them in the context of research artifacts.

Provocative Tasks

The implementation of statistically (mathematically), contextually, and technologically provocative tasks and task sequences (Blind, 2011a) may be instrumental for creating surprise and cognitive conflict for learners, and ultimately result in increased engagement, public discourse, and collective understanding of challenging mathematical ideas. This notion of *provocative tasks* grew from examination of tasks-as-enacted in another study and I have continued to pursue the construction of such tasks for their potential value to communities of learners as well as individual cognition. Most importantly is the notion that some tasks appear to be provocative on their mathematical or statistical face to some learners. Some tasks are bound up in contexts that learners seem to find especially engaging or interesting. Some tasks-as-enacted become provocative through the integration of DCT for exploration. Some tasks live in the intersections of categories (See Figure 1). It appears that not all tasks are provocative for all learners, but what appears necessary for a task to broadly support learning is that it is provocative in at least some way for at least some person. By virtue of this provocation, interesting and challenging aspects tend to come into the public space for interrogation and that provocative quality can spread. Examples of what may make a task provocative as well as classroom discourse during the implementation of provocative tasks will be provided.

Figure 1. Provocative task framework

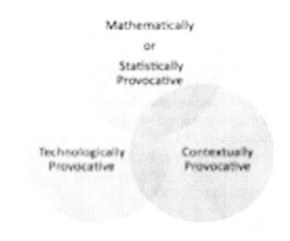

Dynamic Technology Scaffolding (DTS)

DTS (Madden, 2008, 2010) is represented by a sequence of tasks wherein during a mathematical investigation involving modeling, learners navigate from a physical environment (manipulatives) to a dynamic exploration environment (using an exploratory but expert designed tool; e.g. java applet, microworld) to a dynamic construction (using an expressive landscape tool; e.g., dynamic geometry or statistics) environment (See Figure 2). DTS has been utilized to provide learners access to complex ideas and to support technological facility of novice users with *Cabri II Geometry*,

Figure 2. Dynamic technology scaffolding model

Fathom, and *TinkerPlots*, as they have navigated new and challenging content and technological terrain. Several DTS tasks will be illustrated along with transcripts from classroom video during implementation.

Sustained Intellectual Press

Sustained intellectual press is a pedagogical commitment in which a classroom community is co-constructed such that its members come to embrace educative discomfort, cognitive conflict, cognitive overload, undefined endpoints, shared authority for knowledge, individual and group potential, multiple solution paths and ways of knowing, collective intelligence, and sharing not comparing (Madden, 2011b). Sustained intellectual press grew out of a theoretical design focus on Productive Disciplinary Engagement (PDE) (Engle & Conant, 2002). PDE "can be fostered by designing learning environments that support (1) problematizing subject matter, (2) giving students authority to address such problems, (3) holding students accountable to others and to shared disciplinary norms, and (4) providing students with relevant resources" (2002, p. 399). It was through retrospective analyses of three semesters of classroom videotape, student written artifacts, and informal dialogue between students and instructor from the graduate course that all of the dimensions of what I am calling sustained intellectual press emerged.

Technologically rich learning environments, designed to intentionally incorporate these design elements, have been spaces where learners appear to feel safe to take intellectual risks and ultimately support the learning of all members. In the following section, I will elaborate some of the challenges and successes of supporting mathematics teachers' instrumental genesis with several DCTs through the use of careful orchestration of classroom-based activities that embody principles of the design elements of provocative tasks, dynamic technology scaffolding, and sustained intellectual press. Though the research I report is with graduate students, these design elements have promise for designing learning environments for secondary mathematics students as well. Some of my students have been utilizing this modeling approach with their students and reporting productive results. To achieve the vision set forth in CCSSM, well-prepared and highly technologically skilled teachers are essential.

AN EXTENDED DESIGN EXPERIMENT: DESCRIPTION, TRAJECTORY, AND SAMPLE TASKS

For the past four years, I have been designing and studying a learning environment that exists as a one semester, graduate-level course in mathematics education. The course is typically taken by students who are either pre-service teachers in a secondary mathematics teacher-licensing program, in-service teachers pursuing Master's degrees in education, or doctoral students in the Mathematics, Science, and Learning Technology program. Recently, students pursuing Master's degrees in Applied Mathematics have discovered the course. Students tend to have at least the equivalent of an undergraduate degree in mathematics, but this varies somewhat. Reasonably strong mathematical content knowledge is assumed. Pedagogical experience and knowledge varies dramatically, from nearly none to that of very accomplished teachers. This background matters because the setting represents a strangely experientially heterogeneous mixture of students, relatively speaking. On one dimension, however, these students are quite homogeneous—their familiarity with tools, beyond pencil and paper, for exploring mathematics tends to be extremely limited.

For the most recent three of the past four years, students have completed a survey at the beginning of the course. When asked about their familiarity

with technology, students tend to mention things like *HeyMath!, Quizlet, TeacherTube, Illuminations,* Pearson's video, *Delicious, Kidblog, iPod, Windows Movie Maker,* clickers, *Smart Boards,* document cameras, graphing calculators, and overhead projectors. They also say things like, "I've tended to view technology as an add-on and not essential" or "I find graphing calculators annoying and non-intuitive," or "I am in favor of technology so long as it is not interfering with what is considered the 'normal' baseline" (all from 2012). Students are asked to rate their personal comfort level on a scale from 1 (low) to 10 (high) with a set of technological tools (the list includes: *Cabri II Geometry, Geometers' Sketchpad, GeoGebra, Fathom 2, TinkerPlots, TI-Nspire, TI-83/84 Graphing Calculator, CPMP-Tools, National Library of Virtual Manipulatives*). With the exception of TI-83/84 graphing calculators, aggregate ratings for the other tools are uniformly low (*mean* < 3, *median* < 2, $n = 36$). When asked about the frequency with which they use any of these tools in teaching, as might be expected, the ratings were even lower. Each semester, it has been clear that students in this course have not had the opportunity to learn with, or use some very powerful DCTs for exploring mathematics and consequently, when teaching students in their own classrooms, these tools are notably absent.

The course is not a technology course per se, but learning to use DCTs is a strong component of the experience. From the syllabus, students completing this course are expected to:

- Communicate knowledge of local, state and national professional recommendations for mathematics at the secondary level and use this knowledge to inform curriculum development, instruction, and assessment.
- Demonstrate an emerging understanding of how secondary students may learn mathematics with technological tools.

- Develop facility with a number of dynamic technological tools for teaching and learning mathematics.

- Utilize an increasingly sophisticated pedagogical toolkit for supporting mathematics learning for all secondary students.

- Integrate contemporary technological tools into mathematical investigations in appropriate ways to support students' learning of big mathematical ideas.

- Understand current research perspectives on student learning with technology and become cognizant of potential research in this area.

- Appreciate the challenging and important work of mathematics teaching and adopt the position that teaching is a lifelong learning endeavor worthy of spirited, intellectual engagement.

Students' initial positions about the use of technology in the mathematics classroom range from "somewhat agnostic" to "open to considering the possibility" to "I rather like mathematics the way I learned it." These beliefs coupled with limited prior opportunity to learn with DCT set the stage for the course. You may be wondering what we do in the course to move forward. Let me make one design assumption explicit here before proceeding: Given what I have come to know about learners with whom I work and the short time we have together, I choose to introduce students to dynamic geometry and dynamic statistics environments. A working conjecture that I continue to accumulate evidence to support is that once students understand the nature of constructing relationships and hot-linking virtual objects, their experiences in one environment tend to port rather seamlessly to another environment (e.g., from *Cabri II* to *Geometers Sketchpad*, *GeoGebra*, *Fathom*, and *TinkerPlots)*. One caveat to this: learning in dynamic geometry seems to be the most challenging for learners, but once instrumental

genesis occurs in this environment, moving to another DCT seems less demanding. From this standpoint and given the ubiquitous presence of graphing calculators in many schools, I devote the vast majority of technological exploration to two tools: *Cabri II Geometry* and *Fathom 2 Dynamic Statistics*. I will refer to them as *Cabri* and *Fathom* hereafter. We do explore other software tools and more advanced features of graphing calculators as appropriate during investigations.

Mathematical investigations form the basis for utilizing technology and highly demanding investigations begin the first day of class. Innovative curriculum materials are utilized periodically (e.g., *Core-Plus Mathematics Project*, *Mathematics Modeling Our World*) to explore contemporary mathematics topics in light of CCSSM and other professional recommendations. The course incorporates critical evaluation of research and practitioner literature from which to examine many aspects of mathematics teaching and learning, particularly with DCT. Students construct written responses to articles and classroom investigations; they design task sequences which might embody aspects of what we are learning; they critique each other's work and have choices to follow a practitioner or researcher path in the course.

From the retrospective analysis of four iterations of this course, design commitments common to each iteration of the course have included:

- Introductory DCT tours are completed independently by students (self-paced guides/videos).

- Community of learners and productive disciplinary engagement are fostered in the class (classroom norms).

- Non-routine, mathematically or statistically worthwhile/provocative task(s) are explored (high cognitive demand).

- Dynamic technology scaffolding experiences are implemented with multiple tools and in multiple contexts.

What follows are four selected examples that serve to illustrate the nature of some of the mathematical work explored in the course along with student examples and reflections. All of these examples relate to mathematical modeling and were selected to provide a sense of the ways in which tasks, such as these, appeared useful in supporting learners' instrumental genesis with DCT. In particular, the first three tasks are presented in an order in which they occurred during the first weeks of the semester and the final task is a student presented solution to a task that appeared near the end of the course. What you will see is the evolution of mathematical and technological skills and dispositions of learners in this environment. There were many other tasks explored both in between and after those described here. Pseudonyms are used for all student names.

Soda Can

The inspiration for the first mathematical investigation, which now begins Day 1 of the course, came from the NCTM Illuminations Website (http://illuminations.nctm.org/LessonDetail. aspx?ID=U175).

Fourteen soda cans are placed in a bin that is slightly wider than four cans, but not as wide as five cans. A first row of four cans is placed on the bottom; a second row of three cans is placed on top of the bottom row; a third row of four cans is placed next; and finally a row of three cans is placed on top.

The Illuminations task was designed to support student investigation of the properties of the top row of cans as the two middle cans on the bottom row are shifted in the bin. The reader is encouraged to explore this relationship fully at their leisure, but there are a host of potential connections to CCSSM, most notably mathematical modeling with geometric and algebraic objects. A task like this could support students' making sense of

problems and persevering in solving them, reason abstractly and quantitatively, construct and critique mathematical arguments, use appropriate tools strategically, look for and make use of structure, and perhaps even looking for and expressing regularity in repeated reasoning.

In the research environment, this task was modified to engage students in mathematical investigation while also tapping into the work of teaching. Ultimately, this task launched the class into initial investigations in a dynamic geometry environment. Through yearly design modifications, the physical aspect of the task evolved from the instructor presenting an already created physical model for students to explore (year 1), to students creating physical models with resources provided by the instructor (years 2 and 3), to students having to find resources on their own to model this phenomenon (year 4). Some of these artifacts can be seen in Figure 3 and illustrate a variety of material representations to model the situation.

The experience of creating the models always generated lively discussion about the merits of certain materials. For example, a student spoke of trying to find a balance between elegance and toughness (inability to get messed up) of the model. Regardless of materials, students consistently found constructing a model much more challenging than they imagined. Their publicly communicated struggles began the process of sharing difficulties with one another and beginning to bond as a fledgling community. Mathematically, the process of constructing a physical model highlighted issues of measurement and relative size of "cans" to "container" that would serve them later as they attempted to construct a virtual model of their own. It also served to help students make initial conjectures as to the underlying mathematical relationships constraining the top row of cans. Following some discussion, they were shown an exploratory model (Doerr & Pratt, 2008) from the Illuminations Website, which provided a virtual soda can simulation that could

Figure 3. Physical models of the soda can task

be manipulated. This seemed to help students further refine their mathematical conjectures about the top row of cans. Part of the instructional goal was to move students to a dynamic geometry software environment where they could construct a model that functioned as the physical and exploratory models appeared to. This would be their first project in *Cabri* and the first attempt at expressive modeling (Doerr & Pratt, 2008). The cognitive demand of this task is extremely high in a new software environment and this was a purposeful move.

Students had done three initial guided tours using the *Cabri II* manual and were able to utilize the construction tools in *Cabri* that might be needed to create a working soda can model. What they didn't necessarily have was a connection from the physical and exploratory models that nicely linked with the desired expressive model. Some initial screenshots of students' work and statements from students with their constructions illustrate varying levels of facility with the tool in this mathematical context at the beginning of the

course (See Figure 4). Instrumental genesis with *Cabri* was not yet in sight for these students, but the journey had begun. By this time, students had been reading, *Research on Technology in Mathematics Education: A Perspective of Constructs* (Zbiek, et al., 2007) from the *Second Handbook of Research on Mathematics Teaching and Learning* (Lester, 2007) and grappling with new language and constructs related to technology.

In an email to me while reflecting on the construction experience in *Cabri,* one student, whom I'll call Alexander, began mocking the term instrumental genesis in a somewhat playful manner when he wrote,

. . .mathematize in the context of the tool. I'm still groping in the dark banging into the furniture a lot of the time. This issue of cognitive fidelity is really coming home to me. People have ideas of what they want to do (or could do with a compass and pencil) but can't make happen the way they want to in the tool. Weird things happen and then you have to figure out why the tool is doing that.

Figure 4. Student-constructed expressive soda can models in Cabri illustrating a range of mathematical and technical facility

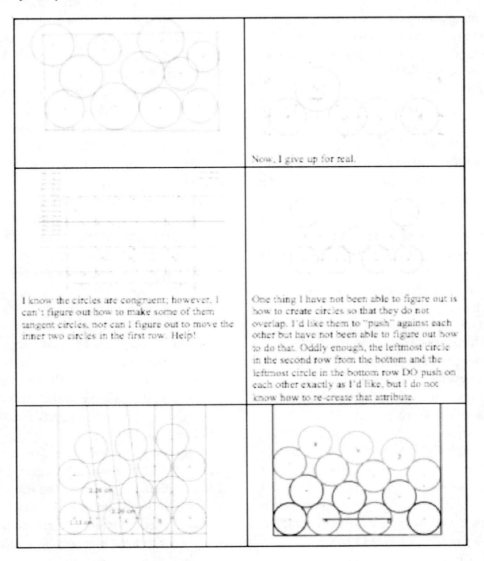

Sometimes it's really just an annoying non-feature and sometimes it's something that is important. Ultimately we will all evolve and adapt the way we solve problems to the customary methods (and perhaps some newly invented ones) that work within Cabri and then you just forget all these things that drove you crazy at first. Until you have to teach someone else and you watch them go through it! (Alexander, personal communication, January 27, 2010).

This same student, nearly two years later, continued to joke about instrumental genesis as exemplified in the following portion of an email where he provided the following multiple choice assessment question, entirely unsolicited, for me to use in my class:

What is instrumental genesis?

1.   When God created light over the void using the sun as his instrument.

2. When a person first starts to learn to play French Horn.
3. Becoming proficient with a tool.
4. An overly complex name for a simple idea (Alexander, personal communication, December 14, 2011).

This type of unsolicited, extended, and often playful communication has been common among students over the years. Many such instances of discourse with nearly every student exists both within student-constructed artifacts during the course and in many cases, after the course was completed. Communications among students, with me and each other, contained significant evidence of the community of learners that developed in which autonomy, competence, relatedness, and creativity were valued, exhibited, and intellectually nourishing.

These types of communications were augmented with continued refinement of digital soda can constructions that, in some cases, lasted the semester or beyond. Periodically, students would share progress and thinking about their models with one another. From my standpoint, it was mission accomplished: the task appeared engaging; facility with *Cabri* was developing; community was forming; and interesting mathematical connections were emerging. The task appeared mathematically and technologically provocative for students, it was their first exposure to DTS, and a commitment to sustained intellectual press was begun. This task may feel too open and lacking closure for some tastes; however, it has been the source of perturbing my students' thoughts about mathematical modeling and mathematics in general. More connections between the soda can task and CCSSM will become evident in a future section of this chapter.

Paper Folding and the Parabola

A second task sequence explored in each course was the paper folding task (See Figure 5). The task was constructed as a second experience with DTS, to introduce paper folding as a mathematical tool, and to support further construction facility with Cabri. Beyond many of the standards for mathematical practice, this task sequence supports the CCSSM Content Standard, Expressing Geometric Properties (G-GPE) and the equation of a conic section. In particular, Translate between the geometric description and the equation for a conic section: "Derive equation of a parabola given a focus and directrix" (p.78). If one knows the focus and directrix, then finding the vertex of the parabola is trivial. Using the vertex form of a quadratic equation, $y = (x - h)^2 + k$, with (h, k) the vertex point, becomes a straightforward exercise. The task sequence also addresses:

Modeling with Geometry (G-MG): "Use geometric shapes, their measures, and their properties to describe objects" (p. 78) is addressed. In this case the object is the parabola.

Congruence (G-CO), Make geometric constructions: Make formal geometric constructions with a variety of tools and methods (compass and straightedge, string, reflective devices, paper folding, dynamic geometric software, etc.); and "Apply geometric methods to solve design problems" (p. 76).

Only one of 36 students had prior experience with paper folding, which meant that this was a novel medium for students. The patty paper creation was accessible to all students and interesting to most. Then, a dynamic demonstration of an already constructed parabola-generating mechanism in *Cabri* provided an existence proof that it could be done and students quickly went into *Cabri* to see if they could construct some type of mechanism create a working model. Confidence was high, *Cabri* facility was getting better and students appeared eager to get to work. As students' constructions evolved, many students began to exhibit signs of cognitive conflict. What they thought to do was not working. Trying to replicate the paper folding actions in *Cabri*, students could generate the "paper fold," but they tended not to realize that the locus of paper folded lines that generates the appearance of the parabola does not

Figure 5. The paper folding parabola task

Paper Folding and Technology Investigation

Part I

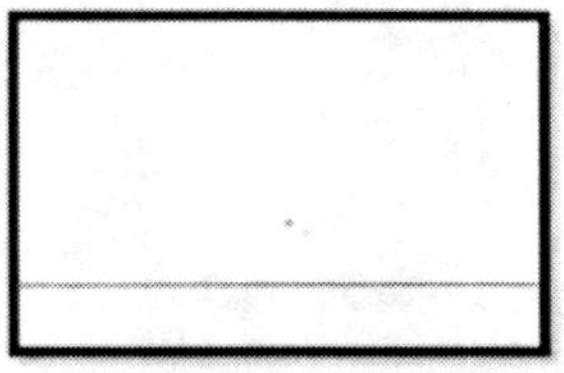

Materials needed:
Patty Paper
Pencil
Ruler

Directions:
On a sheet of patty paper, draw a thick line close to the bottom of the paper (should extend from one side to the other of the paper). Somewhere above the line, within an inch or so of the line and near the horizontal center of the paper, mark a point with a dot and label the point P. Mark at least 12 distinct points on the line.

At each point on the line, neatly fold the paper so that point P lies directly over the point on the line. Crease the paper at the fold and then repeat with the remaining points on the line.

Once you have completed the paper folding for all of your points, examine your patty paper. What do you notice? Have you generated a familiar mathematical object? Describe what you see. What mathematical relationships help to explain the object that was generated?

If time permits, you may try additional paper folding by varying the location of point P with respect to your line segment and try to notice the impact of result compared to the relative placement of the line segment and point. When P is closer to the line or further away, how does the outcome change?

Part II
You will see a dynamic model of the physical model you just constructed. You are encouraged to make connections between Part I and Part II in preparation for Part III.

Part III
Materials needed:
Cabri II Plus or other dynamic geometry software

Directions:
Your task is to use the tools available in the software to construct a mechanism to model the relationship you discovered in part one. Be prepared to discuss your construction and any difficulties you had while working on this task

generate the set of points that actually comprise the parabola. This turns out to be a particularly elusive relationship at first, for most students. Because locus definitions were less familiar to students and because of the unintended, but fortuitous epistemological obstacle created by the paper folding activity, the construction required a great deal of mathematizing and testing in *Cabri*. See Figure 6 for DTS representations of this task. The task took on a contextually, mathematically, and technologically provocative quality for students.

As will be evidenced in a classroom discussion that occurs several weeks after the paper folding task and several additional DTS experiences (in 2012), the paper folding task served as an anchor and a source of extended reflection. As a course requirement and about midway through the semester, students were asked to design two DTS sequences using any tools and any content that made sense for them. The project was wide open, but a chance for the students to grapple with the work of teaching in this capacity. What constitutes a big idea? What is big enough? What tools support this work? What could the sequence look like so that students are making meaningful connections from one level to the next and such that each task serves as a scaffold for the next? Students struggled to generate what they considered worthwhile DTS sequences for their projects. As this shared struggle was voiced, the 2012 class engaged in a discussion of DTS sequences that had been explored in class. A student mentioned the paper folding parabola activity and the following dialogue commenced.

SM: So, we already had an idea of what was going on with this phenomenon (dragging the free point on the directrix and seeing the

Figure 6. *Illustrations of the dynamic technology scaffolding artifacts from the paper folding parabola task*

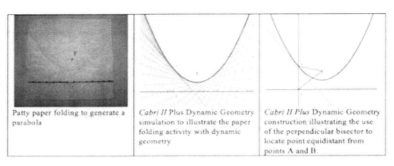

locus of points making up the parabola), in some ways. I wonder what mathematical ideas you gained through the construction in Cabri. You already knew what a parabola was. At this point, you were grappling with the locus definition, but you kind of had a sense of "how did it work?" But what were the mathematical ideas that were gained in addition to learning about the locus points of the parabola that you had already kind of figured out? (pause) Because we messed around with that for a while.

Connor: *Well, I could think that one of the mathematical ideas has to do with just how mathematical knowledge is formed, in general. Just in terms of how we all worked on it together. And um, and built up the construction of the model as a group. So as far as the mathematical idea, I'd say that it's, um, it reflects how math is done in general, as a part of just offering ideas, you know, talking about them, maybe changing them a bit, building them up, and then eventually understanding, coming to a general conclusion as a whole.*

SM: *OK. So you're talking about the whole process of mathematizing.*

Connor: *Um hum. The process.*

SM: *All right, fair enough.*

According to Radford, Schubring, and Seeger (2011), "in mathematics learning, it is not easy to find how meaning is related to the world of objects partly because the meaning is not related to more

or less material objects but to the activity itself. The key to meaning-making can only be to base it on the development of a communal practice of meaning making" (p. 155). Here we see evidence from the perspective of Connor who recognizes the importance of the activity in the public space as ideas and representations were being explored. Another student then mentions construction versus drawing in a dynamic geometry environment.

Alyse: *Constructing versus just drawing. I could have easily just drawn the parabola, but having to construct it so that that definition is true--it's a definition I'd never even, maybe had heard at one point, but didn't know.*

SM: *Yeah. So that construction/drawing thing, that was in play maybe still at that point for us. OK.*

Adriana: *I think when we did it as a group and we tried to do it with the circles, because I think, you know how we talked, people wanted to do it with the circles [referring to the construction]? We had that point of challenging our cognitive fidelity, when the right hand of the parabola went up and we were all like, "Yeah!" But then we went the other way and it didn't do the other half. We were like, "Nooooo!" (laughter) Because we knew what we expected to happen, but it didn't and then, so we knew we had to go back to the drawing board and sort of start again and see if we could get the other half to come in to play with the circles.*

Cathy: I think, like what Connor was saying about learning, like this process, it just helps it stick for later. Maybe, I don't know if we learned, like, new mathematical ideas through that activity, but I feel like that definition of parabola will now be stuck in my mind forever because I went through that process. And if you just kind of showed it on the board, and said oh, "this definition," I might have forgotten it by now.

SM: So something about you actually constructing that, and that's kind of what you were saying too (Connor), you're constructing those ideas. You're making those connections personally for yourself.

Cathy: Yeah, just really engaged.

Johann: We ah, we also like were, I mean, even though we were talking about parabolas, which are traditionally sort of an algebraic structure, in like, traditional high school math, we were looking at isosceles triangles, we were looking at like, tangent lines, slope lines, tangent points on the parabola, bisectors, and seeing how this one definition leads into a lot of other interesting, um, pieces of geometry that we address in high school.

This exchange illustrates students being willing to voice their mathematical vulnerabilities with one another and it captures the reflective nature of one class of students. Collectively, students reconstructed both process and content components of the task and confirmed the challenges and successes that they remembered. The DTS experience, and particularly the construction in *Cabri*, was more complex than they had imagined, but the benefit was that they clearly constructed mathematical and technological meaning from the experience. And according to their own words, the meaning appears robust.

Varignon Parallelogram

A third example is the result of the following question: What happens when you construct the midpoints of the sides of a quadrilateral and join consecutive midpoints with segments? Students physically modeled this situation (See Figure 7). Four students volunteered to be vertices of a random quadrilateral that would be formed using a long loop of ribbon. Four more students volunteered to be midpoints of each side of the quadrilateral. The group needed to determine a strategy for locating the midpoints of each side. After some debate and without measuring tools, students arrived at a plan where students representing adjacent vertices would come together, allowing the ribbon to be folded in half, thus identifying a midpoint. Each pair of adjacent vertices followed suit. With the midpoints determined, a long elastic loop was used to form the quadrilateral formed by joining adjacent midpoints. Students conjectured about the nature of the quadrilateral formed in this way and then proceeded to explore the non-rigidity of the original ribbon quadrilateral and resultant midpoint quadrilateral. Conjectures continued and new quadrilateral constructions were created and explored. All students in the class were actively

Figure 7. Two separate groups of students physically modeling the Varignon parallelogram construction

engaged, either as vertices, conjecturers, or both. Mathematical arguments began to be formed. Students then moved to the *Cabri* environment, where, they readily constructed a dynamic quadrilateral and midpoint quadrilateral to interrogate the relationships further, eventually resulting in a proof that the resultant quadrilateral was indeed a parallelogram.

This task was well within the skill level of students with *Cabri* at this point in the semester, but it served to extend a physical exploration that had "construction" limitations to a more flexible space. It also served as pedagogical modeling regarding the structure of a physical activity, the use of cheap and available resources, and student engagement in ways not necessarily typical in their prior experiences. Given that the "Varignon Parallelogram Kit" cannot be ordered from stores, a healthy discussion about the work of teaching that includes thinking about materials that may be used to provide access to tasks like this was pivotal to some students. The fact that "we" did it may have influenced their thinking about how they might do something like it. Maybe even more significantly, the experience gave them some kind of permission to pursue these types of tasks with students. It was interesting to them. They saw how it might go with real humans, and they were making meaning through the mathematical experience. The task had a contextually provocative nature during the physical modeling phase and by this point in the course, students could readily construct and explore these mathematical relationships in *Cabri,* so their sense of competency was high. Instrumental genesis with *Cabri* was evident from students' use of the software to investigate and eventually prove Varignon's Parallelogram Theorem. The artifact had become an instrument for exploring mathematical relationships for these students.

Approximately 60% of course time was devoted to exploring mathematical tasks and curricula that would align with the use of *Cabri,* such as those presented so far. The remaining 40% of the course targeted mathematical tasks and curricula

for which dynamic statistics software would be relevant. Using *Fathom* as the primary software tool, students would encounter instrumental genesis in a different DCT. The same design principles were used to select and implement tasks when introducing this new tool. Due to space limitations, I will not illustrate the trajectory, but rather fast-forward to an example of what students were able to do within a very short time of working in the new DCT environment. My working conjecture is that the experiences in *Cabri,* involving hot-linking mathematical objects via dynamic constructions provided scaffolding for work in a new tool.

Semi Circle Problem

Three points are chosen at random on the unit circle. Find the probability that all three points lie on some semicircle.

Some students pursued this task after reading, *Can You Fathom This? Connecting Data Analysis, Algebra, and Probability Simulation* (Edwards & Phelps, 2008). Figure 8 is one students' simulation to solve this problem. This student created a powerful construction in which she generated 100 sets of three random angle measures between 0 and 2π, computed *sin* and *cos* for each to establish unit circle coordinates and so she could generate a visual geometric representation, computed side lengths of each side of the triangle from coordinates using the distance formula, set up a set of decision rules invoking the Pythagorean Theorem to determine whether a random triad of points would result in a triangle within a semicircle. Finally, she used this logic to set up an empirical sampling distribution in order to accurately approximate the probability of a random triangle lying on a semicircle. Mathematical modeling? Statistical modeling? Problem solving? Persistence? Powerful 21st century computational thinking? All of the above.

When you see many students taking up the use of DCT to invoke the kind of thinking represented in Figure 8 and when you acknowledge that these same students began the semester with

Figure 8. A sample simulation in Fathom2 to model the semi-circle problem

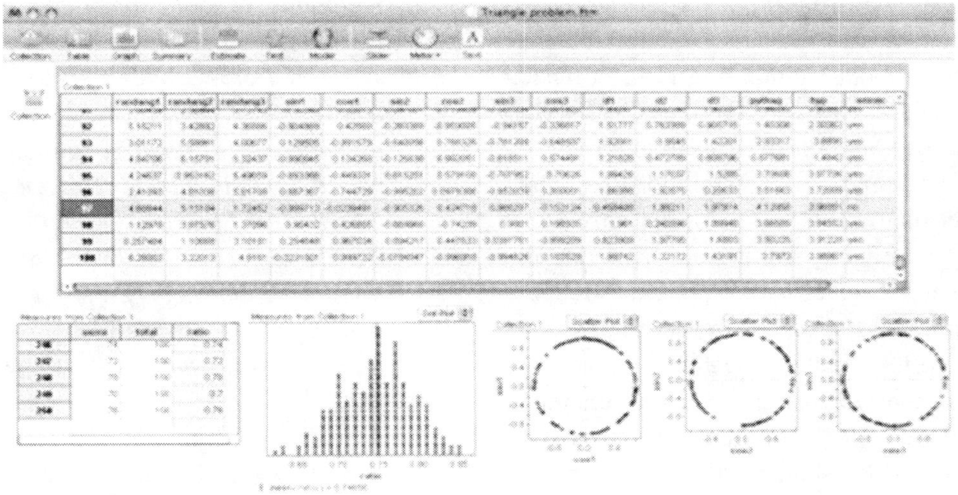

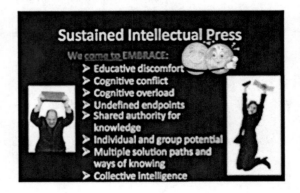

typically very limited technological facility with the kinds of tools explored, you develop a sense that something powerful and transformative is happening. At the end of the course in 2010, I began to systematically explore this phenomenon.

The Genesis of Sustained Intellectual Press

The following exchange takes place in 2011 with a group of graduate students who had been studying with me in the course that is the setting from which this writing emerged. I had been retrospectively analyzing videotape and other classroom artifacts and dialogue from several iterations of the course trying to unpack and understand what might be contributing to what I was seeing as unusually positive results. Given that students appeared to develop strong facility with several DCTs and that they demonstrated what I would consider to be strong evidence of instrumental genesis and powerful mathematical thinking, I sought to understand this apparently robust phenomenon. Using methods of grounded theory (Strauss & Corbin, 1998), I identified a construct I called "sustained intellectual press," and I wanted to

share my analysis and thinking with students and to solicit their feedback and to serve as a member check. I presented them with a slide, which at the time looked like Figure 9. I asked them to think about whether what I was claiming fit with their experience and whether they had alternate claims or other things that made sense from their view.

Students agreed with what had emerged from the research, but helped me to amend the text on the slide to include a characteristic that I had overlooked. They used the language of, "In this class, it's about sharing, not comparing." They were right. My experience was consistent with

Figure 9. Draft slide representing characteristics of sustained intellectual press

their assessment and the videotapes confirmed it. In my terms it had lived implicitly among some of the other characteristics, but given that students were emphatic about including it, I did. It made sense to all of us. That was an important aspect of our work together. Through the exploration of tasks with undefined endpoints and all of the other conditions listed, we created a space together where meaning making and negotiation were the norm. We shared authority for knowledge.

A two minute, fifty second transcript of video is provided to illuminate the nature of negotiating conversations in this space. Unfortunately, transcript alone cannot capture the emotion and the tone of the discussion, but it provides strong evidence of things that repeatedly surfaced during this course experience: students share their professional vulnerability, they publically challenge their own conceptions of mathematics and beliefs about what it means to learn and teach mathematics, and they begin to recognize that DCTs may afford learners, including themselves, opportunities to make important mathematical connections in ways they may have never imagined.

Allen: I definitely agree with that [referring to the slide]. It's about the amount of time that we had, but I don't think it's just like because we had time here [during class]. I mean, if we had half an hour and then you set us free. There was no, "this is the end of the chapter [slapping hand on the table to indicate closure], now we're going to work on this." There was never a packaged finish to anything. You know, like you bring back up the soda can thing, and I'm like, "Oh yeah, I was thinking about that and how I was going to figure out the stupid vectors." You know, like it's still going.

SM: Well and then, I have people writing to me saying, "I need to take a break and I went out and walked the dog and I figured this out" or they write, "I was in the shower and I was still thinking about this." So that's

what I mean by that [referring to undefined endpoints]. There's something, like it's still working, it's still playing.

Laura: I don't know about anybody else, but I can't get away from it. I think about that now, that dynamic technology scaffolding, every single time [laughter]. I mean, no matter where I am. I'm walking, and I'm thinking, "OK, I've got to do more physical things for my kids so that I can get to the exploratory and hopefully get to the expressive. . .It's non-, it's gotta stop. It's non-stop [laughter].

SM: Well, but even if. . .

Laura: But I never thought of it before. I never thought of it before and now I'm constantly thinking about it.

SM: Is it because it was important for you?

Laura: I think it's important for me, yes, but as an educator I'm just trying to. . ., I have to give my kids, I have to provide my kids more opportunities, activities, to construct on many levels [hand gestures to indicate this]. Not only physically, but mentally [pointing to her head] too. And I'm, I'm not doing that now [voice quivering].

SM: OK.

Laura: So I'm constantly thinking of, "OK, I've got to get better. I've got to get better. I've got to. . . there's got to be more hands on, more physical, to get to the next level, because I seem to be just jumping into, OK, this is the theorem, this is what we do, and that's the way we do it and so and then the next day they come in and there's no recall at all [gesture indicates strong feeling]. It's like, yeah, because it means nothing to you, you're not taking ownership, it's not going in here [pointing to her head], you're not connecting.

Yvonne: I feel not understood by my husband [lots of laughter]. I open the fridge and we have like this thing to put cans [gesturing with hands to describe cans going in], and I took one and it's like [gesturing with arm to indicate motion of shifting cans] [lots of laughter], you know that we're doing this problem with the soda cans where they go like this [motions with hands]. He looks at me like [makes funny face indicating something like, are you crazy?] [Lots more laughter], "Forget about it" [apparently said affectionately].

Laura: *Yeah, I walk around the house thinking, "OK, can I use that for something?" and "Don't throw that out yet, wait a minute, I've got to wash that out—that may come in handy."*

IMPLICATIONS, CHALLENGES, FUTURE DIRECTIONS

Most students in the learning environment described herein teach or will be teaching mathematics to secondary students under the auspices of CCSSM. To support the work of teaching, as tasks were debriefed and sometimes along the way, connections to CCSSM were made explicit. Students became familiar with the document as they searched for myriad ways in which each of the mathematical tasks that they explored embodied content and practice standards. For each task, usually long lists of possibilities were generated. Students began to understand new possibilities of using a single task sequence to support many content and practice standards simultaneously. They also began to think about ways in which a task may simply plant a seed to be germinated and grown later.

There is, however, a tension between how the content standards in CCSSM are perceived and the possibility of harnessing technology for reasoning and sense making. There is a tension between learning to think and reason mathematically and having to be tested without the tools you may have come to appreciate and utilize in powerful ways. There is a tension about being judged using some obsolete metric and preparing children

for life in the 21st century. Teachers with whom I have worked have come to value DCT as they have lived instrumental genesis with them for doing mathematics because of the powerful images and representation they have been able to construct, manipulate and interrogate. Many highly trained learners in my classroom have bumped into mathematics in ways that have been profoundly new and initially uncomfortable for them.

When given choices for projects near the end of the course, some students have elected to independently explore additional DCTs in order to present alternatives to the class (e.g., *GeoGebra, TI-Nspire, TinkerPlots, CPMP-Tools*). It has been fascinating to witness the flexibility with which these learners operate once they "become one" with *Cabri* and *Fathom*. Though transfer is not direct, it appears that work with dynamic geometry and dynamic statistical tools is portable. Some students explored *Cabri 3D* while constructing a response to a written case study of a teacher attempting to provide instruction around surface area and volume problems of cylinders. Others explored innovative instructional materials and modified lessons to incorporate DCT where appropriate. Some students worked in teams to construct, implement, and analyze lessons where they incorporated DCTs.

CCSSM provides a framework for thinking about opportunities all students should have to learn mathematics, but it does not provide a road map for how to offer those opportunities. Though work on learning progressions is being done to create some maps, I suggest that there is not a one-size fits all learning progression or textbook or tool that will be the panacea. Rather, good instructional materials, including DCT resources in the hands of well prepared, thoughtful, and flexible teachers is a necessity. The research discussed herein is encouraging because it suggests that there is hope in achieving this. The learners with whom I worked repeatedly demonstrated a newfound appreciation for what insights tools could offer, whether physical manipulatives, existing expert exploratory models, or environments where individuals had flexibility to construct. They demonstrated flexibility navigating among DCTs and an eagerness to use these tools with their own students.

Over the course of several studies, data have accumulated to suggest that the nature of the experiences in the graduate course may have had a profound effect on the students. One student said, "I like figuring out things in the dynamic geometry environment because I feel like I have a chance" (Alexander, personal communication, June 1, 2012). This represents powerful affect and alludes to issues to self-determination. Another student, from 2010, was a self-proclaimed geometry-averse, technology skeptic at the beginning of the course. She was a particularly reluctant learner in terms of her disposition to some of the initial tasks. About halfway through the course, she decided to try using dynamic geometry software with her students while she was in the middle of her intern teaching. One notable aspect of this was that it was not required and she was electing to try something of her own volition. Completely unsolicited, she sent the following email message to me. It is this kind of sharing with the instructor and with peers that appears contagious. It seems that other students that may have been reticent to go live with technology with their own students, are encouraged by their peers' experiences. Perhaps success breeds success.

Just wanted to write you a quick note to tell you that our use of Geometer's Sketchpad in the classroom yesterday was quite successful! There were some kids that acted just as I predicted - hesitant to try any of it and literally needing a step-by-step guide to prevent mental/mathematical breakdown; but there were also a bunch of kids who acted as you and others in the class have said - eager and willing to try, discovering functions on their own, etc. It was especially beneficial to me that the first class of the day (of four to use the program) was

a bright class that fell into the latter category, and so I learned a lot about the activity before our 'problem' class came around.

Some of the positive comments I got:

"Ms. Baggley, we should have math class in here from now on".

"THIS WAS AWESOME!!!" [literally screaming at the end of class, haha!]

"I couldn't really get it on paper but now I see it".

A few kids even asked if they could access the program at home, and I told them about Cabri's free download [hopefully they would have more success than I did!].

Anyway, that's all I wanted to share:) See you later on in class (Evelyn, personal communication, March 20, 2010).

This is but one of many examples of a person who leaned into her own vulnerability and decided to take a risk. She managed to construct a beginning existence proof of what might be possible with children in her classroom. From a research perspective, it continues to be important to ask questions about how to increase the likelihood that our teachers and future teachers come to see the importance of DCT for learning mathematics. Moreover, if we can engineer learning environments for this to happen, we still have issues of equity and scaling up to better understand.

CONCLUSION

I share this work because there appears a certain robustness in the ideas presented here. What has happened in this learning environment appears not random; it has become predictable to a great degree. To support students' mathematical opportunities to learn, we must have teachers who have both an appreciation of what that might mean, especially in light of the powerful digital technologies available and constantly evolving today. We want to engage all students in mathematical meaning making endeavors and that means having tools and dispositions with promise for doing this. CCSSM supports standards for mathematical practice that include using tools strategically, among others. In my work, I have routinely been working with students who have come to my courses with very little exposure to powerful DCT for mathematical exploration. The use of provocative tasks, dynamic technology scaffolding, and sustained intellectual press have been characteristics of our work together that have positively impacted students' beliefs about mathematics and technology, and their facility with tools. Instrumental genesis has occurred for my students as they have "become one" with *Cabri* and *Fathom* software and have used these tools, and others, as instruments for their mathematical excursions. Many of these students have gone on to pursue the use of these tools with their own students.

Brene Brown says, "Stories are just data with a soul." My students and I share and bare our mathematical souls because together we achieve great things. We learn, we grow, and we wonder. We have the courage to dream of a productive mathematical future for ALL of our students. We are empowered and self-determined and sometimes we are even in flow. I will leave you with a few examples of parts of students' final reflections at the end of the course. Do not take my word for it; take theirs (HSIRB approved research).

Student 1 Reflection

My views on the use of technology for teaching and learning of mathematics have drastically changed since the beginning of the course. I never even knew some of this technology even existed until I encountered it in this course. Also, since

I am taking undergraduate mathematics classes simultaneously with this course, I have really been able to see what benefits the technology offers as well as what the profound effect if can have on learning and understanding. For example, I will probably never forget the moment I realized the relationship between a function and its derivative. It was not until I was working in *Cabri II Plus*, and its drag and trace functions, that I realized the relationship. Not only did it help me make sense of mathematical concepts I learned in my first calculus class, but it also helped me understand concepts like integrals and area that I might never have realized without the use of this technology. I cannot begin to imagine all the positive benefits this dynamic software can have in a classroom when it is utilized regularly. Students can extend their knowledge to areas they might never have dreamed of. (Melissa, personal communication, May 2009)

Student 2 Reflection

This course has brought to my attention just how inadequate the technology at the school I work in is for the purposes of teaching mathematics. The classrooms are not equipped with the technology and the current staff has little knowledge of dynamic technology. (I am changing that) Since I began the course I have pushed for a set of graphing calculators and am now the proud owner of a set of 30 TI-84 Plus calculators. I have convinced the technology department to download *GeoGebra* onto the computer in the computer lab and onto one of the laptop carts. My next challenge will be to obtain the monies to acquire Fathom. . . .The introduction to *Fathom* was my favorite part of the course. I was introduced to a new type of instruction that combined more than one area of mathematics and lead to a direction that I would not have anticipated in the first couple of units. Fathom actually helped me in understanding sampling distributions (Lacy, personal communication, May 2009).

Student 3 Reflection

This course has made me rethink and re-evaluate my views about the use of technology in teaching and learning mathematics. I had limited exposure to interactive mathematical software before taking this class. . . .

While getting exposed to more interactive software such as *Cabri, Geogebra*, and *Fathom* during this course, learning about the software, their history, reading the manuals etc. was helpful, what helped most in convincing me of the usefulness of these software was engaging with the software as a middle or high school student would; that is, learning about the software while engaging in tasks designed for middle and high school students. Especially in tasks that involved physical models, we (the students in class) used the interactive software to explore relationships and conjectures we had made using the physical models. We also made lots of connections that sometimes worked and other times didn't. While struggling through the tasks, trying to build models in *Cabri* for example, we realized how many of us perceived things differently, or tried to solve the same task in different ways, and we learned when our own models worked, or did not work, or somebody else's model worked. That whole process of struggling and learning together was probably the most convincing part. We were trying to make sense of math on our own, using the software, but also learning from each other while doing so. I think the way class activities and class discussions were designed lent itself to more of a "community-learning" experience, if you may, than it would be if students were learning just by themselves. It was very obvious how "learners with a broad range of mathematical backgrounds and technological sophistication [could] access powerful mathematical ideas, make new connections, and develop confidence in figuring things out. In addition, they [could] develop productive habits of mind as they explore, persevere, and problem solve" (Madden 2010: 282). . . .

The use of technology in teaching mathematics will also make it much more accessible to a larger proportion of students. It will also help them see the magic and beauty of mathematics as Lockhart says, something that students hardly ever get to experience. I could see that sense of awe in my students' eyes when I showed them a geogebra app depicting Archimedes method of calculating the value of pi, and I could feel that sense of awe when we, in class, were showed some of the things that *Cabri 3-d* was capable of doing. I end this semester wanting so badly to be in my own classroom and for my students to experience that feeling of awe, of how amazingly cool mathematics can be. What's so promising about these software that we explored is that they offer so much potential whether you are using it for something as "simple" as the tasks described in Lockhart's Lament, or more complicated investigations from the *Core-Plus* curriculum. Such software should be made an integral part of the math curriculum, not to be used just 3 or 4 times during the year, but rather to be part of the daily or weekly routines (Sarah, personal communication, May 2012).

REFERENCES

Brown, B. (2007). *I thought it was just me: Women reclaiming power and courage in a culture of shame*. New York: Gotham Books.

Brown, B. (2010). *The gifts of imperfection: Let go of who you thinnk you're supposed to be and embrace who you are*. Center City, MN: Hazelden.

Cobb, P., Confrey, J., DiSessa, A., Lehrer, R., & Schauble, L. (2003). Design experiments in educational research. *Educational Researcher, 32*(1), 9–13. doi:10.3102/0013189X032001009.

Csikszentmihalyi, M. (1990). *Flow: The psychology of optimal experience*. New York: Harper and Row.

Csikszentmihalyi, M., & Csiksentmihalyi, I. S. (Eds.). (2006). *A life worth living: Contributions to positive psychology.* New York: Oxford University Press.

Cuoco, A., Goldenberg, E. P., & Mark, J. (1996). Habits of mind: An organizing principle for mathematics curricula. *The Journal of Mathematical Behavior, 15,* 375–402. doi:10.1016/S0732-3123(96)90023-1.

Doerr, H. M., & Pratt, D. (2008). The learning of mathematics and mathematical modeling. In M. K. Heid & G. W. Blume (Eds.), Research on technology and the teaching and learning of mathematics: Volume 1: Research syntheses (Vol. 1, pp. 259-286). Charlotte, NC: Information Age Publishing, Inc.

Edwards, M. T., & Phelps, S. (2008). Can you fathom this? Connecting data analysis algebra, and probability simulation. *Mathematics Teacher, 102*(3), 210–217.

Engle, R., & Conant, F. (2002). Guiding principles for fostering productive disciplinary engagement: Explaining emerging argument in a community of learners classroom. *Cognition and Instruction, 20*(4), 399–483. doi:10.1207/S1532690XCI2004_1.

Frykholm, J. (2004). Teachers' tolerance for discomfort: Implications for curricular reform in mathematics. *Journal of Curriculum and Supervision, 19*(2), 125–149.

Guin, D., & Trouche, L. (1998). The complex process of converting tools into mathematical instruments: The case of calculators. *International Journal of Computers for Mathematical Learning, 3*(3), 195–227. doi:10.1023/A:1009892720043.

Leont'ev, A. N. (1978). *Activity, consciousness, and personality.* Englewood Cliffs, NJ: Prentice-Hall.

Leontyev [or Leont'ev], A. N. (2009). *Activity and consciousness.* Pacifica, CA: MIA.

Lester, F. K. (Ed.). (2007). *Second handbook of research on mathematics teaching and learning (Vol. 2).* Charlotte, NC: Information Age Publishing.

Madden, S. R. (2008). *Dynamic technology scaffolding: A design principle with potential to support statistical conceptual understanding.* Paper presented at the ICME, Monterrey, Mexico.

Madden, S. R. (2010). Designing mathematical learning environments for teachers. *Mathematics Teacher, 104*(4), 274-282.

Madden, S. R. (2011a). Statistically, technologically, and contextually provocative tasks: Supporting teachers' informal inferential reasoning. *Mathematical Thinking and Learning, 13*(1-2), 109-131.

Madden, S. R. (2011b). *Supporting teachers developing instrumental genesis with dynamic mathematical software.* Paper presented at the National Council of Teachers of Mathematics Research Presession.

Mishra, P., & Koehler, M. J. (2006). Technological pedagogical content knowledge: A framework for teacher knowledge. *Teachers College Record, 180*(6), 1017–1054. doi:10.1111/j.1467-9620.2006.00684.x.

National Governors Association and State Education Chiefs. (2010). *Common core state standards initiative: Preparing America's students for college & career.* Author.

National Research Council. (2001). *Adding it up: Helping children learn mathematics.* Washington, DC: National Academy Press.

Niess, M. L. (2005). Preparing teachers to teach science and mathematics with technology: Developing a technology pedagogical content knowledge. *Teaching and Teacher Education, 21*(5), 509–523. doi:10.1016/j.tate.2005.03.006.

Pea, R. (1985). Beyond amplification: Using the computer to reorganize mental functioning. *Educational Psychologist, 20*(4), 167–182. doi:10.1207/s15326985ep2004_2.

Radford, L., Schubring, G., & Seeger, F. (2011). Signifying and meaning-making in mathematical thinking, teaching, and learning. *Educational Studies in Mathematics*, (77): 149–156. doi:10.1007/s10649-011-9322-5.

Ryan, R. M., & Deci, E. L. (2000). Self-determination theory and the facilitation of intrinsic motivation, social development, and well-being. *The American Psychologist, 55*(1), 68–78. doi:10.1037/0003-066X.55.1.68 PMID:11392867.

Strauss, A. L., & Corbin, J. M. (1998). *Basics of qualitative research: Techniques and procedures for developing grounded theory*. Thousand Oaks, CA: Sage.

Verillon, P., & Rabardel, P. (1995). Cognition and artifacts: A contribution to the study of thought in relation to instrumented activity. *European Journal of Psychology of Education, 10*(1), 77–101. doi:10.1007/BF03172796.

Vygotsky, L. S. (1962). *Thought and language* (Hanfmann, E., & Vakar, G., Trans.). New York: John Wiley & Sons, Inc. doi:10.1037/11193-000.

Vygotsky, L. S. (1978). *Mind in society: The development of higher psychological processes*. Cambridge, MA: Harvard University Press.

Zbiek, R. M., Heid, M. K., Blume, G. W., & Dick, T. P. (2007). Research on technology in mathematics education: A perspective of constructs. In Frank, J., & Lester, K. (Eds.), *Second Handbook of Research on Mathematics Teaching and Learning (Vol. 2*, pp. 1169–1208). Charlotte, NC: Information Age Publishing.

Zbiek, R. M., & Hollebrands, K. (2008). A research-informed view of the process of incorporating mathematics technology into classroom practice by in-service and prospective teachers. In M. K. Heid & G. W. Blume (Eds.), *Research on technology and the teaching and learning of mathematics: Volume I, research syntheses*. Charlotte, NC: Information Age Publishing, Inc.

KEY TERMS AND DEFINITIONS

Dynamic Technology Scaffolding: A modeling task sequence in which learners begin by exploring with a physical model, then move to an exploratory (expert) model frequently in a microworld or applet environment, and finally to an expressive model in which learners construct dynamic mechanisms to explore a mathematical phenomenon.

Flow: The psychological state achieved when the challenge of a task matches the skill level of the individual, thus resulting in a pleasurable experience.

Instrumental Genesis: The process by which an artifact becomes an instrument for a user. I refer to instrumental genesis as "becoming one with the tool".

Provocative Task: A task which creates cognitive conflict, surprise, or interest such that it increases engagement and supports learning for a community of learners.

Sustained Intellectual Press: A pedagogical commitment to support a community of learners through purposely embracing educative discomfort, cognitive conflict, cognitive overload, undefined endpoints, shared authority for knowledge, individual and group potential, multiple solution paths and ways of knowing, collective intelligence, and sharing not comparing.

Chapter 21

A Framework for Developing Robust Online Professional Development Materials to Support Teacher Practice under the Common Core

Theodore Kopcha
University of Georgia, USA

Keri Duncan Valentine
University of Georgia, USA

ABSTRACT

The purpose of this chapter is to present a framework for developing online professional development materials to support teachers as they adopt the Common Core standards. The framework builds conceptually from the principles associated with successful mathematics professional development on the teaching practices that support productive mathematical discourse in the classroom. The framework was applied to online materials developed from an emergent perspective (Cobb & Yackel, 1996) in the context of the Common Core fractions standards at the elementary level. Implications for the use of the framework to guide the selection, development, and implementation of mathematics professional development are discussed.

PROBLEM STATEMENT

With the impending adoption of the Common Core standards and assessments in the majority of states, there is a tremendous need for resources and professional development (professional development)

materials that support elementary teachers as they transition to a standards-based approach to teaching mathematics. The new standards emphasize conceptual understanding of mathematics through problem solving rather than learning mathematics as isolated computational procedures. Specifically,

DOI: 10.4018/978-1-4666-4086-3.ch021

the Common Core standards promote instruction that creates opportunities to learn mathematical content as it is used in real world practices. These practices draw heavily on the National Council of Teachers of Mathematics (NCTM) (2000) process standards, such as promoting mathematical reasoning and communication, using mathematical representations, solving problems, and connecting across mathematical concepts.

One way in which these standards can be met is by teaching with cognitively demanding tasks (CDTs). CDTs are rich tasks that create opportunities for teachers and students to explore and discuss mathematics, develop multiple solution strategies, connect across mathematical concepts, and often embed computational practice within the larger context of higher-order thinking (Boston & Smith, 2009; Franke, Kazemi, & Battey, 2007; Smith & Stein, 1998; Stein, Grover, & Henningsen, 1996). The NCTM (2012) strongly promotes teacher use of problem solving activities with the characteristics of CDTs in an effort to increase student understanding of mathematical concepts. Teaching with CDTs has the potential to meet the goal of the Common Core to bring mathematical content and practice together in the context of authentic problems.

There are key teaching practices associated with successful implementation of CDTs in the classroom and in a manner that meets the Common Core standards. Generally, these practices facilitate rich mathematical discussion that sustains cognitive demand throughout the exploration or solving of a problem. Stein, Engle, Smith, and Hughes (2008) identified five practices that support effective mathematical discourse in the classroom. Those practices are described briefly:

- **Anticipating:** Anticipating involves teachers predicting possible student responses as they explore mathematical tasks. This includes anticipating appropriate mathematical thinking around a task, misinterpretations of a problem, and possible mis-

conceptions that students might hold. An important aspect of this practice is anticipating the questions that a teacher might use to address possible student responses to sustain cognitive demand.

- **Monitoring:** Monitoring involves listening to students' mathematical thinking during classroom activity and determining appropriate responses to that thinking. Teachers may circulate the classroom as they monitor to assess the types of thinking that are present, introduce questions to sustain cognitive demand, and begin to plan the focus of the later practice of connecting.

- **Selecting:** When selecting student responses, the teacher assesses the variety of strategies used in the classroom with the goal of determining which strategies to make public to the class. This is an opportunity for teachers to probe the mathematical thinking underlying each solution strategy to determine which types of thinking help support the objectives of the task. When selecting, a teacher may choose strategies that expand on a given concept or expose common misconceptions in a way that the students are capable of dealing with as a group.

- **Sequencing:** Once specific student strategies are selected, the teacher then determines a sequence for making those strategies public to the entire class. The sequence purposefully conveys mathematical ideas in a way that supports the goals of the task. In some cases, this may be to expose similar types of thinking, while in others it may be to expose students to multiple representations or contradictory strategies in an effort to better understand an underlying concept.

- **Connecting:** Finally, the teacher must help students make deliberate and specific connections among the ideas that are presented to the class. This may include having students make connections among the ideas within a task, or to previously learned mathematics. Connecting may also include follow-up or extension activities that continue mathematical thinking on a given concept.

Emerging research on student learning through problem solving has shown that such practices can impact student learning in measurable ways (Kazemi & Stipek, 2001; Wood, Williams, & McNeal, 2006). A teacher's ability to implement effective teaching practices when using CDTs, however, is highly dependent on his/her own mathematical content knowledge and understanding of teaching mathematics (Franke et al., 2007; Hill & Ball, 2009). Elementary teachers are typically unprepared to teach in this manner, favoring traditional approaches to teaching mathematics that emphasize computations and procedures and de-emphasize conceptual understanding. As a result, they inadvertently reduce the complexity of problem-solving tasks and their students learn mathematics in a way that fails to meet the new standards. Since elementary teachers teach across multiple subject areas (e.g., National Mathematics Advisory Panel [NMAP], 2008), they will need guidance and support focused on refining their understanding of mathematics and the effective practices associated with employing problem-solving tasks in the classroom. This is not likely to occur under the Common Core standards without professional development.

These issues become more problematic when teaching fractions at the elementary level under the new standards. Elementary teachers rely more heavily on procedural approaches to teaching fractions, especially when they lack an understanding of the underlying concepts and the connections among those concepts (Isiksal & Cakiroglu, 2011; Ma, 1999; Tirosh, 2000). Teachers who primarily understand fractions in a procedural way are most likely to continue favoring procedural approaches

while enacting cognitively demanding tasks (Ball, Thames, & Phelps, 2008; Franke et al., 2007; Ma, 1999). In addition, Levenson, Tsamir, and Tirosh (2010) found that elementary school teachers generally prefer to use mathematical explanations that are procedural rather than those that develop or connect concepts because they are most easily and immediately understood by students. An emphasis on procedural understanding is ineffective when teaching under the goals of the Common Core standards because it fails to draw on and connect the mathematical concepts that are associated with that task.

Although face-to-face methods of mathematics professional development have been found to be successful, they are costly and place high demands on school resources. In addition, a recent study by Garet et al. (2010) indicates that they do not always lead to improved teacher practice or student achievement. Teachers in that study received one year of face-to-face mathematics professional development that focused on using visual representations, eliciting student thinking, and focusing on mathematical reasoning as part of classroom activity. After one year, there was little difference in teacher practice and no difference in student achievement for teachers who received significantly more professional development contact hours, including in-classroom coaching. While in-class and face-to-face support is undoubtedly important, the viability, feasibility, and scalability of such methods for broader implementation have been questioned (Stiles, Mundry, Loucks-Horsley, Hewson, & Love, 2009). Matos, Powell, Sztajn, and Ejersbo (2009) similarly noted that new digital technologies in the classroom create an opportunity to explore a wider variety of approaches to supporting teachers in the classroom. With the technologies that are widely available in today's classrooms, there is an opportunity to develop support that is readily available to teachers via the Internet while reducing the costs associated with face-to-face methods.

DESIGN FRAMEWORK

Our goal was to develop online professional development materials to support the teaching of fractions under the Common Core standards at the elementary level. Specifically, we targeted the Common Core's goal to connect the standards for mathematical practice with the standards for content. Through an interdisciplinary effort among *Universities (we will name them later, but omitted for review to keep the process 'blind')*, we created a design framework to support the development of online professional development materials. Specifically, the materials introduce the Stein et al. (2008) teaching practices in the context of fraction CDTs at the fourth grade level.

The framework draws heavily on our current knowledge of effective face-to-face and online professional development to maximize the potential to change teacher practices in the classroom while being flexible enough to complement existing professional development strategies and mathematics curriculum (e.g. Investigations, Connected Math Project, etc.). The framework includes a total of five features that are described:

- **Concepts in the Context of CDTs:** Grounding teacher learning in CDTs addresses the need to develop a teacher's own understanding of mathematical concepts and practices. Teachers whose professional development focuses on math concepts as part of learning to teach with CDTs are more likely to understand how to sequence mathematics with greater curricular cohesion (Ferrini-Mundy, Burrill, & Schmidt, 2007). By focusing on fraction concepts as part of a meaningful teaching activity like CDTs, we are likely to improve teachers' ability to ask students effective questions, understand a wider variety of student-generated approaches to a task, and engage students in mathematical reasoning using a variety of representations (Ball, Thames, et al., 2008; Lampert, Beasley, Ghousseini, Kazemi, & Franke, 2010).

- **Visual Representations:** A teacher's ability to use visual representations to promote student learning is critical to instruction under the Common Core. Learning fraction concepts through reasoning and logic with representations rather than abstract rules provides a tangible context in which to ground more advanced mathematics and promote student thinking about mathematics (Burns, 2001; National Mathematics Advisory Panel, 2008; Van de Walle & Lovin, 2006). At the elementary level, Ball, Hill, and Bass (2005) and others (Borko, Roberts, & Shavelson, 2008; Hill & Ball, 2004) have stressed the importance of teachers' use of representations to express and explain mathematical reasoning, as well as to demonstrate how algorithms work conceptually.

- **Question Strategies:** Teachers often lower the cognitive demand of a CDT through the questioning strategies they use to promote student thinking. Typical ways of doing this include shifting the emphasis from exploring key concepts to identifying correct answers, de-emphasizing problematic aspects by giving students the solution, and not pressing students for clear, logical arguments (Stein, Grover, et al., 1996). Structuring professional development materials around questioning strategies such as those presented in the *Thinking Through a Lesson Protocol* (TTLP) (Smith, Bill, & Hughes, 2008) provides teachers with planning support aligned to the nature of CDTs and standards-based practice (Boston & Smith, 2009).

- **Student Thinking:** Teachers can lower the cognitive demand associated with CDTs by failing to anticipate a wide variety of student responses, both correct and incorrect (Stein, Grover, et al., 1996). Researchers (Isiksal & Cakiroglu, 2011; Ma, 1999; Tirosh, 2000) have suggested that a teachers' ability to teach fractions would be improved through greater exposure to examples of student misconceptions, as well as potential student difficulties when solving problems. To effectively implement CDTs, teachers will need examples of student work, implementation strategies, and analogous activities that expose them to a variety of student thinking.

- **Effective Teaching Practice:** Teacher practice improves when their learning includes models of best practice (Boston & Smith, 2009; Lampert et al., 2010; Sherin, Linsenmeier, & van Es, 2009). Providing video of actual teaching situations or voice-over accounts of specific practices can help teachers visualize each practice and support their own practice in the classroom.

APPLYING THE FRAMEWORK

The framework was used to develop online professional development materials that support the teaching of fractions at the elementary level. The materials, contained in a Website entitled *Fractions to the Core* (http://tothecore.coe.uga.edu) were created through design based research. Specifically, the materials were developed in close coordination with three teachers at a local elementary school. Our work is situated in what Cobb and Yackel (1996) refer to as an emergent perspective – a perspective that attempts to coordinate individual activity with the social context in which it occurs. The emergent perspective, the development process, and the application of the framework to *Fractions to the Core* are described next.

Emergent Perspective: Cobb and Yackel (1996) present what they call an emergent perspective during their developmental research with elementary mathematics teachers. The emergent perspective is a form of social constructivism that assumes learning is a reflexive relationship between psychological and social perspectives, not merely one or the other. The psychological perspective aims to account for individual student or teacher learning. For example, the researcher may try to analyze cognitive restructurings of the child in reaction to perturbations during problem solving activity. On the other hand, the social perspective aims to analyze interactions at the classroom level (or school/cultural levels) to account for learning. Referring to the classroom microculture, they identify these as classroom social norms, sociomathematical norms, and classroom mathematical practices.

Cobb and Yackel (1996) argue that these perspectives move between the foreground and background of research conducted in the mathematics classroom. One can choose to analyze the psychological aspects of learning while recognizing the social context as background and vice versa. The authors stress the use of a coordinated analysis, stating that classroom social norms, "evolve as students reorganize their beliefs, and, conversely, the reorganization of these beliefs is seen to be enabled and constrained by evolving social norms" (p. 178). Although one may choose students beliefs as the unit of analysis, it is important to see how these beliefs form as a result of the classroom culture and also help shape this culture simultaneously.

By aligning our development process with this perspective, we recognize the role of this continuum between individual activity and the social context. In the process of teacher professional development, we believe one cannot place attention solely on students' individual cognition without also addressing how these are supported within the classroom community. No matter how well suited the creation or selection of tasks, the classroom norms and practices play an equal role in determining the degree to which the task is successfully implemented.

Development Process: The materials were developed in conjunction with three fifth-grade teachers at a local elementary school. The teachers volunteered to work with the design team to receive professional development aligned to the framework and implement CDTs in their own classrooms. The teachers worked with the designers to develop and implement prototypes of the online materials, including three CDTs with lesson plans organized around the Stein et al. (2008) practices, interactive whiteboard files that accompanied the lesson plans, information about student thinking, and visual representations (e.g. blank 100's grids, number lines, and fraction bars). Teachers also received face-to-face professional development sessions on those practices in the context of the specific CDTs. The goal of working with paper-based materials and face-to-face professional development was to test a variety of professional development strategies aligned with the framework before developing them fully as online materials.

In total, the designers worked with the teachers over a three-month period and implemented three CDTs with the teachers. This process included initial interviews and observations with the teachers, three one-hour professional development sessions on teaching the CDTs, in-classroom support including live modeling of the practices, and follow-up interviews after each implementation. The teachers worked closely with the designers to select tasks and professional development activities that were most appropriate and pertinent to the teachers' needs and tasks being implemented.

This process provided key design information from the emergent perspective – that is, both the psychological and social perspective about the manner in which teachers used the materials to implement the Stein et al. (2008) practices and meet the Common Core standards. Table 1 contains a description of the design information gained during the development process. Initial observations and interviews revealed that classroom instruction focused heavily on mathematical procedures, even when teaching with CDTs. This created a teacher-centered environment where students had little opportunity to engage in mathematical reasoning or communication as part of problem

Table 1. Description of the design information gained during the development process

Event	Description	Design Information Gained
Initial Interview and Observation	Designers met with teachers to introduce the Stein et al. (2008) practices and CDTs. Teachers were observed teaching mathematics for one 90-minute period.	Teachers were concerned over the mathematical knowledge needed to teach using CDTs, as well as students' ability to engage in such tasks. The mathematics classroom was primarily teacher-centered. Student had little opportunity to express their thinking and instruction focused on memorizing procedures and processes.
Observation of first CDT and follow-up interview	Teachers were observed delivering a 90-minute mathematics lesson involving the representation of ½ on a geoboard. Prior to the lesson, teachers met with the designers to select the task and receive professional development about the Stein et al. practices in the context of the task (about 60 minutes total).	Students had limited opportunity to express mathematical thinking, both in written and spoken words. They struggled to divide shapes in half, work with peers, and explain their thinking. Teachers' use of questions to sustain cognitive demand was limited and they often provided solutions and procedures outright. Teachers were uncomfortable with allowing students to struggle with mathematics and conducted the lesson in a teacher-centered manner.
Observation of second and third CDT and follow-up interview	Teachers team-taught a 90-minute lesson with designers, who modeled effective practices and question strategies. The CDTs involved placing benchmark fractions on the number line and playing Burn's (2001) Comparing Game.	Students struggled to place benchmark fractions on the number line. Students continued to struggle with expressing mathematical thinking and using visual representations to complete tasks involving fractions. Teachers continued to express their beliefs that having students struggle with mathematics would negatively affect standardized test scores.

solving activities. Overall, students had difficulty expressing their mathematical thinking and using visual representations of benchmark fractions (e.g. unable to use fraction bars to place ¼ between 0 and 1 on a number line or divide a geoboard shape in half). At the same time, the teachers preferred to avoid mathematical struggle (for themselves and their students) and were concerned that any student confusion would result in poor standardized test performance in the future. At the conclusion of our work, the teachers were interested in learning more about teaching mathematics with CDTs but felt they needed additional support with the use of question strategies and visual representations.

This information was used to inform our application of the framework as we developed *Fractions to the Core*. The most apparent implication was that, while the Stein et al. (2008) practices strongly align with the Common Core standards, teachers needed explicit and clear examples of how the two connect. While not explicit in our framework, we realized that this could be achieved by putting the idea of mathematical struggle in a learner-centered classroom at the forefront of the professional development materials. The practices and the Common Core standards both imply that this struggle is important, but our work made it clear that this idea was complex and multifaceted in the actual classroom. Teachers missed opportunities to allow students to struggle, and lacked the strategies for making effective use of that struggle.

This had major implications for the development of our videos of best teaching practices and, in turn, the documents needed to support teacher practice. Specifically, we focused on isolating and presenting specific instances of struggle, including examples of what typical struggle looks like, strategies for sustaining struggle with questions and visual representations, and illustrations of student-centered instruction in the mathematics classroom. In addition, we realized that the practices of selecting, sequencing, and connecting were strongly connected and difficult to present as

discrete practices. As a result, our videos integrate selecting and sequencing into the practice of connecting. Finally, teachers struggled with the fact that the process of learning to teach with CDTs was difficult and required practice. The videos and support materials would need to attend to the classroom environment, student activities, and teacher pedagogy as part of demonstrating best practices.

Fractions to the Core: The professional development materials housed on the *Fractions to the Core* Website present a sequence of professional development around three related CDTs: 1. Exploring benchmark fractions using 100's grids, 2. ordering benchmark fractions on the number line, and 3. the Comparing Game (Burns, 2001). These address Common Core standards 4.NF.1 (equivalence) and 4.NF.2 (comparing). These materials are open in that they are available for free on a public Website. Figure 1 contains a screen shot of the *Fractions to the Core* home page, which contains an introductory video about the Stein et al. (2008) practices.

To create the materials found on the Website, we converted the paper-based prototypes to an online format. The professional development that was delivered in a face-to-face manner during the development process was converted into a series of videos. The Website contains a separate page for each CDT containing the following professional development materials:

- Videos of anticipating student thinking and question strategies, monitoring student work, and connecting, which includes selecting and sequencing student responses.
- A full lesson plan built around the practices in the videos.
- The *Thinking Through a Lesson Plan* protocol (blank).
- Question ideas for each phase of the CDT.
- An interactive whiteboard file for the CDT.
- Printable visual representations (in the Resources).

Figure 1. Fractions to the core homepage containing a video introduction to the Stein et al. (2008) practices

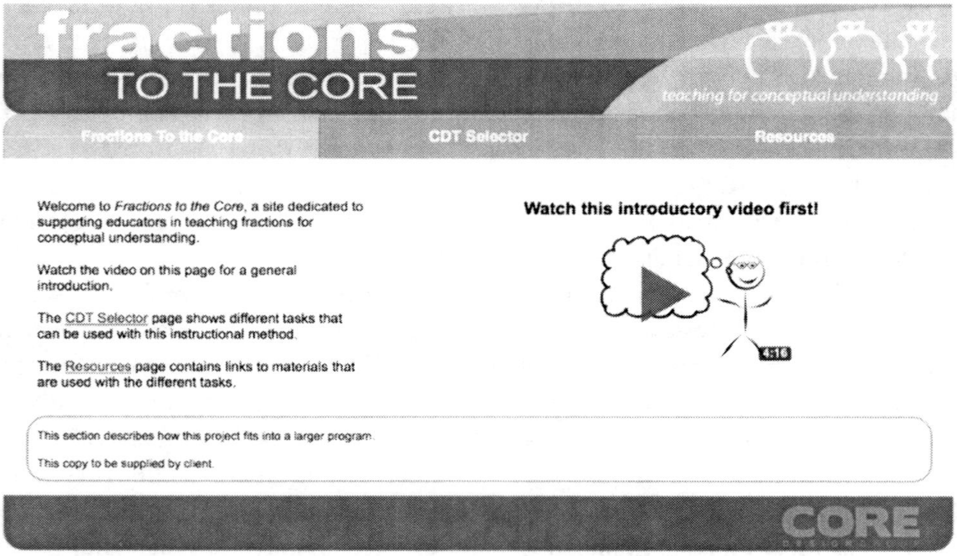

Figure 2 contains a screen shot of the professional development provided for the *Number Line* task. As noted in Figure 2, the professional development is grounded in the context of specific CDTs (Framework 1). Within each specific CDT, they then find the materials needed to effectively teach that specific CDT. Question strategies are promoted by providing both the *Thinking Through a Lesson Plan* protocol and a set of question ideas tailored to specific CDT (Framework 3). The teaching practices are presented in video format such that each video contains exemplars of each practice in the context of the specific CDT (Framework 5). A short assessment is available for teachers to complete a knowledge check regarding the practices in the videos.

Unlike many online professional development materials for mathematics, the videos on *Fractions to the Core* do not showcase live classrooms. Video of live classrooms can be problematic in professional development situations. Student-teacher interactions are often difficult to hear, important student activity may not be visible, and key teaching strategies may not be immediately apparent. The videos in *Fractions to the Core*

instead recreate the real problems and situations that occurred during our development process through animated video with voice-over narration. This allowed us to isolate and expand on the use of question strategies and visual representations to promote student struggle, make visible a wider variety of teacher activity and student thinking, and illustrate the classroom environment that supports CDT use.

Figure 3 contains screen shots from the *Anticipating* video, which illustrate common student issues with the Number Line task (Framework 4). Specifically, the figure contains a sequence of images describing how a strategy for ordering fractions that works in one situation may not work in another similar situation. Figure 4 contains a screen shot from the *Monitoring* video that depicts a teacher using fraction bars to support student thinking as they complete the task (Framework 2). Figure 5 contains a sequence of screen shots from the *Connecting* video, which visually depicts the teacher selecting, sequencing, and presenting student work at the conclusion of the CDT (Framework 5).

Figure 2. The application of the framework (1, 3, and 5) to the number line investigation and supporting materials as they appear in the fractions to the core site

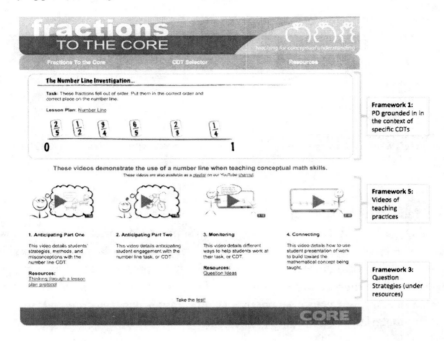

Figure 3. The application of the framework (4) to the anticipating video for the number line investigation

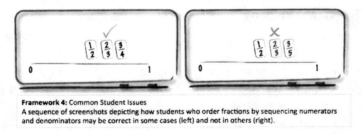

Framework 4: Common Student Issues
A sequence of screenshots depicting how students who order fractions by sequencing numerators and denominators may be correct in some cases (left) and not in others (right).

Evaluation: Three inservice and 15 preservice teachers participated in an evaluation of the Website and the materials housed there. Participants completed a pre- and post-treatment survey that assessed their interest in learning more about CDTs, their attitudes about the videos and Website materials, and their suggestions for improving the materials. Overall, the majority of participants found the site interesting, clear, and effective at demonstrating effective teaching practices associated with CDTs. Preservice teachers indicated that the videos increased their comfort with implementing CDTs, including anticipating possible

Figure 4. The application of the framework (2) to the monitoring video for the number line investigation

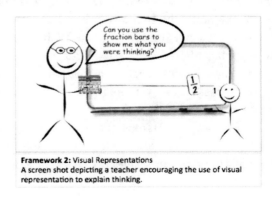

Framework 2: Visual Representations
A screen shot depicting a teacher encouraging the use of visual representation to explain thinking.

Figure 5. The application of the framework (5) to the connecting video for the number line investigation

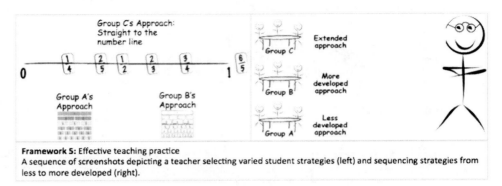

Framework 5: Effective teaching practice
A sequence of screenshots depicting a teacher selecting varied student strategies (left) and sequencing strategies from less to more developed (right).

student responses and methods for supporting students as they engaged in CDTs. In contrast, inservice teachers noted that they needed time to try the practices in the classroom before determining whether the videos and materials were helpful to them. Both inservice and preservice teachers commented that the materials would be helpful for planning and implementing CDTs.

EXTENDING THE FRAMEWORK

Fractions to the Core represents an attempt to capitalize on the affordances of online technology to provide elementary school teachers with readily available, robust professional development around the Common Core standards. The framework that guided our development, which draws heavily on the research on effective professional development, created materials that both inservice and preservice teachers found accessible, clear, and helpful. As design-based research, the next step in extending the framework is to learn more about how teachers make use of the Website and the materials offered there. To do this, we intend to work closely with teachers as they attempt to use the Website as they adopt the Common Core standards in their classrooms.

In addition, the framework may be used to guide the work of teacher educators facing the challenge of preparing teachers to adopt the Com-

mon Core standards. Educational leaders looking to support Common Core standards may use the framework for planning and making decisions about the professional development they offer to teachers. Leaders, including coaches, may use the framework to locate and implement existing professional development resources as they work with teachers to adopt Common Core standards. The framework may be used to develop resources outright, or in an effort to generate a comprehensive library of professional development support or for the purpose of creating customized professional development materials. In either case, the framework encourages the use of professional development materials that not only explain key mathematical content, but also situate that content in the context of mathematical practice. *Fractions to the Core* is offered as an example of such materials and serves as a resource for supporting teachers in the classroom as they adopt the Common Core Standards.

CONCLUSION

The Common Core standards emphasize teaching mathematics content and processes as a unified curriculum and promoting understanding in the mathematics classroom. Professional development on the Common Core will need to illustrate specific teaching practices that foster this emphasis.

Unfortunately, developers of online professional development may choose to separate content from pedagogy in order to address specific standards more fully. For example, the materials contained on the Website for the Southeast Comprehensive Center [SECC] seek to "clarify the meaning of the individual standard rather than to be a guide on how to teach each standard, although the examples can be adapted for instructional use" (Southeast Comprehensive Center [SECC], 2012, p. 1). Both content and pedagogy are undoubtedly important aspects of any teacher professional development. However, professional development materials that focus solely on one without addressing the other may ultimately fail to support teachers fully in the process of enacting the Common Core standards in the classroom. The NMAP (2008) noted this, stating "conceptual and procedural knowledge of fractions reinforce one another and influence such varied tasks as estimation, computation, and the solution of word problems" (p. 28).

To meet the vision of the Common Core, teachers will need strategies for supporting students as they make sense of problems, express mathematical reasoning, and use questions and visual representations to better understand the content associated with each standard. By taking an emergent perspective, we acknowledge that this is most likely to occur when professional development focuses both on what teachers know *and* what they and their students do within the context of the classroom. The framework detailed in this chapter is an attempt to provide teachers and teacher educators with a guide for selecting, developing, and implementing online professional development that sits at the intersection of practice and content. *Fractions to the Core* demonstrates how the framework can be used to develop robust online professional development materials that can be used in a variety of ways by individual teachers, math coaches, and professional developer alike.

REFERENCES

Ball, D. L., Hill, H. C., & Bass, H. (2005). Knowing mathematics for teaching: Who knows mathematics well enough to teach third grade, and how can we decide? *American Educator, 29*(1), 14–46.

Ball, D. L., Thames, M. H., & Phelps, G. (2008). Content knowledge for teaching: What makes it special? *Journal of Teacher Education, 59*(5), 389–407. doi:10.1177/0022487108324554.

Borko, H., Roberts, S. A., & Shavelson, R. J. (2008). Teachers' decision making: From Alan J. Bishop to today. In Clarkson, P., & Presmeg, N. (Eds.), *Critical issues in Mathematics Education* (pp. 37–67). New York, NY: Springer. doi:10.1007/978-0-387-09673-5_4.

Boston, M. D., & Smith, M. S. (2009). Transforming secondary mathematics teaching: Increasing the cognitive demands of instructional tasks used in teachers' classrooms. *Journal for Research in Mathematics Education, 40*(2), 119–156.

Burns, M. (2001). Lessons for introducing fractions (grades 4-5). Sausalito, CA: Math Solutions Publications.

Cobb, P., & Yackel, E. (1996). Constructivist, emergent, and sociocultural perspectives in the context of developmental research. *Educational Psychologist, 31*(3-4), 175–190. doi:10.1080/00 461520.1996.9653265.

Ferrini-Mundy, J., Burrill, G., & Schmidt, W. H. (2007). Building teacher capacity for implementing curricular coherence: Mathematics teacher professional development tasks. *Journal of Mathematics Teacher Education, 10*(4), 311–324. doi:10.1007/s10857-007-9053-9.

Franke, M. L., Kazemi, E., & Battey, D. (2007). Mathematics teaching and classroom practice. In Lester, F. K. (Ed.), *Second Handbook of Research on Mathematics Teaching and Learning* (2nd ed., Vol. 1, pp. 225–256). Charlotte, NC: Information Age Publishing.

Garet, M. S., Wayne, A. J., Stancavage, F., Taylor, J., Walters, K., & Song, M. et al. (2010). *Middle school mathematics professional development impact study: Findings after the first year of implementation (No. NCEE 2010-4009)*. Washington, DC: National Center for Education Evaluation and Regional Assistance, Institute of Education Sciences, U.S. Department of Education.

Hill, H., & Ball, D. L. (2009). The curious – and crucial – case of mathematical knowledge for teaching. *Phi Delta Kappan, 91*(2), 68–71.

Hill, H. C., & Ball, D. L. (2004). Learning mathematics for teaching: Results from California's mathematics professional development institutes. *Journal for Research in Mathematics Education, 35*(5), 330–351. doi:10.2307/30034819.

Isiksal, M., & Cakiroglu, E. (2011). The nature of prospective mathematics teachers' pedagogical content knowledge: The case of multiplication of fractions. *Journal of Mathematics Teacher Education, 14*(3), 213–230. doi:10.1007/s10857-010-9160-x.

Kazemi, E., & Stipek, D. (2001). Promoting conceptual thinking in four upper-elementary mathematics classrooms. *The Elementary School Journal, 102*(1), 59–80. doi:10.1086/499693.

Lampert, M., Beasley, H., Ghousseini, H., Kazemi, E., & Franke, M. (2010). Using designed instructional activities to enable novices to manage ambitious mathematics teaching. In Stein, M. K., & Kucan, L. (Eds.), *Instructional Explanations in the Disciplines* (pp. 129–141). Boston, MA: Springer US. doi:10.1007/978-1-4419-0594-9_9.

Levenson, E., Tsamir, P., & Tirosh, D. (2010). Mathematically based and practically based explanations in the elementary school: Teachers' preferences. *Journal of Mathematics Teacher Education, 13*(4), 345–369. doi:10.1007/s10857-010-9142-z.

Ma, L. (1999). *Knowing and teaching elementary mathematics: Teachers' understanding of fundamental mathematics in China and the United States*. Mahwah, NJ: Lawrence Erlbaum Associates.

Matos, J. F., Powell, A., Sztajn, P., Ejersbø, L., & Hovermill, J. (2009). Mathematics teachers' professional development: Processes of learning in and from practice. In Even, R., & Ball, D.L. (Eds.), *The professional education and development of teachers of mathematics* (Vol. 11, pp. 167–183). Boston, MA: Springer US. doi:10.1007/978-0-387-09601-8_19.

National Council of Teachers of Mathematics. (2000). *Principles and standards for school mathematics*. Reston, VA: NCTM.

National Council of Teachers of Mathematics. (2012). *Why Is teaching with problem solving important to student learning? Brief*. Retrieved June 4, 2012, from http://www.nctm.org/news/content.aspx?id=25713

National Mathematics Advisory Panel. (2008). *Foundations for success: The final report of the national mathematics advisory panel*. Washington, DC: U.S. Department of Education.

Sherin, M. G., Linsenmeier, K. A., & van Es, E. A. (2009). Selecting video clips to promote mathematics teachers' discussion of student thinking. *Journal of Teacher Education, 60*(3), 213–230. doi:10.1177/0022487109336967.

Smith, M. S., Bill, V., & Hughes, E. K. (2008). Thinking through a lesson: Successfully implementing high-level tasks. *Mathematics Teaching in the Middle School, 14*(3), 132–138.

Smith, M. S., & Stein, M. K. (1998). Selecting and creating mathematical tasks: From research to practice. *Mathematics Teaching in the Middle School, 3*(5), 344–350.

Southeast Comprehensive Center [SECC]. (2012, June 4). Southeast and Texas comprehensive centers at SEDL - Common core videos. *Common Core State Standards Video Series*. Retrieved June 4, 2012, from http://secc.sedl.org/common_core_videos/

Stein, M. K., Engle, R. A., Smith, M. S., & Hughes, E. K. (2008). Orchestrating productive mathematical discussions: Five practices for helping teachers move beyond show and tell. *Mathematical Thinking and Learning, 10*(4), 313–340. doi:10.1080/10986060802229675.

Stein, M. K., Grover, B. W., & Henningsen, M. (1996). Building student capacity for mathematical thinking and reasoning: An analysis of mathematical tasks used in reform classrooms. *American Educational Research Journal, 33*(2), 455–488. doi:10.3102/00028312033002455.

Stiles, K. E., Mundry, S., Loucks-Horsley, S., Hewson, P. W., & Love, N. (2009). *Designing professional development for teachers of science and mathematics* (3rd ed.). Thousand Oaks, CA: Corwin Press.

Tirosh, D. (2000). Enhancing prospective teachers' knowledge of children's conceptions: The case of division of fractions. *Journal for Research in Mathematics Education, 31*(1), 5–25. doi:10.2307/749817.

Van de Walle, J. A., & Lovin, L. H. (2006). Teaching student-centered mathematics (grades 5-8). Boston, MA: Pearson Education, Inc.

Wood, T., Williams, G., & McNeal, B. (2006). Children's mathematical thinking in different classroom cultures. *Journal for Research in Mathematics Education, 37*(3), 222–255.

Chapter 22
The Use of Digital Resources to Support Elementary School Teachers' Implementation of the Common Core State Standards

Amy Jensen Lehew
Charlotte-Mecklenburg Schools, USA

Drew Polly
UNC Charlotte, USA

ABSTRACT

This chapter describes the process of developing Web-based resources to support elementary school teachers' implementation of the Common Core State Standards in Mathematics in a large urban school district in the southeastern United States. Based on a learner-centered approach to teacher professional development the authors describe a three-fold process of supporting teachers: providing opportunities for teachers to deepen their understanding of the CCSSM, providing curricular resources that align with the CCSSM, and providing ongoing support through teachers' implementation of the CCSSM. Implications for the development of Web-based resources and researching these types of endeavors are also shared.

INTRODUCTION

Change is an inevitable part of life for educators. Regularly, school districts, states, and nations, are modifying such things as the academic standards that students are expected to master, the achievement scores that must be reached on large-scale tests, the ways that teacher performance is evaluated, and the expectations and duties that are placed on classroom teachers. How teachers adapt to change is a vital component of their success over the course of their career. Further, how

DOI: 10.4018/978-1-4666-4086-3.ch022

educational leaders at school, district, and state levels support their teachers is a crucial component of the success of those educational organizations.

In order to ensure all students have access to rich curriculum resources, more and more schools have adopted the notion of Professional Learning Communities (PLCs; Dufour, Dufour, & Eaker, 2008). The era of "close your door and teach what you want" is coming to an end as schools develop schedules that allow teachers at a grade level to meet periodically to plan instruction. In American schools, teachers have become heavily dependent on both their curricular resources and pacing guide for direction on when to teach specific topics and concepts (David & Greene, 2007).

As the Common Core State Standards in Mathematics (CCSSM; CCSSI, 2011) continue to be rolled out through the early phases of implementation in schools, there is a drastic need for educational leaders to support teachers by:

1. Providing opportunities for teachers to deepen their understanding of the CCSSM.
2. Providing curricular resources that align with the CCSSM.

In this paper we will describe our process of addressing both areas of need in a large, urban school district in the southeastern United States. This process has been a multi-year endeavor, and is by no means an exemplar model. Rather, we offer a description of our experience to provide ideas that may be used, modified, or further examined in an attempt to find the most effective ways to best prepare teachers for the implementation of the CCSSM in elementary school mathematics classrooms.

The projects that we describe here took place in a large, urban school district in the southeastern United States. There are approximately 3,600 elementary school teachers who teach Kindergarten through Grade 5. Teachers in the district have had access to the standards-based

curriculum, *Investigations in Number, Data, and Space* (TERC, 2008) since the 2009-2010 school year, when the district adopted that curriculum as their primary resource. The implementation of the CCSSM has taken place over a few years, with every Kindergarten, Grade 1, and Grade 2 teacher implementing the CCSSM during the 2011-2012 year, and teachers in Grades 3, 4, and 5 starting implementation in the 2012-2013 school year. Teachers have access to multiple professional development opportunities in mathematics during the school year and during the summer. Some of these are detailed in this chapter.

THEORETICAL FRAMEWORK

Our work is informed by a notion of teacher-learning referred to as learner-centered professional development (National Partnership for Educational Accountability and Teaching, 2000; Polly & Hannafin, 2011). Briefly, this construct claims that the most effective ways to support teachers' work and teacher learning are to provide opportunities:

1. That are directly relevant to teachers' classroom practice.
2. That are comprehensive and occur over time instead of one-time workshops.
3. That simultaneously deepen teachers' knowledge of both the content they teach and instructional pedagogies.
4. To collaborate with other teachers from their grade level, school, or others that they come in contact with outside of the professional development.
5. That address student-learning issues by helping teachers to identify low areas of student performance and devise a strategy to address them.
6. To reflect repeatedly about the teaching and learning processes.

During this entire endeavor, we and all of our teacher-leaders kept asking ourselves the driving question: "How will this work and these resources support our teachers?" In the next section we describe how this concept of learner-centered professional development influenced our initiatives to support elementary school teachers' work with the Common Core State State Standards.

MODES OF SUPPORT

1. Providing Opportunities for Teachers to Deepen their Understanding of the CCSSM

Our process of supporting teachers' understanding of the CCSSM has occurred and is occurring primarily through a variety of professional development projects. These professional development projects have included both a variety of face-to-face, online and classroom-based projects.

A. Face-to-Face Professional Development

Through both grant and district-funded support, over 900 of the district's approximate 3,600 elementary school teachers have participated in at least 80 hours of professional development, while each elementary school teacher has participated in at least 12 hours of professional development. Table 1 describes the various professional development activities and how they align to the various elements of Learner-Centered Professional Development (LCPD).

This professional development design has been described in more detail (Polly & Lehew, 2012). Further, evaluation studies of the grant-funded professional development initiatives found that the professional development led to statistically significant shifts in teachers' beliefs in favor of more reform-oriented pedagogies, a greater enactment of reform-based pedagogies in classrooms,

Table 1. Professional development activities

Professional Development Activity	Element(s) of LCPD
Exploring cognitively-demanding mathematical tasks	Deepening knowledge of content and pedagogy Collaboration
Discussing how to implement cognitively-demanding mathematical tasks in classrooms	Relevant to classroom practice Deepening knowledge of content and pedagogy Collaboration
Unpacking the major work of the CCSSM at each grade level, including primary and supporting clusters within each domain.	Deepening knowledge of content and pedagogy Collaboration Examining student learning issues
Examining resources, such as *Progressions* and *Unpacking* documents, which explain the CCSSM Standards and effective pedagogies in more detail.	Deepening knowledge of content and pedagogy Collaboration
Mapping curricula to the Standards and identifying standards where additional resources were needed	Relevant to classroom practice Deepening knowledge of content and pedagogy Collaboration
Examining student work from their students and other students in the district	Relevant to classroom practice Collaboration Examining student learning issues Reflecting on classroom practice

and some statistically-significant gains in student learning outcomes on curriculum-based assessments (Polly, Wang, McGee, Lambert, Martin, & Pugalee, in press).

B. Online Professional Development Materials

In addition to face-to-face professional development, we also provided online materials for teachers and building level coaches to explore on their own, as well as professional development materials from face-to-face meetings for redelivery. One of the most popular resources provided is a set of modules that address how to incorporate the CCSSM Standards for Mathematical Practice in each grade level. They are linked here: https://

elementarymathematics.org/Math_Facilitators. php. Within each module are resources for teachers to incorporate the mathematical practices on a consistent basis including mathematical tasks, examples from the district's curriculum *Investigations in Number, Data, and Space* (TERC, 2008), and professional readings. These materials have been used by groups of teachers at the same grade level (PLCs), administrators and others to conduct professional development in their own building, as well as by individual teachers.

As a district we also have monthly district-wide professional development sessions for our mathematics coaches/facilitators/lead teachers. Following each session we all of the PowerPoints and resources onto the district math Website. In many instances, the materials that we use with coaches/facilitators/lead teachers are then in turn reused by them in their own buildings during staff meetings, grade level planning meetings, or other professional development opportunities.

Further, by putting professional learning materials and resources online on an open Website, numerous districts in North Carolina have accessed, used and also shared with us professional development materials. The Internet and open nature of Web-based materials has led to increased access and use of these educational resources.

C. Classroom-Based Projects

In order to support teachers' ongoing access to professional learning experiences and embed their learning in their work in the classroom, we have utilized classroom-based projects as a venue of professional learning. This has primarily occurred through the use of student assessment projects and videos of classroom discussions.

Student Assessment: Our student assessment projects that have been part of Common Core professional development have differed by grade level. One project required teachers to pose the same cognitively-demanding tasks to students who encompassed a variety of abilities. Teachers posed the tasks, compared students' responses,

and designed instructional strategies based on what they noticed. Teachers have also posed curriculum-based assessments from *Investigations*, and analyzed student work to determine where students need more support.

Most recently, Kindergarten through Second Grade teachers involved in a professional development program are using the Math Perspectives Assessing Mathematics Concepts Web-based tool AMC Anywhere to assess students' work. Using the tool, teachers conduct brief interviews with students which focus on the Counting and Cardinality and Numbers in Base Ten domains of the CCSSM. During the professional development workshops, teachers were instructed on how to use the data from these assessments to plan developmentally-appropriate instruction.

Videos of Classroom Discussions: As part of a grant-funded professional development project, teacher-participants were required to video record a 10 minute mathematical discussion twice during the school year. During the workshops, teachers learned about varying levels of questioning and discussed strategies that they could use to facilitate discussions in which students described their mathematical thinking and conceptual understanding.

After watching the video, teachers shared their video with a colleague. Then teachers met in pairs or small groups to discuss the videos, focusing on evidence of student learning, and the questions that teachers posed during the discussion. All of these classroom-based projects have been well received by teachers in the district. Many have cited the benefit of being able to learn and spend time on projects that were directly connected to their classroom teaching and their students' learning.

2. Providing Curricular and Assessment Resources that Align with the CCSSM

The selection and creation of curricular and assessment resources has been one of the most time consuming aspects of supporting teachers with the implementation of the CCSSM. Using the district's Website (http://elementarymathematics. org), there was a need to create a user-friendly, easy to read, Web-based location for pacing guides, teacher support resources, and other curricular resources.

A. Curricular Resources

Prior to setting this Website up, though, there was a need to determine which curricular resources were the most effective at supporting teachers' work with the CCSSM. Key mathematics facilitators and classroom teachers from the district met with us across several days to unpack the CCSSM, align our curriculum *Investigations* with the Standards, identify gaps in the alignment, and then determine what resources can be used to address those gaps. This work occurred in the spring and summer before the first year teaching the Standards (2011 for Grades K-2 and 2012 for Grades 3-5), and has continued since as we get more feedback from teachers and facilitators about concepts that students need more experiences with, and feedback about what has worked and what hasn't worked with resources that teachers are currently using.

Our work has focused on developing a set of curricula resources that is coherent and cohesive (Goldsmith, Lynn, & Kantrov, 2000; Watanabe, 2007), while maintaining a focus on standards-based pedagogies with cognitively-demanding tasks, and offering high-level questions and opportunities for students to explore mathematical concepts and discuss their strategies and ideas about mathematics.

Technology has supported the housing of these resources in a Web-based environment as well as access to numerous resources. Albeit many resources on the Internet which claim alignment to the CCSSM do not support standards-based pedagogies, but some, such as the curriculum frameworks of the Georgia Department of Education (https://www.georgiastandards.org/Common-Core/Pages/Math-K-5.aspx), tasks on Inside Mathematics (http://www.insidemathematics.

org/index.php/tools-for-teachers/7th-grade-math/mars-tasks-scoring-rubrics-a-analysis), and lessons written by the North Carolina Department of Public Instruction (http://maccss.ncdpi.wikispaces.net/Elementary) have been valuable. While these resources have been beneficial, work has been required to determine where to include these resources in the curriculum, and what format to use to provide these to teachers so that they will be easily accessible and usable.

B. Assessment Resources

The release of various types of assessment items by the Smarter Balance Assessment Consortium (SBAC) caught the attention of us and our teacher-leaders. Of special note were the SBAC Extended Performance tasks (see http://commoncoremathtasks.wikispaces.com/Smarter+Balanced+Tasks), which include multiple parts, authentic contexts, and a combination of problem solving, computation, and writing about mathematical ideas. Our work of educating teachers about this began by including these tasks in professional development. Teachers, math leaders, and administrators engaged in the "Storage Facility" task, shared their problem-solving strategies, and communicated their reasoning with their peers.

Following this, we began providing teachers with access to these items that SBAC released and encouraging teachers to try them with their students, and discuss their experiences.

After working with these released tasks with students, and also having teachers complete them during workshops, a group of teacher-leaders began working with us to write examples of these extended performance tasks, which we could embed into curriculum. Our goal is to have 5-6 of them focused on the major work of each grade level available for teachers to use from Grades 2 through Grade 5. An example can be found here (https://elementarymathematics.org/uploads/3rd_grade_unit_3_Performance_Task.rtf).

Each of these extended performance tasks written by our team includes an authentic context, multiple parts, and a task in which students need to write and communicate about mathematical ideas. Most of these tasks address at least 5 of the CCSSM Standards for Mathematical Practice. As we continue to prepare for the SBAC assessment in 2014-2015, we hope that these tasks will support students' mathematical understandings.

IMPLICATIONS AND CHALLENGES

There are numerous implications and challenges for our work as we continue through the early stages of implementing the CCSSM. These include: 1) providing ongoing support to teachers, facilitators, and administrators, 2) constantly refining resources, and 3) preparing for the implementation of large-scale assessments.

1. Providing Ongoing Support

Our professional development work this year has focused on extending teachers' work with addition and subtraction problem structures in Grades K-2 and introducing teachers to the grade level standards in Grades 3-5. Work with mathematics facilitators/coaches has focused on fractions, and the need to provide them with opportunities to deepen their content knowledge as well as understanding of pedagogies used to effectively teach fractions concepts.

Future work is needed to reexamine teachers and facilitators/coaches needs as well as reexamine ways to most effectively support their work. As professional development resources are minimal, models such ones shared earlier, where facilitators/coaches participate in workshops and then engage their teachers in those activities may be the most feasible method of delivery in such a large district.

2. Constantly Refining Resources

Our work identifying the gaps between our district mathematics curriculum, *Investigations*, and the CCSSM was time consuming, and while we felt prepared for the first year, we know that there is a critical need to reevaluate this work, obtain feedback from teachers, and continue to refine our selection, design, and development of curricular resources. The goal of maintaining a cohesive, coherent curriculum in which standards-based pedagogies are included in every lesson is central to our work, and must remain that way. To that end, there is a need to provide teachers and coaches/facilitators with education and resources that can help them if they go off examining various Internet-based curricula resources. For example, if a teacher feels the need to go find more opportunities for their fifth grade students to multiply and divide decimals, how can we as a district provide either resources or suggested guidelines for teachers to choose and implement appropriate mathematical tasks and related pedagogies?

3. Preparing for Large-Scale Assessments

As the Smarter Balance and PARCC assessment consortia continue to develop, test, and revise items, our work with extended performance tasks that we shared earlier needs more attention. While we have started down this road by having teachers engage in these tasks, and have created a few tasks for teachers to use with their students, there is a need to revise existing tasks, create new tasks, and explore ways to best prepare students for these rigorous mathematical tasks. As we work with teachers, many voice their complaints about the amount of reading and writing involved, the difficulty students will have determining how to begin each aspect of the multi-part tasks, and the amount of endurance that students need to persevere through each task. While teachers need to pose these types of tasks to their students to give them experiences with this work, we must continue to examine what types of supports would help teachers and students during this process.

REFERENCES

Common Core State Standards Initiative. (2011). *Common core state standards-mathematics*. Retrieved from http://www.corestandards.org/Math

David, J. L., & Greene, D. (2007). *Improving mathematics instruction in Los Angeles high schools: An evaluation of the PRISMA pilot program*. Palo Alto, CA: Bay Area Research Group.

Dufour, R., Dufour, R., & Eaker, R. (2008). *Revisiting professional learning communities at work: New insights for improving schools*. Bloomington, IN: Solution Tree.

Goldsmith, L. T., Mark, J., & Kantrov, I. (2000). *Choosing a standards-based mathematics curriculum*. New York: Heinemann.

Polly, D., & LeHew, A. J. (2012). *Supporting elementary teachers' retention through professional development: Developing teachers' understanding of the common core state standards in mathematics*. Los Angeles, CA: California Mathematics Project. Retrieved from http://cmpstir.cmpso.org/monograph

Polly, D., Wang, C., McGee, J. R., Lambert, R. G., Martin, C. S., & Pugalee, D. K. (2013). Examining the influence of a curriculum-based elementary mathematics professional development program. *Journal of Research in Childhood Education*.

TERC. (2008). *Investigations in number, data, and space* (2nd ed.). New York: Pearson.

Watanabe, T. (2007). In pursuit of a focused and coherent school mathematics curriculum. *The Mathematics Educator*, *17*(1), 2–6.

ADDITIONAL READING

David, J. L. (2008). Pacing guides. *Educational Leadership*, *66*(2), 87–88.

Polly, D., & LeHew, A. J. (2012). *Supporting elementary teachers' retention through professional development: Developing teachers' understanding of the common core state standards in mathematics*. Los Angeles, CA: California Mathematics Project. Retrieved from http://cmpstir.cmpso.org/monograph

Watanabe, T. (2007). In pursuit of a focused and coherent school mathematics curriculum. *The Mathematics Educator*, *17*(1), 2–6.

Chapter 23
Digitizing Students' Voices:
Assessing Mathematical Justification

Christine Browning
Western Michigan University, USA

Alden Edson
Western Michigan University, USA

Diane Rogers
Western Michigan University, USA

ABSTRACT

This chapter focuses on how assessment for learning can be used to promote the development of student understanding of mathematics and mathematical practices as described in the Common Core State Standards for Mathematics while emphasizing the affordances of digital technologies. The mathematical focus centered on the families of functions connected to the mathematical practice of constructing viable arguments when using the digital technology tool, VoiceThread. The chapter describes an iterative model for implementing assessment for learning practices where VoiceThread gave voice to preservice teachers' mathematical justifications. Findings are taken from a study set in an algebra course designed for preservice elementary teachers working towards a minor in mathematics. Preservice teachers noted the positive impacts of using VoiceThread in improving their justification skills and the benefits of assessment for learning practices on their learning process.

INTRODUCTION

Assessment is a key factor in the teaching and learning process. The general process of assessment has evolved from only examining the "end game" results (summative) to a process that permeates learning from the beginning and carries forward (formative); from a process where teachers were the only catalysts to promote the design and enactment of assessment to one where students and teachers are both engaged. Language regarding assessment has evolved as well, to help

DOI: 10.4018/978-1-4666-4086-3.ch023

reflect the change in thinking about the process. Assessment for learning is described by Black, Harrison, Lee, Marshall, and Wiliam (2004) as:

Any assessment for which the first priority in its design and practice is to serve the purpose of promoting students' learning. It thus differs from assessment designed primarily to serve the purposes of accountability, or of ranking, or of certifying competence. An assessment activity can help learning if it provides information that teachers and their students can use as feedback in assessing themselves and one another and in modifying the teaching and learning activities in which they are engaged. Such assessment ... is actually used to adapt the teaching work to meet learning needs (p. 10).

Based upon this thinking, we envision assessment for learning as a teaching practice involving students in a dynamic process that includes the following three components: (1) teachers and students have a shared understanding of expectations for learning and assessment, (2) teachers use student assessments to make instructional changes, and (3) teachers and students use assessment information

to provide continual feedback about the teaching and learning process (Engelman, Noakes, & Rogers, 2011). Engelman, Rogers, and Noakes (2013) performed a summary of research on formative assessment and assessment for learning in mathematics education in an attempt to differentiate and clarify the definitions of assessment for learning and formative assessment. From their research summaries, they developed a three-dimensional model (See Figure 1) that displays a relationship between four assessment-for-learning practices: *Learning and Assessment Expectations, Instructional Changes and Feedback* with *Student Involvement* as the base of the pyramid. The *Feedback* component was a key feature in our work as the preservice teachers developed their self- and peer-assessment abilities. We believe there is a strong connection between these assessment for learning practices and students' proficiencies with doing mathematics.

The Common Core State Standards for Mathematics (CCSSM) initiative intends to bring a set of more *focused* and *coherent* mathematics standards into the United States school mathematics curriculum, minimizing the number of mathematical topics presented to students within a given

Figure 1. Assessment for learning model (Engelman, Rogers, & Noakes, 2013)

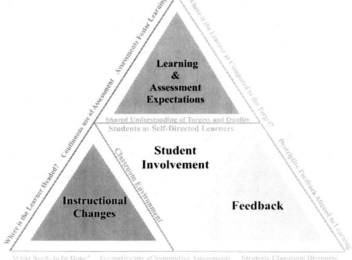

school year, allowing for more depth of study within these fewer topics. (National Governors Association Center for Best Practices [NGACBP] and Council of Chief State School Officers [CCSSO], 2010)

These Standards define what students should understand and be able to do in their study of mathematics. Asking a student to understand something means asking a teacher to assess whether the student has understood it. But what does mathematical understanding look like? One hallmark of mathematical understanding is the ability to justify, in a way appropriate to the student's mathematical maturity, why a particular mathematical statement is true or where a mathematical rule comes from (NGACBP & CCSSO, 2010, p. 4).

In addition to being a hallmark of understanding mathematics, justification permeates the Standards for Mathematical Practice, standards that focus on using and doing mathematics and include: (1) make sense of the problems and persevere in solving them; (2) reason abstractly and quantitatively; (3) construct viable arguments and critique the reasoning of others; (4) model with mathematics; (5) use appropriate tools strategically; (6) attend to precision; (7) look for and make use of structure; and (8) look for and express regularity in repeated reasoning (NGACBP & CCSSO, 2010).

In order to understand a mathematical concept, students need to engage with the mathematics, making use of the mathematical practices. To help clarify what this engagement could or should look like, teachers and students should develop a shared understanding of expectations. These shared expectations can lead to the development of rubrics for how students will justify their understanding. Thus learning, justification, and assessment are interwoven threads in the tapestry of understanding. In our work, another strand in

the weaving of this understanding involved the use of digital tools.

The use of digital tools was important in our study for two reasons. One, we wanted to examine how students made use of the tools and begin to assess how such tools impacted the students' learning; and two, since our students were elementary school (Grades K-8) preservice teachers, we wanted them to reflect on the use of digital tools for their own subsequent teaching of mathematics, developing their Technology, Pedagogy, And Content Knowledge (TPACK) in mathematics (Mishra & Koehler, 2006; Niess, 2005). Thus, this chapter will describe, through a lens of assessment for learning, how we used digital technologies to support the implementation of Standards for Mathematical Practice (NGACBP & CCSSO, 2010) in order to promote the learning of algebra.

BACKGROUND

The content of this chapter is based on data taken from a Spring 2012 study exploring the implementation of assessment for learning strategies mediated by the use of digital technologies in an algebra course designed for elementary preservice teachers. Collected data consisted of course work that included exams and quizzes, writing assignments, projects, mathematical tasks making use of digital technology and responses taken from semi-structured interviews.

The preservice teachers in this course are those who are seeking an elementary mathematics minor at a large mid-western university. This minor, along with successfully completing a state certification test, makes the preservice teachers eligible for a middle school endorsement in mathematics. The course focuses on algebraic content knowledge necessary to teach middle school mathematics in an era of the CCSSM. In particular, students work through algebraic problems, discuss their justifications and approaches to solving problems, use technological tools to support and extend their thinking, and work in groups to peer- and self-assess. This type of instruction is intended to help prospective mathematics teachers further develop their mathematical content knowledge for teaching.

The authors investigated the impact of a more deliberate use of assessment for learning practices in the algebra course. The implementation of assessment for learning practices centered on the three components described earlier. Briefly, they are to develop a shared understanding of clear learning expectations, base instructional changes on assessment tasks, and provide continual feedback for teaching and learning through assessments.

Clear Learning Expectations

An example of a task that was designed to help the teacher and students have a shared understanding of expectations for learning and assessment provided learning targets corresponding to particular CCSSM standards and were written in "student-friendly" language, referred to as "I Can" statements. The "I Can" documents were

used throughout the semester (e.g., prior, during, closing of the unit as well as for the final exam). Students would rank their understanding and/or ability for each statement throughout the course, encouraging students to take ownership of their learning of course content. Table 1 provides an example of two learning targets, "I Can" statements, and the corresponding CCSSM content standards for an exponential functions unit of the course.

Instructional Changes

An example related to the teacher using student assessments to make instructional changes, occurred when the instructor used the TI-Navigator™ to "capture" screens from the graphing calculators. Students would be engaged in their groups, completing a problem. The instructor would ask students to, perhaps, have a graph of their solution on their calculators. Using the Navigator™ software, the instructor could capture their screens, projecting them at the front of the class, making all calculator screens visible to the class. This would make it "easier to see what everyone else was thinking" (participant code, G1P3), capturing

Table 1. Learning targets and "I Can" statements as well as corresponding CCSSM standards

Learning Target and "I Can" Statements	Corresponding CCSSM Standards
Know and apply the properties of integer exponents to generate equivalent numerical expressions. • I can define the meaning of an exponent. • I can make sense of and justify the properties of exponents. • I can represent ideas related to properties of exponents using tables. • I can apply the properties of exponents to generate equivalent numerical expressions.	**Work with radicals and integer exponents.** 1. Know and apply the properties of integer exponents to generate equivalent numerical expressions. For example, $3^2\ 3^{-5} = 3^{-3} = 1/3^3 = 1/27$.
Create equations and use them to solve problems. Include equations arising from exponential functions. • I can describe basic patterns of exponential growth and decay, including determining the factor of change (growth/decay factor) and the growth or decay rate. • I can see and describe the patterns of change in a table, a graph, or an equation (both recursive and explicit). • I can express those patterns in symbolic rules (equations), using both recursive and explicit forms. • I can modify the symbolic rules to model other similar patterns of change. • I can determine and describe the difference between linear and exponential functions shown in tables, graphs, or symbolic rules. • I can find approximate solutions to exponential equations using tables and graphs to a given degree of accuracy.	**Create equations that describe numbers or relationships** 1. Create equations and inequalities in one variable and use them to solve problems. *Include equations arising from linear and quadratic functions, and simple rational and exponential functions.*

the variation of graphs and solutions across the class. Instructional decisions, such as questions to ask, mathematical directions to take, pacing of lesson, etc., would need to be made in-the-moment based on what the students provided through these screen captures. The graphing calculator screens were, in some sense, "windows" into the students' mathematical thinking.

Continual Feedback

An affordance of a continual feedback process is that students are aware of what they understand, how well they understand it, and what they still need to work on. In this process of developing their own self-assessment skills, feedback does not only have to come from the teacher but should be provided by preservice teachers' peers as well. In our study, we found that VoiceThread helped to mediate the development of the self- and peer-assessment skills of the preservice teachers. Therefore, the implementation of the assessment for learning practices encourages preservice teachers to be more self-directed and motivated learners.

For this chapter, we attend primarily to the third component of the assessment for learning model, namely, teachers and students using assessment information to provide continual feedback about the teaching and learning process. Although we recognize the dynamic nature of the three components of assessment for learning, we will focus on preservice teachers' self- and peer-assessment on mathematical tasks.

IMPLEMENTING ASSESSMENT FOR LEARNING PRACTICES USING DIGITAL TECHNOLOGIES

As depicted in Figure 2, an iterative process beginning with the negotiation of a whole-class rubric and involving problem solving, recording, reflecting, and refining was used several

Figure 2. Model for implementing assessment for learning practices using digital technologies, giving a voice to student justification

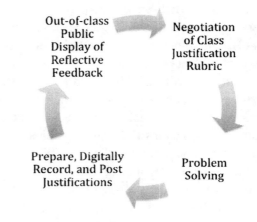

times through the second-half of the semester. A single iteration consisted of the following activities: preservice teachers engaged in different problem-solving situations involving functions in their small groups using a teacher and student co-constructed justification rubric. Each group of preservice teachers were asked to present their mathematical justifications of problem solutions while being video-recorded using a digital camera. These recordings were then posted online using a digital tool, VoiceThread. Each VoiceThread posting was both peer- and self-assessed outside of class using the co-constructed rubric. In class, preservice teachers discussed online video postings and comments and made modifications to the co-constructed rubric.

The Iterative Cycle

Negotiation of Class Justification Rubric

Justification is a common thread in the CCSSM Standards for Mathematical Practice. Therefore, a significant portion of the course was spent on mathematical justification of algebraic function tasks. Preservice teachers first discussed the process of mathematical justification in this course, as they read an article entitled, "Why, Why, Should I Justify?" (Lannin, Barker, & Townsend, 2006), which was used to help preservice teachers begin to understand "what constitutes a valid justification?" (p. 440). Through reading this article and class discussion, preservice teachers considered that a justification should be constructed to convince oneself, a friend, and a skeptic, that their reasoning made sense. Additionally, justifications should include generalizations that can help connect to other contexts and problems; thus, justification is more than just an explanation of solving a problem.

Midway through the semester, the instructor facilitated a class discussion designed to develop a working draft of a justification rubric. This initial draft, displayed in Table 2, was generated using the preservice teachers' language and ideas of quality justification.

Through the discussion, preservice teachers came to consensus and instructed a peer as to what to record. The rubric was then placed on the class Wiki for public access and for future modification. The process of co-constructing a rubric is aligned

to the assessment for learning practice of making *clear learning expectations*. The involvement of students in this process encouraged motivation and engagement in the learning process as students have buy-in or ownership of the learning goals.

In order to develop a deeper understanding of justification, preservice teachers were asked to use the justification rubric as they completed a group problem-solving task. Following the recording of their group's justification, preservice teachers were asked to watch their own video and two other groups' videos. They were instructed to critique their justification based on the working rubric and their observation of all videos watched and provide suggestions of potential modifications of the rubric. The following class period, the instructor facilitated a discussion with the aim to improve the justification rubric. The modified rubric is displayed in Table 2.

Preservice teachers discussed their various ideas for modifying the rubric. One student reflected that, "it is important that the response in our justification are *(sic)* clear, complete and correct" (G1P1). Other students agreed and thus

Table 2. First and second iteration of the class justification rubric

Class Justification Rubric				
First Iteration			**Second Iteration**	
Points	**Criteria**	**Points**	**Criteria**	
2	To receive full points your justification should include: • Making connections from the context of the problem to the mathematics or from a solution to a property if there is no context. • A complete verification through describing each of the variables and what them mean. • A general rule that addresses all components of the model, formula, equation, expression, and/or rule.	5	To receive full points your justification should include: • Making connections from the context of the problem to the mathematics or from a solution to a property if there is no context. When in a context, be sure to use appropriate units. • A complete verification through describing each of the variables and what they mean. • A general rule that is explicit. Recursive formulas can be included but are not necessary if not stated in the problem set up. • Response addresses all components of the model, formula, equation, expression, and/or rule. • Response is clear/concise/organized.	
1	To receive partial credit your justification would include Only a general rule **OR** only a few of the above things mentioned.	0 - 4	To receive partial credit your justification would include only parts of the full justification. For each criterion not clearly addressed, a point is lost.	
0	No credit will be given without some of the above things mentioned.			

the additional criterion was added in the second iteration (See Table 2). Another preservice teacher wrote,

If I were to modify the rubric, I would add a bullet point for the use of examples. I noticed that several groups used examples within their justifications to help explain the variables and to demonstrate the effectiveness of the model. I feel that the use of examples strengthens justifications, and should be included in a rubric for assessing this skill (G6P3).

Although this specific modification was not added to the rubric, preservice teachers gained more clarity about what was meant by "Making connections from the context of the problem to the mathematics." Preservice teachers decided to specifically add wording about attending to units to clarify a solution in context. This rubric was used for subsequent work involving justification.

Problem Solving

Throughout the course, preservice teachers engaged in problems within their small groups situated around proportionality and linear, quadratic, and exponential functions. The instructor drew the mathematical tasks from the Connected Mathematics Project and the Core-Plus Mathematics Project. Preservice teachers used the co-constructed rubric and graphing calculators in their groups as they solved problems, often times working through each question prompt together discussing their strategies and solution-processes. Two mathematical tasks, adapted from the *Core-Plus Mathematics Course 1* (Hirsch, Fey, Hart, Schoen, and Watkins, 2008), are indicated in Table 3, which correspond to the exponential and quadratic units in the course.

The instructor selected mathematical tasks to promote justification in preservice teachers' work as well as to connect preservice teachers' learning to the CCSSM Standards for Mathematical Practice. For instance, consider the Mold Problem

Table 3. Sample mathematical tasks (adapted from Hirsch, et al., 2008)

Mold Problem (Adapted from Hirsch, et al., 2008)
The drug Penicillin was discovered by observation of mold growing on biology lab dishes. Suppose a mold begins growing on a lab dish. When first observed, the mold covers 7 sq. cm of the dish surface, but it appears to double in area every day.
a) What rules can be used to predict the area of the mold patch
i. using NOW – NEXT form?
ii. using "y = ..." form
b) How much mold was present on days 2, 5, and 20?
c) On what day will there be more than 2 million sq. cm of mold?

Basketball Problem (Adapted from Hirsch, et al, 2008)
In game 3 of the 1970 NBA championship series, the LA Lakers were down by two points with three seconds left in the game. The ball was inbounded to Jerry West, whose image is silhouetted in todays' NBA logo. He launched and made a miraculous shot from beyond midcourt, a distance of 60 feet, to send the game into overtime (there were no 3-point shots at that time). Through careful analysis of the game tape, one could determine the height at which Jerry West released the ball, as well as the amount of time that elapsed between the time the ball left his hands and the time the ball reached the basket. This information could then be used to write a rule for the ball's height h in feet as a function of time in flight t in seconds.
a. Suppose the basketball left West's hands at a point 8 feet above the ground. What does that information tell about the rule giving h as a function of t?
b. Suppose also that the basketball reached the basket (at a height of 10 feet) 2.5 seconds after it left West's hands. Use that information to help in writing the rule giving h as a function of t.
c. What final rule do you have for giving h as a function of t?

shown in Table 3. When preservice teachers made sense of the contextual problem, they reasoned about the area of the mold on day zero and described how the growth occurs on a daily basis. Further, students provided a recursive formula and a general rule for bacteria mold area, justifying their reasoning for how they developed their rules and formulas by making connections to the bacteria mold context. For the Basketball Problem shown in Table 3, preservice teachers modeled phenomenon mathematically, often times providing multiple representations for describing the movement of the basketball in relation to the basket. Students reasoned abstractly and quantitatively by connecting the equation to values on the graph when persevering to find missing values. Students use the co-constructed rubric to justify their solutions when making connections to the basketball context.

Prepare, Digitally Record, and Post Justifications

After each group believed they adequately solved the mathematical tasks, the preservice teachers began to prepare to organize their work as well as their explanations and justification to be video-recorded. In general, the preparation process varied as some groups thought carefully about the process whereas other groups simply "winged it," showing no obvious forethought. Groups made decisions in the preparation process based upon (1) the readability of each preservice teacher's written work, (2) overall quality of justification from individual's work, and (3) confidence of speakers for each group. The scaffolded nature of the mathematical tasks and corresponding preservice teachers' solutions were taken to be the script or storyboard structure of the video presentations. No rehearsals of preservice teachers' presentations occurred for the first video recording.

After preservice teachers engaged in the preparation process, each group video-recorded their presentations using a digital camera, providing justification throughout their explanation process. The video-recordings captured written work for each problem, technology use, and their oral explanations and justifications when solving the task. The instructor uploaded these videos online using a free Web 2.0 tool, VoiceThread. VoiceThread is a "collaborative, multimedia slide show that holds images, documents, and videos and allows people to navigate slides and leave comments in 5 ways - using voice (with a mic or telephone), text, audio file, or video (via a Webcam)" (VoiceThread, 2012, p. 1). Each VoiceThread was posted on the course Wiki where students accessed, watched, and posted comments using the justification rubric. The use of VoiceThread permitted students to reflect on their own work as well as their peers' work outside of the classroom and conduct assessments on their own time.

In general, video length ranged from one to four minutes. Each video also ranged in the number of voices from one to all members of the group speaking. Figure 3 depicts the Website http://bit.ly/digitizingmathvoices that includes the adapted mathematical tasks and sample student VoiceThread work. Note that all comments posted on the VoiceThreads are removed to protect the identity of the participants.

Out-of-Class Public Display of Reflective Feedback

It is clear to the authors, based on the data collected, that the third mathematical practice (*construct viable arguments and critique the reasoning of others*) is particularly highlighted in this component of our model. Preservice teachers created their justifications with this critiquing process in mind; thus, preservice teachers self-assessed as

Figure 3. Sample student VoiceThread, available at http://bit.ly/digitizingmathvoices

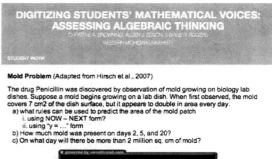

Mold Problem (Adapted from Hirsch et al., 2007)

The drug Penicillin was discovered by observation of mold growing on biology lab dishes. Suppose a mold begins growing on a lab dish. When first observed, the mold covers 7 cm2 of the dish surface, but it appears to double in area every day.
a) what rules can be used to predict the area of the mold patch
   i. using NOW – NEXT form?
   ii. using "y = ..." form
b) How much mold was present on days 2, 5, and 20?
c) On what day will there be more than 2 million sq. cm of mold?

they were problem solving and continued to self- and peer-assess as they moved into the recording and commenting phases of the cycle. Preservice teachers continually referenced the justification rubric throughout these processes to compare their own and other's work with class expectations.

Once group justification videos were posted, preservice teachers were asked to watch their own group as well as two others and make comments that aligned with the justification rubric. Preservice teachers could see any comments made previously since all comments were posted immediately for public viewing. This feedback process was completed asynchronously outside of class, which provided the affordance of extending mathematical thinking outside of class.

VoiceThread allows for verbal, text, and video comments that can be inserted as the video is playing or at the end of the video. A majority of students provided text comments that were one to two sentences in length. In general, the comments seemed to align with three different continua: (1) answer-oriented to process-oriented, (2) mathematical details to contextual connections, and (3) surface level/evaluative to constructive/descriptive comments. For example, one preservice teacher

focused on the connection to the context in the comment to his peers, in that the group had a:

Really solid explanation on the steps to solving the equation. I understood the process of building the equation using the information, but you might make it a little more clear as to exactly what 'initial Height and Velocity' mean in the context of the problem. For instance 'The Instant the ball left his hands.' Great Job! (G4P2).

Another preservice teacher self-assessed at a more surface level and process-oriented comment as she reflects, "It seemed like I was more thorough while I was actually talking. I could have explained each part of the equation more clearly – connections were good but actualy (*sic*) meaning could definitely be improved" (G6P3). Figure 4 shows an example of a VoiceThread video and a descriptive comment about the connection between a term in the group's equation and the context.

The feedback loop created by the process of commenting and facilitated by the digital tool, allowed students to both peer- and self-assess; thus, preservice teachers continued the learning process outside of class as they reflected, compared

Figure 4. Sample student descriptive comment in a VoiceThread

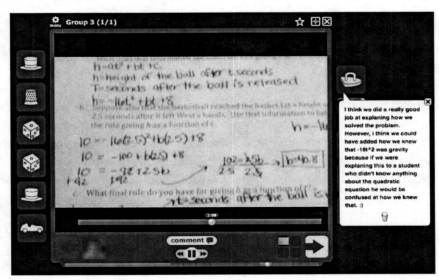

and contrasted justifications, and articulated their critique in a public forum.

Students completed the iterative process twice, making use of the recordings and VoiceThread, and a final third time completing a problem-solving task independently making use of their co-constructed rubric. The next section provides more details on what we learned from the VoiceThreads ourselves and student interviews where preservice teachers reflected on their last problem-solving task as well as ideas related to assessment for learning mediated by digital tools.

IMPLICATIONS, CHALLENGES, AND FUTURE DIRECTIONS

Implications: What Does our Data Suggest?

In analyzing the VoiceThreads and preservice teacher interviews, we find the Standards for Mathematical Practice permeate the iterative cycle that describe our model for implementing assessment for learning practices. In setting up the class justification rubric, preservice teachers had to determine criteria that would define what they would accept as a "viable argument" or a senseable justification. During the problem solving in their groups, they made sense of what was asked and persevered in finding solutions. The problems themselves required preservice teachers to engage in several areas of mathematical practice such as reasoning abstractly and/or quantitatively, using mathematics to create relevant models, choosing appropriate tools, attending to precision, looking for and making use of mathematical structure, and looking for and express regularity through their recursive rules. VoiceThread allowed preservice teachers to give voice to many of these practices as well as providing an alternative medium for relaying their justifications and critiquing the reasoning of their peers. We also believe it is important to note that in every case where we indicate "preser-

vice teacher" we could easily substitute "student"; we believe the iterative cycle is practical for any elementary or secondary classroom. A "free" education-version of VoiceThread is available at the school level as well.

The iterative cycle also attends to all components of our assessment for learning definition and can be used to give student voice to mathematical thinking across a variety of mathematical domains beyond algebra. Students can generate rubric criteria allowing student involvement in setting clear expectations for learning and assessment. Teachers can make use of the public display of student thinking and critiques to inform their instructional changes, as students use the public display of critiques and peer thinking to inform their learning. In the first iteration of this cycle, this was evident as preservice teachers reworked the class justification rubric based on critiques of their own work as well as what they observed in the work of their peers. Preservice teacher interviews also provided further indications of how the rubric impacted their work, with preservice teachers stating how they attended to components within the rubric, making sure they were doing "quality work" (G1P1). Overall, preservice teachers seemed to find the co-construction of the justification rubric as a helpful process in developing their ability to justify their answers. As one preservice teacher shared,

I think it was helpful to like create it as a class, because ... a lot of the classmates brought up a lot of things that I didn't think about that should be included in a justification. It was nice to make it halfway through the course and then go back to it towards the end before we did this [the pumpkin problem] and really make it like more specific. It was helpful to like help make it and then use it to do my own work with (G1P3).

Having a medium to give voice to student thinking was also critical to many preservice teachers:

If I know that I'm going to be using something on VoiceThread, I want to make it so that I explain things clearly. I write ya know neatly and show all my work. But, a lot of times, as a student, when I'm doing my work, I'll take short cuts and stuff like that, but that's not what you want to do on the VoiceThread because you want to show all your work, show how you got each step, showing how you looked at the graph, showing the lines, showing what each line is, the points on the table, like you are showing more specifically, how you got that (G1P1).

[VoiceThread] helps me think through it more when I talk about, because I'll say something and I'll realize that that didn't really make sense. Like let me re-word that. Versus like when I'm writing it down, I'm just going to write the facts and I'm not really going to write down like why I thought that. But like talking through it, I guess it's just the way that I learned, but when I talk through it, I learn more from it. Um, so I feel like I kind of, I would have learned more, had a better understanding, if I was able to talk through my justifications versus just writing them (G1P3).

Further, Using VoiceThread facilitates a:

Trifecta of the inquiry-based process: we are analyzing it (the VoiceThread) ourselves, and then we are going and putting it out there. We are looking at other people's interpretations of it so that we can make connections of our own, and then doing an entire class discussion about why they think it was that way. … we are getting out of the lectures and actually having students get into the, you know, grit and bones of the concepts and VoiceThread is really good at doing that (G4P2).

The use of the digital technology tool, VoiceThread, extended the classroom in productive mathematical ways that was engaging to the preservice teachers. Partial evidence for the engaging nature of the VoiceThread tasks was based on

the fact that all out-of-class VoiceThread tasks were completed with not one preservice teacher complaining about the assignments, assignments that were not graded and were more for student learning and the authors' investigative purposes. Generally our preservice teachers want to be given "credit" for the work they do, so having such support for the VoiceThread tasks was very encouraging.

Challenges Implementing Assessment for Learning Practices Using Digital Technologies

As with all experimentation, we were presented with unforeseen challenges. Again, we will work through the components of our iterative model, sharing what speed bumps came across our path and offering some suggestions for alterations. In a sense, we are working through the iterative model ourselves and redefining our expectations for the next iteration of having students voice their thinking.

Negotiation of Class Justification Rubric

Preservice teachers feedback suggests that the justification rubric process should have been implemented earlier in the course, with construction of the rubric following the reading of the "Why, Why, Should I Justify?" (Lannin, Barker, & Townsend, 2006) article. The complexity of constructing a rubric is often taken for granted. The structure of the rubric requires pre-planning in reference to how the rubric will be used and what information is desired from its use. In this case, the justification rubric was not intended to be used to provide evaluative feedback, such as a grade, but rather constructive feedback that would allow preservice teachers to take action to improve their justification skills. The introduction of point values in the initial design of the rubric may have distracted students to focus on point values rather than on the process of improving their justifications. It is often advantageous to develop a holistic rubric that addresses broader concepts and skills rather than an analytic rubric that attends to specific criteria for a given assignment or problem. The rubric developed in this case tends to blur the line between holistic and analytic, at times causing preservice teachers to treat the rubric as a checklist of ingredients rather than a reflective tool to think more deeply about their mathematical justifications.

It is important to clarify and develop shared definitions for the particular language used to describe the rubric criteria. For example, class work suggests that preservice teachers struggled to find balance between being clear, concise, and complete in their mathematical justifications. At times preservice teachers seemed to sacrifice important mathematical details for the sake of brevity. An extended conversation about the difference between completeness and conciseness may help students further differentiate between an explanation and a justification.

Problem Solving

Although the problems selected in this case allowed classroom students to choose from various problem-solving approaches, the scaffolding of the tasks seemed to direct them towards a particular approach. In the future, the authors encourage instructors to select or adapt more open-ended tasks that could employ multiple representations and use multiple function families for capturing students' mathematical justifications. Each mathematics classroom develops norms and socio-mathematical norms related to student collaboration as well. It may be important to discuss expectations for roles and individual contributions when implementing collaborative groupings.

Digitally Recorded Justifications

No specific directions or requirements were given to groups about the recording process other than to attend to the justification rubric. It may be helpful to discuss the process and view previously collected examples of VoiceThread justifications so that students are encouraged to plan their recording process more thoroughly. Often preservice teachers did not mention the use of graphing calculator technology, mistakes, or misconceptions in their videos. Additionally, preservice teachers left out key decisions such as why a quadratic equation was chosen to model the situation, or why a certain representation was used to justify the solution. Watching a video of a problem that is unfamiliar to students may help them see things that have been overlooked more readily. This process may help students navigate the difference between explanation and justification.

All of the preservice teachers used work that was written prior to the recording process. At times, preservice teachers struggled to follow and/or read their peers' work as they were presenting. It may be advantageous to encourage classroom students to do the problem live so that all pieces of the solution process are clearly included. In this study, one camera was used to record each group at the back of the room or hallway. Depending on resources available, the process could be sped up through the use of cell phones, flip video cameras, and/or iPads. As students get used to the process, they can also be given the responsibility of posting videos, which can even be done outside of class.

Out-of-Class Public Display of Reflective Feedback

Although the intention was to design a holistic justification rubric that could be used throughout the semester to improve students' work, the preservice teachers often used the co-constructed rubric as a list of ingredients that could be checked off as proof of attending to the scoring criteria. Future use of the rubric should encourage students to frequently provide constructive and descriptive details in their comments about how the criteria were addressed and what could be improved. An instructor should intentionally introduce these concepts to students and help them understand the difference between evaluative and descriptive feedback. In addition to improving the quality of the content of the comments, it may be helpful to encourage comments involving other modalities than text such as verbal and video comments. Preservice teachers often mentioned the ease of verbal recordings in comparison to written work. Specifically, VoiceThread provides students the ability to mark on the video with a drawing tool to illustrate a viewer's point.

Future Directions

The preliminary analysis of our findings provide several areas for us to focus on in future classes. Listening to all of the course groups' VoiceThreads, we see how we could refine the problems they work through to further assist preservice teachers' learning. For example, we could minimize the amount and/or alter the type of scaffolding provided in the problems to elicit different kinds of thinking and perhaps allow for more freedom in the choice of mathematical representations preservice teachers choose in solving the problems.

By having subsequent classes observe VoiceThreads created by this current class, perhaps preservice teachers will note different features they believe to be critical for constructing a strong justification. Perhaps other Standards for Mathematical Practice could be made evident by observing the VoiceThreads, helping preservice teachers understand the importance of precision, for example.

Based on student interviews, we plan on implementing VoiceThread early in the semester and using it throughout the term but we need to determine a reasonable number of problems for students to complete and critique. It was not intentional that we began the VoiceThreads in the second half of the semester; it was more by necessity in that we needed to prepare to make use of the digital tool. We are also curious if these VoiceThread tasks continue to be ungraded, if preservice teachers will still value their completion as they did in this study. Will preservice teachers eventually want to create an evaluation rubric for the VoiceThread tasks?

Analyses also provided other questions we would like to pursue. With respect to VoiceThread:

- What are the connections between what is written on the paper and what is said in the video?
- How are decisions made on who will speak, whose paper is used to present from, and how do these decisions influence the speaker(s)?
- How do comments on VoiceThread relate to individual/group's performance (e.g. notice things they did well or poorly and make changes)?
- Does VoiceThread help the students and instructor know more quickly in the timeline of the course students' strengths and weaknesses so that they can be remedied or attended to more quickly?

With respect to assessment for learning:

- How do the rubric labels for indicating success at meeting each criteria impact the use? (e.g. points vs. categories such as proficient).
- How do varied contexts of problem tasks posted on VoiceThread impact performance on tasks? (The problem tasks used in this study all involved concepts related to physical or biological science).

CONCLUSION

Our chapter described how assessment for learning practices fostered growth in preservice teachers' justification skills as well as the use of the CCSSM Standards for Mathematical Practice.

VoiceThread, combined with the iterative model of the assessment for learning practices, gave voice to preservice teachers' justification and opportunities for self- and peer-assessment. Preservice teacher interview comments overwhelming supported the use of VoiceThread as an engaging and motivating tool and how having to communicate their thinking was very powerful to their own learning; as one student voiced, the VoiceThread tasks promoted "a trifecta of the inquiry-based process".

REFERENCES

Black, P., Harrison, C., Lee, C.-H., Marshall, B., & Wiliam, D. (2004). Working inside the black box: Assessment for learning in the classroom. *Phi Delta Kappan, 86*(1), 9–21.

Engelman, J., Noakes, L. J., & Rogers, D. R. (2011, April). *Assessment for learning and formative assessment: Establishing a common definition for mathematics education*. Paper presented at the research pre-session of the National Council of Teachers of Mathematics Annual Meeting. Indianapolis, IN.

Engelman, J., Rogers, D. R., & Noakes, L. J. (2013). *Assessment for learning and formative assessment: Establishing a common definition for mathematics education*. Unpublished manuscript.

Hirsch, C. R., Fey, J. T., Hart, E. W., Schoen, H. L., & Watkins, A. E. (2008). *Core-plus mathematics: Contemporary mathematics in context* (2nd ed.). New York: Glencoe McGraw-Hill.

Lannin, J., Barker, D., & Townsend, B. (2006). Why, why should I justify? *Mathematics Teaching in the Middle School, 11*(9), 438–443.

Mishra, P., & Koehler, M. J. (2006). Technological pedagogical content knowledge: A new framework for teacher knowledge. *Teachers College Record, 108*(6), 1017–1054. doi:10.1111/j.1467-9620.2006.00684.x.

National Governors Association Center for Best Practices (NGACBP) & Council of Chief State School Officers (CCSSO). (2010). *Common core state standards for mathematics*. Washington, DC: National Governors Association Center for Best Practices and the Council of Chief State School Officers.

Niess, M. L. (2005). Preparing teachers to teach science and mathematics with technology: Developing a technology pedagogical content knowledge. *Teaching and Teacher Education, 21*(5), 509–523. doi:10.1016/j.tate.2005.03.006.

VoiceThread. (2012). *VoiceThread overview*. Retrieved June 1, 2012, from http://voicethread.com/about/features/

Chapter 24

TPACK Pathways that Facilitate CCSS Implementation for Secondary Mathematics Teacher Candidates

Nathan Borchelt
Western Carolina University, USA

Kathy Jaqua
Western Carolina University, USA

Axelle Faughn
Western Carolina University, USA

Kate Best
Western Carolina University, USA

ABSTRACT

Implementation of the Common Core State Standards in Mathematics has provided teacher educators a great opportunity to reexamine whether teacher preparation programs adequately provide the experiences to develop the base of knowledge and 21st century skills necessary to be effective teachers. The Mathematics TPACK Framework provides a roadmap for a series of pathways to integrate three knowledge components that are essential in teacher development: content knowledge, pedagogical knowledge, and technological knowledge. In this chapter, the authors examine how a teacher preparation program has evolved to integrate meaningful uses of digital technologies in content and pedagogy that are relevant to the teaching and learning of mathematics through the lens of implementing the Common Core State Standards.

INTRODUCTION

When examining the components of a teacher preparation program, one of the most pressing implications for practice is a need for meaningful experiences for teacher candidates similar to those provided through in-service professional devel-opment. Teacher candidates must be prepared to establish learning environments that emphasize 21st century skills.

People in the 21st century live in a technology and media-suffused environment, marked by various characteristics, including: (1) access to an

DOI: 10.4018/978-1-4666-4086-3.ch024

abundance of information, (2) rapid changes in technology tools, and (3) the ability to collaborate and make individual contributions on an unprecedented scale. To be effective in the 21st century, citizens and workers must be able to exhibit a range of functional and critical thinking skills related to information, media, and technology (Partnership for 21st Century Skills, Information, Media, and Technology Skills, 2011).

To that effect, technology should be an integral part of teacher candidates' experiences learning mathematics, or else they may not value the benefits of technology integration. They must also understand what the Common Core State Standards in Mathematics say about students' experiences with digital technologies in order to meet professional standards used to evaluate teachers.

Technology is valuable in leveraging and enhancing classroom experiences for students which promote mathematical reasoning and sense making (Dick & Hollebrands, 2011). In this chapter, we examine how a teacher preparation program has evolved to integrate meaningful uses of digital technologies in content and pedagogy which are relevant to the teaching and learning of mathematics. The Mathematics Technological Pedagogical and Content Knowledge (TPACK) Framework (Mishra & Koehler, 2006; Koehler & Mishra, 2008; 2009; Association of Mathematics Teacher Educators (AMTE), 2009) provides a roadmap for a series of pathways to integrate three knowledge components, which are essential in teacher development: content knowledge, pedagogical knowledge, and technological knowledge. We argue the necessity of moving teacher candidates through these pathways to help them promote in their students the types of mathematical practices described in the Common Core documents (Common Core State Standards Initiative (CCSSI), 2010).

BACKGROUND

Program Description

Our undergraduate pre-service mathematics education program includes extensive work both in mathematics and in education. Because of the comprehensive nature of our program, each of our teacher candidate graduates receives two degrees—a Bachelor of Science in Education, Mathematics and a Bachelor of Science, Mathematics. As part of this program teacher candidates complete 15 hours of education and mathematics methods courses, 42 hours of mathematics content courses, and at least 12 hours of full-time field experience. These degrees reflect the North Carolina Professional Teaching Standards (North Carolina Professional Teaching Standards Commission, 2006) and the 21st century knowledge, skills, and dispositions embedded in them.

Early classroom experience is a key component of our program. School partners are actively and continuously involved in providing multiple field experiences for our teacher candidates in the form of field observations and pre-service lesson study cycles. During internship and student teaching, school partners help evaluate teacher candidates' performance through observation protocols. As part of a prior evaluation of the program, a group of 58 teachers from local middle schools and high schools attended a presentation on our mathematics education program. Specific topics of discussion addressed what teacher candidates need to know and be able to do in the classroom upon graduation from a teacher education program. As a result of this evaluation, we designed a new course to enhance the connection of content, technology, and pedagogy. The new course, *Math 414: Introduction to Secondary Mathematics Teaching Methods*, has an emphasis on connecting technology and pedagogy. This course serves as a springboard to the second methods course, *Math 415: Methods and Materials for Teaching*

Mathematics in Secondary Schools. Now *Math 415* takes a more holistic approach to instructional design in which teacher candidates make instructional choices that integrate technology, pedagogy, and content.

TPACK Framework

As a guiding framework for promoting teacher candidates' acquisition of 21st Century skills and dispositions with respect to digital technologies, we use TPACK constructs that emerged from research in recent years. In this section, we provide a brief introduction to the TPACK Knowledge Bases, Standards, and Stages of Development.

As described by Koehler (2011), there are three Knowledge Bases:

Technology Knowledge is knowledge about standard technologies such as books and chalk and blackboard, as well as more advanced technologies such as the Internet and digital video. This would involve the skills required to operate particular technologies. In the case of digital technologies this would include knowledge of operating systems, and computer hardware, as well as the ability to use standard set of software tools such as word processors, spreadsheets, browsers, email etc. (TK)

Pedagogical Knowledge is deep knowledge about the processes and practices or methods of teaching and learning and how it encompasses (among other things) overall educational purposes, values and aims. This is a generic form of knowledge that is involved in all issues of student learning, classroom management, lesson plan development and implementation, and student evaluation. Pedagogical knowledge requires an understanding of cognitive, social and developmental theories of learning and how they apply to students in their classroom. (PK)

Content Knowledge is knowledge about the actual subject matter that is to be learned or taught. Clearly, teachers must know and understand the subjects they teach, including: knowledge of central facts, concepts, theories and procedures within a given field; knowledge of explanatory frameworks that organize and connect ideas; and knowledge of the rules of evidence and proof. (CK)

The TPACK framework focuses on essential knowledge created in the intersections of these three knowledge bases as illustrated in Figure 1 (Mishra & Koehler, 2006):

In addition to the framework, which provides a way to examine and categorize our course sequence in the light of overlapping sections of the diagram in Figure 1, the TPACK Standards listed provide a set of goals that proficient teacher candidates should strive to achieve by the end of their program. The following four TPACK Standards are suggested by AMTE (2009):

Figure 1. TPACK Image (rights free image (http://tpack.org/))

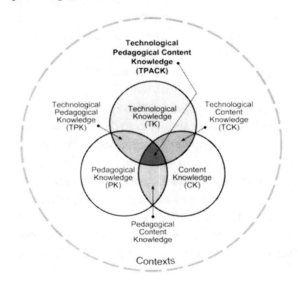

1. Design and develop technology enhanced mathematics learning environments and experiences.
2. Facilitate mathematics instruction with technology as an integrated tool.
3. Assess and evaluate technology enriched mathematics teaching and learning.
4. Engage in ongoing professional development to enhance technological pedagogical content knowledge (Information, Media, and Technology Skills).

In practice, these standards permeate the classroom culture and the everyday work of teachers who use technology to enhance students' comprehension of the subject matter through carefully designed "instruction, organization, and classroom management specific to the application of technology in the mathematics classroom." In particular, these teachers "understand their content areas with both breadth and depth as a result of using technology as part of their instruction" (Guerrero, 2010).

Finally, the TPACK Stages of Development allow us to identify strategic places in the program that present opportunities for teacher candidates to transition from one stage to the next when using a specific technology in the teaching of mathematics. It is our goal as Mathematics Educators to facilitate these transitions through a carefully designed sequence of courses and experiences. In order for teacher candidates to demonstrate proficiency in the previously mentioned standards by the time they transition to the classroom, teacher educators need to select learning opportunities that promote TPACK acquisition in teacher preparation courses. In turn, the framework can be the basis for an in-depth examination of areas of growth for teacher candidates in relation to the use of technology as they move through the following stages of TPACK development when learning to use specific technology in the mathematics classroom (Niess et al., 2009):

- **Recognizing (Knowledge):** Where teachers are able to use the technology and recognize the alignment of the technology with mathematics content yet do not integrate the technology in teaching and learning of mathematics.
- **Accepting (Persuasion):** Where teachers form a favorable or unfavorable attitude toward teaching and learning mathematics with an appropriate technology.
- **Adapting (Decision):** Where teachers engage in activities that lead to a choice to adopt or reject teaching and learning mathematics with an appropriate technology.
- **Exploring (Implementation):** Where teachers actively integrate teaching and learning of mathematics with an appropriate technology.
- **Advancing (Confirmation):** Where teachers evaluate the results of the decision to integrate teaching and learning mathematics with an appropriate technology.

Mishra argues that teachers must "learn technology not by learning specific computer programs, but rather by designing technological solutions to pedagogical problems." (Mishra, 2012, May 12, para. 5). Likewise, the learning of a technology for technology's sake has been well documented as providing little support for students to attain reasoning and sense-making in the mathematics classroom (Jones, 2002). Furthermore, exposure to the use of technology through the modeling and observation of exemplary practice in the field will mold teacher candidates' beliefs and attitudes regarding the use of instructional technologies to enhance mathematical inquiry-based learning tasks (Meagher, et al., 2011a). Therefore successful TPACK acquisition requires moving teacher candidates along pathways through intersecting sections of the TPACK diagram, as well as through the Stages of Development as they engage in technology-intensive mathematics classes, in mathematics teaching methods classes, and in appropriate field experiences that model instruction specifically catered to the needs of 21st century learners.

CCSS-M Implementation and Technology (Secondary Education Focus)

The Common Core State Standards in Mathematics (CCSS-M) was developed as a state-led initiative out of concerns that existing sets of different standards across the country were not adequately providing students with knowledge and skills essential to compete in an increasingly mobile society.

The Standards for Mathematical Practices provide descriptions of the proficiencies with process that CCSS-M advocates for all students. Students need to be able to do the following:

1. Make sense of problems and persevere in solving them.
2. Reason abstractly and quantitatively.
3. Construct viable arguments and critique the reasoning of others.
4. Model with mathematics.
5. Use appropriate tools strategically.
6. Attend to precision.
7. Look for and make use of structure.
8. Look for and express regularity in repeated reasoning (CCSSI, 2010).

While the CCSS-M focuses heavily on the content proficiencies of students, it does acknowledge the role of technology as a tool for mathematics learning and constructing knowledge. "Strategic use of technology is expected in all work. This may include employing technological tools to assist students in forming and testing conjectures, creating graphs and data displays and determining and assessing lines of fit for data" (CCSSI, 2010, Appendix A).

Implementation of the Common Core State Standards in mathematics requires that teachers of mathematics must have deep content knowledge to teach mathematics effectively and that content preparation needs to be tied closely with pedagogical training. But where do teacher candidates get the practice and experience that they need to develop strong pedagogy using technology? Preparing future teacher for 21st century classrooms makes it essential for all educators to work together in providing adequate experiences and opportunities for future teachers throughout their program of study. This needs to be evident in content courses as well as methods courses. This chapter proposes a model for teacher preparation that seeks to develop strong content knowledge, pedagogical knowledge, technological knowledge, and intersections of these knowledge bases necessary for teacher candidates to be successful as secondary mathematics teachers.

MOVING TEACHER CANDIDATES ALONG TPACK PATHWAYS TO SUPPORT CCSS-M IMPLEMENTATION

The TPACK framework serves as a foundation for analyzing our program and identifying places where we provide teacher candidates with opportunities to advance their understanding of each intersection of Knowledge Bases. At the same time, we recognize different people will progress through the TPACK Stages of Development differently and will respond to a specific technology in various ways. Our goal is to provide learning experiences that allow exploration of all Knowledge Bases and their intersections with an emphasis on early and ongoing experiences in the center of the framework. These experiences help teacher candidates start on their journey of progressing towards advancing stages of TPACK. Figure 2 is an adaptation of the TPACK image that includes

Figure 2. Program components that help form TPACK pathways

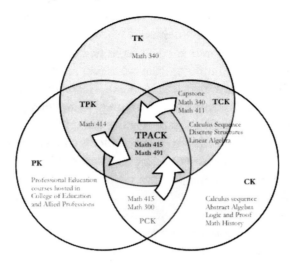

the most pertinent experiences in our program that help form the necessary pathways towards the center of the framework. The sections that follow will describe those pathways.

Beginning from Technology and Content Knowledge

In looking at the interplay of technological knowledge and content knowledge, it is clear that there are instances where these two areas are distinct. For instance, teacher candidates must have sufficient technological knowledge to access information on a particular network that may not involve any mathematical content knowledge. They must also have content knowledge that is primarily abstract in nature, such as what constitutes a group. There is evidence, however, to show that students can learn mathematics more deeply with appropriate use of technology (Jones, 2002; Ellington, 2003; Fey, Cuoco, Kieran, McMullin, & Zbiek, 2003). Therefore, it is very important that teacher candidates experience how to embrace the power of technology to better understand mathematics that challenges them during their teacher preparation program. Not only will teacher candidates experience how to use technology to do mathematics

but also how to use technology to communicate mathematical thought and reasoning abilities.

In parallel with the CCSS-M Standards for Mathematical Practices #2 and #4, our teacher candidates are learning college level mathematics both abstractly and quantitatively with an emphasis on modeling. Our program requires several mathematics courses that integrate technology as a tool for learning. While instructors of each course determine exactly how much technology is used, it is a common tool. For example, graphing calculators are required for the three courses in the calculus sequence, and these courses tend to incorporate graphical and numerical techniques in conjunction with theoretical ones. Some instructors choose to use computer algebra systems in these courses to enhance the various ways of understanding. As teacher candidates move into higher-level mathematics classes, their ability to use a variety of technologies becomes important.

To ensure that teacher candidates have a sufficient background and proficiency with a variety of technologies, our program requires all of our majors to complete a course entitled *Math 340: Introduction to Scientific Computing*. The main goal of this course is to provide teacher candidates with a basis for using technology appropriately to aid in their own learning of higher-level mathematical content. In this way, they are moving into the intersection of content knowledge and technological knowledge within the TPACK framework from a learner's point of view as evidenced by its learning outcomes:

Math 340 (Introduction to Scientific Computing)

By the end of the course we expect students to be able to:

- Model problems mathematically and use mathematical software to solve or simulate these problems.

- Develop algorithms and implement them in the appropriate software or programming language.
- Present algorithms and solutions to problems in a mathematically sophisticated manner using a scientific documentation environment.
- Know the benefits and drawbacks of each of the computational tools used during the semester.

After successfully completing this course, teacher candidates are expected to be able to use a variety of mathematical software in other upper level mathematics courses without explicit instruction. In this way, teacher candidates in numerical analysis, linear algebra, discrete mathematics, and other courses are able to choose appropriate technologies to aid them in understanding the mathematical content. They also have developed the skills to present their understandings in mathematical ways. Through this integration, we encourage all of our teacher candidates to move into the zone that allows technology and content knowledge to interact seamlessly from the student point of view. They are trying to enhance their own understanding of the content through a technological lens.

Further integration of technology and content knowledge from the teacher perspective occurs as teacher candidates complete Capstone projects and prepare presentations of their work using technology, a part of the required course *Math 479: Capstone Seminar.* In this course, each teacher candidate chooses problems to explore and/or to solve. Often this work entails use of statistical analysis packages, computer algebra systems, dynamical graphing programs, or other digital technologies. What is common to all teacher candidates is the requirement to present their findings in print and as presentations using appropriate software. As each project is specific to the individual, each teacher candidate must demonstrate the integration of choosing appropriate technologies to aid in his or her understanding and in the presentation of that

understanding to others. In this way, they begin to consider the intersection of technological and content knowledge from a teacher view.

In the required geometry class, *Math 411: Foundations in Geometry,* a more advanced level course, teacher candidates are introduced to *Geometer's Sketchpad*, a dynamical graphical software package, through an exploratory unit on transformational geometry. As teacher candidates explore particular examples and topics, they are asked to develop theorems that they then prove formally based on their experiences with the technology.

This allows students to play with shapes and form, making it easier to construct standard geometry proofs. In this regard, the software program merely emulates what was done earlier when learning geometry. However, the computer program does more than that. By allowing students to "play" with geometrical constructions, it also changes the nature of learning geometry itself – proofs by construction are a form of representation in mathematics that was not available prior to this technology (Koehler, 2011, TCK).

In this instance, teacher candidates experience how they can learn particular content with technological assistance and how that interaction allows for a different type of understanding. Through comparison of their own work in earlier parts of this course, teacher candidates are encouraged to consider the differences in the ways of understanding that are possible.

These examples demonstrate the incorporation of particular technologies for specific purposes in mathematics courses. Through these experiences, teacher candidates move along the early pathways from content knowledge and technological knowledge into the intersection of these two zones from both a student point of view and a teacher point of view. Furthermore, their continued work with content and technology aid our teacher candidates in moving from the early TPACK stage of Recognizing towards the next stage of Accepting in their TPACK development. Thus, additional steps on the pathway of TPACK development also help lead teacher candidates towards more sophisticated stages, Adapting and Exploring, as they begin to choose the software that would be most useful to their own learning and teaching.

Beginning from Technology and Pedagogical Knowledge

Pedagogical knowledge is the information we gather from research and experience of expert educators that helps us understand connections between teaching and learning. Effective teachers will use pedagogical knowledge to make decisions regarding how to convey and reveal subject matter to students. They are aware of the preconceptions and background knowledge that students typically bring to each subject and of strategies and instructional materials that can be of assistance. In addition, they understand and solve the possible difficulties likely to arise in the classroom and modify their practice accordingly. Their instructional repertoire allows them to create multiple paths to knowledge, in general, and to the subjects they teach, in particular. Obviously, this is not possible without specifically addressing the area in which the use of technology and pedagogical knowledge converge. Since the presence of technology is unavoidable in 21st century classrooms, what do teacher candidates need in order to be prepared for integrating technology appropriately into their teaching practices? As teacher candidates move into their methods courses, it is essential for them to develop a solid Technological Pedagogical Knowledge (TPK) which is described as "knowledge of the existence, components and capabilities of various technologies as they are used in teaching and learning settings, and conversely, knowing how teaching might change as the result of using particular technologies" (Koehler, 2011, TPK).

The CCSS Standard for Mathematical Practice #5 emphasizes that all students must be able to consider available tools and use them appropri-

ately in their problem solving. This must include knowing how and when to embrace technological tools such as graphing calculators, dynamic geometry software, computer algebra systems, etc. If students are to be proficient in using the tools appropriately, then it is of the utmost importance that their teachers feel comfortable doing the same. Technology should be introduced and utilized to deepen understanding or reduce reliance on routine tasks so that students engage in higher-level mathematical reasoning. Teacher candidates need to spend significant time becoming familiar with the standards, considering multiple ways of presenting content addressed in the standards, and building technological knowledge necessary to support development of connections between and across those standards. Our teacher candidates begin a two-course sequence with *Math 414*. In this course, we want our teacher candidates to achieve four major learning outcomes:

Math 414 (Introduction to Secondary Mathematics Teaching Methods)

The future teacher will be able to:

- Understand and be familiar with the Common Core State Standards for secondary mathematics as well as the NCTM Principles and Standards.
- Identify mathematical connections among various topics and can apply content, processes, and reasoning to real world situations.
- Identify mathematics curricular goals and plan instruction to meet these goals, and identify appropriate uses of technology.
- Identify appropriate uses of technology and plan instruction that uses technology to enhance teaching and learning, and use technology to assess learning.

This course is taught based on a learning community model. Wenger and Lave (1991) proposed a model of situated learning that involves engagement in a community of practice. They argue that communities of practice are everywhere and that as individuals we are included in many of them – whether at work, school, home, or leisure activities. These communities evolve around things that matter to the people that are involved (Wenger, 1998). In keeping with this idea, we believe the shared experiences both in and out of the classroom can serve the development of a learning community in which teacher candidates and professor work collaboratively to explore technologies and develop strong TPK. The teacher candidates are all responsible for presenting and sharing their thoughts and ideas related to the Common Core State Standards.

This course is the first time during their program that teacher candidates are introduced to the Common Core State Standards in grades 9-12 and their implications for teaching. At the same time, teacher candidates are exposed to various forms of technologies that may be used to teach mathematics. Teacher candidates are given opportunities through presentations and written assignments to use technology productivity tools to complete required professional tasks. While not yet using the tools themselves in authentic teaching experiences, teacher candidates do begin to make meaningful connections between their own technological knowledge and how to teach. Through practice and demonstration using technology, they begin to align the content with the integration of technology. Teacher candidates are asked to develop lesson plans based on standards. While doing so, there is a focus on differentiating between appropriate and inappropriate uses of technology for teaching and learning as well as using electronic resources to design and implement learning activities.

Through purposeful class activities in *Math 414* involving various technologies as a tool for mathematical sense making, it is hoped that the teacher candidates move to a level of acceptance in which decisions are made regarding the ben-

efits or risks involved with using technology for instruction. It is important that teacher candidates begin to realize the capabilities of using technology as a cognitive tool to maximize student learning and to facilitate higher order thinking skills. To do so requires time to research and evaluate the accuracy, relevance, and appropriateness of these technologies. Teacher candidates also need time to explore electronic information resources that complement their developing pedagogical styles. The community of learning encourages valuable debate and open discussions that help each individual develop positive attitudes toward teaching and learning mathematics with an appropriate technology.

The course provides several experiences where technology is used to move between and within multiple representations of functions (numerical, graphical, verbal, and symbolic). For example, one activity involves using TI-Nspire technology to explore geometric relationships between the height of a vase and the volume of water in the vase by changing the values dynamically. The shape of the vase can be manipulated as well as the height of the water in the vase so that the relationships can be explored. The teacher candidates also get experience using data collection devices to collect information such as distances and temperatures for the purposes of developing mathematical models based on the data.

Additionally, teacher candidates are expected to explore and review numerous virtual manipulative and electronic resources to analyze whether they might be appropriate tools to use with students to address Common Core State Standards in grades 9-12. As the manipulatives are explored, the teacher candidates have a chance to investigate the use of interactive whiteboards for active teaching and learning. Ample time is allowed for discussion of how, when, and why to use the technologies to advance student thinking. As the course progresses, the teacher candidates have their first experiences developing lesson plans that address specific standards in the Common Core for which technology can play an important role. This aids in their development of recognizing the role of technology and adapting activities that can engage their students.

Strong technological knowledge is not enough when it comes to teaching mathematics effectively. Teachers must apply their skills in using technology with understanding of teaching strategies which engage students in mathematics. "The value of technology to the teacher lies not so much in the answers technology provides but rather in the questions it affords" (Dick & Hollebrands, 2011, p. xvi). It is the teaching pedagogy employed by the teacher that defines whether or not technology opens doors to understanding or becomes an instrument of distraction that diminishes mathematical sense-making. The experiences students have in *Math 414* create another pathway that aids our teacher candidates in moving toward the intersection of pedagogy, technology, and content. As teacher candidates progress in their program of study, they will begin to apply teaching strategies using technology that support the construction of content knowledge.

Beginning from Content and Pedagogical Knowledge

The notion of Pedagogical Content Knowledge was first described by Shulman (1986) as a way to consider pedagogy and content as inclusive components of a teacher's knowledge that inform the teaching decisions that best fit a specific subject matter. This includes knowing the different representations commonly used to present and make sense of curricular material, understanding the connections necessary to unveil so that students may overcome difficulties in learning a concept due to prior misconceptions, and making pedagogical decisions that promote students' mathematical proficiency.

Because of the strong emphasis on content inherent in most secondary education teacher preparation courses, there are often many factors that make it difficult for teacher candidates

to gain access to authentic classroom experiences prior to their field placements. In order to provide additional opportunities for teacher candidates to plan lessons, Mathematics and Mathematics Education faculty work together to personalize end of course projects in several of our mathematics content courses. While applied mathematics students might be focused on a modeling project, teacher candidates will often be asked to develop an activity that integrates the course material into a secondary mathematics lesson plan. These recurring connections between higher level mathematics courses such as Discrete Structures or Linear Algebra, and the mathematics they will be expected to teach in high school, help teacher candidates understand the value of deeper content understanding that serves the purpose of sense making for appropriately challenging task design. This is a connective pathway from viewing mathematics as learners to constructing new knowledge of mathematics as teachers.

Another course specifically geared towards future mathematics teachers is *Math 300,* a problem-solving course in which teacher candidates are actively engaged in collaborative group work that helps them improve their problem solving abilities, while encouraging them to argue solutions with their peers in a constant open-communication atmosphere. In *Math 300,* teacher candidates have to simultaneously assume the roles of doers of mathematics, trusting members of a learning community where they learn to listen and to understand others' ways of thinking, and at times, teachers for their peers. This course specifically addresses the CCSS-M Standard for Mathematical Practice #1 where students are expected to "make sense of problems and persevere in solving them", as well as Standard #3 focused on constructing "viable arguments and critique the reasoning of others". Content standards addressed in *Math 300* cover a wide range of secondary mathematics topics across all major content strands of the CCSS-M, therefore providing teacher candidates with a collection of problem solving situations that they may immediately pull from once in the classroom. When exploring a variety of problem solving approaches, teacher candidates are also exposed to Standards for Mathematical Practices #7 and #8, which permeate all the mathematics content courses in the program. Learning outcomes for *Math 300* include:

Math 300 (Methods and Techniques for Problem Solving in Mathematics)

The future teachers will be able to:

- Identify and apply methods and techniques that are helpful in solving problems.
- Solve problems using problem solving steps.
- Explain and discuss problem solving strategies.
- Create problems that may be solved using a variety of strategies.

Using the TPACK framework to analyze our program has helped us identify areas where technology can be better integrated. For example, *Math 300* has previously been taught in ways that provided teacher candidates with limited opportunity to integrate technology in their reasoning and solutions. However it is an obvious place for us to move teacher candidates along a major pathway from pedagogical content knowledge experiences to more integrated TPACK experiences, therefore placing the course in the center of the TPACK diagram. In particular the use of Computer Algebra software can reinforce the nature of mathematical inquiry and investigation, conjecture building, conjecture testing, and developing logical arguments.

To build on the introductory methods course *Math 414*, seniors in our program take a second methods class, *Math 415*, which can be taken concurrent to a first semester internship, and directly precedes the full time student teaching semester. Learning outcomes for *Math 415* are as follows:

Math 415 (Methods for Teaching Mathematics in the Secondary Schools)

The future teachers will be able to:

- Reflect upon and discuss contemporary issues in teaching mathematics at the high school level.
- Identify mathematics curricular goals.
- Plan instruction to meet these goals.
- Implement lesson presentation skills.
- Evaluate mathematics instruction.

Following a similar community-based model as *Math 414*, students in *Math 415* routinely engage in lesson planning and teaching activities following discussions of important components of teaching, such as classroom management, questioning and student engagement, technology integration, assessment, curriculum, and mathematics. The community-modeling approach of the course assumes teacher candidates are actively involved in designing rubrics for the purpose of course assessments, leading and facilitating discussions, and taking turns teaching their peers. The students who are simultaneously enrolled in an internship experience often bring to class discussion topics which allow the community to provide a "just-in-time" model of trouble shooting professional development that is one of the highlights of communities of practice when implemented in the schools. A variety of teaching methods are enacted and discussed in the light of benefits they may bring to teaching, learning, and curricular concerns; these include interactive lecturing, inquiry-based practice, and collaborative group work.

As an overall course project, students are asked to design a full unit plan that will be one of the evidences required by the North Carolina Department of Public Instruction for obtaining a teacher credential. Within this unit, curricular goals must be clearly identified, alignment to the Common Core State Standards is required, and a variety of teaching and assessment strategies must be used, including integration of technology in instruction.

Through this unit planning, teacher candidates begin to comprehend the bigger picture of curricular alignment, incorporation of multiple representations in instruction, and purposeful planning for promoting their future students' reasoning and sense-making. For teacher candidates, these tasks go beyond their own knowledge of mathematics and how to solve a particular problem, to include identifying student learning objectives, researching best ways to present a particular concept, becoming knowledgeable of high school students' common misconceptions, questioning for inquiry into students' prior knowledge, and students' understanding of new material. Regarding technology, the work started in *Math 414* expands to the necessity for reflections on when the use of a particular technology is appropriate depending on the content presented and student learning objectives. Teacher candidates are now asked to make choices that will have consequences for their instructional practices. Through these activities, teacher candidates are actively engaged in the center of the TPACK diagram with opportunities to reach Adapting, and perhaps Exploring, Stages of Development when deciding to incorporate specific technologies in their plans. Open sharing of these explorations into lesson planning and task design positions teacher candidates as active members of a 21st Century learning community.

When researching pre-service teachers' acquisition of TPACK in a teacher preparation program, Meagher, Özgün-Koca, and Edwards (2011) found that "if pre-service teachers are to develop a positive attitude to the use of advanced digital technologies in their instructional practice, they require more than a methods class to develop TPACK" (p. 259). They emphasize the role of field experiences in shaping teacher candidates' attitudes and dispositions towards using technology. With such findings in mind, we recently decided to address a need for increased collaboration between practicing teachers and teacher candidates earlier in the program through an adaptation of lesson study cycles into *Math 415* that will help teacher candidates better understand the importance of technology and curriculum integration.

Research on models of professional development interventions that best promote transfer of new teaching knowledge into the classroom shows that a lesson study approach is most efficient in ensuring teachers will actually implement the new ideas and materials in their teaching (Faughn, Brown, Kent, & Tuba, 2011). At the teacher preparation level, one way to adapt lesson study is to have teacher candidates commonly plan lessons during class time and receive feedback on those lesson plans from a practicing master teacher through a back and forth discussion until the lesson is ready to be implemented. Video recordings and conference calls can then be used in order for teacher candidates to view and reflect upon the teaching of their lesson by this experienced master teacher, who will also provide feedback on the lesson once implemented in the classroom. Teacher candidates can then revise the lesson once again in light of what went well and what needs to be changed (Meagher et al., 2011b).

We hope that requiring the use of technology in the lesson planning stage of the lesson study cycle and the teacher candidate-Master teacher feedback loops will move some of our teacher candidates to the Exploring Stage of Development with that particular piece of technology, while the post-lesson reflection with feedback from the mathematics education faculty teaching the course will facilitate reaching this stage with the technology used during the lesson. This is the first activity that our teacher candidates will engage in prior to their student teaching experience, where they may begin to observe and understand the different learning approaches of high school students when faced with having to use technology. It will be a crucial experience in reinforcing CCSS-M Standard for Mathematics Practice #5.

Reaching the Center: Technological, Pedagogical, and Content Knowledge

We have now argued the necessity of moving teacher candidates through multiple TPACK pathways to help them promote students' mathematical practices described in the Common Core documents.

Finally, at the intersection of all three elements is Technological Pedagogical Content Knowledge (TPACK). True technology integration is understanding and negotiating the relationships between these three components of knowledge. A teacher capable of negotiating these relationships represents a form of expertise different from, and greater than, the knowledge of a disciplinary expert (say a mathematician or a historian), a technology expert (a computer scientist) and a pedagogical expert (an experienced educator). Effective technology integration for pedagogy around specific subject matter requires developing sensitivity to the dynamic, [transactional] relationship between all three components (Koehler, 2011, TPACK).

As discussed in earlier sections, examples of early experiences in the center are included in courses throughout the program. Early opportunities for moving along pathways towards the center will position teacher candidates in our program to embrace digital technologies and the type of inquiry-based practices that accompany their use in the classroom. Table 1 summarizes activities that we identified as places where teacher candidates are introduced to the center with specific technological tools that support Common Core Mathematical Practices.

Based on the experiences summarized in Table 1, by the time teacher candidates go out for field placement, our goal is for them to demonstrate readiness to work in the TPACK center. During their last semester, all teacher candidates are enrolled in internship/student teaching, which serves as a culminating experience with the following outcomes:

Math 491 (Supervised Student Teaching – Mathematics 9-12)

By the end of the course we expect students to be able to:

- Demonstrate proficiency in teaching mathematics at the high school level.
- Be able to identify mathematics curricular goals, plan instruction to meet these goals, implement lesson presentation skills, and evaluate mathematics instruction.
- Reflect on teaching experiences addressing the following dimensions of teaching: (1) Classroom Management; (2) Planning; (3) Questioning and Student Engagement; (4) Technology; (5) Assessment and Grading;

Table 1. Pre-field placement experiences that move teacher candidates along pathways to the center

Pathways	Courses	CCSS Experiences	Technology Examples
Content and Pedagogy to Center	Math 300 re-visited with technology Math 415	Revisiting Algebra Lesson study and unit plan	CAS, Graphing Calculators Student choice
Technology and Content to Center	Math 340 Capstone Math 411	Projects Projects Revisiting Geometry	Variety Variety Dynamic Geometry Software
Technology and Pedagogy to Center	Math 414	Lesson planning and curricular study	Graphing Calculators, Software, Interactive Whiteboards

(6) Curricular Choices and Pacing; (7) Knowledge of Mathematics for Teaching.

Once in the classroom, teacher candidates are able to directly experiment with the integration of technology in working with their own students. As they develop into reflective practitioners and define their identity as educators, it is expected that they will move toward the TPACK center and advance to higher Stages of Development.

IMPLICATIONS, CHALLENGES, AND FUTURE DIRECTIONS

Technology is an integral part of society, and it is essential that we embrace and explore opportunities for developing higher-order reasoning and thinking skills for secondary mathematics teacher candidates. All stakeholders have a responsibility to encourage appropriate uses of technology to engage students and develop mathematical understanding. We would like to offer a word of caution, however, that unequal access may exist from one placement school to another, which in turn will shape opportunities and development in the use of digital technologies. While the model presented here is a step in the right direction, there is much more work to be done. Wilson (2008) suggests that teacher education programs must serve as the conduit for connecting research and innovations in technology with practice and curriculum in mathematics (p. 425). Additional questions to be answered include:

1. Do our teacher candidates actually progress through the TPACK Stages of Development as we intend?
2. How do we assess teacher candidates' experiences with digital technologies as a means to enhance their students' experiences in support of the Common Core State Standards?
3. What means of support are necessary to encourage continued use of technology to further develop 21st century skills teaching and learning after graduation in classrooms with differing technology resources?

Addressing question #1 can take place within our program. There are several TPACK surveys (Koehler, 2011, TPACK surveys) that can be used as assessment instruments for evaluating teacher candidates' level of TPACK acquisition at various points in our program. This will help us gauge teacher candidates' changes in attitudes towards technology and towards its use for teaching and learning mathematics. These same instruments can help us to begin answering Question #2. According to Niess et al. (2009), the Stages of Development can be targeted to four specific themes to help us further unpack the levels of TPACK acquisition our teacher candidates may demonstrate: Curriculum and Assessment, Teaching, Learning, and Access. Indicators for these themes can serve as a tool for evaluating how accomplished our teacher candidates have become in using the technologies they were introduced to in their courses for the purpose of TPACK implementation in their own classrooms. In particular, analysis of teacher candidates' levels of TPACK acquisition before graduation can become part of the student teaching/internship review process. Continuing that assessment and addressing question #3 will be more difficult because of issues of access and control of external factors once teacher candidates have graduated and moved into the teacher role fulltime. Longitudinal research that follows these teacher candidates through their early years of teaching is clearly indicated. We can begin this process through surveys and other self-reporting instruments, but a more focused research design should be developed. It is only through following our teacher candidates' into their classrooms that we will be able to assess the long-term efficacy of our efforts to guide them along the pathways of TPACK acquisition.

CONCLUSION

The Conference Board of Mathematical Sciences insists that teacher candidates of mathematics be exposed to specific mathematical topics and progressions as well as applications of mathematics, modeling, and connections with other disciplines such as engineering and computational biology. This necessitates building strong 21st century skills to enhance mathematics teaching and learning. In addition, teacher preparation programs should immerse teacher candidates in various experiences throughout their program of study that challenge mathematical habits of mind, incorporate sound mathematical practices, and place a greater emphasis on field and clinical experiences. To ensure that teacher candidates are provided with these type of experiences, professional learning communities must develop including teachers at all levels, mathematicians (at two- and four-year institutions), and mathematics educators (Conference Board of Mathematical Sciences (CBMS), 2011, p. 15).

We have described a model for teacher preparation that emphasizes the importance of developing 21st century skills. The TPACK Framework provides a foundation to develop a series of pathways to integrate content knowledge, pedagogical knowledge, and technological knowledge. We argue the necessity of moving teacher candidates through these pathways to help them promote in their students the types of mathematical practices described in the Common Core documents.

REFERENCES

Association of Mathematics Teacher Educators. (2009). *Mathematics TPACK (technological pedagogical content knowledge) framework*. Retrieved from http://www.amte.net/sites/all/themes/amte/resources/MathTPACKFramework.pdf

Common Core State Standards Initiative (CCSSI). (2010). *Common core state standards for mathematics*. Washington, DC: National Governors Association Center for Best Practices and the Council of Chief State Officers. Retrieved from http://www.corestandards.org

Conference Board of Mathematical Sciences. (2011). *Common standards and the mathematical education of teachers* (White Paper). Retrieved from http://www.cbmsWeb.org/Forum3/CBMS_Forum_White_Paper.pdf

Dick, T. P., & Hollebrands, K. F. (2011). Introduction to focus in high school mathematics: Technology to support reasoning and sense making. In Dick, T. P., & Hollebrands, K. F. (Eds.), *Focus in high school mathematics: Technology to support reasoning and sense making* (pp. xi–xvii). Reston, VA: National Council of Teachers of Mathematics.

Ellington, A. J. (2003). A meta-analysis of the effects of calculators on students' achievement and attitude: Levels in precollege mathematics classes. *Journal for Research in Mathematics Education, 34*, 433–463. doi:10.2307/30034795.

Faughn, A. P., Brown, K., Kent, N., & Tuba, I. (2011). *Supporting beginning mathematics teachers with technology-based professional development*. Paper presented at the 2011 meeting of the American Educational Research Association. New Orleans, LA.

Fey, J. T., Cuoco, A., Kieran, C., McMullin, L., & Zbiek, R. M. (Eds.). (2003). *Computer algebra systems in secondary school mathematics education*. Reston, VA: National Council of Teachers of Mathematics.

Guerrero, S. (2010). Technological pedagogical content knowledge in the mathematics classroom. *Journal of Digital Learning in Teacher Education*, *26*(4), 132–139.

Jones, K. (2002). Research on the use of dynamic geometry software: Implications for the classroom. *MicroMath*, *18*(3), 18–20.

Koehler, M. J. (2011). TPACK – Technological *pedagogical and content knowledge*. Retrieved from http://tpck.org/

Meagher, M., Edwards, M. T., & Koca, A. (2011b). *Project CRAFTeD: An adapted lesson study partnering preservice mathematics teachers with a master teacher*. Paper presented at the 33rd annual meeting of the North American Chapter of the International Group for the Psychology of Mathematics Education. Reno, NV.

Meagher, M., Özgün-Koca, S. A., & Edwards, M. T. (2011a). Preservice teachers' experiences with advanced digital technologies: The interplay between technology in a preservice classroom and in field placements. *Contemporary Issues in Technology & Teacher Education*, *11*(3), 243–270.

Mishra, P. (2012). *Design and pedagogy*. Retrieved from http://punya.educ.msu.edu/research/design-pedagogy/

Mishra, P., & Koehler, M. J. (2006). Technological pedagogical content knowledge: A framework for teacher knowledge. *Teachers College Record*, *108*(6), 1017–1054. doi:10.1111/j.1467-9620.2006.00684.x.

Niess, M. L., Ronau, R. N., Shafer, K. G., Driskell, S. O., Harper, S. R., & Johnston, C. et al. (2009). Mathematics teacher TPACK standards and development model. *Contemporary Issues in Technology & Teacher Education*, *9*(1), 4–24.

North Carolina Professional Teaching Standards Commission. (2006). *North Carolina professional teaching standards*. Retrieved from http://www.ncpublicschools.org/docs/profdev/standards/teachingstandards.pdf

Partnership for 21st Century Skills. (2011). Information, media and technology skills. Retrieved from http://www.p21.org/overview/skills-framework/61

Shulman, L. S. (1986). Those who understand: Knowledge growth in teaching. *Educational Researcher*, *15*(2), 4–31. doi:10.3102/0013189X015002004.

Wilson, P. S. (2008). Teacher education: A conduit to the classroom. In G.W. Blume & M.K. Heid (Eds.), Research on Technology and the Teaching and Learning of Mathematics: Volume 2: Cases and Perspectives (pp. 415-426). Charlotte, NC: Information Age Publishing, Inc.

ADDITIONAL READING

(2008). In Blume, G. W., & Heid, M. K. (Eds.). Research on technology and the teaching and learning of mathematics: *Vol. 2. Cases and perspectives*. Charlotte, NC: Information Age Publishing, Inc..

Conference Board of Mathematical Sciences. (2011). *Common standards and the mathematical education of teachers* (White Paper). Retrieved from http://www.cbmsWeb.org/Forum3/CBMS_Forum_White_Paper.pdf

(2008). InHeid, M. K., & Blume, G. W. (Eds.). Research on technology and the teaching and learning of mathematics: *Vol. 1. Research synthesis.* Charlotte, NC: Information Age Publishing, Inc..

Koehler, M. J. (2011). *TPACK – Technological pedagogical and content knowledge.* Retrieved from http://www.tpck.org/

Partnership for 21st Century Skills. (2011). Information, media and technology skills. Retrieved from http://www.p21.org/overview/skills-framework/61

KEY TERMS AND DEFINITIONS

21st Century Skills: Learning a profession in the 21st Century requires a specific set of skills that reflect an ability to solve problems collaboratively while communicating with and navigating evolving digital technologies. Examples of such skills include: Sharing and critically adopting knowledge, ideas and resources; addressing challenges as members of a team; and using social networks and other 21st century technologies to make individual contributions. Higher order and critical thinking skills will be demonstrated in a classroom where 21st Century skills are encouraged and developed.

Content Knowledge (CK): Or mathematical content knowledge in our case, refers to a teacher's understanding of mathematical ideas including concepts, procedures, and reasoning skills, as well as an understanding of the connections that serve as the underlying structure of the discipline.

Pedagogical Content Knowledge (PCK): Is more than just the intersection of knowledge about particular content and knowledge about particular pedagogies. It is the interaction of these two knowledge bases to create a separate type of knowledge that encompasses how to choose, organize, and present specific content so that learning occurs.

Pedagogical Knowledge (PK): Is familiarity with techniques, approaches, and strategies that may be used in a classroom to engage students and support the teaching and learning of mathematics.

Technological Content Knowledge (TCK): Develops when students have the opportunity to integrate technology with mathematical content in meaningful ways. Mathematics is not simply the backdrop in which technology is used but is an organizer and shaper of students' technological experiences. Likewise, the constraints and affordances that are offered by a particular mathematical technological tool help define the boundaries of mathematical learning.

Technological Pedagogical Content Knowledge (TPACK): Is the blending of all three knowledge bases to create new knowledge that is more than the sum of the individual parts. This new type of knowledge integrates aspects of all three knowledge bases with particular emphasis on the relationships created by those interactions.

Technological Pedagogical Knowledge (TPK): Refers to the interplay between pedagogical and technological knowledge bases. This entails being able to negotiate all aspects of how and when to use certain technologies to advance student learning. Moreover, it involves a teacher's understanding about how pedagogical choices and preferences inform the use of technology in the classroom.

Technology Knowledge (TK): Includes skills and understanding necessary to use, operate, and demonstrate technologies such as communication tools, software, and hardware to accomplish a variety of tasks.

Chapter 25
Using the iPad to Develop Preservice Teachers' Understanding of the Common Core State Standards for Mathematical Practice

Mary Grassetti
Framingham State University, USA

Silvy Brookby
Framingham State University, USA

ABSTRACT

The Standards for Mathematical Practice as delineated in the Common Core State Standards for Mathematics describe the processes, proficiencies, and habits of mind that students are expected to develop through their engagement with mathematics (Dacey & Polly, 2012). The purpose of this chapter is to discuss, anecdotally, how the iPad, a tablet computer designed by Apple ™, can be used to develop preservice teachers' understanding and implementation of the Standards for Mathematical Practice, most specifically Mathematical Practice Standard 3: Construct viable arguments and critique the reasoning of others. Under examination are the authors' experiences using the iPad as an observational tool during student teaching and as a teaching tool in their mathematics methods courses. The chapter concludes with suggestions for additional uses of the iPad to support preservice teachers as they work to develop their understanding of the Standards for Mathematical Practice.

DOI: 10.4018/978-1-4666-4086-3.ch025

INTRODUCTION

The Common Core State Standards for Mathematics ([CCSSM]; CCSSI, 2010) delineate not only the mathematical content that students need to know and understand but also the mathematical practices that students must develop in order to be successful practitioners of mathematics. The Standards for Mathematical Practice (See Table 1) documented in the CCSSM "describe varieties of expertise that mathematics educators at all levels should seek to develop in their students" (CCSSI, p. 6). The Standards for Mathematical Practice describe the processes, proficiencies, and habits of mind that students are expected to develop through their engagement with mathematics (Dacey & Polly, 2012). For students to be able to develop the processes and habits of mind espoused by the CCSSM, teachers must work intentionally and systematically on their development.

In this chapter we will discuss anecdotally how the iPad, a tablet computer designed by Apple ™, can be used to develop preservice teachers' understanding and implementation of the Standards for Mathematical Practice, most specifically Mathematical Practice Standard 3: *Construct viable arguments and critique the reasoning of others.* Since Practice Standard 3 inherently encompasses discourse practices used by the teacher, the chapter will begin with a review of the literature examining traditional and reform-orientated classroom discourse to examine how classroom discourse shapes students' opportunities to construct viable arguments and critique the reasoning of their peers. Next, the chapter will provide a review of the literature detailing the ways in which new mobile technologies are used to support and enhance the process of teaching and learning. The chapter will then describe how the authors have used the iPad as an observational tool with student teachers and discuss how the iPad has the potential to enhance the observation experience through enhancing collaboration and self-reflection. The authors will share how they have utilized the iPad in tertiary environments such as a mathematics methods class, to develop preservice teachers' understanding of the Standards for Mathematical Practice before they are in the role of student teacher. The chapter will conclude with suggestions for additional uses of the iPad to support preservice teachers as they work to develop their understanding of the Standards for Mathematical Practice as delineated by the Common Core State Standards for Mathematics.

EXAMINING DISCOURSE PRACTICES

Developing a classroom community where rich mathematical discourse unfolds can be a challenging endeavor for teachers (Mendez, Sherin, & Louis, 2007) and especially challenging for preservice teachers during the student teaching internship. Mathematical Practice Standard 3 (MPS3) requires a discourse community where students use their understanding of mathematics content to construct viable arguments, and as importantly examine, compare, and critique the arguments of their peers (CCSSM, 2010). To develop this practice, students must be provided multiple and varied opportunities to "talk through" their understanding whether it be incomplete, developing, or on target because it is through

Table 1. Standards for mathematical practice

1. Make sense of problems and preserve in solving them.
2. Reason abstractly and quantitatively.
3. Construct viable arguments and critique the reasoning of others.
4. Model with mathematics.
5. Use appropriate tools.
6. Attend to precision.
7. Look for and make use of structure.
8. Look for and express regularity in repeated reasoning.

the vehicle of talk that MPS 3 develops. Giving students the necessary *air time* to talk through their thinking provides them with a metacognitive opportunity whereby they can reflect on their thinking and mathematical reasoning (Chapin, O'Connor, Anderson, 2009). Moreover, when a student talks through her mathematical reasoning it provides her peers with another point of view from which to examine and compare each others' thinking and reasoning and subsequently develop and refine their own mathematical arguments in response. Providing such opportunities must be an intentional move on the part of the teacher. Such a move can be difficult to manage and facilitate, especially given that most preservice teachers have experienced a traditional approach to learning mathematics. Examining the ways in which discourse has traditionally been facilitated within the mathematics classroom will provide a foundation for examining the shift that is needed for MPS3 to develop.

Traditional Discourse

Traditionally in classrooms teachers and students interact within a very predictable discourse paradigm, especially during whole class discussions (Wells & Arauz, 2006). Research on classroom discourse reveals that, for-the-most-part, classroom discourse takes the form of a three-part sequence wherein the teacher asks a question, a student is selected by the teacher to respond, and finally the teacher evaluates the student's response. This pattern of discourse has been labeled the initiation-reply-evaluation sequence (IRE) (Mehan, 1979) and is a pervasive form of discourse found in many classrooms across the United States and abroad (see Abd-Kadir & Hardman, 2007; Inagaki, Morita, & Hatano, 1999; Nassaji & Wells, 2000).

Such a pattern of discourse is counter to the types of discourse proposed by the CCSSM (2010) and delineated in the Standards for Mathematical Practice. The practice standards require teachers

to provide students with opportunities to make sense of problems and preserve in solving them, reason abstractly and quantitatively, construct viable arguments and critique the reasoning of others, and attend to precision in their explanations and justifications. Engaging in such deep and worthwhile mathematics will require a shift in how discourse is orchestrated within classrooms.

Traditionally in the United States the mathematics classroom has been teacher-directed with the teacher showing students how to solve problems using traditional algorithms. An international comparison study by Ma (1999) compared the procedural and conceptual understanding of mathematics teachers from China and the United States. Ma found that the Chinese teachers possessed a deeper conceptual and procedural understanding of the elementary mathematics curriculum than did their American counterparts. The U.S. teachers tended to be procedurally focused. Most teachers showed competence in the area of algorithmic manipulation of whole number subtraction and multidigit multiplication. However, when it came to more advanced topics, such as division with fractions, area and perimeter, the U.S. teachers lacked the procedural skills as well as the conceptual understanding needed to solve such problems. In contrast, the Chinese teachers demonstrated not only a strong procedural understanding of all four topics but a conceptual understanding as well. In addition, the Chinese teachers were adept at delineating the relationship between the conceptual and procedural aspects of the elementary mathematics curriculum.

Since mathematics classrooms in the U.S. have traditionally focused on rote memorization of standard algorithms, preservice teachers enter teacher education programs with a limited understanding of different ways to solve even the most basic of mathematics problems. A study documenting the discourse practices used by novice teachers as they attempted to enact mathematics reform practices (Grassetti, 2010) found that eliciting different solutions was a foundational practice from which other reform orientated practices could emerge. However, the study also revealed the novice teachers were weary of allowing students to solve problems differently because they themselves only understand mathematics using traditional algorithms. As one study participant revealed, "I think being annoyed is only coming from my own insecurities or my own confusion, so if I'm teaching something one way and I've come to understand it that one way and someone does something different, it throws me off (Grassetti, 2010, p. 116).

Although preservice teachers in college classrooms today were educated during the height of the reform movement, reform initiatives have had little impact on how mathematics is taught (Hardy, 2004). The changes that have been made in school mathematics have been superficial and "students persistently experience a fundamental curriculum of fact learning and routinized computations where they are expected to be consumers of established mathematical truths" (p. 104). In her book documenting her attempt to change her mathematics teaching practice Heaton (2000) poignantly describes, through her own self-reflection, how mathematics is often taught in schools. She reflected:

I taught mathematics the way I had learned it up through college calculus. Whether I was the learner or the teacher the routine was the same – memorizing rules and procedures, computing problems in silence, and checking answers with the teacher's guide (p. 2).

If, as Heaton asserts, we teach as we were taught, it is clear that the preservice teachers currently enrolled in teacher education programs will need to be supported and guided as they learn to use discourse practices different from those they are familiar with. Such support and guidance will subsequently help their future students develop the processes and dispositions advocated by the Standards for Mathematical Practice. The follow-

ing section will examine the types of discourse practices that are necessary for teachers to utilize if we want students to develop the Standards for Mathematical Practice.

Reform-Orientated Discourse

In 1989 and again in 1991 and 2000 the National Council of Teachers of Mathematics proposed standards that called for teachers to orchestrate discourse so that "reasoning and arguing about mathematical meanings" (NCTM 1991, p. 2) becomes the norm. In such classrooms students are expected to actively engage in the role of *talker* rather than only in the traditional role of passive *listener*. Teachers, whose classrooms are oriented toward reform, expect students to make conjectures, explain, and justify their divergent methods of solution; argue for the appropriateness of their methods; and attempt to understand and critique the methods posed by their classmates and teacher. Similarly, the Standards for Mathematical Practice, documented in the CCSSM (2010), expect students to develop the same types of dispositions or practices as they work with and build their mathematical proficiency. Moreover, such dispositions and practices developed in the mathematics classroom can and should be "transferable skills that students can develop and keep with them for a lifetime" (Sommers & Olsen, n.d., p. 10).

The teacher is responsible for facilitating the development of the practice standards in her students and within the mathematics classroom. As such, she must orchestrate discussions so that students have opportunities to explain and justify their mathematical thinking and reasoning as well as provide them with opportunities and space to listen to the divergent solution strategies of others. Additionally, for mathematical practice standards to take shape, the teacher must ask higher order questions rather than questions with a known answer (Mehan, 1979) and provide students with opportunities to think critically about the mathematics they are learning. The teacher is therefore responsible for guiding mathematics discussions as well as developing her students' abilities to "engage in productive mathematical discourse" (McClain & Cobb, 2001, p. 236). However, as previously noted, research indicates that most teachers experienced a very traditional and teacher-directed form of classroom discourse as students, thus facilitating the CCSSM and more specifically, Mathematical Practice Standard 3, may prove problematic for an experienced teacher and quite daunting for the inexperienced preservice teacher.

According to Ernest (1988), the mental models that teachers possess regarding mathematics teaching and learning significantly impact their ability to implement the reform initiatives. Ernest articulates the relationship between what a teacher believes about the nature of mathematics and the teacher's developing mathematical teaching practice as being recursive in nature. What a teacher believes about the nature of mathematics is "transformed into classroom practices" (Ernest, 1988, p. 3). Feldman (2000) argues that being dissatisfied with one's own educational experience and being engaged in reform-oriented methods during preservice teacher education may not be enough to bring about the "practical paradigm shifts" (p. 622) needed to enact reform-oriented practices. Feldman suggests that for a practical paradigm shift to occur, a teacher must first be dissatisfied with a practical theory that she holds. Once dissatisfied, it is possible, according to Feldman, for a new theory to be taken up, if it proves to be "sensible... and ...as beneficial" (p. 621), as other reasoned, practical theories may seem in a given situation. Lastly, for a paradigm shift to take root, a theory must also be "enlightening" (p. 621) when applied to a particular situation.

Practical conceptual change theory provides a lens from which to examine how the iPad can help facilitate a practical conceptual shift from traditional classroom discourse to the more conceptual classroom discourse proposed by the CCSSM. The iPad with its powerful audio and video capabilities, numerous applications, portability,

and ease of use make it a productive tool to use to examine and reflect upon the preservice student teaching experience. Using the iPad provides student teachers with immediate opportunities to critically examine their discourse patterns with their university supervisor soon after teaching a lesson and again later with their peers in a university practicum seminar. Examining ways in which mobile technology can support preservice teachers as they develop their teaching practice around the CCSSM is a critical line of inquiry.

USING TECHNOLOGY TO SUPPORT TEACHER DEVELOPMENT

Technology has been used as a means to examine and support teacher development and continues to do so with new and emerging technologies. Importantly, mathematics teacher educators have consistently been on the cutting edge of developing and using ever-changing technologies to support and enhance preservice teacher development (Morris & Easterday, 2008). However, according to Borko, Whitcomb, and Listen (2008a) there is limited knowledge on how new technologies can support the development of teachers work. Since the 1989 inception of the NCTM standards, teachers have been exposed to and encouraged to use different and more novel pedagogical approaches to teaching and learning mathematics (Morris & Easterday, 2008). However, as noted previously, moving away from traditionally used practices in the mathematics classroom has proven to be a difficult task for teachers. Shifting from a teacher-directed classroom to a student-centered one where students engage in problem solving within a community that encourages the use of argument requires a shift in the ways in which teachers facilitate classroom discourse.

In student-centered classrooms, the teacher is no longer considered the sole mathematical authority; rather, with the advent of the NCTM standards and now the CCSSM (2010), students are expected to propose viable arguments, explain, justify, defend, and critique their own arguments and the arguments of others. Consequently, teachers must have opportunities to examine the discourse that unfolds in their own practice as student teachers, so as to reflect upon how their discourse practices foster or inhibit the development of the Standards for Mathematical Practice. Mobile technologies such as the iPad with its powerful audio and video capabilities, are tools that can be used by university supervisors to develop and refine preservice teachers abilities to establish classroom environments where rich and worthwhile discussion can flourish.

On November 10, 2001 Apple ™ introduced the iPod technology to the public and in the last twelve years the advances and uses of Apple ™ technologies have permeated our lives in ways that ten years ago were only imagined. The iPod, a powerful audio and video player, became, according to Pasnik (2007), "a cognitive and cultural tool" (p.2) that allowed "students to explore symbols and meanings" (p. 2). With the introduction of the iPod in 2001, technology has become a part of our everyday lives both personally as well as professionally (Pasnik, 2007).

Similarly, the iPad, introduced in 2010, is quickly changing our modes of communication as well as how we interact with others. Moreover, the iPad is rapidly changing the ways in which we learn. According to Murphy (2011) literature discussions on learning have shifted from "e-learning, to m-learning (mobile learning), and now more recently, the idea of ubiquitous learning" (p. 19). Mobile devices such as the iPad, along with competing devices have taken learning and made it ubiquitous in that content is readily available anywhere and anytime day or night (Murphy, 2011). Moreover, m-learning, with devices such as the iPad, has the functionality to be situated in real contexts, personalized, learner centered, collaborative, ubiquitous, and a lifelong endeavor (Sharple, Taylor, & Vavoula, 2005). Mobile devices are changing the way in which learning is conceived (Sharple, et al. 2005) and subsequently delivered.

Just as the iPod had the "power to extend and reinforce students' understanding of content areas in specific disciplines" (Pasnik, p. 2) the iPad has the capacity to develop and support preservice teachers' understanding of how their students engage with mathematical content and how their teaching practices support and/or inhibit students' abilities to develop and internalize the Standards for Mathematical Practice. In the following sections we will describe how we have used the iPad to facilitate preservice teachers understandings of the practice standards during the student teaching semester and in a mathematics methods course. We will discuss how the iPad has helped us develop and enhance preservice teachers' understanding of the Standards for Mathematical Practice in a way that is personalized, learner centered, situated in real contexts, and ubiquitous thus tapping into the reconceived notion of learning and ultimately teaching.

FROM THEORY TO PRACTICE

At Framingham State University and other teacher education programs around the country, once preservice teachers have completed their educational course work, they move into what is referred to as the *student teaching semester*. The sixteen-week student teaching semester includes a fulltime-supervised internship in an elementary classroom and a corresponding practicum seminar. It is during this internship experience that preservice teachers begin to transition from the theoretical to the practical side of teaching in an elementary classroom. The student teaching semester provides preservice teachers with a hands-on experience working with children, under the direct supervision of the classroom teacher, and an opportunity to put theory learned in the university classroom into practice in the elementary setting.

This transition period can be inspirational and uplifting, and it can be difficult and tumultuous (Goldstein, 2005). Some student teachers demonstrate strong teaching skills that surface immediately once in the elementary classroom, while others have difficulty making the transition from student of education to student teacher, responsible for developing curriculum and teaching elementary aged students. Both groups of student teachers need differentiated guidance and support from their university supervisor and from the classroom teachers in whose classrooms they have been assigned. As university supervisors, we have guided many student teachers through this transitional period and have used various methods in an effort to personalize the experience for each preservice teacher under our supervision. With the advent of mobile technologies, we contest that a new focus on the use of iPads in aiding with this transition will make for a more personalized teaching and learning experience for the student teacher and help to foster critical reflection on their developing teaching practice with regard to the Standards for Mathematical Practice. As Crichton, Pegler, and White (2012) noted after researching the use of iPod Touch and iPad devices in the classroom, "personal wireless devices might be those nimble, shape shifters, capable of putting opportunity and access into the hands of learners, significantly changing teaching and learning" (p. 2). We too see the iPad as a game changer in terms of providing preservice teachers with timely and personalized feedback on their teaching practice. The following section will highlight some of the ways in which we have used the iPad to conduct classroom observations of preservice teachers.

USING THE IPAD AS AN OBSERVATIONAL TOOL

We began using the iPad simply as a tool to record observational data during our visits to classrooms where student teachers were completing their student teaching internship. Previously, when conducting classroom observations of student teachers, we either hand wrote notes about the teaching episode or brought in a lap top computer to record our notes. When we transitioned in Fall 2011 to using the iPad for classroom observations, we immediately found the device to be a useful and productive tool as it allowed us to capture in more detail what was happening during each observed lesson. Moreover, the preservice teachers we have worked with have found the iPad to be beneficial to their developing teaching practice and much less intrusive than a laptop computer. As one student teacher noted, "The iPad seems to be less distracting when teachers [university supervisors] are using them during an observation. I can't hear the clicking of the keys in the background on an iPad and wonder what is being typed, like on a laptop." (Email communication, March 7, 2012)

There are multiple benefits to using the iPad as an observational tool during classroom observations and mobility is first and foremost one of the advantages. According to Sharples et al. (2005) mobility refers to the user rather than the technology itself and we have found this to be true. As university supervisors, we supervise student teachers placed in different schools, often in different towns, with some as many as forty miles apart, thus we are quite mobile with respect to supervision. Having technology that can move along with us is highly advantageous. First, the iPad is compact, light, and portable. We can easily put the iPad in our purse or carry it in a light bag–taking the technology from school to school, and place to place, seamlessly. The iPad has an on screen keyboard, or a wireless keyboard and stand, which can be purchased to accompany the device for ease of typing longer documents. Additionally, the iPad has a long battery life (Sharples et al., 2005), thus making multiple observations in any given day a possibility without the need to recharge.

With an iTunes account, users can purchase applications (apps) that serve to make the iPad a powerful word processing tool. For example, the "Pages" app can be downloaded and used to create templates and folders that automatically store documents on the iPad. Pages quickly converts the iPad document into a Word document or PDF, and if your are in a wireless area or you have the 3 or 4-G models, the document can be immediately emailed to the student teacher after the observation and post-conference. We have found that the iPad has helped to shorten the time between observation and feedback in that we now type our observation notes on-site and send them via email to the student teacher immediately after post-conferencing. Because of this our student teachers can reflect on the feedback provided shortly thereafter or when they have a break in their teaching day. As one student teacher commented, "They [observation write-ups] also come so much quicker and I think you can write so much more when you're typing" (Email communication, March 7, 2012). The timely use of feedback is essential in helping student teachers learn from their immediate practice.

Another feature of the iPad 2 and later models is the front and rear-facing camera, which can be used to take pictures during observations and later saved as artifacts documenting the student teacher's progress throughout the student teaching internship. Pictures are quickly and seamlessly embedded into observation write-ups, to give student teachers a more personalized and meaningful look at what took place during each observation. When discussing the value of seeing pictures that compliment the text write-up one student teacher noted:

There are so many positives from using this technology! I think my favorite part is that you are able to photograph us while you are in the classroom and add that to our observation write-ups. It adds such a special touch that I don't think you can get from just writing on a page (Email communication, March 7, 2012).

The adage, a "picture is worth a thousand words," describes the complexity of meaning that can be found in pictures that words alone cannot convey, thus using photographs of student teachers engaged in the work of teaching and learning has the potential to reveal a complexity that cannot be found in words alone. For example, one of our observational write-ups described the way in which a particular preservice teacher had developed a community of learners who respected the learning environment and worked together in a productive and thoughtful manner. The picture accompanying the text was that of the student teacher with a warm and inviting smile, sitting in a circle surrounded by her students who were intently listening as she engaged them in an activity. The photo of the student teacher and her students conveyed a sense of community much more so than the words written on the page. Moreover, the photo was used by the student teacher in her professional portfolio to document her ability to establish an environment conducive to learning.

Another important feature of the iPad is its powerful and seamless video capability. Although video in teacher education is not a novel idea and research indicates video reflection enhances the experience for student teachers (e.g., Baecher, & Shiao-Chuan, 2011; Borko, Jacobs, & Eiteljorg, 2008; Borko, Whitcom, & Listen, 2008), the iPad makes such recording work almost effortless on the part of the supervisor. Moreover, taking video with the iPad makes the transition from recording to viewing seamless and instant, as the videos are stored on the iPad, which can also be used as the viewing device. Previously, we have used video cameras, and more recently Flip ™ cameras, to record teaching episodes, however, we have found the iPad a much more efficient tool to use for recording and subsequent viewing. Digital and Flip ™ camera videos could be watched immediately afterward; however, the small screen size and weak audio made the experience less than optimal. The iPad, on the other hand, makes the experience pleasurable as the screen is large enough for both student teacher and supervisors to view simultaneously, the picture is clean and crisp, and the audio feature is crystal clear.

Using the video function of the iPad, university supervisors can videotape segments of a lesson or the lesson in its entirety and use the footage immediately afterward, during the post conference meeting, to stimulate critical and collaborative reflection with the student teacher. Supervisors can very easily select particular segments of the video thus focusing the post conference meeting on important features of the student teacher's mathematical teaching practice (Marsh, 2011). We have just begun to use the video function of the iPad to take short video clips of our student teachers as they converse mathematically with students and then use the clips for subsequent collaborative analysis. As a result, we have been able to discuss instances in their teaching where the Standards for Mathematical Practice are emerging. For example, we have collaboratively examined the video with our student teachers to discern if the student teacher is asking questions with a known answer, which lend themselves to lower levels of cognitive demand, or if they ask questions such that students have opportunities to explain and justify their mathematical thinking and reasoning. The iPad has provided us with the means to collaboratively reflect on the Standards for Mathematical Practice as they emerge within practice thereby making the experience a personalized and meaningful one for the student teacher.

The ability to capture teaching episodes as they unfold and seamlessly send the clips to student teachers is a dynamic feature of the iPad and lends itself to collaborative reflection as well as sustained self-reflection because the student teacher can store the video clips on her computer or iPad and continue to reflect upon each episode as a stand alone one, or in comparison to other teaching episodes thus documenting growth over time. Video taken with the iPad offers student teachers a snapshot in time of their teaching practice and the opportunity to reflect on their developing teaching practice immediately and collaboratively with their university supervisor, which is more practical and meaningful than try-

ing to reconstruct a lesson from memory hours or days removed from the experience.

The iPad is also instrumental in fostering collaborative reflection between student teachers and their peers within a practicum seminar. During seminar the iPad can very easily be connected to a large screen TV and selected segments from student teachers' videos can be used, with their permission, as springboards to stimulate reflective collaborative discussion on the practice of teaching and learning mathematics. During this viewing we can point out and highlight places where the Standards for Mathematical Practice are being developed and as importantly, where opportunities are lost. Murphy's (2011) research on the uses of "post PC devices" (p. 18) such as the iPad, led him to develop of a typology that documents the functionality of mobile devices beyond their technical specifications. Through his research, Murphy found that collaboration was an essential feature of post PC. He said:

PPCs such as the iPad enable collaboration in two ways, in a physical sense when students are in close geographical proximity, and in a virtual sense whereby students can gain and generate knowledge within a broader social network via interactive technologies (Murphy, 2011, pp. 22-23).

This broader social network can be found when using observation applications, such as Common Core Look Fors (CCL4s), developed for the iPhone and iPad. The application can be downloaded onto the iPad and used to observe a mathematics lesson, specifically focused on the Standards for Mathematical Practice. The application gives the observer the ability to take a running record of students using the Standards for Mathematical Practice and a running record of the moves the teacher makes that encourage the development of the practice standards in students. Observers can also take video clips and still images, which become part of the observation documentation and reports that can be run regarding the use of various practices.

When post conferencing, the CCL4 provides an opportunity to view the data gathered during the observation collaboratively with the supervisor. Moreover, data from previous observations can be merged to provide a cumulative look at the student teacher's practice over time. Additionally, the application has a feature that links the observation to additional Internet video resources of teachers implementing particular practice standards as well access to more in-depth information on each of the Standards for Mathematical Practice. This application provides student teachers with a broader social community from which to draw inspiration and resources to help shape and challenge her teaching practice. We have not yet used the CCL4 during observations but have plans to integrate this new application in Fall 2012 (See Figure 1).

As university supervisors, we have found the use of the iPad, with its powerful audio, video, and still picture capabilities and its numerous applications, instrumental in helping student teachers examine their teaching practice in context, thus facilitating a more meaningful and productive reflection process. With the iPad, we have the ability to easily capture their teaching practice as it unfolds and then use the video footage and still pictures to collaboratively examine places where the Standards for Mathematical Practice are emerging or actually happening and as importantly, places in their teaching where they missed opportunities to develop a particular practice standard in a meaningful and productive way. The student teachers under our supervision have also found value in our using the iPad as an observational tool. As one student noted:

You are able to absorb what is going on in the classroom and seamlessly, as if a stream of consciousness, put your thoughts of my performance on your iPad. I know you are not missing a beat as you are typing away about my performance. You are able to capture a moment of my day, and evaluate its strengths and points of challenge through words and images. (Email communication, March 7, 2012)

Figure 1. Screen shot of common core look-fors application

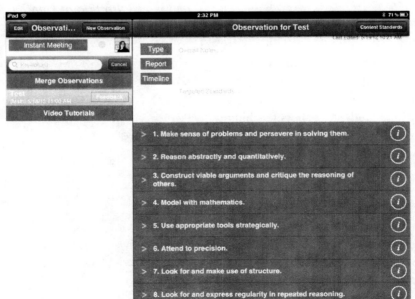

The iPad has been instrumental in efficiently and unobtrusively allowing us to capture the improvising nature of classroom communities working to develop dispositions associated with the Common Core State Standards for Mathematical Practice.

As university supervisors we are at the beginning stages of understanding and harnessing the power of the iPad to enhance the student teaching observation and reflection process. Figure 2 is a model of our current conceptual framework, as to the way in which the iPad facilitates collaborative and sustained self-reflection.

As new applications are developed our model will change to reflect these new and ever emerging technologies. Currently, we use the iPad as a tool to observe, record, and collaboratively reflect with student teachers on the practice of teaching and learning mathematics. We look forward to learning new and more innovative ways to use the device to enhance the student teaching experience. In the following section we will discuss our beginning work using the iPad as a tool for engaging students enrolled in our mathematics methods course.

USE OF THE IPAD IN METHODS COURSES

To stimulate productive discussion among students enrolled in our mathematics methods course, we have used the iPad to show short video clips, with permission, of current student teachers teaching mathematics lessons, as a way to bring the tertiary elementary classroom environment into our methods course. Students in our methods course often know the student teachers featured in the video clips and experience a personal connection when watching their peer's teach lessons. Such an experience empowers students in the methods course as they watch their peers teaching and practicing the methods they are currently learning about in their university classes. After viewing the

videos the students often comment on the positive nature of the experience. They find viewing their contemporaries engaged in the act of teaching as a formative, inspiring, and challenging experience. They comment on connections they see between the videos and the theoretical ideas discussed in class and in their textbooks, as well as comment on the inspiration they gained and the awesome challenge they see in the work of teaching and learning. We have found the comments students make are personalized, as they seem to see themselves within their fellow education students' videos. Again, it is the ease of use and the many functions and applications that make the iPad a powerful and easily integrated learning tool that has the power to seamlessly bring the tertiary elementary classroom to life for students who are not yet enrolled in the student teaching internship.

The iPad has been beneficial in helping methods students develop an understanding of the tertiary elementary classroom environment by facilitating the development of tacit knowledge. According to Murphy (2011), tools such as the iPad:

...provide a mechanism that facilitates tacit knowledge transfer through both socialization and internalization of knowledge. This appears

Figure 2. Model of the reflection cycle using the iPad

particularly relevant in tertiary environments populated by students building knowledge within their own groups, but perhaps unaware of potentially valuable developments in other groups that may also assist in their learning (Murphy, 2011, p. 23).

Viewing video of one's peers is a social experience and helps to develop tacit knowledge of the elementary classroom for methods students not yet involved in the student teaching experience. In the future we plan to invite student teachers to present selected video clips from the video libraries as a way to extend the reflection cycle and include students enrolled in our mathematics methods course. Because we will be able to house each student teachers video clips on our iPads the design and production of such an experience will be seamless and efficient for us as the course instructors and for the student teacher who will present her video clips.

SUPPORTING MATHEMATICS UNDERSTANDING

The use of the iPad to record and playback video clips of student teachers as they teach, as well as teaching experiences in the classroom before student teaching, support mathematics understanding in multiple ways. First, visually watching a teacher teach and having the ability to stop, replay and discuss the mathematics at hand is critical. Connecting the theoretical aspects of teaching to the practical is seamless in a university classroom, as the iPad easily connects to the overhead projectors and/or interactive whiteboards. University students can observe mathematics moments where either student teachers or young students make connections and display understandings on the screen. As one methods student noted on an exit card, "It's fun to see how she was able to field questions and not answer them directly but encourage the students to find out on their own. Also how she made many connections through-

out the unit." This quote taken from a student towards the end of the semester shows that she is recognizing the importance of not being the sole mathematical authority in the classroom. She also recognizes the interdisciplinary nature of the presented lesson. University students also express doubts about their ability to recreate the teaching that they see on the screen. "It leaves me wondering if I will ever be able to do this." Clearly the student recognizes good teaching, but is nervous about her own ability to teach in such a way. Most students have positive experiences, however. "I find it inspirational to see the strong relationships between the teacher and students. It's also nice to see her comfort level and teaching style." These types of responses to the teaching have been much more common.

Using the iPad to continue to show students that their peers are successfully teaching, just one semester after engaging in a mathematics methods course, we feel will only increase their confidence in teaching mathematics. We would like to expand our video and image experience with the use of iPad's so that students in our methods course can watch themselves teaching a lesson and begin the self-reflection process even earlier in their teacher preparation career. In this way, students will not just be watching models of others, but will have an opportunity to reflect on their own teaching and examine their teacher moves in comparison to experts, their own university professors, their supervising practitioners, and their peers. The broader the practical experience the students have before they begin student teaching, the more confident they will be in their teaching of mathematics and other subjects as well.

USING THE IPAD TO STIMULATE PRODUCTIVE DISCUSSIONS

The iPad has also been beneficial in helping to facilitate rich mathematical discussions within our methods course. We use the camera feature of the iPad to take pictures of students as they work to develop ways to model mathematics situations using manipulatives (e.g. Unifix ™ cubes and base ten blocks). For example, in one class students were asked to design a model to represent the product of 23 x 10. Most groups modeled the problem as ten groups of twenty-three (See Figure 3). However, one group modeled the problem as twenty-three groups of ten (See Figure 4). Being able to take photos with the iPad of both models and display each effortlessly on the document camera for all members of the class to examine, discuss, and critique led to a meaningful and substantial conversation about the commutative property of multiplication. Moreover, showing both models on a big screen for group analysis and critique became a shared experience with students

examining, discussing, and analyzing each model with the support of their peers. Those who had difficulty seeing Figure 4 as a way to model 23 x 10 were supported by their peers as the conversation ensued. This robust discussion housed more critical arguments and questions as advocated by the Standards for Mathematical Practice. Because the critical discussion focused on student work a greater understanding of the concepts developed. Moreover, because the photos were up on the screen for an extended period, students were able to use the manipulatives at their tables and reconstruct what they were seeing, rather than only being able to listen to someone explain each model. In this particular instance a picture was most defiantly worth a thousand words. We have

Figure 3. Model of 23 x 10

Figure 4. Model of 23 x 10

found with our use of the iPad that we are able to more easily and frequently use student work to stimulate productive mathematics conversations within our mathematic methods course. We no longer have to ask students to draw their models on a large sheet of chart paper for group viewing or try and fit the whole class around one groups' model. Rather, we now snap a photo and within minutes display it for all to examine and discuss.

IMPLICATIONS, CHALLENGES, AND FUTURE PLANS

As teacher educators, we would like to expand our experience with using iPads with student teachers completing the student teaching internship as well as with students enrolled in our mathematics methods courses to examine the Standards for Mathematical Practice in more detail and depth. Focusing on specific topics or modes of teaching helps our students watch the videos with a focused lens of meaning. We will continue to use the methods we have just begun to use this year, and have students use iPads more and more for their learning experiences. It would also be meaningful to ask students to track their teaching mathematics lessons over the course of their student teaching semester and keep a journal based on the videos and still images taken during scheduled observations to reflect on their attitudes and anxieties affiliated with teaching of mathematics in their classroom. Further it would be meaningful to note changes in attitude, anxiety and beliefs as the semester progresses. Video analysis is a critical piece in the student teaching process (Baecher, L. & Kung, S. C., 2011) and the iPad makes video analysis a much more seamless, efficient, and enriching experience for the university supervisor as well as the student teacher.

For student teachers having difficulty or anxiety teaching mathematics, it could also be meaningful to use the application Face Time or similar ap-

plications to conduct off site observations. With this application we could conduct an observation from our university office in real time and provide immediate feedback following the observation. The Face Time application would afford us more directed interactions with the student teachers and more opportunities to reflect with them about their teaching as we would not have to be onsite for each and every classroom observation. The iPad, with its many communication applications, can help to support and facilitate communication between university supervisors and their student teachers, making the student teaching experience more manageable and rewarding for all.

CONCLUSION

Mathematics Practice Standard 3 of the Common Core State Standards for Mathematics (2011) states that students should be able to, "construct viable arguments and critique the reasoning of others." The use of iPad technology provides university supervisors and student teachers with a powerful and user-friendly audio video tool to capture discourse as it unfolds in the classroom. The very nature of the technology makes communication more robust through the ease of use, quick response time, and integrated video and picture capability. Students and teachers alike are able to critique and self-reflect on teaching that occurs in the pre-service students' classroom instantly and at later times. The integration of the iPad's video, picture, writing, emailing and portability make it an ideal technology to aide in the continuing discourse between student teachers, their peers, and their university supervisors.

As university supervisors, we have successfully used the iPad and plan to expand its use in the upcoming academic year. Our plan includes managing and exploring further the iPad's observational capabilities with the next group student teachers we are assigned to and with the students enrolled in our mathematics methods courses. Students will be encouraged to expand their reflections and self-assessments in relationship to the Standards for Mathematical Practice. Moreover, we intend to use the application Common Core Look Fors to gather data on student teachers use of the Standards for Mathematical Practice.

The use of iPad's in the classroom has increased the meaningful discourse and critical analysis of mathematics teaching and learning that is occurring at our small university. Clearly, our university students and the young students they will teach in the future will benefit the most from this exciting ever-changing technology-based living experience.

REFERENCES

Abd-Kadir, J., & Hardman, F. (2007). The discourse of whole class teaching: A comparative study of Kenyan and Nigerian primary English lessons. *Language and Education*, *21*(1), 1–15. doi:10.2167/le684.0.

Baecher, L., & Kung, S. C. (2011). Jumpstarting novice teachers' ability to analyze classroom video: Affordances of an online workshop. *Journal of Digital Learning in Teacher Education*, *28*(1).

Borko, H., Jacobs, J., & Eiteljorg, E. (2008b). Video as a tool for fostering productive discussions in mathematics professional development. *Teaching and Teacher Education: An International Journal of Research and Studies*, *24*(2), 417–436. doi:10.1016/j.tate.2006.11.012.

Borko, H., Whitcomb, J., & Liston, D. (2008a). Wicked problems and other thoughts on issues of technology and teacher learning. *Journal of Teacher Education*, *60*(1), 3–7. doi:10.1177/0022487108328488.

Chapin, S., O'Connor, C., & Anderson. (2009). *Classroom discussion: Using math talk to help student learn*. Sausalito, CA: Math Solutions.

Cobb, P., Stephan, M., McClain, K., & Gravemeijer, K. (2001). Participating in classroom practices. *Journal of the Learning Sciences*, *10*(1/2), 113–163. doi:10.1207/S15327809JLS10-1-2_6.

Common Core State Standards Initiative. (2010). *Common core state standards for mathematics*. Retrieved from http://www.corestandards.org/assets/CCSSI_Math%20Standards.pdf

Crichton, S., Pegler, K., & White, D. (2012). Personal devices in public settings: Lessons learned from an iPod touch/Ipad project. *The Electronic Journal of e-Learning*, *10*(1), 23-31.

Dacey, L., & Polly, D. (2012). Common core state standards for mathematics: The big picture. *Teaching Children Mathematics*, *19*(6), 378–383.

Ernest, P. (1988). *The impact of beliefs on the teaching of mathematics*. Paper presented at the Sixth Annual Meeting of the International Congress of Mathematical Education. Budapest, Romania.

Feldman, A. (2000). Decision making in the practical domain: A model of practical conceptual change. *Science Education*, *84*, 606–632. doi:10.1002/1098-237X(200009)84:5<606::AID-SCE4>3.0.CO;2-R.

Goldstein, L. S. (2005, Winter). Becoming a teacher as a hero's journey: Using metaphor in preservice teacher education. *Teacher Education Quarterly*.

Grassetti, M. T. (2010). Engaging students in mathematics conversations: Discourse practices and the development of social and socialmathematical norms in three novice teachers' classrooms. *Open Access Dissertations*. Paper 196. http://scholarworks.umass.edu/open_access_dissertations/196

Heaton, R. M. (2000). *Teaching mathematics to the new standards: Relearning the dance*. New York, NY: Teachers College Press.

Inagaki, K., Morita, E., & Hanto, G. (1999). Teaching-learning of evaluative criteria for mathematical arguments through classroom discourse: A cross-national study. *Mathematical Thinking and Learning*, *1*(2), 93–111. doi:10.1207/s15327833mtl0102_1.

Marsh, B. (2011). *The evaluation of a university in-school teacher education program in science (INSTEP)*. (Unpublished dissertation). University of Sussex, Sussex, UK.

Maxfield, M., & Romano, D. (2012). The role of video in pre-service teacher first day of school observations: Peer review on learning of teaching concepts and future application. In P. Resta (Ed.), *Proceedings of Society for Information Technology & Teacher Education International Conference 2012* (pp. 636-641). Chesapeake, VA: AACE.

McClain, K., & Cobb, P. (2001). An analysis of the development of social and social mathematical norms in one first grade classroom. *Journal for Research in Mathematics Education*, *32*(3), 236–266. doi:10.2307/749827.

Mehan, H. (1979). What time is it Denise? Asking known information questions in classroom discourse. *Theory into Practice*, *18*(4), 285–294. doi:10.1080/00405847909542846.

Mendez, E. P., Sherin, M. G., & Louis, D. A. (2007). Multiple perspectives on the development of an eighth-grade mathematical discourse community. *The Elementary School Journal*, *108*(1), 41–61. doi:10.1086/522385.

Murphy, G. D. (2011). Post pc devices: A summary of the early iPad technology adoption in tertiary environments. *E-Journal of Business and Scholarship of Teaching*, *5*(1), 18–32.

Nassaji, H., & Wells, G. (2000). What's the use of triadic dialogue? An investigation of teacher-student interaction. *Applied Linguistics*, *21*(3), 376–406. doi:10.1093/applin/21.3.376.

National Council of Teachers of Mathematics. (1989). *Curriculum and evaluation standards for school mathematics*. Reston, VA: NCTM.

National Council of Teachers of Mathematics. (1991). *Professional standards for teaching mathematics*. Reston, VA: NCTM.

National Council of Teachers of Mathematics. (2000). *Principles and standards of school mathematics*. Reston, VA: NCTM.

Pasnik, S. (2007). *iPod in education: The potential for teaching and learning* (White paper). Retrieved May 23, 2012 from http://64.25.222.20/resource/iPod_in_Education_Whitepaper.pdf

Sharples, M., Taylor, J., & Vavoula, G. (2005). Towards a theory of mobile learning. In *Proceedings of mLearn 2005 Conference*. Cape Town, South Africa: mLearn. Retrieved May 18, 2012 from http://www.iamlearn.org/public/mlearn2005/www.mlearn.org.za/CD/papers/Sharples%20Theory%20of%20Mobile.pdf

Sommers, W. A., & Olsen, W. (n.d.). *Habits of mind: Teacher's companion*. Retrieved May 25, 2012 from http://www.mindfulbydesign.com/sites/default/files/HOM-Sampler.pdf

Wells, G., & Arauz, R. M. (2006). Dialogue in the classroom. *Journal of the Learning Sciences*, *15*(3), 379–428. doi:10.1207/s15327809jls1503_3.

KEY TERMS AND DEFINITIONS

CCSSM: Common Core State Standards for Mathematics.

Reform-Oriented Discourse: Serious discussion between people or groups that includes the use of reasoning and arguing about mathematical meanings (NCTM).

IRE: Initiation-Reply-Evaluation, traditional discourse model (Mehan, 1979).

iPad: Portable tablet computer designed by Apple.

MPS3: Mathematical Practice Standard 3 of the CCSSM, "Construct viable arguments and critique the reasoning of others."

Student-Teacher: A university student who is presently completing their final course in their Education series by spending all day in an elementary classroom observing, co-teaching and teaching.

University Supervisor: An individual responsible for supervising student teachers completing a fulltime internship in an elementary classroom.

Compilation of References

Aamodt, A. (2005). A computational model of knowledge-intensive learning and problem solving. In Wielinga, Boose, Gaines, Schreiber, & Van Someren (Eds.), Current Trends in Knowledge Acquisition. Amsterdam: IOS Press.

Abd-Kadir, J., & Hardman, F. (2007). The discourse of whole class teaching: A comparative study of Kenyan and Nigerian primary English lessons. *Language and Education*, *21*(1), 1–15. doi:10.2167/le684.0.

Acker, S. (1999). *The realities of teachers' work: Never a dull moment*. New York: Cassell & Continuum.

Adams, W. K., Reid, S., LeMaster, R., McKagan, S. B., Perkins, K. K., Dubson, M., & Wieman, C. E. (2008a). A study of educational simulations part I - Engagement and learning. *Journal of Interactive Learning Research*, *19*(3), 397–419.

Adams, W. K., Reid, S., LeMaster, R., McKagan, S. B., Perkins, K. K., Dubson, M., & Wieman, C. E. (2008b). A study of educational simulations part II – Interface design. *Journal of Interactive Learning Research*, *19*(4), 551–577.

Ada, T., & Kurtlus, A. (2010). Students' misconceptions and errors in transformation geometry. *International Journal of Mathematical Education in Science and Technology*, *41*(7), 901–909. doi:10.1080/0020739X.2010.486451.

Anderman, E. M., & Maehr, M. L. (1994). Motivation and schooling in the middle grades. *Review of Educational Research*, *64*(2), 287–310. doi:10.3102/00346543064002287.

Archambault, L. M., & Barnett, J. H. (2010). Revisiting technological pedagogical content knowledge: Exploring the TPACK framework. *Computers & Education*, *55*, 1656–1662. doi:10.1016/j.compedu.2010.07.009.

Ares, N., Stroup, W. M., & Schademan, A. R. (2009). The power of mediating artifacts in group-level development of mathematical discourses. *Cognition and Instruction*, *27*(1), 1–24. doi:10.1080/07370000802584497.

Arnold, S. (2004). Integrating technology in the middles school: Years 5-9. *Australian Primary Mathematics Classroom*, *9*(3), 15–19.

Association of Mathematics Teacher Educators. (2006). *Preparing teachers to use technology to enhance the learning of mathematics: A position of the association of mathematics teacher educators*. Retrieved from http://www.amte.net/sites/all/themes/amte/resources/ AMTETechnologyPositionStatement.pdf

Association of Mathematics Teacher Educators. (2009). *Mathematics TPACK (technological pedagogical content knowledge) framework*. Retrieved from http://www.amte. net/sites/all/themes/amte/resources/MathTPACKFramework.pdf

Baecher, L., & Kung, S. C. (2011). Jumpstarting novice teachers' ability to analyze classroom video: Affordances of an online workshop. *Journal of Digital Learning in Teacher Education*, *28*(1).

Ball, D. L., Hill, H. C., & Bass, H. (2005). Knowing mathematics for teaching: Who knows mathematics well enough to teach third grade, and how can we decide? *American Educator*, *29*(1), 14–46.

Ball, D. L., Thames, M. H., & Phelps, G. (2008). Content knowledge for teaching what makes it special? *Journal of Teacher Education*, *59*(5), 389–407. doi:10.1177/0022487108324554.

Ball, D., & Forzani, F. (2009). The work of teaching and the challenge for teacher education. *Journal of Teacher Education, 60*(5), 497–511. doi:10.1177/0022487109348479.

Basham, K. L., & Katrlik, J. W. (2008). The effects of 3-dimensional CADD modeling on the development of the spatial ability of technology education students. *Journal of Technology Education, 20*(1), 32–47.

Battista, M. T., & Clements, D. H. (2007). *Constructing geometric concepts in logo*. Retrieved from http://investigations.terc.edu/library/bookpapers/constructing_geo_concepts.cfm

Battista, M. T. (2007). The development of geometric and spatial thinking. In Lester, F. (Ed.), *Second Handbook of Research on Mathematics Teaching and Learning* (pp. 843–908). Reston, VA: NCTM.

Baxter, J. A., Woodward, J., & Olson, D. (2005). Writing in mathematics: An alternative form of communication for academically low-achieving students. *Learning Disabilities Research & Practice, 20*(2), 119–135. doi:10.1111/j.1540-5826.2005.00127.x.

Beck, C., & Kosnik, C. (2006). *Innovations in teacher education: a social constructivist approach*. Albany, NY: State University of New York Press.

Becker, J. R. (2001). Classroom coaching: An emerging method of professional development. In *Proceedings of the Annual Meeting of the North American Chapter of the International Group for the Psychology of Mathematics Education*. Snowbird, UT: PME.

Begle, E. G. (1973). Some lessons learned by SMSG. *Mathematics Teacher, 66*, 207–214.

Ben-Zvi, D. (2000). Toward understanding the role of technological tools in statistical learning. *Mathematical Thinking and Learning, 2*, 127–155. doi:10.1207/S15327833MTL0202_6.

Ben-Zvi, D., & Garfield, J. (2004). Statistical literacy, reasoning, and thinking: Goals, definitions, and challenges. In Ben-Zvi, D., & Garfield, J. (Eds.), *The challenge of developing statistical literacy, reasoning and thinking* (pp. 3–16). Springer.

Berthold, K., & Renkl, A. (2009). Instructional aids to support a conceptual understanding of multiple representations. *Journal of Educational Psychology, 101*(1), 70–87. doi:10.1037/a0013247.

Biesinger, K., Crippen, K., & Muis, K. (2008). The impact of block scheduling on student motivation and classroom practice in mathematics. *NASSP Bulletin, 92*(3), 191–208. doi:10.1177/0192636508323925.

Bitter, G. G., & Hatfield, M. M. (1994). The calculator project: Assessing school-wide impact of calculator implementation. In Bright, G. W., Waxman, H. C., & Williams, S. E. (Eds.), *Impact of calculators on mathematics instruction* (pp. 49–66). Lanham, MD: University Press of America.

Black, P., Harrison, C., Lee, C.-H., Marshall, B., & Wiliam, D. (2004). Working inside the black box: Assessment for learning in the classroom. *Phi Delta Kappan, 86*(1), 9–21.

Bliss, J., & Ogborn, J. (1989). Tools for exploratory learning. *Journal of Computer Assisted Learning, 5*, 37–50. doi:10.1111/j.1365-2729.1989.tb00196.x.

Boaler, J., & Staples, M. (2008). Creating mathematical futures through an equitable teaching approach: The case of railside school. *Teachers College Record, 110*(3), 608–645.

Boaler, J., Wiliam, D., & Brown, M. (2000). Students' experiences of ability grouping - Disaffection, polarisation and the construction of failure. *British Educational Research Journal, 26*(5), 631–648. doi:10.1080/713651583.

Borko, H., Jacobs, J., & Eiteljorg, E. (2008b). Video as a tool for fostering productive discussions in mathematics professional development. *Teaching and Teacher Education: An International Journal of Research and Studies, 24*(2), 417–436. doi:10.1016/j.tate.2006.11.012.

Borko, H., Roberts, S. A., & Shavelson, R. J. (2008). Teachers' decision making: From Alan J. Bishop to today. In Clarkson, P., & Presmeg, N. (Eds.), *Critical issues in Mathematics Education* (pp. 37–67). New York, NY: Springer. doi:10.1007/978-0-387-09673-5_4.

Borko, H., Whitcomb, J., & Liston, D. (2008a). Wicked problems and other thoughts on issues of technology and teacher learning. *Journal of Teacher Education, 60*(1), 3–7. doi:10.1177/0022487108328488.

Bos, B. (2007). The effect of the Texas instrument interactive instructional environment on the mathematical achievement of eleventh grade low achieving students. *Journal of Educational Computing Research*, *37*(4), 351–368. doi:10.2190/EC.37.4.b.

Boston, M. D., & Smith, M. S. (2009). Transforming secondary mathematics teaching: Increasing the cognitive demands of instructional tasks used in teachers' classrooms. *Journal for Research in Mathematics Education*, *40*(2), 119–156.

Bottge, B. A., Grant, T. S., Stephens, A. C., & Rueda, E. (2010). Advancing the math skills of middle school students in technology education classrooms. *NASSP Bulletin*, *94*(2), 81–106. doi:10.1177/0192636510379902.

Bransford, J., Brown, A. L., & Cocking, R. R. (Eds.). (2000). *How people learn: Brain, mind, experience, and school*. Washington, DC: National Academy Press.

Brinkman, P. (1997). Students build math skills by visualizing problems. *Christian Science Monitor, 89*(251).

Broers, N. J. (2008). Helping students to build a conceptual understanding of elementary statistics. *The American Statistician*, *62*(2), 161–166. doi:10.1198/000313008X 302091_a.

Brotherton, S., Bruckhart, G., & Reed, J. (1975). *Transformations: Geometry module for use in a mathematics laboratory setting*. Denver, CO: Regional Center for Pre-College Mathematics, University of Denver.

Brown, R. E. (2009). *Community building in mathematics professional development*. (Doctoral dissertation). University of Georgia, Athens, GA.

Brown, A. (1992). Design experiments: Theoretical and methodological challenges in creating complex interventions in classroom settings. *Journal of the Learning Sciences*, *2*(2), 141–178. doi:10.1207/s15327809jls0202_2.

Brown, B. (2007). *I thought it was just me: Women reclaiming power and courage in a culture of shame*. New York: Gotham Books.

Brown, B. (2010). *The gifts of imperfection: Let go of who you thinnk you're supposed to be and embrace who you are*. Center City, MN: Hazelden.

Brown, J. S., & Duguid, P. (1991). Organizational learning and communities-of-practice: Toward a unified view of working, learning, and innovation. *Organization Science*, *2*(1), 40–57. doi:10.1287/orsc.2.1.40.

Bruner, J. (1991). The narrative construction of reality. *Critical Inquiry*, *18*(1), 1–21. doi:10.1086/448619.

Burke, J., Cowen, S., Fernandez, S., & Wesslen, M. (2006). Dynamic gliding. *Mathematics Teacher*, *195*, 12–14.

Burns, M. (2001). Lessons for introducing fractions (grades 4-5). Sausalito, CA: Math Solutions Publications.

Burns, B. A., & Hamm, E. M. (2011). A comparison of concrete and virtual manipulative use in third- and fourth-grade mathematics. *School Science and Mathematics*, *111*(6), 256–261. doi:10.1111/j.1949-8594.2011.00086.x.

Burrill, G., Allison, J., Breaux, G., Kastberg, S., Leatham, K., & Sanchez, W. (2002). *Handheld graphing technology in secondary mathematics*. Retrieved from http://education.ti.com/sites/UK/downloads/pdf/References/Done/Burrill,G.%20(2002).pdf

Calkins, L. (1983). *Lessons from a child: On the teaching and learning of writing*. Portsmouth, NH: Heinemann.

Capraro, M. M., & Joffrion, H. (2006). Algebraic equations: Can middle-school students meaningfully translate from words to mathematical symbols? *Reading Psychology*, *27*, 147–164. doi:10.1080/02702710600642467.

Carter, S. (2009). Connecting mathematics and writing workshop: It's kinda like ice skating. *The Reading Teacher*, *62*(7), 606–610. doi:10.1598/RT.62.7.7.

Chai, C., Koh, J., & Tsai, C. (2010). Facilitating preservice teachers' development of technological, pedagogical, and content knowledge (TPACK). *Journal of Educational Technology & Society*, *13*(4), 63–73.

Chance, B. (2002). Components of statistical thinking and implications for instruction and assessment. *Journal of Statistics Education*, *10*(3). Retrieved from http://www.amstat.org/publications/jse/v10n3/chance.html.

Chapin, S., O'Connor, C., & Anderson. (2009). *Classroom discussion: Using math talk to help student learn*. Sausalito, CA: Math Solutions.

Chen, C. L. (2012). *Learning to teach from anticipating lessons through comics-based approximations of practice.* (Unpublished doctoral dissertation). University of Michigan, Ann Arbor, MI.

Chi, M., Feltovich, P., & Glaser, R. (1981). Categorization and representation of physics problems by experts and novices. *Cognitive Science, 5*(2), 152, 121.

Chief Council of State School Officers. (2011). *Common core state standards for mathematics.* Retrieved from http://www.corestandards.org

Chieu, V. M., Kosko, K. W., & Herbst, P. (2013). Enhancing mathematics teachers' online discussions with animated classroom stories as reference objects. *International Journal of Computer-Supported Collaborative Learning.*

Clark, R. C., & Mayer, R. E. (2007). e-Learning and the science of instruction: Proven guidelines for consumers and designers of multimedia learning (2nd ed.). Pfeiffer.

Clements, D. H. (1998). *Geometric and spatial thinking in young children* (White paper). Washington, DC: National Science Foundation.

Clements, D. H., & Battista, M. T. (1989). Learning of geometric concepts in a logo environment. *Journal for Research in Mathematics Education, 20,* 450–467. doi:10.2307/749420.

Clements, D. H., & Battista, M. T. (2001). Logo and geometry. *Journal for Research in Mathematics Education,* 10.

Cobb, P. (1994). *Learning mathematics: Constructivist and interactionist theories of mathematical development.* New York: Springer.

Cobb, P., Confrey, J., DiSessa, A., Lehrer, R., & Schauble, L. (2003). Design experiments in educational research. *Educational Researcher, 32*(1), 9–13. doi:10.3102/0013189X032001009.

Cobb, P., Stephan, M., McClain, K., & Gravemeijer, K. (2001). Participating in classroom practices. *Journal of the Learning Sciences, 10*(1/2), 113–163. doi:10.1207/S15327809JLS10-1-2_6.

Cobb, P., Wood, T., & Yackel, E. (1993). Discourse, mathematical thinking, and classroom practice. In Forman, E., & Stone, A. (Eds.), *Contexts for learning: Sociocultural dynamics in children's development* (pp. 91–119). New York: Oxford University Press.

Cobb, P., & Yackel, E. (1996). Constructivist, emergent, and sociocultural perspectives in the context of developmental research. *Educational Psychologist, 31*(3-4), 175–190. doi:10.1080/00461520.1996.9653265.

Cobb, P., Yackel, E., & McClain, K. (2000). *Symbolizing and communicating in mathematics classrooms: Perspectives on discourse, tools, and instructional design.* Mahwah, NJ: Lawrence Erlbaum Associates.

Cohen, D., Raudenbush, S., & Ball, D. (2003). Resources, instruction, and research. *Educational Evaluation and Policy Analysis, 25*(2), 119–142. doi:10.3102/01623737025002119.

Collins, A. (1992). Toward a design science of education. In Scanlon, E., & O'Shea, T. (Eds.), *New directions in educational technology* (pp. 15–22). New York: Springer-Verlag. doi:10.1007/978-3-642-77750-9_2.

Common Core Standards Initiative. (2010). *The common core state standards for mathematics.* Retrieved from http://www.corestandards.org/assets/CCSSI_Math%20Standards.pdf

Conference Board of Mathematical Sciences. (2011). *Common standards and the mathematical education of teachers* (White Paper). Retrieved from http://www.cbmsWeb.org/Forum3/CBMS_Forum_White_Paper.pdf

Conference Board of the Mathematical Sciences (CBMS). (1983). *The mathematical sciences curriculum K–12: What is still fundamental and what is not.* Report to National Science Board Commission on Precollege Education in Mathematics, Science, and Technology. Washington, DC: CBMS.

Confrey, J., & Krupa, E. E. (2010). *Curriculum design, development, and implementation in an era of common core state standards: Summary report of a conference.* Arlington, VA: Center for the Study of Mathematics Curriculum.

Costa, A., & Kallick, B. (2008). *Learning and leading with habits of mind*. Alexandria, VA: Association for Supervision and Curriculum Development.

Coulter, B. (2007, March-April). Sketching a path into geometry. *Connect*, 16-17.

Crichton, S., Pegler, K., & White, D. (2012). Personal devices in public settings: Lessons learned from an iPod touch/Ipad project. *The Electronic Journal of e-Learning, 10*(1), 23-31.

Croitoru, A., & Doytsher, Y. (2004). Right-angle rooftop polygon extraction in regularized urban areas: Cutting the corners. *The Photogrammetric Record, 19*(108), 311–341. doi:10.1111/j.0031-868X.2004.00289.x.

Csikszentmihalyi, M. (1990). *Flow: The psychology of optimal experience*. New York: Harper and Row.

Csikszentmihalyi, M., & Csiksentmihalyi, I. S. (Eds.). (2006). *A life worth living: Contributions to positive psychology*. New York: Oxford University Press.

Cuoco, A., Goldenberg, E. P., & Mark, J. (1996). Habits of mind: An organizing principle for mathematics curricula. *The Journal of Mathematical Behavior, 15*(4), 375–402. doi:10.1016/S0732-3123(96)90023-1.

Dacey, L., & Polly, D. (2012). Common core state standards for mathematics: The big picture. *Teaching Children Mathematics, 19*(6), 378–383.

D'Ambrosio, B., Johnson, H., & Hobbs, L. (1995). Strategies for increasing achievement in mathematics. In Cole, R. W. (Ed.), *Educating everybody's children: Diverse teaching strategies for diverse learners: What research and practice say about improving achievement* (pp. 121–137). Alexandria, VA: Association of Supervision and Curriculum Development.

David, J. L., & Greene, D. (2007). *Improving mathematics instruction in Los Angeles high schools: An evaluation of the PRISMA pilot program*. Palo Alto, CA: Bay Area Research Group.

Davis, R. B. (1984). *Learning mathematics: The cognitive science approach to mathematics education*. Praeger Pub Text.

Design-Based Research Collective. (2003). Design-based research: An emerging paradigm for educational inquiry. *Educational Researcher, 32*(1), 5–8. doi:10.3102/0013189X032001005.

Deusing, B. (2006, April). Automotive design program inspires creative students. *Tech Directions*, 12–14.

Dick, T. P., & Hollebrands, K. F. (2011). Introduction to focus in high school mathematics: Technology to support reasoning and sense making. In Dick, T. P., & Hollebrands, K. F. (Eds.), *Focus in high school mathematics: Technology to support reasoning and sense making* (pp. xi–xvii). Reston, VA: National Council of Teachers of Mathematics.

Doering, A., Veletsianos, G., Scharber, C., & Miller, C. (2009). Using the technological, pedagogical, and content knowledge framework to design online learning environments and professional development. *Educational Computing Research, 41*(3), 319–346. doi:10.2190/EC.41.3.d.

Doerr, H. M., & Pratt, D. (2008). The learning of mathematics and mathematical modeling. In M. K. Heid & G. W. Blume (Eds.), Research on technology and the teaching and learning of mathematics: Volume 1: Research syntheses (Vol. 1, pp. 259-286). Charlotte, NC: Information Age Publishing, Inc.

Doerr, H. M., & Zangor, R. (2000). Creating meaning for and with the graphing calculator. *Educational Studies in Mathematics, 41*(2), 143–163. doi:10.1023/A:1003905929557.

Doyle, W. (1977). Learning the classroom environment: An ecological analysis. *Journal of Teacher Education, 28*(6), 51–55. doi:10.1177/002248717702800616.

Doyle, W. (1979). Classroom effects. *Theory into Practice, 18*(3), 138–144. doi:10.1080/00405847909542823.

Dreyfus, H. L. (2007). The return of the myth of the mental. *Inquiry: An Interdisciplinary Journal of Philosophy, 50*(4), 352–365. doi:10.1080/00201740701489245.

Drijvers, P., & Trouche, L. (2008). From artifacts to instruments: A theoretical framework behind the orchestra metaphor. In Heid & G. W. Blume (Eds.), Research on technology and the teaching and learning of mathematics (Vol. 2, pp. 363–392). Academic Press.

Dufour, R., Dufour, R., & Eaker, R. (2008). *Revisiting professional learning communities at work: New insights for improving schools*. Bloomington, IN: Solution Tree.

Dunham, P., & Hennessy, S. (2008). Equity and use of educational technology in mathematics. In Heid, M. K., & Blume, G. (Eds.), *Research on technology and the teaching and learning of mathematics* (Vol. 1, pp. 345–418). Charlotte, NC: Information Age Publishing.

Durmus, S., & Karakirik, E. (2006). Virtual manipulatives in mathematics education: A theoretical framework. *The Turkish Online Journal of Educational Technology, 5*(1).

Duschl, R. A., Schweingruber, H. A., & Shouse, A. W. (Eds.). (2007). *Taking science to school: Learning and teaching science in grades K-8*. Washington, DC: National Academies Press.

Dweck, C. S. (2000). *Self-theories: Their role in motivation, personality, and development*. Philadelphia, PA: Psychology Press.

Easa, S. M., & He, W. (2006). Modeling driver visual demand on three-dimensional highway alignments. *Journal of Transportation Engineering, 132*(5), 357–365. doi:10.1061/(ASCE)0733-947X(2006)132:5(357).

Economopoulos, K., Mokros, J., & Russell, S. J. (1998). *From paces to feet*. Glenview, IL: Scott Foresman.

Ediger, M. (2005). Struggling readers in high school. *Reading Improvement, 42*, 34–39.

Edwards, M. T., & Phelps, S. (2008). Can you fathom this? Connecting data analysis algebra, and probability simulation. *Mathematics Teacher, 102*(3), 210–217.

Ellington, A. J. (2003). A meta-analysis of the effects of calculators on students' achievement and attitude: Levels in precollege mathematics classes. *Journal for Research in Mathematics Education, 34*, 433–463. doi:10.2307/30034795.

Engelman, J., Noakes, L. J., & Rogers, D. R. (2011, April). *Assessment for learning and formative assessment: Establishing a common definition for mathematics education*. Paper presented at the research pre-session of the National Council of Teachers of Mathematics Annual Meeting. Indianapolis, IN.

Engle, R., & Conant, F. (2002). Guiding principles for fostering productive disciplinary engagement: Explaining emerging argument in a community of learners classroom. *Cognition and Instruction, 20*(4), 399–483. doi:10.1207/S1532690XCI2004_1.

Ernest, P. (1988). *The impact of beliefs on the teaching of mathematics*. Paper presented at the Sixth Annual Meeting of the International Congress of Mathematical Education. Budapest, Romania.

Ernest, P. (1996). Varieties of constructivism: A framework for comparison. In Steffe, L. P., Nesher, P., Cobb, P., Goldin, G. A., & Greer, B. (Eds.), *Theories of mathematical learning* (pp. 389–398). Hillsdale, NJ: Erlbaum.

Ertmer, P., & Ottenbreit-Leftwich, A. (2009). *Teacher technology change: How knowledge, beliefs and culture intersect*. Paper presented at the Annual Meeting of the American Educational Research Association. Denver, CO.

Ertmer, P. A. (1999). Addressing first- and second-order barriers to change: Strategies for technology integration. *Educational Technology Research and Development, 47*(4), 47–61. doi:10.1007/BF02299597.

Faughn, A. P., Brown, K., Kent, N., & Tuba, I. (2011). *Supporting beginning mathematics teachers with technology-based professional development*. Paper presented at the 2011 meeting of the American Educational Research Association. New Orleans, LA.

Feldman, A. (2000). Decision making in the practical domain: A model of practical conceptual change. *Science Education, 84*, 606–632. doi:10.1002/1098-237X(200009)84:5<606::AID-SCE4>3.0.CO;2-R.

Fendel, D. M., Resek, D., Alper, L., & Fraser, S. (2011). *Interactive mathematics program: Integrated high school mathematics*. Key Curriculum Press.

Ferrini-Mundy, J., Burrill, G., & Schmidt, W. H. (2007). Building teacher capacity for implementing curricular coherence: Mathematics teacher professional development tasks. *Journal of Mathematics Teacher Education, 10*(4), 311–324. doi:10.1007/s10857-007-9053-9.

Fey, J. T., Atchison, W. F., Good, R. A., Heid, M. K., Johnson, J., Kantowski, M. G., & Rosen, L. P. (1984). *Computing and mathematics: The impact on secondary school curricula*. College Park, MD: National Council of Teachers of Mathematics and the University of Maryland.

Fey, J. T., Cuoco, A., Kieran, C., McMullin, L., & Zbiek, R. M. (Eds.). (2003). *Computer algebra systems in secondary school mathematics education*. Reston, VA: National Council of Teachers of Mathematics.

Fey, J. T., & Hirsch, C. R. (2007). The case of core-plus mathematics. In Hirsch, C. R. (Ed.), *Perspectives on the design and development of school mathematics curricula*. Reston, VA: National Council of Teachers of Mathematics.

Finzer, W. (2000). *Design of fathom™, a dynamic statistics environment for the teaching of mathematics*. Paper presented at the International Congress on Mathematical Education (ICME). Tokyo, Japan.

Finzer, W., & Erickson, T. (1998). Dataspace: A computer learning environment for data analysis and statistics based on dynamic dragging, visualization, simulation and networked collaboration. In *Proceedings of the Fifth International Conference on Teaching Statistics*. Voorburg, The Netherlands: International Statistical Institute.

Franke, M. L., Kazemi, E., & Battey, D. (2007). Mathematics teaching and classroom practice. In Lester, F. K. (Ed.), *Second Handbook of Research on Mathematics Teaching and Learning* (2nd ed., *Vol. 1*, pp. 225–256). Charlotte, NC: Information Age Publishing.

Franz, D., & Hopper, P. F. (2007). Is there room in mathematics reform for pre-service teachers to use reading strategies? National implications. *National FORUM of Teacher Education Journal, 17*(3).

Friedlander, A., & Tabach, M. (2001). Promoting multiple representations in algebra. In Cuoco, A. A. (Ed.), *The roles of representations in school mathematics: 2001 yearbook of the national council of teachers of mathematics (NCTM)* (pp. 173–185). Reston, VA: NCTM.

Friel, S. (2007). The research frontier: Where technology interacts with the teaching and learning of data analysis and statistics. In Blume, G. W., & Heid, M. K. (Eds.), *Research on technology and the teaching and learning of mathematics: Case and Perspectives* (Vol. 2, pp. 279–331). Greenwich, CT: Information Age Publishing, Inc..

Frykholm, J. (2004). Teachers' tolerance for discomfort: Implications for curricular reform in mathematics. *Journal of Curriculum and Supervision, 19*(2), 125–149.

Garafalo, J., & Sharp, B. D. (2003). Teaching fractions using a simulated sharing activity. *Learning and Leading with Technology, 30*(7), 36–39, 41.

Garet, M. S., Porter, A. C., Desimone, L., Birman, B. F., & Kwang Suk, Y. (2001). What makes professional development effective? Results from a national sample of teachers. *American Educational Research Journal, 38*(4), 915–945. doi:10.3102/00028312038004915.

Garet, M. S., Wayne, A. J., Stancavage, F., Taylor, J., Walters, K., & Song, M. et al. (2010). *Middle school mathematics professional development impact study: Findings after the first year of implementation (No. NCEE 2010-4009)*. Washington, DC: National Center for Education Evaluation and Regional Assistance, Institute of Education Sciences, U.S. Department of Education.

Garfield, J., & Burrill, G. (Eds.). (1997). *Research on the role of technology – Teaching and learning statistics*. Voorburg, The Netherlands: International Statistical Institute.

Geometer's Sketchpad Resource Center. (n.d.). Retrieved May 10, 2012 from http://www.dynamicgeometry.com/General_Resources.html

Goldenberg, E. (2000). *Thinking (and talking) about technology in math classrooms*. Newton, MA: Education Development Center, Inc..

Goldsmith, L. T., Mark, J., & Kantrov, I. (2000). *Choosing a standards-based mathematics curriculum*. New York: Heinemann.

Goldstein, L. S. (2005, Winter). Becoming a teacher as a hero's journey: Using metaphor in preservice teacher education. *Teacher Education Quarterly*.

Gordon, M. (2009). The misuses and effective uses of constructivist teaching. *Teachers and Teaching: Theory and Practice, 15*, 737–746. doi:10.1080/13540600903357058.

Gordon, S. P., & Gordon, F. S. (2009). Visualizing and understanding probability and statistics: Graphical simulations using Excel. *PRIMUS (Terre Haute, Ind.), 19*(4), 346–369. doi:10.1080/10511970701882891.

Gow, G. (2008, February). Tips on creating complex geometry using solid modeling software. *Tech Directions*, 18–20.

Graham, C. R. (2011). Theoretical considerations for understanding technological pedagogical content knowledge (TPACK). *Computers & Education, 57*, 1953–1960. doi:10.1016/j.compedu.2011.04.010.

Graphing Calculator (NuCalc). (n.d.). Retrieved June 13, 2012 from http://www.nucalc.com/WhatsNew.html

Gravemeijer, K. (1994). Educational development and developmental research in mathematics education. *Journal for Research in Mathematics Education, 35*(5), 443–471. doi:10.2307/749485.

Graves, D. H. (1983). *Writing: Teachers and children at work.* Portsmouth, NH: Heineman.

Grow, G. (1990). *Writing and multiple intelligences.* Paper presented at the Annual Meeting of the Association for Educators in Journalism and Mass Communication. Retrieved from http://www.longleaf.net/ggrow

Guerrero, S. (2010). Technological pedagogical content knowledge in the mathematics classroom. *Journal of Digital Learning in Teacher Education, 26*(4), 132–139.

Guin, D., & Trouche, L. (1998). The complex process of converting tools into mathematical instruments: The case of calculators. *International Journal of Computers for Mathematical Learning, 3*(3), 195–227. doi:10.1023/A:1009892720043.

Hadlock, C. R. (2007). Practicing mathematics in the public arena: Challenges and outcomes in some prominent case studies. *The American Mathematical Monthly, 114*(10), 849–870.

Hallinen, N. R., Chi, M., Chin, D. B., Prempeh, J., Blair, K. P., & Schwartz, D. L. (2013). Applying cognitive developmental psychology to middle school physics learning: The rule assessment method. In *Proceedings of 2012 Physics Education Research Conference.* Academic Press.

Hannafin, R. D., Burruss, J. D., & Little, C. (2001). Learning with dynamic geometry programs: Perspectives of teachers and learners. *The Journal of Educational Research, 94*(3), 132–144. doi:10.1080/00220670109599911.

Hannafin, R., Truxaw, M., Vermillion, J., & Liu, Y. (2008). Effects of spatial ability and instructional program on geometry achievement. *The Journal of Educational Research, 101*(3), 148–157. doi:10.3200/JOER.101.3.148-157.

Harris, J. (1998). Using literature to investigate transformations. *Teaching Children Mathematics, 4*(9), 510–513.

Harris, J. B., & Hofer, M. J. (2011). Technological pedagogical content knowledge (TPACK) in action: A descriptive study of secondary teachers' curriculum-based, technology-related instructional planning. *Journal of Research on Technology in Education, 43*(3), 211–229.

Hart, E. W., Hirsch, C. R., & Keller, S. A. (2007). Amplifying student learning in mathematics using curriculum-embedded Java-based software. In Martin, W. G., & Strutchens, M. (Eds.), *The learning of mathematics: 2007 yearbook of the national council of teachers of mathematics* (pp. 175–202). Reston, VA: NCTM.

Heaton, R. M. (2000). *Teaching mathematics to the new standards: Relearning the dance.* New York, NY: Teachers College Press.

Hegedus, S. J., & Penuel, W. R. (2008). Studying new forms of participation and identity in mathematics classrooms with integrated communication and representational infrastructures. *Educational Studies in Mathematics, 68*(2), 171–183. doi:10.1007/s10649-008-9120-x.

Heid, M. K. (1997). The technological revolution and the reform of school mathematics. *American Journal of Education, 106*, 5–61. doi:10.1086/444175.

Heid, M. K. (2005). Technology in mathematics education: Tapping into visions of the future. In Masalski, W. J. (Ed.), *Technology-supported mathematics learning environments: Sixty-seventh yearbook of the national council of teachers of mathematics* (pp. 345–366). Reston, VA: NCTM.

Heid, M. K., & Blume, G. W. (Eds.). (2008). *Research on technology in the teaching and learning of mathematics: Research syntheses (Vol. 1).* Charlotte, NC: Information Age Publishing.

Henningsen, M., & Stein, M. K. (1997). Mathematical tasks and student cognition: Classroom-based factors that support and inhibit high-level mathematical thinking and reasoning. *Journal for Research in Mathematics Education, 28*(5), 524–549. doi:10.2307/749690.

Herbst, P., & Chazan, D. (2004). *Thought experiments in mathematics teaching.* Grant proposal to the National Science Foundation, funded 2004-2011.

Herbst, P., & Chieu, V. M. (2011). *Depict: A tool to represent classroom scenarios*. Technical report. Retrieved from http://hdl.handle.net/2027.42/87949

Herbst, P., Chazan, D., Chen, C., Chieu, V.M., & Weiss, M. (2011). Using comics-based representations of teaching, and technology, to bring practice to teacher education courses. *ZDM—The International Journal of Mathematics Education, 43*(1), 91-103.

Herbst, P., Nachlieli, T., & Chazan, D. (2011). Studying the practical rationality of mathematics teaching: What goes into installing a theorem in geometry? *Cognition and Instruction, 29*(2), 1–38. doi:10.1080/07370008.2011.556833.

Hiebert, J., Carpenter, T. P., Fennema, E., Fuson, K. C., Wearne, D., Murray, H., & Human, P. (1996). *Making sense: Teaching and learning mathematics with understanding*. Portsmouth, NH: Heinemann.

Hiebert, J., Carpenter, T. P., Fennema, E., Fuson, K., Human, P., & Murray, H. et al. (1996). Problem solving as the basis for reform in curriculum and instruction: The case of mathematics. *Educational Researcher, 25*(4), 12–21. doi:10.3102/0013189X025004012.

Hill, H. C., & Ball, D. L. (2004). Learning mathematics for teaching: Results from California's mathematics professional development institutes. *Journal for Research in Mathematics Education, 35*(5), 330–351. doi:10.2307/30034819.

Hill, H. C., Rowan, B., & Ball, D. (2005). Effects of teachers' mathematical knowledge for teaching on student achievement. *American Educational Research Journal, 42*(2), 371–406. doi:10.3102/00028312042002371.

Hill, H., & Ball, D. L. (2009). The curious – and crucial – case of mathematical knowledge for teaching. *Phi Delta Kappan, 91*(2), 68–71.

Hirsch, C. R., Fey, J. T., Hart, E. W., Schoen, H. L., & Watkins, A. E. (2008). *Core-plus mathematics: Contemporary mathematics in context* (2nd ed.). New York: Glencoe McGraw-Hill.

Hobden, P. (1998). The role of routine problem tasks in science teaching. In Fraser, B. J. T. (Ed.), *International Handbook of Science Education* (*Vol. 1*, pp. 219–231). Dordrecht, The Netherlands: Kluwer Academic Publishers. doi:10.1007/978-94-011-4940-2_14.

Hogg, R. (1991). Statistical education: Improvements are badly needed. *The American Statistician, 45*(4), 342–343.

Hokanson, B., & Hooper, S. (2004). *Integrating technology in classrooms: We have met the enemy and he is us*. Paper presented at the convention of the Annual Meeting of the Association for Educational Communication and Technology. Chicago, IL.

Hollebrands, K. F., Laborde, C., & StraBer, R. (2008). Technology and the learning of geometry at the secondary level. In M. K. Heid & G. W. Blume (Eds.), *Research on technology in the teaching and learning of mathematics: Research syntheses* (Vol. 1, pp. 155–205). Charlotte, NC: Information Age Publishing.

Hollingworth, R. W., & McLoughlin, C. (2001). Developing science students' metacognitive problem solving skills online. *Australian Journal of Educational Technology, 17*(1), 50–63.

Honey, M., & Moeller, B. (1990). *Teachers' beliefs and technology integration: Different values, different understandings*. New York, NY: Center for Technology in Education.

Hoyles, C., Morgan, C., & Woodhouse, G. (1999). *Rethinking the mathematics curriculum*. Philadelphia, PA: Falmer. doi:10.4324/9780203234730.

Hoyles, C., Noss, R., & Kent, P. (2004). On the integration of digital technologies into mathematics classrooms. *International Journal of Computers for Mathematical Learning, 9*(3), 309–326. doi:10.1007/s10758-004-3469-4.

Huck, S. W. (2007). Reform in statistical education. *Psychology in the Schools, 44*(5). Retrieved from http://onlinelibrary.wiley.com/doi/10.1002/pits.20244/pdf doi:10.1002/pits.20244.

Hufferd-Ackles, K., Fuson, K. C., & Sherin, M. G. (2004). Describing levels and components of a math-talk learning community. *Journal for Research in Mathematics Education, 35*(2), 81–116. doi:10.2307/30034933.

Illustrative Mathematics. (2012). *A-REI the circle and the line.* Retrieved May 14, 2012, from http://illustrativemathematics.org/illustrations/223

Inagaki, K., Morita, E., & Hanto, G. (1999). Teaching-learning of evaluative criteria for mathematical arguments through classroom discourse: A cross-national study. *Mathematical Thinking and Learning, 1*(2), 93–111. doi:10.1207/s15327833mtl0102_1.

International Society for Technology in Education. (2000). *National educational technology standards for students: Connecting curriculum and technology.* Eugene, OR: ISTE.

International Society for Technology in Education. (2011). *ISTE NETS.* Retrieved from http://www.iste.org/standards.aspx

Isiksal, M., & Askar, P. (2005). The effect of spreadsheet and dynamic geometry software on the achievement and self-efficacy of 7th-grade students. *Educational Research, 47*(3), 333–350. doi:10.1080/00131880500287815.

Isiksal, M., & Cakiroglu, E. (2011). The nature of prospective mathematics teachers' pedagogical content knowledge: The case of multiplication of fractions. *Journal of Mathematics Teacher Education, 14*(3), 213–230. doi:10.1007/s10857-010-9160-x.

ITEST Learning Resource Center. (2004). Retrieved from http://www2.edc.org/itestlrc/

Ives, S. E., Lee, H. S., & Starling, T. (2009). Preparing to teach mathematics with technology: Lesson planning decisions for implementing new curriculum. In *Proceedings of Research in Undergraduate Mathematics Education.* Raleigh, NC: Academic Press. Retrieved from http://mathed.asu.edu/crume2009/Ives_LONG2.pdf

Ivy, J. T. (2011). *Secondary mathematics teachers perceptions of their integration of instructional technologies.* (Doctoral dissertation). University of Mississippi, Starkville, MS.

Jackiw, N. (2009). *Dynamic geometry® Sketchpad's big idea. Spark! Teaching Mathematics with The Geometer's Sketchpad.* Emeryville, CA: Key Curriculum Press.

Jingzi, H., & Normandia, B. (2009). Students' perceptions on communicating mathematically: A case study of a secondary mathematics classroom. *International Journal of Learning, 16*(5), 1–21.

Jingzi, H., Normandia, B., & Greer, S. (2005). Communicating mathematically: Comparison of knowledge structures in teacher and student discourse in a secondary mathematics classroom. *Communication Education, 54*(1), 34–51. doi:10.1080/14613190500077002.

Johnson, C. D. (2002). The effects of the geometer's sketchpad on the van Hiele levels and academic achievement of high school students. *ETD Collection for Wayne State University.* Retrieved from http://digitalcommons.wayne.edu/dissertations/AAI3071795

Jones, K. (2002). Research on the use of dynamic geometry software: Implications for the classroom. *MicroMath, 18*(3), 18–20.

Jurdak, M., & Shahin, I. (2001). Problem solving activity in the workplace and the school: The case of constructing solids. *Educational Studies in Mathematics, 47*(3), 297–315. doi:10.1023/A:1015106804646.

Kadijevich, D. M. (2012). TPACK framework: Assessing teachers' knowledge and designing courses for their professional development. *British Journal of Educational Technology, 43*(1), E28–E30. doi:10.1111/j.1467-8535.2011.01246.x.

Kafai, Y. B. (2002). Constructionism. In Sawyer, R. K. (Ed.), *Cambridge handbook of the learning sciences.* West Nyack, NY: Cambridge University Press.

Kaput, J. J. (1992). Technology and mathematics education. In Grouws, D. A. (Ed.), *Handbook of research on mathematics teaching and learning* (pp. 515–556). New York, NY: Macmillan.

Karadag, Z., Martinovic, D., & Frieman, V. (2011). Dynamic and interactive mathematics learning environments. In L. R. Wiest & T. Lamberg (Eds.), *Proceedings of the thirty-third annual conference of the North American Chapter of the International Group for the Psychology of Mathematics Education.* Reno, NV: PME-NA.

Kazemi, E., & Stipek. (2001). Promoting conceptual thinking in four mathematics classrooms. *The Elementary School Journal, 102*(1), 59–80. doi:10.1086/499693.

Kazemi, E., & Stipek, D. (2001). Promoting conceptual thinking in four upper-elementary mathematics classrooms. *The Elementary School Journal, 102*(1), 59–80. doi:10.1086/499693.

Kebritchi, M., Hirumi, A., & Bai, H. (2010). The effects of modern mathematics computer games on mathematics achievement and class motivation. *Computers & Education, 55*(2), 427–443. doi:10.1016/j.compedu.2010.02.007.

Keller, B. A., & Hirsch, C. (1998). Student preferences for representations of functions. *International Journal of Mathematical Education in Science and Technology, 29*, 1–17. doi:10.1080/0020739980290101.

Key Curriculum Press. (2001). *The geometer's sketchpad: Dynamic geometry software for exploring mathematics.* Berkeley, CA: Key Curriculum Press.

Key Curriculum Press. (2012a). *Exploring expressions and equations with the geometer's sketchpad® version 5: Addressing the common core state standards for mathematics.* Emeryville, CA: Steven Rasmussen.

Key Curriculum Press. (2012b). *Exploring geometry and measurement with the geometer's sketchpad® version 5: Addressing the common core state standards for mathematics.* Emeryville, CA: Steven Rasmussen.

Key Curriculum. (2012). *Online courses.* Retrieved from www.keycurriculum.com/online-courses

Kieran, C. (1992). The learning and teaching of school algebra. In Grouws, D. (Ed.), *Handbook of research on mathematics teaching and learning* (pp. 390–419). New York: Macmillan Library Reference.

Kilpatrick, J., & Izsak, A. (2008). A history of algebra in the school curriculum. In Greenes, C. E. (Ed.), *Algebra and algebraic thinking in school mathematics* (pp. 3–18). Reston, VA: National Council of Teachers of Mathematics.

Kilpatrick, J., Swafford, J., & Findell, B. (2001). *Adding it up: Helping children learn mathematics.* Washington, DC: National Academy Press.

Kimmins, D. (1995). *Technology in school mathematics: A course for prospective secondary school mathematics teachers.* Paper presented at the Eighth Annual International Conference on Technology in Collegiate Mathematics. Houston, TX.

King-Sears, M. (2009). Universal design for learning: Technology and pedagogy. *Learning Disability Quarterly, 32*(4), 199–201.

Knuth, E. J., Stephens, A. C., McNeil, N. M., & Alibali, M. W. (2006). Does understanding the equal sign matter? Evidence from solving equations. *Journal for Research in Mathematics Education, 37*(4), 297–312.

Koehler, M. J. (2011). TPACK – Technological *pedagogical and content knowledge.* Retrieved from http://tpck.org/

Koehler, M. J., & Mischra, P. (2008). Introducing technological and pedagogical knowledge. In AACTE Committee on Innovation and Technology (Eds.), The handbook of technological pedagogical content knowledge for educators. New York: Routledge/Taylor & Francis Group for the American Association of Colleges of Teacher Education.

Konold, C. (2006). Designing a data tool for learners. In M. Lovett & P. Shah (Eds.), *Thinking with data: The 33rd Annual Carnegie Symposium on Cognition,* (pp. 267-292). Hillside, NJ: Lawrence Erlbaum Associates.

Konold, C. (2005). *Exploring data with TinkerPlots.* Emeryville, CA: Key Curriculum Press.

Kostos, K., & Shin, E. (2010). Using mathematics journals to enhance second graders' communication of mathematical thinking. *Early Childhood Education Journal, 38*(3), 223–231. doi:10.1007/s10643-010-0390-4.

Kumar, G. P., & Mathew, L. (2010). Three-dimensional computer-aided design-based geometric modeling of a new trileaflet aortic valve. *Artificial Organs, 34*(12), 1121–1124. doi:10.1111/j.1525-1594.2009.00973.x PMID:20545658.

La Pierre, S. D. (1993). *Issues of gender in spatial reasoning.* Paper presented at the Annual Conference of the National Art Education Association. Chicago, IL.

La Pierre, S. D., & Fellenz, R. A. (1988). *Spatial reasoning and adults.* Bozeman, MT: Center for Adult Learning Research, Montana State University.

Lampert, M., Beasley, H., Ghousseini, H., Kazemi, E., & Franke, M. (2010). Using designed instructional activities to enable novices to manage ambitious mathematics teaching. In Stein, M. K., & Kucan, L. (Eds.), *Instructional Explanations in the Disciplines* (pp. 129–141). Boston, MA: Springer US. doi:10.1007/978-1-4419-0594-9_9.

Lancaster, K., Moore, E., Parson, R., & Perkins, K. (2013). Insights from using PhET's design principles for interactive chemistry simulations. In *Proceedings of Pedagogic Roles of Animations and Simulations*. ACS.

Lannin, J., Barker, D., & Townsend, B. (2006). Why, why should I justify? *Mathematics Teaching in the Middle School, 11*(9), 438–443.

Lawrence, V. (2002). Teacher-designed software for interactive linear equations: Concepts, interpretive skills, applications & word-problem solving. In *Proceedings from ED-MEDIA 2002 World Conference on Educational Multimedia, Hypermedia & Telecommunications*. Denver, CO.

Lee, C.-Y., & Chen, M.-P. (2010). Taiwanese junior high school students' mathematics attitudes and perceptions towards virtual manipulatives. *British Journal of Educational Technology, 41*(2), E17–E21. doi:10.1111/j.1467-8535.2008.00877.x.

Lee, H., & Hollebrands, K. (2008). Preparing to teach mathematics with technology: An integrated approach to developing technological pedagogical content knowledge. *Contemporary Issues in Technology & Teacher Education, 8*(4). Retrieved from http://www.citejournal.org/vol8/iss4/mathematics/article1.cfm.

Lei, J. (2010). Quantity versus quality: A new approach to examine the relationship between technology use and student outcomes. *British Journal of Educational Technology, 41*(3), 455–472. doi:10.1111/j.1467-8535.2009.00961.x.

Leong, Y. W., & Lim-Teo, S. K. (2003). Effects of geometer's sketchpad on spatial ability and achievement in transformation geometry among secondary two students in Singapore. *The Mathematics Educator, 7*(1), 32–48.

Leont'ev, A. N. (1978). *Activity, consciousness, and personality*. Englewood Cliffs, NJ: Prentice-Hall.

Leontyev [or Leont'ev], A. N. (2009). *Activity and consciousness*. Pacifica, CA: MIA.

Lesh, R., & Sriraman, B. (2005). John Dewey revisited—Pragmatism and the models-modeling perspective on mathematical learning. In A. Beckmann, C. Michelsen, & B. Sriraman (Eds.), *Proceedings of the 1st International Symposium on Mathematics and its Connections to the Arts and Sciences* (pp. 32–51). Berlin: Franzbecker Verlag.

Lesh, R. (1979). Mathematical learning disabilities: Considerations for identification, diagnosis, and remediation. In Lesh, R., Mierkiewicz, B., & Kantowski, M. G. (Eds.), *Applied Mathematical Problem Solving* (pp. 111–180). Columbus, OH: ERIC/SMEAC.

Lester, F. K. (Ed.). (2007). *Second handbook of research on mathematics teaching and learning (Vol. 2)*. Charlotte, NC: Information Age Publishing.

Levenson, E., Tsamir, P., & Tirosh, D. (2010). Mathematically based and practically based explanations in the elementary school: Teachers' preferences. *Journal of Mathematics Teacher Education, 13*(4), 345–369. doi:10.1007/s10857-010-9142-z.

Liang, H., & Sedig, K. (2010). Role of interaction in enhancing the epistemic utility of 3D mathematical visualizations. *International Journal of Computers for Mathematical Learning, 15*, 91–224. doi:10.1007/s10758-010-9165-7.

Li, Q., & Ma, X. (2010). A meta-analysis of the effects of computer technology on school students' mathematics learning. *Educational Psychology Review, 22*(3), 215–243. doi:10.1007/s10648-010-9125-8.

Lopez, L. D., Ding, Y., & Yu, J. (2010). Modeling complex unfoliaged trees from a sparse set of images. *Computer Graphics Forum, 29*(7), 2075–2082. doi:10.1111/j.1467-8659.2010.01794.x.

Lowrie, T., & Logan, T. (2006). Using spatial skills to interpret maps: Problem solving in realistic contexts. *Australian Primary Mathematics Classroom, 12*(4), 14–19.

Ludwigs, A. (2009). Mental models and problem solving: Technological solutions for measurement and assessment of the development of expertise. In Blumschein, P., Hung, W., Jonassen, D., & Strobel, J. (Eds.), *Model-Based Approaches to Learning: Using Systems Models and Simulations to Improve Understanding and Problem Solving in Complex Domains* (pp. 17–40). Boston: Sense Pub..

Lundeberg, M. A., Levin, B. B., & Harrington, H. L. (Eds.). (1999). *Who learns what from cases and how? The research base for teaching and learning with cases*. Hoboken, NJ: Lawrence Erlbaum.

MacGregor, M., & Price, E. (1999). An exploration of aspects of language proficiency and algebra learning. *Journal for Research in Mathematics Education, 30,* 449–467. doi:10.2307/749709.

Ma, L. (1999). *Knowing and teaching elementary mathematics: Teachers' understanding of fundamental mathematics in China and the United States.* Mahwah, NJ: Lawrence Erlbaum Associates.

Manizade, A. G., & Mason, M. M. (2011). Using Delphi methodology to design assessments of teachers' pedagogical content knowledge. *Educational Studies in Mathematics, 76*(2), 183–207. doi:10.1007/s10649-010-9276-z.

Manouchehri, A., & Enderson, M. C. (1999). Promoting mathematical discourse: Learning from classroom examples. *Mathematics Teaching in the Middle School, 4,* 216–222.

Markovits, Z., & Smith, M. S. (2008). Cases as tools in mathematics teacher education. In Tirosh, D., & Wood, T. (Eds.), *The international handbook of mathematics teacher education: Tools and processes in mathematics teacher education* (Vol. 2, pp. 39–64). Rotterdam, The Netherlands: Sense Publishers.

Marsh, B. (2011). *The evaluation of a university in-school teacher education program in science (INSTEP).* (Unpublished dissertation). University of Sussex, Sussex, UK.

Marti, E., Gil, D., & Julia, C. (2006). A PBL experience in the teaching of computer graphics. *Computer Graphics Forum, 25*(1), 95–103. doi:10.1111/j.1467-8659.2006.00920.x.

Martin, T. (2008). Physically distributed learning with virtual manipulatives for elementary mathematics. In Robinson, D. H., & Schraw, G. (Eds.), *Recent innovations in educational technology that facilitate student learning* (pp. 253–275). Charlotte, NC: Information Age Publishing.

Masalski, W. J. (Ed.). (2005). *Technology-supported mathematics learning environments: Sixty-seventh yearbook of the national council of teachers of mathematics.* Reston, VA: NCTM.

Mason, J. (1996). Expressing generality and routes of algebra. In N. Bednarz, C. Kieran, & L. Lee (Eds.), *Approaches to algebra: Perspectives for research and teaching* (pp. 65-86). Dordrecht, The Netherlands: Kluwer Academic.

Matos, J. F., Powell, A., Sztajn, P., Ejersbø, L., & Hovermill, J. (2009). Mathematics teachers' professional development: Processes of learning in and from practice. In Even, R., & Ball, D. L. (Eds.), *The professional education and development of teachers of mathematics* (Vol. 11, pp. 167–183). Boston, MA: Springer US. doi:10.1007/978-0-387-09601-8_19.

Maxfield, M., & Romano, D. (2012). The role of video in pre-service teacher first day of school observations: Peer review on learning of teaching concepts and future application. In P. Resta (Ed.), *Proceedings of Society for Information Technology & Teacher Education International Conference 2012* (pp. 636-641). Chesapeake, VA: AACE.

Mayes, R. L. (1995). The application of a computer algebra system as a tool in college algebra. *School Science and Mathematics, 95*(2), 61–67. doi:10.1111/j.1949-8594.1995.tb15729.x.

McClain, K., & Cobb, P. (2001). An analysis of the development of social and social mathematical norms in one first grade classroom. *Journal for Research in Mathematics Education, 32*(3), 236–266. doi:10.2307/749827.

McCloud, S. (1994). *Understanding comics.* New York: Harper.

McCrory, M. R. (2010). *An exploration of intial certification candidates' TPACK and mathematics-based applications using touch device technology.* (Unpublished doctoral dissertation) University of Mississippi, Oxford, MS.

McIntosh, M. E., & Draper, R. J. (2001). Using learning logs in mathematics: Writing to learn. *Mathematics Teacher, 94*(7), 554–557.

McLeod, S. A. (2008). *Simple psychology.* Retrieved from http://www.simplypsychology.org/bruner.html

McNeil, N. M., & Uttal, D. H. (2009). Rethinking the use of concrete materials in learning: Perspectives from development and education. *Child Development Perspectives, 3*(3), 137–139. doi:10.1111/j.1750-8606.2009.00093.x.

Meagher, M., Edwards, M. T., & Koca, A. (2011b). *Project CRAFTeD: An adapted lesson study partnering preservice mathematics teachers with a master teacher.* Paper presented at the 33rd annual meeting of the North American Chapter of the International Group for the Psychology of Mathematics Education. Reno, NV.

Meagher, M., Özgün-Koca, S. A., & Edwards, M. T. (2011a). Preservice teachers' experiences with advanced digital technologies: The interplay between technology in a preservice classroom and in field placements. *Contemporary Issues in Technology & Teacher Education, 11*(3), 243–270.

Mehan, H. (1979). What time is it Denise? Asking known information questions in classroom discourse. *Theory into Practice, 18*(4), 285–294. doi:10.1080/00405847909542846.

Mendez, E. P., Sherin, M. G., & Louis, D. A. (2007). Multiple perspectives on the development of an eighth-grade mathematical discourse community. *The Elementary School Journal, 108*(1), 41–61. doi:10.1086/522385.

Meng, C., & Sam, L. (2011). Enhancing pre-service secondary mathematics teacher's skills of using the geometer's sketchpad through lesson study. *Journal of Science and Mathematics Education in Southeast Asia, 34*(1), 90–110.

Microsoft Excel Features and Benefits. (n.d.). Retrieved June 1, 2012 from http://office.microsoft.com/en-us/excel/excel-2010-features-and-benefits-HA101806958.aspx

Miller, J. E. (2010). Quantitative literacy across the curriculum: Integrating skills from English composition, mathematics, and the substantive disciplines. *The Educational Forum, 74*(4), 334–346. doi:10.1080/0013 1725.2010.507100.

Mills, G. E. (2011). *Action research: A guide for the teacher researcher* (4th ed.). Boston, MA: Pearson.

Mishra, P. (2012). *Design and pedagogy.* Retrieved from http://punya.educ.msu.edu/research/design-pedagogy/

Mishra, P., & Koehler, M. J. (2006). Technological pedagogical content knowledge: A framework for teacher knowledge. *Teachers College Record, 108*(6), 1017–1054. doi:10.1111/j.1467-9620.2006.00684.x.

Moore, A. M., & Baer, T. (2010). *Research put into practice.* Apex Learning Curriculum & Pedagogy.

Moore, D. S. (1997). New pedagogy and new content: The case of statistics. *International Statistical Review, 65*, 123–137.

Moyer, P., Bolyard, J. J., & Spikell, M. A. (2002). What are virtual manipulatives? *Teaching Children Mathematics, 8*, 372–377.

Moyer-Packenham, P. S., & Westenskow, A. (2012). *Effects of virtual manipulatives on student achievement and mathematics learning.* Paper presented at the Annual Meeting of the American Educational Research Association (AERA). Vancouver, Canada.

Moyer-Packenham, P. S., & Suh, J. (2011). Learning mathematics with technology: The influence of virtual manipulatives on different achievement groups. *Journal of Computers in Mathematics and Science Teaching.*

Murphy, G. D. (2011). Post pc devices: A summary of the early iPad technology adoption in tertiary environments. *E-Journal of Business and Scholarship of Teaching, 5*(1), 18–32.

Murray, D. (1968). *A writer teaches writing: A practical method of teaching composition.* Boston: Houghton Mifflin.

Myers, R. Y. (2009). The effects of the use of technology in mathematics instruction on student achievement. *FIU Electronic Theses and Dissertations.* Retrieved from http://digitalcommons.fiu.edu/etd/136

Nassaji, H., & Wells, G. (2000). What's the use of triadic dialogue? An investigation of teacher-student interaction. *Applied Linguistics, 21*(3), 376–406. doi:10.1093/applin/21.3.376.

National Center for Education Statistics. (2011). *The nation's report card.* Reading: National Center for Education Statistics.

National Council for Teachers of Mathematics. (2010). *NCTM public comments on the common core standards for mathematics.* Retrieved from http://www.nctm.org/about/content.aspx?id=25186

National Council of Teachers of Mathematics. (1989). *Curriculum and evaluation standards for school mathematics.* Reston, VA: NCTM.

National Council of Teachers of Mathematics. (2000). *Principles and standards for school mathematics.* Reston, VA: National Council of Teachers of Mathematics.

National Council of Teachers of Mathematics. (2008). *The role of technology in the teaching and learning of mathematics.* Retrieved from http://www.nctm.org/standards/content.aspx?id=26809

National Council of Teachers of Mathematics. (2009). *Focus in high school mathematics: Reasoning and sense making.* Reston, VA: National Council of Teachers of Mathematics.

National Council of Teachers of Mathematics. (2011). *Technology in teaching and learning mathematics: A position statement of the national council of teachers of mathematics.* Retrieved from http://www.nctm.org/about/content.aspx?id=31734

National Council of Teachers of Mathematics. (2012). *Why Is teaching with problem solving important to student learning? Brief.* Retrieved June 4, 2012, from http://www.nctm.org/news/content.aspx?id=25713

National Council of Teachers of Mathematics. (2012a). *Data sets.* Retrieved May 14, 2012, from http://www.nctm.org/standards/content.aspx?id=32705

National Council of Teachers of Mathematics. (2012b). *Relating leg length to stride length.* Retrieved May 14, 2012, from http://www.nctm.org/uploadedFiles/Statistics%20and%20Probability%20Problem%202.pdf

National Council of Teachers of Mathematics. (2012c). *Waiting for blood donors.* Retrieved May 14, 2012, from http://www.nctm.org/uploadedFiles/Waiting%20for%20Donor_2(2).pdf

National Curriculum Board. (2009). *Shape of the Australian curriculum: Mathematics.* Retrieved from http://www.acara.edu.au/verve/_resources/Australian_Curriculum_-_Maths.pdf

National Governor's Association/Chief Council of State School Officers. (2010). *Common core state standards for mathematics.* Retrieved from http://corestandards.org/assets/CCSSI_Math%20Standards.pdf

National Governors Association and State Education Chiefs. (2010). *Common core state standards initiative: Preparing America's students for college & career.* Author.

National Library of Virtual Manipulatives. (2010). *National library of virtual manipulatives.* Retrieved January 2, 2011, from http://nlvm.usu.edu/en/nav/vlibrary.html

National Mathematics Advisory Panel. (2008). *Foundations for success: The final report of the national mathematics advisory panel.* Washington, DC: U.S. Department of Education.

National Research Council. (2001). *Adding it up: Helping children learn mathematics.* Washington, DC: National Academy Press.

National Research Council. (2005). *How students learn: History, mathematics, and science in the classroom.* Washington, DC: National Academies Press.

National Research Council. (2011). *Successful k-12 stem education: Identifying effective approaches in science, technology, engineering, and mathematics.* Washington, DC: The National Academies Press.

National Staff Development Council. (2012). *Standards for professional learning.* Retrieved from http://www.learningforward.org/standards/standards.cfm

Newkirk, T., Atwell, N., & Northeast Regional Exchange, I. A. (1982). *Understanding writing: Ways of observing, learning & teaching.*

Nguyen, D., Hsieh, Y., & Allen, G. (2006). The impact of web-based assessment and practice on students' mathematics learning attitudes. *Journal of Computers in Mathematics and Science Teaching, 25*(3), 251–279.

Niess, M. L. (2005). Preparing teachers to teach science and mathematics with technology: Developing a technology pedagogical content knowledge. *Teaching and Teacher Education, 21*(5), 509–523. doi:10.1016/j.tate.2005.03.006.

Niess, M. L., Ronau, R. N., Shafer, K. G., Driskell, S. O., Harper, S. R., & Johnston, C. et al. (2009). Mathematics teacher TPACK standards and development model. *Contemporary Issues in Technology & Teacher Education, 9*(1), 4–24.

Norman, D. A. (2002). *The design of everyday things.* Basic Books.

North Carolina Professional Teaching Standards Commission. (2006). *North Carolina professional teaching standards.* Retrieved from http://www.ncpublicschools.org/docs/profdev/standards/teachingstandards.pdf

Obara, S. (2009). Where does the formula come from? *Australian Mathematics Teacher, 65*(1), 25–33.

Obudo, F. (2008). *Teaching mathematics to students with learning disabilities: A review of literature.* Retrieved from http://www.eric.ed.gov/ERICWebPortal/contentdelivery/servlet/ERICServlet?accno=ED500500

Olive, J., & Lobato, J. (2008). The learning of rational number concepts using technology. In M. K. Heid & G. W. Blume (Eds.), Research on technology and the teaching and learning of mathematics: Volume 1 – Research syntheses. Charlotte, NC: Information Age Publishing.

Olson, A. T. (1969). *High school plane geometry through transformations: An exploratory study.* Whitewater, WI: The Wisconsin State Universities Consortium of Research Development, Wisconsin State University-Whitewater.

Orrill, J. (2003). *Fraction bars.* [software]. Retrieved from http://www.transparentmedia.com/software.php

Palmer, L. (1994). *It's a wonderful life: Using public domain cinema clips to teach affective objectives and illustrate real-world algebra applications.* Paper presented at the Annual Conference of the International Society for Exploring Teaching Alternatives. Salt Lake City, UT.

Partnership for 21st Century Skills. (2011). Information, media and technology skills. Retrieved from http://www.p21.org/overview/skills-framework/61

Partnership for Assessment of Readiness for College and Careers (PARCC). (2012). *Press release: New technology readiness tool.* Retrieved May 15, 2012, from http://www.parcconline.org/press-release-new-technology-readiness-tool

Pasnik, S. (2007). *iPod in education: The potential for teaching and learning* (White paper). Retrieved May 23, 2012 from http://64.25.222.20/resource/iPod_in_Education_Whitepaper.pdf

Pea, R. (1985). Beyond amplification: Using the computer to reorganize mental functioning. *Educational Psychologist, 20*(4), 167–182. doi:10.1207/s15326985ep2004_2.

Pea, R. D. (1987). Cognitive technologies for mathematics education. In Schoenfeld, A. H. (Ed.), *Cognitive science and mathematics education* (pp. 89–122). Hillsdale, NJ: Lawrence Erlbaum Associates.

Pearson. (2010). *Research into application: How scientifically-based research findings apply to investigations and the interactive whiteboard.* Glenview, IL: Pearson Education, Inc. Retrieved May 15, 2012, from http://www.pearsonschool.com/index.cfm?locator=PS1cHy

Pearson. (2011). *Implementing guide for the interactive whiteboard.* Glenview, IL: Pearson Education, Inc. Retrieved May 15, 2012, from http://rebekahvictoria.com/resume.pdf

Perkins, K., Moore, E., Podolefsky, N., Lancaster, K., & Denison, C. (2012). Towards research-based strategies for using PhET simulations in middle school physical science classes. *AIP Conference Proceedings, 1413*(1), 295–298. doi:10.1063/1.3680053.

Pew Internet & American Life Project. (2009, September). *Parent-teen cell phone survey.* Retrieved from http://www.pewInternet.org/Reports/2009/Teens-and-Sexting/Survey/Topline.aspx

PhET Interactive Simulations. (2012a). *PhET publications.* Retrieved from http://phet.colorado.edu/en/research

PhET Interactive Simulations. (2012b). *PhET's teacher resources: Goals, facilitation, and activity design.* Retrieved from https://phet.colorado.edu/en/contributions/view/3610

Piaget, J. (1926). *The language and thought of the child.* New York: Harcourt, Brace, Jovanovich.

Piaget, J., & Inhelder, B. (1973). *Memory and intelligence.* London: Routledge and Kegan Paul.

Ploger, D., & Hecht, S. (2009). Enhancing children's conceptual understanding of mathematics through chartworld software. *Journal of Research in Childhood Education, 23*(3), 267–278. doi:10.1080/02568540909594660.

Podolefsky, N. S., Rehn, D., & Perkins, K. (2013). Affordances of play for student agency and student-centered pedagogy. In *Proceedings of the 2012 Physics Education Research Conference.* Academic Press.

Podolefsky, N. S., Paul, A., Moore, E., & Perkins, K. K. (2013). *Implicit scaffolding as a design approach for interactive simulations: Theoretical foundations and empirical evidence.* Academic Press.

Podolefsky, N. S., Perkins, K. K., & Adams, W. K. (2010). Factors promoting engaged exploration with computer simulations. *Physical Review Special Topics - Physics. Education Research, 6*(2), 020117.

Polly, D., & LeHew, A. J. (2012). *Supporting elementary teachers' retention through professional development: Developing teachers' understanding of the common core state standards in mathematics.* Los Angeles, CA: California Mathematics Project. Retrieved from http://cmpstir.cmpso.org/monograph

Polly, D. (2011). Technology to develop algebraic reasoning. *Teaching Children Mathematics, 17*(8), 472–478.

Polly, D., McGee, J. R., & Martin, C. S. (2010). Employing technology-rich mathematical tasks in professional development to develop teachers' technological, pedagogical, and content knowledge (TPACK). *Journal of Computers in Mathematics and Science Teaching, 29*(4), 455–472.

Polly, D., Wang, C., McGee, J. R., Lambert, R. G., Martin, C. S., & Pugalee, D. K. (2013). Examining the influence of a curriculum-based elementary mathematics professional development program. *Journal of Research in Childhood Education.*

Polya, G. (1945). *How to solve it: A new aspect of mathematical method.* Princeton, NJ: Princeton University Press.

Poon, K., & Leung, C. (2010). Pilot study on algebra learning among junior secondary students. *International Journal of Mathematical Education in Science and Technology, 41*(1), 49–62. doi:10.1080/00207390903236434.

Porter, A., McMaken, J., Hwang, J., & Yang, R. (2011). Common core standards: The new U.S. intended curriculum. *Educational Researcher, 40*(3), 103–116. doi:10.3102/0013189X11405038.

Porter, M., & Masingila, J. (2000). Examining the effects of writing on conceptual and procedural knowledge in calculus. *Educational Studies in Mathematics, 42*(2), 165–177. doi:10.1023/A:1004166811047.

Preston, R. V., & Garner, A. S. (2003). Representation as a vehicle for solving and communication. *Mathematics Teaching in the Middle School, 9*(1), 38–43.

Qualifications and Curriculum Authority (QCA). (2007). *Mathematics: Programme of study for key stage 4.* London: Qualifications and Curriculum Authority. Retrieved from http://orderline.qcda.gov.uk/gempdf/1847215408.PDF

Radford, L., Schubring, G., & Seeger, F. (2011). Signifying and meaning-making in mathematical thinking, teaching, and learning. *Educational Studies in Mathematics,* (77): 149–156. doi:10.1007/s10649-011-9322-5.

Rasmussen, C., & Marrongelle, K. (2006). Pedagogical content tools: Integrating student reasoning and mathematics instruction. *Journal for Research in Mathematics Education, 37*(5), 388–420.

Reimer, K., & Moyer, P. S. (2005). Third-graders learn about fractions using virtual manipulatives: A classroom study. *Journal of Computers in Mathematics and Science Teaching, 24*(1), 5–25.

Roberts, D. M. (1980). The impact of electronic calculators on educational performance. *Review of Educational Research, 50*(1), 71–98. doi:10.3102/00346543050001071.

Robitaille, D. F., & Travers, K. J. (1992). International studies of achievement in mathematics. In Grouws, D. A. (Ed.), *Handbook of research on mathematics teaching and learning* (pp. 687–709). Reston, VA: National Council of Teachers of Mathematics.

Rojano, T. (2002). Mathematics learning in the junior secondary school: Students' access to significant mathematical ideas. In English, L. (Ed.), *Handbook of international research in mathematics education.* Mahwah, NJ: Lawrence Erlbaum Associates.

Roschelle, J., Shechtman, N., Tatar, D., Hegedus, S., Hopkins, B., & Empson, S. et al. (2010). Integration of technology, curriculum, and professional development for advancing middle school mathematics three large-scale studies. *American Educational Research Journal, 47*(4), 833–878. doi:10.3102/0002831210367426.

Rosenthal, I. G. (1999). New teachers and technology. *Technology & Learning, 19*(8), 22–27.

Rowell, J., & Mansfield, H. (1980). The teaching of transformation geometry in grade eight: A search for aptitude-treatment interactions. *The Journal of Educational Research, 74*(1), 55–59.

Rubin, A., & Hammerman, J. K. (2006). Understanding data through new software representations. In Burrill, G. (Ed.), *Thinking and reasoning with data and chance: Sixty-eighth yearbook* (pp. 241–256). Reston, VA: NCTM.

Rudmann, D. S. (2002). *Solving astronomy problems can be limited by intuited knowledge, spatial ability, or both.* Paper presented at the Annual Meeting of the American Educational Research Association. New Orleans, LA.

Russell, S. J., & Economopoulos, K. (2012a). *Implementing investigations in grade 3.* Glenview, IL: Pearson Education, Inc..

Russell, S. J., & Economopoulos, K. (2012b). *Investigations and the common core state standards.* Glenview, IL: Pearson Education, Inc..

Ryan, R. M., & Deci, E. L. (2000). Self-determination theory and the facilitation of intrinsic motivation, social development, and well-being. *The American Psychologist*, *55*(1), 68–78. doi:10.1037/0003-066X.55.1.68 PMID:11392867.

Sarama, J., & Clements, D. H. (2009). Concrete computer manipulatives in mathematics education. *Child Development Perspectives*, *3*(3), 145–150. doi:10.1111/j.1750-8606.2009.00095.x.

Schmidt, W. H., McKnight, C. C., & Raizen, S. A. (1997). *A splintered vision: An investigation of U.S. science and mathematics education.* Dordrecht, Netherlands: Kluwer.

Schoenfeld, A. H. (2005). On learning environments that foster subject-matter competence. I L. Verschaffel, E. De Corte, G. Kanselaar, & M. Valcke (Eds.), Powerful environments for promoting deep conceptual and strategic learning, (pp. 29-44). Leuven, Belgium: Studia Paedagogica.

Schoenfeld, A. (1994). Reflections on doing and teaching mathematics. In Schoenfeld, A. (Ed.), *Mathematical Thinking and Problem Solving* (pp. 53–69). Hillsdale, NJ: Lawrence Erlbaum Associates.

Schoenfeld, A. H. (1987). What's all the fuss about metacognition. In Schoenfeld, A. H. (Ed.), *Cognitive Science and Mathematics Education* (pp. 189–215). Hillsdale, NJ: Lawrence Erlbaum Associates.

Schoenfeld, A. H. (1992). Learning to think mathematically: Problem solving, metacognition, and sense making in mathematics. In *Handbook of research on mathematics teaching and learning* (pp. 334–370). Academic Press.

Schoenfeld, A. H. (2002). Making mathematics work for all children: Issues of standards, testing, and equity. *Educational Researcher*, *31*(1), 13–25. doi:10.3102/0013189X031001013.

Schoenfeld, A. H. (2007). What is mathematical proficiency (and how can it be assessed)? In Schoenfeld, A. H. (Ed.), *Assessing Mathematical proficiency* (pp. 59–73). Cambridge, UK: Cambridge University Press. doi:10.1017/CBO9780511755378.008.

Schuster, L., & Anderson, N. C. (2005). *Good questions for mathematics teaching: Why ask them and what to ask.* Sausalito, CA: Mathematics Solutions.

Sedig, K. (2008). From play to thoughtful learning: A design strategy to engage children with mathematical representations.

Sewall, J., Wilkie, D., Merrell, P., & Lin, M. C. (2010). Continuum traffic simulation. *Computer Graphics Forum*, *29*(2), 439–448. doi:10.1111/j.1467-8659.2009.01613.x.

Sharples, M., Taylor, J., & Vavoula, G. (2005). Towards a theory of mobile learning. In *Proceedings of mLearn 2005 Conference.* Cape Town, South Africa: mLearn. Retrieved May 18, 2012 from http://www.iamlearn.org/public/mlearn2005/www.mlearn.org.za/CD/papers/Sharples%20Theory%20of%20Mobile.pdf

Sherin, M. G., Linsenmeier, K. A., & van Es, E. A. (2009). Selecting video clips to promote mathematics teachers' discussion of student thinking. *Journal of Teacher Education*, *60*(3), 213–230. doi:10.1177/0022487109336967.

Show Me. (2012). *ShowMe.* Retrieved from http://www.showme.com

Shulman, L. S. (1986). Those who understand: A conception of teacher knowledge. *American Educator*, *10*, 9–15, 43.

Shulman, L. S. (1986). Those who understand: Knowledge growth in teaching. *Educational Researcher*, *15*(2), 4–11. doi:10.3102/0013189X015002004.

Siegler, R. S. (2003). Implications of cognitive science research for mathematics education. In Kilpatrick, W. B. Martin, & D. E. Schifter (Eds.), A research companion to principles and standards for school mathematics (pp. 219-233). Reston, VA: National Council of Teachers of Mathematics.

Silver, E. A. (1985). Research on teaching mathematical problem solving: Some under-represented themes and needed directions. In Silver, E. A. (Ed.), *Teaching and learning mathematical problem solving: Multiple research perspectives* (pp. 247–266). Hillsdale, NJ: Lawrence Erlbaum Associates.

Silverman, J., & Thompson, P. W. (2008). Toward a framework for the development of mathematical knowledge for teaching. *Journal of Mathematics Teacher Education, 11*, 499-511. DOI: 0857-008-9089-5

Simon, M. A. (1996). Beyond inductive and deductive reasoning: The search for a sense of knowing. *Educational Studies in Mathematics, 30*(2), 197–210. doi:10.1007/BF00302630.

Singapore Ministry of Education. (2007). *Singapore mathematics syllabus*. Retrieved from http://www.moe.sg/education/syllabuses/sciences/files/maths-primary-2007.pdf

Skemp, R. (1976). Instrumental understanding and relational understanding. *Mathematics Teacher, 77*, 20–26.

Smith, M. S., Bill, V., & Hughes, E. K. (2008). Thinking through a lesson: Successfully implementing high-level tasks. *Mathematics Teaching in the Middle School, 14*(3), 132–138.

Smith, M. S., & Friel, S. (Eds.). (2008). *Cases in mathematics teacher education: Tools for developing knowledge needed for teaching*. Association of Mathematics Teacher Educators.

Smith, M. S., & Stein, M. K. (1998). Selecting and creating mathematical tasks: From research to practice. *Mathematics Teaching in the Middle School, 3*(5), 344–350.

Snee, R. D. (1990). Statistical thinking and its contribution to total quality. *The American Statistician, 44*(2), 116–121. doi:10.2307/2684144.

Sokolowski, A., & Rackley, R. (2011). Teaching harmonic motion in trigonometry: Inductive inquiry supported by physics simulations. *Australian Senior Mathematics Journal, 25*(1), 45–53.

Sommers, W. A., & Olsen, W. (n.d.). *Habits of mind: Teacher's companion*. Retrieved May 25, 2012 from http://www.mindfulbydesign.com/sites/default/files/HOM-Sampler.pdf

Southeast Comprehensive Center [SECC]. (2012, June 4). Southeast and Texas comprehensive centers at SEDL - Common core videos. *Common Core State Standards Video Series*. Retrieved June 4, 2012, from http://secc.sedl.org/common_core_videos/

Sriraman, B., & English, L. (2010). *Theories of mathematics education: Seeking new frontiers. Belrin*. Springer-Verlag. doi:10.1007/978-3-642-00742-2.

Stahlhut, R. G. (1992). *Math student teachers: How well prepared are they?* Paper presented at the Annual Conference of the National Council of Teachers of Mathematics. Nashville, TN.

Star, J. (2005). Research Commentary: Reconceptualizing procedural knowledge. *Journal for Research in Mathematics Education, 36*, 404–411.

Star, J. (2010). Reconceptualzing procedural knowledge in mathematics. *Journal for Research in Mathematics Education*.

Steen, K., Brooks, D., & Lyon, T. (2006). The impact of virtual manipulatives on first grade geometry instruction and learning. *Journal of Computers in Mathematics and Science Teaching, 25*(4), 373–391.

Stein, M. K., Engle, R. A., Smith, M. S., & Hughes, E. K. (2008). Orchestrating productive mathematical discussions: Five practices for helping teachers move beyond show and tell. *Mathematical Thinking and Learning, 10*(4), 313–340. doi:10.1080/10986060802229675.

Stein, M. K., Grover, B. W., & Henningsen, M. (1996). Building student capacity for mathematical thinking and reasoning: An analysis of mathematical tasks used in reform classrooms. *American Educational Research Journal, 33*(2), 455–488. doi:10.3102/00028312033002455.

Stein, M. K., Smith, M. S., Henningsen, M. A., & Silver, E. A. (2009). *Implementing standards-based mathematics instruction: A casebook for professional development* (2nd ed.). New York: Teachers College Press.

Stigler, J. W., & Heibert, J. (2004). Improving mathematics teaching. *Educational Leadership, 61*(5), 12–17.

Stiles, K. E., Mundry, S., Loucks-Horsley, S., Hewson, P. W., & Love, N. (2009). *Designing professional development for teachers of science and mathematics* (3rd ed.). Thousand Oaks, CA: Corwin Press.

Stohl, H. (2005). *Probability explorer*. Retrieved from http://www.probexplorer.com

Story Jumper. (2012). *Story jumper*. Retrieved from http://www.storyjumper.com

Strauss, A. L., & Corbin, J. M. (1998). *Basics of qualitative research: Techniques and procedures for developing grounded theory*. Thousand Oaks, CA: Sage.

Suh, J., Moyer, P. S., & Heo, H.-J. (2005). Examining technology uses in the classroom: Developing fraction sense using virtual manipulative concept tutorials. *Journal of Interactive Online Learning, 3*(4), 1–21.

Sweller, J. (1988). Cognitive load during problem solving: Effects on learning. *Cognitive Science, 12*, 257–285. doi:10.1207/s15516709cog1202_4.

Technologies, K. C. P. Inc. (2011a). *Fathom® dynamic data software (version 2.11)*. [Software]. Retrieved from http://www.keycurriculum.com/fathom/download

Technologies, K. C. P. Inc. (2011b). *The geometer's sketchpad® dynamic geometry® software for exploring mathematics (version 5.04)*. [Software]. Retrieved from http://www.keycurriculum.com/sketchpad/download

Telese, J. A. (1999). *The role of social constructivist philosophy in the teaching of school algebra and in the preparation of mathematics teachers*.

Teoh, S. H., Koo, A. C., & Singh, P. (2010). Extracting factors for students' motivation in studying mathematics. *International Journal of Mathematical Education in Science and Technology, 41*(6), 711–724. doi:10.1080/00207391003675190.

Tepper, A. B. (1999). A journey through geometry: Designing a city park. *Teaching Children Mathematics, 5*(6), 348–352.

TERC. (2008). *Investigations in number, data, and space* (2nd ed.). New York: Pearson.

The Learning Principle. (2000). Retrieved from http://www.nctm.org/standards/content.aspx?id=26807

Thinglas, T., & Kaushal, D. R. (2008). Three-dimensional CFD modeling for optimization of invert trap configuration to be used in sewer solids management. *Particulate Science and Technology, 26*, 507–519. doi:10.1080/02726350802367951.

Tirosh, D. (2000). Enhancing prospective teachers' knowledge of children's conceptions: The case of division of fractions. *Journal for Research in Mathematics Education, 31*(1), 5–25. doi:10.2307/749817.

Tirosh, D., & Wood, T. (Eds.). (2008). *Tools and processes in mathematics teacher education*. Rotterdam, The Netherlands: Sense Publishers.

Totten, S. (2005). Writing to learn for pre-service teachers. *The Quarterly of the National Writing Project, 27*, 17-20, 28.

Treiguts, E. (2012, May 17). *Waiting for a bus? Math may help*. Retrieved from www.lightyears.blogs.cnn.com

U. S. Department of Education. (2008). *Foundations for success: The final report of the national mathematics advisory panel*. Retrieved from http://www.ed.gov/about/bdscomm/list/mathpanel/report/final-report.pdf

University of Massachusetts. (2012). *Tinkerplots® dynamic data exploration (version 2.0)*. [Software]. Retrieved from http://www.keycurriculum.com/tinkerplots/download

US Department of Education. (2010). *Evaluation of evidence-based practices in online learning*. Retrieved June 15, 2012, from http://www2.ed.gov/rschstat/eval/tech/evidence-based-practices/finalreport.pdf

Usiskin, Z. (1985). We need another revolution in secondary school mathematics. In Hirsch, C. R. (Ed.), *The secondary school mathematics curriculum: 1985 yearbook of the national council of teachers of mathematics (NCTM)* (pp. 1–21). Reston, VA: NCTM.

Vahey, P., Lara-Meloy, T., Moschkovich, J., & Velazquez, G. (2010). Representational technology for learning mathematics: An investigation of teaching practices in Latino/a Classrooms. In *Proceedings of the 9th International Conference of the Learning Sciences*. Chicago, IL: Academic Press.

Van de Walle, J. A., & Lovin, L. H. (2006). Teaching student-centered mathematics (grades 5-8). Boston, MA: Pearson Education, Inc.

Van De Walle, J. A., Karp, K. S., & Bay-Williams, J. M. (2013). *Elementary and middle school mathematics: Teaching developmentally* (8th ed.). Boston: Pearson.

van Es, E. A., & Sherin, M. G. (2008). Mathematics teachers' learning to notice in the context of a video club. *Teaching and Teacher Education, 24,* 244–276. doi:10.1016/j.tate.2006.11.005.

Varelas, M., Pappas, C. C., Kokkino, S., & Ortiz, I. (2008). Methods and strategies: Students as authors. *Science and Children, 45*(7), 58–62.

Verillon, P., & Rabardel, P. (1995). Cognition and artifacts: A contribution to the study of thought in relation to instrumented activity. *European Journal of Psychology of Education, 10*(1), 77–101. doi:10.1007/BF03172796.

Vlassis, J. (2008). The role of mathematical symbols in the development of number conceptualization: The case of the minus sign. *Philosophical Psychology, 21,* 555–570. doi:10.1080/09515080802285552.

VoiceThread. (2012). *VoiceThread overview.* Retrieved June 1, 2012, from http://voicethread.com/about/features/

Vygotsky, L. (1978). *Mind in society: The development of higher psychological processes.* Boston: Harvard University Press.

Vygotsky, L. S. (1962). *Thought and language* (Hanfmann, E., & Vakar, G., Trans.). New York: John Wiley & Sons, Inc. doi:10.1037/11193-000.

Vygotsky, L. S. (1978). *Mind in society: The development of higher psychological processes* (Cole, M., John-Steiner, V., Scribner, S., & Souberman, E., Eds.). 14th ed.). Boston: Harvard University Press.

Wadsworth, B. (1996). *Piaget's theory of cognitive and affective development.* New York: Longman Publishers.

Wallman, K. K. (1993). Enhancing statistical literacy: Enriching our society. *Journal of the American Statistical Association, 88*(421), 1–8.

Wander, R., & Pierce, R. (2009). Marina's fish shop: A mathematically- and technology-rich lesson. *Australian Mathematics Teacher, 65*(2), 6–12.

Watanabe, T. (2007). In pursuit of a focused and coherent school mathematics curriculum. *The Mathematics Educator, 17*(1), 2–6.

Watson, J. M., & Moritz, J. B. (2000). Developing concepts of sampling. *Journal for Research in Mathematics Education, 31,* 44–70. doi:10.2307/749819.

Weber, B., Muller, P., Wonka, P., & Gross, M. (2009). Interactive geometric simulation of 4D cities. *Computer Graphics Forum, 28*(2), 481–492. doi:10.1111/j.1467-8659.2009.01387.x.

Wells, G., & Arauz, R. M. (2006). Dialogue in the classroom. *Journal of the Learning Sciences, 15*(3), 379–428. doi:10.1207/s15327809jls1503_3.

Wenglinsky, H. (1998). Does it compute? The relationship between educational technology and student achievement in mathematics. *Educational Testing Service Policy Information Center.* Retrieved from http://www.mff.org/pubs/ME161.pdf

Wenglinsky, H. (2005). *Using technology wisely: The keys to success in schools.* New York: Teachers College Press.

Wilcox, B., & Monroe, E. (2011). Integrating writing and mathematics. *The Reading Teacher, 64*(7), 521–529. doi:10.1598/RT.64.7.6.

Wilson, J. W. (2005). *Technology in mathematics teaching and learning.* Retrieved June 13, 2012 from http://jwilson.coe.uga.edu/texts.folder/tech/technology.Paper.html

Wilson, J. W. (2012a). *Intermath project.* Retrieved from http://intermath.coe.uga.edu/

Wilson, J. W. (2012b). *Technology and secondary school mathematics.* Retrieved from http://jwilson.coe.uga.edu/emt668/emt668.html

Wilson, P. S. (2008). Teacher education: A conduit to the classroom. In G.W. Blume & M.K. Heid (Eds.), Research on Technology and the Teaching and Learning of Mathematics: Volume 2: Cases and Perspectives (pp. 415-426). Charlotte, NC: Information Age Publishing, Inc.

Wood, K. C., Smith, H., & Grossnicklaus, D. (2001). Piaget's stages of cognitive development. In M. Orey (Ed.), *Emerging perspectives on learning, teaching, and technology.* Retrieved from http://projects.coe.uga.edu/epltt/

Wood, T., Williams, G., & McNeal, B. (2006). Children's mathematical thinking in different classroom cultures. *Journal for Research in Mathematics Education, 37*(3), 222–255.

Yuan, Y., Lee, C.-Y., & Wang, C.-H. (2010). A comparison study of polyominoes explorations in a physical and virtual manipulative environment. *Journal of Computer Assisted Learning, 26*(4), 307–316. doi:10.1111/j.1365-2729.2010.00352.x.

Zahner, W., Velazquez, G., Moschkovich, J., Vahey, P., & Lara-Meloy, T. (2012). Mathematics teaching practices with technology that support conceptual understanding for Latino/a students. *The Journal of Mathematical Behavior, 31*(4), 431–446. doi:10.1016/j.jmathb.2012.06.002.

Zbiek, R. M., & Hollebrands, K. (2008). A research-informed view of the process of incorporating mathematics technology into classroom practice by in-service and prospective teachers. In M. K. Heid & G. W. Blume (Eds.), Research on technology and the teaching and learning of mathematics: Volume I, research syntheses. Charlotte, NC: Information Age Publishing, Inc.

Zbiek, R. M., & Heid, M. K. (2012). Using computer algebra systems to develop big ideas in mathematics with connections to the common core state standards for mathematics. In Hirsch, C. R., Lappan, G. T., & Reys, B. J. (Eds.), *Curriculum issues in an era of common core state standards for mathematics* (pp. 149–160). Reston, VA: National Council of Teachers of Mathematics.

Zbiek, R. M., Heid, M. K., Blume, G. W., & Dick, T. (2007). Research on technology in mathematics education: A perspective of constructs. In Lester, F. (Ed.), *Second handbook of research on mathematics teaching and learning* (pp. 1169–1207). Charlotte, NC: Information Age.

Zhou, J., & Li, B. (2011). Rapid modeling of cones and cylinders from a single calibrated image using minimum 2D control points. *Machine Vision and Applications, 22,* 303–321. doi:10.1007/s00138-009-0241-8.

Zimmerman, B., Fritzla, T., Haapasalo, L., & Rehlich, H. (2011). Possible gain of IT in problem oriented learning environments from the viewpoint of history of mathematics and modern learning theories. *The Electronic Journal of Mathematics and Technology, 5*(2).

Zinsser, W. K. (1988). *Writing to learn.* New York: Harper & Row.

About the Contributors

Drew Polly is an Associate Professor in the Elementary Education program at the University of North Carolina at Charlotte. His research interests include examining how to best support teachers' use of learner-centered pedagogies and educational technologies in mathematics teaching.

* * *

Wendy Rose Aaron is an assistant professor of Education at Oregon State University and former graduate student and postdoctoral fellow at the University of Michigan. Wendy's research interests include the work that students do in secondary classrooms, the use of representations of instruction in teacher education and educational research, and the mathematical knowledge required to effectively teach mathematics.

Sandra Alon is an Assistant Professor for Teaching Children Mathematics at William Paterson University, College of Education. Alon's work draws on her many years of experience as a Mathematics classrooms teacher, Mathematics Supervisor, and teacher educator. Her main areas of research are the acquisition and development of mathematical concepts. Dr. Alon received her Ed.D. in Mathematics Education in 1997 from Teachers College, Columbia University.

Lisa Ames graduated from Bucknell University in 2007 with a B.A. in Mathematics and a minor in Education. Since then, she has been a middle and high school mathematics teacher at Wood-Ridge High School in Wood-Ridge, New Jersey. Lisa received her M. Ed. in Curriculum and Learning, concentrating in Teaching Children Mathematics in 2011 at William Paterson University.

Heejung An is an Associate Professor of Learning Technologies and the Director of the M. Ed in Curriculum and Learning at the College of Education, William Paterson University. Her main areas of research explore how technology impacts cognition and how K-12 teachers can use technology effectively for teaching and learning. Dr. An received her Ed.D. in Instructional Technology and Media in 2004 from Teachers College, Columbia University.

Kate Best is a Visiting Assistant Professor of Mathematics Education in the Department of Mathematics and Computer Science at Western Carolina University in Cullowhee, North Carolina. She earned an M.A. in Mathematics from Miami University. She has completed significant doctoral work towards a Ph.D. in Mathematics Education at Portland State University. Her current research interests focus on equity in mathematics education, mathematical agency, and assessment.

Linda Boland has worked for Pearson as the Product/Marketing Manager of *Investigations in Number, Data, and Space* for the past 11 years. She works closely with the TERC authors of Investigations, and the Pearson editors as they develop copyright updates and new editions of the product. She also provides marketing collateral for the account executives who sell the program, and provides product support for the customers who purchase *Investigations*. Ms. Boland has been a publishers' educational consultant to provide implementation support to customers, and an independent consultant providing teachers' professional development in math and science in Arizona. She has taught elementary grades, and supported district teachers as a Specialist in Mathematics and Gifted Education. She was awarded the Presidential Award for Excellence in Teaching Elementary Mathematics, Arizona, 1996.

Nathan Borchelt is an Assistant Professor of Mathematics Education in the Department of Mathematics and Computer Science at Western Carolina University in Cullowhee, North Carolina. He holds a M.S.T. in Mathematics from the University of Florida and a Ph.D. in Teaching and Learning: Mathematics Education from Georgia State University. His research interests are focused on the scholarship of teaching and learning, especially with respect to the role of technology as a cognitive tool.

Silvy Brookby is an assistant professor at Framingham State University in Framingham, Massachusetts. She received her bachelor's degree from Northwestern University, her master's degree from Stanford University and her doctorate from University of Missouri (Kansas City). She teaches early childhood and elementary mathematics and science methods courses as well as monitoring student teachers. Her research interests' center around mathematics teaching and learning as well as mathematics anxiety affiliated with pre-service elementary and early childhood teachers.

Christine A. Browning is a professor of mathematics education in the Department of Mathematics at Western Michigan University based in Kalamazoo, Michigan. She teaches undergraduate and graduate mathematics content courses for K-8 preservice teachers, and undergraduate and graduate mathematics education courses that focus on middle school. Christine is interested in developing mathematics curriculum for preservice elementary/middle school teachers that a) makes appropriate use of digital tools and b) incorporates artifacts of children's thinking. She is also interested in the use of digital tools that extend the walls of the mathematics classroom and engage preservice teachers with mathematics, teaching and learning. Her research areas of interest are on mathematical content knowledge for teaching K-8, and Technology, Pedagogy, And Content Knowledge (TPACK).

Vu Minh Chieu is a researcher at the School of Education, University of Michigan. Chieu is interested in the research of learning technologies, including multimedia, Web-based learning platforms, simulations, intelligent tutoring systems, and computer-supported collaborative learning, for higher education and professional development.

Jennifer Czocher is an Assistant Professor of Mathematics at Texas State University. She received her doctoral degree in mathematics education from The Ohio State University in 2013 where she also received her master's degree in mathematics. Her research interests are in students' mathematical thinking and their development of mathematical modeling skills.

Alden J. Edson is a doctoral fellow in the Center for the Study of Mathematics Curriculum and a Ph.D. student studying K-12 Mathematics Education at Western Michigan University. He is currently a research assistant with the Core-Plus Mathematics Project and with the Transition to College Mathematics and Statistics Project. AJ is interested in school mathematics curriculum development, the emergence of innovative technologies in mathematics education, the impact of highly interactive digital resources on students' mathematical learning, and the professional development of mathematics teachers at the secondary school level. His research interests center on the learning and teaching of mathematics in technology-rich environments.

A. Kursat Erbas is an Associate Professor in the Department of Secondary Science and Mathematics Education at Middle East Technical University in Turkey. His research interests include examining the knowledge base for teaching mathematics at the middle and secondary grades and modeling, technology, and problem solving in mathematics education.

Axelle Faughn is an Assistant Professor of Mathematics Education at Western Carolina University, North Carolina. She holds a secondary mathematics teacher certification from France, and a Ph.D. in Computer Algebra from North Carolina State University. Her research focuses on mathematics teacher retention, including opportunities and challenges professional development interventions provide for beginning mathematics teachers. Specific interests include using technology to support the work of secondary mathematics teachers, professional learning communities, and enhancing classroom mathematical inquiry.

Nicole L. Fonger was a doctoral fellow in the Center for the Study of Mathematics Curriculum and earned her PhD in mathematics education at Western Michigan University. For her dissertation research she collaborated with a ninth-grade teacher in investigating algebra students' change in representational fluency in a computer algebra systems and paper-and-pencil environment. On a broader scale, she is interested in secondary school algebra curriculum development with an emphasis on supporting a meaningful connection between students' experiences in arithmetic and the study of algebra. An overarching goal of her research agenda is to pursue new ways to link research and practice in secondary school mathematics.

Dana Pomykal Franz is an Associate Professor in Curriculum Instruction and Special Education at Mississippi State University. She teaches both secondary mathematics education methods courses curriculum, instruction, and assessment courses. Her research interests include middle level mathematics education and the implementation of the Common Core State Standards in mathematics. Her public school teaching experience includes over 12 years of high school mathematics, specifically specializing in working with academically at-risk students.

Chris Gordon is the Assistant Director of the Center for Education in Science, Technology, Engineering and Mathematics (CESTEM) at the University of North Carolina Wilmington.

Mary T. Grassetti is an assistant professor of education at Framingham State University in Framingham, Massachusetts. She earned a bachelor of arts in psychology from Mount Holyoke College and a doctorate in education from the University of Massachusetts Amherst. Dr. Grassetti teaches elementary mathematics and science methods courses and supervises student teachers completing a professional practicum. Her research interests focus on examining the discourse practices novice teachers use to engage students in productive mathematics conversations.

Karen Greenhaus has been a math educator for the past 22 years. In her 17 years in public education, she taught middle school, high school and was a district administrator. She has been involved in professional development for the past 18 years, supporting teacher's integration of technology and instructional strategies through face-to-face workshops, conference presentations, online courses, and Webinars. Karen is currently completing her doctoral dissertation in Curriculum and Education Technology from the College of William and Mary in Williamsburg, VA, with a projected finish date of May, 2014. She has been in education for the past 23 years, as a teacher, administrator, and professional development provider. Her professional development experience supports teacher's integration of technology and instructional strategies through face-to-face workshops, conference presentations, online courses and webinars. Karen most recently worked for Key Curriculum as their Director of Education Technology Outreach, and McGraw-Hill Education, as a Senior Product Sponsor for Professional Development. She is currently an independent consultant in edtech professional development.

Karina K. R. Hensberry is a Postdoctoral Research Associate with the PhET Interactive Simulations project, where she contributes to the development of mathematics simulations and conducts research on simulation design and use in middle schools. She earned her PhD in curriculum and instruction (mathematics education) from the University of Florida in 2012. Dr. Hensberry is particularly interested in the role of PhET sims in supporting marginalized students to learn mathematics.

Patricio Herbst is an associate professor of education and mathematics at the University of Michigan. His research interests include mathematics teaching and learning at the secondary and tertiary level, offline and online, teacher thinking and decision-making, teacher knowledge, teacher preparation in mathematics, and the design and use of information technology in education research and practice.

Christian R. Hirsch is Professor and Distinguished Faculty Scholar in the Department of Mathematics at Western Michigan University. His interests include secondary school mathematics curriculum design and development, the impact of innovative curricula on student learning, and the use of innovative curriculum materials as a context for teacher learning. Since 1992, he has directed the Core-Plus Mathematics Project, a high school curriculum development and research project, formerly funded by the National Science Foundation. Christian is also Co-Director of the Center for the Study of Mathematics Curriculum and of the Core Math Tools Project, each supported by the NSF. He presently is Chair of the NCTM Core Tools Task Force. eHE He also currently directs the NSF-funded Transition to College Mathematics and Statistics Project to design, develop, and evaluate the efficacy of a new fourth-year course for non-STEM college-bound students.

Jessica Ivy is a Visiting Assistant Professor at Mississippi State University, where she teaches undergraduate elementary and secondary mathematics methods and general education courses. Her current and recent research interests include instructional technology integration in secondary mathematics classrooms, professional experiences which enhance the quality of secondary mathematics instruction, and secondary mathematics teachers' perceptions of their Technological Pedagogical Content Knowledge. Additionally, Jessica is interested in the pursuit of initiatives which form and strengthen partnerships between faculty members of Mississippi institutions of higher learning who have a common goal of improving opportunities for K-12 students in mathematics classrooms, and in projects which consider revisions of pre-service mathematics teacher programs to foster a better development of TPACK prior to beginning classroom experiences.

Kathy M. C. Jaqua is an Associate Professor of Mathematics at Western Carolina University in Cullowhee, NC. She holds a B.S. in Mathematics and English from East Tennessee State University, an M.S. in Mathematics and Mathematics Education from Oregon State University, and a Ph.D. in Mathematics Education from Washington State University. She is director of WCU's undergraduate program in secondary mathematics education, and her research interests include the sociology of mathematics classrooms and how students become teachers.

Brin A. Keller is an Associate Professor of Mathematics at Michigan State University. Her research interests over the last 20 years have resided at the intersection of mathematics, science, and technology. She was Co-director of the National Council of Teachers of Mathematics (NCTM) Illuminations Project from 2000-2003. Brin's current work is as a curriculum and software developer for the Core-Plus Mathematics Project and for the Transition to College Mathematics and Statistics Project funded by the National Science Foundation. She also is currently Co-Director of the Core Math Tools Project also funded by NSF and a member of the NCTM Core Tools Task Force.

Dong-Gook (DK) Kim is a faculty member in the School of Business at Dalton State College, Dalton, Georgia. Kim received his Ph.D. degree in Decision Sciences from Georgia State University, Atlanta. He is currently teaching Business Statistics and Quantitative Methods at Dalton State College. His research interests include human decision-making and pedagogical improvement in teaching statistics.

Theodore (TJ) Kopcha is an assistant professor in Learning, Design, and Technology at the University of Georgia. He received his Ph.D. from Arizona State University and has written several papers on teacher professional development. This research was conducted through the support of a research grant from the Office of the Vice President for Research at the University of Georgia.

Sarah Ledford is an Assistant Professor at Kennesaw State University in Georgia. Her research agenda focuses on how to best support secondary mathematics teachers' use of standards-based pedagogies. She is currently a co-Principal Investigator of the North Metro Mathematics Collaborative project funded by the Georgia Teacher Quality grant program.

Carl Lee earned his BA degree in Mathematics from Yale University with conditional certification to teach secondary math, and his MS and PhD degrees in Applied Mathematics from Cornell University. He joined the Department of Mathematics at the University of Kentucky in 1980, where he is now Professor. He is presently a Chellgren Endowed Professor associated with the University of Kentucky Chellgren Center for Undergraduate Excellence. His research interests include polyhedra, discrete geometry, and mathematics education. He has served as a PI or co-PI for a variety of NSF grants, including a Center for Learning and Teaching (ACCLAIM), a Math Science Partnership (AMSP), and a DRK-12 project on Geometry Assessments for Secondary Teachers, and he collaborates in many projects on the teaching and learning of mathematics.

Amy Jensen LeHew is the Elementary Mathematics Specialist for Charlotte-Mecklenburg Schools in Charlotte, NC. LeHew directs, plans, and designs professional development and other projects to support teaching and learning of mathematics in the district's 104 elementary schools.

Woong Lim is an assistant professor of mathematics education at Kennesaw State University. He is primarily concerned with investigating what teachers learn about teaching and learning and how pre-service teachers develop professional teaching practices. Prior to joining the faculty at Kennesaw State University, Lim taught high school and college mathematics. He studied mathematics at Northwestern University and received his doctorate at the University of Houston.

Jayme Linton is the Director of Teacher Education at Lenoir-Rhyne University in Hickory, North Carolina. Previously, she has held positions as Instructional Technology Facilitator, Staff Development Coordinator, and Instructional Coach for Newton-Conover City Schools. Jayme is a doctoral student in the Teacher Education Ph.D. program at the University of North Carolina at Greensboro. She received a bachelor's degree in elementary education from Western Carolina University and a master's degree in curriculum and instruction from Appalachian State University. Jayme is a SimpleK12 Webinar leader and has presented for the Global Education Conference and K-12 Online Conference.

Yating Liu is an assistant professor of mathematics education at Old Dominion University. His research focuses on understanding and enhancing students' proof and reasoning ability.

Sandra Madden is Assistant Professor of Mathematics Education at the University of Massachusetts Amherst. She pursues several lines of related research including statistics education, by supporting the development and understanding of statistical ideas by secondary teachers and students; mathematics curriculum design and implementation; pre-service and in-service teacher education as evidenced through content knowledge for teaching, beliefs, and practices; and the use of dynamic cognitive tools for teaching and learning. Improving all students' opportunities to engage with and come to understand powerful mathematical ideas is her ambition.

Robin Magruder earned her doctorate of instruction and administration from the University of Kentucky, where she is a part-time instructor in the STEM department. Her interests include the effective use of manipulatives, both concrete and virtual, in the mathematics classroom. Also, she is interested in developing conceptual understanding on the part of middle school mathematics students. She enjoys sharing knowledge and experiences from over 12 years in the mathematics classroom with preservice and inservice mathematics teachers.

Azita Manouchehri completed her doctorate in mathematics education under the guidance of Dr. James W. Wilson at the University of Georgia. Her scholarly work in the past decade has concentrated on identifying factors that enhance or impede successful implementation of reformed based mathematics teaching in classroom settings. More specifically, her research focuses on understanding the anatomy of inquiry-based mathematics instruction and factors that contribute to the development of generative mathematical discourse among learners. Her current research focuses on three interpenetrating domains. Firstly, she is involved in developing research based, pedagogically powerful contexts that successfully engage mathematical inquiry among middle and secondary teachers. Dr. Manouchehri has conducted close to 100 professional development sessions and seminars on various topics including: technology in mathematics, mathematical problem solving, mathematical problem posing, the role and features of inquiry in mathematics classroom, authentic assessment in mathematics for middle, high school, university faculty, and researchers across the country.

Christie Sullivan Martin is an Assistant Professor in Elementary Education at the University of South Carolina. She earned in Ph.D. in 2013 in Curriculum and Instruction with a focus on literacy from the University of North Carolina at Charlotte. Her research agenda focuses on examining the impact of writing across the curriculum and effectively preparing teachers to design these opportunities.

Mahnaz Moallem is a Professor of Instructional Technology and the Coordinator of the Instructional Technology Master's Degree Program at the University of North Carolina Wilmington.

Margaret Mohr-Schroeder joined the University of Kentucky faculty in 2006 and is currently an associate professor of middle/secondary mathematics education and chair of the secondary mathematics education program. She holds a BSEd and MS in Mathematics from Pittsburg State University (Kansas), and a PhD in Curriculum and Instruction – Mathematics Education from Texas A&M University. As a native of Kansas, she began her career as a junior high, high school, community college, and college mathematics instructor. Since her arrival to UK, Dr. Mohr-Schroeder has been involved in over $13 million in NSF funding, expanding STEM Education through various initiatives including the creation of a STEM Education major, and has been instrumental in garnering internal and external funding to support transdisciplinary teacher preparation. When she is not boating, camping, or using her mathematical abilities to remodel her home, she enjoys researching pre-service teacher Mathematics Education, Mathematics Knowledge for Teaching, and Assessment.

Emily B. Moore is a Postdoctoral Researcher with the PhET Interactive Simulations project. In addition to designing PhET chemistry simulations, Dr. Moore studies the use and effectiveness of PhET simulations in classrooms from elementary to undergraduate levels. She is particularly interested in understanding the role of PhET simulations in supporting effective guided-inquiry learning in group environments.

Shelby P. Morge is an Associate Professor in the Department of Elementary, Middle Level, and Literacy Education at the University of North Carolina Wilmington. She teaches mathematics education courses for pre-service and in-service elementary and middle school teachers. Her research focuses on mathematics-related beliefs, understanding, and assessment. Shelby received her doctorate in mathematics education from Indiana University. She is a former middle school and high school mathematics teacher.

Sridhar Narayan is Professor of Computer Science and Department Chair in the Department of Computer Science at the University of North Carolina Wilmington. He received his M.S. and Ph.D. degrees in Computer Science from Clemson University. He also holds an M.S. in Mechanical Engineering from Clemson University, and the B.Tech degree in Mechanical Engineering from the Indian Institute of Technology, Madras, India. Dr. Narayan's research interests are primarily in the area of computational intelligence: neural networks, genetic algorithms, and their applications. He also has an active interest in object-oriented technology, a nascent interest in mobile computing, and he enjoys introducing learners of all ages to the joys of computer programming. He has published research papers in several of these areas and has served as the PI or co-PI on grants exceeding $1.5 million.

Chandra Orrill is an Assistant Professor in STEM Education at UMass Dartmouth where she also serves as a Research Associate in the Kaput Center for Research and Innovation in STEM Education. Her research focuses on teacher knowledge and professional development.

Ariel J. Paul is a Research Associate with the PhET Interactive Simulations project where he works on designing and studying interactive simulations for middle school math and science. Prior to joining PhET, he earned his PhD in experimental physics from CU-Boulder in 2007 and then worked as a scientific instrument maker in JILA. During his undergraduate, graduate, and subsequent work experience, he kept a constant interest in education; tutoring and teaching at high school, and college levels.

Katherine K. Perkins is Director of the PhET Interactive Simulations Project at University of Colorado Boulder (CU). She also directs CU's Science Education Initiative and serves as a faculty member in Physics. She was trained as an experimental physicist and atmospheric scientist at Harvard University, and transitioned to physics education research in January 2003 as a post-doctoral researcher with Carl Wieman. Since then, her work in science education research has focused on advancing STEM education through several avenues, including work and research on pedagogically-effective design and use of interactive simulations, sustainable course reform, students' beliefs about science, and institutional change.

Noah S. Podolefsky is a research associate with the PhET Interactive Simulations Project and the Physics Education Research Group at University of Colorado Boulder (CU). He earned a PhD in physics at the University of Colorado, Boulder in 2008, with a focus on student use of analogy and representation in learning physics. His current research on interactive simulations examines the nature of learning through play and exploration.

Diane R. Rogers is a secondary mathematics teacher and a doctoral student in the Interdisciplinary Ph.D. in Evaluation program at Western Michigan University. She is currently a research fellow for a National Science Foundation funded Assessment *for* Learning project designed to improve K-12 student assessment practices and preservice teacher education in the Science, Technology, Engineering, and Mathematics (STEM) fields. Diane is interested in building the capacity of pre-service and in-service educators in the areas of assessment for learning, technology integration, databased decision making, and anti-bias education in order to better meet the educational needs of our diverse student bodies.

D. Craig Schroeder holds dual BS degrees in Physics and Mathematics from Centre College, a MS and PhD in Mathematics Education and an EdS in Educational Leadership from the University of Kentucky. He began teaching high school in Kentucky in 2002 and served as a middle school mathematics coach for a grant project in Fayette County in 2011-2012. He is presently a middle school mathematics and science teacher at Beaumont Middle School and director of the See Blue™ STEM Camp for middle school students. His interests include using technology effectively in the mathematics and science classroom, developing self-regulated learning, and helping students to explore and apply real world STEM concepts in informal learning settings.

Milan Sherman is Assistant Professor of Mathematics Education at Portland State University. He received his EdD in Mathematics Education at the University of Pittsburgh in 2011, and also holds an MS in Mathematics from the University of Pittsburgh (2002). His research interests are in the areas of the teaching and learning of school algebra, and the use of technology the teaching and learning of mathematics at the secondary level. In particular, his research has focused on the influence of instructional technology on students' mathematical thinking in secondary classrooms. His teaching interests include teacher education courses aimed at supporting teachers in designing and implementing instruction that can support students' high-level mathematical thinking using technology, and the use of dynamic geometry software to promote conceptual understanding in calculus.

Ravi Somayajulu is an Assistant Professor of Mathematics Education at Eastern Illinois University. He completed his doctoral degree in mathematics education from The Ohio State University in 2012 and a master's degree in mathematics from Bowling Green State University in 2006. His research interests lie in the area of mathematics teaching and teacher education.

David Stegall is the Associate Superintendent for Newton-Conover City Schools. He previously served Newton-Conover as the Director of Elementary Curriculum, ESL (English as a Second Language) and AIG (Academically and Intellectually Gifted). In February 2012, he was named the Outstanding Young Educator for North Carolina by NCASCD. David joined the Newton-Conover City School system from Iredell-Statesville Schools in July 2007. He has presented at the state, national, and international levels on professional learning communities and teacher empowerment. David received a bachelor's degree in elementary education from the University of North Carolina at Charlotte; a master's degree in education from Gardner-Webb University; an education specialist degree in education administration from Appalachian State University; and a doctorate degree in educational leadership from Appalachian State University.

Gene A. Tagliarini, Professor of Computer Science at UNCW, received the BA and MA in Mathematics from the University of South Florida and the PhD in Computer Science from Clemson University. He served as Principal Investigator or Co-PI for Department of Defense, National Science Foundation, Department of Education, and industry grants and contracts in excess of $2M. As an active researcher in the field of biologically inspired computing, he developed neural networks for sonar signal classification, fingerprint matching, image compression, combinatorial optimization, and constraint satisfaction.

He developed a genetic algorithm to design chemical structures, and he has applied wavelet processing techniques, with emphasis upon combining wavelet and neural processing paradigms. Recently, he has engaged in research that uses computing to integrate STEM instruction into 7th -12th grade curricula. Dr. Tagliarini has published over 65 technical papers in the areas of computing for primary education, multimedia software, and biologically inspired computing.

Jenna Tague is a doctoral student in mathematics education at The Ohio State University. She received her B.S. Mathematics and M.S. Mathematics from Bucknell University and Colorado State University, respectively. Her research interests include problem solving and mathematical thinking.

P. Mark Taylor is a mathematics teacher educator at Carson-Newman University. Dr. Taylor studies inservice and preservice mathematics teacher learning as well as curriculum implementation.

Keri Duncan Valentine is a doctoral student at the University of Georgia in the Educational Psychology and Instructional Technology Department within the Learning, Design, and Technology program. Her background as an elementary and middle school mathematics teacher have led her to an interest in designing mathematics learning environments focused on complex geometric and spatial reasoning.

Pingping Zhang is a doctoral candidate in mathematics education at the Ohio State University. My research interest lies in the area of epistemology of mathematics. Most specifically, I study individuals' mathematical thinking processes as exhibited during their engagement in mathematical problem solving, aiming to provide guides for how mathematical thinking might be nurtured and enhanced in instruction. I also examine ways in which knowledge about children's mathematical thinking might be utilized in courses designed for teachers so to increase their pedagogical and mathematical understandings.

Index